CLASSIFIERS

OXFORD STUDIES IN TYPOLOGY AND LINGUISTIC THEORY

SERIES EDITORS: Ronnie Cann, *University of Edinburgh*, William Croft, *University of Manchester*, Mark Durie *University of Melbourne*, Anna Siewierska, *University of Lancaster*

This series offers a forum for orginal and accessible books on language typology and linguistic universals. Works published will be theoretically innovative and informed and will seek to link theory and empirical research in ways that are mutually productive. Each volume will also provide the reader with a wide range of cross-linguistic data. The series is open to typological work in semantics, syntax, phonology, and phonetics or at the interfaces between these fields.

Published:

Indefinite Pronouns
Martin Haspelmath

Intransitive Predication
Leon Stassen

Classifiers: A Typology of Noun Categorization Devices
Alexandra A. Aikhenvald

Anaphora
Yan Huang

In preparation:

The Noun Phrase
Jan Rijkhoff

Double Object Constructions
Maria Polinsky

CLASSIFIERS

A Typology of Noun Categorization Devices

ALEXANDRA Y. AIKHENVALD

OXFORD
UNIVERSITY PRESS

Great Clarendon Street, Oxford OX2 6DP
Oxford University Press is a department of the University of Oxford.
It furthers the University's objective of excellence in research, scholarship,
and education by publishing worldwide in

Oxford New York

Auckland Bangkok Buenos Aires Cape Town Chennai
Dar es Salaam Delhi Hong Kong Istanbul Karachi Kolkata
Kuala Lumpur Madrid Melbourne Mexico City Mumbai Nairobi
São Paulo Shanghai Taipei Tokyo Toronto

Oxford is a registered trade mark of Oxford University Press
in the UK and certain other countries

Published in the United States
by Oxford University Press Inc., New York

© A. Y. Aikhenvald 2003

The moral rights of the author have been asserted
Database right Oxford University Press (maker)

First published 2000
First published in paperback 2003

All rights reserved, No part of this publication may be reproduced,
stored in a retrieval system, or transmitted, in any form or by any means,
without the prior permission in writing of Oxford University Press,
or as expressly permitted by law, or under terms agreed with the appropriate
reprographics rights organizations. Enquiries concerning reproduction
outside the scope of the above should be sent to the Rights Department,
Oxford University Press, at the address above

You must not circulate this book in any other binding or cover
and you must impose this same condition on any acquirer

British Library Cataloguing in Publication Data
Data available

Library of Congress Cataloging in Publication Data
Data applied for
ISBN 0–19–823886–X
ISBN 0–19–926466–X (pbk.)

1 3 5 7 9 10 8 6 4 2

Typeset in Times
by J&L Composition, Filey, North Yorkshire
Printed in Great Britain
on acid-free paper by
Biddles Ltd, Guildford & King's Lynn

For Bob, okojibotee

Preface

This book aims at providing a cross-linguistic analysis of noun classification systems across the languages of the world, also dealing with a variety of other problems such as the morphological status of the markers of these categories, agreement phenomena, and the syntactic and semantic classification of adjectives and numbers. It is generally accepted that linguistic categorization of nouns is a reflection of human mind and culture. The present study thus has far-reaching implications for cross-cultural as well as cross-linguistic studies of human cognition, and will provide new insights concerning the mechanisms by which human language functions.

Languages with extensive systems of noun classification devices, especially those which combine classifiers and genders, present a true challenge for the typologist. My first encounter with these unusual systems was through fieldwork on Tariana and Baniwa, two closely related North Arawak languages spoken in Northwest Amazonia. The more I worked on the topic, the more exotic and unusual systems I encountered, especially among little-known South American languages, and languages of the South Pacific. This book came into being as an attempt to integrate these systems into a cross-linguistically based typological framework.

This study is an up-to-date introduction to the field, and will be of value not only to a wide variety of linguists and linguistic students but also to anthropologists, cognitive psychologists, and philosophers who are interested in language and the mind. It can be used both as a sourcebook for further typological studies, and as a textbook. The discussion in the book is in terms of basic linguistic theory, the framework of linguistic analysis in terms of which most grammars are cast, and in terms of which significant typological generalizations are postulated. (I have avoided using any of the more specific formalisms, which come and go with such frequency.)

Some terminological clarifications are in order. First, my conception of a lexical entry for 'noun' roughly corresponds to the notion of 'lexeme' as outlined by Lyons (1977 vol. 1: 19). Second, throughout the book 'linguistic categorization of a noun' is used to mean 'linguistic categorization of the referent of a noun', just as in many linguistic usages 'human noun' is a short way of saying 'noun with a human referent'. Third, the term 'noun categorization' is used here in a sense close to the 'noun classification' (cf. Craig 1986a; Derbyshire and Payne 1990) or 'nominal classification' (cf. Harvey and Reid 1997) employed by other authors. The term 'classifier system' refers to a grammatical system of noun categorization device(s) in a particular language.

In order to limit the book to a reasonable size, I have only been able to refer to a portion of the available literature. There are many other sources that I have consulted, which only provide additional exemplification for points that are already well covered. When a language is introduced for the first time, its genetic affiliation and the source of information on it are given in parentheses; further on, this information is only repeated where relevant. Examples, tables and diagrams are numbered separately within each chapter.

The orthography used in the examples and language names follows that of the sources (unless indicated otherwise).

A study like this could only be definitive when good and thorough descriptions have been provided for most of the world's languages; we are at present a long way from this situation. Nevertheless, I hope that this study will provide a framework within which fieldworkers and typologists will be able to work, and which can be amended and adjusted as new data and new insights emerge.

It is my hope that this book will encourage people to study noun classification devices, especially in little-known or undescribed languages, going out into the field and documenting languages threatened by extinction (before it is too late to do so).

Acknowledgements

My gratitude goes to all those native speakers who taught me their languages and their unusual classifier and gender systems: Cândido, José, Jovino, Graciliano, and Olívia Brito (Tariana); Humberto Baltazar and Pedro Ângelo Tomas (Warekena); the late Candelário da Silva (Bare); Afonso, Albino and João Fontes, Celestino da Silva, Cecília and Laureano da Silva, and the late Marcília Rodrigues (Baniwa); the late Tiago Cardoso (Desano, Piratapuya); Alfredo Fontes (Tucano); Marilda and Carlito Paumarí (Paumarí); Raimunda Palikur (Palikur); Simone Nientao (Tamachek) and—last but not least—Pauline and James Laki (Manambu).

I am also indebted to students in the Federal University of Santa Catarina, Brazil, and in the Australian National University. I learned a lot from working with Rute Amorim, Lilias Chun, Christiane Cunha de Oliveira, Tim Curnow, Michael Dunn, Catriona Hyslop, Dorothy Jauncey, Yunseok Lee, Eva Lindström, Peita Littleton, Rina Marnita, Silvana Martins, Kazuko Obata, Kristina Sands, Eva Tatrai, Angela Terrill, Simoni Valadares, and Jacki Wicks. My warmest thanks go to Silvana and Valteir Martins and Lenita and Elias Coelho de Assis, without whose friendship and assistance a great deal of my fieldwork would have been impossible. Special gratitude goes to Diana Green, who revealed to me the beauty of genders and classifiers in Palikur.

I am most grateful to those people who helped me by sending copies of their papers, answering my questions and commenting on various parts of this manuscript: José Alvarez, Mengistu Amberber, Felix Ameka, Peter van Baarle, Janet Barnes, Cândida Barros, Edith Bavin, Walter Bisang, Kim Blewett, Paula Boley, John Boyle, Friederike Braun, Lea Brown, Bill Callister, Lyle Campbell, Eugene Casad, Meiyun Chang-Smith, Adam Chapman, Shirley Chapman, Hilary Chappell, Helen Charters, Bernard Comrie, Bob Conrad, Grev Corbett, Tim Curnow, Des Derbyshire, Connie Dickinson, Tony Diller, Gerritt Dimmendaal, Mark Donohue, Nancy Dorian, Mark Durie, Tom Dutton, Nora England, Nick Evans, Cindi and Jim Farr, Bill Foley, Lys Ford, David Foris, Paul Frank, David Gil, Cliff Goddard, Elsa Gomez-Imbert, Ian Green, Rebecca Green, Colette Grinevald (Craig), Geoff Haig, Mark Harvey, Rie Hasada, Bernd Heine, Debbie Hill, Chu-Ren Huang, Rodney Huddleston, Suanu Ikoro, Liisa Järvinen, Jae Jung Song, Aleksandr J. Kibrik, Harold Koch, Antonina I. Koval', Randy LaPolla, Jason Lee, Jennie Lee, Jeff Leer, W. P. Lehmann, Adrienne Lehrer, Frank Lichtenberk, Eva Lindström, Elizabeth Löbel,

Acknowledgements

Ivan Lowe, Harriet Manelis-Klein, Jack Martin, Marianne Mithun, Catherine McGuckin, Ulrike Mosel, Otto Nekitel, Bee Chin Ng, Johanna Nichols, Masayuki Onishi, Patricia Pacioni, Helma Pasch, Peter Paul, Andrew Pawley, David Payne, Vladimir Plungian, Bill Poser, Kostantin Pozdnjakov, Bruce Rigsby, Phil Quick, Susan Quigley, Katya Rakhilina, Henri Ramirez, Nick Reid, Keren Rice, Aryon Rodrigues, Malcolm Ross, Carl Rubino, Alan Rumsey, Filomena Sândalo, Risto Sarsa, Hansjakob Seiler, Lucy Seki, Gunter Senft, Beatriz and Rodolfo Senn, Gi-Hyun Shin, Tim Shopen, Edgar Suter, Chad Thompson, Irina Toporova, Joe Tsonope, Ione Vasconcelos, Alejandra Vidal, Tiit-Rein Viitso, Viktor A. Vinogradov, Julie Waddy, Bruce Waters, Laurel Watkins, Anna Wierzbicka, Mary Ruth Wise, Stephen Wurm, and Roberto Zavala.

I am most grateful to those who read through the whole draft of this book, or parts of it, and provided comments, corrections and ideas—Peter Denny, Nancy Dorian, David Foris, Cliff Goddard, Nikolaus Himmelmann, Frank Lichtenberk, Edith Moravcsik, Patricia Pacioni, Helma Pasch, Doris Payne, Nick Reid, Malcolm Ross, Fritz Serzisko, and Roberto Zavala. Invaluable comments on almost every page came from R. M. W. Dixon, Keith Allan, Walter Bisang, Lyle Campbell, Gerritt Dimmendaal, Mark Durie, Ulrike Mosel, and Gunter Senft.

My deepest gratitude goes to the SIL Library in Ukarumpa, and to Paul Frank, the director of the Summer Institute of Linguistics (Colombia), who provided me with invaluable materials on languages of Papua New Guinea and Colombia respectively.

I am also grateful to the members of Eesti Noorte Grupp of Canberra—Reet Bergman, Krista Gardiner, and Reet Vallak—who helped me realize that communicating in a language without genders or classifiers can be great fun.

Suzanne Kite carefully read through several drafts of this book and corrected it with her usual skill, dedication, and good humour. Thanks are equally due to her.

Jennifer Elliott provided a wonderful working atmosphere at the Research Centre for Linguistic Typology. This book would have been scarcely possible without her.

Plea

This book is far from being the last word on noun categorization devices. I welcome reactions, counterexamples, new ideas and data, to further develop, refine, and improve the generalizations put forward here. Please send them to me at Research Centre for Linguistic Typology, La Trobe University, Bundoora Vic., 3083 Australia.

Contents

List of Maps	xx
List of Tables	xxi
List of Diagrams	xxiv
List of Abbreviations	xxv
1. Preliminaries	1
1.1 General remarks	1
1.2 Classifiers: an illustration	1
1.3 Theoretical framework, data, and sources	4
1.4 Approaches to the typology of classifiers	5
1.5 Parameters for the typology of classifiers	13
1.6 The structure of this book	16
2. Noun Class and Gender Systems	19
2.1 General remarks	19
2.2 Properties of noun class systems	20
2.3 Principles of noun class assignment	22
2.3.1 Semantic assignment	22
2.3.2 Morphological assignment	25
2.3.3 Phonological assignment	25
2.3.4 Mixed principles of assignment	25
2.4 Noun classes and agreement	28
2.4.1 A working definition of agreement and agreement properties	28
2.4.2 Principles of noun class agreement	31
2.4.3 Variability in noun class assignment and variable agreement	41
2.4.4 Determining the number of noun classes in a language	45
2.5 Markedness and resolution in noun classes	50
2.5.1 Markedness	50
2.5.2 Noun class resolution	52
2.5.3 Markedness relationships in noun classes	54
2.6 Realization of noun classes	56
2.6.1 Overt and covert noun class marking	57
2.6.2 Morphological realization of noun classes	58
2.6.3 Double marking of noun classes	63

xiv *Contents*

    2.7 Languages with more than one kind of noun class   67
        2.7.1 Nominal and pronominal noun class   68
        2.7.2 Different kinds of noun class in the same environment   70
        2.7.3 Languages with more than one kind of noun class: a summary   76
    2.8 Distribution of noun classes in the languages of the world   77

3. Noun Classifiers   81
    3.1 Properties of noun classifiers   81
    3.2 Noun classifiers: discussion and exemplification   82
        3.2.1 The choice of noun classifiers and the cooccurrence of several classifiers within one noun phrase   82
        3.2.2 Semantic functions of noun classifiers   84
        3.2.3 Size of inventory and degree of grammaticalization of noun classifiers   84
        3.2.4 Syntactic functions of noun classifiers   87
    3.3 Noun classifiers and numeral classifiers   90
    3.4 Realization and grammaticalization of noun classifiers   91
    3.5 Overt noun class marking and noun classifiers   92
    3.6 Distribution of noun classifiers in the languages of the world   97

4. Numeral Classifiers   98
    4.1 Properties of numeral classifiers   98
    4.2 Numeral classifier constructions and morphological realization of numeral classifiers   101
        4.2.1 Numeral classifiers as independent lexemes   101
        4.2.2 Numeral classifiers attached to numerals   105
        4.2.3 Numeral classifiers attached to the head noun   110
    4.3 Languages with more than one morphological type of numeral classifier   112
        4.3.1 Different types of numeral classifier in complementary distribution   112
        4.3.2 Different types of numeral classifier which occur together   113
    4.4 Problems with numeral classifiers   114
        4.4.1 Mensural and sortal classifiers: distinguishing classifiers from quantifying expressions   114
        4.4.2 Incipient numeral classifiers   120
    4.5 Distribution of numeral classifiers in the languages of the world   121

Contents xv

5. Classifiers in Possessive Constructions — 125
   - 5.1 Categorization in possessive constructions — 125
   - 5.2 Possessed classifiers — 126
   - 5.3 Relational classifiers — 133
     - 5.3.1 Relational classifiers and their properties — 133
     - 5.3.2 Types of possession and relational classifiers — 137
   - 5.4 Possessor classifiers — 139
   - 5.5 Interaction of possessed and relational classifiers — 140
     - 5.5.1 Integrating relational and possessive classifiers — 140
     - 5.5.2 Languages with two types of classifier in possessive constructions — 142
   - 5.6 Contrasting classifiers in possessive constructions — 144
   - 5.7 Distribution of classifiers in possessive constructions in the languages of the world — 147

6. Verbal Classifiers — 149
   - 6.1 Properties of verbal classifiers — 149
   - 6.2 Realization of verbal classifiers — 149
     - 6.2.1 Classificatory noun incorporation — 150
     - 6.2.2 Verbal classifiers as affixes — 152
     - 6.2.3 Suppletive 'classificatory verbs' — 153
     - 6.2.4 The interaction of the three types of verbal classifier — 160
   - 6.3 Verbal classifiers and syntactic function of the argument — 162
   - 6.4 Combinations of different types of verbal classifier — 163
     - 6.4.1 Different types of verbal classifier in complementary distribution — 163
     - 6.4.2 Distinct systems of verbal classifiers — 167
   - 6.5 Distribution of verbal classifiers — 169

7. Locative and Deictic Classifiers — 172
   - 7.1 The structure of this chapter — 172
   - 7.2 Properties of locative classifiers — 172
   - 7.3 Properties of deictic classifiers — 176
     - 7.3.1 Examples of deictic classifiers — 177
     - 7.3.2 Conclusions and discussion — 181

8. Different Classifier Types in One Language — 184
   - 8.1 General observations — 184
   - 8.2 Coexisting classifier sets in different environments — 185
   - 8.3 Different classifier sets in the same environment — 198
   - 8.4 Conclusions — 201

xvi Contents

- 9. Multiple Classifier Languages — 204
  - 9.1 Noun categorization in multiple classifier languages — 204
  - 9.2 Multiple classifier languages and noun class agreement on multiple targets — 228
  - 9.3 Fuzzy types: overlapping classifiers in multiple environments — 230
    - 9.3.1 Multiple classifiers in Baniwa — 230
    - 9.3.2 Multiple classifiers in Tariana — 235
    - 9.3.3 Fuzzy types and borderline cases — 240

- 10. Classifiers and Other Grammatical Categories — 242
  - 10.1 Classifiers and number — 243
    - 10.1.1 Noun classes and number — 243
    - 10.1.2 Number and other classifier types — 249
  - 10.2 Classifiers and person — 252
  - 10.3 Classifiers and grammatical function — 255
    - 10.3.1 Noun classes and grammatical function — 255
    - 10.3.2 Verbal classifiers and grammatical function — 257
  - 10.4 Classifiers and types of possession — 257
    - 10.4.1 Noun classes and types of possession — 258
    - 10.4.2 Classifiers in possessive constructions and types of possession — 259
  - 10.5 Classifiers and politeness — 260
  - 10.6 Classifiers and declensional classes — 262
  - 10.7 Classifiers and verbal categories — 263
  - 10.8 Classifiers and deictic categories — 266
  - 10.9 Classifiers, derivation, and lexicon — 266
  - 10.10 Conclusions — 268

- 11. Semantics of Noun Categorization Devices — 271
  - 11.1 Semantic parameters in noun categorization — 271
    - 11.1.1 Basic parameters of categorization — 271
    - 11.1.2 Additional semantic characteristics — 274
    - 11.1.3 Semantic relationship between a classifier and the referent — 275
  - 11.2 Semantics of classifier types — 275
    - 11.2.1 Semantics of noun classes — 275
    - 11.2.2 Semantics of noun classifiers — 283
    - 11.2.3 Semantics of numeral classifiers — 286
    - 11.2.4 Semantics of classifiers in possessive constructions — 293
    - 11.2.5 Semantics of verbal classifiers — 295

	11.2.6 Semantics of locative and of deictic classifiers	300
	11.2.7 Semantic parameters in languages with several different types of classifier	301
	11.2.8 Semantic parameters in multiple classifier systems	303
	11.2.9 Conclusions	305

12. Semantic Organization and Functions of Noun Categorization — 307

  12.1 Semantic organization and functions of classifier systems — 307
    12.1.1 Semantic complexity in classifier systems — 308
    12.1.2 Semantic roles of classifiers — 317
    12.1.3 Discourse-pragmatic functions of classifiers — 320
    12.1.4 Applicability of classifiers and default classes — 334
  12.2 Human cognition and classifiers — 337
    12.2.1 Perceptual correlates of noun categorization — 337
    12.2.2 Cognitive mechanisms and noun categorization — 339
  12.3 Social and cultural issues in noun categorization — 340
    12.3.1 Social structure in noun categorization — 342
    12.3.2 Environment and culture in noun categorization — 343
    12.3.3 Culture-specific metaphorical extensions — 346
    12.3.4 Socio-cultural motivations for change in noun categorization — 347
  12.4 Conclusions — 350

13. Origin and Development of Noun Categorization Devices — 352

  13.1 Lexical sources for classifiers — 353
    13.1.1 From a noun to a classifier — 353
    13.1.2 Repeater phenomena and the origin of classifier constructions — 361
    13.1.3 From a verb to a classifier — 362
    13.1.4 Classifiers from deverbal nominalizations — 365
    13.1.5 Classifiers of mixed origin — 366
  13.2 From a closed class to a noun categorization system — 367
  13.3 Languages with several classifier types, and the relative age of noun categorization devices — 370
  13.4 Internal evolution of noun categorization — 372
  13.5 Grammaticalization and reanalysis in noun categorization systems — 374
    13.5.1 Grammaticalization in the development of noun categorization — 374
    13.5.2 Reanalysis in noun categorization — 377

xviii   Contents

13.6	Reduction and loss of noun categorization devices	379
13.7	Language-external motivations for the development and decay of noun categorization	382
	13.7.1 Language contact and noun categorization	383
	13.7.2 Creolization and noun categorization	388
	13.7.3 Language obsolescence and noun categorization	389
	13.7.4 Language-external motivations and their impact on noun categorization	391
13.8	Development and loss of agreement	391
	13.8.1 The genesis and development of agreement	391
	13.8.2 Decline and loss of agreement	398
13.9	Semantic changes in noun categorization devices	400
	13.9.1 From lexical item to classifier: principles of semantic change	401
	13.9.2 Further changes in noun categorization devices	407
13.10	Sources of noun categorization devices: a summary	411

14. Noun Categorization Devices in Language Acquisition and Dissolution — 413

14.1	Acquisition and development of noun classes	413
14.2	Acquisition of numeral classifiers	417
14.3	Dissolution of noun classes and of numeral classifiers	422
14.4	Conclusions	423

15. Conclusions — 425

15.1	Properties of classifier types	425
15.2	Cooccurrence of classifier types and multiple classifier languages; prototypes and continua	432
15.3	Prospects for future studies	434

Appendix 1. Noun Categorization by Means Other than Classifiers — 436

Appendix 2. From Nouns to Classifiers: Further Examples of Semantic Change — 442
    (A) Body parts as sources for classifiers: semantic extensions — 442
    (B) Sources for shape-based numeral classifiers — 446

Appendix 3. Fieldworker's Guide to Classifier Languages — 447

References — 452

List of Languages — 489

List of Language Families, Linguistic Areas, and Proto-languages — 504

Index of Languages, Linguistic Areas, and Language Families   509
Index of Authors   519
Subject Index   525

List of Maps

1. Distribution of noun classes and genders in the languages of the world — 78
2. Distribution of noun classifiers in the languages of the world — 96
3. Distribution of numeral classifiers in the languages of the world — 122
4. Distribution of classifiers in possessive constructions in the languages of the world — 148
5. Distribution of verbal classifiers in the languages of the world — 170

List of Tables

1.1	Shopping list in Japanese	2
1.2	Differences between noun classes and classifiers	6
1.3	Classifiers, their morphological realization, and semantics	7
1.4	Classifiers and their functions	8
2.1	Semantics of noun classes in Proto-Bantu	24
2.2	Semantic features for the gender assignment of inanimate nouns in Cantabrian Spanish	27
2.3	Inflection and derivation	30
2.4	Gender marking in Rumanian	46
2.5	Gender marking in Telugu	46
2.6	Gender agreement in Khinalug	47
2.7	A fragment of the Russian nominal paradigm	48
2.8	Noun classes in Ingush	49
2.9	Noun classes in Ndali	64
2.10	'Pronominal' and 'nominal' noun class systems	68
2.11	*Ka*-class assignment in Paumarí	73
2.12	Two types of noun class (genders) in Mba	75
4.1	Numeral classifiers used with humans in Assamese	102
4.2	Numeral classifiers in Telugu	108
4.3	Classifiers fused with numerals in Kusaiean	108
4.4	Numeral classifiers in Nivkh	109
4.5	Numeral classifiers in Warekena	109
4.6	Numeral classifiers in Squamish	110
5.1	Possessed classifiers in Panare	128
5.2	Systems of two relational classifiers	134
5.3	A system of relational classifiers in Boumaa Fijian	134
5.4	Sample of classifiers in Puluwat	141
5.5	Differences between possessed and relational classifiers	145
5.6	Relational, possessed, and possessor classifier: a comparison	146
6.1	Mescalero Apache classificatory verb categories	155
6.2	Classificatory verbs in Ojibway	155
6.3	Classificatory verbs in Ika	156
6.4	Examples of the use of 'give' in Mescalero Apache	157
6.5	Classificatory verbs in Koyukon: an example	157
6.6	Classificatory verbs in Nevome	158
6.7	Classificatory verbs in Enga	159
6.8	Classificatory verbs in Ku Waru	159
6.9	Verbal classifiers in Waris	166

xxii List of Tables

6.10	Classificatory verbs in Waris	167
6.11	Affixed verbal classifiers in Koyukon	167
7.1	Locative classificatory suffixes in three Carib languages	175
7.2	Article classifiers in Ponca	178
7.3	A sample of demonstratives in Proto-Guaicuruan	181
7.4	Deictic classifiers in Eskimo	182
8.1	Noun classes and noun classifiers in Ngan'gityemerri	186
8.2	Classifiers in Mokilese	187
8.3	Numeral classifiers in Akatek	188
8.4	Noun classifiers in Akatek	188
8.5	Numeral, verbal, and locative classifiers in Palikur	193
8.6	Demonstratives in Palikur (singular)	194
8.7	Gender marking on verbs in Palikur	194
8.8	Properties of classifiers and genders in Palikur	195
8.9	Semantic and functional properties and origin of classifiers in Palikur	197
8.10	Different classifier sets in different environments in one language	202
8.11	Different classifier sets in the same environment in one language	202
9.1	Same set of classifiers in several environments (A–D)	207
9.2	Locative and verbal classifiers in Eyak	209
9.3	Same morphemes in several classifier environments	225
9.4	Environments in which genders and classifiers are used in Baniwa and Tariana	230
9.5	Classifiers in Baniwa	232–4
9.6	Classifiers in Tariana	236–8
9.7	Agreement forms of *kwa-* in Tariana	240
10.1	Personal pronouns in Tamachek	245
10.2	Personal pronouns in Lithuanian	245
10.3	Personal pronouns in Slovene	246
10.4	Personal pronouns in Resígaro and in Bora	247
10.5	Gender in Malto	248
10.6	Classificatory verbs in Tewa and their semantics	251
10.7	Animacy marking on verbs in Jarawara (Arawá)	251
10.8	Personal pronouns in Minangkabau (singular)	253
10.9	Personal pronouns in Spanish	254
10.10	Personal pronouns in Tariana	254
10.11	Paradigm of Latin *is* 'this'	256
10.12	Possessed classifiers and speech styles in Ponapean	261
10.13	Examples of possessed classifiers in common and humiliative speech in Ponapean	261
10.14	Paradigm of *dela-t'* 'do' in past tense in Russian	264
10.15	Paradigm of *katav* 'write' in Modern Hebrew	264
10.16	Variable noun class assignment in Maung	267
10.17	Classifiers and their interaction with other grammatical categories	269

11.1	Examples of physical properties in noun class assignment	277
11.2	Semantic basis of gender choice in German: an illustration	280
11.3	Noun classes in Bantu	282
11.4	Shape-based classes in ChiBemba	282
11.5	Size-based classes in ChiBemba	282
11.6	Noun classifiers for humans and deities in Jacaltec	284
11.7	Noun classifiers for non-humans in Jacaltec	285
11.8	Hole classifiers in Tzeltal	289
11.9	Function-based classifiers in Burmese	291
11.10	Verbal classifiers in Ojibway and Cree	297
11.11	Chipewyan (Athabaskan) classificatory verbs	298
11.12	Classificatory existential verbs in Kamoro (Asmat)	299
11.13	Preferred semantic parameters in classifiers	306
12.1	Burmese numeral classifiers for inanimate objects	312
12.2	Animate classifiers in Burmese	315
12.3	Verified superordinate–subordinate pairs in Japanese numeral classifiers	317
12.4	Reclassification of an inanimate noun in Burmese	319
13.1	Groups of nouns which tend to develop to classifiers	354
13.2	Numeral classifers from body parts in Totonac	356
13.3	Noun classifiers derived from common nouns in Mam	357
13.4	Generic classifiers in Minangkabau	359
13.5	Semantic groups of verbs which develop into classifiers	362
13.6	A sample of verbal classifiers in Imonda	363
13.7	Historical changes in Mandarin Chinese classifiers	410
13.8	Typical sources for noun categorization devices	412
15.1	Scope of classifier types	427
15.2	Assignment of classifiers	429
15.3	Morphological realization of classifiers	430

List of Diagrams

2.1	Tendencies for animacy-based and shape-based noun classes	76
6.1	Verbal classifiers in Palikur	164
7.1	Locative classifiers in Palikur	173
7.2	Classifiers with spatial semantics in Toba	179
8.1	Semantics of numeral classifiers in Minangkabau	189
9.1	Semantics and form of demonstratives with classifiers in Tariana	239
9.2	Semantics and form of articles with classifiers in Tariana	240
10.1	Animacy hierarchy and expression of number	247
11.1	Gender assignment in Manambu	278
11.2	Extendedness in Proto-Bantu noun classes	283
11.3	Numeral classifiers in Totonac	289
11.4	Numeral classifiers for inanimates in Palikur	290
11.5	Interaction of semantic domains in numeral classifiers in Minangkabau	292
11.6	Classificatory verbs in Western Apache	298
11.7	Semantics of fourteen numeral classifiers in Akatek	302
11.8	Semantics of fourteen noun classifiers in Akatek	302
11.9	Polygrammaticalization of *batang* 'tree' in Minangkabau	302
11.10	Classifiers in Nambiquara	304
11.11	Semantics of classifiers in Kilivila	304
12.1	Structure of the *tua* category in Thai	314
12.2	Factors regulating the use of classifiers in Malay	324
12.3	Semantic network of the *nge*-class in Maasina Fulfulde	346
12.4	Gender pronouns in former and contemporary prescribed English usage	350
13.1	Evolution of gender markers (1)	367
13.2	Evolution of gender markers (2)	368
13.3	Phonological reduction in the development of noun classifiers in Mixtec	376
13.4	Singular and plural noun classes in Grebo	377
13.5	Gender in Proto-Dravidian (singular)	378
13.6	Gender in Proto-South-Dravidian (singular)	378

List of Abbreviations

A	subject of a transitive verb	DEF	definite
		DEIC	deictic
ABL	ablative	DEM	demonstrative
ABS	absolutive	DER	derivational
ACC	accusative	DET	determiner
ADJ	adjectivizer	DIM	diminutive
ADV	adverb	DIR	directional
AFF	affix	DIST	distal
AGR	agreement	DS	different subject
ALIM	alimentary possession	DU	dual
AN, ANIM	animate	DUR	durative
ANA	anaphoric	EMPH	emphatic
ARG.MAN	argument manipulating derivation	ERG	ergative
		EXCL	exclusive
ART	article	EXT	extended
ASP	aspect	EYEW.PRES	eyewitness present
ATT	attributive		
AUG	augmented	F, FEM, f, fem	feminine
AUX	auxiliary	FRUST	frustrative
BENEFACT	benefactive	FUT	future
CAUS	causative	GEN	generic
CL	classifier	GN	genitive
CL:HAB	classifier: habitat	HAB	habitual
CMPL	completed	HON	honorific
COLL	collective	HORIZ	horizontal
COMIT	comitative	HUM	human
COMPL	completive	HUMIL	humiliative
CONC	concordial	IMAG	imaginary
CONJ	conjunctive	IMP	impersonal
CONT	continuous	IMPF	imperfective
CONTR	contrast	INAN, INANIM	inanimate
CURV	curved	INCL, incl	inclusive
CV	connective	INDEF	indefinite
CYLIDR	cylindrical	INS	instrumental
DAT	dative	INT	intensifier
DEC	declarative	INTER	interrogative
		IRREG	irregular form or shape

List of Abbreviations

LIG	ligature vowel	PRED	predicative
LINK	linker	PREF	prefix
LIV.BEING	living being	PRES	present
LOC	locative	prim	primary
M, MASC, m, masc	masculine	PRO	1/2/3 person proform
MENS	mensural classifier	PROB	probablility
MIN	minimal	PROGR	progressive
MOD	modal	pron	pronoun
N, NEUT	neuter	PURP	purposive
NCL	noun class	PX	proximity
NEG	negative	QUAL	qualifier
NF, nf	non-feminine	QUANT	quantifier
NOM	nominative	RE	referential
NONPOSS, NPOSS	non-possessed	REC	reciprocal
NP	nonpast	REFL	reflexive
NUM.CL	numeral classifier	REL	relativizer
O	object of a transitive verb	REL.CL	relational classifier
		REM.P.INFR	remote past inferred
		RES	resultative
		S	subject of an intransitive verb
OBJ	object	sec	secondary
PART	participle	sg, SG	singular
PASS	passive	sp	species
pcl	paucal or plural number	SUBJ	subject
		SUBORD	subordinating
		SUFF	suffix
		TA	tense-aspect marker
PERF	perfective	TAM	tense-aspect-mood marker
pf	perfect		
PI	past imperfective	TH	thematic
		THEM.CONTR	thematic contrast
PL	plural	TNS	tense
POSS	possessive	TOP	topic
POSS.CL	possessive classifier	TOP.ADV	topic advancing voice
PP	past perfective	TOP.O	topical O
		VB	verbalizer
PRECONT	precontemporary tense	VCL	verbal classifier
		VERT	vertical

1 Preliminaries

1.1. General remarks

Almost all languages have some grammatical means for the linguistic categorization of nouns and nominals. The term 'classifiers' will be used here as an umbrella label for a wide range of noun categorization devices. Different types of classifier can be distinguished by their grammatical status, degree of grammaticalization, conditions for use, meaning, kinds of origin, mode of acquisition, and tendencies towards loss.

Classifiers and noun categorization devices have long been a particular focus of interest in functional typology. The urgent need to establish a comprehensive typology of classifiers is motivated by a number of factors. First, a large amount of new data on classifier systems has been produced during the past decades; on the one hand, this data needs to be systematized, and on the other hand, its existence creates the opportunity of providing a typology with reasonable scope and validity. Second, due to the lack of an overarching unified analysis of classifier systems in the languages of the world, there exists a pervasive terminological confusion in the literature which makes difficult the cross-linguistic comparison of noun categorization devices as well as the analysis of new data. This book is an attempt to provide such a comprehensive approach insofar as this is possible at our present stage of knowledge about the structure and mechanisms of human languages and human cognition. The book is also intended to serve as a guide for analytic work on previously undescribed languages and their mechanisms for noun categorization.

Examples of different kinds of classifier are provided in §1.2. In §1.3 I briefly describe the theoretical framework used in this study, together with the database and sources. The next section provides a short overview of previous approaches to noun categorization which are precursors to the approach adopted here. The methodological basis for this approach is outlined in §1.5. The structure of this book is outlined in §1.6.

1.2. Classifiers: an illustration

Classifiers come in different guises.

Some languages have grammatical agreement classes, based on such core semantic characteristics as animacy, sex, or humanness. These are called

2 Classifiers

NOUN CLASSES, or GENDERS. The number of noun classes varies—from two, as in Portuguese (examples below), to ten, as in Bantu, or even to several dozen, as in some South American languages. Examples 1.1 and 1.2, from Portuguese, illustrate masculine and feminine genders which are marked on the noun itself and on the accompanying article and adjective.

1.1. o   menin-o   bonit-o
     ART:MASC.SG   child-MASC.SG beautiful-MASC.SG
     'the beautiful boy'

1.2. a   menin-a   bonit-a
     ART:FEM.SG   child-FEM.SG beautiful-FEM.SG
     'the beautiful girl'

A classifier can just categorize the noun by itself, as in the following example from Yidiny, an Australian language (Dixon 1982: 192 ff.). This is a NOUN CLASSIFIER.

1.3. bama   waguja
     CL:PERSON   man
     'a man'

Other languages have special morphemes which only appear next to a numeral, or a quantifier. They may categorize the referent of a noun in terms of its animacy, shape, and other inherent properties. These are NUMERAL CLASSIFIERS. The way they are used is exemplified with a shopping list in Japanese (Rie Hasada 1995) given in Table 1.1.

TABLE 1.1. *Shopping list in Japanese*

Shopping list	Numeral	Classifier	Meaning of classifier
nasu (eggplant)	*nana* (7)	*-ko*	CL:SMALL.EQUIDIMENSIONAL
kyuuri (cucumber)	*hachi* (8)	*-hon*	CL:ELONGATED
hamu (ham)	*juu* (10)	*-mai*	CL:SHEETLIKE

A special morpheme may characterize a possessed noun in a possessive construction, as in 1.4, from Tariana, a South American language from the Arawak family. This is a POSSESSED classifier.

1.4. tʃinu   nu-ite
     dog   1SG-CL:ANIMATE
     'my dog'

A special morpheme in a possessive construction may characterize the way in which the referent of a possessed noun relates to that of the possessor. This is illustrated in 1.5 and 1.6, from Fijian, an Austronesian language (Lichtenberk 1983a: 157–8). Such morphemes, underlined in 1.5 and 1.6, are called RELATIONAL CLASSIFIERS.

1.5. na   me-qu   yaqona
     ART CL:DRINKABLE-my kava
     'my kava' (which I intend to drink)

1.6. na   no-qu   yaqona
     ART CL:GENERAL-my kava
     'my kava' (that I grew, or that I will sell)

VERBAL CLASSIFIERS appear on the verb, but they categorize a noun, which is typically in S (intransitive subject) or O (direct object) function, in terms of its shape, consistency, and animacy. Example 1.7, from Waris, a Papuan language (Brown 1981: 96), shows how the classifier *put-* 'round objects' is used with the verb 'get' to characterize its O argument, 'coconut'.

1.7. sa   ka-m   put-ra-ho-o
     coconut 1SG-to VCL:ROUND-GET-BENEFACT-IMPERATIVE
     'Give me a coconut' (lit. 'coconut to-me round.one-give')

There are two more, much rarer, kinds of classifiers. Those which occur on locative adpositions, are called LOCATIVE CLASSIFIERS. This is illustrated with 1.8 and 1.9, from Palikur, an Arawak language from Brazil.

1.8. pi-wan   min
     2SG-arm   on+VERT
     'on your (vertical) arm'

1.9. ah   peu
     tree on+BRANCH.LIKE
     'on (branch-like) tree'

Classifiers which are associated with deictics and articles are called DEICTIC CLASSIFIERS. Examples of deictic classifiers, from Mandan, a Siouan language (Barron and Serzisko 1982: 99), are given in 1.10 and 1.11.

1.10. dɛ-mãk
      'this one (lying)'

1.11. dɛ-nak
      'this one (sitting)'

The term 'classifier systems' is used to denote a continuum of methods of noun categorization. Well-known systems, such as the lexical numeral classifiers of Southeast Asia, on the one hand, and the highly grammaticalized gender agreement classes of Indo-European languages, on the other, are the extremes of this continuum. They can have a similar semantic basis; and one type can develop out of the other. Parameters used for the proposed typology of classifiers are discussed in §1.5.

1.3. Theoretical framework, data, and sources

The aim of this book is to present a functional-typological, empirically based account of noun categorization devices across the languages of the world. The analysis is cast in terms of basic linguistic theory, 'the fundamental theoretical apparatus that underlies all work in describing languages and formulating universals about the nature of human language', where 'justification must be given for every piece of analysis, with a full train of argumentation' (Dixon 1997: 132; see also Dixon 1994: p. xvi). The categories, and their properties, considered here are developed inductively.[1]

This study is based on examination of the grammars of about 500 languages representing each major language family and each linguistic area across the globe. A large database has been used, since the presence or absence of a particular kind of classifier system is often an inherited property of a language family or a diffusional property of a linguistic area. Special attention has been paid to data that has recently become available on the languages of South America (which by and large have not been included in previous typological studies of classifier systems). Data on the following languages come from my own fieldwork: Tariana, Baniwa, Warekena, Bare (Arawak family), Tucano, Piratapuya (East Tucano family), Paumarí (Arawá family), from Brazil; and Manambu (Ndu family, East Sepik) from Papua New Guinea.

I have not restricted myself to considering just some samples of the available set of languages. Rather, I have looked at every language on which I could find data and which has noun categorization devices. This approach (sometimes called 'sample of convenience') allowed me to make the typology proposed here as comprehensive as it could be at our present level of knowledge about the languages of the world, without imposing artificial limitations dictated by this or that 'sampling strategy'. Owing to limitations of space, I could not cite all the examples of occurrence of every particular phenomenon. I usually provide a particularly illustrative example, and mention others. If a certain phenomenon is found in more than half of the languages under consideration I call it 'relatively frequent'; if it is found

---

[1] Cf. Bloomfield (1933: 20) 'The only useful generalizations about language are inductive generalizations. Features which we think ought to be universal may be absent from the very next language that becomes accessible. . . . The fact that some features are, at any rate, widespread, is worthy of notice and calls for an explanation; when we have adequate data about many languages, we shall have to return to the problem of general grammar and to explain these similarities and divergences, but this study, when it comes, will not be speculative but inductive.'

in a restricted number of languages (one to ten), I cite all of them and indicate its rarity. Note, however, that what appears rare to us at the present stage of knowledge may turn out to be frequent when we start learning more about hitherto little-known languages and areas. This is the reason why I choose not to give any statistical counts at this stage. Five hundred is no more than about one-tenth of all human languages, and it seems most judicious to follow a qualitative approach at the present time, postponing quantitative analysis until more data is available and can be assessed.

Lists of languages, of language families, and of linguistic areas considered, are given in the index. I chose not to enumerate classifier types found in each particular language referred to in the index in order not to impose my analytic solution onto a language which is not my area of expertise (readers can do this for themselves). Examples which come from my own work are not followed by the indication of a source. I preserve the orthography of the source (or use an accepted practical orthography, transcription, or transliteration) unless otherwise indicated.

1.4. Approaches to the typology of classifiers

Classifiers and noun categorization systems have long been a particular focus of interest in functional typology. They provide a unique insight into how people categorize the world through their language. The study of classifiers and noun categorization systems is intrinsically connected with many issues which are crucial in modern linguistics, such as agreement; processes in language development and obsolescence; the distinction between inflection and derivation; and types of possessive construction.

Noun classes and genders, on the one hand, and numeral classifiers, on the other, have been the object of linguistic investigation for as long as languages with these categories have been studied. The first overview full of fascinating insights—albeit preliminary—was provided by Royen (1929). A number of linguists have had ideas about similarities between different systems of noun categorization devices; for instance, Worsley (1954) pointed out functional similarities between Bantu-type noun class systems and noun classes and numeral and verbal classifiers in Anindilyakwa, an Australian language.

The systematic typological study of classifiers started only about two decades ago. Studies of classifiers divide into two kinds: attempts to create a general typological picture, and studies of individual types. The two cannot be easily separated, since each discovery of a new type provides feedback into the general typological picture.

6   Classifiers

During the last two decades, there have been a number of proposals for a semantic and grammatical typology of noun categorization systems (often also called 'noun classification'; e.g. Dixon 1968; 1982; Denny 1976; Allan 1977; Craig 1986a). Recently the typological parameters of classifiers and other agreement categories have had to be revised in the light of new data, especially those from previously undescribed South American Indian languages (e.g. Derbyshire and Payne 1990; Craig 1992, forthcoming; Corbett 1991).

Greenberg undertook a pioneering study of classifiers, in his paper on numeral classifiers and substantival number (1972). Though this paper does not overtly suggest any typology of noun categorization devices, various classificatory phenomena are mentioned alongside numeral classifiers (e.g. relational classifiers in Oceanic languages and verbal classifiers); he also suggested a correlation between the existence of numeral classifiers in a language and other grammatical categories, such as obligatory expression of number.

Further attempts at global typologies of classifiers include Adams and Conklin (1973), Denny (1976), Allan (1977), and Serzisko (1982). Dixon (1982) put forward an important suggestion for distinguishing between the two extremes of noun categorization devices: obligatory grammatical noun class systems, and semi-open lexical-like systems of classifiers (e.g. noun classifiers and numeral classifiers). Dixon (1982; 1986) was also the first to have explicitly stated a correlation between language type and noun categorization devices (that classifiers tend to be a property of isolating languages, while noun classes tend to be present in fusional and agglutinating languages); he showed how one type (noun classifiers) can develop into another (noun classes). The distinctions he drew between noun classes and classifiers are shown in Table 1.2.

TABLE 1.2. *Differences between noun classes and classifiers*

	Noun classes	Classifiers
Size	Small finite set	Large number
Realization	Closed grammatical system	Free forms
Scope	Marking is never entirely within the noun word	Never any reference outside the noun phrase

Source: Dixon (1982; 1986).

Allan (1977) provided a useful overview of noun categorization, for the first time explicitly stating that the following types of noun categorization device belong to the same domain: noun classes (or concordial classifiers), numeral classifiers, verbal classifiers (including separate morphemes and suppletive classificatory verbs), possessive and intralocative classifiers.

Serzisko (1982) considered gender, noun class, and numeral categorization as a part of a continuum of 'classificatory techniques' (under the typological dimension of 'apprehension'), working out correlations between these and other categories (such as number), and comparing them as to their grammaticality, semantic complexity, and variability.

A very important though frequently underestimated contribution to the typology of noun categorization is found in Seiler and Stachowiak (1982) and Seiler and Lehmann (1982), followed by a summary in Seiler (1986), and also in Seiler's (1983) book on possession. These volumes are full of insightful case studies; also, Barron and Serzisko (1982), followed by a summary in Seiler (1986), provided the first consistent evidence in favour of the existence of deictic (or article) classifiers in Siouan languages. Seiler (1986) was the first to put forward the view of various kinds of classificatory techniques—including numeral classifiers, verbal classifiers, noun classes and 'article' classifiers—as continua within the broad dimension of apprehension.

Craig (1986a) was a major contribution to typological studies on noun categorization, their role in cognition and culture. In particular, noun classifiers as a special type have been established on the basis of her work. A new view on the typology of noun categorization devices was provided by Derbyshire and Payne (1990) in their survey of typologically unusual systems of noun categorization devices in Lowland Amazonian languages. Amazonian languages were shown to systematically allow more than one— and often more than two—types of noun categorization simultaneously.

Further typological studies on classifiers include Nichols (1989b), Kiyomi (1992), and Croft (1994). These focused on different parameters. Nichols concentrated on the morphosyntactic realization of classifiers, pointing out the differences between agreeing and non-agreeing noun categorization devices. Kiyomi (1992) attempted to establish morphosyntactic correlates of classifier realization (with free or with bound morphemes) for the main classifier types, and argued that neither animacy nor shape can be established as defining semantic parameters for a typology of noun categorization devices. See Table 1.3.

TABLE 1.3. *Classifiers, their morphological realization, and semantics*

Free morpheme classifiers	Bound morpheme classifiers
Numeral classifiers (Animate, Shape)	Concordial classifiers (Animate, Shape)
Non-numeral classifiers (Animate only)	Predicate classifiers (Animate, Shape)
	Intralocative classifiers (Shape only)

Source: Kiyomi (1992: 33).

Croft (1994) reanalysed classifier types, associating each of them with semantic and pragmatic functions (he disregarded a few problematic classifier types, such as locative and deictic classifiers, and systems of verbal classifiers with no animacy distinctions; see Chapters 6, 7, and 11 below). See Table 1.4.

TABLE 1.4. *Classifiers and their functions*

Classifier type	Semantic/pragmatic function
Noun class	Determination (reference)
Numeral classifiers	Enumeration
Possessive classifiers	Possession
Predicate classifiers	Spatial predication

Source: Croft (1994: 147).

Recent overviews of the typology of classifier systems can be found in an in-depth study of Japanese numeral classifiers by Downing (1996), and in a detailed analysis of classifiers in Kilivila (Austronesian) by Senft (1996).

Craig (1992; forthcoming) argued for the existence of the following types of classifiers based primarily on the morphosyntactic loci in which they occur: numeral classifiers; noun classifiers; noun class and gender; verbal classifiers; genitive classifiers. Craig (forthcoming: 42) also mentioned the existence of a 'marginal' classifier type—classifiers which occur with articles or deictics. Further arguments in favour of this morphosyntactic typology include cooccurrence of types within one language, different semantics for distinct classifier types, and different degrees of grammaticalization of classifiers. Importantly, classifiers are not presented as discrete types, but rather as focal points on various continua. This prototype-continuum approach, which implies a gradient rather than categorical treatment of properties of classifier systems, is taken up in the present study (see §1.5).

Craig's approach was elaborated upon in a case study of classifiers in Tariana by Aikhenvald (1994a), and in Palikur by Aikhenvald and Green (1998). The typology proposed in this book is largely based on the schema established by Craig.

However, the current literature is somewhat confusing as far as generally adopted definitions and concepts are concerned. The way linguists of different traditions and theoretical trends use different terms, such as GENDER, NOUN CLASS, CLASSIFIER, can be misleading.

The terms GENDER and NOUN CLASS are sometimes used interchangeably (see §2.1). Corbett (1991) uses 'gender' as a cover term for agreement classes, while Evans (1997: 109) opts for 'noun class' to cover the same phenomenon. GENDER has also been used in a quite different way. In the Athabaskan linguistic tradition the term 'gender' is used to refer to verbal classifiers which mark agreement with intransitive subject or transitive object, and characterize the referent noun in terms of shape and form (Thompson 1993). In the Bantuist tradition, the term 'noun class' is used to refer to a set of singular and of corresponding plural forms of a noun and the agreement markers they trigger on modifiers and on the predicate, while the pairs of singular and plural markers are considered 'genders'. For instance, Singular Noun Class 1 forms one 'gender' with its plural counterpart, Noun Class 2 (see e.g. Table 2.1).

The term 'verbal classifier' is sometimes used by Australianists (Silverstein 1986; Green 1989; Reid 1990 and p.c.; Rumsey 1982; Donaldson 1980 and others) to refer to a closed class of inflected verbs which typically carry grammatical marking, and 'classify' the lexical verb by delimiting its aspect or scope (e.g. 'do something on the surface', 'do something with hands', 'do moving up'). There is typically a small class of inflected verbs with fairly generic meanings (often called 'simple' verbs, e.g. Rumsey 1982, for Ungarinjin; Silverstein 1986) which together with a 'main verb' (or 'co-verb') form a complex verb. In Ngiyambaa (Donaldson 1980: 201–24; Dixon 2002: 183) a main verb 'dig', 'sew', or 'spear' takes the classifier 'pierce'; and a verb such as 'take', or 'pick up' requires a classifier 'do with hands'. This usage of 'classifier' has some similarity with noun categorization via generic noun classifiers: a simple, or 'classifier' verb defines the generic scope of action, and the main verb specifies it; similarly, a noun classifier indicates general reference (e.g. 'person' for people or 'animal' for animates), and the specific noun following it further specifies this reference. This usage is completely different from the one adopted here; however, as pointed out by Ian Green and Nicholas Reid (p.c.), simple verbs may develop further semantic specifications whereby they start being used to characterize the particular kind of instrument or location. Further study is needed to delineate 'noun classifying' functions of simple verbs in Australian languages.

The term 'verbal classifiers' is used in another, completely different way by some specialists in the languages of South and Southeast Asia. Haas (1942: 205) calls 'words indicating how many times an event takes place' verbal classifiers; i.e. in a sentence like 'he ran twice' 'twice' is considered a verbal classifier. This term is employed in a similar way for Newari (Tibeto-Burman) by Bhaskararao and Joshi (1985: 17), and for Mulao, a Tai language, by Jun and Guoqiao (1993: 48).

The term 'classifier' is used in yet another way in the Athabaskan linguistic tradition, where it refer to markers of voice and change of transitivity which have nothing to do with categorization of nouns.

Some authors simply avoid the term 'classifier'. Moussay (1981) uses the term 'spécificatif' for numeral classifiers and 'catégoriel' for noun classifiers in Minangkabau.

A number of the general statements about different types of classifier have recently been shown to be erroneous. Some of the previously accepted universals and general tendencies do not, in fact, hold. For example, Dixon (1982: 220) suggested that languages could not have classifiers and gender as separate categories, and stated: 'no example is known of a language with two distinct systems of noun classes' (see also Craig 1986a; 1986b; 1986c). Recent work on South American and Papuan languages has shown that classifiers and genders do cooccur, and that languages can have two distinct systems of noun classes. For instance, Baniwa, a North Arawak language from Brazil, has a system of two genders, and also a system of over 40 noun classes (see Chapters 8 and 9 below).

The dichotomy between a concordial noun class as an 'obligatory grammatical system where each noun chooses one from a small number of possibilities' and noun categorization as a system where 'noun classifiers are always separate lexemes which may be included with a noun in certain syntactic environment' (Dixon 1986: 105) appears to be rather simplistic, especially in the light of the data from Amazonian languages. The presence of noun classes had often been associated with a fusional or agglutinating morphological type, and classifiers (especially numeral classifiers) were viewed as a typical property of isolating languages—a premise that also appears to be a little simplistic when viewed cross-linguistically.

Finally, particular terms, such as 'classifier', 'noun classifier', or 'noun categorization system', are frequently used by different authors either in a different way for different types of system or as a cover term for any kind of system. Thus, it is not always clear what is a classifier and what is a concordial noun class in each particular case.

During the last two decades, a number of studies of specific classifier types and individual languages have made an important contribution to an overall typological picture. Corbett's (1991) book on GENDER (which is used as a cover term for NOUN CLASS SYSTEMS) is an important, almost encyclopedic, overview of this type of noun categorization. It is almost impossible to enumerate all the studies of noun class systems in African languages; however, the collection *La Classification nominale dans les langues négro-africaines* (1967) and Hyman's (1980) book on noun classes in Grasslands Bantu languages remain the main reference on the subject. Heine's (1982a) article 'African Noun Class Systems' remains the main reference for the typology of noun classes in African languages. Noun class systems in Papuan languages are described by Foley (1986); some of these are extremely unusual—their assignment may be largely based on phonological form (see Foley 1986; 1991; Conrad 1996; Dobrin 1999; Nekitel ms). Work on noun classes in Australian languages includes ground-breaking studies by Dixon (1972; 1982), Sands (1995), and the papers in Harvey and Reid (1997).

NOUN CLASSIFIERS have been introduced into the typological picture comparatively recently; their properties have been discussed at length by Dixon (1982), Craig (1986a; 1992; 2000), and in more specific case studies, e.g. Zavala (1992; forthcoming), Reid (1997), and Sands (1995). In addition, Payne (1990) and Derbyshire and Payne (1990) considered the problem of noun classifiers in Amazonian languages.

There is an immense corpus of literature on NUMERAL CLASSIFIERS, especially in Southeast and East Asian languages. Adams (1989) and Downing (1996) provide in-depth discussions of problems relevant for the cross-linguistic definition of numeral classifiers (further, more language-specific, or area-specific case studies include Barz and Diller 1985; Goral 1978; Bisang 1993; 1996; Pe 1965; T'sou 1976; Conklin 1981).

The existence of CLASSIFIERS IN POSSESSIVE CONSTRUCTIONS in Oceanic languages was first recognized by Codrington (1885). The credit for the first systematic study of relational classifiers and how they differ from numeral classifiers in Oceanic languages goes to Lichtenberk (1983a); among further studies one must mention Harrison (1976) for Mokilese; Dixon (1988) for Fijian; Pawley and Sayaba (1990) for Wayan, a Western Fijian dialect; and Rehg (1981) and Keating (1997) for Ponapean. Seiler (1983) provides an insightful analysis of noun categorization in possessive constructions and of the differences which can be noted between classification devices which characterize the ways in which nouns can be possessed, or handled (relational classifiers) and devices which describe properties of possessed nouns (possessed classifiers, in our terminology). Carlson and Payne (1989) attempted a broader survey of relational classifiers in some North American Indian languages (Yuman, Uto-Aztecan) and some South American Indian languages (some Carib, Tupí-Guaraní, and Jê languages); further data on relational and possessive classifiers in South American languages can be found in Rodrigues (1997, on Kipeá, an extinct language of the Kariri family, Macro-Jê, South America), Rodrigues (1999), Barnes (1990), Martins (1994), and Aikhenvald (1994a).

VERBAL CLASSIFIERS and SUPPLETIVE CLASSIFICATORY VERBS have been the subject of extensive study based on the facts of specific language families. Seminal studies of classificatory verbs in Athabaskan languages include Hoijer (1945), Davidson et al. (1963), Krauss (1968), Basso (1968), Carter (1976), and Thompson (1993); also see Mithun (1986) and Seiler (1986). There is extensive literature on classificatory verbs in other North American Indian languages, e.g. Kiowa-Tanoan (Speirs 1974) and Cherokee (Blankenship 1996; 1997). Verbal classifiers in South American languages are discussed in Derbyshire and Payne (1990); verbal classifiers in Papuan languages are considered by Lang (1975), Brown (1981), and Merlan et al.

(1997). For verbal classifiers in Mesoamerican and South American Indian languages see also Suárez (1983), Gonçalves (1987), and Mithun (1984; 1986).

A few studies have been undertaken on rare and problematic classifier types. The existence of DEICTIC classifiers as a special type has been shown by Klein (1979), Vidal (1995; 1997), and Céria and Sândalo (1995), for the languages of the Guiacuruan family of Argentina and Brazil. Barron and Serzisko (1982) describe article classifiers for Siouan languages. Further data from South American languages in support of the existence of deictic classifiers are given by Aikhenvald (1994a; 2000). The existence of a special type of LOCATIVE classifier was first suggested by Allan (1977) (the term he used was 'intralocative'); his results were criticized by Croft (1994). In fact, locative classifiers have only been found in a limited number of South American languages (to which Croft did not have access), e.g. Palikur (Arawak), Dâw (Makú), and Carib languages (see Aikhenvald 1994a; 1996b).

Up until now no systematic attempt has been made to consider multiple classifier systems in a cross-linguistic perspective (see Chapter 8 below). Previous studies have not taken account of the unusual types of multiple classifier system found in South American Indian languages. (Systems of this kind were only briefly mentioned by Dixon 1982; Craig 1992; forthcoming; and Lichtenberk 1983a.) Among descriptions of multiple classifier systems from other parts of the world one should mention Hurd (1977) on the Nasioi language from Bougainville, and Worsley (1954) on Anindilyakwa, an Australian language from Groote Eylandt. Recently, the number of studies of multiple classifier languages has increased, e.g. Gonçalves (1987), on Munduruku, a Tupí language from Amazonia; Bisang (1993) on Hmong, a Miao-Yao language from China; Onishi (1994) on Motuna, a Papuan language; Foris (1993, 2000) on Sochiapan Chinantec from Mexico; Vidal (1997) on Pilagá, a Guaicuruan language from Argentina; Shepard (1997) on Machiguenga, an Arawak language from Peru; and the survey of multiple classifier systems in Arawak languages in Aikhenvald (1996b). Another problem for multiple classifier systems is 'fuzzy' boundaries between types which makes it difficult to attribute a given language to a particular type (see e.g. the discussion in Vidal 1997).

To summarize—in spite of the considerable work already accomplished, a new, integrated typological framework is needed to account for all the types of noun categorization device and the new language data which have appeared on the linguistic scene during the last decades. This is attempted in the present volume.

1.5. Parameters for the typology of classifiers

All human languages have some ways of categorizing nouns and their referents in terms of their semantic and syntactic properties. The purpose of this book is to investigate how languages employ classifiers to provide a semantically based categorization, which may have far-reaching implications concerning human cognitive mechanisms.

Classifiers are defined as morphemes which occur 'in surface structures under specifiable conditions', denote 'some salient perceived or imputed characteristics of the entity to which an associated noun refers' (Allan 1977: 285), and are restricted to particular construction types known as 'classifier constructions'. Classifier constructions are understood as morphosyntactic units (which may be noun phrases of different kinds, verb phrases, or clauses) which require the presence of a particular kind of a morpheme, the choice of which is dictated by the semantic characteristics of the referent of the head of a noun phrase.

Nouns and their referents can also be categorized in various other ways, e.g. by choosing different number forms for nouns with different semantics; by assigning the nouns to different declension classes; or by using different pronominalization strategies. These strategies of noun categorization (sometimes also called 'noun classification') are not considered classifiers. However, they may be used in a way functionally similar to classifiers, and they often reflect comparable semantic parameters. Historically, they may go back to classifier systems. Examples are given in Appendix 1.

The main purpose of this book is to present a typology of classifiers primarily based on the morphosyntactic loci (or environments) of classifier morphemes (elaborating on the approach in Craig 1992; forthcoming). This implies establishing types of noun categorization system which acquire surface realization in natural languages. As a result, the typology is inclusive in that it covers types of classifier morpheme and construction types in which they are required, and categorization types. We start with a typology of classifier morphemes and the constructions in which they are employed, and then proceed to uncover a link between these and universal and language specific parameters of categorization types. This is the basis for distinguishing definitional properties and contingent characteristics of classifier types.

The terminology chosen for each classifier type relies as much as possible on currently accepted terminology. If there are several terms in use, I employ the one which is most current and most transparently describes the morphosyntactic locus of a classifier type (e.g. I use 'verbal classifier' rather than 'verb-incorporated classifier').

Following Craig (forthcoming: 43), classifier types are not viewed as discrete entities, but rather as focal points on continua of various properties used for the present typology (see below). As the result, definitional as well

14   Classifiers

as secondary, or contingent, properties of different classifier types will be shown to be gradient rather than categorical; this accounts for the existence of instances of classifier systems which 'do not fit squarely into any of the types' (Craig forthcoming: 43). As Frawley (1992: 30) puts it,

if we look at ordinary language, we find that it is full of gradient phenomena, more technically known as *fuzziness*. . . . The insight behind fuzziness indicates that categories have vague boundaries and are internally organised from central focal values, the *prototype* (Rosch 1973, 1975a, b), to less focal instances and fringe values. As the centrality of the category fades, . . . criteria for membership in the category are less decisively applied, and categories merge into each other.

Consequently, classifier types outlined and argued for in this study correspond to *prototypes*, or *focal instances*, which display all the definitional and most of the contingent properties of a type. Less focal instances represent various points on *continua* for different parameters of a typology of noun categorization; these display varying degrees of the prototypical properties of each type. In describing and analysing the data on noun categorization devices in a given language, it is important to situate them within the continua of various gradient properties rather than to try and fit them into the mould of cross-linguistically established 'types'.

This prototype-continuum approach is also justified by historical facts about classifier systems—it is well known that distinct classifier types 'blend into one another through time' (Craig forthcoming: 43). These points will be amply illustrated within the present study; they are summarized in Chapter 15.

The following dimensions will be employed to establish focal points on the typological continuum of noun categorization devices.

(A) Morphosyntactic locus of coding

A noun categorization device can be realized in different morphosyntactic loci, that is, on the head, or on all—or just some—of the dependents. We will pay particular attention to languages which use different sets of classifier morphemes (often with different semantic and other properties) in several morphosyntactic environments. The coexistence of these sets in one language constitutes a strong argument in favour of the proposed typology, since this indicates the independent existence and independent development of different noun categorization devices in several morphosyntactic environments in one language.

Some kinds of noun categorization device have several distinct subtypes coexisting within one language: one set of noun classes may be used in one environment, and a somewhat different set in another. For instance, many Arawak languages of South America have a small system based on the masculine/feminine distinction realized on verbal cross-referencing markers and on demonstratives, while adjectival modifiers show a large system of agreement noun classes. Systems of this kind are called 'split' systems; they may represent potential new 'focal points' for developing further classifier types.

(B) Scope, or domain of categorization

Noun categorization devices can refer to nouns within noun phrases of different structures (modifier-head, possessive noun phrases, or adpositional noun phrases), or within a verb phrase. They can also refer to different constituents (e.g. possessed noun or possessor; A, S, O, or an oblique argument). Thus, one can say that in 1.7 it is the O constituent, 'coconut', that is being categorized by the morpheme *put* 'classifier: round', and thus it constitutes the scope, or domain, of this classifier morpheme.

(C) Principles of choice, or 'assignment' of noun categorization devices

The choice of a classifier may depend on some semantic properties of the referent of the noun they categorize. However, it can also depend on other properties of a noun (e.g. morphological or phonological).

(D) Kind of surface realization

Some noun categorization devices are realized with an affix or a clitic, while others often appear as separate words.

(E) Agreement

Some noun categorization devices involve agreement, and some do not. Agreement is understood as a requirement in covariance between grammatical meanings of grammatical morphemes (cf. Steele 1978: 610; Lehmann 1982: 203; see §2.4 below). Categories which involve agreement are 'syntactic' (or 'inflectional') in nature.

(F) Markedness Relations

Some noun categorization devices have a functionally and/or a formally unmarked term; while others tend not to.

(G) Degree of Grammaticalization and Lexicalization

Some noun categorization devices are highly grammaticalized closed sets while others tend to involve a lexical choice. A more lexical kind of noun categorization can become grammaticalized.

(H) Interaction with other grammatical categories

Different types of noun categorization device tend to show different dependencies with other grammatical categories (such as number, or case, or verbal categories).

(I) Semantic organization of the system

Noun categorization in the languages of the world is based on a number of universal parameters (e.g. 'human' versus 'non-human'). However, noun categorization devices differ in terms of a number of other parameters, termed their 'preferred semantics'. They also differ as to the organization of their systems: in some, but not in others, every noun has to be assigned a classifier. They also differ in the degree of their semantic transparency and in the syntactic and discourse-pragmatic functions they perform. Classifiers of different types differ in how they respond to socio-cultural influence.

(J) Evolution and decay

Distinct types of noun categorization devices differ in their etymological sources, and in the ways they develop and how they fall out of use. Classifiers of one type can develop into another.

(K) Language Acquisition and Dissolution

Distinct noun categorization devices show fundamental differences in how they are acquired by children, and what processes they undergo under language dissolution in aphasia.

Properties (A–G) are definitional properties of classifiers, in agreement with the morphosyntax-prior approach to classifiers adopted here. Properties (H–K) are contingent properties. Once the types of classifiers are established with respect to characteristics (A–G), they will be shown to display correlations with properties (H–K).

Quite a few languages use different sets of morphemes in different classifier environments. Many languages employ the same (or almost the same) set of classifier morphemes in different morphosyntactic loci. In this case, the question to ask is whether we should consider them as instances of distinct, albeit homophonous, classifier types, or as basically one type extended to other environments. These and other related issues will be discussed together with the problems of multiple classifier systems.

The structure of this book, as outlined in the next section, follows the above order: we discuss the definitional properties of classifiers first, and then proceed to consider the contingent ones.

1.6. The structure of this book

We will first discuss the proposed types, or 'focal points' on the continuum of noun categorization devices with respect to their definitional properties (A–G above) in the following order.

NOUN CLASSES and GENDERS are noun categorization devices realized outside the noun itself within a head-modifier noun phrase. They are realized, as agreement markers, on modifiers such as adjectives, but may also appear on modifiers from closed classes such as demonstratives and interrogatives. They can also be realized outside the noun phrase, e.g. be marked on the predicate, or even on adverbs. They are most often affixes. They usually contain reference to inherent properties of nouns, such as animacy and sex, and sometimes also shape, structure etc. Some languages have a special smallish set of noun classes/genders restricted to closed classes of modifiers (demonstratives, and others) along with a different set which appears on modifiers from other classes. These are discussed in Chapter 2.

NOUN CLASSIFIERS are associated with the noun itself, and are independent of any other element in an NP, or in a clause. They may be independent words, or, more rarely, affixes attached to nouns. They refer to inherent properties of nouns. Noun classifiers are free forms. Noun classes and noun classifiers differ in their synchronic properties; however, noun classes often develop from noun classifiers. These are discussed in Chapter 3.

NUMERAL CLASSIFIERS are another kind of noun categorization device which operate within an attributive NP. These are realized outside the noun in a numeral NP, and/or in expressions of quantity. Numeral classifiers can be free forms, or affixes, typically to the numeral or quantifier. They refer to the noun in terms of its inherent properties. These are discussed in Chapter 4.

Noun categorization devices which operate within a possessive NP are considered in Chapter 5. They can be of three kinds:

(i) The scope of categorization is the possessive relation itself, i.e. the way a noun can be possessed, or treated. These markers are called RELATIONAL CLASSIFIERS; they refer to the function of a noun, and not to its inherent properties.

(ii) The scope of categorization is the possessed noun itself. Classifiers which categorize the possessed noun are called POSSESSED CLASSIFIERS. The noun is categorized in terms of its inherent properties.

(iii) The scope of categorization is the possessor, and its inherent properties. These are POSSESSOR CLASSIFIERS.

Another type of classifiers which have a clause as their scope are VERBAL (or VERB-INCORPORATED) CLASSIFIERS discussed in Chapter 6. Their scope is an argument of the predicate, usually in S/O function, more rarely in an oblique function, and they are realized on the verb. They refer to inherent properties of the noun; and may also convey information on its position in space.

There are a few further, rare and rather problematic kinds of noun categorization devices with an NP as their scope. LOCATIVE CLASSIFIERS appear in adpositional NPs attached to an adposition, and characterize the head noun in terms of its inherent properties. Some languages have DEICTIC classifiers—morphemes which appear on deictics within an NP and qualify the noun in terms of its inherent properties and its orientation, such as horizontal or vertical. These are considered in Chapter 7.

Some languages have more than one kind of noun categorization—these are discussed in Chapter 8. The same set of morphemes can be used in several classifier environments—see discussion in Chapter 9.

We then consider contingent properties of classifiers. The ways in which different classifier types interact with other grammatical categories are discussed in Chapter 10. Parameters for the semantic categorization of referents of nouns and the preferred semantics of different classifiers are considered in Chapter 11.

The semantic organization of classifier systems and their functions are dealt with in Chapter 12, together with a discussion of socio-cultural parameters and mechanisms of human cognition reflected in noun categorization. This chapter demonstrates the unitary basis for noun categorization devices, providing support for considering them as variant realizations of one phenomenon.

The origins, evolution, and decay of different noun categorization devices are discussed in Chapter 13. The processes noun categorization devices undergo in language acquisition and dissolution are considered in Chapter 14. The results of the proposed typology and perspectives for further studies are given in the concluding Chapter 15.

Appendix 1 describes noun categorization by means other than classifiers, i.e. through marking number, grammatical relations, and other categories. Appendix 2 contains additional examples of semantic changes in the process of development from nouns to classifiers.

Suggestions for linguists undertaking fieldwork on classifier languages are provided in Appendix 3.

2 Noun Class and Gender Systems

2.1. General remarks

NOUN CLASSES and GENDERS are grammaticalized agreement systems which correlate—at least in part—with certain semantic characteristics (particularly in the domain of human and animate referents). They are sometimes called concordial classes; they include grammaticalized 'gender' systems of the Indo-European type. They are realized outside the noun itself, usually on modifiers which most often include adjectives, but may also include modifiers from closed classes (demonstratives, interrogatives, possessives, etc). They can also be realized outside the noun phrase, i.e. be marked on the predicate, or even on adverbs. Some languages have a special smallish set of noun classes/genders restricted to closed classes of modifiers (demonstratives, and others) along with a different set which appears on modifiers from other classes.

A terminological clarification is in order. The term GENDER was first used in the 5th century BC by the Greek philosopher Protagoras, when he divided Greek nouns into three classes: 'feminine', 'masculine', and 'inanimate' (nowadays called 'neuter'). This is a typical gender system, which is found in many Indo-European languages. Latin had a similar system; later, neuter nouns were redistributed between the other two genders, giving the modern system of masculine and feminine in French and Italian.

When Europeans came to study African languages, they discovered larger gender-like systems with eight or more distinctions in languages like Swahili; these often did not include a masculine/feminine distinction. The term NOUN CLASS came to be used for systems of this type.

NOUN CLASS, GENDER, and sometimes GENDER CLASS are often used interchangeably, depending on the linguistic tradition (some examples are given in §1.4). Here I shall use 'noun class' as a cover term for noun class and gender. In agreement with the linguistic tradition, I shall reserve the term gender for small systems of two to three distinctions (always including masculine and feminine), like the ones typically found in Indo-European, Afroasiatic, and Dravidian languages.

Since gender systems show some correlation with sex, many non-linguists (and a few linguists) erroneously confuse 'linguistic' gender and sex. However, sex represents biological categorization, and gender represents grammatical categorization. Feminine and masculine genders often include inanimate nouns with no connection to female or male sex, e.g. French *maison* 'house' (feminine), *château* 'castle' (masculine).

The languages of the world differ in the number of noun classes they have, how much semantic transparency there is to noun class assignment, where and how noun class gets expressed, and whether it is possible to change the noun class of a given noun.

Noun class systems are typically found in languages with a fusional or agglutinating (not an isolating) profile. Noun class agreement is often a major criterion for distinguishing nouns from other word classes. In a language where noun and adjective have similar morphology, an adjective can usually take any noun class marking whereas a noun is normally restricted to one class.

Because of the limitations of space, it is impossible to cover all the literature on noun class systems. To avoid an overlap with Corbett's (1991) study of noun class systems (for which he uses a cover term 'gender'), I will concentrate on the issues and examples which have not been considered there, and briefly mention the ones for which Corbett (1991) provides detailed coverage.

The properties of noun class systems are considered in §2.2. Noun class assignment is discussed in §2.3. Noun class agreement is dealt with in §2.4. The next section discusses markedness relations and resolution in noun class systems. Realization of noun classes is analysed in §2.6. Some languages have two noun class systems. These may be in a complementary distribution with respect to the modifiers with which they are used; they may display peculiar agreement properties—see §2.7. Finally, §2.8 surveys the distribution of noun classes in the languages of the world.

2.2. Properties of noun class systems

A noun class system is the most grammatical means a language can use for the semantic categorization of nouns. As we shall see later, other noun categorization mechanisms are more lexical and often more semantically based.

Noun class systems have the following definitional properties.

1. Some constituent outside the noun itself must agree in noun class with a noun. Agreement can be with other words in the noun phrase (adjectives, numbers, demonstratives, articles etc.) and/or with the predicate of the clause or with an adverb. That is, noun class can be realized in a number of morphosyntactic loci (depending on the agreement rules in the language) and its scope can be a noun phrase and/or a clause. Noun classes are defined syntactically. They constitute a closed obligatory grammatical

system (which often arises as the result of grammaticalization of some other noun categorization device: see Chapter 13).

Noun classes are realized with affixes or with clitics, and in most cases there is a limited, countable number of noun classes (see §2.6).
2. Noun class membership is assigned on semantic—and sometimes also morphological and phonological—principles. Each noun in the language belongs to one (or occasionally more than one) class(es).

There is always some semantic basis to the grouping of nouns into classes, but languages vary in how much semantic transparency there is. This semantic basis usually includes animacy, humanness and sex, and sometimes also shape and size. We will return to this in Chapter 11.

In some languages, in addition to the realization of noun classes through agreement, there is a marker of noun class on the noun itself, or on some nouns; in other languages nouns bear no overt marker.

Languages often have portmanteau morphemes combining information about noun class with number, person, case, etc. This is considered in Chapter 10.

Some systems based on animacy and sex (and traditionally called 'gender systems') do not, in fact, satisfy the criteria set out here. English distinguishes three genders just in 3rd person pronouns, *he/she/it*. They involve the opposition: male, female, inanimate. There are a few conventionalized metaphorical extensions, e.g. ships are commonly referred to with the feminine pronoun *she* (see further examples in §12.3.3). There is no gender agreement within a noun phrase or with a verb in a clause.[1] Gender markers in English simply have an anaphoric function, as they also do in Japanese where masculine and feminine forms are distinguished only in 3rd person pronouns with a human referent *kare* 'he', *kanojo* 'she' (recently introduced, possibly, under the influence of European languages: Walter Bisang, p.c.).[2] Many languages of the world also have animacy-based distinctions in interrogative and indefinite pronouns (see Haspelmath 1997), e.g. English *anybody* or *anything* which can be used anaphorically. Strictly speaking, these are not noun classes.

The presence of agreement is the main definitional property of a noun class. Some languages have singular/plural alternations which can be shown as at least partially conditioned by the semantics of nouns. However, these pairings do not correspond to different agreement classes. Such appears to be the case with singular/plural alternations in Eastern Sudanic

---

[1] However, if we follow Lehmann's (1982: 219) view of agreement, the use of these pronouns to 'agree' in animacy/sex with their antecedent can be considered 'anaphoric agreement'; see §2.4.1.
[2] There can also be complicated relations between sex of speaker and form of other pronouns, e.g. first person; these relate to the category of politeness: cf. Chapter 10.

languages (Dimmendaal 2000). This is a system of classifying nouns and their referents; however, it cannot be considered a system of noun classes. In contrast, Bantu languages have large systems of noun class affixes which are portmanteau morphemes of noun class with number; since they appear both on the noun itself and on the agreeing constituents they 'qualify' as noun classes. Modern Hebrew distinguishes two genders, masculine and feminine, both in the singular and in the plural (see §2.3.4) which are realized in agreement within a noun phrase and on the verb. Nouns also fall into several classes depending on their number and case forms (Aikhenvald 1990: 48); this second kind of classification lies outside the scope of the present study.

2.3. Principles of noun class assignment

The principles by which nouns are 'assigned' to different classes can be governed by semantics (§2.3.1), or formal morphological (§2.3.2) or phonological (§2.3.3) properties of a noun, or a combination of these (§2.3.4) (also see Corbett 1991: 7–69). In a sense all systems of noun class assignment are mixed, since there is always a semantic core which involves the universal semantic parameters (see §11.2.1) of sex, humanness, animacy but this is never the entire story.

Noun class systems were defined above as obligatory grammatical systems, such that every noun has to belong to a noun class. However, noun class assignment is sometimes impossible for a smallish group of nouns. These are exceptions to the statement that every noun in a language with a noun class system has to be assigned to a noun class. For example, Russian does not distinguish genders in the plural. Then, the gender of pluralia tantum, i.e. nouns which are used only in the plural and always have plural agreement, cannot be determined, e.g. *sani* 'sledge', *brjuki* 'trousers', *seni* 'entrance into a hut'.[3]

The psycholinguistic reality of gender assignment has been confirmed by recent studies of child language acquisition (Connelly 1984; Mills 1986; Tsonope 1988). We shall return to this in Chapter 14.

2.3.1. Semantic assignment

In languages with purely semantic assignment the class of a noun can be inferred from its meaning. In Tamil (Dravidian) all nouns divide into what are traditionally called 'rational' and 'non-rational' classes. 'Rational' nouns comprise humans, gods, and demons (Asher 1985: 136). Other

---

[3] These nouns do distinguish animacy; see (C) in §2.4.4 on subgenders in Russian.

Dravidian languages, Malto, Kolami, Ollari, and Parji distinguish male humans as distinct from other nouns which refer to 'rational' beings. From the Northeast Caucasian family, Godoberi, Akhvakh, and Bagval distinguish male 'rational', female 'rational', and the rest (Corbett 1994b). Diyari (Australian), Kaingáng (Jê), and the North Arawak subgroup divide nouns into female humans and the rest.

Semantic assignment can be more complex. Dyirbal (Dixon 1972: 306–12) has four classes. Three are associated with one or more basic concepts: gender 1—male humans, non-human animates; gender 2—female humans, water, fire, fighting; gender 3—non-flesh food. Gender 4 is a residue class, covering everything else. There are also two rules for 'transferring' gender membership. By the first, an object can be assigned to a gender by its mythological association rather than by its actual semantics. Birds are classed as feminine by mythological association since women's souls are believed to enter birds after death. The second transfer rule is that if a subset of a certain group of objects has a particular important property, e.g., being dangerous, it can be assigned to a different class from the other nouns in that group. Most trees without edible parts belong to gender 4, but stinging trees are placed in gender 2.

Mythological association plays an important role in class assignment in other languages, too. In the Western Torres Strait language all nouns denoting males are masculine, with the remainder being feminine. However, the moon is masculine, due to its mythological association with masculinity (Bani 1987). This is also characteristic of other Australian languages. The assignment of masculine and feminine noun classes in Abu' Arapesh (Papuan; Nekitel 1985, 1986, ms) can sometimes be explained by mythological associations; for instance, cassowary is feminine because it used to be a mythological woman, and the moon is masculine—it is a mythological man who engages in a sexual intercourse with women (making them menstruate).

In Ket (Krejnovič 1961, Dul'son 1968: 62ff.), all sex-differentiable nouns are masculine or feminine. Among non-sex-differentiable nouns, those which show a higher degree of activity or are particularly important for Ket culture are masculine, e.g. wood, large wooden objects, growing trees. Gender assignment of sun (feminine) and moon (masculine) is determined by their role in myths.[4] Other inanimate nouns are treated as neuter.

The degree of semantic motivation for noun classes varies from language to language. Systems with a larger number of noun classes tend to have

---

[4] Also see Harvey (1997) for an insightful overview of semantic parameters employed in gender assignment in Australian languages. In this and other cases it can also be argued that the mythological role was originally determined by gender assignment, and not the other way round. Indeed, in many cases it is impossible to prove which line of argument is better founded.

more semantic motivation; however, this is not necessarily so. Languages of the Ndu family (East Sepik, Papua New Guinea) have two semantically assigned genders (see §2.4.3). In Babungo (Grassfields Bantu, Benue-Congo: Schaub 1985: 172; Croft 1995) there are significant correlations between 14 noun classes and semantic categories, but none of them is absolute. The meanings ascribed to some reconstructed Proto-Bantu noun classes by Denny and Creider (1986: 232–9) are shown in Table 2.1 (a somewhat different version is given in Table 11.3). In the Bantuist tradition, every countable noun is assigned to two classes: one singular and one plural (see §1.5 on terminology and §10.1.1 on the correlations between noun classes and number).

TABLE 2.1. *Semantics of noun classes in Proto-Bantu*

Noun class (SG/PL)	Semantics
Class 1/2	Human, person
Class 3/4	Extended (long) (e.g. body, river)
Class 5/6	Fruits; non-extended (e.g. stone, spot, nose)
Class 7/8	Utilitarian artefacts, despised objects and beings
Class 9/10	Animal
Class 14/6	Differentiated internal structure (e.g. bridge, bow, canoe)

In modern Bantu languages, however, noun class assignment is often much less semantically motivated, though the semantic 'nucleus' is still discernible. Thus, in Babungo, class 1/2 is basically human; however, it is a much bigger class than it was in Proto-Bantu, and also contains many animals, some birds and insects, body parts, plants, household and other objects, e.g. necklace, pot, book, rainbow (Schaub 1985: 175) (also see Tables 11.4 and 11.5, and Diagram 11.2).

It has often been stated that there is no real semantic basis for gender assignment of the better-known Indo-European languages. However, in a seminal study, Zubin and Köpcke (1986) provided a semantic rationale for gender assignment of nouns of different semantic groups in German (see (D) in §11.2.1). Masculine and feminine genders mark the terms for male and female adults of each species of domestic and game animals (following the 'natural sex' principle), and neuter is assigned to non-sex-specific generic and juvenile terms. Masculine gender is used for types of cloth, of precipitation and wind, and of minerals. Types of knowledge and discipline have feminine gender, and games and types of metal—with the exception of alloys—have neuter gender.[5]

---

[5] Paul (1972) also demonstrated a partial semantic motivation for the gender assignment of English borrowings into German; for instance, drinks are mostly masculine, while fruits and flowers are feminine.

2.3.2. Morphological assignment

A connection between derivational suffix and noun class can form a morphological basis for noun class assignment. In German at least some derivational affixes are each associated with one gender, e.g. *-ung* 'action noun' is feminine and *-chen* 'diminutive' is neuter (Zubin and Köpcke 1986; Plank 1986). In Portuguese, a number of derivational suffixes (e.g. *-ção* 'action noun', as in *marca-ção* 'marking') indicate feminine gender.

In a language with a number of nominal declensions, each may correlate with a gender. In Russian the semantic assignment is restricted to human and higher animate referents. Otherwise, gender assignment is linked to declension: all nouns of declension 1 are masculine, nouns of declensions 2 and 3 are feminine, and all the rest are neuter (Corbett 1991: 40).

2.3.3. Phonological assignment

No noun class system in the world is assigned by phonological principles only. The application of phonological principles of assignment is usually restricted to nouns with inanimate referents. In some languages every noun which ends or begins with a certain vowel or consonant must belong to a particular gender. In Qafar (Saho-Afar, East Cushitic: Corbett 1991: 51–2) nouns with inanimate reference whose citation form ends in a vowel are feminine; all the rest are masculine. In Hausa all non-sex-differentiable nouns which end in *-aa* are feminine. In Katcha (Kordofanian: Heine 1982a: 200), any noun—unless it has a male referent—belongs to the feminine gender if it begins with *m-*. Phonological noun class assignment is found in Limilngan (Australian: Harvey forthcoming: §3.2): nouns whose initial segment is /l/ or /d/ tend to be assigned to Class 2 (which includes animals), and nouns with the initial /m/ tend to be assigned to Class 3 (which covers plants), even if their reference lies outside the semantic domain of these classes.

2.3.4. Mixed principles of assignment

No system of noun classes is completely devoid of semantic motivation. If a language has non-semantic principles of noun class assignment the assigment principles will be mixed, since there is always a 'core' where semantics operates. This 'core' includes humans in some languages and animates in others (see §11.2.1).

In the Harar dialect of Oromo (East Cushitic: Clamons 1993: 271) nouns referring to females are feminine, and noun referring to males are masculine. Nouns referring to inanimates, or animates for which sex is not important, are feminine if they end in a non-low vowel; otherwise they are masculine. Russian has predominantly morphological gender assignment (§2.3.2). However, sex-differentiable nouns are assigned gender according to their semantics, and not their form. Thus, nouns like *mužčina* 'man' or *detina* 'big man' belong to the second declension, and should be feminine; but in fact they are masculine as far as agreement goes.[6]

An interesting interaction of semantic and phonological principles is found in Yimas (Sepik, Papua New Guinea, Foley 1986: 86 ff.; 1991), where the first four classes are assigned by their semantics: I—human males; II—human females; III—animals; class IV—culturally important plants. Classes 5–11 are motivated phonologically: the agreeing constituent repeats the last consonant of the nominal root.

Arapesh languages (Torricelli phylum, Papua New Guinea) appear to have a similar system. The assignment of two human classes, which comprise males and females respectively, is considered semantic by most scholars. Nekitel (1985; 1986; ms) has convincingly argued against a 'purely phonological' assignment of noun classes in Abu' Arapesh (cf. Fortune 1942 and the analysis of Muhiang Arapesh by Conrad 1978: 92).[7] A strong argument in favour of the semantic assignment of the human classes comes from loans. Most nouns which belong to Class 1 'masculine' contain either a final or an initial segment *n* (e.g. *aleman* 'man', *Nekitel* 'male name'). However, words like *Spiritu Santu* 'Holy Spirit' and *ankelo* 'angel' are attributed to Class 1 'masculine', although they do not contain the 'marker' *n*; similarly, *siste* 'nun' (from English *sister*) is assigned to the Class 2 'feminine' (though it does not contain ʔ- or *kw*-, initial sounds typical of this class). Morphological and phonological assignment may be hard to distinguish. There is a strong tendency to assign nouns which end in -*n* (e.g. *aun* 'moon') to the masculine class (unless they have a female referent, e.g. *nes* 'nurse', a loan from English); this is sometimes interpreted as a fossilized affix (cf. Conrad 1996).

Many languages display more complicated mixed principles of 'assignment' mingling semantic, morphological, and phonological criteria. Iraqw (South Cushitic; Heine 1982a: 200) has masculine and feminine genders. All nouns denoting singular male and female animates and male and female agentive nouns are masculine and feminine respectively. Singular

---

[6] Loan words provide a few more exceptions to morphological assignment in Russian. *Kofe* 'coffee' is indeclinable, ends in -*e*, and does not denote a sex-differentiable being; these are usual properties of neuter nouns. The archaic form of this word (borrowed from Dutch or English: Vasmer 1953) was *kofej*, and it was assigned masculine gender since nouns ending in -*ej* are masculine; later it became *kofe*. In prescriptive Russian grammar, this noun is still considered masculine, while in substandard colloquial language it triggers neuter agreement.

[7] For an attempt to account for Arapesh noun classes as an exclusively phonologically based system, see Aronoff (1991; 1994).

nouns ending in *-mo* and *-aŋw* are masculine. Nouns derived from Class 1 verbs are masculine while those from Class II verbs are feminine.[8]

A more 'grammatical' system of gender assignment can move towards a more 'semantically' oriented one. In Cantabrian Spanish a number of semantic features have been introduced for the assignment of inanimates to masculine or feminine gender (Holmquist 1991: 69), e.g. feature large/small: masc. *montón* 'stack of hay' vs fem. *montona* 'very big stack of hay'; feature deprecatory/approbatory, neutral: masc. *carreteru* 'a bad road' vs. fem. *carretera* 'a road'; feature coarse/smooth: masc. *espinu* 'mountain thorn, dark coarse bark' vs. fem. *espina* 'mountain thorn, light smooth bark'—see Table 2.2. These oppositions are mostly absent from standard Spanish.

TABLE 2.2. *Semantic features for the gender assignment of inanimate nouns in Cantabrian Spanish*

Masculine	Feminine
Male	Female
Small	Large
Narrow	Wide
Vertical	Horizontal
Tall	Squat
Phallic	Supine
Coarse	Smooth
Dark	Light
Deprecatory	Approbatory, neutral
Derived	Primary
Occasional	Familiar

For nouns with animate reference, semantic assignment often overrides morphological or other principles. In Alamblak (Lower Sepik) (Bruce 1984: 97) all nouns which denote females and short, squat, or wide objects are feminine and can have a form marked with a feminine suffix. There is one exception, the word for canoe, *doh-t*, which has a feminine marker *-t*, but is always treated as masculine in agreement, in accordance with its typical 'masculine-like' slender dimensions.[9]

---

[8] A similar system is found in Punjabi (Indo-Aryan: Bantia 1993: 216–18). In Chechen and Ingush (Nakh-Daghestanian: Nichols 1989a) the distribution of nouns into five classes is partially semantically motivated; there is also a dependency between class assignment and the initial consonant of the noun. Semantic and phonological principles of noun class assignment interact in Bowili (Togo Remnant, Eastern Ghana: Heine 1982a: 199–200). See also Aikhenvald and Green (1998) for a detailed description of mixed semantic and phonological principles of gender assignment in Palikur, a North Arawak language from Brazil.

[9] The word *Mädchen* 'girl' in German may be considered an exception to this. It is neuter since it contains a diminutive suffix *-chen* which, like other diminutive suffixes, determines the assignment of neuter. However, the situation in the modern spoken language is more

Semantic, morphological, and phonological principles account for the great majority of the assignment of nouns to gender classes in any given language, but there will often be a small residue of unexplained exceptions. Modern Hebrew has two genders, masculine and feminine. The principles of assignment are semantic and morphological. Sex-differentiable nouns are assigned gender in agreement with their semantics; nouns which contain suffixes -*t* and -*a* are feminine. Nouns which refer to cities and land, and paired and some non-paired body parts, are feminine. There are a few nouns which belong to feminine gender as unexplainable exceptions: *even* 'stone', *kos* 'goblet', *eš* 'fire' (Aikhenvald 1990: 44).[10]

Nouns which display a conflict between different rules of gender/noun class assignment are called HYBRIDS (Corbett 1991). In Russian *mužčina* 'man' is feminine by its morphology (it belongs to the 2nd declension: see §2.3.2) but masculine according to semantics. Semantics often takes precedence in agreement, as it does here. In Russian, in the case of most nouns denoting professions which are morphologically masculine (they belong to the first declension), such as *professor* 'professor', the agreement is feminine when focusing on the female sex of the person. In Portuguese, some nouns denoting professional occupations which end in -*a* or -*e* can also be assigned either gender depending on the sex of the referent, e.g. *dentista* 'dentist', *estudante* 'student'. The issue of variable noun class assignment and agreement is taken up in §2.4.3.

2.4. Noun classes and agreement

The presence of agreement is a definitional property of noun classes which distinguishes them from a number of other noun categorization devices. The presence of agreement is linked to the opposition between inflection and derivation. A working definition of agreement is given in §2.4.1. Principles of noun class agreement are discussed in §2.4.2. Variability in agreement, and variable noun class assignment are considered in §2.4.3. Then, in §2.4.4, I discuss the problem of how to determine the number of noun classes within a language.

2.4.1. A working definition of agreement and agreement properties

Agreement is defined by Matthews (1997: 12) as a 'syntactic relation between words and phrases which are compatible, in a given construction,

---

complicated: *Mädchen* may trigger feminine agreement with a relative clause marker and with a possessive pronoun; neuter is preferred when the antecedent is a child rather than a grown-up girl (Fritz Serzisko, Geoff Haig, Helma Pasch p.c.).

[10] See also Clamons (1995) on semantic residue in gender assignment in Oromo, a Cushitic language.

by virtue of inflections carried by at least one of them'.[11] Agreement implies a systematic covariance between the grammatical meanings of grammatical morphemes (cf. Durie 1986). In a study of agreement systems the questions to be answered are:

(A) Domain of agreement

What elements agree with what elements in what grammatical configurations?

It is useful to distinguish two basic types of agreement domain: (a) agreement within an NP between modifiers and heads (head-modifier type), and (b) agreement within a clause between a predicate and its arguments (predicate-argument type).[12]

Morphosyntactic loci on which agreement markers appear are called AGREEMENT TARGETS (see Corbett 1991). Noun classes can have a noun phrase, and/or a clause, as their domain of agreement.

(B) Features and principles of agreement

In what grammatical properties do grammatical elements agree and how is it marked?

The principles of agreement are linked to the assignment of agreement features. The assignment may be either purely semantic, or mixed semantic and syntactic (cf. the distinction between 'grammatical' agreement and 'notional' agreement in Matthews 1997). These issues are discussed in §2.4.2. Conditions which may allow neutralization or variation in the agreement, and limitations on the agreement, are considered in §2.4.3.

---

[11] A similar definition of agreement is provided by Steele (1978: 610): 'The term *agreement* commonly refers to some systematic covariance between a semantic or formal property of one element and a formal property of another. For example, adjectives may take some formal indication of the number and gender of the noun they modify.' See further attempts at defining agreement by Keenan (1978: 167); Lehmann (1982: 203; 1988); further analysis of the basic parameters in terms of which agreement phenomena can or should be characterized is given by Barlow and Ferguson (1988a: 3); also see Lapointe (1985: 84), and discussion in Anderson (1992: 103–18). Agreement can be taken in a wider sense to include the so-called anaphoric agreement, i.e. the 'determination of the form of personal and relative pronouns' by their antecedents (Corbett 1991: 112; cf. Lehmann 1982). Barlow (1992) has shown that there are no reasons to make a sharp distinction between agreement within a noun phrase, and antecedent–anaphora relations. Historically, grammatical agreement often comes from grammaticalized anaphoric markers (see §13.8; also see Givón 1976; Bresnan and McChombo 1986). A number of languages, including English, distinguish different forms of personal pronouns conditioned by the gender and animacy of the antecedent. If agreement is understood in a wider sense, English can be considered a language with genders (as it was done by Corbett 1991: 112, 169).

[12] Following the distinction in Anderson (1992: 106 ff.). The important difference between Anderson's approach, and the one suggested here lies in the treatment of adpositional and possessive constructions. For the reasons which will become obvious in the course of this chapter, I will consider the principles of agreement within a noun phrase under head-modifier type; and the principles of agreement within a clause under predicate-argument type (unlike Anderson, who groups together agreement of verb with its arguments, and agreement in possessive and adpositional constructions).

Some languages have different noun class/gender agreement systems depending on the domain of agreement (head-modifier vs. predicate-argument) and on the morphological class of the agreeing element. These systems, called 'split agreement', are discussed in §2.7.

Correlations between noun classes and other grammatical categories which may also influence the ways agreement operates are considered in Chapter 10; correlations with discourse-pragmatic functions are discussed in Chapter 12.

An important distinction in the morphology of many languages is that between inflectional and derivational processes. These are summarized in Table 2.3 (cf. Payne 1990; Anderson 1992: 77 ff.; Aikhenvald forthcoming b).

TABLE 2.3. *Inflection and derivation*

Inflection	Derivation
1. Usually obligatory	Optional
2. Final process (if affix, on rim of word)	Pre-final process (if affix, between root and inflection)
3. Forms a complete word	Derives a stem which takes inflections
4. Defining characteristic of a word class (e.g. nouns inflect for case)	Usually specific to a word class
5. Do not change word class	May derive a stem of a different word class, or may add some semantic specification to a root without changing class
6. May indicate grammatical relationship between words, and/or participate in agreement	Never indicate grammatical relationship between words or participate in agreement
7. Tend to be smallish systems	May be large systems
8. Tend to have high frequency in language	Likely to have lower frequency
9. Tend to be monosyllabic likely to undergo phonological processes when combined with stem (such as assimilation, or fusion)	May be longer and are less likely to undergo phonological processes

By virtue of being realized as agreement markers, noun classes have to be treated as an inflectional category. Note that noun classes marked on the head noun ('head classes': see §2.6.1, and Evans 1997) can have a derivational function, since they may derive a stem of a different word class, e.g. Kikongo (Bantu) Ø/ba[13]-*bakála* (CL1/2-male) 'man', *ki-bakála*

---

[13] Note that here and in other examples from Bantu languages the two numbers correspond to singular and plural class markers.

(CL7/8-male) 'maleness'; Swahili *kúbwa* 'big', *u-kúbwa* 'size' (Mufwene 1980: 248–9). Similarly, in Portuguese—and in numerous other Indo-European languages—gender is used to mark agreement, e.g. *agua branca* (water: FEM white-FEM.SG) 'white water'; it is also used as a derivational device, e.g. *professor* (teacher: MASC.SG) 'he-teacher', *professor-a* (teacher-FEM.SG) 'she-teacher'; *ministro* 'he-minister', *ministr-a* 'she-minister'.

2.4.2. Principles of noun class agreement

Noun class agreement can be a property of a noun phrase or of a clause. In A–E below we consider possible morphosyntactic loci of agreement marking and interrelations between them. Semantic versus syntactic agreement is discussed in F. Factors which may constrain agreement are summarized under G.

(A) Noun class agreement in head-modifier (attributive) noun phrases

Noun class agreement can be marked on any type of modifier—adjectives, including numeral and deverbal adjectives (participles), demonstratives, or articles.

The head determines noun class agreement within an NP (there may not necessarily be an overt noun class marker on the head noun itself—see §2.6.2). This is a major criterion for recognizing which word is the head of an NP (Nichols 1986). In 2.1, from Baniwa (North Arawak), *inaʒu* 'woman' is the head since it determines the form of the proximate demonstrative.

2.1. ʃua inaʒu
     DEM:FEM woman
     'this woman'

In 2.2, from Mayali (Australian: Evans 1997: 129), an adjective 'good' shows noun class agreement with the noun.

2.2. al-makkawarri   al-mak
     CLII(FEM)-lesser.salmon.catfish CLII(FEM)-good
     'that good male lesser salmon catfish'

(B) Noun class agreement in possessive noun phrases

Noun class agreement is rarer in possessive constructions. In numerous Bantu languages, a possessive, or 'associative' morpheme is marked for the noun class of the possessed noun, e.g. 'knife', as in 2.3 from Swahili (Welmers 1973: 175).

2.3. kisu   ch-a   Hamisi
     NCL7-knife   NCL7-POSS Hamisi
     'Hamisi's knife'

Possessed nouns can show noun class agreement with the possessor. This is illustrated with 2.4, from Paumarí (Arawá: my own data). The possessed noun, 'house', shows agreement with the feminine possessor, Bajara.[14]

2.4. Bajara   gora-ni
     female.name   house-3SG.FEM
     'Bajara's house'

The possessor noun can take a marker of agreement with the possessed one. This is the case in Chamalal (Northeast Caucasian: Magomedbekova 1967: 388). Chamalal has five noun classes. In 2.5, the possessor, *hek'wa* 'man', belongs to Class 1 and the possessed noun, *ĩsa* 'cheese', belongs to Class 4; the Class 4 agreement marker appears on the possessor.[15]

2.5. hek'wa-ssu-l   ĩsa
     man(CL1)-GN-CL4 cheese (CL4)
     'man's cheese'

In Manambu, a Ndu language from the East Sepik province of New Guinea, possessive constructions mark noun class agreement with the possessor, and with the possessed noun within a a possessive morpheme (cf. Aikhenvald 1998a). This is illustrated with 2.6. Agreement is shown with arrows.

2.6. Pauline   lə-kə-də   ma:j
     Pauline(feminine) 3SGFEM-POSS-3 SGMASC story(masculine)
     'Pauline's story'

Double agreement—with the possessor and with the possessed noun—is also found in a few Bantu languages. In Shona, the possessive morpheme is marked for the class of both possessor and possessed (Welmers 1973: 178). *Tuvana* 'child' belongs to class 13 (diminutive plural), and *imbwa* 'dogs' belongs to class 10 (animal plural).

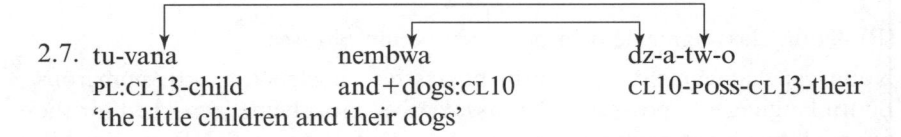

2.7. tu-vana   nembwa   dz-a-tw-o
     PL:CL13-child   and+dogs:CL10 CL10-POSS-CL13-their
     'the little children and their dogs'

---

[14] A similar phenomenon is found in Abkhaz (Northwest Caucasian: Hewitt 1979: 116; Corbett 1991: 108), and in Wari' (Everett and Kern 1997).

[15] A similar agreement pattern is reported for Kuot (non-Austronesian, New Ireland: Eva Lindström p.c.), where there are two genders.

Noun class agreement in possessive constructions may depend on the morphological subclass of a noun. In many Australian languages inalienably possessed nouns display unusual agreement patterns and unusual correlations between overtly marked noun classes and agreement types (Evans 1994: 2; Kirton 1971: 13).[16] The agreement of an inalienably possessed noun 'name' with possessor in noun class is illustrated with 2.8a and 2.8b, from Yanyuwa:

2.8a. nya-ganymarda   niya-wini
       MALE-two   CL:MASC-name
       'his two names'

2.8b. rra-mangaji   nanda-wini
       FEMALE-that   CL:FEM-name
       'that name of hers'

In some languages noun class agreement is marked on adpositions, as in Abkhaz (Northwest Caucasian: Hewitt 1979: 113–14), e.g. Áxra yə-zə́ (Axra 3SG.HUMAN.MALE-for) 'for Axra'.

Noun classes are very rarely marked on interrogative pronouns. This is the case in Tariana (North Arawak), e.g. ku-ite tʃãri-tha (what-CL:AN man-PRES.INTER.VISUAL) 'what (person) is this?', kwaka-whya namia-ni-whya (what:INAN-CL:CANOE 3PL+sink-TOP.ADV-CL:CANOE) 'Which canoe was (the canoe) they sank?' In Baining, a non-Austronesian language from East New Britain, interrogatives 'who' and 'which' take noun class agreement markers (Parker and Parker 1977: 21).[17]

(C) Noun class agreement outside a noun phrase

If there is noun class agreement outside a noun phrase, the verb agrees with core constituents: subject (S and/or A) and/or direct object. There is often agreement with just one core argument, more frequently with the subject than with a direct object (see Corbett 1991: 110 ff. for more examples). Bantu languages show consistent gender agreement with subject and direct object; the subject agreement marker usually comes before the tense

---

[16] There may also be occasional lexical 'exceptions'. In Tiwi, like in Yanyuwa, body parts are assigned the gender/noun class of their possessor (Osborne 1974), but genitals are assigned the gender of the opposite sex (Evans 1994: 2). Some Australian languages have several patterns of agreement depending on body part lexemes. One of the most striking and complicated examples is Gurr-goni (Evans 1994: 6; and R. Green 1995: 109 ff.).

[17] Gender and number are marked on interrogatives in Bine, a Fly river language of New Guinea with two genders (Fleischmann and Turpeinen 1975: 13) and in Kuot (Eva Lindström p.c.); also see Pasch (1986: 154–5; 175) for the agreement on interrogatives in Mba (Ubangi, Niger-Congo). Most Australian languages with agreement noun classes mark them on at least some interrogatives; e.g. in Ngalakan noun classes are marked only on 'who', while in Nunggubuyu they are marked on 'where'; see Dixon (2002: 479) for a detailed description.

marker, while the object agreement marker comes between the tense prefix and the root. In Swahili, the occurrence of the object prefix is optional when the object is inanimate, but obligatory when it is animate. Example 2.9 shows verb agreement with animate subject (Maryamu) and object ('children'), from Swahili (Bresnan and McChombo 1986: 293).

2.9. Maryamu$_A$ a-li-wa-onyesha wa-toto$_O$ ki-su
Maryamu CL1$_A$-PAST-CL2$_O$-show CL2$_O$-children CL7-knife
'Maryamu showed the children a/the knife.'

Noun class agreement with both subject (A/S) and object is found in some prefixing Australian languages (Dixon 2002: 479–85). In the North Kimberley languages (Worrorra, Ungarinjin, Wunambal) agreement is found with S/O, and not with A, while Jingulu has noun class agreement with A, and not with S/O (see §10.7, for interactions between clausal or predicate categories and noun class).

In Paumarí (Arawá), there is agreement either with A, or with S/O, depending on the type of construction and constituent order (Aikhenvald MS; Chapman and Derbyshire 1991; see §2.7.2 below).

Noun class agreement with a peripheral constituent is rare. In Lak (Northeast Caucasian), there is noun class agreement on adverbs. This is illustrated with 2.10: *ars* 'son' belongs to Noun Class 1 which includes human males; the numeral 'two' takes Noun Class 1 agreement marker -*j*-, while the locative adverb 'at home' takes the agreement marker -*w*-; the marker on the verb 'be' is Ø (markers are underlined) (Khaidakov 1980: 206).

2.10. k'i-*j*a ars ša-*w*a *Ø*-ušar
two-NCL1:MALE son at.home-NCL1:MALE NCL1:MALE-be
'Two sons are at home'

Agreement is very rarely marked on complementizers. However, these agree in gender with the subject of the complement clause in West Flemish (Corbett 1991: 113).[18]

Noun class agreement may take place with a topical constituent, independently of its syntactic function. Motuna (non-Austronesian, Bougainville: Onishi 1994 and p.c.) has five noun classes. The verb in a clause takes obligatory subject and object cross-referencing, and also agrees in noun class with the topical constituent. In 2.11, the object *nii* 'I

---

[18] Garifuna (North Arawak, Central America) is reported to have neutral, or default agreement on complementizers; thus complementizers can be said to agree with the clause they introduce (Munroe MS: 7):

busé-tina l-ún n-abínaha
want-TI.SERIES:1SG 3SG.NF-DATIVE 1SG-dance
'I want to dance'

(masculine)' is topical and its masculine noun class is cross-referenced on the verb (Masa Onishi, p.c.).

2.11. nii   Aanih-ki   tangu-mu-u-ng
      I(MASC):ABS Aanih(FEM)-ERG   slap-1sGO+3sGA-NEAR.PAST-MASC
      'Aanih (a female name) slapped me (topic).'

In contrast, in 2.12 the subject, *Aanih*, is topical and its feminine gender is cross-referenced on the verb (Masa Onishi, p.c.).

2.12. Aanih   nii   tangu-mu-i-na
      Aanih(FEM)   I(MASC):ABS   slap-1sGO+3sGA-NEAR.PAST-FEM
      'Aanih (a female name) (topic) slapped me.'

(D) Noun class agreement on several targets

The majority of languages mark noun class in more than one place in the clause. Dyirbal marks gender on determiners and interrogatives. Burushaski marks gender on pronouns, adjectival modifiers, and verbs. In Anindilyakwa (Australian: Leeding 1989) gender is marked on head nouns, verbs, adjectives, and all types of pronoun. Bantu, some West Atlantic languages, and the North Kimberley languages of Australia (Worrorra, Ungarinjin, and Wunambal) mark gender on every type of noun modifier and on the verb.

A remarkable property of Bantu languages is ALLITERATIVE CONCORD, whereby the same noun class marker is repeated on modifiers and on the predicate, as in 2.13, from Swahili (Corbett 1991: 117; Welmers 1973: 171).

2.13. ki-kapu   ki-kubwa   ki-moja   ki-li-anguka
      CL7-basket   CL7-large   CL7-one   CL7-PAST-fall
      'One large basket fell.'

!Xóõ, a Southern Khoisan language, has five noun classes (Traill 1994: 20–2). They are marked by suffixes on nouns and also realized through agreement on various targets (adjectives, relativizers, object markers). Noun suffixes bear a strong phonological similarity to agreement markers; an example of such an 'alliterative' concord is given in 2.14 (Traill 1994: 21). Noun class markers are underlined.

2.14. ñ à |nà-i̠ |à-i̠   !xà-i̠   t-i̠
      I PAST   see-NCL1:O   lion-NCL1   big-NCL1   which-NCL1
      |'áa |îi   k-i̠
      dead   is   which-NCL1
      'I saw a large dead lion'

Only some nouns from classes 1–4 can take a noun class prefix. Others do not, e.g. *dào* 'road' in 2.15; concord is then not alliterative.

2.15. ñ à |nà-i̱   dào   xà-i̱   t-i̱
    I past   see-NCL1:O   road big-NCL1   which-NCL1
    !nólisí |îi   k-ì
    broken   is   which-NCL1
    'I saw the broken up big road.'

In many Bantu languages the original alliterative character of the concord has been obscured by phonological changes, and so prefixes retain some phonological similarities without being exactly the same, as in Zulu (Herbert 1991: 106):

2.16. uku-dla   kw-ethu   ko-nke   ku-phelile
     CL15-eat   CL15-our   CL15-all   CL15-is.finished
     'All our food is finished.'

Lowland Amazonian languages with large systems of noun classes which can be overtly marked on the head noun as nominalizers (see (F) in §9.1) do not allow multiple affixation on agreeing constituents. To mark agreement, just the last classifier on the head noun is repeated on all the agreeing constituents. Example 2.17 is from Tariana (North Arawak). The last classifier, -*puna* 'stretch' (underlined), appears as an agreement marker on the adjective and on the verb.

2.17. kaɾa-ka-whya-puna   hanu-puna
     REL+fly-THEME-CL:CANOE-CL:STRETCH   big-CL:STRETCH
     na-ni-ni-puna
     3PL-do-TOP.ADV-CL:STRETCH
     'A big flying strip (i.e. a stretch (of land) for flying canoes = planes) was made.'

The presence of agreement on multiple targets does not imply the existence of a multiple classifier system. We return to this in §9.2.

(E) Interrelations between different morphosyntactic loci of noun class agreement

For the time being, it appears impossible to establish any hierarchy in agreement preferences between members of closed classes, e.g. demonstratives or personal pronouns, such that 'if agreement is marked in class X, it must also be marked on class Y'. In many languages of the world noun classes/genders are found only in personal pronouns (e.g. English; Kaingáng, a Jê language from South Brazil: Wiesemann 1972; Rikbaktsa, a Macro-Jê language from Central Brazil: Wiesemann 1986; Guahibo languages from Colombia). In other languages, such as Dyirbal, noun classes are restricted to determiners, deictics and locative interrogatives.

It should be noted, however, that 3rd person pronouns and deictics are often used interchangeably.

The existence of correlations between different morphosyntactic loci of noun class agreement is another intriguing question. According to Greenberg's Universal 31 (Greenberg 1963: 112; Corbett 1991: 111), 'a language which has agreement of the verb in gender with subject or object will also have agreement of the adjective with its head noun'. In other words, the existence of predicate-argument noun class/gender agreement presupposes the existence of head-modifier agreement. This appears to be true in the vast majority of cases. In just a few cases noun class agreement is found outside a noun phrase but not within it. Most such examples come from prefixing Australian languages: in Marrithiyel (Green 1989) and Murrinhpatha (Walsh 1976) noun classes (masculine and feminine) are marked only on dative bound pronouns and on free pronouns, while in Iwaidja (Pym and Larrimore 1979) noun classes are marked exclusively on bound pronouns referring to the transitive subject (A).

This dependency may take a more complicated form. For instance, not all modifiers may agree in gender with their head noun; there may also be different systems of noun classes/genders in head-modifier and predicate-argument agreement. We will return to this in §2.7.

If there is head-modifier agreement, then the following 'hierarchy' operates: agreement on modifiers from open classes > agreement on modifiers from closed classes > agreement in possessive constructions > agreement on peripheral constituents.

These correlations do not necessarily mean that the agreement rules are the same in terms of strictness or variability, or in terms of correlation with discourse-pragmatic and semantic functions. Thus, Manambu distinguishes two genders both in head-modifier and in predicate-argument construction; a correlation between topicality of a noun and its agreement in gender is restricted to non-subject (A/S) participants in predicate-argument constructions, and head-modifier constructions. In Baniwa, agreement in pronominal noun class correlates with topicality of a noun only in predicate-argument constructions, but not in head-modifier ones. In this case different agreement types differ in their discourse-pragmatic properties and variability—though they are marked in a similar way and involve the same semantic oppositions (see Aikhenvald 1995b and (G) below).

(F) Semantic and non-semantic agreement

Noun class can be assigned on the basis of semantic parameters, or a combination of formal and semantic features (see §2.3). These principles of assignment correspond to the notion of 'semantic' and 'syntactic', or 'mechanical' agreement, respectively (Corbett 1991: 225–6; Heine 1982a:

194). A typical example of semantic agreement would be feminine agreement of a modifier with a noun like Russian *vrač* 'doctor'—a noun which can equally refer to a man or to a woman. In this case, there is a choice between feminine and masculine agreement; the feminine agreement will be preferred if the sex of a particular doctor is known, and is important for the speaker. Otherwise the functionally unmarked masculine agreement will be used (see §2.5 on markedness). Semantic agreement is found in many Bantu and non-Bantu languages of Africa, and in Papuan languages. We often get semantic agreement with animate nouns and syntactic agreement with other nouns, e.g. Swahili *ki-faru m-kubwa* (CL7-rhinoceros CL1-big) 'a big rhinoceros' where the head noun, 'rhinoceros', is marked for Class 7 but it governs agreement in Class 1 which covers animates. Syntactic or 'mechanical' agreement is agreement which goes with non-semantic principles of assignment (see Heine 1982a: 194).

The problem of a choice between semantic and syntactic agreement often arises in the case of morphological 'mismatches' between the noun class marked on the noun itself, and the agreement class it is assigned to.[19] In Mayali (Australian: Evans ms: 107–16) the noun classes marked on nouns and agreement class markers on modifiers are often isomorphic, *na-rangem na-kimuk* (CL:MASC-boy CL:MASC-big) 'big boy', *ngal-kohbanj ngal-kimuk* (CL:FEM-old woman CL:FEM-big) 'big old woman'. Nouns without prefixes are assigned to the appropriate agreement classes according to their semantics, e.g. *bininj na-kimuk* (man CL:MASC-big) 'big man' (or on other principles: for instance, manner adverbials derived from nouns and adjectives belong to Class 3 (which is basically the vegetable class) (Evans ms: 105–7)).

The regular 'mismatch' between noun class marked on the noun and the agreement class it belongs to has been referred to as 'quirky' agreement (Evans ms; R. Green 1995). In Mayali quite a few nouns are assigned agreement Class 1 (masculine) or 3 (non-flesh food) which is different from their overt noun class marking. For instance, *kun-(r)ak* 'fire' has a Class 4 prefix but always requires Class 3 agreement (Evans ms: 109). (The quirky agreement is one of the indications in favour of functional unmarkedness of Class 1, for animates, and Class 3, for inanimates; see §2.5.3.) In Gurr-goni (Australian: R. Green 1995: 62) 'quirky' agreement shows a tendency towards a semantic 'regularization' of an otherwise opaque noun class system. The majority of plants and plant parts belong to Class 3, non-flesh food; but a very small number are in Class 1 and 2, e.g. *wartbirritji* 'a white yam', *gurlpuru* 'a yellow yam'. All these nouns require Class 3 agreement. Green reports an opposite tendency as well. Yams which do not have any

---

[19] To account for them, Evans (1997) suggested a useful distinction between *head class* (overtly marked on the noun itself) and *agreement class* (realized in agreement).

overt marking of class usually belong to Class 3. Some speakers occasionally use Class 1 agreement markers for these yams. According to R. Green (1995: 63), 'both patterns of reclassification act to unite yams within one noun class'. 'Double' agreement in noun class is another instance of non-semantic agreement; it will be discussed in §2.6.3, together with double noun class marking.

The Agreement Hierarchy suggested by Corbett (1979: 204; 1991: 226–42) presents constraints for the choices between semantic and non-semantic agreement. There are four types of agreement position (or agreement target): attributive < predicate < relative pronoun < personal pronoun, and 'as we move rightwards along the hierarchy, the likelihood of semantic agreement will increase monotonically (that is, with no intervening decrease)' (Corbett 1991: 226). The Agreement Hierarchy accounts for the use of neuter on adjectives with *Mädchen* 'girl' in German, and the occasional anaphoric use of the personal pronoun *sie* 'feminine'.[20]

(G) Constraints on agreement

Agreement can be constrained by various language specific factors. In some languages agreement only occurs in certain constructions. In North Berber languages which have two genders (masculine and feminine) the verb agrees in gender with its subject; however, there is no agreement in cleft constructions (Laoust 1928: 201–3). In Palikur (North Arawak: Aikhenvald and Green 1998) gender agreement shows up only in some tense-aspect forms. Members of a given word class can show different gender distinctions depending on their syntactic function; in Tamazight and Kabyle (North Berber: Laoust 1928: 40; Vincennes and Dallet 1960) demonstratives used as modifiers do not distinguish gender; they do distinguish genders when used as noun phrase heads.

'Referential' constraints involve dependencies between agreement and such discourse properties of nouns as definiteness and topicality. In some Arawak languages of South America the form of noun class agreement on a modifier is associated with the topicality of the head noun and with focusing on a particular property. This is often the case in languages with a large number of noun classes. In Baniwa (North Arawak: Aikhenvald 1996c), *-ñapi* 'bone' can be considered part of the human body, in which case it triggers agreement in the 'human' noun class, as in 2.18. If it is considered as a vertical object, it triggers agreement in the 'vertical' class, as in 2.19; and if it is looked at as a long object (e.g. a bone used to make a flute), it triggers agreement in the noun class for 'long' objects, as in 2.20.

---

[20] See Corbett (1991: 235–41) for further examples; reformulations of the Agreement Hierarchy have been suggested by Barlow (1992).

2.18. ɾi-ñapi   maka-dari
     3SGNF-bone   big-NCL:NON.FEM.ANIM
     'a bone' (seen as an attribute of human body)

2.19. ɾi-ñapi   maka-ne
     3SGNF-bone   big-NCL:VERT
     'a big bone' (considered as a long vertical object, e.g. a leg bone)

2.20. ɾi-ñapi   maka-pi
     3SGNF-bone   big-NCL:LONG.THIN
     'a long bone'

In North Arawak languages, and in Abkhaz-Abaza, agreement in gender is neutralized if the subject is preposed to the verb, as a means of focusing the agent (Aikhenvald 1995b). In Garifuna, from the North Arawak subgroup, predicate-argument agreement with the subject is obligatory; agreement with an object depends on its definiteness: only definite objects agree (Munroe MS: 2).

In Motuna (see 2.11 and 2.12) gender agreement on the verb depends on the topicality of a noun. In classical Arabic agreement in gender in predicate-argument constructions depends both on constituent order and on definiteness. In verb-initial sentences, agreement in gender is optional (Corbett 1991: 125; Russell 1984: 124–5); it is more likely to occur if the noun phrase is definite. If the subject precedes the predicate, agreement in gender is obligatory.[21]

There may be morphological constraints; for instance, agreeing modifiers can divide into different morphological classes which determine their noun class agreement possibilities. In Latin, adjectives fall into three classes: those which distinguish three genders (masculine, feminine, neuter), those which distinguish two (neuter vs. non-neuter), and those which have just one form for all genders.

Phonological constraints on agreement imply that there is no agreement because of some phonological property of a modifier. As pointed out by Corbett (1991: 134), many adjectives in the spoken French of Paris which end in a vowel do not distinguish genders. In Tsez (Northeast Caucasian) noun classes are overtly marked only on verbs which begin with a vowel (Bernard Comrie, p.c.). In Portuguese, adjectives which end in -e do not distinguish gender agreement forms, e.g. *um homem gigante* 'a giant man', *uma mulher gigante* 'a giant woman'.

Finally, there may be lexical constraints; some modifiers simply fail to show agreement, often due to some 'historical accident'. Many examples of this sort are found among numerals. Cross-linguistically, smaller numbers

---

[21] See also Corbett (1991: 124), for examples of referential constraints on agreement in Swedish.

are more likely to display agreement in gender/noun class than larger ones. In most Berber languages of North Africa, only the numerals 'one' and 'two' agree with the head noun in gender. In the Nakh languages of the Caucasus (Chechen, Ingush, and Tsova-Tush) only the numeral 'four' shows gender agreement. In a number of Dravidian languages (Kolami, Parji, Naiki) which have two basic genders (male human and the rest) lower numerals have special female human forms. In Russian *odin* 'one' distinguishes three genders, as do all adjectives, but *dva* 'two' and *oba* 'both' distinguish only two genders (one form is used for masculine/neuter, the other one for feminine). Historically they are residues of duals, and fewer gender distinctions were present in the dual than in the singular (see §10.1.1). Other numerals do not distinguish genders.[22]

2.4.3. Variability in noun class assignment and variable agreement

Variability in noun class agreement is often due to the semantic reassignment of noun class, for instance, in the case of HYBRID nouns (see §2.3.4) denoting professions.[23]

Variability in noun class assignment is found in systems with semantically transparent noun classes. In Australian languages, nouns with sex-differentiable referents can trigger agreement in accordance with the natural gender (note that the noun class marked on the noun itself remains the same), e.g. Mayali *na-garndegin na-rangem* (CL:MASC-dingo CL:MASC-male) 'male dingo'; *na-garndegin al-daluk* (CL:MASC-dingo CL:FEM-female) 'female dingo' (Evans 1997: 128).

(A) Semantic groups of nouns with variable noun classes

Many languages allow variable noun class marking on a number of nouns like 'baby' and 'child', on some kinship terms and some inanimates. In Dyirbal, *bimu* is both 'father's elder sister' (taking a feminine gender marker) and 'father's elder brother' (masculine marker). *Jaja* 'baby' can be specified as either masculine or feminine. (Alternately, these may be viewed as different lexemes.)

---

[22] In a way, one can say that numbers from 2 to 10 agree in animacy with the head noun (Corbett 1991: 135). They have special collective forms optionally used with animate nouns, e.g. *dva mužčiny* (two:MASC/NEUT man-SG.COUNTING.FORM) 'two men', *dve žentschin-y* (two:FEM woman-SG.COUNTING.FORM) 'two women', *dvoe muzčin/žentschin* (two:ANIM.COLL man/woman-PL.COUNTING.FORM), *dvoe okon 'two:ANIM.COLL windows+PL.COUNTING.FORM'. Another group of constraints on agreement forms comes from interaction between classifiers and other categories, e.g. noun class and number. See Chapter 10.

[23] Some generic terms for animate beings take one agreement form though they denote beings of either sex (termed 'epicenes'). It is up to the language as to what gender epicenes are formally assigned to. In Russian, *kit* 'whale' takes masculine agreement, and *akula* 'shark' always takes feminine agreement, though both can denote beings of either sex (Corbett 1991: 67).

Noun classes and genders can vary in different ways for different semantic groups of nouns. In Brazilian Portuguese, this is widespread for nouns with a human referent, especially the ones which refer to professions. Masculine forms also have generic reference and are used when the sex of a referent is not in focus: *juiz* 'judge (male, or generic)', *juiz-a* 'female judge'; *ministro* 'minister (male, or generic)', *ministra* 'female minister'. In the colloquial language, variable gender is sometimes extended to sex-differentiable non-humans, e.g. *peixe* 'fish (male or generic)', *peix-a* 'female fish (which has caviar inside it)'.

In Ket gender can vary only for inanimates (Dul'son 1968: 62 ff., Krejnovič 1961). Then, for instance, a growing tree is masculine, a cut-down tree is inanimate; an upright tree is masculine, and a tree with a curved trunk is feminine. In languages with shape-based genders spoken in the East Sepik region of New Guinea, change in (covert) gender of most inanimate nouns signals change in shape (see Bruce 1984, on Alamblak). In Manambu (Ndu family) nouns which denote male humans and higher animates and long and thin inanimate objects are masculine, while those which denote female humans and higher animates, and short and round objects, are feminine. Consequently, *nəma-də wi* (big-MASC house) is used to refer to 'a big house' (which is extraordinarily long, or high, or both); and *nəma wi* (big+FEM house) describes 'a big house' (which is not necessarily long, or high).[24]

Along similar lines, in Kxoe (Khoisan; Heine 1982a: 198) an inanimate noun stem can be allocated to masculine or feminine gender depending on its shape: masculine is associated with big, long, rectangular, and feminine with small, round, broad, e.g. *ngú* 'hut', *ngú-mà* 'big rectangular hut (masc.)'; *ngú-hè* 'small, round hut (fem.)'.

Semantic choices may be more complex. Turkana (East Nilotic: Dimmendaal 1983: 220) has three genders: masculine, feminine, and neuter. By changing the gender of an animate noun, specific reference can be made to a male, female or a young of the species:

fem. a-gete'		'female antelope'
masc. e-gete'		'male antelope'
neut. i-gete'		'small antelope of either sex'

A number of nouns referring to inanimates allow variable gender. Some have two forms—masculine and feminine, e.g. 'grass' and 'tree'. Masculine

---

[24] A smallish woman-like man can occasionally be treated as feminine, and a largeish woman can be treated as masculine. The use of a different gender is impossible when the shape cannot be changed (turtles are 'round' and always feminine), or when the 'masculinity' is culturally important. Descent is strictly patrilineal, and so the word *gwalugw* 'patrilineal clan' is masculine. Morphologically, *gwal-ugw* is the plural form of *gwal* which means 'father's child (female or male)' and 'father's father'.

forms mean 'growing, green', and feminine forms mean 'dead, dry state', e.g.

masc. ŋi-ɲaˋ   'green grass'
fem. ŋa-ɲaˋ   'dry grass'

Some inanimate nouns have three gender forms. The opposition of the three is by size, e.g.

masc. e-mor-uˋ   'rocky mountain, big stone'
fem. a-mor-uˋ   'hill stone'
neut. i-mor-uˋ   'pebble'

The degree of variability in agreement class assignment depends on the language. In Dyirbal, variable class assignment is restricted to sex-differentiable animals; the Class 1/Class 2 correlation with male/female is obligatory for humans. Each name of an animal has a fixed class membership; however, exceptionally, noun class assignment can be changed to stress the sex of a particular animal, e.g. 'to point out that a certain dog is male *bayi guda* can be used' (Dixon 1982: 182). Usually, *guda* 'dog' belongs to Class 2 (Dixon 1982: 180), and so the 'unmarked' usage would be *balan guda*. Very occasionally, changing noun class can create a pragmatic effect. In Dyirbal, *yara* 'man' belongs to Class 1, and so would be referred to as *bayi yara*. However, Dixon (1982: 166) reports that a hermaphrodite was once jokingly referred to as *balan yara*, with a feminine Class 2 marker, pointing out his female characteristics. In this case, the manipulation of noun class realized in agreement has pragmatic, as well as semantic effect (see C below).

In these cases variability of noun class assignment is linked to a semantic superclassing of nouns (see C in §2.4.4), most often into animate and inanimate, or human and non-human.

Change in noun class agreement can be employed to distinguish distinct lexical entries. In Anindilyakwa (Australian) *dirija* 'dress' is treated as feminine when understood as a piece of female clothing; it is treated as a member of inanimate *m*-class when seen as a material (Julie Waddy, p.c.).[25] These nouns are said to have double or multiple gender, depending on their semantics. In Russian, Portuguese, or Anindilyakwa, only a limited number of nouns can be assigned more than one gender. In other languages, such 'reclassification' (which is reminiscent of the use of noun classifiers—see Chapter 3—for disambiguating polysemous referents) is much more widespread; this typically happens in languages with semantic

---

[25] Just as in Turkana discussed above. Similarly, in Archi (Northeast Caucasian), *lo* can be assigned to three classes, with a corresponding change in meaning. When assigned to Class 1, it means 'boy'; when assigned to Class 2, it means 'girl', and when assigned to Class 4, it means 'young animal'.

gender assignment which involves parameters other than just sex or animacy.

Variability in 'overt' noun class marking on the same root is the way of creating new words, in languages with overt noun class marking. In Bantu languages, e.g. Swahili, most stems usually occur with a prefix of one class. Prefixes can be substituted to mark a characteristic of an object. *M-zee* means 'old person' and has the human class prefix *m-*. It can be replaced by *ki-* (inanimate class) to yield *ki-zee* 'scruffy old person' (Dixon 1982: 166; also see Shepardson 1982 on the correlations between diminution and choice of class prefix in Swahili).

(B) Limits of variability of noun classes

Variable gender assignment may be restricted to a few random exceptions, and have no semantic content. In Hebrew, a few nouns can have either feminine or masculine gender, without any change in semantics, e.g. *dereh* 'road, way', *lašon* 'language', *ruah* 'spirit, wind'.[26] Variable gender can be found with recent loans. In Russian, *kivi* 'kiwi-fruit', a recent loanword, is sometimes treated as neuter (since it is an undeclinable noun which ends in a vowel), and sometimes as masculine, by association with the superordinate noun *frukt* 'fruit' which is masculine.

(C) Functions of noun class variation

The choice of noun class agreement depends on what aspect of the noun is highlighted. Some northern Australian languages allow different agreement possibilities for certain nouns depending on the 'viewpoint' from which the referent is seen (Evans ms: 108). In Gunwinjgu *kukku* 'water, drink' triggers Class 4 ('neuter') agreement when it is seen as a part of the landscape:

2.21. kun-ekke   kukku   kun-bo-gimuk
       CLIV:NEUTER-that   water   CLIV:NEUTER-CL:LIQUID-big
       'That water (i.e. river) is big.'

When considered a drink, it is assigned to Class 3 (which also covers vegetable food).

2.22. yun   yi-bongu-n   man-ih   kukku
       don't   2SG-drink-NON.PAST   CLIII:NON.FLESH.FOOD-this.here water
       'Don't drink this water!'

---

[26] Garifuna (North Arawak) is reported to have a different kind of variable gender assignment. A subclass of nouns which covers plant names and body parts changes gender according to the sex of the speaker (Taylor 1952). This requires further investigation.

Variable agreement is reported for other semantic groups. *Kun-waral* 'spirit' usually belongs to neuter Class 4 (which is also its 'head class', *kun-* being the prefix of this class). When it refers to 'certain types of spirit', especially malignant spirits, this noun takes agreement with Class 1, since malignant spirits are a subclass of this class. Along similar lines, *delek* 'white ochre, white clay' takes Class 3 agreement when it is not associated with art; but in association with painting, which is considered a typically male activity, it takes masculine Class 1.

Gender variation is often used metaphorically to describe unusual situations (see A above, on the use of the word *yara* 'man' with the feminine class marker, instead of the masculine one, to point out the female characteristics of a hermaphrodite, in Dyirbal). In Manambu, *ab* 'head' is usually feminine because of its round shape, but it is treated as masculine when a person has a headache, since then the head feels heavy and unusually big (properties associated with the masculine gender). Spontaneous manipulation of gender variation is widely used in jokes, and to describe unusual situations, in Cantabrian Spanish. A speaker may use the masculine *hiju miu* 'my son' in a deprecatory reference to a young girl, i.e. a female not yet fully developed, or masculine *oveju* 'male sheep' with a reference to a particularly meagre and unattractive animal independently of its sex (Holmquist 1991: 59–60; see Table 2.2 above).

Different gender agreement systems for different word classes can coexist in one language. Languages with distinct noun class systems used for different types of modifier often allow variable assignment only for one of the systems; usually, the largest one (see §2.7).

2.4.4. Determining the number of noun classes in a language

The number of genders in a language is determined by the types of agreement (Corbett 1991; 1994a; 1994b; Chapter 10 below). For instance, Spanish and Portuguese have two types of agreement, which correspond to feminine and masculine genders. However, a number of problems may create difficulties with establishing how many noun classes and noun class agreement types a language has.

(A) Target genders and controller genders

The number of surface realizations of genders (TARGET GENDERS: Corbett 1991: §6.3) can be different from types of agreement (CONTROLLER GENDERS: Corbett 1991: §6.3). In Rumanian nouns divide into three gender classes. There are two surface markers of genders in singular and two in the plural, but three combinations of these (Corbett 1991: 151). See Table 2.4.

TABLE 2.4. *Gender marking in Rumanian*

SG		PL
-a	F ⎫	-e
-Ø	N ⎬	
	M ⎭	-i

Thus, nouns divide in three classes: (I) those which take -Ø in the singular and -*i* in the plural, e.g. *bărbat* 'man' as in *bărbatul e bun* (man.DEF is good) 'the man is good'; *bărbaţii sînt buni* (men.DEF are good) 'the men are good'; (II) those which take -Ø in the singular and -*e* in the plural, e.g. *scaun* 'chair' as in *scaunul e bun* (chair.DEF is good) 'the chair is good', *scaunele sînt bune* (chairs.DEF are good) 'the chairs are good'; and (III) nouns which take -*a* in the singular and -*e* in the plural, e.g. *fata* 'girl' as in *fata e bun-ă* (girl.DEF is good) 'the girl is good', *fetele sînt bune* (girls.DEF are good) 'the girls are good' (Corbett 1991: 150–1). Thus, there are two target genders and three controller genders (or agreement classes).

The gender system in the Dravidian language Telugu (Krishnamurti and Gwynn 1985: 56–8) works on a similar principle (Table 2.5).

TABLE 2.5. *Gender marking in Telugu*

SG		PL
-ḍu	males, moon, sun ⎫	-ru
-di	females ⎬	
	neuter ⎭	-yi

This is illustrated with the agreement on the verb 'to be' in 2.23–6.

2.23. waaḍ(u)   unnaaḍu
     he   be+MASC.SG
     'He is'

2.24. ad(i)   unnadi
     she/it   be+FEM/NEUTER.SG
     'She/it is'

2.25. waaru   unnaaru
     they   be+MASC/FEM.PL
     'They (those persons: M,F) are'

2.26. aw(i)   unnaayi
     they   be+NEUTER.PL
     'They (those things) are'

Khinalug (Northeast Caucasian: Kibrik *et al.* 1972: 154–5; 118 ff.) has a more complicated system. Nouns divide into four classes: 1: males; 2: females; 3: most non-human animates and some inanimates; 4: all the rest (including abstract nouns and other nouns, e.g. *nimts* 'louse'). Gender agreement is found on demonstrative pronouns, headless adjectives, and verbs. There are two sets of surface agreement markers. Set 1 is used with past and future tenses of resultative and non-resultative aspects. Set 2 is used to mark gender/number agreement on different verbs depending on their morphological class (Table 2.6).

TABLE 2.6. *Gender agreement in Khinalug*

Gender	Set 1		Set 2	
	Singular	Plural	Singular	Plural
1	-du	-dur	Ø/j/h-	b/v/f-
2	-dæ	-dur	z/z/s-	b/v/f-
3	-dæ	-ʒi(tʰ)	b/v/f-	Ø/j/h-
4	-ʒi	-ʒi(tʰ)	Ø/j/h-	Ø/j/h-

In Set 1 singular, genders 2 and 3 have identical marking. In Set 2 singular, genders 1 and 4 group together. And in both plurals, Genders 1 and 2, and 3 and 4, have the same marking. See further discussion in Corbett (1991: 147–70).

(B) Restricted and residual genders

Some languages have genders with a very small number of members. In Archi (Northeast Caucasian) there is a class which takes Gender 3 agreement markers when singular and Gender 1/2 when plural; it consists of just two nouns ('people' and 'population'). In Tsova-Tush (Nakh) there is a gender which contains only four nouns (Corbett 1991: 171).

In Spanish, Romansch, and Portuguese there is a residual neuter gender which is only used for anaphoric agreement (cf. Corbett 1991: 214–15). Portuguese has two genders realized in agreement within a noun phrase (see examples 1.1 and 1.2). However, demonstrative pronouns have three forms: masculine, feminine, and the third one, which goes back to an original neuter in Latin, e.g. masculine *este*, feminine *esta*, neuter *isso* 'this'. These neuter forms are used as resumptive anaphoric pronouns for 'default' agreement (see §2.5). They are also used in fixed expressions, e.g. *por isso* (for this:NEUT) 'this is why', *isto é* 'that is, i.e.', *isto!* 'This is what it is, you are right'. Obviously, neither Portuguese, Spanish, nor Romansch can be said to have three genders synchronically; however, the residual 'anaphoric' gender is a useful indication of the previous stage of the language.

In some languages gender distinctions are restricted to a subclass of nouns and adjectives. In Ayacucho Quechua only a few nouns with human referents require agreement with a closed class of adjectives borrowed from Spanish, e.g. *loko maqta* 'crazy:MASC boy', *loka sipas* 'crazy:FEM girl'. A few borrowed nouns with a human referent distinguish feminine and masculine forms, e.g. *biyudo* 'widower', *biyuda* 'widow' (Parker 1969: 34–5). There is no agreement elsewhere in the language. It is problematic whether such 'exceptions' should be considered separate noun classes at all.[27]

(C) Subgenders and superclassing

Further grouping of noun classes and genders involves SUBGENDERS and SUPERCLASSING. Subgenders can be defined as 'minor agreement classes which control minimally different sets of agreement' (Corbett 1991: 163). Innovative subgenders based on the feature of animateness and personality are characteristic of Slavic languages (Laskowski 1988). Russian has three genders: masculine, feminine, and neuter. Masculine nouns fall into two further subclasses, animate and inanimate. In the animate subclass, accusative singular (on nouns and modifiers) coincides with genitive singular. In the inanimate subclass, accusative singular (on nouns and modifiers) coincides with nominative (as is also the case for neuter nouns) (see Table 2.7).

TABLE 2.7. *A fragment of the Russian nominal paradigm*

	Masculine animate	Masculine inanimate	Neuter	Feminine
NOM SG	*bol'š-oj mal'čik* 'a big boy'	*bol'š-oj dom* 'a big house'	*bol'š-oe selo* 'a big village'	*bol'š-aja košk-a* 'a big cat'
ACC SG	*bol'š-ogo mal'čik-a*	*bol'š-oj dom*	*bol'š-oe selo*	*bol'š-uju košk-u*
GN SG	*bol'š-ogo mal'čik-a*	*bol'š-ogo dom-a*	*bol'š-ogo sel-a*	*bol'š-oj košk-i*

Northwest Caucasian languages (Abkhaz-Abaza) have a basic distinction between human and non-human noun classes. This distinction is manifested in the choice of plural morpheme and agreement with numerals and with adjectives in the plural. Male and female subclasses are distinguished within 3rd person possessive and cross-referencing morphemes (Hewitt 1979: 44–8).

---

[27] A similar phenomenon in Tagalog has been pointed out to me by Randy LaPolla. Certain nouns referring to humans and adjectives used to modify them, most or possibly all of which are loans from Spanish, distinguish two genders, e.g. *loko-ng Pinoy* (crazy:MASC-ATT Philippine) 'a crazy Philippine man', *loka-ng Pinay* (crazy:FEM-ATT Philippine) 'a crazy Philippine woman'.

Chechen and Ingush (Nichols 1989a) has five lexically determined noun classes, formally marked by the appearance of an agreement prefix. There are two human classes, which can be grouped into a human 'macroclass' (or macrogender: Nichols 1989a: 162). For other classes, only a few semantic generalizations can be made (e.g. fruiting trees and fruits and wild animals are in the J class; non-fruiting trees are in the D class; names of manufactured items are distributed among the D, J, and B classes). On the whole, semantics is not a good predictor of gender. Surface markers used for these classes partially overlap (see Table 2.8).

TABLE 2.8. *Noun classes in Ingush*

Class	Prefix singular	Prefix plural
Human feminine	j-	b(ld)-
Human masculine	v-	b(ld)-
J	j-	j-
D	d-	d-
Bd	b-	d-
Bb	b-	b-

An unmarked agreement class may replace the inherent class of the noun. In Ngalakan (Merlan 1983) demonstratives can agree with the head noun, or can simply show the unmarked prefix *rnu-* 'masculine gender', unless the referent of the head noun is female.

This is described as CONCORDIAL SUPERCLASSING (Evans 1997; Harvey 1997; Sands 1995: 264–5). Concordial superclassing may result in the creation of 'macroclasses', which are superimposed onto the system of noun agreement classes. For example, Gaagudju (Australian: Harvey 1997: 153) has four noun agreement classes, with distinct class prefixes: 1: human males, most animates, European material objects, rain; 2: human females, some animates; 3: plants and their parts, weapons; 4: abstract entities, body parts, fire, geographical features, temporals. Noun class is marked on adjectives, demonstratives, quantifiers, and in absolutive pronominal prefixes on the verb. With demonstratives as modifiers, all nouns with an animate referent tend to have Class 1 agreement, and all the inanimates Class 3 agreement. Thus, Gaagudju can be said to have two macroclasses: animate and inanimate.[28]

---

[28] Alternatively, one may say that there are homophonous class markers used just with demonstratives. This solution does not help us solve the problem concerning the 'number' of noun classes in this language.

50   Classifiers

Superclassing does not necessarily reduce the number of classes. In some languages 'superclassing' indicates the overlap of different classes.

Lokono (North Arawak: Pet 1987: 25–7) distinguishes two genders, masculine and feminine, in the singular (see (C) in §11.2.1, on the semantics of gender in Lokono). There are three distinctions in singular and in plural which are based on an interaction of feminine and masculine gender, and the feature human/non-human. All non-humans regardless of their sex or number are referred to with an anaphoric pronoun *tho* and require feminine agreement on modifiers and on the verb. Plural humans are referred to with a plural anaphoric pronoun *ne* and require plural agreement. Singular masculine nouns are referred to with *li* and require masculine agreement, while singular feminine nouns require feminine agreement and are referred to with *tho*.

2.5. Markedness and resolution in noun classes

Markedness relations in noun class systems are different from those in other noun classification devices. I discuss markedness in §2.5.1. The notion of noun class resolution is explained in §2.5.2. Then, in §2.5.3, I consider different markedness relations in noun class systems.

2.5.1. Markedness

There are two main types of markedness—formal and functional. A term in a system is formally unmarked if it has zero realization or a zero allomorph. If the terms in a system, save one, are only used in specified circumstances, and the remaining term is used in all other circumstances, then it is said to be functionally unmarked (cf. Dixon 1994: 56–7; Aikhenvald and Dixon 1998: 60).

A useful summary of criteria found relevant to markedness was provided by Greenberg (1966); also see Croft (1990: 71).[29] Only criteria relevant to functional markedness are given here (Greenberg 1966: 25–30).

---

[29] See Croft (1996) and Andrews (1990) on further issues concerning markedness relations. When grammatical categories have more than two values, one value is marked relative to another (cf. Croft 1990: 66; 1996). Markedness relations may be dependent on other categories which correlate with them, and may be restricted to grammatical subclasses. For instance, in the vast majority of the world's languages singular numbers are less marked than non-singular ones (e.g. Tsonope 1988, on the relative markedness of singular and plural noun classes in Setswana, a Bantu language). In some languages, the unmarked form is the collective one; and the singular noun has a special singulative marker. This is an areal feature shared by a number of families in the Northwest Amazon—Arawak (Resígaro, Tariana), East Tucano, and Guahibo (e.g. Cuiba: Kerr 1995). There, noun classifiers are used as singulative markers; and a noun can be pluralized only if it contains a noun classifier. In this case, formally

(i) The unmarked value of the form will refer to either value (marked or unmarked one) in certain contexts—e.g. the unmarked term can be used for a supercategory which covers all the terms.

(ii) In certain grammatical environments, only the unmarked value will appear (see below on gender resolution and neutral, or default agreement).

(iii) The unmarked category is the one most frequently used (or the one that is used at least as frequently as each marked one).

(iv) The marked category displays syncretization of its inflectional possibilities with respect to the unmarked member; i.e. there are 'at least as many distinct forms in the paradigm with the unmarked value as in the paradigm with the marked value' (Greenberg 1966: 27).

(v) The unmarked category is realized in neutralized contexts.

Formal markedness and functional markedness may correlate, but they do not necessarily always go together (see Corbett 1991: 291; Hayward and Corbett 1988, for discussion of Qafar, an East Cushitic language; Bulygina and Shmelev 1996, for Russian[30]). There are systems in which all noun classes are equally formally marked and no relations of functional markedness can be established.

A noun class can be considered functionally unmarked under the following conditions:

(a) It is used as a generic term and for indefinite reference.

(b) It is used when the noun class distinction is neutralized or is of no relevance.

(c) It may be used in default, or neutral agreement (see Corbett 1991: 206 ff., and below).

A functionally unmarked noun class is likely to be one of the largest classes.

Noun class systems may have a special agreement form with heads, or controllers which are not specified for any agreement class. This is called neutral or default agreement (Corbett 1991: 203 ff.). These controllers are called 'non-prototypical'. The range of non-prototypical controllers varies. These may include infinitive phrases, nominalizations, and dummy

---

unmarked nouns are also functionally unmarked: they are used if number does not have to be specified. This is called 'local markedness' or 'markedness reversal' by Croft (1990: 66, 144–5). This may be limited to certain semantic subclasses. In some languages this 'reversal' is limited to objects that 'naturally occur in groups and are difficult to individuate' (Croft 1990: 66, 144–5), as in Semitic, Berber and Nilo-Saharan languages. In Amazonian languages, this is found with inanimate nouns whose referents are easily individuated, and never with nouns which have a collective referent. There may be different markedness relations between noun classes and classifiers for animate and inanimate nouns.

[30] For further discussion of relative markedness of Russian genders, see Jakobson (1984).

elements. The use of one of the noun classes for default agreement is an indication of the functional unmarkedness of this class. In a two-gender system, Hebrew uses masculine form for neutral agreement. Masculine gender is unmarked—both formally, and functionally. In Zayse (Omotic: Hayward 1989), feminine gender is unmarked and is used for default agreement (see Fraser and Corbett 1997, for the notion of default gender in Arapesh).

There may be unique forms used just for default agreement, e.g. neutral resumptive pronouns in Spanish and Portuguese (discussed in §2.4.4; cf. discussion of Spanish in Corbett 1991: 214–15).

2.5.2. Noun class resolution

Languages differ in the ways in which they deal with the coordination of nouns belonging to different noun classes/genders, or associated with different classifiers. This choice of a noun class for coordination can be referred to as a 'resolution rule' (Givón 1970). The choice of the agreeing form has to do with the functional markedness of one, or more than one, form.[31] Resolution rules in coordinating nouns which belong to different classes also provide evidence in favour of the relative markedness of noun classes.

The problem of noun class/gender resolution is sometimes solved semantically, and sometimes syntactically, or by a combination of these methods. In some languages it cannot be solved at all; then markedness relations cannot be established.

SEMANTIC RESOLUTION involves exclusive reference to the meaning of the conjoined noun phrases (Corbett 1991: 269–78). It usually involves grouping nouns into larger classes, based on more general semantic features, usually dividing nouns into animate, or human and the rest.

In Luganda and ChiBemba conjoined nouns with human referents are treated as plural class 2 (human), even if none of the referents actually belongs to this class (Givón 1970: 253–4; 1971: 38–9): see 2.27, from ChiBemba.

2.27. omu-kazi es-sajja ne olu-ana
 CL1-woman CL5-fat.man and CL11-thin.child
 ba-alabwa omusajja
 CL2-were.seen (by).the.man
 'The woman, the fat man and the thin child were seen (by) the man.'

If neither of the conjuncts denotes a human, class 8 is used on the predicate:

---

[31] Features which require resolution are person, number, and gender/noun classes. Person resolution rules and person hierarchies have been discussed at length by Zwicky (1977: 718, 725), and summarized by Corbett (1991: 262–3). Number resolution rules are stated in Corbett (1991: 263–4).

2.28. en-te   omu-su   eki-be   ne   ely-ato
     CL9-cow   CL3-wild.cat   CL7-jackal   and   CL5-canoe
     bi-alabwa   omusajja
     CL8-were.seen   (by).the.man
     'The cow, the wild cat, the jackal and the canoe were seen (by) the man.'

Conjoining nouns denoting a human and a non-human is considered 'less natural', or 'less grammatical' and tends to be avoided (see Givón 1970: 253).

In some Northern Australian languages resolution principles are directly associated with superclassing (also see C in §2.4.4). The functionally unmarked masculine noun class 1 is used to mark agreement of conjoined plurals of any class in Mayali (Nick Evans, p.c.).

In SYNTACTIC RESOLUTION, one of the existing forms will be used, as in Portuguese, French, Modern Hebrew, or Hindi, and it can then be considered the unmarked one. In Portuguese, when the conjuncts are of different genders, the masculine form of the adjective is used:[32]

2.29. um   menino   e   uma   menina   bonit-os
      INDEF:MASC   boy   and   INDEF:FEM   girl   beautiful-PL:MASC
      'beautiful boy and girl'

The use of a default, or neutral form is another means of resolution. Lama (Gur) has a default class—the resumptive *wa* is used to refer to conjoined elements of any two classes if they undergo left dislocation, as in 2.30 (Yu 1988: 332–3):

2.30. yo   ŋka   na   nawu   ŋkʉ   me   hem   wa
      child   DET.CL5   and   bull   DET.CL3   I   pulled   PRONOUN
      'The child and the bull, I pulled them.'

There may be MIXED SEMANTIC AND SYNTACTIC RESOLUTION. In Latin, semantic resolution is found with nouns denoting persons; and syntactic resolution is used with other nouns. Masculine agreement is used when conjuncts of different genders denote persons; if not, neutral agreement is used (Corbett 1991: 284 ff.).[33]

---

[32] Another strategy which is alternative to syntactic resolution is agreement with just one conjunct (see a discussion on Swahili in Corbett 1991: 265–6; see also Steinberg and Caskey 1988: 301; Bokamba 1985).

[33] Languages can combine several strategies of syntactic resolution, as does Hausa (Schwartz *et al.* 1988), or several semantic and syntactic principles, as does Spanish (Steinberg and Caskey 1988). A very complicated example of mixed semantic and syntactic noun class resolution is found in Gurr-goni (Australian: R. Green 1995). Gender resolution may even be determined on phonological principles, as in Xhosa, a Bantu language; see Voeltz (1971) and Pullum and Zwicky (1986).

Some languages have no resolution strategies: nouns which belong to different classes cannot be conjoined. Then, markedness relations cannot be established (see C in §2.5.3).

2.5.3. Markedness relationships in noun classes

The following situations can be distinguished with respect to the functional markedness of noun classes.

(A) In a system with several classes, one is marked and the others are unmarked

The unmarked gender is often masculine, as in Indo-European or Afroasiatic languages; more rarely feminine, as in Guajiro, Lokono (Arawak: Aikhenvald 1999a), Jarawara (Arawá: Dixon 1995); Wangkumara and Wagaya (Australian: Alpher 1987: 174; Breen 1976a: 336; 1976b: 340, 590).

A term—or an agreement form used as generic, and for indefinite reference—may be functionally unmarked. In traditional English, the masculine pronoun *he* was used as an unmarked generic term for human reference (see the discussion in Alpher 1987), and so was functionally unmarked. In French, masculine gender can be considered functionally unmarked since it is used in the case of generic reference. Masculine plural like *les américains* can refer to a mixture of the sexes, while feminine plural *les américaines* refers only to female Americans (Schane 1970; cf. also Greenberg 1966: 30–1; Corbett 1991: 291). Indefinites and interrogatives require masculine agreement in Manambu, a Ndu language from the East Sepik region of New Guinea, with two genders (masculine and feminine). This shows that masculine is functionally unmarked—see 2.31. The use of the feminine agreement form (*ha-l*) would imply that the speaker already has some idea about the shape, or the sex of the referent.

2.31. agua-jap   ha-d
      what-thing   DEM-MASC
      'What is this?'

In Russian, the choice of masculine agreement with interrogative and indefinite pronouns indicates the functional unmarkedness of masculine (Bulygina and Shmelev 1996: 103).

In Gurr-goni, a northern Australian language with a 'typical' Australian system of four noun classes, class prefixes used on the indeterminates *-nji* 'what/which/any thing' and *-njatbu* 'whatsitsname' provide interesting evidence in favour of the relative functional markedness of noun classes. All the four noun classes are formally marked with prefixes (R. Green 1995: 64–7). If the semantic domain of a referent is known, the appropriate noun class prefix is used. Class I 'masculine' is used only when the referent is not known, as in 2.32.

2.32. a-nji   nji-na-ni
      3CL1-what   2MIN.A.3MIN.O-see-PRECONT
      'What did you see?'

In contrast, in 2.33 the indefinite/interrogative takes the Class 3 prefix *mu-* 'vegetable food', because the domain of the referent is known: the speaker is trying to remember a plant name. The indefinite/interrogative form is underlined.

2.33. mu-njatbu   muwu-me-nji
      3CL3-whatsit   3AUG.A.3CL3:O-get-PRECONT
      awurr-ni-Ø
      3AUGS-be-PRECONT
      'What's that CL.3 thing (vegetable food) they were getting?'

Class 1 agreement is also used as 'generic' agreement with reference to a group of referents of a different class. In 2.34 the speaker enumerates members of Class 3, 'vegetable food', but refers to them with the Class 1 prefix on the indefinite pronoun (underlined).

2.34. njiwu-ba-rri   mitja   a-nji
      1AUG.A.3MINO-eat-PRECONT vegetable.food(CL3)   3CL1-what/which
      djuka   dilip . . .
      sugar(CL3)   tea-leaves(CL3)
      'We ate vegetable food, which one (kind), sugar, tea-leaves . . .'

If a language has concordial superclassing (when one agreement class can be used to replace some, or all other), the class which is used as the superclass can be considered unmarked (Sands 1995: 264, and C under §2.4.4). Australian languages with superclassing typically use masculine as the superclass (cf. (C3) in §12.1.3).

(B) Noun classes can have different properties with respect to markedness relations depending on semantics, and on syntactic contexts

Concordial superclassing in Australian languages often provides evidence in favour of different functionally unmarked classes for animates and for inanimates. Mayali (Evans 1997) has a 'typical' Australian system of four noun classes. In the case of a mismatch between head class and agreement class the class assigned to animates is always Class 1 'masculine', and the class assigned to inanimates is always Class 3 'vegetable food'.

Different classes of modifiers can have different markedness relations. In Gurr-goni Class I 'masculine' is used as the functionally unmarked choice with indefinites and interrogatives. But there are also instances in which

Class IV is used as a functionally unmarked one (R. Green 1995: 66). There are two adjectives whose 'scope of reference is universal: everything or nothing': -*marrman* 'good, well' and -*yalang* 'not having anything'. Thus, *gun-yalang* (3CLIV-not.having.anything) can be used to deny the possession or existence of something from any of the four noun classes. In the same way, *gun-marrman* (3CLIV-good, well) can be used to refer to the state of any person, or anything independently of its class.

Some languages provide contradictory evidence for markedness. The Western Torres Strait language has two semantically assigned 'genders', feminine and masculine. The feminine gender is the obvious 'candidate' to be considered an unmarked gender, since it is the one used for the majority of instances of default agreement (Bani 1987). All plurals are treated as 'feminine'. However, agreement with an unidentified human being (at a distance) will always be masculine (for comparable data from Slovene, a Slavic language with a three-gender system, see Corbett 1991: 291).

Different word classes can display different relations of markedness. In Ngalakan masculine gender is used as a superclass only for demonstrative modifiers (Merlan 1983).

(C) None of the noun classes can be considered unmarked

This is the case for Ungarinjin (Rumsey 1982), Tiwi (Osborne 1974), Alamblak (Bruce 1984), or Dyirbal (Dixon 1972). In Tamil, rational nouns (which include humans, gods, and other mythical beings) cannot be conjoined with irrational ones. The Australian language Ungarinjin does not allow conjunction of nouns belonging to different classes. Then the same verb must simply be repeated with each conjunct, as in 2.35 (Rumsey 1982: 137).

2.35. uŋgaḷu m-iniŋani
 beet.like.tuber M.CLASS.OBJECT-she.put
 banimbum w-iniŋani
 carrot.like.tuber W.CLASS.OBJECT-she.put
 'She put down a beet-like tuber and a carrot-like tuber (lit. she put down a beet-like tuber, she put down a carrot-like tuber).'

2.6. Realization of noun classes

In a language with noun classes, noun class is realized through agreement outside the noun itself. In some languages the noun class of some, or all nouns can be inferred from its form. These languages are said to have an 'overt' noun class. In contrast, languages in which the form of a noun tells us nothing about its class are said to have a 'covert' noun class. These, and related problems, are discussed in §2.6.1. Morphological means used to mark noun classes are discussed in §2.6.2. Double marking of noun class is considered in §2.6.3.

2.6.1. Overt and covert noun class marking

Overt noun class marking is common in Bantu languages. They have large systems of affixes which are typically portmanteau morphemes of noun class and number (see D in §10.1.1), e.g. Sesotho *mọ*–*thọ* 'person' (Class 1), *ba-thọ* 'people' (Class 2), *sẹ*–liba 'spring, well' (Class 7), *li-liba* 'springs, wells' (Class 8) (Demuth *et al.* 1986: 455); Kikuyu *ha-ndũ* 'place' (Class 16), *ũ-ndũ* 'event' (Class 14) (Denny and Creider 1986: 217).

In Apurinã (Arawak, Brazil) feminine nouns tend to end in *-ro*, and masculine nouns tend to end in *-ri* (Facundes 1994: 38). In Portuguese, similar to many other Romance languages, nouns which end in *-a* are feminine, and those which end in *-o* are masculine (with a few exceptions, e.g. *dia* 'day' which is masculine, and *mão* 'hand', which is feminine).

Chechen-Ingush languages have a strong correlation between the initial consonant of a noun and its gender. For instance, nouns beginning with *d* or *t* favour D-class, and nouns beginning with *b* or *m* favour B-class (Nichols 1989a: 165; see §2.3.4).

Overt and covert marking can be viewed as two extremes of a continuum. The degree of 'overtness' of a noun class may depend on case and number. In Russian, gender is almost always shown in the nominative case. In oblique cases there is a certain amount of syncretism between the inflections of nouns of different genders, and so it is more difficult to tell from the form of the noun what gender it belongs to.

Overt marking of noun class may depend on other factors. In numerous Australian languages the degree of overtness of noun class marking is related to its morphological transparency. In Wardaman (Australian) many nouns have a prefix of one of three classes: *yi-* 'animate and human beings, meat, body parts'; *ma-* 'flora', *wu-* 'the rest'. However, prefixes are often morphologically fused with the root, and are then synchronically inseparable from it, e.g. *wuja* 'fire', *magulu* 'cheeky yam'; only a few nouns can occur with either *ma-* or *wu-* prefix (Merlan *et al.* 1997). And numerous nouns, e.g. names for animals, trees, and flora, do not occur with a class prefix (Merlan 1994: 61).

Not all nouns in a language have to be overtly marked. Babungo (Grassfields Bantu, Benue-Congo; Schaub 1985: 172) has fourteen noun classes which differ as to the degree of their overt marking on the noun. Only eight of them require a noun class prefix, one has a noun class suffix, and five classes have no overt marker on the noun at all.

In Anindilyakwa (Australian) only inherited nouns (not loans) are overtly marked for noun class; the borrowings receive no overt class marking. This may be an indication that overt noun class marking was productive at an earlier stage, but then ceased to be productive; any noun which was borrowed into the language after the noun class marking stopped being productive does not have a prefix (Leeding 1989; Sands 1995: 260).

Some languages seldom or never mark gender on the noun itself, e.g. Arawá languages (South Amazon), Ndu languages (East Sepik region of Papua New Guinea), Zande (Niger-Congo), or !Xu (North Khoisan) (Heine 1982a: 193). This is 'covert' gender.

In some languages nouns can be either marked or unmarked for gender. The marked form tends to be more specific than the unmarked form. The presence of a gender marker may correlate with definiteness in discourse (as in Gola: West Atlantic; see A in §12.1.3). In Turkana (Eastern Nilotic: Dimmendaal 1983: 221) the gender prefix is frequently omitted from names of animals in folk tales when the names are used generically. Overt gender marking in Alamblak (Lower Sepik) is used to focus on the sex of an animate referent, or indicate a change in size of an inanimate one.

The overt noun class marking on the noun can be omitted in Baniwa, Tariana (North Arawak) and in Tucano languages. The overt marking correlates with the individuation of the item and the focusing of a criterial property, usually related to shape and size. In Tariana, *sawari* means 'thread (in general)'; and *sawari-kha* (thread-CL:CURVILINEAR) means 'long and thin thread'. In Baniwa, *tʃinu* means 'dog (of any size or sex, usually non-feminine)', *tʃinu-da* (dog-CL:ROUND) means 'smallish dog'.

Languages with semantically transparent noun class assignment tend not to mark class on the noun. In languages of this type, only nouns with human and, more rarely, with animate referents are likely to have their gender overtly marked. For instance, in Manambu masculine and feminine gender (assigned according to transparent semantic principles) are not marked on the noun.[34]

'Mismatches' between the overt noun class marking and the agreement class were discussed under F in §2.4.2.

2.6.2. Morphological realization of noun classes

Noun classses are never marked with free morphemes (unlike other noun categorization devices). Various types of morphological processes are used for noun class marking: (A) external affixation, (B) apophony, or vowel

---

[34] The lexemes *ta:kw* 'woman' and *du* 'man' are used with a few kinship nouns and a few other nouns with a human referent for specification of sex, e.g. *yanan* 'grandchild', *yanan-takw* 'granddaughter', *yanan-du* 'grandson'. In Tariana (North Arawak) a number of derivational affixes are used to distinguish masculine and feminine nouns with human referents, e.g. *ha-niri* 'father (parent-MASC)', *ha-dua* 'mother (parent-FEM)'.

changes. Suprasegmental processes (tone patterns, or change of stress) are almost never used (see (C)). Noun classes are never realized suppletively, or via reduplication. Another, very rare, method of morphological realization of noun classes is via repeaters (see (D)).

(A) External affixation

Suffixes and prefixes are the most frequent realizations of noun classification. In the majority of Indo-European and South American Indian languages, noun class agreement in noun phrases is realized with suffixes. Some languages use a prefix and a suffix together (sometimes called circumfixes, confixes, or simulfixes), e.g. *t-* . . . *-t* 'feminine marker' in Berber languages.

Suffixes are more common than prefixes across the world's languages, and noun class suffixes are found more frequently than noun class prefixes. Languages sometimes employ either suffixes or prefixes depending on the type of agreement target and the type of modifier. In Papuan languages of the Torricelli family, head-modifier agreement on adjectives is marked with suffixes, and predicate-argument agreement is realized through prefixes (e.g. Arapesh, Yimas, Monumbo, Olo: Foley 1986: 85). In Baïnouk (West Atlantic) some demonstratives take prefixed agreement, and some take suffixed agreement in noun class; agreement markers with adjectives, numerals, and interrogatives are prefixes (see (D) below). Limilngan (Australian: Harvey forthcoming) has four noun classes: one for humans, one for animals, one for plants, and one residual. Noun class agreement is marked with prefixes on adjectives and pronominal possessives, and with suffixes on demonstratives. Tiwi (Australian: Osborne 1974: 51) has two noun classes, masculine and feminine; these are marked with suffixes on nouns, adjectives and the interrogative 'who/what', and with prefixes to verbs and demonstratives. In Nunggubuyu, an Australian language with four noun classes (Heath 1984: 163, 274), noun class is marked with prefixes to adjectives, nouns, and demonstratives, and with suffixes to demonstratives used as predicates (Heath 1984: 272).

Prefixes mark noun classes in most Benue-Congo, Togo Remnant, West Atlantic and Eastern Nilotic languages. Suffixes are used for marking noun class in Gur (Voltaic), some West Atlantic (e.g. Ful), a few Niger-Congo, Khoisan, and Afroasiatic languages (Heine 1982a: 194).

(B) Apophony, or vowel changes

Languages rarely use vowel change to mark noun class agreement. However, in Jarawara (Arawá) vowel changes are used to mark feminine and masculine agreement (Dixon 1995; Dixon forthcoming). Typically for an Amazonian language, gender is not overtly marked on nouns. It is marked on some adjectival and deictic modifiers, and on some possessed nouns within a possessive NP—these cross-reference the gender of the possessor. There is also gender cross-referencing on most types of verbal suffix (and on a verb root itself when no suffix follows). For possessed nouns, there are six types of gender marking which involve vowel alternation and external affixation, e.g. *i/o* alternation in the last syllable, e.g. fem. *noki*, masc. *noko* 'eye, face', or *e/a* alternation in non-final syllable(s), e.g. fem. *tame*, masc. *teme* 'foot'; fem. *anate*, masc. *enete* 'chin'.[35]

Another notable example of noun classes marked by vowel alternation is Marind, spoken in southern Irian Jaya (Drabbe 1955: 22–3; Foley 1986: 82–3). Marind has four noun classes which trigger head-modifier type agreement with demonstratives and adjectives. Noun class is indicated by the vowel of the stem-final syllable of some nouns, and of modifiers. The first class, with a characteristic vowel *e*, contains male humans; the second class, with vowel *u*, contains female humans and animals; the third class mainly consists of plants and trees, and is characterized by *e*, *a*, or *o*. The fourth class is a residual class which contains decorations, clothing, body parts, some plants and trees, etc., and its characteristic vowel is *i*, e.g. *haz<u>e</u>z* 'weak' (1 class), *haz<u>u</u>z* 'weak' (2 class), *haz<u>a</u>z* 'weak' (3 class), *haz<u>i</u>z* 'weak' (4 class).[36]

Elements of ablaut are used for gender marking in several Pamir languages (Southeastern Iranian languages spoken in Tadjikistan and Afganistan: Rastorgueva 1978), e.g. Roshani *rāšt māwn* 'red:FEM apple', *rošt kurtā* 'red:MASC shirt' (Sokolova 1966: 372).[37]

Warekena (North Arawak: Aikhenvald 1998b) has one of the most morphologically varied systems of gender agreement marking. Distal spatial demonstratives obligatorily mark gender agreement with the head noun through an infix: masc. *eta* (from *ayta*), fem. *ay-u-ta* 'that'. The proximate demonstrative is semi-suppletive: masc. *eni*, fem. *ayupalu* 'this'. Agreement with adjectives is marked with a suffix, masc. Ø fem. *-yawa*; predicate-argument agreement is marked with prefixes for A and S_a and with suffixes for O and S_o.

(C) Suprasegmental processes (tone patterns, or change of stress)

Suprasegmental processes are very rarely used in noun classification marking. An example of a suprasegmental realization of noun classes marked on the noun itself comes from Rendille (East Cushitic: Heine 1982a: 201). In

---

[35] This unusual fusional pattern of gender marking in possessed nouns in Jarawara can be explained in terms of a number of regular diachronic changes from an entirely agglutinative, suffixing structure in Proto-Arawá (Dixon 1995: 281), with possessed nouns marked with the suffixes *-ni* 'feminine' and *-ne* 'masculine'.

[36] There are further examples for how this ablaut pattern works in complex adjectives in Drabbe (1955: 23).

[37] Vowel ablaut and infixation mark absolutive gender agreement in Budukh (Lezgian branch of Daghestanian, Northeast Caucasian: Nichols 1989a: 159).

this language every noun is overtly marked for masculine or feminine gender. Masculine nouns have the tone pattern high–low, and feminine nouns have low–high pattern on the last two syllables; all preceding syllables are low in both genders, e.g. *maxábal* 'man, husband', *maxabál* 'woman, wife' (where ´ marks high tone and low tone is unmarked).

(D) 'Repeaters' as noun class agreement markers

In very few languages noun class agreement is marked via partial or total 'repetition' of a noun. ('Repeaters' of this sort are a rare and frequently neglected means of marking agreement.) Similarly to free forms used as repeaters for numeral classifiers (see Chapter 4), or in multiple classifier systems (see Chapter 9), they are never the only agreement type, being limited to a semantically or morphologically defined subset of nouns. 'Repeaters' are a kind of counterexception to the statement that there is a limited countable number of noun classes (see §2.2).

This phenomenon has been described for Baïnouk, a West Atlantic language spoken in Senegal and in Guinea Bisau (Sauvageot 1967).[38] Baïnouk has two structural types of noun—those which contain overt noun class prefixes[39] and those which do not. Agreement in noun class is obligatory in head-modifier constructions (a modifier can be a demonstrative, an adjective, an interrogative, or a numeral up to nine). If a noun is marked for class, 'head class' prefixes are also used as agreement markers. Then they are suffixed or prefixed to demonstratives of different types, as in 2.36, and prefixed to adjectives, interrogatives and numerals, as in 2.37 (Sauvageot 1967: 230–1).

2.36. si-dēn-o   in-si
     NCL4-canoe-DEM   this-NCL4
     'this canoe'

2.37. gu-sɔl   gu-fɛr
     NCL7-boubou   NCL7-white
     'a white boubou (a kind of clothing)'

Some nouns with no overt noun class marking[40] require prefix *a*- with adjectives and numerals, and (-)*no*(-) with demonstratives. Examples given

---

[38] A similar system has been mentioned for a few other West Atlantic languages, e.g. Badyaranké and Landuma (Volodja Plungian, Antonina I. Koval', and Viktor A. Vinogradov, p.c.).

[39] As in many other West Atlantic languages, noun classes interact with number: there are fewer classes in the plural than there are in the singular (Sauvageot 1967: 227). The assignment of noun classes is opaque in most cases, e.g. *si-dēn* (NCL4-canoe) 'a canoe'; in some cases, however, semantics is straightforward, e.g. *da-dēn* (NCL13:AUGMENTATIVE-canoe) 'a big canoe'; *ko-dēn* (NCL11:DIM-canoe) 'a small canoe' (Sauvageot 1967: 229).

[40] There are about 200 nouns which have no prefixes. They constitute a quarter of the vocabulary on which Sauvageot's analysis is based (1967: 229). No information is given about how many prefixless nouns require repeating agreement.

by Sauvageot (1967: 232) include nouns with animate referents, e.g. ḍiboṇ a-fɛr 'a white horse', ḍiboṇ in-no 'this horse'.

Other prefixless nouns mark agreement on modifiers by REPEATING the first CV sequence of their stem on the agreeing constituent, e.g. 2.38–41. All the examples given by Sauvageot (1967: 232) are nouns with inanimate referents.

2.38. katāma-ŋɔ   in-ka
      river-DEM   this-REPEATER
      'this river'

2.39. katāma   ka-wayi
      river   REPEATER-big
      'a wide river'

2.40. ḍapɔṇ-ɔ   in-ḍa
      grass-DEM   this-REPEATER
      'this grass'

2.41. ḍapɔṇ   ḍa-wuri
      grass   REPEATER-long
      'long grass'

Thus, in Baïnouk phonologically determined 'repeating' agreement is restricted to a morphologically defined subclass of nouns.[41] According to Sauvageot (1967: 233), prefixless nouns appear to be loans, or at least 'foreign-sounding' words.

This example of repeaters used for noun class agreement shows that:

(a) repeaters are just one of the mechanisms of marking agreement; it will be shown in Chapter 9 that no example has been found so far of a language where this is the only mechanism;[42]

(b) repeaters have some semantic and/or morphological constraints on their use (and sometimes discourse constraints as well: see Chapter 9); they are often used just with inanimates.

---

[41] But see objections to this raised by Doneux (1967: 235).

[42] 'Repeaters' as an agreement device have some similarities with phonologically conditioned noun class agreement systems, e.g. those found in the languages of the Arapesh family in the East Sepik province of New Guinea (Arapesh: Fortune 1942; Aronoff 1991; Conrad 1996; Bukiyip: Conrad and Wogiga 1991; Mufian: Conrad 1978; 1996), and in Yimas (Foley 1986). Elements of repetition are also found in the noun class assignment of loan words in Wolof (described as 'the copy process' by McLaughlin 1997: 16–17), e.g. galaas gi 'the ice' (from French glace), waliis wi 'the suitcase' (from French valise), soble si 'the onion' (from Portuguese cebola).

2.6.3. Double marking of noun classes

Some languages allow double marking of noun class. Examples of these unusual strategies are found (A) in a few Bantu languages and (B) in some Australian languages. Their properties are summarized in (C).

(A) Double marking of noun classes in Bantu languages

A number of Bantu languages with multiple noun class systems allow two noun classes to be marked on a morphological word. Certain nouns that already contain a noun class prefix which determines their agreement properties may take a further noun class prefix.

In Kikuyu, if a noun is diminutivized, it can receive two noun class prefixes: if a noun of noun class 1/2 (singular/plural) is diminutivized, it acquires the diminutive class 12/13 which is then prefixed to the original 1/2 class marker, e.g. *mũ-ndũ* (Prefix1:CL1/2-person) 'a person'; *ka-mũ-ndũ* (Prefix2:CL12/13-Prefix1:CL1/2-person) 'a small person' (Stump 1993: 171). A similar strategy is found in Swahili (Shepardson 1982; Helma Pasch, p.c).

Not all noun class prefixes can occupy the pre-prefixal position. The set of prefixes which can occur in this position (termed 'secondary' prefixes by Vail 1974: 24) are typically associated with degree, or value: they include diminutives and augmentatives, and sometimes pejoratives and honorifics.

Ndali (a Bantu language spoken in Malawi and in Tanzania) has 21 noun class prefixes which correspond to 14 classes: of the 21 prefixes, 14 are singular vs. plural pairs, and thus correspond to seven classes; the remaining seven classes do not have plural counterparts (they contain abstract nouns and locatives). The system of noun classes in Ndali is illustrated in Table 2.9 (adapted from Vail 1974: 25–47). Noun classes are numbered in accordance with Vail (1974: 25).

As in the majority of Bantu languages, noun class assignment is only partly based on semantic principles, and is partly opaque; there are also some morphological principles in operation, e.g. all verbal infinitives belong to Class 15. It can be seen from this table that secondary noun prefixes correspond to augmentatives, pejoratives, and diminutives, and also locatives, e.g. *uØ-kaβwɣa* 'dog (CL1a)', *icokaβwɣa* (from *ic(i)-uØ-kaβwɣa*) 'very dirty dog' (sec. CL7) (Vail 1974: 33). If the same prefix is used as a primary, and as a secondary marker, the semantics of the primary marker may be opaque; but the semantics of the secondary one is always associated with augmentatives/pejoratives, or diminutives, as is the case with Classes 3/4, 7/8, 12/13 above.

Double prefix structures in Ndali, and a few other languages (e.g. Kikuyu: Stump 1993) are restricted to marking the overt noun classes; this is to say, they appear on head nouns only.

TABLE 2.9. *Noun classes in Ndali*

No.	Prefix SG	Prefix PL	Status	Semantics
1/2	umu	aβa	prim	Persons; kinship terms
1a/2b	uØ	awo	prim	Mostly animates and persons
3/4	umu	imi	prim, sec	Prim.: inanimates, natural phenomena Sec: augmentative, pejorative
5/6	iØ	ama	prim	Natural phenomena, body parts, plant names, etc.
7/8	ici	ifi	prim, sec	Prim: miscellaneous, generally impersonal Sec: pejorative
9/10	iN	iN[43]	prim	Impersonal; animals; tools, implements, etc.
11	ulu	–	prim	Impersonal objects, body parts, plants, insects, abstract concepts
12/13	aka	utu	prim, sec	Prim: body parts, manners of action Sec: diminutives
14	uβu	–	prim	Abstract nouns; names of geographical areas, miscellaneous
15	uku	–	prim	Verbal infinitives
16	pa	–	sec	Motion to/from, situation; proximity to someone or something near the speaker
17	ku	–	prim	Motion to/from, situation; proximity to someone or something far from the speaker
18	mu	–	prim	Situation inside something
21	ili	–	sec	Augmentation, pejorative

The preprefixed structures in Kikuyu display the following possibilities of agreement.

(i) Most frequently, the prefix 2, or the 'outmost' one, overrides the prefix 1 and determines agreement of any type, as in 2.42 from Kikuyu (Stump 1993: 174):

2.42. tũ-mĩ-rũũthi   tũ-nini   (*mĩ-nini)
      CL13:PL-CL2:PL-lion   CL13-little   (*CL4-little)
      'little lions'

(ii) There are a few cases when the agreement properties of a noun with double prefixing are determined either by prefix 1, or by prefix 2. In all these cases prefix 2 marks a locative noun class. Variable agreement with a

---

[43] N stands for a homorganic nasal.

demonstrative modifier 'that' in Ndali is shown in 2.43 and 2.44 (Vail 1974: 42). There is no information as to semantic consequences of the differences in agreement.[44]

2.43. p. -iØ-liŋga   il-yo
LOC.CL16-CL5-fortress   CL5-that
'at that fortress'

2.44. p. -iØ-liŋga   apo
LOC.CL16-CL5-fortress   LOC.CL16+that
'at that fortress'

(iii) A few Bantu languages have 'pre-prefixation' in marking agreement. In Nyanja, a Bantu language of Malawi, some adjectives regularly take one agreement prefix, as in 2.45 (Stump 1993: 175).

2.45. ci-manga   ca-bwino
NCL7-maize   NCL7-good
'good maize'

Other adjectives mark agreement with two sets of prefixes if the head noun has two prefixes (Stump 1993: 176). One is labelled qualifying (restricted to head-modifier agreement) and the other concordial (also used in verb-argument agreement). This is illustrated with 2.46. The division of adjectives into two agreement types appears to be lexically determined.

2.46. ka-n-khuku   ka-ka-kulu
CL12-CL9-chicken   QUAL12-CONC12-large
'a large chicken'

All these cases can be considered instances of non-semantic agreement.

(B) Double marking of noun class in Australian languages

A similar but somewhat different example of double marking of noun class on a head noun comes from Australian languages. Gender/noun class assignment to body parts and other inalienably possessed items in Australian languages is often problematic (Evans 1994). The noun class can be assigned according to the 'intrinsic' properties of a body part. If a body part belongs to neuter gender, it is assigned neuter gender and takes the appropriate gender prefix, e.g. Maung *kun-ngey* (CLIV:NEUT RESIDUAL-name) 'her name', but not **ngal-ngey* (CLII:FEM-name) (Evans 1994: 1). In other languages inalienably possessed items take the 'inherited' gender/noun class, i.e. the noun class of the possessor (which is then to be considered the head of a possessive NP), e.g. 2.8 from Yanyuwa. Yet another strategy is found in Nungali. In this

---

[44] Similar examples from the Zezuru dialect of Shona are given by Stump (1993: 173).

language, possessed body parts take two prefixes—the 'inner' prefix (i.e. the one which comes closer to the root) corresponds to the noun class/gender of the possessor, while the 'outer' prefix (the one which precedes the inner prefix) corresponds to the gender of the possessed noun itself. In 2.47 (Evans 1994: 3; Bolt *et al*. 1971: 70) the possessed noun 'ear' has two noun class prefixes: the Class 4 prefix marks its inherent class and the Class 1 prefix marks agreement with the possessor, 'man'.

2.47. ni-ya-manga   d-uŋunin
   CL4:NEUT-CL1:MASC-ear   CL1:MASC:ABS-man
   'the man's ear'

The examples of double marking of noun classes with body parts in Nungali are limited to masculine vs. feminine 'inherited' gender, and vegetable and neuter 'intrinsic' gender. This is perfectly understandable from the semantics of morphosyntactic contexts in which possessed body part terms occur. Typically, possessors are animate (and thus belong to the masculine or feminine class), and body part terms belong to either the neutral or vegetable class.

In Yanyuwa (Evans 1994: 2; Kirton 1971) and Anindilyakwa (Leeding 1996) the multiple-marking strategy is found with kin terms. This multiple marking of noun class is restricted to overt noun class marking only. Languages differ as to the strategies of agreement: some agree with the 'intrinsic' gender only (i.e. the gender of the possessed noun, not that of the possessor), as in Nungali, and some show more complicated agreement patterns, as do Nunggubuyu, and Gurr-goni. This double marking is related to the head noun; it does not correspond to agreement.

(C) Double marking of noun classes: a summary

Overt noun class morphemes in Bantu languages which allow multiple noun class markers fall into two groups which correspond to primary and secondary prefixes. In a way, they can be considered as two noun class systems which coexist in a language. They can be marked simultaneously on a head noun. However, they differ from systems described in §2.7 in that they are used in the same morphosyntactic environments.

In Nungali semantic restrictions on cooccurrence of noun class prefixes with possessed body parts which take double noun class marking are linked to the semantics of possessive constructions. Unlike Bantu languages, only body parts (which are inalienably possessed) have this double marking; double marking is associated with a specific type of possessive construction and a specific type of noun semantics.

It will be shown in §2.7 that, unlike the cases described here, 'split' noun class systems allow 'double' agreement which is not attested in Bantu, or in Australian languages.

2.7. Languages with more than one kind of noun class

It was possible at one time to state that 'no example is known of a language with two distinct systems of noun classes' (Dixon 1982: 220; cf. Craig 1986a; 1986b; 1986c). The discussion in this section is based mainly on the data from languages which have been described only recently. This is an example of a certain 'progress' in typology: the access to new, previously unknown data broadens the scope of the typological generalizations we can achieve.

Languages which have more than one type of noun class fall into two groups. On the one hand, there can be more than one noun class type, with different semantics, used with different modifiers, and/or for different agreement types. This type is sometimes referred to as 'nominal' and 'pronominal' noun classes (or genders)—see §2.7.1. On the other hand, there can be more than one system of noun classes, with different semantics, which are used, at least partly, in the same environment, e.g. with the same modifiers—see §2.7.2. Both kinds of systems involve 'split agreement'; i.e. different agreement rules operate for different morphological classes (cf. Aikhenvald 1994a). A summary is given in §2.7.3.

The possibility of coexistence of 'noun classes' and 'semantic' gender was in fact discussed by Dixon (1982: 169), for Mba (Niger-Congo) and for Wogamusin and Chenapian (Papuan, based on Laycock and Z'graggen 1975: 743–4), and by Corbett (1991: 168–75). Corbett considers cases like the South Dravidian languages Kolami, Parji, Naiki, which have two genders (male human and others). In these languages, some lower numerals have additional forms for female humans. Similarly, Wogamusin and Chenapian have at least five noun classes, shown by different forms of numerals; in addition, the number 'one' has distinct masculine and feminine forms (Laycock and Z'graggen 1975: 744). Given the scarcity of information, these data can be reinterpreted in such a way as to avoid admitting the existence of more than one noun class, as Dixon does for Wogamusin and Chenapian (positing 'ten noun classes, arranged in masculine/feminine pairs, with neutralisation between pairs beyond the number "one"').[45] Corbett considers similar cases as 'overdifferentiated targets', with a somewhat 'exceptional' behaviour.

The data from South American, Papuan, African, and Australian languages discussed below show quite a few regularities as to the ways in which more than one noun class system can operate in a language.

---

[45] Another possibility would be to say that these languages have a set of numeral classifiers fused with numbers 1–4 and an independent set of noun classes, or genders. This analysis was adopted by Lock (forthcoming) for Abau, an isolate spoken in the same area as Wogamusin and Chenapian.

2.7.1. Nominal and pronominal noun class

Different noun class systems can coexist in one language for different types of modifier; this distinction was first outlined by Heine (1982a) for African languages. One system of noun classes is used with personal, demonstrative, and other pronouns, and for verbal cross-referencing; this is called 'pronominal' gender/noun class (Heine 1982a: 195). The other is used with adjectives (and sometimes other modifiers, such as numerals); this is called 'nominal' gender/noun class (Heine 1982a: 195).

(A) Properties of pronominal and nominal noun classes

In each case the two types have all the properties of noun class systems. They differ, with respect to:

(i) morphosyntactic loci (i.e. grammatical context of occurrence);
(ii) size of system;
(iii) semantics;
(iv) transparency of semantic basis;
(v) variability in assignment;
(vi) overlap with other classifier types in multiple classifier systems (see Chapter 9);
(vii) possible interrelations with other categories.

These differences are summarized in Table 2.10.

TABLE 2.10. *'Pronominal' and 'nominal' noun class systems*

Properties	Pronominal noun class	Nominal noun class
(i) Morphosyntactic loci	Personal pronouns and demonstratives as modifiers; verbal cross-referencing	Adjectives, more rarely numerals, as modifiers
(ii) Size of system	Smaller systems	Bigger systems
(iii) Semantics	Animacy/sex/humanness	Animacy/sex/shape/size
(iv) Transparency of semantic basis	Always clear	May be opaque
(v) Variability in assignment	None	Possible
(vi) Use in multiple classifier systems	None	Possible
(vii) Interrelations with other categories	Interrelate with other nominal and verbal categories, e.g. number, person, and tense (see Chapter 10).	Interrelate only with number (Baniwa, Tariana: see §10.1)

(B) Examples of coexisting noun class systems

In Motuna (Papuan language of Southern Bougainville, Papua New Guinea: Onishi 1994) a five-term gender opposition (masculine, feminine, diminutive, local and manner) governs agreement in head-modifier constructions with articles, demonstratives and some adjectives. Gender agreement with a topical constituent in verb-argument agreement was illustrated in 2.11 and 2.12. A system of 51 agreement morphemes, based on shape, size, and animacy, is used with other modifiers (see (D) in §9.1).

Many languages of South America—including languages of the Arawak, Tucano, and Harakmbet families, and Yagua—have a small gender system for personal pronouns, articles, and verbal agreement, and a largeish system of classes for adjectival and numeral modifiers. The smaller system of classes involves sex and animacy distinctions. Among Arawak languages, Tariana has a feminine/non-feminine distinction; Palikur and Ignaciano have feminine, masculine, and inanimate (see Aikhenvald and Green 1998 on gender marking and gender assignment principles in Palikur). The larger system consists of several dozen classes based on shape and sometimes also animacy and sex; the classifying morphemes can be used in other classifier environments (see §8.3).

Demonstratives may behave differently in different languages that have two types of noun class system. In the majority of Arawak languages, demonstratives usually distinguish two (more rarely three) genders. In Tariana and Resígaro (both Arawak), Tucano and Bora-Witoto languages, and in Yagua (Payne 1990: 139) they take noun class agreement markers.

Baniwa (North Arawak: Aikhenvald 1995a; see Table 9.5 below) has two genders, feminine/non-feminine in demonstratives, personal pronouns, and verbal cross-referencing markers. A closed set of 44 noun classes is used with adjectives; these are based on shape, form, structure, sex, and animacy; there is a feminine class which is marked differently from the way feminine is marked in demonstratives. Variable noun class assignment only occurs within a larger system, and is only possible for inanimate nouns. It is used to focus on a particular shape. 2.48 and 2.49 illustrate the possibility of variable noun class assignment, depending on the shape of a *river* in Baniwa.

2.48. hliehẽ uni maka-peki
   DEM:NF water big-NCL:EXTENDED.LONG.STRETCH
   'this long river'

2.49. hliehẽ uni maka-khay
   DEM:NF water big-NCL:CURVILINEAR
   'this long (curved) river'

2.49a is ungrammatical: the system of 'pronominal' noun class does not allow variability in class assignment.

2.49a. *ʃuahã   uni
       DEM.F   water

Two systems of noun class—one restricted to pronominal modifiers and verbal cross-referencing, and the other used for the remaining modifiers—can be reconstructed for Proto-Arawak (Aikhenvald 1996b).

In the Australian language Gaagudju a two-term gender system is restricted to verb-argument agreement and free pronouns, and a larger system of four classes is used with adjectives. In Gurr-goni (R. Green 1995) and Warray (Harvey 1987) a system of four classes is found in all head-modifier and verb-argument constructions, and a smaller system with only two distinctions is found in independent personal pronouns. Malak-Malak (Birk 1976: 97–101) has four noun classes, with obligatory agreement in some head-modifier and all verb-argument constructions, and a feminine/non-feminine distinction in 3rd person singular pronouns and object bound pronouns.

In African languages agreement in pronominal gender is most likely to be semantic, while nominal gender agreement is most likely to be syntactic, as in Iraqw (South Cushitic: Heine 1982a: 195–6).

There are usually no more than two coexisting noun class systems. A possible case of three systems is found in Barasano (East Tucano: Jones and Jones 1991: 29, 74). This language distinguishes masculine, feminine, and inanimate for personal pronouns (used anaphorically); masculine, feminine, animate, and inanimate in verbal cross-referencing; a large system of shape and animacy based classes is used with other modifiers, and in other classifier environments (as in numerous other East Tucano languages—cf. examples 9.54–7 below).

This situation is totally unlike concordial superclassing (see §2.4.4), because different systems are used for different modifiers and agreement types, and their semantics may partially overlap. In concordial superclassing, different choices are made from essentially the same system.

2.7.2. Different kinds of noun class in the same environment

There are fewer examples of languages with different noun classes in the same environment than of those with two noun class systems in complementary distribution. The only example appears to be Paumarí (Arawá) (possibly, a similar system is found in Dení, from the same family: Paula Boley, p.c.). It will be discussed in some detail in (A). Two noun class systems which partially overlap are found in Mba; this is discussed in (B).

(A) Noun classes in Paumarí

Paumarí (Arawá: Chapman and Derbyshire 1991: 254 ff. and my field data) has two types of agreement class. One is based on a feminine/masculine opposition, feminine being the unmarked term. This is called 'gender' by Chapman and Derbyshire (1991). The other, the so-called *ka-* vs. *non-ka-* noun class, has its semantics partially based on shape and structure. Both systems are only partly semantically motivated. Both have no overt marker and are realized only through agreement.

'Gender' agreement in Paumarí is marked on demonstratives (e.g. *ada* 'this:MASC'; *ida* 'this:FEM'), on suffixes of inalienably possessed nouns which agree in gender with the possessor (the head of a construction), and on just three verbal suffixes. Gender agreement in an NP denoting inalienable possession is illustrated in 2.50. Gender agreement through verbal suffixes is illustrated in 2.51. Note that the functionally unmarked agreement is feminine.[46]

2.50. kahami 'dama
 palm.tree(NON-KA,MASC) foot(FEM)+MASC
 'foot of a palm tree'

2.51. voroni-'a-ha ada kahami
 fall-ASP-TH:MASC this+MASC palm.tree(NON-KA,MASC)
 'The palm tree fell down.'

The other system of noun classes involves the inclusion or lack of inclusion of *ka-* as a prefix to the verb, marking agreement with the S or O constituent. The *ka-* class agreement with the S constituent is illustrated in 2.52. *Ka-* is also used to mark agreement with the possessor in a construction of inalienable possession, as illustrated in 2.53. The absence of *ka-* agreement with a non-*ka*-class noun is illustrated in 2.54.

2.52. ka-voroni-'a-hi ida ojoro
 NCL-fall-ASP-TH:FEM this+FEM turtle(KA-CLASS,FEM)
 'The turtle fell down.'

2.53. kaira ka-bono-ni
 guava(KA-CLASS,FEM) NCL-fruit(NON-KA-CLASS,FEM)-FEM
 'guava fruit'

2.54. sinari bono-ni
 buriti.palm(NON-KA-CLASS,FEM) fruit(NON-KA-CLASS,FEM)-FEM
 'fruit of a buriti palm'

---

[46] First and second person (singular and plural) pronouns have inherent feminine gender: that is, they trigger feminine agreement; and those of third person plural have inherent masculine gender (trigger masculine agreement).

(A1) Gender assigment in Paumarí All nouns with female referents belong to the feminine gender. All body parts, parts of plants and the vast majority of artefacts and their parts are feminine. Of 52 names for cultivated plants (Chapman MS: A.g.1), 17 are feminine. Of 92 names for wild plants and trees (A.g.4), 53 are feminine. Out of 45 mammals, 27 are feminine; out of 80 bird names, 41 are feminine; out of 15 reptiles, one is feminine; out of 34 amphibians (turtles, lizards, crocodiles), 25 are feminine; all the 8 molluscs are masculine; out of 74 insects, 14 are feminine; and out of 84 fish, 8 are feminine. Nouns denoting terrestrial natural phenomena, such as 'earth', 'lake', 'beach', are feminine. Nouns denoting celestial bodies are mostly masculine (e.g. 'star', 'moon', 'sun'); the word for 'sky' is feminine. Some nouns denoting weather phenomena are masculine (e.g. 'rain', 'fog'), and some are feminine ('rainbow', 'wind'); all names of seasons are feminine.

Many nouns which denote higher animals can be of either gender according to the sex of the referent, e.g. *ojoro* 'turtle', *hotairi* 'deer'.

Thus, gender assignment in Paumarí is only partially semantically motivated.

(A2) The *ka*-class assignment in Paumarí Nouns with human referents, abstract nouns (e.g. nominalizations) and nouns which refer to natural objects and phenomena, never belong to the *ka*-class. The assignment is partially semantic, and the principles vary, depending on the semantic field to which the referent belongs. These principles are given in Table 2.11.

Some body parts distinguish two forms—a *ka*- class and a non-*ka*- class one (see (1) in Table 2.11).

The masculine-feminine gender and *ka*-class interact in certain ways. The vast majority of nouns with non-human inanimate referents which belong to the *ka*-class are inherently feminine. Few *ka*-class nouns are inherently masculine; these include *kasi'i* 'crocodile', *vahajari* 'alligator', *maoba* 'the ritual building'.

Gender and *ka*-class cooccur with non-demonstrative modifiers and on verbs. (Note that all numerals are stative verbs in Paumarí.) Demonstratives distinguish only feminine and masculine forms (they do not take the *ka*- prefix).

2.55. ada   kawina   hoara-na
      DEM:MASC   monkey(NON-KA-CLASS,MASC)   one-MASC
      'one monkey'

2.56. ida   hotairi   hoara-ni
      DEM:FEM   deer(NON-KA-CLASS,FEM)   one-FEM
      'this one deer'

TABLE 2.11. Ka-*class assignment in Paumarí*

Semantic group	*Ka*-class	Non-*ka*-class
1. Body parts	a. Whole, extended: *sa'ay* 'hand', *'damay* 'foot' b. Inner (i.e. more vital) organ: *moroboy* 'inner ear', *viridi* 'inner part of the nose', *kajoi* 'intestines'.	Singular parts: *sa'ay* 'finger', *'damay* 'toe' Outer organ: *moroboy* 'outer part of the ear', *viridi* 'outer part of the nose'
2. Plants, fruit, artefacts	a. Larger size/extension and/or flat in shape, e.g. *mesa* 'table', *sandalia* 'sandals', *vanami* 'paddle', and most containers, e.g. *kanawa* 'canoe', *kojira* 'spoon', *carro* 'car' b. Substances which consist of small particles, e.g. *ka'ija* 'pepper', *jokira* 'salt'; or are thick in texture, e.g. *kojahari* 'banana mash'; fruit with many seeds, e.g. *barasia* 'watermelon', *jaro'oa* 'corn'	Small, thin, long objects, e.g. *dono* 'pestle', *hado* 'knife' Other substances and fruit, e.g. *paha* 'water', *simaka* 'manioc', *sipatihi* 'banana'
3. Animals	Big, flat, e.g. *ojoro* 'turtle', *ba'dana* 'lizard'	Others, e.g. *hotairi* 'deer', *jomahi* 'jaguar'

2.57. ada   kasi'i   ka-hoara-na
       DEM:MASC   crocodile(KA-CLASS,MASC)   NCL-one-MASC
       'one crocodile'

2.58. ida   kanawa   ka-hoara-ni
       DEM:FEM   canoe(KA-CLASS,FEM)   NCL-one-FEM
       'this one canoe'

Some stative verbs used as modifiers have the *ka*-class agreement, but no gender agreement.

2.59. vanami   ka-pororo-ki
       paddle(KA-CLASS,FEM)   NCL-black-DESCRIPTIVE
       'a black paddle'

Further differences concern the agreement in gender, and *ka*- noun class predicate argument constructions. Agreement in genders and in the *ka*-class goes along different lines. The predicate agrees in gender with O in one type of transitive construction (of structure AVO) illustrated in 2.60, where *sinari bono-ni* 'fruit of buriti palm' is feminine, and it triggers feminine agreement on the aspect and thematic markers -*'i-hi* (underlined).

2.60. ada   ojoro   bi-kamitha-'i-hi
       DEM:MASC   turtle(KA-CLASS, MASC)   3sGA-hear-ASPF-THF
       ida   sinari   bono-ni
       DEM:FEM   buriti.palm(NON-KA-CLASS, FEM)   fruit(NON-KA-CLASS, FEM)
                                                    -POSSF
       'The turtle heard the buriti-fruit fall.'

In a different type of transitive construction, of structure OVA, it is the A that triggers gender agreement. In 2.61, *makhira* 'man' is masculine, and it triggers masculine agreement on the aspect and thematic marker *-a-ha* (underlined).

2.61. ida   ojoro-ra   ka-karaga-'a-ha   ada
       DEM:FEM   turtle(KA-CLASS, FEM)-OBJ NCL-find-ASPM-THM   DEM:MASC
       makhira
       man(NON-KA-CLASS, MASC)
       'A man found a turtle.'

In intransitive sentences, gender agreement on the verb is with S:

2.62. oniaroa   ajihi-'a-ha   ada   jomahi
       then   go away-ASP-THM   DEM:MASC   jaguar(NON-KA-CLASS, MASC)
       'Then the jaguar went away.'

Ka- noun class agreement is always obligatory for O and S only. There is never *ka-* class agreement with A. This can be seen in 2.52 and in 2.61 (agreement with S and with O is signalled by *ka-* on the predicate). Note that in 2.60 there is no agreement with the *ka-* class noun, *ojoro* 'turtle', in A function.

Another basic difference between gender and *ka-*class agreement in Paumarí is that gender agreement applies only to singular nouns. Masculine and feminine are neutralized in the plural. In contrast, *ka-* class agreement does not depend on number, i.e. there is here no neutralization of noun class agreement in the plural. Thus, the *ka-* class marking is independent of plural, and cooccurs with it. This is shown in 2.63.

2.63. ada-ni   kasi'i   vi-ko-bami-ki
       DEM:MASC-PL   crocodile   PL-NCL-two-DESCRIPTIVE
       'those two crocodiles (*ka*-class, masculine)' (*-ko* here is a phonologically conditioned allomorph of *ka-*.)

The two types of noun classification are only partially semantically motivated and constitute distinct agreement systems. They correlate with the grammatical categories of number in different ways (see §10.1).

The *ka-* agreement class is more likely to be lost first in a gradual language death situation (Aikhenvald MS). Gender agreement is more stable in the situation of language death. A tendency towards maintaining gender agreement, but not noun class agreement may be due (wholly or partly) to the influence of Portuguese in which all the young speakers of Paumarí are bilingual; Portuguese has masculine and feminine genders, but nothing corresponding to the *ka*-class.

(B) Noun classes in Mba

Mba (Ubangi, Niger-Congo: Serzisko 1981: 114 ff.; Heine 1982a: 208–9; Pasch 1986) has two noun class systems which partially overlap. It distinguishes seven 'gender' classes in the singular, and three pronominal genders. Nominal genders have opaque semantics; nouns indicating human beings occur in Classes 1, 2, 7; body parts occur in Classes 3 and 4. Pronominal genders have a clear semantic basis: (i) masculine, (ii) feminine, (iii) non-human animate and inanimate. They are used only to mark agreement with animate nouns. Agreement in pronominal gender is semantic, and agreement with nominal gender is syntactic. The distribution of genders with different modifiers is shown in Table 2.12, where + indicates obligatory occurrence of gender in the given environment and (+) indicates optional occurrence.

TABLE 2.12. *Two types of noun class (genders) in Mba*

	Nominal gender	Pronominal gender (with animate NP head)
Nouns	+	–
Adjectives	+	–
Demonstratives	+	(+)
Genitive	(+)	–
Interrogative 'which?'	+	+
Interrogative 'how much?'		
Numerals	(+)	+
Personal pronouns	–	+

The two systems of gender marking can cooccur on the same modifier in a noun phrase (Serzisko 1982: 115 ff.). In 2.64, the numeral 'one' has a prefix *bì*- showing pronominal gender agreement followed by a prefix *ú*- showing nominal gender agreement.

2.64. ju bì-ú-ma
 woman PRON:FEM-NOMINAL.GENDER-one
 'one woman'

Pronominal gender agreement is said to 'intensify' a demonstrative.

2.7.3. Languages with more than one kind of noun class: a summary

We have considered two kinds of situation. Different systems of noun classes involving agreement can be independent and employed with different kinds of modifiers used in distinct morphosyntactic contexts; two different noun classes cannot then be marked within one morphological word. This is the case in African, Australian, and a number of South American languages (§2.7.1). Alternatively, different noun class systems may partially overlap; then two noun classes can be marked within one morphological word, as in Paumarí (Arawá), or Mba (Ubangi, Niger-Congo); see §2.7.2.

These two kinds of systems are similar in that, in each case, one type of noun class is used for pronouns and a different type for other modifiers.

If a language has a closed set of animacy-based noun classes, these are more likely to appear associated with third person pronouns and demonstratives (see §10.2 on the link between person and noun class). A larger set of animacy and shape-based noun classes are more likely to be used for common nouns. This tendency, indicated in Table 2.10, is shown in Diagram 2.1 (Aikhenvald 1994a).

3rd person pronouns	Demonstratives	Common nouns

Animacy-based noun classes
◄─────────────────────────

                                                    Shape-based noun classes
─────────────────────────►

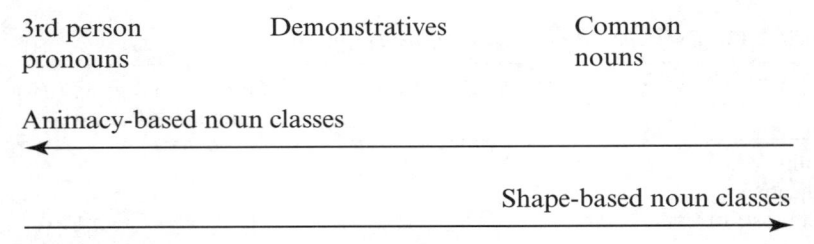

DIAGRAM 2.1. *Tendencies for animacy-based and shape-based noun classes*

If a language distinguishes a system of nominal and of pronominal noun classes, members of a closed class of modifiers (e.g. demonstratives, articles, etc.) will agree in pronominal noun classes (with a smallish number of members). For instance, Waurá (Xinguan Arawak: Richards 1988, Aikhenvald 1996a) distinguishes two genders—masculine and feminine—only in deictics. Gender marking is fused with demonstratives, e.g. masc. *eze*, fem. *izi* 'this'. There are no gender oppositions elsewhere in the system, unlike for other Arawak languages. Waurá also has a largeish set of morphemes used as numeral, verbal, and noun classifiers, and possibly, as noun class markers on modifiers from open classes.

In languages with two systems of noun classes there is also a correlation between head-modifier and predicate-argument agreement. In a language with split agreement the predicate will tend to agree with its arguments in pronominal noun class, while nominal noun class is more likely to be found in head-modifier constructions. This is typically the case in North Amazonian languages with large multiple classifier systems and two genders (e.g. Baniwa: Aikhenvald 1996c, or Tariana: Aikhenvald 1994a).

2.8. Distribution of noun classes in the languages of the world

NOUN CLASSES (which include GENDER) constitute one of the most frequent types of classifier system—see Map 1.

A system of two or three genders is present in most Indo-European and Northwest Caucasian languages. Some Indo-European languages (Armenian, some Indic, e.g., Bengali, and some Iranian, e.g. Persian) have lost gender agreement. The vast majority of Afroasiatic languages have two genders: masculine and feminine. Munda languages, spoken in Northeast India, have animate and inanimate genders.

More complicated systems of three to five genders are present in Northeast Caucasian languages (Comrie 1981: 208). Burushaski (an isolate spoken in Northwestern Kashmir) has four genders. The Dravidian languages of South India have from two to four genders (Krishnamurti 1975). Ket (a Paleosiberian isolate) has three genders.

Noun classes and genders are present in the majority of African languages. Eastern Nilotic languages distinguish masculine and feminine gender (Dimmendaal 1983). Khoisan languages distinguish three to four genders (Welmers 1973: 248; Köhler 1962; 1971). The majority of Niger-Congo languages have extensive noun class systems (up to 20 agreement noun classes combined with number). Some Nilo-Saharan languages do not have gender, but instead employ systems of noun classification through nominal derivational suffixes and plural markers which do not trigger agreement. Some African languages lack noun classes, but have categorization of nouns which goes back to noun class systems in the proto-languages (Pozdniakov 1995; Ducos 1979). For instance, Mande languages have an opposition of alienable and inalienable nouns, Yoruba of human and non-human, and Igbo of animate and inanimate (Welmers 1973: 211-21; Heine 1982a: 190), but there is no agreement, and thus these are not noun classes.

Noun classes are widespread in Papuan languages of the Sepik basin and adjoining lowland areas of Irian Jaya. Languages spoken in the Sepik area—e.g. all languages of the Ndu family and distantly related Kwoma/Washkuk (Kooyers n.d.), Sepik Hill family, or Abau (Lock forthcoming)—tend to have two genders, feminine and masculine, which correlate with shape and size of the referent noun. Ok languages (see e.g. the description of Yonggom by Christensen 1995: 9-10) spoken in the Western province of Papua New Guinea and the adjacent areas of Irian Jaya have two genders, as does Marind (Marind family, Southern Irian Jaya). The languages of the

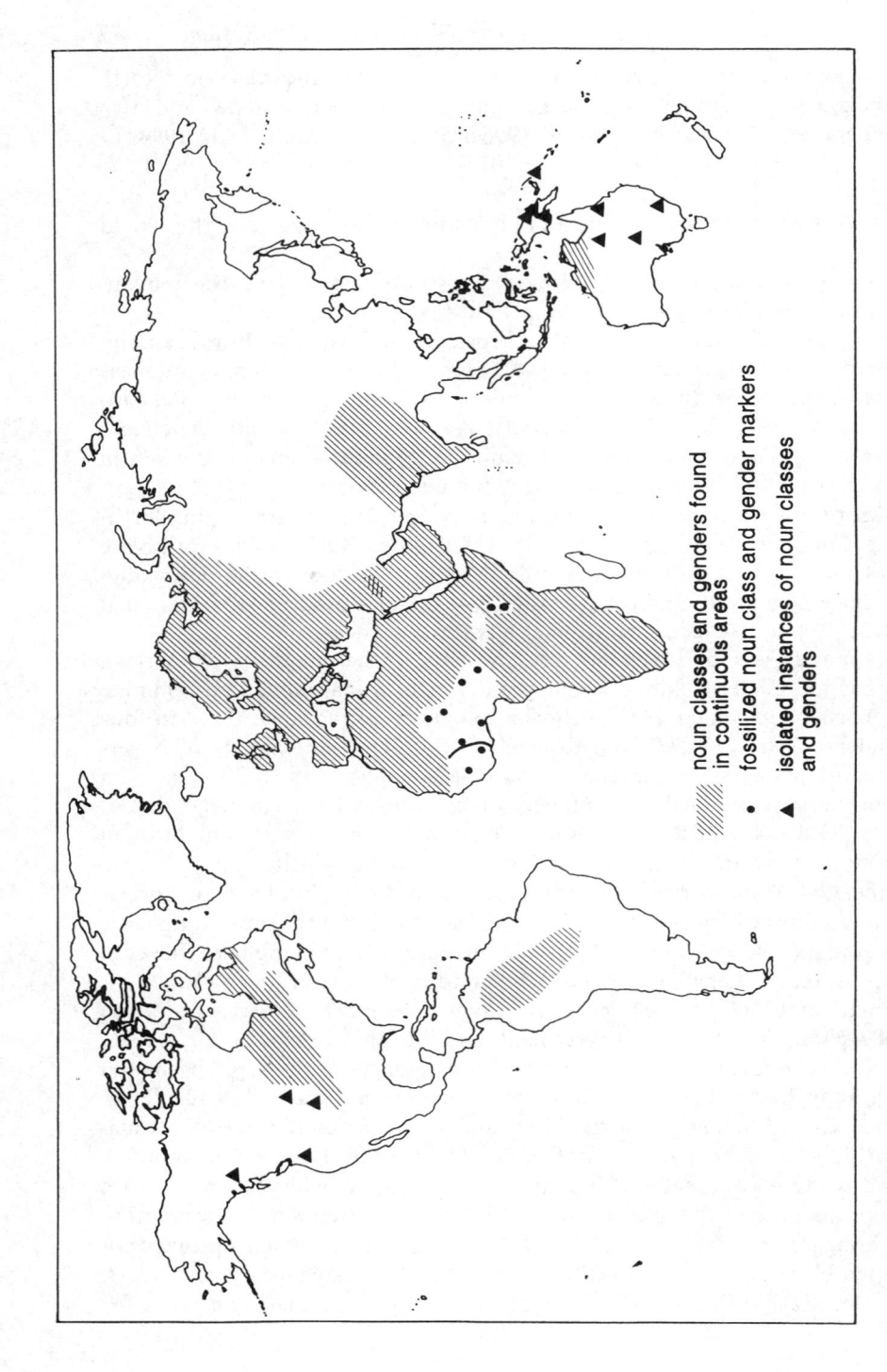

MAP 1. *Distribution of noun classes and genders in the languages of the world*

noun classes and genders found in continuous areas
• fossilized noun class and gender markers
▲ isolated instances of noun classes and genders

Torricelli family and some of those of the Lower Sepik family have fascinating systems of about a dozen classes (see Foley 1986: 85 ff.; 1991 for information on Yimas; Fortune 1942; Nekitel 1985; 1986; Conrad 1978 on the Arapesh languages). Angan languages spoken at the junction of the Eastern Highlands, Morobe, and Gulf Provinces, have up to ten noun classes (see Whitney n.d., for Akoye; Speece n.d., for Angave; Carlson 1991 for Taenae). Extensive systems with several dozen agreement classes are found in the Papuan languages of Southern Bougainville: Nasioi, Motuna (Foley 1986: 83 ff.; Onishi 1994) and in those of Central Bougainville: Napues (or Kunua), Eywo, Keriaka and Rotokas (Kim Blewett, p.c.), and in Reef-Santa Cruzan languages (Wurm 1992a; 1992b).

Small gender systems (with two or three members) are found in the non-Austronesian languages of the Solomon Islands (Bilua: Kazuko Obata, p.c.; Lavukaleve: Angela Terrill, p.c.; Savosavo), in Kuot, the only Papuan language of New Ireland (Eva Lindström, p.c.) and in most languages of the Fly river (Bine: Fleischmann and Turpeinen 1975; Wipi: Dondorp and Shim 1997; Wära: Risto Sarsa, p.c.). Some non-Austronesian languages of East New Britain (e.g. Baining and possibly also Taulil) have a complicated system of agreement noun classes (Parker and Parker 1977 for Baining; Lindrud and Nicholson n.d., for Taulil).

The typical noun class system in Australian languages contains four terms which can be broadly labelled as masculine, feminine, edible vegetable, and residual. Individual languages range from two noun classes to six. The majority of languages with noun classes are spoken in a continuous region of the central north 'prefixing' area with two outliers, Dyirbal and Banjalang, on the east coast (Sands 1995; Dixon 2002: 464–508). A few other languages have a gender distinction just in the third person singular pronoun (Sands 1995: 257).

American Indian languages north of Mexico (Sherzer 1976; Campbell 1997) divide into a number of linguistic areas, some of which show genders/noun classes and classifiers, and some of which do not. Gender systems are typically small (with two to three members). The most frequent oppositions are masculine/feminine, animate/inanimate, or human/non-human.

Algonquian languages—spoken in the Eastern Subarctic, the Northeast, and in the Plains linguistic area—distinguish animate and inanimate genders. Chemakuan and Salish languages of the Northwest Coast linguistic area distinguish masculine and feminine genders, and Lower Chinook distinguishes between human and non-human. The distinction between masculine and feminine is an areal feature of the Northwest Coast area (Campbell 1997: 332). In the Plateau area, Upper Chinook has an opposition between masculine and feminine. Among Californian languages, only Pomoan distinguishes feminine and masculine (this is considered an innovation). Animate and inanimate nouns are distinguished in the plural in Pacific Coast Athabaskan, in Yuki (Yukian), in Karok and Yana, and in Miwok and Costanoan.

Of the Pueblo languages, Hopi (Uto-Aztecan) distinguishes three genders (animate, inanimate, and vegetable) in the plural. Kiowa-Tanoan languages (with Kiowa spoken in the Great Plains) have up to four classes of nouns based on distinctions between number, animacy, and individuation (Watkins 1984, 1995). In the Great Basin area, Southern Paiute (Numic branch of Uto-Aztecan) has animate and inanimate 3rd person pronouns. In the Plains, the opposition between animate and inanimate genders is (as mentioned above) present in all Algonquian languages, in a number of Siouan languages, and in Comanche (Numic branch of Uto-Aztecan). Iroquoian languages fall into two subgroups: those of the Northeast have masculine, feminine, and neuter for the 3rd person pronoun, while Cherokee, in the Southeast, distinguishes only masculine and feminine. In the Southeast linguistic area, masculine and feminine are distinguished in nouns and pronouns in Tunica (Gulf), and only in 3rd person pronouns in Yuchian languages.

In Central America, two genders (animate vs. inanimate) are present in a few Otomanguean languages and in Tequislatec (Costenla 1991: 117). Many Central American languages have numeral classifiers and a few have noun classifiers, rather than genders/noun classes (see Chapters 3 and 4).

More than half of the languages of South America show genders and/or noun classes. A system of two genders, masculine and feminine, is characterictic of languages of the Jê, Guahibo, and Arawá families, some Arawak languages, the languages of Gran Choco and related families, e.g. Guaicuruan and Maká. Chapacuran languages distinguish three genders (Everett and Kern 1997). The coexistence of two noun class systems for different types of modifier is characteristic of Arawak and Tucano languages, Yagua (Peba-Yagua), Zaparoan, Bora-Witoto and Harakmbet, and a number of isolates, such as Waorani, Sáliba, Itonama and Movima (see Derbyshire and Payne 1990; Dixon and Aikhenvald 1999). One of these noun class systems has two or three members, while the other is larger. The Tupí, Pano, Carib, Yanomami, Makú,[47] Tacana, Quechua, Pirahã, Aymara, Jivaro and Ticuna families, isolates Aikana, Koaia, and four of the Arawak languages (Terêna, Amuesha, Chamicuro, Bahwana) of South America have no genders or noun classes; however, they often have classifiers of other types. No noun classes or classifiers of any other type have been reported for the isolates Jabutí, Trumai, Yaruro, and Warao (see Aikhenvald and Dixon 1999).

---

[47] Kakua is the only Makú language which is reported to have a gender distinction in pronominal cross-referencing (Martins and Martins 1999).

3 Noun Classifiers

3.1. Properties of noun classifiers

Noun classifiers characterize the noun and cooccur with it in a noun phrase. They have been recognized in Australian (Dixon 1977; 1982; Wilkins 1989; Sands 1995: 269–70) and in Mesoamerican languages (Craig 1986b; 1986c). Their properties have been discussed by Craig (1992; forthcoming; §3.2.3 below). In the Australianist tradition, they are called 'generic classifiers', or 'generics' (Sands 1995: 269–70; Harvey and Reid 1997: 9–10).

The definitional property of noun classifiers is that their presence in a noun phrase is independent of other constituents inside or outside it. Their 'scope' is a noun phrase. They are a type of non-agreeing noun categorization device, their choice being determined by lexical selection, and not by matching any inflectional properties of nouns with any other constituents of a noun phrase.

Additional, contingent, properties of noun classifiers are:

(i) The choice of a noun classifier is based on semantics. Every noun in a language does not necessarily take a noun classifier (§3.2.1).

(ii) Languages may allow the cooccurrence of several noun classifiers within one noun phrase (§3.2.1).

(iii) One noun can be used with different classifiers, with a change in meaning (§3.2.2).

(iv) The size of the inventory of noun classifiers can vary, from a fairly small closed set to a fairly large open set. Consequently, noun classifiers can be grammaticalized to varying extents (§3.2.3).

(v) Noun classifiers are often used anaphorically; they may grammaticalize as markers of syntactic functions (§3.2.4).

§3.3 deals with the relationship between noun classifiers and numeral classifiers. The realization of noun classifiers is considered in §3.4, and their functional similarities and historical links with overt noun class marking in §3.5. The distribution of noun classifiers across the languages of the world is surveyed in §3.6.

3.2. Noun classifiers: discussion and exemplification

Noun classifiers are found in a fair number of Australian languages, as well as in some Mesoamerican languages and in some Western Austronesian and Amazonian languages. They are also found in a few isolating languages of East and Southeast Asia[1] (see §3.6). The existence of noun classifiers does not seem to correlate with the degree of synthesis or head- or dependent-marking morphology in a language.

3.2.1. The choice of noun classifiers and the cooccurrence of several classifiers within one noun phrase

The choice of a noun classifier is semantic (unlike noun classes described in §2.3). Example 3.1 illustrates the use of a noun classifier in Jacaltec (Kanjobalan Mayan: Craig 1992: 284). The noun classifiers, *naj* 'man' and *no7* 'animal', categorize the nouns with which they form one NP as belonging to a class of 'humans' and of 'animals', respectively.

3.1. xil [naj xuwan] [no7 lab'a]
    saw CL:MAN John CL:ANIMAL snake
    '(man) John saw the (animal) snake'

Noun classifiers correlate with inherent semantic characteristics of nouns, such as 'animal', 'human', 'plant'; form, shape and structure of the referent. There is often a generic-specific relationship between the classifier and the noun (see §11.2.2). Classifiers can also refer to the social status, or a kinship relation of people. Some Australian languages have 'social status' noun classifiers with the meanings such as 'initiated man' (see Goddard 1985: 94 for Yankuntjatjara, and a slightly different system in Mparntwe Arrernte described by Wilkins 1989: 106). Social status classifiers are widespread in East and Southeast Asian languages (e.g. Adams 1989: 47 ff. for human classification in Palaungic). DeLancey (1998) discusses noun classifiers referring to social status in Tibetan.

The choice of a classifier is usually semantically transparent; in some cases, however, the semantic link between a noun classifier and a noun is not obvious. In most languages of the Daly area in Australia 'honey' takes the noun classifier for 'flesh food' (maybe due to the way in which 'honey'

---

[1] An interesting example of noun classifiers of a different sort are 'graphical' classifiers, also known as 'semantic determiners', in the hieroglyphic writing of Ancient Egyptian and cuneiform writing systems of ancient languages of the Middle East (Rude 1986). These languages had no classifiers. Semantic determiners were used to disambiguate polysemous signs, or to specify the meaning of a noun, e.g. Hittite ^{KUR}*Hatti* '(land of) Hatti', ^{URU}*Hatti* city of Hatti'. Apparently, they were not pronounced.

is conceived as a source of energy: Lys Ford, p.c.). The choice of noun classifier in Jacaltec is often 'obscured' by extension through perceptual analogy; for instance, 'ice' is assigned to 'rock' class (see Craig 1986c: 275–6). Similarly to numeral classifiers (Chapter 4), proficiency in noun classifiers can vary from one speaker to another.

The most thoroughly described system of classifiers in an Australian language is that in Yidiny (Dixon 1977: 480 ff.; 1982: 192 ff.).

Yidiny has a closed set of about twenty classifiers. They fall into two groups. INHERENT NATURE classifiers divide into humans (*waguja* 'man', *bunya* 'woman', and a superordinate *bama* 'person'); fauna (*jarruy* 'bird', *maŋgum* 'frog', *munyimunyi* 'ant'); flora (*jugi* 'tree', *narra* 'vine'); natural objects (*buri* 'fire', *walba* 'stone', *jabu* 'earth'); and artefacts (*gala* 'spear', *bundu* 'bag', *baji* 'canoe'). FUNCTION classifiers are *minya* 'edible flesh food', *mayi* 'edible non-flesh food', *bulmba* 'habitable', *bana* 'drinkable', *wirra* 'movable', *gugu* 'purposeful noise'.

3.2. jarruy   durrguu   'mopoke owl'
     CL:BIRD   owl

3.3. buri   birmar   '(hot) charcoal'
     CL:FIRE   charcoal

Among classifiers referring to humans, *bama* 'person' can cooccur with *waguja* or with *bunya*, as shown in *bama waguuja wurgun* 'a teenage boy', lit. CL:PERSON CL:MAN boy, in 3.4. This is the only instance of a 'hierarchical' relation among generic classifiers in Yidiny (Dixon 1977: 484).

3.4. ŋanyji   bama   waguuja
     we+NOM CL:PERSON+ABS CL:MAN+ABS
     wurgun   muyŋga   gunda:alna
     pubescent.boy+ABS cicatrice+ABS cut+PURP
     'We must cut tribal marks [on] the teenage boy.' (lit. person man pubescent boy)

The classification is cross-cutting. This means that different classifiers have to be used depending on whether the focus is an inherent property, or on function. Thus, all ants are covered by the inherent nature classifier *munyimunyi*; only some ant species are edible, and these are also covered with function classifier *minya* 'edible flesh food' (Dixon 1982: 198).

Cooccurrence of classifiers is governed by the following principle. If two classifiers cooccur, one of them must be an inherent nature classifier, and the other has to refer to 'function/use' (Dixon 1982: 203), e.g. *bulmba walba malan* (CL:HABITABLE CL:STONE flat rock) 'a flat rock for camping' (Dixon

1982: 200); *jugi mayi badil* (CL:TREE CL:EDIBLE.NON.FLESH.FOOD rickety nut) 'rickety nut tree and its fruit' (Dixon 1982: 199).[2]

Noun classifiers can fall into different subgroups, as in Yidiny (and see Wilkins 1989: 106, on how social status noun classifiers differ from noun classifiers of other groups). However, so far no language has been reported to have several distinct sets of noun classifiers.

The cooccurrence of two noun classifiers is not permitted in all languages; for instance, it does not happen in Mayan languages, or Minangkabau.

3.2.2. Semantic functions of noun classifiers

In languages with noun classifiers, distinct classifiers can be used with the same noun to specify its meaning, e.g. Minangkabau *batang limau* (CL:TREE lemon) 'lemon-tree', *buah limau* (CL:FRUIT lemon) 'lemon-fruit' (Marnita 1996). Similarly, in Yidiny, 'a piece of hot charcoal (*nirgil*), say, can be described as *buri* (CL:FIRE) or as *wirra* (CL:MOVABLE.OBJECT), and a plot of ground either as *jabu* (CL:GROUND) or as *bulmba* (CL:HABITABLE) (Dixon 1977: 203), focusing on different properties of the referent of the noun. Cooccurrences of nouns with different classifiers may be less obvious; 'a tree species, *diwiy*, holds water inside its bark (which can be tapped and drunk) yielding *bana* (CL:DRINKABLE) *diwiy* in addition to *jugi* (CL:TREE) *diwiy*' (Dixon 1982: 203). Walsh (1997: 275) provides further examples of changing meanings of a polysemous noun with noun classifiers in Murrinhpatha: *nanthi* (CL:GENERIC) *kamarl* (eye) 'eye/face', *kura* (CL:AQUATIC) *kamarl* (eye) 'water-hole', *kardu* (CL:HUMAN) *kamarl* (eye) 'sweetheart', *mi* (CL:VEGETABLE) *kamarl* (eye) 'seed'.

These noun classifiers are not semantically redundant (*pace* Craig 1992: 292). Their behaviour is similar to the derivational functions of noun class markers (see §2.6; also see §3.5).

3.2.3. Size of inventory and degree of grammaticalization of noun classifiers

Systems of noun classifiers differ in the size of the inventory and their degree of grammaticalization. We have seen that Yidiny has a closed class of around twenty classifiers. Mparntwe Arrernte (Australian: Wilkins 1989) has 19; Ngan'gityemerri (Australian: Reid 1997) has about twelve 'generic' noun classifiers, and Murrinhpatha (Australian: Walsh 1997) has ten. In contrast, Emmi (Australian: Ford 1998) has two, and Patjtjamalh has three (Lys Ford, p.c.). Acehnese (Western Austronesian) has eleven noun classifiers. Some languages of East and Southeast Asia have as many as several hundred noun classifiers.

---

[2] The order of two classifiers appears to be relatively free. There are no examples of cooccurrence of more than two classifiers (Dixon 1982: 203).

In other languages, almost any generic noun can be used as a classifier. This appears to be the case in Minangkabau (Austronesian: Marnita 1996) and in Dâw (Makú: Martins 1994), where any noun with generic reference can be used as a noun classifier. A generic noun classifier *dâw* 'human' in Dâw is illustrated in 3.5 (Martins 1994: 51).

3.5. dâw tɨúm
 NOUN.CL:HUMAN eye
 'a human eye'

Language-internal criteria have to be established to distinguish a free form classifier from a noun. In Yidiny, a test for what can be used as a classifier is provided by the way interrogative-indefinite pronouns are used. *Wanyi* 'what, something' is used 'to refer to an object concerning which nothing is known—it enquires about the genus' (Dixon 1982: 190–1). There is another interrogative pronoun, *wanyirra*, which is used 'when it is known which generic classifier the object comes under, and the actual species name is being sought'. That is, *wanyirra* occurs with a generic classifier, and 'a criterion for whether a word belonged to the set of generic classifiers was whether it could occur with *wanyirra*' (Dixon 1982: 191). This is illustrated with 3.6. The classifier *minya* 'animal' is underlined.

3.6. person A: wanyi gali-ŋ
 what.genus-ABS go-PRES
 'What is that going [along there]?'
 person B: minya gali-ŋ
 CL:ANIMAL-ABS go-PRES
 'It's an animal going [along].'
 person A: [wanyirra minya] juŋga-ŋ
 what.species-ABS CL:ANIMAL-ABS run-PRES
 'What sort of animal is it running [along there]?'
 person B: [minya-ABS ganguul] warri-ŋ
 CL:ANIMAL-ABS wallaby-ABS jump-PRES
 'It's a wallaby jumping [along].'

Further syntactic properties of noun classifiers in Yidiny are discussed in §3.2.4.

In Minangkabau (Western Austronesian: Marnita 1996), generic noun classifiers can be distinguished from parts of compounds. A generic noun classifier can be omitted under certain discourse conditions (see Chapter 12), but a part of a compound can not be. Thus, *buruang balam* 'NCL:BIRD turtledove' is a construction Classifier—Noun; *buruang* can be omitted if the referent has been previously established. *Buruang antu* 'ghost bird' (lit. bird ghost) is a compound noun since the omission of *buruang* is impossible.³

It is often hard to decide whether a language has established noun classifiers, or whether there is just a discourse device which consists in occasional pairing of generic and specific nouns. Awa Pit (Barbacoan: Curnow 1997: 121) has a generic-specific construction which can be used just for plants and animates (it is never obligatory). For instance, *wisha* is a generic term for 'person', and so a white person can be referred to as *wisha awa* (white.person person). More study of their discourse and syntactic properties is needed to decide whether they are noun classifiers, or just a stylistic device (also see discussion in Sands 1995: 270). It is often difficult to ascertain whether a language has a given type of classifier or not, because of the limited productivity of a classifying device. For instance, Pilagá (Vidal 1997: 61) has generic-specific noun compounding which seems similar to noun classifiers, e.g. *pagela-lapaɣat* (wasp-insect) 'a wasp', *piyoq-lapaɣat* (flea-insect) 'flea'. These are comparable to derivational components in class nouns, such as *berry* in English *strawberry*, *blackberry*, etc.; because of their limited productivity, high degree of lexicalization, and the fact that they are restricted to a closed class of noun roots they should not be considered part of a classifier system.⁴ Similar problems arise with respect to class nouns and noun classifiers in languages of other types (cf. DeLancey 1986); in each case a decision should be made based on language-internal criteria. Problems of the same sort appear when one has to decide whether a language has classificatory verbs or just a set of lexical verbs the choice of which is determined by the properties of S or O (e.g. *drink*, or *chew*: see §6.2.3).

The decisive criterion is how obligatory the generics are, and whether it is possible to formulate explicit rules of their omission. For instance, in the Australian language Emmi (Ford 1998) generic classifiers have evolved into a grammatical device, since there are identifiable discourse conditions under which either generics, or specific nouns can be omitted. Incipient structures of this sort can be found in Indo-European languages. For instance, in English it is possible to use a proper name together with a descriptive noun phrase, such as *that evil man Adolf Hitler*, but this type of apposition is rather marked and used to achieve rhetorical effect.⁵ Lexico-

---

³ Walsh (1997) provides criteria distinguishing noun classifiers from compounds in Murrinhpatha.

⁴ Denny Moore (p.c.) informs that noun classifiers in Gavião (Tupí) are also better analysed as markers of class nouns (see Moore 1984: 203–4), *pace* Carlson and Payne (1989).

⁵ In a famous poem 'Lullaby' ('Kolybel'naya'), Nikolai Zabolocki used generic-specific combinations such as 'fish flounder' (*ryba kambala*), 'plant potato' (*rastenie kartoška*) and 'animal dog' (*zhivotnoe sobaka*) in describing a fantastic and absurd reality. This 'generic-specific' construction is just a lexico-syntactic mechanism employed for stylistic effect.

syntactic mechanisms of this kind may well be a historical source of noun classification devices.

Noun classifiers are also different from nouns such as 'berry' in the English combinations *straw-berry*, *blue-berry*, *black-berry*. These are sometimes called class nouns, and are usually restricted to few lexical fields (generally a few floral and/or faunal domains) while noun classifiers are more extensive in that they cover most of the lexicon. Class nouns do not constitute a syntactic construction as classifier-noun constructions do, and they do not have the contingent properties (i–iv) outlined in §3.1.

3.2.4. *Syntactic functions of noun classifiers*

Noun classifiers are typically used with anaphoric function, as in 3.7 (Craig 1992: 284), where the corresponding nouns, 'John' and 'snake', are omitted.

3.7. xil   naj   no7
     saw CL:MAN CL:ANIMAL
    'he (man) John saw it (animal)'[6]

Classifiers are employed anaphorically in Yidiny. They are often used in answers to a question, in order to avoid the repetition of the head noun. In 3.8, the question contains a noun *duguur* 'house'. The answer contains the corresponding function classifier *bulmba* 'habitable' (Dixon 1982: 187).

3.8. *Question*: nyundu   duguur-mu   gada-any
                   you+NOM house-ABL come-PAST
                'Have you just come from the house?'
     Answer: (yiyi)   ngayu   bulmba-m
                 (yes)   I+NOM   CL:HABITABLE-ABL
               gada-any
               come-PAST
              '(Yes), I've just come from the camp'

In subordinate clauses, a specific noun is often stated in the main clause, and its classifier in the subordinate clause, as in 3.9, or vice versa (Dixon 1982: 188–9).

3.9. ngayu   ganguul   bugaany   nyundu
     I+NOM wallaby+ABS   eat+PAST   you+NOM
     minya   baga-lnyunda
     CL:EDIBLE.FLESH.FOOD+ABS spear-SUBORD
     'I ate the wallaby, which animal you speared.'

---

[6] Mam (Mayan: England 1983: 158–9) has a dozen noun classifiers which are only used anaphorically when the head noun is omitted. They involve such meanings as *baby*, *non-human*, *young man*, and *young woman*.

Noun classifiers are used anaphorically in most other Australian languages (see Wilkins 1989 for Mparntwe Arrernte, and Goddard 1985 for Yankuntjatjara).

Akatek (Kanjobal Mayan: Zavala 1993: 25–7, and p.c.) has 14 noun classifiers; they are obligatory as nominal adjuncts, and can be used anaphorically. 3.10 illustrates the use of the noun classifier *no?* 'animal' in a noun phrase.

3.10. no?   tšitam   tu?
      CL:ANIMAL pig   distal
      'those pigs'

3.11 illustrates *nax* 'CL:MAN' used anaphorically. The head noun *tšownom* 'merchant' is introduced in the first sentence, and is later referred to just by a noun classifier.

3.11. yeešin   ši   nax   tšonwom   š?ey   tšotan
      all right said   CL:MAN   merchant   sat   down
      nax   smaxa   šyetšmane
      CL:MAN   waiting waited
      nax   satk'al k'am   tšen   tumin
      CL:MAN   long.time there.was.no CL:ROCK   money
      'All right, said the merchant, and sat down to wait, he waited, he waited a long time, but there was no money.'

Noun classifiers can have a number of syntactic functions as the result of their grammaticalization as anaphoric devices.

In a number of languages classifiers realized as independent words can be used to mark relative causes, in a function similar to relative pronouns. There is a link between an anaphoric function of classifiers and their use as heads of relative clauses: the passage from anaphoric demonstrative pronoun to a relative pronoun is typologically well attested (see Zalizniak and Paducheva 1976).

An extension of anaphoric and pronominal use of noun classifiers in Jacaltec is their function as markers of coreferentiality (Craig 1986b: 276). Pronominally used noun classifiers can be deleted under coreferentiality within certain syntactic boundaries, e.g. 3.12a, b.

3.12a. xil   [naj]   pel]   [s-mam   naj]
       saw   CL:MALE.NON.KIN   Peter POSS-father CL:MALE.NON.KIN
       'Peter$_i$ saw his$_j$ father' (cannot mean 'his$_i$ father')

3.12b. xil   [naj]   pel]   [s-mam]
       saw   CL:MALE.NON.KIN   Peter POSS-father
       'Peter$_i$ saw his$_i$ father' (cannot mean 'his$_j$ father')

The anaphoric classifier cannot be coreferential with the NP to its left. Classifier deletion is important in determining complement clause boundaries, and it is the major way of encoding a relative clause. 3.13a shows how a classifier inside the relative clause is deleted under coreference with a classifier in the main clause (Craig 1986b: 279; example from Craig 1977: 165). 3.13b shows an underlying full clause which corresponds to the relative clause in 3.13a.

3.13a. mat yohtajoj   ix
       not knows   CL:FEMALE.NON.KIN
       [naj   xmakni {———— ————   }
       CL:MALE.NON.KIN   hit   {Noun Classifier DELETION}
       yul   parce]
       in   park
       'She$_i$ does not know the man who hit her$_i$ in the park.'

3.13b. smak naj   ix   yul
       hit   CL:MALE.NON.KIN/he   CL:FEMALE.NON.KIN/her   in
       parce
       park
       'He hit her in the park.'

Morphemes which are used in noun classifier constructions can be used to mark relative clauses. For instance, in Lao (Chapman 1996) classifiers—which function as numeral classifiers and as noun classifiers (see Chapter 9)—are used to mark non-restrictive relative clauses.

3.14. [sùa   too   pûan lɛ̂ɛw]$_{Relative Clause}$ mɛ̄ɛn   sùa   khɔ̌ɔj
      shirt   CL:BODY   dirty finish   be   shirt   1SG
      'The shirt that's already dirty is mine.'

The obligatoriness of noun classifiers in a noun phrase differs from language to language. We have seen above that in Yidiny (Australian), noun classifiers and full nouns alternate in relative and other subordinate clauses: if a specific noun is stated in the main clause, its classifier can appear in the subordinate clause (see 3.9). Their use almost always depends on whether the referent is contextually established. In Ngan'gityemerri, nouns can 'stand alone without classifiers'; 'there is a preference, once a specific noun is contextually established', to refer to the noun with a classifier (Reid 1997: 167). In Murrinhpatha (Walsh 1997: 264), noun classifiers are often omitted 'when the specific referent has a norm association with that noun class', as in 3.15.

3.15. (ku)   kulerrkurrk   murntak   ngala   pangu
      (CL:ANIM)   brolga   old   big   that
      'That big old brolga'

Noun classifiers in Murrinhpatha are always included with a noun when it is being cited (Lys Ford, p.c.). Similarly, in Kugu-Ngancara (Australian: Smith and Johnson 1999), the generic is 'normally given along with the noun when vocabulary is being elicited or discussed', but 'may not be present when the noun occurs in a sentence, especially when it has already been mentioned in the discourse'.

The noun can be considered the semantic head of a classifier-noun construction. The question of syntactic headship in noun phrases which consist of a noun classifier and a noun has to be established on a language specific basis. Since the noun can often be omitted (see examples above; and also Walsh 1997: 262–3 for further evidence from Murrinhpatha), the classifier can be used as head. The classifier may alternatively be omitted (as in 3.15 above); then the noun is the head.

3.3. Noun classifiers and numeral classifiers

Noun classifiers are often considered as a subtype of numeral classifiers in the languages of Southeast Asia (e.g. Craig forthcoming; Lichtenberk 1983a; see Chapter 4 for numeral classifiers). The basic difference between the two types is that numeral classifiers occur in numerical—and often in other quantifying—expressions. Noun classifiers occur independently of the presence of other modifiers in a noun phrase. Quite a number of languages have numeral classifiers, and noun classifiers as separate systems. Noun classifiers will then differ from numeral classifiers in a number of grammatical and semantic properties. Noun classifiers may not be obligatory in a noun phrase, unlike numeral classifiers which are generally obligatory in a numerical NP (see Chapter 8).

Minangkabau has numeral classifiers and noun classifiers; the two sets differ in a number of properties such as anaphoric usage and obligatoriness. Noun classifiers can be more readily omitted than numeral classifiers (see §8.2) and are more often used anaphorically. A numeral classifier and a noun classifier may cooccur in one noun phrase, as in 3.16.

3.16. sa-batang   batang   pisang
     one-NUM.CL:LONG.VERT   NOUN.CL:TREE   banana
     'one banana tree'

In Akatek (Kanjobalan Mayan: Zavala 1992)—a Mayan language with numeral classifiers and noun classifiers—noun classifiers are independent lexemes, and numeral classifiers are suffixed to numerical and quantifying expressions (see §8.2). In this language numeral classifiers can also cooccur with noun classifiers in one NP (see example 4.31).

Grammaticalization of generic nouns in different classifier constructions can follow different paths. In Acehnese (Western Austronesian: Durie 1985) eleven nouns may be used as generic classifiers (e.g. *aneuk* 'child', *boh* 'fruit, egg', *ie* 'liquid', *ureueng* 'person': Durie 1985: 135). These nouns can also be used by themselves. There are nine numeral classifiers, some of which are related to generic nouns, e.g. *yue* 'NUM.CL:LEAF.OF.BANANA.OR.PALM', cf. generic noun *yue* with the same meaning. A few generic nouns grammaticalize as numeral classifiers and as noun classifiers, with meaning difference, e.g. generic noun *bak* 'stem trunk', 'NOUN.CL:STEM,TRUNK', NUM.CL:LONG.CYLINDRICAL.THINGS'; generic noun *ôn* 'leafy plant', 'NOUN.CL: LEAFY.PLANT', 'NUM.CL:FLAT.FLEXIBLE.THIN.THINGS' (Durie 1985: 135, 139). (See §13.1 for discussion of the lexical sources for classifiers.)

3.4. Realization and grammaticalization of noun classifiers

The noun classifiers considered so far in this chapter are all free morphemes. They can be cliticized to the noun, as in Acehnese (Durie 1985: 139), and Akatek (Zavala 2000). Noun classifiers can be a subclass of nouns (as in Yidiny or a number of other Australian languages: Sands 1995), or constitute a class of morphemes on their own. For instance, free-form classifiers in Mayan languages are often derived from independent nouns. Of fifteen free-form noun classifiers in Kanjobal Mayan, twelve come from independent nouns (Zavala 2000).[7]

No system has been found with 'repeaters' employed as noun classifiers.

Noun classifiers can undergo grammaticalization and phonological reduction and become affixes to nouns. This has happened in some Australian languages (Dixon 1982: 207; Sands 1995: 252). In Olgolo, some of the optional prefixes to nouns are reduced forms of generic classifiers, e.g. *y-* is based on *úyu-* 'fish' and *nh-* comes from *ínha-* 'animal'. The evolution of overt noun class prefixes from free classifier forms in Olgolo has a phonological motivation: the language is eliminating vowel-initial words (which appeared as the result of consonant-initial dropping) (Dixon 1982: 207–10).

Noun classifiers, once they become affixes to nouns, can further give rise to noun class agreement (see Sands 1995: 253–4; see §13.4 below). The grammaticalization chain: noun classifiers → overt noun class markers → agreement markers, and the genesis of agreement are discussed in §13.8.

---

[7] The development of classifiers from independent nouns involves a few phonological processes (Craig 1986b: 255 ff.; cf. §13.5.1) such as segmental reduction, e.g. loss of the first syllable, as in *winax* 'man' > *nax* 'CL:MALE' and cliticization, i.e. loss of independent stress.

3.5. Overt noun class marking and noun classifiers

Overt noun class markers have a number of functional similarities with noun classifiers (from which they may have derived in the first place: see §3.4, and Chapter 13). Overt noun class markers occur on a noun independently of other constituents in a noun phrase. They often have a similar semantics.[8] Lama Lama dialects (Laycock 1969; Sands 1995) have overt noun class markers (probably derived from grammaticalized classifiers), e.g. *nja-* 'meat food', *mun-* 'starch food', *aR-* 'body parts and nature', *ku*, *kuR-* 'animals', *kuR-, ku-* 'trees'. Combinations of different noun classifiers with the same root result in the creation of new lexical items, e.g. *ku-won* 'kangaroo (living animal)', *nja-won* 'kangaroo (as game)' (cf. the behaviour of noun classifiers discussed in §3.2.2). Overt noun class prefixes are more grammaticalized than noun classifiers, they usually constitute a closed set, and are often less semantically transparent (see e.g. Evans 1997 on overt noun class prefixes in Mayali).

Similarly to noun classifiers which are often used anaphorically and have discourse functions (see §12.1.3), affixed noun class markers have a discourse role in some Australian languages, for example, Nunggubuyu (Heath 1984: 169–70), Warray (Harvey 1987: 53), and Wardaman (Merlan *et al.* 1997).

Ngan'gityemerri (Australian: Reid 1997) has agreement noun classes, overt marking of a noun class on the noun itself and an independent system of generic noun classifiers. Functionally, one of the most striking properties of Ngan'gityemerri noun class markers is that, similarly to noun classifiers, noun class proclitics can nominalize or relativize a clausal constituent or even a whole clause. 3.17 is a 'simple' example of this (Reid 1997: 203):

3.17. wa=[de-pi   kerre]
      MALE=body-head   big
      'the boss' (big-headed man)

The nominal constituent ('big head') is in square brackets; the male noun class proclitic, *wa=*, is used to nominalize this constituent. This device is

---

[8] Numerous languages have several sets of nominal derivational affixes which are semantically similar to genders, or noun classes. In Afroasiatic languages gender markers have derivational functions. Feminine gender is frequently used to form diminutives, as in the majority of Berber langauges (Aikhenvald 1984), and Oromo (Cushitic: Clamons 1993). There is another set of noun classifiers, suffixes to nouns used to mark semantic subgroups of non-humans, such as *-(a)b* 'non-domesticated or harmful animals', *-r* 'domesticated animals' (Diakonoff 1988: 57). Both can cooccur in one word. For instance, Hebrew ʔarn(e)-b-(e)t 'hare' contains a Proto-Afroasiatic noun classifier *-(a)b* 'non-domesticated or harmful animals', and *-t* 'feminine marker'. Tariana (North Arawak) has several sets of derivational gender-sensitive suffixes (see Aikhenvald in prep.). Their analysis lies outside the scope of this book.

productively used to create new names out of nominalized clauses. A more complicated example is in 3.18, with the Ngan'gityemerri name for 'metal detector' (Reid 1997: 205).

3.18. yerr=[tyagani-merrendi   gentyerrmi-gi-baty   knife]
       TREE/THING=[something-LEST   2PL.S:AUX-DU-hold   knife]
       'metal detector' (lit. a thing in case you might have something like a knife)

This usage is very similar to the syntactic functions of noun classifiers as relativizers and anaphoric pronouns described in §3.2.4, indicating an 'intermediary' status for Ngan'gityemerri noun classification devices, on a grammaticalization continuum between noun classifiers and noun classes. The Ngan'gityemerri system can be regarded as, in Reid's words, a 'system in transition', from noun classifiers to noun classes.

In most languages with classifiers in multiple environments (Chapter 9) classifier morphemes occur on the noun itself, adding new meaning to it. In Arawak and Tucanoan languages they have individualizing functions, e.g. Tariana (North Arawak): *episi* 'iron (as substance); iron in general'; *episi-da* (iron-CL:ROUND) 'axe'; *episi-aphi* (iron-CL:HOLLOW) 'iron pan'; *episi-kha* (iron-CL:CURVED) 'long thin piece of iron'; *episi-pukwi* (iron-CL:RING.LIKE) 'metal ring' (see Aikhenvald 1994a). Thus, these morphemes are used as derivational affixes and as noun class agreement markers, and could be analysed as derivational or as inflectional (see §9.1).

In a number of multiple classifier languages from Amazonia, classifiers are also employed as relativizers. In Tuyuca (Central Tucano: Barnes 1990: 286; p.c.), a classifier can be suffixed to a nominalized verb, to yield the predicate of a relative clause. In 3.19 the relative predicate, with a classifier, is underlined.

3.19. ti-bã-ré   ãdõ-pé   kɨ̃ɨ̃
       that-CL:PATH-RE here-THEM.CONTR   3msg
       <u>atí-a-ri-bã-pɨ</u>
       <u>come-recently-SG.NOM-CL:PATH-LOC</u>
       hoá-wa-yigɨ
       start.down.path-go-3msg.PAST.EVIDENTIAL
       'He started down that path over here [that he had recently come on].'

These examples illustrate a functional similarity between noun classifiers and overt class markers on nouns themselves (which can be considered derivational). Similar examples from Nambiquara (Lowe 1999) are given in §9.1.

We have seen in §3.2.1 that in some languages, e.g. Yidiny, several noun classifiers can cooccur within one NP. In Lowland Amazonian languages of the Tucano, North Arawak, and possibly a few other families (such as

Guahibo and Witoto), head nouns can take more than one classifier suffix simultaneously. Several (up to three) classifiers can cooccur on nouns with inanimate referents. Examples below are from Tariana. (Note that 'aeroplane' comes within the scope of the 'canoe' classifier -*hwya*.)

3.20. kara-ka-hwya-puna   hanu-puna
    REL+fly-TH-CL:CANOE-CL:STRETCH   big-CL:STRETCH
    'a big airstrip'

3.21. kara-ka-hwya-puna-way
    REL+fly-TH-CL:CANOE-CL:STRETCH-CL:CORNER
    'corner of an airstrip'

There seem to be no semantic restrictions on which classifiers may and which may not cooccur. The order of classifiers depends on the type of morphological word. If a noun with classifiers is to be presented as a head-modifier construction, the affix which is the head of the morphological construction always occupies the last place in the string of derivational affixes. It also triggers the agreement on an adjective (as in 3.20).

In 3.22, the last derivational affix -*maka* 'cloth-like' is the head of a morphological construction, and so it occupies the last place in the string of morphemes.

3.22. kuda-ma-maka
    garment-CL:FEM-CL:CLOTH.LIKE
    'woman's garment'

In 3.23 the derivational affix -*da* 'round object' is used twice. The first occurrence of -*da* can be interpreted as a modifier to the root *hipa* 'ground, earth', and its second occurrence as a modifier to the derived noun *hipa-da* 'stone'. An alternative ordering of morphemes is possible, but it changes the meaning of the word (as illustrated in 3.24 and 3.25) since the semantics of a derived word in Tariana is connected with bracketing (see Anderson 1992: 264 ff.; and Aikhenvald 1999b, for a fuller account of the possibilities of variable morpheme ordering in Tariana).

3.23. hipa-da-da
    ground-CL:ROUND-CL:ROUND
    'gravel, i.e. a small round stone'

3.24. nu-kapima-da   hanu-da
    1SG-hand+CL:SIDE-CL:ROUND   big-CL:ROUND
    'the big palm of my hand'

or: nu-kapima   hanu-da
    1SG-hand+CL:SIDE   big-CL:ROUND
    'the big side of my hand'

3.25. nu-kapi-da-ma	hanu-ma
1SG-hand-CL:ROUND-CL:SIDE	big-CL:SIDE
'the big side of my finger'

In all the Amazonian languages where this kind of 'stacking' of classifiers occurs, if the same—or almost the same—set of classifiers is used as noun class agreement markers, the noun is assigned to just one agreement class and this is marked on the adjective, as shown in 3.23 to 3.25.

The multiple occurrences of classifiers are reminiscent of 'double marking' of head classes attested in Bantu and in some Northern Australian languages discussed in §2.6.3.

In spite of the functional similarities and possible historical connection, we prefer not to consider the derivational (overt) noun class markers, as in Bantu, Australian, or Amazonian languages (see §2.6.1 and §2.6.3) as instances of noun classifiers, since their scope is a noun, and not a noun phrase. Synchronically, there are significant differences between noun classifiers and overt noun class markers on head nouns in the rare languages which have both. In Ngan'gityemerri (Australian: Reid 1997) noun classifiers are optional and their usage depends on the discourse; the overt noun class markers are obligatory. This is shown in 3.26 (Reid 1997: 175).

3.26. (gagu)	a-matyi	bengin-da
     CL:ANIMAL	NCL:ANIM-kangaroo	3SG.S:AUX-hit
     'He shot a kangaroo.'

Note that the overt noun class markers in Ngan'gityemerri are most often the same as agreement noun class markers on adjectives, as shown in 3.27 (note that = marks a clitic boundary) (Reid 1997: 176).

3.27. a-matyi	a=kerre
     NCL:ANIM-kangaroo	NCL:ANIM-big
     'a big kangaroo'

There is no such correlation between noun classifiers and agreement, at least synchronically. (Note that the absence of agreement is the definitional property of noun classifiers.) However, if we look at the relationships between noun classifiers and noun class markers from a historical perspective the two may be considered as extreme points of a grammaticalization continuum, from the lexico-syntactic mechanism of noun classifiers to closed sets of grammaticalized noun classes (cf. Sands 1995: 249). This shows that the distinct types of noun categorization devices discussed in this book are not independent of each other. We will return to this in Chapter 13.

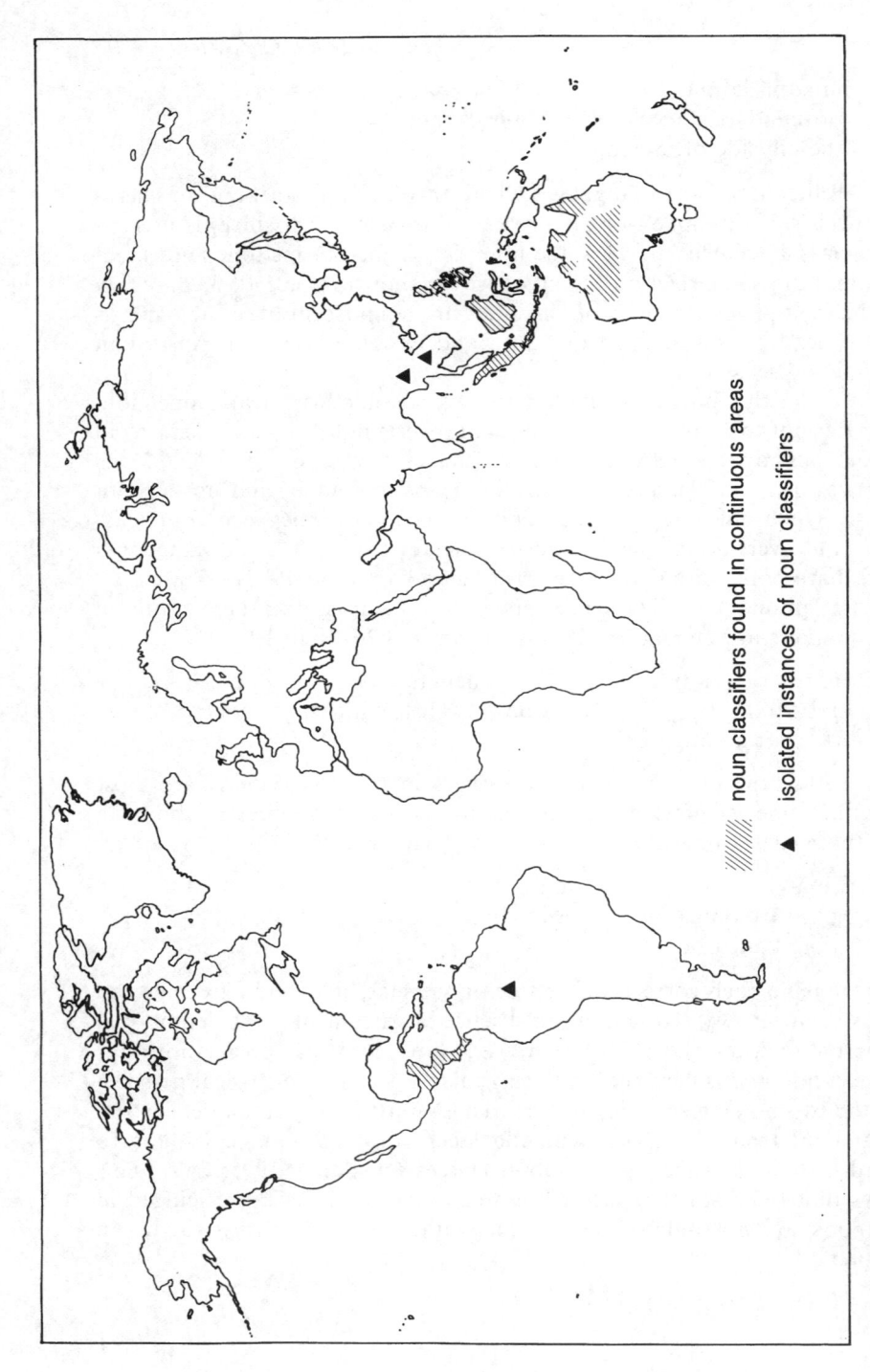

MAP 2. *Distribution of noun classifiers in the languages of the world*

3.6. Distribution of noun classifiers in the languages of the world

Map 2 shows the distribution of noun classifiers in the languages of the world. Numerous Australian languages have noun classifiers (Sands 1995: 269-70; Dixon 2002: 454-60). In particular, noun classifier systems are found in the Daly area languages, e.g. Murrinhpatha (Walsh 1997), Emmi (Ford 1998), and Pattjamalh (Ford 1990). In Ngan'gityemerri (Reid 1997) and Marrithiyel (Green 1997), noun classifier systems coexist with noun classes. Noun classifiers are widespread in the languages spoken along the east coast of the Cape York peninsula of Australia (Dixon 1977: 496). The best described system of noun classifiers in an Australian language is that of Yidiny (Dixon 1977; 1982).

Noun classifiers are found in some Mesoamerican languages, e.g. Mayan languages of the Kanjobalan branch and, possibly, in Chibchan languages (Craig forthcoming).

Examples of noun classifiers are not known for North American Indian or Papuan languages. In South America, noun classifiers are found in a few Makú and possibly in some Jê languages, and maybe also in Awa Pit (Barbacoan: Curnow 1997: 121).

Noun classifiers are found in a number of Western Austronesian languages (such as Minangkabau: Marnita 1996, or Acehnese: Durie 1985; also see Conklin 1981), and in some Oceanic languages (e.g. Yapese: Jensen 1977). They are also found in Tai languages (DeLancey 1986), in Tibetan (DeLancey 1998), and in a number of Austroasiatic languages (Adams 1989).

4 Numeral Classifiers

4.1. Properties of numeral classifiers

Numeral classifiers are perhaps the most commonly recognized type of classifier system. They appear contiguous to numerals in numeral noun phrases and expressions of quantity. Numeral classifiers do not have to appear on any constituent outside the numeral NP; thus, there is no agreement in numeral classifier between the noun and another constituent.

Numeral classifiers have other, contingent properties.

(i) The choice of a numeral classifier is predominantly semantic.

(ii) Numeral classifier systems differ in the extent to which they are grammaticalized. Numeral classifiers can be an open lexical class.

In a language with a large set of numeral classifiers, the way they are used often varies from speaker to speaker, depending on their social status and competence (Adams 1989). It is much more similar to the use of lexical items than to the use of a limited set of noun classes. Zavala (1992: 140) points out the variation in the inventory of independent numeral classifiers for speakers of Akatek (Kanjobal Mayan). In Minangkabau (Rina Marnita, p.c.), several specific classifiers (for example, 'thread-like ornaments', 'arms') are not known to younger people.

(iii) In some numeral classifier languages not every noun can be associated with a numeral classifier. Some nouns take no classifier at all; other nouns may have alternative choices of classifier, depending on which property of the noun is in focus.

The range of semantic oppositions employed in numeral classifiers varies; it most often involves animacy, shape, size, and structure. There may be one 'generic' classifier which can be used with any—or almost any—noun, replacing other more specific classifiers. This happens with the classifier *ge* in Mandarin, which can replace specific classifiers for quite a few speakers (Li and Thompson 1981: 112). Numeral classifiers have varying functions, and may be used anaphorically. These issues will be discussed in Chapter 12.

The presence of numeral classifiers in a language is traditionally associated with a number of typological properties.

Numeral classifiers are frequently independent lexemes, but can be affixes to numerals. Classifiers of these two kinds share almost all properties, except for the fact that in isolating languages numeral classifiers are usually independent items.

A typical example is 4.1, from Mandarin Chinese (Li and Thompson 1981: 104). The classifier is here an independent form.

4.1. sān   ge   rén
     three   CL:GENERIC   person
     'three people'

Numeral classifiers are often found in languages with an isolating typological profile (see Dixon 1982; Adams and Conklin 1973). They are also encountered in non-isolating agglutinating languages, such as Japanese or some Niger-Congo languages; in polysynthetic languages, such as Lowland Amazonian languages (Derbyshire and Payne 1990); and in a few fusional languages, e.g. Indic and South Dravidian.

Example 4.2 illustrates a numeral classifier construction in Ejagham (Benue-Congo: Watters 1981: 310). Ejagham has about nineteen noun classes and five numeral classifiers. Numeral classifiers are marked for noun classes, and the numeral agrees in noun class with the classifier. There is a genitive linker (manifested with a floating tone `) between the classifier and the noun.

4.2. à-mə̀gɛ̀   `   í-čɔ̀kúd
     NCL1/6-CL:SMALL.ROUND   GN   NCL19/3-orange.seed
     á-bá'ɛ́
     NCL1/6-two
     'two orange seeds'

In exceptional cases, numeral classifiers can form a constituent with the noun rather than with the numeral (as in Kana), or appear fused with a modifier within a numerical construction (as in Nauru). Numeral classifiers can constitute an almost open set, due to the presence of 'repeaters'. The structure of numeral classifier constructions and the morphological realization of numeral classifiers are considered in §4.2.

The existence of numeral classifiers in a language presupposes that numerals are a special word class. There are two kinds of numeral system in the languages of the world. Some languages have a large class of numerals, within which it is possible to indicate as high a number as required. Languages of this kind often have numeral classifiers, e.g. isolating languages of East and Southeast Asia, Dravidian, and some agglutinating Turkic languages. Other languages have very few numerals, restricted to 'one', 'two', perhaps 'three' and 'many'. This is the case in numerous languages of New Guinea, in the majority of Australian languages, and in many South American Indian languages. These languages rely on some form of deictic indication for higher numbers (frequently employing body parts), or else borrow higher numbers from neighbouring languages if required. Languages with a small number of numerals tend not to have numeral classifiers. A few South American languages are an exception to this statement. All Arawak languages have two to three numerals, and the vast majority of them also have numeral classifiers (see the discussion of Palikur, Tariana, Baniwa, and Warekena in this and the following chapters).

There are languages which do not have numerals in a strict sense: that is, numerals are not used for counting. Australian languages are often said to have 'one', 'two', perhaps 'three' (which is frequently a compound form) (Dixon 1980: 108). Hale (1975) suggested, however, that in many languages these forms are not really numerals; rather, they are indefinite determiners, comparable to English *a* and *some*. In Jarawara and Paumarí (Arawá) the verb meaning 'be alone' came to be used as a numeral 'one' and the verb meaning 'be a pair' came to be used as a numeral 'two' in the situation of contact with Portuguese culture (R. M. W. Dixon, p.c.).

If numerals belong to a major word class, this may partly account for the absence of numeral classifiers. In some Australian languages, numerals are distributed between the adjective and noun classes; for instance, Gurr-goni (Rebecca Green, p.c.) has only two numerals; 'one' is an adjective, and 'two' a noun. 'One' as an adjective takes noun class agreement. In Bantu languages numerals are a subclass of nouns (Gerrit Dimmendaal, p.c.), and they take noun class markers. These languages have no numeral classifiers.

In languages with elaborate systems of numerals, the use of numeral classifiers can depend on the numeral. Classifiers are likely to be restricted to use with smaller numbers. In many languages, they are obligatory with small numbers, and optional with larger ones. In Minangkabau (Austronesian), numeral classifiers are obligatory with numerals one to three, and optional with other numerals (Marnita 1996). In Nung (Tai; Saul and Wilson 1980: 27) classifiers are optional with multiples of ten. In Burmese classifiers do not occur with multiples of ten, and in Thai classifiers are not used with large numbers like 1000, unless individuation is implied. Classifiers are not used with numerals bigger than ten in Telugu (Emeneau 1964: 649). The possibility of classifier omission is linked to the semantic organization of the system (see §12.1.4).

The absence of obligatory plural marking on nouns and of plural agreement (Greenberg 1972; Sanches and Slobin 1973) is a typological property usually associated with the existence of numeral classifiers in a language. However, South Dravidian languages, Nivkh (Paleosiberian isolate: Panfilov 1968), Algonquian languages (Peter Denny, p.c.) as well as some South American languages (Tucano, North Arawak) and a number of languages which combine numeral classifiers with noun class systems (e.g. Ejagham:

see 4.2) are exceptions to this generalization, since number is obligatory in those languages (see §10.1.2).

Numeral classifiers are often an areal feature. Such is the case for the languages of East and Southeast Asia (Bisang 1999), and for Mesoamerica. Numeral classifiers are extremely rare in African and in Australian languages. Kana and other Kegboid languages (Cross River, Benue-Congo, Ikoro 1994) and Anindilyakwa (Australian, Groote Eylandt) are exceptions.

Languages can have more than one kind of numeral classifiers. See §4.3.

A number of questions typically arise with respect to numeral classifiers. In many languages, distinguishing between numeral classifiers and quantifying expressions is problematic. Some languages can be said to have incipient systems of numeral classifiers. These issues will be treated in §4.4.

In the last section of this chapter, §4.5, we consider the distribution of numeral classifiers in the languages of the world.

4.2. Numeral classifier constructions and morphological realization of numeral classifiers

Morphologically, numeral classifiers come in one of three forms.

(i) They may be independent lexemes. This happens often, but not always, in languages with an isolating structure. See §4.2.1.

(ii) They may be affixes, or clitics, attached to, or fused with, numerals. See §4.2.2.

(iii) They may be attached to, or fused with, the head noun. This extremely rare situation is discussed in §4.2.3.

4.2.1. Numeral classifiers as independent lexemes

Numeral classifiers as independent lexemes often comprise semi-open, lexical classes of morphemes; classifiers of this kind are generally found in isolating languages.

An example of numeral classifiers as independent lexemes from an isolating language of Southeast Asia Mal (Mon-Khmer: Wajanarat 1979: 295–6) is given below. The classifier follows the numeral which is postposed to the noun. Example 4.3 illustrates a classifier which refers to shape, and 4.4 illustrates an animacy-based classifier. Mal has a few dozen numeral classifiers, as do many other languages of Southeast Asia (Adams 1989).

102   *Classifiers*

4.3. ʔən   ʔui   ʔɔɔi   phɛʔ   lɛʔ
     I   have pot   three CL:ROUND.THINGS
     'I have three pots.'

4.4. ʔən   ʔui   khwan thiat   phoon   lɔŋ
     I   have child   four   CL:PERSON
     'I have four children.'

Other languages have fewer classifiers. Numeral classifiers are independent lexemes in Uzbek (Turkic: Beckwith 1998; see also Vietze 1979; Scherbak 1977), an agglutinating language. Examples 4.5 and 4.6 are from Tashkent Uzbek, which has fourteen classifiers (Beckwith 1998: 131–2). Example 4.5 illustrates a special classifier for humans. Inanimate objects are classified by their form, as shown in 4.6.

4.5. bir   nafar   âdam
     one   CL:HUMAN   person
     'one person'

4.6. bir   bâs   karâm
     one   CL:HEAD.SHAPED   cabbage
     'one (head of) cabbage'

It is claimed that Hungarian (Finno-Ugric: Beckwith 1992: 201) also has numeral classifiers (about six) used with inanimate objects. Classifiers categorize the nouns with respect to their shape and form, e.g. *egy szál gyertya* (one CL:LONG.CYLINDRICAL candle) 'one candle'. Not all nouns require a classifier; for example, there are no classifiers for human nouns—one just says *egy ember* 'one person'.

Numeral classifiers are separate lexemes in the fusional languages of the Magadhan subgroup of Indo-Aryan (Bengali, Assamese, Oriya, Bihari, Marathi, some Hindi dialects, Nepali: see Barz and Diller 1985; Emeneau 1964) and in South Dravidian languages, e.g. Malto.

Assamese (Barz and Diller 1985: 169) has about ten classifiers used as independent lexemes. Classifiers *zɔn*, *zɔni*, *zɔna*, and *gɔraki* are used with humans (see Table 4.1). They combine reference to sex, animacy, and politeness.

TABLE 4.1. *Numeral classifiers used with humans in Assamese*

Human males of normal rank (respectful)	Female animals; human females (disrespectful)	High-status humans of any sex	Humans of either sex (respectful)
zɔn	zɔni	zɔna	gɔraki

These classifiers are illustrated in 4.7–4.9.

4.7. tini   zɔn   xɔkhi
     three   CL:HUMAN.MALE   friend
     'three friends' (respectful)

4.8. tini   zɔni   sowali
     three   CL:FEM.DISRESPECTFUL girl
     'three girls' (disrespectful)

4.9. tini   gɔraki   mɔhila
     three   CL:HUMAN.RESPECTFUL woman
     'three women' (respectful)

There is a tendency for isolating languages to have a largeish number of numeral classifiers. According to some estimates (e.g. Hundius and Kölver 1983, for Thai), Thai and Burmese have around 200 classifiers; Vietnamese has about 140 classifiers (Craig forthcoming, Adams 1989, Burling 1965). In contrast, agglutinating languages of the Turkic group and Hungarian, and fusional languages, such as Indic and Dravidian, have much smaller sets of classifiers. However, this is only a tendency. Tzeltal (Mayan: Berlin 1968), an agglutinating language, has several hundred classifiers. Nung, an isolating language from the Tai family, has only four numeral classifiers: áhn 'inanimate', óhng 'human', tú 'animate', and cáh 'general' (Saul and Wilson 1980: 25 ff.).

Numeral classifiers can be considered an open class in languages which use *repeaters* (sometimes called 'self-classifiers', or 'auto-classifiers'[1]). A 'repeater' appears when 'the specific object itself (or part of it) [is] used as a numerative' (see Pe 1965: 166; Benton 1968: 115). In a number of East and Southeast Asian languages, such as Lao and Thai, virtually any noun can be used in the numeral or quantifier NP; so that 'classifiers straddle the boundary between closed class and open class words' (Carpenter 1992: 138). Example 4.10 illustrates a repeater construction from Thai (Hundius and Kölver 1983: 190).

4.10. prathêet   săam   prathêet
      land   three CL:LAND
      'three countries'

If a classifier construction contains a compound, only the head is 'repeated'; this is known as 'semi-repeater' construction. Example 4.11 is from Thai (Bisang 1999).

---

[1] Other terms are: 'echo classifiers' and 'identical classifiers' (Burling 1965: 249).

4.11. ráan-ʔaahǎan   sǎam ráan
     shop-meal,food   three CL:SHOP
     'three restaurants'

The use of repeaters makes the system of classifiers almost open-ended, 'to the point of absurdity' (Kölver 1982a: 178). However, no language has been found so far where repeaters are the only type of classifier (cf. Senft 1996: 7). In every language with repeaters these represent a subclass of a classifier; they are often used for otherwise 'non-classifiable' items.[2] For instance, in Mal, a Mon-Khmer language (Wajanarat 1979), there are ten regular unit numeral classifiers, fourteen group classifiers, and two action classifiers (see 4.3 and 4.4). A subset of nouns can be used as repeaters. All of these have an inanimate referent. They include otherwise unclassifiable nouns, e.g. *ciaŋ* 'house', *duup* 'hut', *bɔh* 'mountain', *ŋe* 'day'. Example 4.12 illustrates a repeater (Wajanarat 1979: 298)

4.12. ʔən   ʔui   ciaŋ   ba   ciaŋ
      I   have   house   one   CL:HOUSE
      'I have one house.'

Grammaticalized repeaters often give rise to classifiers as a closed or semi-closed class of affixes to a numeral (Senft 1996: 353). In Kilivila, *iga* 'name' is a phonologically 'depleted' (shortened) form of the repeater *yegila* 'name' in a classifier function (Senft 1996: 171).[3] See §13.1.2.

The status of numeral classifiers with respect to word class has to be established on language internal grounds. For most languages they are treated as a separate word class (e.g. Bisang 1993; 1999; cf. Cohen 1976, for Jeh (Mon-Khmer), and Saul and Wilson 1980, for Nung (Tai)). In some languages numeral classifiers are treated as a subclass of adjectives, e.g. Malto (South Dravidian: Mahapatra 1979: 121).

Parameters of variation in numeral classifier constructions include constituent order and constituency relations in classifier constructions. Constituent order in classifier constructions usually depends on the general syntactic rules of the language (see Greenberg 1963; 1972; Dryer 1992). Greenberg (1972) established four possible constituent orders in numeral classifier constructions:

(i) [NUM-CL]-N: e.g. Chinese, Vietnamese, Hmong, Miao of Wei Ning, Uzbek, Hungarian;

(ii) N-[NUM-CL]: e.g. Thai, Khmer, Mal (above);

(iii) [CL-NUM]-N: e.g. Ibibio (Niger-Congo: Greenberg 1972);

---

[2] Cf. Jones (1970: 2): 'it is interesting to speculate on the possibility that such usage arises from an inadequate supply of classifiers once their use becomes firmly established.'

[3] In Kilivila, of 88 classifiers which are most frequently used 25 are repeaters.

(iv) N-[CL-NUM]: possibly, Bodo (Sino-Tibetan: Greenberg 1972).

These orders exhaust all the possibilities—numerals and classifiers are always adjacent. As Greenberg pointed out (1990: 228), orders (i) and (ii) are much more frequent than orders (iii) and (iv). (Note that he did not distinguish classifiers as independent lexemes from classifiers as affixes. Suffixes are much more frequent than prefixes in the world's languages; so the preference for suffixed rather than prefixed classifiers could be linked to this.) Languages also permit variation in order between types (i) and (ii) (see Greenberg 1990: 236; 1972). In most Thai languages classifiers usually follow numerals except for the number 'one' which precedes (Bisang 1999; Greenberg 1972).[4]

The classifier usually forms a constituent with the numeral. The noun, and not the classifier, is generally the head (see Greenberg 1972 for discussion and examples). However, in isolating languages it is often difficult to work out syntactic criteria for heads, especially since either a classifier or a noun can be omitted under specifiable discourse conditions (see §12.1.3).

According to Greenberg, no language has the order Classifier-Noun-Numeral or Numeral-Noun-Classifier (where the numeral and the classifier are separated by the noun). The former order is in fact found in Ejagham (Watters 1981: see example 4.2 above). In Ejagham the classifier can be shown to form a constituent with the noun rather than with the numeral (at least prosodically). The classifier, and not the noun, is the syntactic head of the NP since it triggers noun class agreement on the number word.

4.2.2. *Numeral classifiers attached to numerals*

Numeral classifiers can be attached to numerals as suffixes, or, more rarely, as prefixes. Numeral classifier systems of this kind are found in South and North American Indian languages and in inflecting Indic languages. There can be from just two to several hundred classifiers.

Bengali (Masa Onishi, p.c.) has five numeral classifiers which are suffixed to the numeral: *-ṭâ* 'countable non-human'; *-ṭi* 'diminutive of *-ṭâ*; *-jan* 'human'; *-khana* 'solid objects with rectangular or flat shape'; *-khâni* 'diminutive of *-khana*', for example,

4.13. ek-ṭâ bai
     one-CL:NON.HUMAN book
     'one book'

---

[4] In Bodo (Sino-Tibetan) there are two subsystems: the 'indigenous' one has the order CL-NUM, while the one borrowed from Assamese has NUM-CL order (Greenberg 1972).

4.14. ek-ṭi   bai
      one-CL:NON.HUMAN.DIM   book
      'one beautiful small book'

Other nouns do not take any classifier.

Numeral classifiers in Marathi (Emeneau 1964: 648) distinguish masculine and feminine forms: masc. *jaṇ*, fem. *jaṇī* 'human'.

Yucuna (North Arawak: Schauer and Schauer 1978) has eight numeral classifiers referring to form (round, cylindrical, plain, side; symmetrical; concave) and animacy (human and non-human animate). Yucuna, like all Arawak languages, has just a small system of numerals (one, two, and three); see 4.15.

4.15. pajluhua-na   yahui
      one-CL:ANIM   dog
      'one dog'

Japanese has several hundred classifiers attached to numerals, however, speakers of the language typically use only about thirty-eight classifiers (Downing 1986: 346; Masa Onishi, p.c.; also see Denny 1979b: 317). There are two syntactic constructions in which numeral classifiers are used (Denny 1979b: 318). One is a numeral classifier noun phrase; it involves a linker, or 'genitive' particle *-no* (called 'basic' by Martin 1975: 777, and 'individualizing' by Downing 1984: 194), e.g. *ni-dai-no kuruma* (two-NUM.CL:VEHICLE-LINKER car) 'two cars'. The other construction, called 'adverbial' by Denny (1979b), involves a copula clause, e.g. *enpitsu ga san-bon aru* (pencil SUBJECT three-long there are) 'there are three pencils'. Similarly, in Korean attributive or genitive *-uy* is typically used to accompany a numeral+classifier construction, e.g. *sey calwu-uy yenphil* (three NUM.CL:LONG.SLENDER-ATT pencil) 'three pencils'. The form *-uy* can be omitted in a more colloquial speech register (Lee 1997; also see Downing 1984: 199, on genitive particle deletion in Japanese). There are several possible orders in numeral classifier constructions; however, the classifier must remain within the same constituent as the numeral. Japanese has two possibilities of constituent order (Bisang 1999): the classifier-numeral constituent can occur in prenominal position (with the linker *no*) as in 4.16, or following the noun (without *-no*) as in 4.17.

4.16. ni-dai-no   kuruma   o   kai-mashi-ta
      two-NUM.CL:VEHICLE-LINKER   car   ACC   buy-HON-PAST
      '(S/he) bought two cars.'

4.17. kuruma   o   ni-dai   kai-mashi-ta
      car   ACC   two-NUM.CL:VEHICLE   buy-HON-PAST
      '(S/he) bought two cars.'

Numeral Classifiers 107

In Korean there are three possibilities. 4.18 shows the unmarked order in a numeral classifier construction (Lee 1997):

4.18. sey   calwu-uy   yenphil-lul
      three NUM.CL:LONG.SLENDER-ATT pencil-ACC
      sa-ss-ta
      buy-PAST-DEC
      '(I) bought three pencils.'

The classifier can immediately follow the head noun and takes case marking (Sohn 1994: 272), as in 4.19.

4.19. Minca-nun   ecey   chayk   sey   kwen-ul
      Minca-TOP   yesterday book   three   CL:BOOK-ACC
      sa-ss-ta
      buy-PAST-DEC
      'Minca bought three books yesterday.'

4.20 shows a different constituent order, used to focus on the head noun (note the absence of the attributive *-uy*) (Lee 1997). The classifier follows the head noun and both are case-marked. This could be considered a discontinuous noun phrase.

4.20. yenphil-lul   ecey   sey   calwu-lul
      pencil-ACC   yesterday three   NUM.CL:LONG.SLENDER-ACC
      sa-ss-ta
      buy-PAST-DEC
      'I bought three pencils (not other items) yesterday.'

While variations in the ordering of the head noun and the numeral + classifier are acceptable (especially in the colloquial speech register: Yunseok Lee, p.c.), the ordering of the numeral and the classifier is rigid, and no constituent can be inserted between them.

In Yagua (Derbyshire and Payne 1990: 253–4; Payne and Payne 1990: 445 ff.) classifiers are infixed to numerals (usually small numbers), as illustrated in 4.21. (The same morphemes are suffixed to demonstratives, adjectives, and verbs; see §9.1.)

4.21. tá-dasiy-quíí
      one-CL:THIN.POLE-one
      'one (shotgun, blowgun, palm trunk, etc.)'

Classifiers sometimes have a different morphological status depending on whether they occur with a number, or with a quantifier. Bahwana, a nearly extinct North Arawak language from Northern Brazil (Ramirez 1992: 55) has twenty-six classifiers obligatorily suffixed to quantifiers (4.22), and infixed to numbers one and two (4.23).

4.22. yaɸa-<u>da</u>　　　　　　　　　karaka
　　　how.much-CL:ROUND.OR.HOLLOW　hen
　　　'How many hens (are there)?'

4.23. a-<u>da</u>-riñi　　　　　　　karaka
　　　one-CL:ROUND.OR.HOLLOW-one　hen
　　　'one hen'

Numeral classifiers can be fused with a number. This often happens in languages with fusional characteristics. Telugu, a fusional language, has two classifiers, human and non-human, fused with the numeral (Krishnamurti and Gwynn 1985: 106–7). Table 4.2 features a sample of numeral classifiers in Telugu.

TABLE 4.2. *Numeral classifiers in Telugu*

Numbers	Non-human	Human
'two'	reṇḍu	iddaru
'three'	muuḍu	mugguru
'four'	naalugu	naluguru
'five'	aydu	ayduguru

Languages with only little fusion can have numeral classifiers fused with numerals. Kusaiean (Micronesian: Lee 1975) has two sets of cardinal numerals. Set A is used in counting fishes, insects, four-legged animals, plants, means of transportation, and long, pointed objects. Set B is used for everything else; these numerals are morphologically unanalysable and can be considered suppletive—see Table 4.3. Some nouns are used with numerals of both sets with a difference in meaning, e.g. *paip yoko* 'four cigarettes', *paip ahkorr* 'four packs of cigarettes'.

TABLE 4.3. *Classifiers fused with numerals in Kusaiean*

	Set A	Set B
'one'	soko	sie
'two'	lukoac	luo
'three'	tolko(e)	tolu
'four'	yoko	ahkorr

Nivkh (Paleosiberian isolate: Panfilov 1968: 414–15), a polysynthetic language, has twenty-six numeral classifiers fused with a numeral; a sample of these is given in Table 4.4. Most of them are used with numerals from one to five, and some with numerals up to ten.⁵ At least some numeral classifiers in Nivkh originate from nouns, e.g. *ar* 'bunch of firewood', *n'-ar* 'one (bundle of firewood)'; *ču* 'family', *n'iz-ču* 'one (family)' (cf. Chapter 13).

TABLE 4.4. *Numeral classifiers in Nivkh*

	Thin flat objects	Small round objects	People	Animals	Objects of different forms	Sledges	Bundles of firewood	Fishes strung on twigs	Families	Fishnets
'one'	n'rah	n'ik	n'en	n'in	n'aqp	n'irš	n'ar	n'ŋgak	n'izču	n'vor
'two'	merah	mik	men	mor	meqp	mirš	mer	mengaq	mizču	mevor

Warekena (North Arawak, Brazil, and Venezuela: Aikhenvald 1998b) has six numeral classifiers; some are realized with prefixes, and some are portmanteau with a numeral (see Table 4.5). This morphological mechanism is peculiar in a predominantly suffixing agglutinating language like Warekena. Note that there are only two native numerals, 'one' and 'two';⁶ the others are loans from Portuguese.

TABLE 4.5. *Numeral classifiers in Warekena*

Semantics	'One'	'Two'
Human male	peya	e-naba
Human female	peya	tuwa-naba
Animals	pamiña	pamiña-naba
Fish	pe-ɾeyaɾu	eɾe-naba
Curvilinear objects	pa-puɾiaɾuni	e-naba
Periods of time	ba-buya, pa-puya	bu-naba

In Squamish (Salish: Kuipers 1967: 149–51) one of the two sets of numeral classifiers (see §4.3.2) is realized by reduplication. There are three numeral classifiers: for objects, animals, and humans. The form used for classifying inanimate objects is formally unmarked. The numeral classifier used with animals is marked with reduplication of the first consonant, and the one used with humans is marked via reduplication of the first two consonants (Table 4.6).

---

⁵ Young speakers tend not to use classifiers at all (Vladimir P. Nedjalkov, p.c.); it is unknown which form of numerals is used.
⁶ Classifiers are used with numerals 'one' and 'two' in only one dialect of Warekena. Other dialects use the human masculine form *peya* with all nouns.

TABLE 4.6. *Numeral classifiers in Squamish*

	Objects	Animals	Humans
'one'	nč'u?	ni'-nč'u?	nč'-nč'u'?
'two'	?a'n?us	?a'n.n.?us	?n-?a'n?us
'three'	ča'nat	ča'-čn?at	čn-ča'nat

Numeral classifiers can attach to a modifier other than a numeral. In Nauru (Micronesian) numeral classifiers are fused with demonstratives in a numerical noun phrase (Kayser 1993: 41 ff.), e.g. *ṅ-aiquön-oe* 'one this one here' (inanimate), *ṅ-airan-e* 'one this one here' (a flat object).

Repeater affixes to numerals can be used as numeral classifiers, as in Truquese (Melanesian: Benton 1968: 115–17).

4.24. únú-ŋaf   ŋaaf
     three-CL:FATHOM   fathom
     'three fathoms'

An example of partial repeaters used as numeral classifiers comes from Movima (an isolate from Bolivia). This language has three genders (masculine, feminine, and neuter or inanimate) in personal pronouns with cross-referencing, and numeral classifiers. Preliminary fieldwork by Craig (1996) showed that there are a few classifiers the choice of which is based on the semantics of a noun: *-poy* 'quadruped animals', e.g. fox, crocodile, tapir; *-mo* 'biped animals', e.g. rooster, duck, owl; and *-ba* 'fruit', e.g. papaya, guava, orange (cf. also Key 1979: 67–8). For other native Movima nouns, the last syllable is repeated on the numeral as an agreement device, e.g. *-d'o* for *chad'o* 'plate'; *-mas* for *d'imas* 'hay'; *-pi*, for *sukapi* 'belt'. For borrowed nouns, the last two syllables are repeated if a noun consists of more than two syllables, e.g. *-misa* for *kamisa* 'shirt', and *-pato* for *zapato* 'shoe' (both loans are from Spanish). If a loan consists of just two syllables, the reduplicated last syllable is used, e.g. *-sasa* for *mesa* 'table', *-yaya* for *siya* 'seat, chair'.

The use of repeaters as agreement devices in Movima depends on the semantics of nouns and on their origin: agreement with loanwords follows different principles from that with native words.

Affixed repeaters are also used with numerals and in other contexts in multiple classifier languages such as Tucano (East Tucano), Tariana (North Arawak), and Kilivila (Austronesian); see Chapter 9.

4.2.3. *Numeral classifiers attached to the head noun*

The only hitherto known instances of numeral classifiers which form a constituent with the head noun rather than with a numeral are Kegboid languages such as Kana (Cross River, Benue-Congo: Ikoro 1994).

Classifiers in Kana form a single morphological and phonological word with the head noun, and not with the numeral. The order in the NP is Numeral-Classifier-Head. The following criteria confirm that the classifier forms one phonological and morphological word with the noun, and not with the numeral.

(A) Rule of tone sandhi in Kana (Ikoro 1994: 19–21)

The rule of tone sandhi in a numeral NP shows that the classifier forms a single phonological word with the head noun. A tone-lowering sandhi rule operates between components of one phonological word, so that the first component of a phonological word never has raised tone. Classifiers never have raised tone, while numerals do.

(B) Formation of diminutives and adjectives in Kána (Ikoro 1994: 21–3)

The diminutive proclitic *í* is attached to the classifier, and not to the noun, in a numeral-classifier-noun construction, e.g.

4.25. í   nṵ́ṵ́
  DIM rat
  'small rat'

4.26. zḭ̀ḭ̀   í   kà   nṵ́ṵ́
  one DIM CL:GENERIC rat
  'one small rat'

A numeral classifier is placed before a noun-based adjective, e.g.

4.27. zḭ̀ḭ̀   kà   kpáá-bée̋   nḛ̄ḛ̄
  one CL:GENERIC bald-head person
  'one bald person'

Ikoro (1994: 23–5) suggests an areal origin for numeral classifiers in Kana. Proto-Benue-Congo had a noun class system, marked on nouns; Kegboid languages lost this, and acquired numeral classifiers. Noun categorization is still associated with the head noun, as a vestige of the noun class system of the proto-language. This may explain the unusual system of numeral classifiers in this and other Kegboid languages.[7]

---

[7] Alternatively, it is possible that the numeral-classifier construction in Kana historically goes back to a genitive constituent, similar to the one in Ejagham (see example 4.2) (Gerrit Dimmendaal, p.c.).

4.3. Languages with more than one morphological type of numeral classifier

Languages with more than one morphological type of numeral classifier are rare. Similarly to languages with more than one type of noun class system (§2.7), there are two possibilities: different types of numeral classifier may be in a complementary distribution (see §4.3.1), or different types of numeral classifier may cooccur and display different properties (§4.3.2).

4.3.1. Different types of numeral classifier in complementary distribution

Different systems of numeral classifiers can be in complementary distribution depending on the numeral, or on the semantics of the classifier.

In Malto (South Dravidian: Mahapatra 1979: 120) numeral classifiers are independent lexemes when used with the number 'three' or more. The order in a numeral phrase is Numeral-Classifier-Noun:

4.28. tini   maq   o:ydu
      three   CL:INAN   cow
      'three cows'

With the numbers 'one' and 'two', non-human classifiers attach to numerals as prefixes, and the structure of the numeral phrase is: Classifier+Numeral-Noun (4.29). For human nouns, portmanteau forms are used: *ort* 'one (human)', *jo:ṛond* or *irw* 'two (humans)'.

4.29. maq-ond   o:ydu
      CL:INAN-one   cow
      'one cow'

Some dialects of Telugu described by Emeneau (1964: 649–50) have a numeral classifier for humans which appears in different forms with different numbers. Suffix *-aru* appears with the number 'two', e.g. *idd-aru manuṣulu* 'two people'. With numbers from three to seven, *-guru* is used, and it can be suffixed to the numeral, as in *mug-guru manuṣulu* 'three people', or be an independent word, as in *nalu guru manuṣulu'* four people'. With numerals from eight to ten, there is an independent lexeme *mandi* 'CL:PERSON', as in *enimidi mandi manuṣulu* 'eight men'. (Classifiers are not used with numerals bigger than ten.) In Nias (Western Austronesian: Lea Brown, p.c.), numeral classifiers for human nouns are suffixes to the number 'one' but prefixes to other numbers, e.g. *sa-mösa niha* (one-NUM.CL:HUMAN person) 'one person', *da-rua niha* (NUM.CL:HUMAN-two person) 'two people'. In many languages classifiers for humans (and/or animates) have different forms with different numbers; see also Aikhenvald and Green (1998) for examples from Palikur.

A few languages use quite different classifier sets for different numbers. To'aba'ita (Austronesian) uses an optional classifier *fa* 'small objects' with numbers below ten. There are different words for 'ten' whose selection is determined by the semantics of the counted noun, *taafulu, taafuli* 'ten (general)', *qada* 'ten (coconuts)', *akwala* 'ten (people, porpoise teeth)', *finta* 'ten (tubers, fruit, etc.)', *lama* 'ten (birds)', *kobi* 'ten (strings of shell money)', *ai* 'ten (bamboo containers full of canarium nuts)' (Lichtenberk 1995),[8] e.g. 4.30.

4.30. te'e <u>lama'e</u>   sobe   ma   lima   <u>fa</u>   sobe
      one ten:BIRDS   bird.species   and   five   CL   bird.species
      '15 (one ten and five) sobe birds'

A few languages distinguish several sets of numeral classifiers according to their origin. Korean has three sets of classifiers (native, Sino-Korean, and loans); native classifiers are used to enumerate 'natural objects' or items which reflect traditional culture, while Sino-Korean and loan classifiers are used with nouns referring to 'products of modern civilization' (Sohn 1994: 272); see Downing (1996: 46) for a discussion of classifiers of Sino-Japanese origin in Japanese.

4.3.2. Different types of numeral classifier which occur together

In Akatek (Kanjobal of San Miguel Acatán; Mayan: Zavala 1992) there are three classifiers which are affixed to the numeral; more than ten classifiers are used as independent lexemes (see Table 8.3). Affixed classifiers are: *-wan* 'human'; *-k'on* 'animate non-human'; *-eb'* 'inanimate' (Zavala 1992: 130–6). These classifiers are obligatory in a numeral, or quantifier phrase, unless there is another modifier present. Affixed classifiers may cooccur with noun classifiers in a noun phrase (noun classifiers in Akatek are discussed in §3.2.4; see also §8.2), for example:

4.31. noʔ   ʔoš-k'on   tšʼi
      NOUN.CL:ANIMAL   three-NUM.CL:ANIMATE.NON.HUMAN   dog
      'three dogs'

Independent classifiers differ from affixed classifiers in the following ways (Zavala 1992: 139–50). First, the inventory of independent classifiers differs from one speaker to another, while the inventory of affixed classifiers does not. Independent classifiers refer to the shape and form of an object; affixed classifiers characterize the referent of the noun in terms of

---

[8] This is reminiscent of Fijian, which does not have numeral classifiers (Dixon 1988). Old Fijian had special forms, for 'ten' and 'hundred', used for counting different objects; these can be considered as fused numeral classifiers. Churchward (1941: 66–7) lists twenty-one forms for 'ten' and two for 'hundred', e.g. *bī* 'ten (turtles)', *mata* 'ten (fish)', *sava* 'ten (pots)', *uduudu* 'ten (canoes)'; *bola* 'a hundred (canoes)', *koro* 'a hundred (coconuts)'.

its animacy. There is more freedom in the choice of an independent classifier. One noun can combine with more than one independent classifier, depending on a particular, shape-related, property of the referent which is in focus. This is not so for affixed classifiers.

A number phrase may contain both an independent and an affixed numeral classifier plus a noun classifier, as in 4.32 (Zavala 1992: 144).

4.32. ʔoš-eb'   šoyan   ʔišim
      three-NUM.CL:INAN NUM.CL:ROUND   NOUN.CL:MAIZE
      paat
      tortilla
      'three tortillas'

Independent classifiers may be omitted (Zavala 1992: 134), as in 4.33.

4.33. teʔ   ʔoš-eb'   teʔ
      NOUN.CL:WOOD   three-NUM.CL:INAN wood
      'three trees'

An affixed numeral classifier also can be omitted; then the independent numeral classifier forms one phonological word with the numeral, as 4.34. According to Zavala (1992: 144), 4.32 and 4.34 are synonymous.

4.34. ʔoš-šoyan   ʔišim   paat
      three-NUM.CL:ROUND   NOUN.CL:MAIZE   tortilla
      'three tortillas'

The two classifier sets in Akatek also differ in what numbers they are used with. Suffixal numeral classifiers occur with all numbers except for 'one' (Roberto Zavala, p.c.), while the other set is used with all the numbers.

Squamish (Salish: Kuipers 1967: 149–52) also has two sets of numeral classifiers which may cooccur in the same environment. Numerals and numerical interrogative 'how much' distinguish three forms: objects, animals, and humans (see Table 4.6). In addition, numerals cooccur with one of the seven so-called 'lexical suffixes' the choice of which depends on the semantics of the noun, e.g. /-qs/ 'small oblong object' as in /xaʔu'cn-qs čə'mx̌/ (four:OBJECT-CL:SMALL.OBLONG wood) 'four pieces of wood'. (No further data is provided concerning the differences between the two sets.)

4.4. Problems with numeral classifiers

4.4.1. Mensural and sortal classifiers: distinguishing classifiers from quantifying expressions

Two basic types of numeral classifier have been distinguished: sortal classifiers and mensural classifiers. A sortal classifier is 'the one which individuates whatever it refers to in terms of the kind of entity that it is' (Lyons 1977: 463). Examples of sortal numeral classifiers were given above. A mensural classifier is 'the one which individuates in terms of quantity' (Lyons 1977: 463). While sortal classifiers categorize nouns in terms of their inherent properties such as animacy, shape, consistency (see §11.2.3), mensural classifiers are used for measuring units of countable and mass nouns. The choice of a mensural classifier is conditioned by two factors: the quantity, or measure, of an entity, and its physical properties (permanent or, more often, temporary ones). The mensural classifier *han* in Korean is used exclusively for measuring rice wine in terms of an institutionalized measuring cup (Lee 1997).

4.35. makkeli   han   mal
      rice.wine one   MENS.NUM.CL:rice.wine
      'one measure of makkeli (rice wine)'

Mensural classifiers differ from sortal classifiers in their semantics (see (F) in §11.2.3). Since the choice of a mensural classifier is often determined by the temporary state of an object (its quantity, or the arrangement it occurs in) there may be more freedom in choosing a mensural classifier than in choosing a sortal one. For instance, in Tzeltal (Mayan: Berlin 1968: 175) the noun *lagrio* 'brick' is used with just one sortal classifier *pech* 'rectangular, non-flexible object'; when counted it can occur with several different mensural classifiers depending on the arrangement: classifier *latz* is used to refer to a stack of bricks, *chol* to aligned bricks, and *bus* is used for a pile of bricks.

There are further points on which mensural and sortal classifiers differ in their behaviour. Different preferences for the lexical sources of the two kinds of numeral classifiers are discussed in §13.1, and the differences in the modes of obsolescence of mensural and sortal classifiers are discussed in §13.7.

Another problem is distinguishing between numeral classifiers, especially those of the mensural type, and quantifiers (sometimes called 'measure words'). As Ahrens (1994: 204) put it, 'classifiers can only classify over a limited and specific group of nouns, while measure words can be used as a measure for a wide variety of nouns'. Almost every language, whether it has numeral classifiers or not, has quantifiers, the choice of which may depend on the semantics of the noun (e.g. in English *much* is used with non-countable nouns and *many* with countable nouns). Examples include '*head*' in English *five head of cattle* and Russian *golova* 'head' in its equivalent *pjatj golov skota*; *stack* in English *three stacks of books*; *csepp* 'drop' in Hungarian *egy csepp méz* 'one drop of honey'. These quantifying expressions are not numeral classifiers for the following reasons.

116   *Classifiers*

(a) They do not fill an obligatory slot in the numeral-noun construction.

(b) They often have a lexical meaning of their own (unlike mensural classifiers).

(c) Their usage is often related to the distinction between mass and count nouns; for instance, 'honey', a noun with mass reference in Hungarian, has to occur with a quantifier in order to be counted (*egy méz '?one honey' instead of *egy csepp méz* 'one drop of honey' which is ungrammatical); see Lyons (1977) and Craig (forthcoming) for the semantic distinctions involved in dividing nouns into mass and count.

(d) They are used in a type of construction which is also employed for other purposes. For instance, quantifier constructions in English *three heads of cattle* are in fact a subtype of genitive constructions.[9] This is the main reason why English is not a numeral classifier language (see further discussion in Lehrer 1986).

(e) There is a restricted number of such words in a non-classifying language; they also have a restricted distribution (for more discussion, see Dixon 1982: 211; Adams 1989: 5 ff.; Lehrer 1986; Beckwith 1992).

In some languages numeral classifiers may also be used with a quantifying meaning, such as 'half', 'quarter', 'slice'. In Baniwa of Içana (North Arawak) these 'quantifying' classifiers are used as agreement markers on other types of modifiers (Aikhenvald 1996c). This language also has quantifiers as a closed word class. These do not take classifiers, or show any agreement with a noun they refer to, e.g. *manupe tʃinu* 'many dogs', *manupe panṭi* 'many houses' (see Table 9.5 for classifiers in Baniwa).

Classifiers and quantifiers may be hard to distinguish if they occupy the same slot in a noun phrase, as appears to be the case in a number of Austroasiatic languages (cf. Adams 1989: 3).[10] Numeral classifiers, then, have to be distinguished from quantifiers on the basis of language specific criteria.

Quantifying expressions and numeral classifiers can have semantic and grammatical differences, which are considered in (A) and (B) below (further criteria are discussed by T'sou 1976; Bisang 1993: 8–14; Pe 1965).

---

[9] The same construction type is employed independently whether the measure words just quantify the referent of a noun (as in *half of*) or contain some reference to arrangement (as in *row of corn*).

[10] There are also significant differences in the use of such terms as (numeral) classifier and quantifier. Burling (1965) uses the term 'numeral classifier' to refer to all the items which occur in the slot adjacent to a number, as a cover term for both classifiers and measure words. Huffman (1970) refers to this group of items as 'specifiers'.

(A) Semantic and pragmatic criteria for distinguishing classifiers from quantifiying expressions

Classifiers use the unit provided by a count noun, while quantifiers establish the unit to be counted. Classifiers categorize nouns in terms of their size, shape and animacy; they provide no information as to 'quantity' (Allan 1977; Becker 1975; Adams 1989: 6). Quantifiying expressions have fewer restrictions than classifiers on the type of noun they can cooccur with. In Minangkabau (Rina Marnita, p.c.), 'half' is a quantifying expression, and not a numeral classifier, since it can be used with any countable noun.

A distinction between classifiers and quantifying expressions is usually linked to the division of nouns into countable and mass (or uncountable). Mass nouns can only be combined with a numeral through the use of a quantifier (cf. Adams 1989: 9). This is illustrated with Comaltepec Chinantec (Otomanguean: Anderson 1989: 61). Example 4.36 shows a countable noun 'orange' in a numeral phrase, and 4.37 shows a mass noun 'paper' with a classifier (M and L indicate middle and low tones).

4.36. gé^M hi?^{L}
      seven   orange
      'seven oranges'

4.37. tú^M má?^{L} ma^L hí^L
      two   CL:LEAF paper
      'two sheets of paper'

Unlike quantifying expressions, classifiers can have pragmatic uses. For example, in Assamese classifiers mark definiteness-indefiniteness (Barz and Diller 1985), while classifiers in Vietnamese signal definiteness and referentiality of the noun (Löbel 2000: 293–8; cf. §12.1.2). Quantifying expressions usually do not have such functions.

The occurrence of classifiers in numeral phrases may not be obligatory. In Minangkabau classifiers are often omitted in everyday language, and this does not change the semantics of a numeral phrase. In contrast, the omission of a quantifying expression does affect the meaning.

In Khmer, classifiers are obligatory in formal standard language, but not in informal language (the only classifier which is used more or less consistently is the human classifier: Walter Bisang, p.c.); quantifying expressions are 'obligatory' in the sense that their omission alters the sense (Adams 1989: 9).

Unlike quantifying expressions, classifiers may be optional for some numbers, usually for big ones (see §4.1; and §4.3.2 on Akatek).

(B) Grammatical criteria for distinguishing classifiers from quantifying expressions

Classifiers and quantifying expressions can differ in possibilities of use in other classifier environments; in anaphoric use; and in agreement.

The different morphosyntactic behaviour of classifiers and 'quantifying expressions' in Comaltepec Chinantec (Otomanguean: Anderson 1989: 58) is shown by the fact that quantifying expressions agree with the head noun in gender (animate vs. inanimate), while classifiers do not.

In Nung (Thai: Saul and Wilson 1980: 25–9) only classifiers, not quantifiers, can be used anaphorically, i.e. as a 'substitute' for a head noun. A classifier construction is illustrated in 4.38.

4.38. slám   áhn   bọc
     three   CL:GENERIC   flower
     'three flowers'

Anaphoric use of a classifier is illustrated in 4.39. The classifier *óhng* 'HUMAN' is repeated, and it has distributive meaning 'everyone'.

4.39. óhng   óhng   tô   ma   chèu
     CL:HUMAN   CL:HUMAN   also   come   look
     'Everyone also came to look.'

In multiple classifier systems, the same morphemes may be used with numerals and in other environments; quantifiers are not used this way. In Nung classifiers are also used in possessive and demonstrative NPs (Saul and Wilson 1980: 25). In Chinese and Vietnamese classifiers occur with demonstratives (Adams 1989: 10; Goral 1978).

In Akatek (Zavala 1992: 145), some independent numeral classifiers can be used as quantifying expressions (§4.3.2) while affixed numeral classifiers cannot. Example 4.40 illustrates the use of *kupan* 'semi-circle' as a numeral classifier. An affixed numeral classifier can be omitted.

4.40. ʔoš-eb'   kupan   ʔišim
     three-NUM.CL:INAN   NUM.CL:SEMI.CIRCULAR   NOUN.CL:MAIZE
     paat
     tortilla
     'three quesadillas (taco of folded tortillas which form a semi-circle)'

Example 4.41 illustrates the use of the same item as a quantifying expression, 'a heap of semi-circular objects' (Zavala 1992: 145–6). Here, the affixed numeral classifier is required.

4.41. ʔoš-eb'   mimex   kupan
      three-NUM.CL:INAN big   QUANT:SEMI.CIRCULAR.HEAP
      ʔišim   paat
      NOUN.CL:MAIZE   tortilla
      'three big heaps of tortillas'

There are other morphosyntactic differences between quantifying expressions and numeral classifiers in Akatek (Zavala 1992: 143). For instance, a suffixed numeral classifier agrees with the head noun in a number phrase which does not contain a quantifying expression, as illustrated in 4.42.

4.42. ʔoš-wan   k'itan   eb'
      three-NUM.CL:HUMAN   NUM.CL:SEPARATE   PL:HUMAN
      nax   winax
      NOUN.CL:MAN   man
      'three men' (viewed separately)

If a number phrase contains a quantifying expression, the affixed numeral classifier agrees with it. This is illustrated in 4.43. Classifier *-eb'* 'inanimate' refers to *tinan* 'conglomerate'.

4.43. ʔoš-eb'   tinan   eb'
      three-NUM.CL:INAN   QUANT:CONGLOMERATE   PL:HUMAN
      nax   winax
      NOUN.CL:MAN   man
      'three groups of men' (group is 'inanimate')

These examples from Akatek clearly show that while a quantifier 'provides' the unit that is counted, the classifier categorizes this unit.

Löbel (2000: 287) shows that the connection between a quantifier and a noun is not as strong as that between a classifier and a classified noun, in spite of the surface similarity between classifier phrases and measure phrases. A stative verb, e.g. *đây* 'be full of' or a noun *ru'ō'i* 'half of' can come between a quantifier and a noun, as illustrated in 4.44.

4.44. một   cân   rưởi   chó
      one   pound   half   dog
      'one and a half pounds of dog (meat)' (at the butcher's)

This is not possible in classifier phrases; then, these forms have to follow the entire classifier phrase, as shown in 4.45.

4.45. một   con   chó   rưởi
      one   animal   dog   half
      'one and a half dogs' (at the butcher's)

Difficulties with discriminating between quantifiers and classifiers may be due to the fact that these are better viewed as extremes of a continuum. Note Becker's (1975: 114) suggestion that quantity and quality are possibly not discrete semantic classes but rather 'polarities in a semantic continuum'. Similarly to mensural classifiers, quantifiers cooccur with numerals and their choice may also correlate with the properties of the units enumerated (Downing 1996: 13). Consequently, in some languages the two categories simply cannot be clearly distinguished (this appears to be the case in Korean). Some properties which proved to be useful for distinguishing quantifiers and classifiers have been given above; internal linguistic criteria should always be used to establish this differentiation.

There may be a historically attested diachronic process of change from a numeral classifier to a quantifier with a corresponding meaning shift. In Minangkabau *miya* was originally just used as a classifier for 'bread crumbs'; in the modern language this item is used as a quantifier 'a little bit' (Rina Marnita, p.c.; Conklin 1981).[11]

4.4.2. Incipient numeral classifiers

Non-classifier languages can have incipient systems of numeral classifiers.

Numeral classifiers are emerging in the Omani-Zanzibar and in the Egyptian variety of Arabic (Greenberg 1990: 178 ff.; Classical Arabic has no classifiers). Omani Arabic has four classifiers used in noun phrases with numerals: *ra:s* 'head' is used for some animals usable as meat, root crops, and 'slave'; *qarn* 'horn' is used for corn-shaped edibles; *šo:b* 'fruit' is used to classify fruits, and *'o:d* 'branch' to classify flowers. Not all nouns in the language take classifiers. The numeral precedes the classifier, agreeing with it in gender. The construction numeral + classifier is similar to the construction numeral + noun. The classified noun follows the classifier and does not change its form, e.g. *ra:s finda:l* '(one) potato' (lit. head potato); *thala:thit rwa:s finda:l* 'three potatoes' (lit. three head:PL potato). These classifiers are restricted to limited classes of nouns, and they are optional.

In Russian (Greenberg 1990: 181–3) *čelovek*, the genitive plural form of 'man', can be used with numerals bigger than four for a restricted set of

---

[11] Numeral classifiers may be difficult to distinguish from compounding. In the following example from Vietnamese it seems to be virtually impossible to tell a classifier from a part of a nominal compound in a phrase like (i) (Adams 1989: 11). See also Bisang (1999).

(i) môt   ngu̇ờ i   lạ   'a stranger'
    one   person   strange

In this example *ngu̇ờ i* is a general classifier for 'person', and also a member of compound meaning 'stranger'. According to Löbel (2000: 48–51), stress is decisive here: in the case of a compound it is on the first element, while in a classifier construction the last element receives the stress.

human referents. The classifying noun takes genitive case (as do nouns 'governed' by numerals bigger than four), e.g. *pjatj čelovek detej* (five people:GN.PL children:GN.PL) 'five children' (lit. five people children). In this construction, the 'classifier' is governed by the numeral exactly as a head noun is governed by the numeral. This construction may go back to the individualizing use of generics with collective nouns. Similarly to Arabic, the classifier use of *čelovek* 'man:GN.PL' is optional. Noun phrases lacking it, e.g. *pjatero detej* 'five:COLL children:GN.PL', or *pjatj detej* 'five children:GN.PL', are perfectly grammatical. Also, the classifier is used for a very limited class of nouns.

These examples provide evidence in favour of the emergence of numeral classifiers from independent lexical items in inflecting languages (see Chapter 13).

4.5. Distribution of numeral classifiers in the languages of the world

Numeral classifiers are the second most frequent type of classifiers, after noun classes and genders—see Map 3.

Numeral classifiers are widespread across the languages of East and Southeast Asia and Oceania. They are present in many Tibeto-Burman languages, in Chinese languages, and in most Austroasiatic languages. In the Far East, Japanese, Korean, and Ainu have numeral classifiers.

Numeral classifiers are not found in languages of the Afroasiatic family. Among Indo-European languages, some of the Indic and Iranian languages (e.g, Marathi, Hindi, Persian) have numeral classifiers, as do many Dravidian languages. (This is an areal phenomenon in South Asia: see Emeneau 1964.)

Among Uralic languages, Hungarian is said to have numeral classifiers (Beckwith 1992), similar to many Turkic languages (Vietze 1979; Beckwith 1998). Nivkh (or Gilyak; Paleosiberian isolate) has a large set of numeral classifiers.

Numeral classifiers are found in scattered pockets across North America (Sherzer 1976; Campbell 1997). The inventories of classifiers are typically small, and the semantics of their classifiers are based on shape and animacy. In the Eastern subarctic linguistic area, Ojibway (Algonquian) has numeral classifiers (as well as verbal classifiers: Denny 1979a). Numeral classifiers are a central areal trait of the Northwest Coast linguistic area, present in those languages of the Eyak-Athabaskan, Haida, Tlingit, Wakashan, Chemakuan, and Salish families which are spoken in the area (Sherzer 1976: 74). Tsimshian apparently acquired them through contact with its neighbours. The Salishan languages of the Plateau area

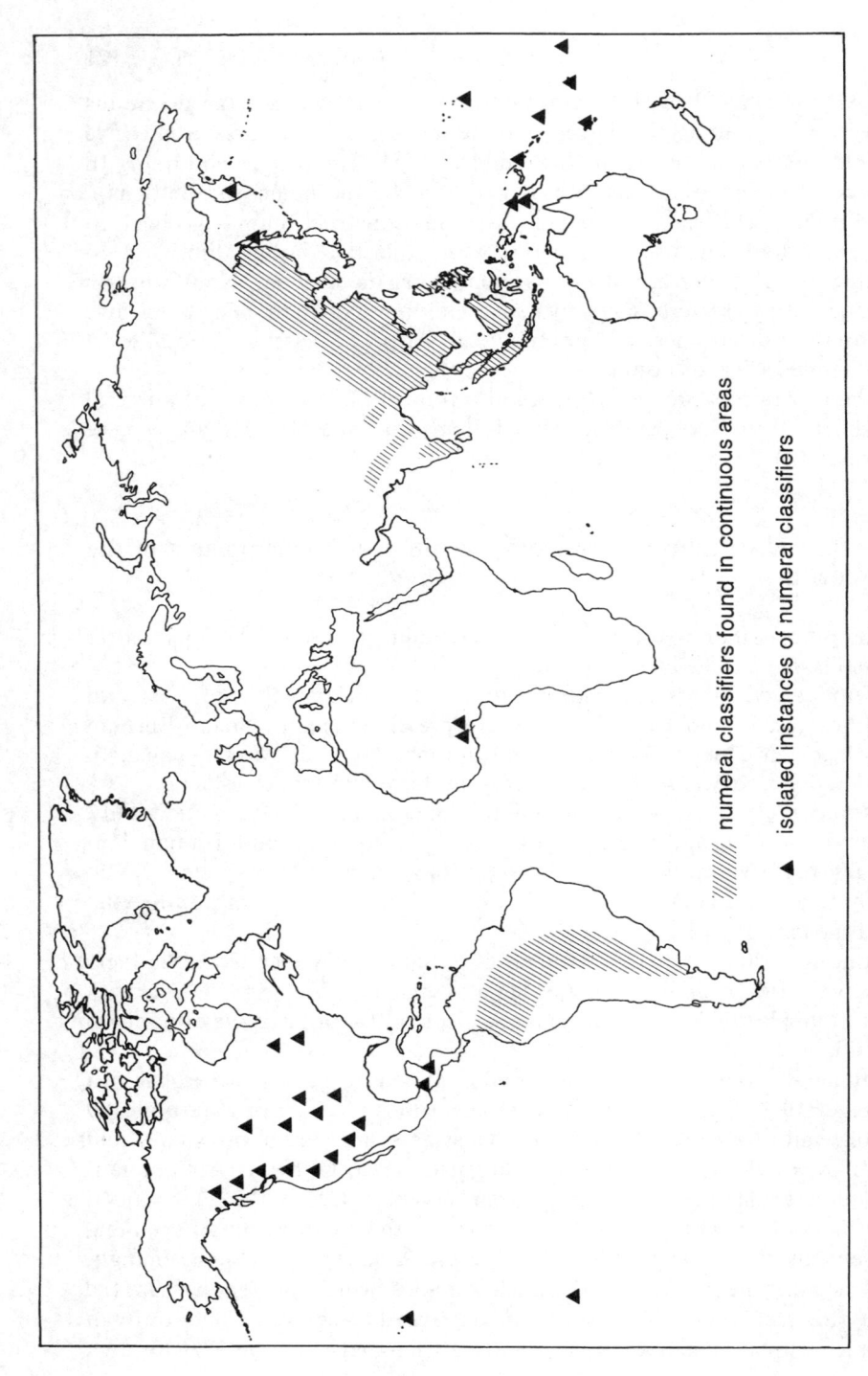

MAP 3. *Distribution of numeral classifiers in the languages of the world*

have shape and form-based numeral classifiers. Human/non-human is distinguished for numerals in Nez Perce, Sahaptin, and Upper Chinook and in one Salish language, Colville. In Sahaptin, number marking in adverbial cases depends on whether or not the nominal refers to a human (Rigsby and Rude 1996).

Numeral classifiers, based on the shape and form of the object, are an areal feature of the extreme northwestern region of California; they are present in Yurok and Wiyot (Algonquian-Ritwan), and in Karok; Hupa (Athabaskan) distinguishes different numerals for humans and non-humans. In the Great Basin linguistic area, numerals distinguish persons, non-persons, and immutable objects only in Washo (isolate). The only language in the Plains with numeral classifiers is Blackfoot (Algonquian), which has two sets of numerals, one for animate and the other for inanimate nouns. In the Northeast linguistic area, Menomini and Potawatomi (Algonquian) have form/shape-based numeral classifiers. Absence of numeral classifiers is a feature of the Pueblo and Southeast linguistic areas.

Numerous Mexican and Central American languages have numeral classifiers, e.g. Aztec (Uto-Aztecan), Huave (isolate), Totonac (isolate), Sierra Popoluca (Zoquean), Zapotec (Otomanguean), Nahuatl (Campbell et al. 1986: 550; Costenla Umaña 1991: 116; Campbell 1997). Mayan languages (especially these of the Kanjobalan branch) have extensive systems of numeral and noun classifiers. Some instances of numeral classifiers in Mayan languages may be the result of diffusion (Hopkins 1970).

Large sets of numeral classifiers are present in numerous languages of South America, especially those of Lowland Amazonia, including the languages of such families as Arawak, Tucano, Guahibo, Peba-Yagua, Chapahuan, Harakmbet, Bora-Witoto, Nambiquara, Tsafiki (Barbacoan: Connie Dickinson, p.c.) and a few isolates, e.g. Waorani and Sáliba (see Derbyshire and Payne 1990; Dixon and Aikhenvald 1999). Some Tupí languages, e.g. Munduruků, also have numeral classifiers. Chimila (Amaya 1997: 139) appears to be the only language with numeral classifiers among the Chibchan languages of Colombia.

Numeral classifiers are found in a number of Papuan languages. In the East Sepik province, Iwam (Conrad and Conrad n.d.; Laycock and Z'graggen 1975: 744) has five numeral classifiers, and Abau (Lock forthcoming; Laycock and Z'graggen 1975: 744) has twelve. Chambri (Lower Sepik area) has five numeral classifiers used with numbers from one to five, while Wogamusin and Chenapian (Laycock and Z'graggen 1975: 743–4) have five numeral classifiers used with numbers up to four. In the Gulf province, some Angan languages have numeral classifiers, also used in other environments (i.e. with adjectives and demonstratives: Speece n.d, for Angave, and Carlson 1991, for Taenae). In the Highlands, Folopa (Podopa), of the Teberan family, has numeral classifiers (Anderson and Anderson 1976). In the Morobe province, the closely related Wantoat (Davis n.d.) and Awará (Susan Quigley forthcoming and p.c.) have a largeish set of numeral classifiers used with the numbers 'one' and 'two' (also employed with demonstratives and as derivational affixes on nouns).

Most Western Austronesian and Oceanic languages[12] have numeral classifiers. However, numeral classifiers appear to be absent from the Austronesian languages spoken in Taiwan. Some Oceanic languages spoken in the Papua New Guinea region have extensive numeral classifier systems (for example, Loniu, an Oceanic language spoken in the Admiralties, has thirty numeral classifiers: Hamel 1994). In contrast, Oceanic languages spoken in Bougainville (e.g. Teop, Halia, or Petats: Ulrike Mosel, Ruth Spriggs, Evelyn Boxall, p.c.) lack numeral classifiers.

Numeral classifiers are very rare in Africa and absent from Australia. In Africa, they are found in a few Kegboid languages (Cross River: Benue-Congo: Ikoro 1994), Ejagham (Watters 1981), and in a few Grassfields languages from Cameroon (e.g. Ngyembɔɔn: Viktor Vinogradov, p.c.).

[12] Pawley (1973) provides a reconstruction of the Proto-Oceanic numeral classifers.

5 Classifiers in Possessive Constructions

5.1 Categorization in possessive constructions

There are three ways of categorizing nouns in possessive constructions and these correspond to three kinds of noun categorization devices.

(A) Categorizing the possessed noun

The choice of classifiers in possessive constructions can be determined by the nature of the referent of the possessed noun in terms of its animacy, shape, form, etc. (cf. Craig forthcoming: 32; 1992). I shall call these classifiers 'possessed' classifiers (see §5.2).

(B) Categorizing the semantic nature of a relation between the possessee and the possessor in a possessive construction

The choice of possessive marker can be determined by the way the possessor handles or owns or otherwise relates to the possessee. I shall call this type of categorization 'relational' classifiers, following Lichtenberk (1983a: 148): 'The crucial property of relational classifiers is that their use is determined . . . by the semantic *relation* between two linguistic elements', e.g., how the possessor might use the possessed.

Relational classifiers (found in Austronesian and in a few American Indian languages; see Carlson and Payne 1989; Croft 1994) are considered in §5.3.

(C) Categorizing the possessor

'Possessor classifiers'—morphemes the choice of which is conditioned by the properties of possessor—are very rare; see §5.4.

The three types of categorization in possessive constructions[1] are relatively independent of each other. Relational classifiers may combine with possessed classifiers to create an integrated system which includes both kinds of categorization (since the way a noun can be 'possessed' may correlate with its inherent properties). This is the case in some Micronesian languages with large systems of classifiers in possessive constructions. There

---

[1] See Heine (1997a), H. Seiler (1986), and Chappell and McGregor (1996) for detailed discussions of possession.

are other languages which have distinct sets of relational and possessed classifiers (see §5.5).

The different types of classifiers in possessive constructions are contrasted in §5.6.[2] Their distribution in the languages of the world is outlined in §5.7.

5.2. Possessed classifiers

Possessed classifiers characterize the possessed term in a possessive construction. They do not involve agreement, and their choice is strictly semantic. They share the following properties with numeral classifiers and noun classifiers.

(i) They characterize nouns in terms of their animacy, shape, size, and structure.

(ii) They are not expressed outside the possessive NP.

(iii) Every noun in a language may not necessarily be able to take a possessed classifier.

(iv) Some languages can have a 'generic' possessed classifier which replaces other, more specific, classifiers.

The size of the inventory of possessed classifiers can vary. Morphologically they can be independent words or affixes to the possessed noun or the possession marker.

Since possessed classifiers do not characterize the type of relationship between the possessor and the possessed, they do not necessarily interrelate with, or depend upon, the distinction between alienable and inalienable possession. In some languages possessed classifiers may be used only with different subclasses of alienably possessed nouns (A); in other languages possessed classifiers are used independently of whether a noun is alienably or inalienably possessed (B). Possessed classifiers of group A are not used in any other environments. Possessed classifiers of group B often are.

(A) Possessed classifiers used only with subclasses of alienably possessed nouns

Possessed classifiers are used with alienably possessed nouns in Yuman and Uto-Aztecan languages.

In Yuman languages inalienable possession is indicated by a prefix on the possessed noun, or a prefix on the possessed noun plus a pronoun. Possession

---

[2] The existing literature is somewhat confusing in distinguishing between different classifier types in possessive constructions. Most typologies consider the three types distinguished here as just one kind of noun categorization (e.g. Lichtenberk 1983a; Craig forthcoming).

of alienably possessed nouns is expressed either by a noun followed by a classifier with affixes indicating possession, or by a noun with possessive suffixes attached to it. There are two classifiers, one for 'pets and domestic animals', and the other a general one (Hualapai, Yavapai, Maricopa -*hat* 'pet'; Yavapai *wi*, Hualapai *-wi:nych*, Maricopa *nywish* 'general possession'). A possessed classifier for 'pet' in Yavapai is exemplified with 5.1; a general classifier in Hualapai is shown in 5.2 (Carlson and Payne 1989).

5.1. qoleyaw ʔ-ñ-hat
chicken 1SG-GENITIVE-CL:PET
'my chicken' (chicken-my pet)

5.2. maḓ ma m-wi:nych
land your 2SG-CL:GENERAL
'your land'

According to Langacker (1977), 'an important feature of Uto-Aztecan languages is a "classifier" construction'. To indicate alienable possession, possessive prefixes are attached to the classifier. Languages typically have two or three classifiers, which distinguish animacy and humanness. Cora (Casad 1982: 236) distinguishes human, animate, and inanimate; Papago and Northern Tepehuan (Bascom 1982; Saxton 1982) have animate and inanimate classifiers.[3] Papago classifier *ṣoi-* with an animate noun is illustrated in 5.3 (Saxton 1982: 186–7).

5.3. has-ču ṣoi-g-ǰ g huan
what-thing CL:ANIMATE-ALIENABLE-GENITIVE ART Juan
'What kind of animal does Juan have?' (lit. what kind of animal of Juan?)

Possessed classifiers in Uto-Aztecan can be used headlessly, in a kind of anaphoric function. This is illustrated in 5.4, from Papago (Langacker 1977: 92), where the noun *miisa* 'table' is included in copula subject function; it is omitted from the NP in the function of a copula complement.

5.4. iida miisa o=ḓ t-'iñi-ga
this table be our-CL:INANIMATE-possessed
'This table is ours'

Panare (Carib: Mattéi-Muller 1974; Carlson and Payne 1989) has twenty-one classifiers which are used with alienably possessed nouns (Carlson and Payne 1989: 19). Classifiers characterize the possessed noun in terms of its shape, structure, and consistency. There are seven

---

[3] Some languages have just one possessed classifier, e.g. Luiseño classifier '*aač* for pets. Chemehuevi (Southern Numic branch of Uto-Aztecan) has two possessed classifiers: *-puŋku* 'pet' and *-igapɨ* 'domesticated plant' (Press 1979: 60–1).

classifiers which are used with a single item each. Four of these are repeaters, i.e. they coincide with the noun which they categorize in a possessive construction: see Table 5.1.

TABLE 5.1. *Possessed classifiers in Panare*

Semantics	Classifier	Examples
General	*iyu*	Soap, gasoline, hammer, paper, table etc.
Edible 1	*yung*	Food items in paste form: mango, corn (mash), manioc
Edible 2	*tä'ma*	Something softer than *yung*: egg, rice, soup
Edible 3	*empa*	Fruit with its pulp, not squeezed out
Edible 4	*yo'/are*	Meat (cooked or raw): fish, chicken, beef
Drinkable/liquid	*uku*	Liquids: coffee, milk, blood
Animal	*yikɨ*	Live animals, including domesticated ones
Vehicle	*kanowa*	Canoe, truck, helicopter, car
Hunting arms	*ko*	Spear, arrow, harpoon
Musical instrument	*ntyën*	Flute, guitar, violin
Body paint	*yanoë*	Body paints
Clothing	*po'*	Necklace, shirt
Container	*mara'pi*	Gourd, etc.
Artificial light	*uyung*	Lantern, flashlight
Single item classes	*ëwɨ'*	House
	tipi'	Swidden garden
	ichi'	Hammock
Repeaters	*pata*	Village, community
	chistë	Hatchet
	wata	Blowgun
	wa'to	Fire

5.5 illustrates the use of the possessed classifier *uku* 'liquid'.

5.5. y-uku-n   wanë
     1SG-CL:LIQUID-GN honey
     'my honey (mixed with water for drinking)'

In Macushí and Apalaí (further Carib languages), the classifiers—which are used with alienably possessed nouns—are themselves in fact a subclass of inalienably possessed nouns. Inalienably possessed nouns can take possessive affixes directly, while the alienably possessed ones cannot. Classifiers are generic terms, which specify nouns that are to be classified. 5.6 illustrates a generic term for food in Apalaí (Koehn and Koehn 1986: 85 ff.).

5.6. a-napy-ry
 2SG-fruit/vegetable-POSS
 'your fruit, vegetable'

Names of plants, animals, and natural phenomena cannot take possessive affixes directly; these must be added to an accompanying possessed classifier with a 'generic' semantics (cf. 'generics' used as noun classifiers: §3), as in 5.7.

5.7. a-napy-ry   paruru
 2SG-fruit/vegetable-POSS banana
 'your banana' (lit. 'your fruit banana')

Similar constructions from Macushi (Abbott 1991: 85–6) are shown in 5.8 and 5.9.

5.8. u-yekîn   kaware
 1SG-pet   horse
 'my horse'

5.9. u-yekkari   ma'pîya
 1SG-FRUIT:FOOD   papaya
 'my papaya'

Classifiers of this kind, in both Macushi and Apalaí, are a semi-open class, since any generic noun can be used as a 'classifier' in a possessive construction. These languages do have an interrelation between possession type and the use of possessed classifier. However, this operates on a different basis from Yuman and Uto-Aztecan languages: both types of possession are involved in a classifier construction in the Carib languages, while possessed classifiers are restricted to constructions with alienable possession in Yuman and Uto-Aztecan. Possessed classifiers which are a subclass of nouns with generic semantics are used with alienably possessed items in other South American languages. Northern Jê languages, such as Timbira (Canela, Krahô), Kayapó, and Panará, have one generic classifier for all alienably possessed items; Bororo (Macro-Jê) has one classifier for pets and another for all other alienably possessed nouns; Tupí-Guaraní languages typically have one classifier for pets and another for game (Rodrigues 1997: 72–3).[4]

(B) Possessed classifiers used independently of possession type

Possessed classifiers can be used independently of possession type both in languages which have a grammatical distinction between alienable and inalienable possession, and in languages which have no such distinction.

---

[4] For possessed classifiers in Urubu-Kaapor (Tupí-Guaraní), see Kakumasu (1986: 371).

'Dongo-ko (Mba group, Ubangi branch of Niger-Congo: Pasch 1985: 75 ff.; 1986: 240 ff.) has ten possessed classifiers. There is an elaborate classification of nouns with classifiers used just in possessive constructions. Example 5.10 illustrates the use of the classifier *dà* 'possession of animals and some inanimate objects' (Pasch 1986: 248). (Note that 'Dongo-ko, similarly to other Mba languages, also has noun class agreement; see §2.4.2.)

5.10. ɓì-gó   Ø-á   dà   rè
leopard-CL7   CL1-POSS   CL:ANIMAL.POSS   1SG
'my leopard'

5.11 illustrates the use of the classifier *kɔ́* which refers to the possession of 'inseparable' body parts (Pasch 1986: 249).

5.11. nzí   m-á   kɔ́   ɓì-gò
blood   CL11-POSS   CL:BODY.PART.POSS   leopard-CL7
'leopard's blood'

Guaicuruan languages (Brazil and Argentina) have no grammatical distinction between alienable and inalienable possession. Some of them do have possessed classifiers (Céria and Sândalo 1995: 14). For instance, Toba and Mocovi each have one possessed classifier (*lo* 'animal classifier'), and Kadiweu has two classifiers; one is used with domestic animals (*wiɠadi*) and the other is used with other nouns (*nebi* 'generic classifier'). The animal possessive classifier agrees in gender (feminine/non-feminine) and number (singular, plural) with the possessed noun, as shown in 5.12, from Kadiweu.

5.12. li-wiɠagi   nigidagiwaɠa
3-CL:ANIMATE:NON.FEM.SG   pig(NON.FEM)
'his (male) pig'

The generic classifier, illustrated in 5.13, shows no agreement (Griffiths and Griffiths 1976: 101–3).[5]

5.13. ɠo-nebi   leyeema
1PL-CL:GENERIC   wheat
'our wheat'

Possession in Kadiweu can also be expressed with a possessive prefix attached to the noun; for emphasis, the possessive prefix may attach both to the classifier and to the possessed noun. This is illustrated in 5.14.

5.14. jabeyagi   ɠa-nibole   ɠa-nebi-tiwaji
already.spoilt   2PL-meat   2PL-CL:GENERIC-PL
'Your meat is already spoilt.'

---

[5] Griffiths and Griffiths (1976: 103) note a certain degree of interchangeability between animate and inanimate classifiers for animate referents.

Possessive prefixes and possessed classifiers occur together in equational copula clauses, illustrated in 5.15. (Examples like this can also be interpreted as instances of the headless use of possessive classifiers.)

5.15. ɟo-dacilo   ɟo-nebi
 1PL-head   1PL-CL:GENERIC
 'The head is <u>ours</u>.'

Classifiers characterize the possessed noun in possessive constructions independently of possession type in a number of multiple classifier languages, including Tariana and Baniwa (North Arawak), East Tucano, Hmong (Miao-Yao: Bisang 1993), and Motuna and Nasioi (Papuan).

Baniwa and Tariana and the East Tucano languages distinguish alienably and inalienably possessed nouns. Kinship terms, body parts, and a few other items, e.g. home, are inalienably possessed; other nouns are alienably possessed. These languages have large sets of classifiers which characterize the noun in terms of animacy, shape, structure, size; classifier morphemes can be used in several environments (see §9.3; Aikhenvald 1994a; 1996c). Possessed classifiers are often employed anaphorically.

Inalienable possession in Tariana is marked with possessive prefixes, as shown in 5.16. Alienable possession is marked by juxtaposition of possessor and possessed, as in 5.17. Note that 5.17a, with a possessive prefix, is ungrammatical.

5.16. nu-pana
 1SG-home
 'my home'

5.17. nuha   tʃinu
 I   dog
 'my dog'

5.17a. *nu-tʃinu

Possessed classifiers can be used with any noun if the fact of a noun being possessed is to be focused on. Example 5.18 illustrates the use of a possessed classifier with an inalienably possessed noun, *panisi* 'home', in Tariana. Example 5.19 illustrates the use of a possessed classifier with an alienably possessed noun, *tʃinu* 'dog'. The head noun is in parentheses (since it can be omitted).

5.18. nu-ya-dapana   (panisi)
 1SG-POSS-CL:HOUSE   (home)
 'my (home)'

5.19. nu-ite   (tʃinu)
     1SG-POSS+CL:ANIM   (dog)
     'my (dog)'

Two Papuan languages of Southern Bougainville, Nasioi (Hurd 1977) and Motuna (Onishi 1994), make no grammatical distinction between alienable and inalienable possession. Possessed classifiers are used in a special 'classifier' possessive construction type, and also in other classifier environments (see §9.1). (§5.4 discusses another possessive construction in Nasioi which is similar to possessor classifiers.) A possessed classifier in Motuna is illustrated in 5.20 (Onishi 1994: 131), and a classifier used in a possessive construction in Nasioi is shown in 5.21.

5.20. ong   moo   ngo-no-mung
      DEM.MASC   coconut   1SG.POSS-LINK-CL:PLANT/FRUIT
      'this/that coconut, (which is) my plant/fruit'

5.21. n-ee-ka-na-va
      US-DU-INTENSE-DER.SUFF-CL:HOUSE
      'our (house)' (Hurd 1977: 155)

In Hmong, a Miao language of China—and in some other Miao languages of the region—possessed classifiers are used with both alienably and inalienably possessed nouns. (The same set of classifiers is used with demonstratives and with numerals: see §9.1.) The possessed classifier can only be omitted from possessive constructions with inalienable possession (Bisang 1993: 29–30). A possessed classifier is used with an inalienably possessed noun in 5.22. It is omitted in 5.23, in a construction with inalienable possession.

5.22. nws   tus   txiv ntxawm
      he   CL:LIV.BEING uncle
            tus   ntxhais
            CL:LIV.BEING daughter
      'the daughter of his uncle'

5.23. kuv   txiv
      I   father
      'my father'

Example 5.24 illustrates the use of a possessed classifier with an alienably possessed noun 'sword'. Here, the possessed classifier cannot be omitted.

5.24. nws   rab   riam ntaj
      he   CL:ARTEFACT   sword
      'his sword'

5.3. Relational classifiers

Relational classifiers are unlike any other classifier type in that, instead of just characterizing a noun, they characterize a possessive relation between nouns. Like possessed classifiers, they do not involve agreement.

They are not marked outside the possessive NP. Every noun in a language does not necessarily take a relational classifier. There may be a generic classifier, and the size of the inventory can vary. Morphologically, they can be realized as independent words or as affixes to the possessed noun or the possession marker.

Relational classifiers are almost always restricted to constructions of alienable possession. I consider examples of relational classifiers in §5.3.1. The distinction between alienable and inalienable possession is another way of categorizing a possessive relationship. In §5.3.2, relational classifiers are compared with the alienable/inalienable distinction.

Unlike possessed classifiers, relational classifiers are not used in other classifier constructions within multiple classifier systems. Their semantics is often different from that of other classifier types: a parameter such as value is more frequent in relational classifiers than in other classifier types (see §11.2.4).

5.3.1. Relational classifiers and their properties

Relational classifiers are found in the Oceanic subgroup of Austronesian,[6] and in a few South American Indian languages (Kipeá, from the Kipeá-Karirí family, South America, extinct: Rodrigues 1997; Baniwa of Içana, from the North Arawak subgroup). Large systems of relational classifiers (integrated with possessed classifiers) will be considered in §5.5.1.

All Oceanic languages distinguish between alienable (indirect) and inalienable (direct) possession. In most languages, inalienable possession is restricted to kinship nouns and parts of a whole; it is indicated by suffixes attached to possessed nouns, e.g. Standard Fijian (Lichtenberk 1983a: 153):

5.25. na   tama-dratou
     ART father-their
     'their (paucal) father'

5.26. na   ulu-qu
     ART head-my
     'my head'

---

[6] The existence of relational classifiers in Oceanic languages was first recognized by Codrington (1885); see Harrison (1976), for Mokilese; Dixon (1988), for Boumaa Fijian; Pawley and Sayaba (1990), for Wayan, a Western Fijian language; for a more general discussion, see Lichtenberk (1983a); Carlson and Payne (1989).

To indicate alienable possession, pronominal affixes are attached to relational classifiers, the special morphemes which indicate the type of relationship between the possessor and the possessed, e.g. Boumaa Fijian (Dixon 1988: 137):

5.27. a o-mu da'ai
ART CL-2SG gun
'your gun' (which belongs to you)

5.28. a 'e-mu da'ai
ART CL-2SG gun
'your gun' (which will be used to shoot you)

Oceanic languages have the following types of systems of relational classifiers (Lichtenberk 1983a).[7]

(a) A system of two relational classifiers involving the opposition: general versus alimentary/consumable (cf. Heine 1997a). This is illustrated for Manam (Lichtenberk 1983a: 151) and Kaliai-Kove (Counts 1969: 100) in Table 5.2. (Two relational classifiers in Baniwa are discussed in §5.5.2.)

TABLE 5.2. *Systems of two relational classifiers*

Language	General	Alimentary
Manam	ne	ʔana
Kaliai-Kove	le	a

(b) A system of four relational classifiers is illustrated in Table 5.3 for Boumaa Fijian (Dixon 1988: 136):

Table 5.3. *A system of relational classifiers in Boumaa Fijian*

Meaning		Form
(a) consumed	(i) drunk/sucked/licked	me-
	(ii) eaten/chewed/smoked	'e-
(b) not consumed	(ii) relating to the 'possessor'	'e-, as in 5.28
	(iii) owned by the 'possessor'	we-lo-, as in 5.27

---

[7] According to Lynch (1993), the distinction between direct and indirect possession and possessive markers, i.e. relational classifiers, can be reconstructed for Proto-Oceanic. Austronesianists (see Lichtenberk 1985) reconstruct three 'indirect' possessive markers: (a) drink possession, Proto-Oceanic *ma-; (b) food and passive possession, Proto-Oceanic *ka-; (c) general possession, marked by Proto-Oceanic *na-. According to Lynch (1993), they have a verbal origin. This is compatible with the derivation of classifiers from independent lexical items; see Chapter 13.

Classifier *'e-* is used for anything which undergoes change of state as it is being consumed; and *me-* is used for anything which does not undergo a change of shape or state as it is being consumed (including a pill that is swallowed).

In Raga, another Oceanic language spoken in Vanuatu, there is a five-term system, including a special classifier for valued possession (Lichtenberk 1983a: 154). This is illustrated in 5.29.

5.29. qoe pila-ma
pig CL:VALUABLE.POSSESSION-2SG
'your valued pig'

Kipeá-Karirí (Rodrigues 1995; 1997) had a system of twelve classifiers characterizing the relationship between the possessor and the possessed in terms of how the possessed could be handled by the possessor. Classifiers used with food items categorize them in terms of (a) acquisition: (i) gathering of wild plants: classifier *uaprú*; (ii) raising of animals: *enkí*; (iii) cultivation of manioc: *uanhí*; (iv) cultivation of other plants: *udjé*; and (b) preparation: (i) boiling: *udé*; (ii) roasting: *upodó*; (iii) maturation at home: *ubó*. Other items are also categorized in terms of (a) acquisition: (i) finding: *uitó*; (ii) sharing: *ukisí*; (iii) gift from outsiders: *ubá*; (iv) booty: *boronunú*, or (b) transportation—carried goods: *e*.

Examples 5.30–3 (Rodrigues 1995) show the same item, *sabuka* 'fowl', with different relational classifiers, to reflect the different ways in which it can be handled by the possessor.

5.30. dz-upodó do sabuka
1SG-CL:ROASTED POSS fowl
'my fowl (roasted)'

5.31. dz-udé do sabuka
1SG-CL:BOILED POSS fowl
'my fowl (boiled)'

5.32. dz-ukisí do sabuka
1SG-CL:SHARING POSS fowl
'my fowl (that was my share)'

5.33. dz-ubá do sabuka
1SG-CL:GIFT. FROM.OUTSIDERS POSS fowl
'my fowl (that was given me)'

Polynesian languages have two relational classifiers (Lichtenberk 1983a: 162), commonly *o* and *a* as basic forms (these may occur with various prefixes, usually an article). *A*-possession implies the control of the possessor over the relationship, or over the initiation of the relationship

(Wilson 1982), and *O*-possession implies the lack of control of the possessor over the relationship.[8] *A* and *O* relational classifiers can be used with the same noun, e.g. examples 5.34 and 5.35 from Hawaiian (Lichtenberk 1983a: 163; examples (84) and (85)).

5.34. k-o-'u   inoa
       ART-CL-my   name
       'my name (that represents me)'

5.35. k-a-'u   inoa
       ART-CL-my   name
       'my name (that I bestow on someone)'

Relational classifiers can be realized as affixes on possession markers, and as independent words or as affixes to nouns. They may form one morphological word with the marker of possession, as in Tolai (Oceanic: Ulrike Mosel, p.c.), some Micronesian languages (e.g. Truquese: §5.5.1) and Kipeá. They may form one morphological word with the possessed noun, as in Baniwa (§5.5.2). Truquese has 'repeaters' (see §5.5.1).

Which relational classifier is to be used in a possessive construction depends on the way the possessed item is to be treated. This is why different relational classifiers can be employed with the same noun.

In Boumaa Fijian, different classifiers can be used with certain nouns, especially with some newly introduced items, such as 'jelly (or jello)', and also some traditional ones, such as tobacco. According to Dixon (1988: 136), 'informants vary as to whether jelly should be *'e-* or *me-*, depending on whether or not they chew it before swallowing'. As far as tobacco is concerned, 'one should use the classifier *'e-* to describe tobacco itself, since it is likely to be rolled and smoked, but *me-* for a pipe which is sucked—thus *a 'e-na tapa'o* 'his tobacco'; but *a me-na paipo ni tapa'o* 'his tobacco pipe' (see Table 5.3). A tripartite system of relational classifiers in Kilivila involves the division of nouns into edible (Series I: 5.36), consumable or closely associated with the possessor (Series II: 5.37), or more distantly associated with the possessor (Series III: 5.38) (Senft 1986: 49–54).

5.36. kagu   tetu
       my:REL.CL:SERIES.I   yam
       'my yams (to eat)'

---

[8] These relationships are described as 'objective' or 'subjective', for Tongan by Churchward (1953: 78). According to some interpretations (H. Seiler 1986; Lichtenberk 1983a), the two relational classifiers in Polynesian can be interpreted as corresponding to alienable and inalienable possession. In some languages, e.g. Tongan, the two different classifiers are used for subject and object nominalizations, e.g. *'e-ne taki* 'his leading', *ho-no taki* 'his being led' (Churchward 1953: 78). This shows how distinction between relational classifiers can also be employed elsewhere in the grammar.

5.37. agu   tetu
my:REL.CL:SERIES.II   yam
'my yams (planted in the garden)'

5.38. ula   tobaki
my:REL.CL:SERIES.III tobacco
'my tobacco (that I will trade or give away)'

5.3.2. Types of possession and relational classifiers

The way possessive relationships can be categorized with relational classifiers shows certain similarities to the grammatical distinction between alienable and inalienable possession. Nichols (1992: 134–5) considers systems with an opposition between alienable and inalienable possession as a subtype of 'non-agreeing' classification.

The similarities between alienable and inalienable possession and relational classifiers can be summarized as follows.

(i) All languages with relational classifiers distinguish alienable and inalienable possession. Relational classifiers are restricted to alienably possessed nouns.

(ii) In languages with a grammatical distinction between alienable and inalienable possession, some nouns can be either alienably or inalienably possessed; there may be a semantic difference. Relational classifiers in these languages are used in a way similar to the alienable/inalienable distinction.

The distinction between alienable and inalienable possession can be used in Kilivila (Oceanic: Senft 1986: 49–54) to indicate different ways in which nouns are possessed (see §5.3.2). Here *doba* 'grass skirt' is treated as inalienably possessed in 5.39, and then it is understood as a piece of clothing.

5.39. doba-gu
grass.skirt-my
'my grass skirt' (when wearing it)

It is understood as a piece of cloth in 5.40, where it is alienably possessed.

5.40. ula   doba
my:REL.CL:SERIES.III grass.skirt
'my grass skirt' (my grass-skirt material)

Similarly, 5.41, from Manam (Oceanic: Lichtenberk 1983a: 158), shows *head* as an inalienably possessed body part. Examples 5.42 and 5.43 show the same noun as alienably possessed with different relational classifiers.

5.41. paŋana-gu
head-my
'my head' (body part; inalienably possessed)

5.42. paŋana ʔana-gu
head CLASS:ALIM-my
'my head' (e.g. fish head: alimentary possession)

5.43. paŋana ne-gu
head CLASS:GENERAL-my
'my head' (the one I found: general possession)

(iii) In some languages with a grammatical distinction between alienable and inalienable possession, but without relational classifiers, some body parts can be marked with either type of possession with a difference in meaning. In Tariana, *kare* means 'breath, heart' when it is inalienably possessed (*nu-kare* 'my breath, my heart'), and 'wind' when alienably possessed. In Paumarí (Arawá: Aikhenvald MS; Shirley Chapman p.c.) *bodi* means 'mouthhole' if inalienably possessed, and 'hole, lair (of an animal)' if alienably possessed. In Boumaa Fijian *yaca* means 'name' when inalienably possessed and 'namesake' when alienably possessed.

However, the analogy between relational classifiers and alienable vs. inalienable possession is not complete. The important difference between relational classifiers and the distinction between alienable and inalienable possession is that relational classifiers are usually semantically transparent; the distinction between alienable and inalienable possession is often much more grammaticalized. For instance, in Paumarí (Arawá) almost all the kinship nouns and body parts are inalienably possessed; but there are three body parts and two kinship nouns which are alienably possessed.

Another difference is that relational classifiers are capable of specifying various distinct ways of handling an object (not just possessive relations). This obviously correlates with properties of the possessed noun, and it results in an interaction between possessed and relational classifiers (see §5.5.1).

Languages which do not have any grammatical opposition between alienable and inalienable possession may have other means of marking a 'closer' possession. 'Closer' possession is claimed to be marked by possessive suffixes in Hebrew (according to Berman 1978): *sifri* 'my book; the one I have written'; with a 'less close' possession being marked by possessive pronouns: *sefer ʃeli* 'my book; the one I own'. So-called possessive adjectives in Russian are used to express a 'closer' possession than possessive genitives (see the final part of §5.4).

5.4. Possessor classifiers

Possessor classifiers are used to categorize the possessor in a possessive construction. They are extremely rare in the languages of the world.[9]

Possessor classifiers are found in Dâw (Martins 1994) and, possibly, in Hupda (Moore and Franklin 1979), languages of the small Makú family spoken on the Brazil/Colombia border.

Dâw distinguishes inalienably and alienably possessed nouns. The first group includes body parts, parts of plants and some kinship terms (Martins 1994: 46). Inalienable possession is expressed by simple juxtaposition of nouns, as shown in 5.44.

5.44. 'yãm   dũm
      tail   dog
      'dog's tail'

Constructions with alienably possessed nouns require classifiers. There are two classifiers: -dee' is used for inanimate possessor, and -ẽj for animate possessor. Both morphemes are clitics (Martins 1994: 138–41).

5.45. yud   dâw   tôg-ẽj
      clothing   human   daughter-CL:ANIMATE.POSSESSOR
      'The clothing is girl's; the girl's clothing'

5.46. yak   kaw-wâ'-dee'
      manioc   garden-up-CL:INANIMATE.POSSESSOR
      'manioc of a garden'

Dâw is unusual in that an inanimate possessor can be used in an alienably possessed construction, as in 5.46. In many languages with a grammatical distinction between alienable and inalienable possession, the possessor in an alienable construction has to be animate.

In Nasioi (Papuan, Bougainville: Hurd 1977), a language with multiple classifiers, classifiers can categorize the possessor in one subtype of possessive constructions: when the possessor is not a personal pronoun. According to Hurd (1977: 138), 'these possessives are the inverse of the possessive pronouns . . . in that the [classifiers] of the latter stand for that which is possessed whereas the [classifiers] of the inverse possessives stand for the possessor'.

These constructions, in which classifiers refer to the possessor, and not to the possessed noun have a special possession marker -po'-. Example 5.47 shows a possessive construction in which the classifier, nono 'village', refers to the possessor, and so can be interpreted as a possessor classifier. The

---

[9] It will be shown in Chapter 9 that the agreement of possessed nouns with the possessor is not an instance of possessor classifiers.

same set of morphemes are used in the function of possessed classifiers, e.g. -*va* 'house' as a possessed classifier in 5.21 above.

5.47. niikanamono toire' mmau'-po'-na-nono
our.village children many-POSS-DS-CL:VILLAGE
'Our village has many children.'

Categorization of possessor[10] in possessive constructions is found in other, non-classifying languages. Possessive marker *'s* in English is predominantly used with a human or at least animate possessor (e.g. *man's leg*, but ?*table's leg*). In Russian, possessive adjectives in *-ov* (masculine possessor) and *-in* (feminine possessor) can be used only if the possessor is animate. One can say *otc-ov-o kreslo* (father-POSS.MASC.ADJ-NEUT.SG.NOM armchair+NEUT) 'father's armchair' (with a human possessor), or *koškin-Ø dom* (cat(FEM)-(POSS.FEM.ADJ-MASC.SG.NOM house+MASC) 'cat's house' (animate possessor). In contrast, *dom-ov-a kryša (house(MASC)-POSS. MASC.ADJ-FEM.SG.NOM roof+FEM) '*house's roof'?, with an inanimate possessor, is unacceptable.[11] Possessive adjectives show gender agreement with the head noun (as all adjectives do in Russian). Boumaa Fijian (Dixon 1988: 120) distinguishes several possessive constructions depending on the type of possessor. All these techniques have functional similarities with possessor classifiers.

5.5. Interaction of possessed and relational classifiers

Possessed and relational classifiers can interact in two ways. Relational classifiers may combine with possessed classifiers to create a single integrated system which marks both kinds of categorization as shown in §5.5.1. Languages which have relational and possessed classifiers as independent systems are considered in §5.5.2.

5.5.1. Integrating relational and possessive classifiers

Largeish systems of classifiers in possessive constructions often characterize both the way an item can be possessed or handled and the item itself.
This is the case in a number of Micronesian languages. Puluwat (Elbert

---

[10] Macushi (Carlson and Payne 1989) appears to have a possessor classifier: *pi-* prefix, which is reported to indicate items which can be 'owned by animate beings'. Mam (Mayan: England 1983: 68) has a possession marker which is restricted to nouns possessible by humans. This can also be interpreted as a kind of possessor classification.

[11] An analytic possessive construction would have to be used: *kryša dom-a* (roof(FEM) house(MASC)-GN) 'a roof of the house'. Note that analytic possessive constructions are equally acceptable as variants for 'father's armchair' and 'cat's house' respectively (*kreslo otca, dom koški*), the differences being pragmatic.

1974: 59–60) has several dozen classifiers, mostly derived from verbal roots. They are a closed class, with the following semantic parameters: general/ default classifier; age with respect to the possessor, kinship; edible/drinkable, preparation of food; function: ornaments, loincloth, etc. A selection is given in Table 5.4. Similarly to Kilivila (5.36–8), nouns in Puluwat can be assigned different classifiers depending on the ways in which they can be handled. Generic classifier *yá-* is used in *yá-án* (CL:GEN-ATT) *Pen wuur* 'bananas raised, owned, or given by Ben'. Classifier *wor* 'raw food, meat' is used in *wor-áy* (CL:RAW.FOOD-ATT) *Pen wuur* 'raw bananas eaten by Ben', and classifier *yán* 'cooked food' is shown in *yán-án* (CL:COOKED.FOOD-ATT) *Pen wuur* 'cooked bananas eaten by Ben' (Elbert 1974: 60–1).

Table 5.4. *Sample of classifiers in Puluwat*

Classifier	Semantics
na-	General classifier for every noun excluding some artefacts
ya-	General classifier for artefacts not taking *na-*
haam-	Senior persons
pwi-	Classificatory sibling of ego's sex
wor-	Raw food, meat
wúnúm-	Beverages, tobacco (things that are not chewed?)
yan-	Cooked food, coconuts
kiy-	Pandanus mat
la-	Bracelets
lim	Sharp tool
méngaak	Clothes
paaŕ	Hat, umbrella
wa-	Canoe, vehicle
wóók	Cane, club, stick, spear
yanúk-	Ropes
yápel	Loincloth

Another Micronesian language, Truquese (Benton 1968: 123 ff.), also has a large system of classifiers which refer to the ways nouns can be possessed, or handled, and also to the physical properties of referents. Since some classifiers are of the repeater type, they form a quasi-open class. Example 5.48 illustrates the use of a classifier *wúnúma* 'potentially drinkable' which relates to the possessed noun, 'water' as something drinkable; it is also similar to relational classifiers such as the ones illustrated for Fijian in Table 5.3 in that it specifies the way in which a referent can be handled. Example 5.49 illustrates the use of repeater *kuusa* 'blanket' in the same slot in a possessive construction (Benton 1968: 124–5).

5.48. wúnúma-yi   we   kkóniki
      CL:DRINKABLE-my DEM   water
      'my water'

5.49. kuusa-yi   we   kuusa
      CL:BLANKET-my   DEM   blanket
      'my blanket'

Tinrin, an Austronesian language of New Caledonia (Osumi 1996: 438), has seven classifiers used in possessive constructions which combine properties of relational and possessed classifiers. They are: *e-* 'starches, to be eaten', *ere-* 'fruit, to be eaten', *hwee-* 'meat or eggs, to be eaten', *odho-* 'things to be drunk', *hwiie-* 'things to be chewed', *êê-* 'plants growing on his/her land, to be planted', *hêê-* 'belongings'.

Palikur (North Arawak; Aikhenvald and Green 1998) has a small set of possessed classifiers. Unlike other classifiers and genders, not all nouns in the language require a possessive classifier. Their use is restricted to alienably possessed referents of nouns which cannot take possessive affixes. Possessed classifiers are in a generic-specific relationship with the noun they refer to (similarly to Apalaí and Macushi: 5.7–9). Referents are classified depending on their functions, or the ways in which they can be handled: fruit can be eaten, or planted; animals can be domesticated, or caught for food. For instance, *-pig* 'pet' is used with domesticated animals, as in *gi-pig pewru* (3M-pet dog) 'his dog'; *gi-pig mutom* 'his sheep'; *-win* is used with animals that are caught to eat, e.g. *nu-win arudiki* (1SG-catch tapir) 'my catch-tapir' (the tapir I caught); and *-kamkayh* 'child' is used with children, e.g. *nu-kamkayh awayg* (1SG-child man) 'my son'. The same noun can be used with different classifiers depending on the way it is going to be treated, e.g. *pi-mana uwas* (2SG-food orange) 'your orange' (the orange you eat), *n-amutra uwas* (1SG-plant orange) 'my plant-orange' (the orange I plant).

5.5.2. *Languages with two types of classifier in possessive constructions*

Languages which have two kinds of classifier in possessive constructions are rare. An example of a language with separate sets of possessed and relational classifiers is Baniwa of Içana (North Arawak: Aikhenvald 1994a).

In Baniwa, a multiple classifier language (§9.3), classifiers are used in possessive constructions independently of possession type; they are very similar to those in Tariana exemplified in 5.16–17. Possessed classifiers in Baniwa are mostly used predicatively. The head is often omitted, as in 5.50.

5.50. (nu-hwida)   nu-dza-da
      (1SG-head)   1SG-POSS-CL:ROUND
      'The head (lit. 'my head') is mine' or 'it is my (own) head'

Baniwa also has relational classifiers which are used only with alienably possessed nouns. These classifiers have no other classifying functions. In the Hohôdene dialect of Baniwa, alienably possessed nouns with animate reference can take either suffix *-ni* or suffix *-te*, depending on the type of possessive relation. In 5.51 *tfinu* 'dog' has a fairly intimate relationship with the possessor; it takes the *-ni* suffix.

5.51. nu-tʃinu-ni
      1SG-dog-POSS.1
      'my dog (the one I brought up)'

In 5.52, *tfinu* 'dog' is less close to the possessor, and it takes the *-te* suffix.

5.52. nu-tʃinu-te
      1SG-dog-POSS.2
      'my dog (the one I found)'

The opposition between relational classifiers is lexicalized in other dialects of Baniwa, e.g. Siuci and Kurripaco; every inalienably possessed noun occurs with just one possessive suffix.[12]

Another example of a language which probably has two independent sets of classifiers in possessive constructions is Cahuilla (Takic branch of Uto-Aztecan: Seiler 1983: 61; Seiler 1977: 299–305). Classifiers in Cahuilla fall into two types. There is a set called 'temporary' ones; these relate to the way an item is 'handled', and are similar to relational classifiers (as illustrated above for Oceanic languages). Certain items can occur with different classifiers, depending on the way they are treated. See 5.53–4 (Seiler 1983: 37).

5.53. ne-ʔáy-ʔa   méñikiš
      1SG-pluck-ABSTRACT   mesquite.beans
      'my (fresh) mesquite beans (to be plucked from the tree)'

---

[12] Possibly, an opposition of this kind goes back to Proto-Arawak. David Payne (1991a) reconstructs the Proto-Arawak possessive markers *-ni*, *-te*, *-re*, labelling them as 'noun classes'. This opposition is blurred in the majority of modern languages, but one cannot exclude the possibility that it might go back to some sort of relational classifiers. A similar situation has been discussed by Facundes (1994) for Apurinã (Pre-Andine Arawak). In some North Arawak languages, e.g., Warekena, the two markers of alienable possession are reinterpreted as proximate vs. remote (Aikhenvald 1998b). Other Arawak languages of the Upper Rio Negro do not use possessive suffixes as relational classifiers; the suffixes are used with different groups of nouns.

5.54. ne-čí-ʔa   méñikiš
     1SG-pick.up-ABSTRACT mesquite.beans
     'my mesquite beans (to be picked from the ground)'

Another set of classifiers refers to 'inherent' properties of a possessed nouns. Such a classifier, 'pet' for dog, is illustrated in 5.55. Similar possessed classifiers in other Uto-Aztecan languages were discussed in §5.2 (examples 5.1–2).

5.55. né-ʔaš   ʔáwal
      1SG-CL:PET   dog
      'my dog'

The system of relational classifiers in Cahuilla is considered a recent innovation by Langacker (1977: 91).

5.6. Contrasting classifiers in possessive constructions

The main difference between relational classifiers and possessed classifiers is that possessed classifiers characterize the possessed item while relational classifiers characterize the possessive relationship. Thus, relational classifiers do not constitute a noun categorization device in the way possessed classifiers do. Often, however, the way a noun can be possessed, or handled, depends on its inherent properties (e.g. a liquid is drinkable, and not chewable). This is why a classifier system may integrate the semantics of relational and of possessed classifiers.

Further differences between relational and possessed classifiers are:

(i) Languages with relational classifiers always have a grammatical distinction between alienable and inalienable possession. This is not always so for languages with possessed classifiers.

(ii) Relational classifiers are necessarily integrated into the system for the marking of possession; they are restricted to alienably possessed nouns. This is not necessarily so for possessed classifiers.

(iii) Possessed classifiers which can be used independently of possession type and integrated systems of possessed and relational classifiers are widespread in multiple classifier languages (e.g. Hmong, and other Miao languages, according to Bisang 1993, as well as the Papuan languages of Bougainville, and South American languages). This is not true of morphemes which are used just as relational classifiers.

(iv) Relational classifiers never occur in other classifier environments in multiple classifier languages (see Chapter 9).

We have also seen that relational and possessed classifiers can coexist as distinct types in one language. Differences between relational and possessed classifiers are summarized in Table 5.5.

TABLE 5.5. *Differences between possessed and relational classifiers*

Properties	Relational classifiers	Possessed classifiers
Which component of a possessive construction is categorized?	Type of possessive relation	Possessed noun
Link with alienable/inalienable possession	Used only with alienable possession	Used independently of possession type
Use in multiple classifier languages	No	Yes

Relational classifiers can be independent lexemes; if not, they may attach to the possessive marker or the noun itself (Baniwa). Possessed classifiers can attach to the possessive marker, or they may be independent lexemes (Hmong). No example has been found so far of a language in which possessed classifiers attach to the possessed noun.

Possessed classifiers are more frequent across the languages of the world than relational classifiers. Indeed, relational classifiers are almost restricted to one genetic group—Oceanic languages, with a very few examples in South America. Possessor classifiers are even rarer.

Inventories of possessed classifiers vary—from smallish, with two to three terms, to largeish, as in South American languages. Inventories of relational classifiers are small; they categorize the way in which items are typically handled or possessed. In languages where relational classifiers are also used as possessed classifiers, such as in Puluwat or Truquese, the inventory can be large. The number of possessor classifiers is always very small; the distinction is between animates and inanimates, or humans and non-humans.

These differences between the three types of classifier in a possessive construction are summarized in Table 5.6.

The differences between the three types of classifier in possessive constructions, in frequency and in size of inventory, are not accidental. They relate to the semantics of these classifiers, and to the type of constituent they categorize.

Possessed classifiers categorize possessed nouns in terms of their shape, size, animacy, and other inherent properties; objects do vary a lot according to these properties, and so possessed classifiers would be expected to be rather frequent, and to come in larger inventories.

TABLE 5.6. *Relational, possessed, and possessor classifier: a comparison*

Type of classifier	Frequency in languages	Size of inventory	Semantics
Possessor classifiers	Rare	Small	Animacy/humanness
Relational classifiers	Medium	Small	The way a noun can be possessed
Relational/possessed classifiers	Medium	May be large	The way a noun can be possessed, animacy, shape, size, etc.
Possessed classifiers	Common	May be large	Animacy, shape, size, etc.

Relational classifiers categorize kinds of institutionalized, culturally relevant relationships between the possessor and the possessed, and these appear to allow fewer possibilities; this is why inventories of relational classifiers are smaller than those of possessed classifiers. Languages outside Oceania and a few languages in South America tend only to use distinctions such as alienable vs. inalienable possession, and kinship possession vs. possession of other kinds.

Inherent properties of possessed nouns do correlate with the ways in which they can be handled, or possessed; this is why possessed and relational classifiers can be integrated into one system. The inventory of these morphemes tends to be largeish, for the same reason as the inventory of possessed classifiers: inherent properties of nouns allow much more variability in categorization.

Finally, the rarity of possessor classifiers in the languages of the world may be due to the fact that the nature of the possessor seems to allow little variation. A prototypical possessor is animate, or at least human (cf. Seiler 1986; and especially Heine 1997a: 5, 39; Taylor 1989). In many languages inanimate nouns cannot be used as possessors in constructions with alienable possession[13] (a part–whole structure is used instead). Thus, there is little need to categorize the possessor; and if such categorization takes place, the only distinction that appears to be likely to occur in a classifier construction is that of animate/inanimate and/or human/non-human.

---

[13] It is true that in many languages the possessed noun is the head in the possessive construction. Classifiers would be expected to characterize the head of the construction, as happens in modifier constructions. Possessor classifiers which characterize the possessor would be expected in languages where the possessor has at least some properties of the head in possessive constructions. However, this is not necessarily so. In Paumarí possessor is the head of constructions with inalienable possession; Paumarí does not have any possessor classifiers.

5.7. Distribution of classifiers in possessive constructions in the languages of the world

Classifiers in possessive constructions are rarer across the world's languages than noun classes or numeral classifiers—see Map 4 below.

POSSESSED CLASSIFIERS are found in some North American Indian languages (Yuman, Uto-Aztecan), a number of South American Indian languages (Nadëb, from the Makú family; Carib, Tupí-Guaraní, Jê, some North Arawak and some Guaicuruan languages), and in 'Dongo-ko (Mba, Ubangi; Niger-Congo). Classifiers are used in possessive constructions in some multiple classifier languages, e.g. Hmong and other Miao-Yao languages spoken in Northern China and Indochina, and Papuan languages of Central and Southern Bougainville (Kim Blewett, p.c.).

RELATIONAL CLASSIFIERS are found in Oceanic languages and in Micronesian languages (where they often coexist with numeral classifiers), and in two South American languages—Kipeá (Kipeá-Kariri family; extinct) and Baniwa of Içana (North Arawak). Reduced sets of relational classifiers are found in Austronesian languages spoken in Papua New Guinea (e.g. Takia: Bruce Waters, p.c., Missima: Bill Callister, p.c., and Gapapaiwa: Catherine McGuckin, p.c.).

POSSESSOR CLASSIFIERS are found only in Dâw and, possibly, Hupda (Makú languages of Northwest Amazonia).

Complicated systems of classifiers in possessive constructions which categorize possessive relationship, possessed noun, and possessor, are reported for Reef-Santa Cruzan languages spoken in the Solomons (Stephen Wurm, p.c.).

No special classifiers in possessive constructions are found in Australian or Eurasian languages.

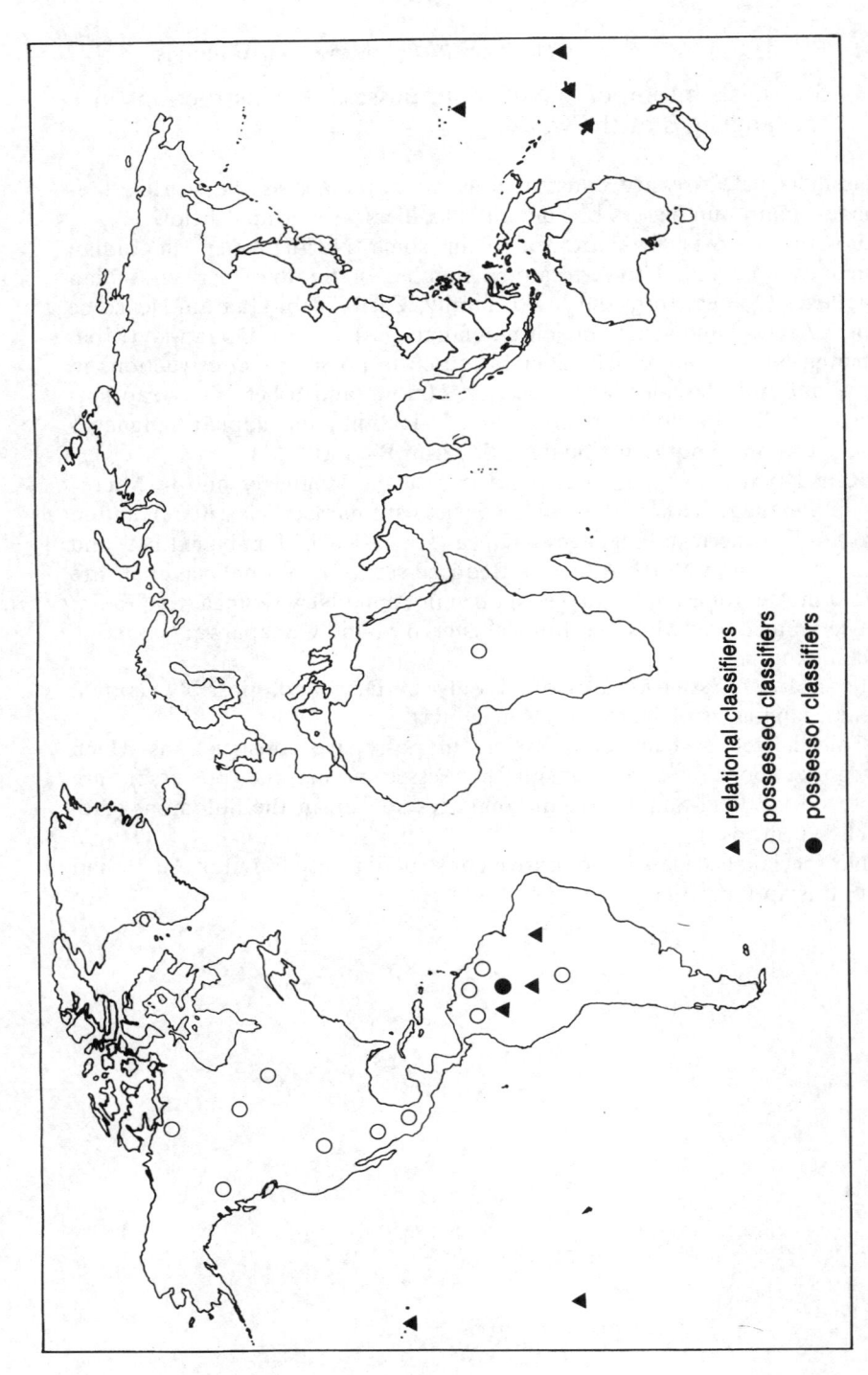

MAP 4. *Distribution of classifiers in possessive constructions in the languages of the world*

▲ relational classifiers
○ possessed classifiers
● possessor classifiers

6 Verbal Classifiers

6.1. Properties of verbal classifiers

Verbal classifiers appear on the verb, categorizing the referent of its argument in terms of its shape, consistency, size, structure, position, and animacy (cf. example 1.7, from Waris, a Papuan language). Verbal classifiers always refer to a predicate argument (usually, S in an intransitive or O in a transitive clause) and can cooccur with it. Their choice is predominantly semantic. Every noun in a language does not necessarily require a verbal classifier; some nouns may be associated with more than one classifier.

The inventory of verbal classifiers varies from two to several score. The choice of verbal classifiers is based on lexical selection rather than grammatical agreement (see §2.4; cf. Rushforth 1991: 255). Verbal classifiers are thus a subclass of non-agreeing noun categorization devices. The use of verbal classifiers is often limited to certain semantic groups of verbs.

The ways verbal classifiers are realized are dealt with in §6.2. Syntactic functions of arguments categorized by verbal classifiers are considered in §6.3. Some languages have more than one kind of verbal classifier—see §6.4. The distribution of verbal classifiers in the languages of the world is presented in §6.5.

6.2. Realization of verbal classifiers

Verbal classifiers come in three forms. Classificatory noun incorporation, whereby a noun is incorporated into a verb to categorize an extra-predicate argument, is discussed in §6.2.1. Verbal classifiers affixed to the verb are described in §6.2.2. Suppletive 'classificatory verbs' are considered in §6.2.3.

Affixed verbal classifiers often develop from classificatory noun incorporation. Sometimes the two coexist, reflecting different stages of grammaticalization. Classificatory noun incorporation, affixed verbal classifiers, and how they can interact, are discussed in §6.2.4.

In many languages, verbal classifiers are optional, and are determined by the discourse function of the extra-predicate noun. Verbal classifiers can be used to maintain reference to the noun within a narrative. Participants can be reintroduced with the help of verbal classifiers in Papuan languages (Merlan *et al.* 1997). In South American Indian languages, verbal classifiers are often used anaphorically (see Aikhenvald 1996b, for examples from the Arawak language family; also see Aikhenvald and Green 1998); see §12.1.3.

6.2.1. Classificatory noun incorporation

Classificatory noun incorporation is the incorporating of a noun into the verb to characterize an external argument, usually, in S or O function. This phenomenon was first recognized by Mithun (1984: her Type 4). There is frequently a relationship of generic-specific between the incorporated NP and the 'external' NP which accompanies it (Mithun 1984: 863; see Dixon 1980: 436–7; 2002: 423–9). This relation is reminiscent of noun classifiers, such as in Yidiny and other Australian languages discussed in Chapter 3. Otherwise incorporated verbal classifiers characterize the referent of a noun in terms of its animacy, shape, and consistency.

In some prefixing languages from Northern Australia, a generic noun—which specifies the corresponding specific noun in S or O function—can be incorporated into the verb. Mayali (Australian: Evans 1996; ms) has a closed class of about forty verbal classifiers. Example 6.1 shows a verbal classifier referring to a noun in O function, and 6.2 shows a verbal classifier referring to an S.[1]

6.1. ga-yaw-garrm-e   al-daluk
     3/3-GEN.CL:BABY-have-NP   CLII-woman
     'She has a baby girl.'

6.2. ga-rrulk-di   an-dubang
     3NP-GEN.CL:TREE-stand(NP) CLIII-ironwood.tree
     'An ironwood tree is there' (lit. a tree-is there an ironwoodtree)

6.3, from Tiwi, illustrates an incorporated verbal classifier referring to S, and 6.4 illustrates a classifier referring to O (Jennifer Lee, p.c.).

6.3. warta a-watu-wuji-ngi-mangi-rr-akupuraji   yiripuwarta$_S$
     bush   3SG.MASC-morning-CONT-CV-VCL:WATER$_S$-CV-fall   high.tide
     'The high tide is falling (lit. water-falling) [exposing the] land (bush).'

6.4. ninkiyi   arlitunga   nga-ri-kunjingi-kirimi
     then   skewer   1PL.AUG-CV-CL:COOKED.FOOD$_O$-make
     [awarra   yinkiti   jirraka]
     that.masc food   wallaby
     'Then we put the cooked food (wallaby) on skewers.'

---

[1] Incorporated nouns may be used to categorize themselves, e.g. the classifier *rruga* 'stone' in Nunggubuyu (Australian: Sands 1995: 273; Heath 1984: 463), used to refer to the S argument: *ma-rruga-ŋu-burra? mana-rruga* (3SG+NCLIII-stone-linker-sits NCLIII-stone) 'The stone sits'.

Noun incorporation and verbal classifiers can be shown to be distinct categories. This is the case in Mayali (Evans 1996; ms). This language has non-productive lexical compounding (Mithun 1984: Type 1), body part incorporation, and also verbal classifiers (called 'generic' classificatory incorporation by Evans 1996). Lexical compounding (Evans 1996: 72–4) is a non-productive process, and constitutes an obligatory closed system, since 'stems with lexically incorporated nominals lack unincorporated paraphrases' (p. 73). In contrast, body part incorporation and verbal classifiers ('generic incorporation') are optional: the choice between incorporated and unincorporated constructions depends on the discourse status of the constituent. The differences between body part incorporation and verbal classifiers are as follows.

(i) Verbal classifiers are a closed class of about 40 members the majority of which are inanimate (the exception being *yaw* 'child, baby', and, used more rarely, *daluk* 'woman' and *binij* 'man'), while body parts are a semi-open class.

(ii) Two body parts in a part–whole relationship may be incorporated together into one verb, as in 6.5, while two classifiers cannot cooccur.

6.5. ngan-garre+mok-bukka-ng
    3/1M-calf+sore-show-PP
    'He showed me the sore on his calf'

Lexical compounding and generic incorporation can cooccur in the same word, as in 6.5 (Evans ms: 266; example 7-537). Of the incorporated nominals, one, *-mim* 'fruit, seed of', can be omitted but the other one, *bo-* 'liquid', cannot be since it forms a part of a lexical compound.

6.6. an-barnadja   ngarri-mim-bo+wo-ni
    CL:III-Owenia.vernicosa   1A-fruit-water+put(=put.in.water)-PI
    'We used to put the fruit of Owenia vernicosa in the water (to poison the fish)'

Besides the syntactic differences mentioned above, incorporated body parts terms and incorporated verbal classifiers have a number of semantic contrasts, e.g. *gun-gaj* as a body part noun means 'flesh, muscle', and as a classifier it means 'meat' (Evans 1996: 78).[2]

---

[2] In other cases, it may be more difficult to distinguish incorporated verbal classifiers from other cases of incorporation and compounding. In Anindilyakwa, a prefixing Australian language from Groote Eylandt, about 100 'bound roots' are used as verbal classifiers and as numeral classifiers. The same morphemes are used to form compounds. There are semantic and syntactic differences which allow one to distinguish the two processes—see Leeding (1996) for details.

6.2.2. Verbal classifiers as affixes

Verbal classifiers can be realized with prefixes (in Waris: see 1.7, or in Athabaskan languages discussed in §6.4), or with suffixes (in North Arawak languages). Verbal classifiers are never expressed with repeaters.

Imonda (Papuan, Waris language family: W. Seiler 1985: 120 ff., 132 ff.; 1986: 197 ff.) has about 100 verbal classifiers; not all verbs take a classifier. Classifiers characterize a noun, in O or in S function, in terms of its inherent properties, such as shape. In 6.7 a classifier *põt* 'fruit which can be picked from trees' refers to O. There is also a verb *põt* which means 'pick fruit from trees'; the classifier *põt* is derived from this verb (see §13.1.3; Table 13.6). It appears that verbal classifiers in Imonda developed from the reanalysis of serial verb constructions.

6.7. sa ka-m põt-ai-h-u
 coconut 1SG-GOAL CL:FRUIT-give-RECIPIENT-IMPERATIVE
 'Give me the coconut.'

Systems of verbal classifiers as affixes vary in their size and semantics. Terêna (South Arawak; Ekdahl and Butler 1979) has several dozen verbal classifiers which characterize the S/O argument in terms of its shape, size, form, and animacy, e.g. *-pu'i* 'round' in 6.8.

6.8. oye-pu'i-co-ti
 cook-CL:ROUND-THEME-PROGR
 'He is cooking (round things).'

In multiple classifier languages, classifiers are often used on verbs (see §9.1). Mundurukú (Tupí; Gonçalves 1987: 42) has a multiple classifier system of over 100 morphemes which refer to shape and form. In 6.9 the classifier *-ba^4* 'banana-like' refers to S, and in 6.9 it refers to O. The same morphemes appear suffixed on the nouns (*-ba^4* 'LONG RIGID OBJECT'[3] is used as a suffix with the root *a^{2}ko^3-* 'banana').

6.9. a^{2}ko^3-ba^4 i^3-ba^2-dom^3
 banana-CL:LONG.RIGID 3SG.POSS-CL:LONG.RIGID-stay+FUT
 ko^{4}be^3 be^3
 canoe LOC
 'A banana will remain in the canoe.'

6.10. be^{3}kit^{2}kit^2 a^{2}ko^3-ba^4 o'^{3}-su^2-ba^2-do^{3}bu^{2}xik^3
 child banana-CL:LONG.RIGID 3SG-POSS-CL:LONG.RIGID-find
 'A child found a banana.'

---

[3] Here and in other examples raised numbers indicate tones.

6.2.3. Suppletive 'classificatory verbs'

Suppletive verbal stems, usually referred to as CLASSIFICATORY VERBS, are comparatively rare in the languages of the world. The selection of a stem is conditioned by properties of the referent of the S or O constituent.

Unlike the verbal classifiers discussed in §6.2.2, classificatory verbs cannot be used in other classifier functions. However, classificatory verbs do show certain correlations with number and with other verbal inflectional categories (see §10.1.2).

Classificatory verbs fall into two categories.

(i) They can be used to categorize the S/O argument in terms of its inherent properties (shape, animacy, etc.; see also §11.2.5).

(ii) They can be used to categorize the S/O argument in terms of its orientation or stance in space, with its inherent properties.

That classificatory verbs should combine reference to inherent properties of referents and to their orientation is not surprising. Shape, form, and other inherent properties of objects correlate with their stance in space. Certain positions and states are only applicable to objects of certain kinds; for instance, a tree usually 'stands', and only liquids can 'flow'. This interaction between the inherent properties of a referent and the spatial position it typically occupies is reminiscent of the way some languages combine typical properties of possessed and of relational classifiers in one system (see §5.5.1).

Classificatory verbs differ from the lexical selection of a verb in terms of physical properties or the position of an object. Most languages have lexical items similar to English *drink* (which implies a liquid O), or *chew* (which implies an O of chewable consistency). Unlike these verbs, classificatory verbs (which typically include verbs of location and handling: see below and §11.2.5) make consistent paradigmatic distinctions in the choice of semantic features for their S/O argument throughout the verbal lexicon. In other words, while English distinguishes liquid and non-liquid objects only for verbs of drinking, classificatory verbs provide a set of paradigmatic oppositions for the choice of verb sets depending on the physical properties of S/O. Similarly, posture verbs in many languages tend to occur with objects of a certain shape. For instance, in Russian, long vertical objects usually 'stand', and long ones 'lie' (Rakhilina 1998); see Borneto (1996), on similar phenomena in German. However, the correlations between the choice of the verb and the physical properties of the object are not paradigmatic; these verbs cannot be considered 'classificatory' (see also §13.1.3).[4]

---

[4] For some languages more work is needed to determine whether they have classificatory verbs, like Athabaskan, or just lexical pairs, like English (e.g. the Mesoamerican languages cited by Suárez 1983: 90–1).

(A) Classificatory verbs categorizing the S/O argument according to its inherent properties

Classificatory verbs of this sort are predominantly found in North American Indian languages, in Tibeto-Burman languages, and in Ika, a Chibchan language from Northern Colombia (Frank 1990).

According to Carter (1976: 24), suppletive classificatory verbs in Athabaskan languages refer to concrete objects, and they describe 'objects at rest, in motion, being handled, being dropped, or falling'. Similarly, in Ika classificatory verbs have to do with the way of handling physical objects ('put', 'carry', 'drop', etc.) or with their position and location, or existence ('lie', 'hang', 'fall', etc.). In Cora (Uto-Aztecan: Casad 1996: 246) classificatory verbs 'indicate the shape of an object that is being transported or the manner in which the object is being moved'; transportable entities are grouped into six classes: (i) long rigid things; (ii) round things; (iii) flat, squareish rigid things; (iv) long, flexible things; (v) domesticated animals; (vi) humans.

Suppletive classificatory verbs in Athabaskan languages go back to Proto-Eyak-Athabaskan (Krauss 1968: 200); they did not develop from affixed classifiers. They categorize the S/O constituent in terms of its shape, form, animacy, number, and consistency (see Chapter 11). Chipewyan (Carter 1976) distinguishes the following semantic oppositions in classificatory verb stems: round objects, long or stick-like objects, living beings (animate or human), containers with contents, fabric-like objects, a collection of objects or rope-like objects, granular mass, dough-like or mud-like object, piled-up fabric (blankets). Similar semantic oppositions are also found in Slave (Rice 1989: 779 ff.). Examples 6.11 and 6.12, from Chiricahua Apache (Hoijer 1945: 14), illustrate the use of classificatory verbs.

6.11. hà-n̄-ʔàˑh
out of-2SUBJ.IMPF-handle.a.round.object:IMPF.MOMENTANEOUS
'you take a round object (out of enclosed space)'

6.12. hà-n̄-ł-cóˑs
out.of-2SUBJ.IMPF-VOICE.MARKER-
handle.a.fabric.like.object:IMPF.MOMENTANEOUS
'you take a fabric-like object (out of enclosed space)'

Table 6.1 illustrates classificatory verb categories from Mescalero Apache (Rushforth 1991: 253). (The stem given here means 'be located').

In Ojibway (Algonquian: Denny 1979a: 106–7), the semantic characterization in classificatory verbs is similar to Athabaskan: the choice of the verb is conditioned by the shape of a noun. Examples of classificatory verbs in Ojibway are in Table 6.2.

TABLE 6.1. *Mescalero Apache classificatory verb categories*

1. -'ą 'single, solid, round inanimate object'
2. -tį 'single animate object'
3. -la 'dual objects of any kind; a ropelike object'
4. -tą 'elongated, rigid object; a stick-like object'
5. -ł-tsuus 'flexible object; a cloth-like object'
6. -ka 'contents of a shallow, open container; a cup- or dish-like object with its contents; a rigid container with its contents'
7. -jaash 'plural objects of any kind; uncontained dry and loose or granular substance, uncontained sand- or flour-like substance; a dry mass
8. -tłe 'uncontained wet or damp mass; dough- or mud-like substance'
9. -ł-tą 'flexible container with its contents'
10. -'a 'indefinitely shaped single solid object'

TABLE 6.2. *Classificatory verbs in Ojibway*

Verb	Semantics
sak-īk-inān (extended two-dimensional flexible)	to hold on to something sheet-like
sakit-āpī-ssin (extended one-dimensional flexible	be sticking out [string-like object]
kotako-minak-ipitōn (non-extended)	to roll over something round-like
kotako-minak-issē (non-extended)	something round-like rolls over

In Tibeto-Burman languages classificatory existential or locative verbs typically distinguish animate and inanimate forms if there are only two of them (as in Idu, with i^{55} 'animate existential verb' and kha^{55} 'inanimate existential'—LaPolla 1994: 75). Other languages distinguish up to seven existential verbs; for instance, Queyu has tfi^{55} for animals; $tçy^{13}$ for location in a vessel or enclosed area; RO^{31}, for non-movable objects $çi^{13}$ for movable objects, lo^{13} for an object mixed with another object, ru^{13} for abstract objects; and tfe^{13}, for possession by a person (LaPolla 1994: 75). (Animate/inanimate distinction in existential verbs is also found in Japanese; this may be an areal typological feature shared with Tibeto-Burman languages—LaPolla 1994: 76.)

Qiang (LaPolla forthcoming: 120–1) has four existential verbs: ṣə for inanimate referents, zi for animate referents, le for referents located in a container of some type, and we for immovable referents or referents inalienably connected to a larger entity. Their use is illustrated in the following examples. In 6.13, the 'inanimate' existential verb is used to refer to a book.

6.13. tsṣuŋtsə̂-məq-ta   ləɣz-e-pen   ṣə
      table-top-LOC:ON book-one-CL exist:INANIM
      'There is a book on the table.'

156   *Classifiers*

In 6.14, the animate verb is used to refer to fish.

6.14. tsə-ʀɑ   ʀzə   ʐi
      water-LOC:IN fish exist:ANIM
      'There are fish in the water.'

Different existential verbs can be used with the same referent, with a difference in meaning. In 6.14 the fish is considered an animate being; while in 6.15 the situation is presented 'from the point of view of the fish being in the water' (LaPolla forthcoming: 121):

6.15. tsə-ʀɑ   ʀzə   le
      water-LOC:IN fish exist:REFERENT.LOCATED.IN.A.CONTAINER
      'There are fish in the water.'

Hani (LaPolla 1994: 75) has six classificatory existential verbs: dza^{33} 'general existential', dzo^{55} 'an existential for people and animals', bo^{33} 'an existential for people and their body parts', $dɔ^{31}$ 'an existential for liquids', $d\underline{e}^{31}$ 'an existential for animates', and $k\underline{x}^{31}$ 'existence within a group'.

This phenomenon is widespread in Tibeto-Burman languages; for an account of this as a recent innovation, see LaPolla (1994: 75).[5]

In the cases illustrated above classificatory verbs are suppletive and not analysable synchronically. In Ika (Chibchan, Colombia: Frank 1990: 55) classificatory verbs (used for location and handling) are partly analysable (one could argue that this is an intermediary case between classificatory verbs and affixed verbal classifiers). In Ika, different semantic parameters interact to yield semantically complicated systems where dimensionality and shape correlate with consistency, form and directionality (see §11.2.5, Table 6.3, and Examples 6.16 and 6.17.)

TABLE 6.3. *Classificatory verbs in Ika*

	Long	Flat	Three-dimenional	Liquid	Holders	Upright
Exist/loc	gaka	pa	sa	–	–	tšo
Be in	aʔ-geikua	aʔ-pʌnkua	aʔ-nikua	aʔkua	aʔžu	aʔnuk
Be up on	i-geikua	i-pʌnkua	i-nikua	–	ižu	i-nuk
Be on	geikua	pʌnkua	nikua	–	–	nuk
Put up on	igeika	i-pan	isa	idos	–	itšo
Put down	gaka (gakó)	pan (pa)	sa	dos	–	tšoʔs
Put in	kʌgaka	kʌpas	kʌssa	kʌdos	kʌžus	kʌtšoʔs

---

[5] As pointed out by William Croft, these systems are different from those in Athabaskan languages in that they classifiy the Ground as well as the Figure, or even the Path (following the terminology of Talmy 1985).

6.16. kʌn gakó ú
stick put.down:LONG.OBJECT AUX
'Put down the stick!'

6.17. ribru pa ú
book put.down:FLAT.OBJECT AUX
'Put down the book!'

Classificatory verbs can be used anaphorically as referent tracking devices (Rushforth 1991: 255–7). They are also employed to highlight different meanings of a polysemous noun in a similar way to noun classifiers discussed in §3.2.2 (see examples from Mescalero Apache in Table 6.4). Different 'arrangements' of tobacco are reflected in the form of the classificatory stems of the verb with the basic meaning 'give'.

TABLE 6.4. *Examples of the use of 'give' in Mescalero Apache*

1. *Nát'uhí shán'aa* 'Give me (a plug of) tobacco'
2. *Nát'uhí shánkaa* 'Give me (a can, box, pack) of tobacco'
3. *Nát'uhí shánłtįį* 'Give me (a bag) of tobacco'
4. *Nát'uhí shántįį* 'Give me (a stick) of tobacco'
5. *Nát'uhí shánjaash* 'Give me (loose, plural) tobacco'

Source: Rushforth (1991: 254).

Table 6.5 gives an idea of the range of meaning of classificatory verbs in Koyukon (Northern Athabaskan: Axelrod forthcoming: 5), and how they can be used to specify the referent of *boogee* 'flour, dough'.

TABLE 6.5. *Classificatory verbs in Koyukon: an example*

Example	Meaning
boogee le'onh	'a lump of flour is there'
boogee daal'onh	'a canister of flour is there'
boogee daaltonh	'a box of flour is there'
boogee etltonh	'a bag of flour is there'
boogee lekkonh	'a bowl of flour is there'
boogee ledlo	'lumps of flour are there'
boogee etlkoot	'flour is there (stored as provision)'
boogee ełetlaakk	'dough is there'
boogee daałenokk	'loose flour is there'

'Non-literal' uses of classificatory verbs can be of two kinds. The use of classificatory verbs can be extended to apply to abstract nouns as a kind

158   *Classifiers*

of metaphorical extension; or an unexpected classificatory verb is used, for instance, the stem for 'single round object' is employed in reference to a person (Rushforth 1991: 262–4), as a kind of 'pun' (Sapir 1932). This is reminiscent of the metaphorical use of gender variation (see (C) in §2.4.3); cf. §12.3.3.

(B) Classificatory verbs characterizing the S/O argument in terms of its orientation in space and its inherent properties

Suppletive classificatory verbs involve reference to the orientation and stance of S/O in a number of North American Indian languages, e.g. Dakota (Siouan: Boas and Deloria 1941: 126; Croft 1994: 157), and Nevome (Uto-Aztecan: Shaul 1986: 12). The categorization involves reference to the orientation and stance, standing or lying, and to the animateness of the S/O argument (Table 6.6).

TABLE 6.6. *Classificatory verbs in Nevome*

	Inanimate referent	Animate referent
be lying	*catu/vutu*	*voho/vopo*
be standing	*cuhca/tutu*	*cuhca/guguhuca*

Complicated systems of suppletive existential verbs are found in Muskogean languages (also see Haas 1978: 306). In Koasati (Kimball 1991: 452–9) five different positional verbs are used depending on the shape of the referent. These verbs have suppletive plural forms. The verb 'stand' is used for tall, vertical things, such as posts, trees, and objects with legs; 'sit' is used for globular objects, such as ball, hill, sun, and heaps of objects; three different verbs, all glossed as 'lie' are used for large, long, thin things; for small, long, thin things; and for objects covering a broad area. In Creek the use of suppletive dual and plural forms of some verbs correlates with shape and consistency of objects (Haas 1978; Jack Martin, p.c.; see §10.1.2). According to Haas (1978: 306):

the only categories of classification that have developed are those which distinguish cloth-like objects from liquids, and these in turn from all other types of objects. Cloth-like objects are treated as duals when the verb has a distinctive dual form; otherwise they are treated as plurals. Liquids are treated as plurals. All other types of objects are treated as singulars, duals or plurals depending upon the actual number of entities involved.

Classificatory verbs which combine reference to the orientation of the noun and to its inherent properties are widespread in Papuan languages of the Engan family (New Guinea Highlands: Foley 1986: 89 ff.). Enga itself (Lang 1975; Foley 1986: 89–91) has seven classificatory verbs, shown in

Table 6.7. When used as existential predicates they classify a noun (S argument) in terms of its orientation in space and its inherent properties. (Their lexical meaning is given in brackets in the first column of the table.)

TABLE 6.7. *Classificatory verbs in Enga*

Verb	Semantics of classified nouns	Examples of nouns
katengé ('stand')	Referents judged to be tall, large, strong, powerful, standing or supporting	men, house, tree
pentengé ('sit')	Referents judged to be small, squat, horizontal and weak	woman, possum, pond
lyingí ('hang')	Referents hanging or protruding out of another object	wasp, fruit, seed
palengé ('lie inside')	Referents internal or subterranean	worm, heart, sweet potato
epengé ('come')	Referents which are intermittent, but capable of growth; or liquid or gas	rain, fur, blood
sínge ('lie')	Referents which are orifices, locations, or crawling or aquatic	ground, eels, mouth
mandenge ('carry')	Referents of sexual production	penis, vagina, testicles

Ku Waru (Waris family, Papuan: Merlan *et al.* 1997: 75) has a similar, somewhat smaller system of classificatory existential verbs (Table 6.8). Unlike Engan, these are not employed as just posture verbs.

TABLE 6.8. *Classificatory verbs in Ku Waru*

Verb	Semantics of nouns
mol	Liquids, certain inanimate objects, e.g. shoes when being worn; almost all living things (including plants)
pe	Abstract nouns referring to sources of trouble (e.g. 'grievance', 'property dispute', 'trouble')
le	Inanimate nouns, prototypically nouns referring to wealth objects
angaly	Body parts and certain artefacts (e.g. 'house')

When classificatory verbs in Ku Waru are used with human beings, they indicate only the orientation of the referent, e.g. *mol*: 'staying', *pe*: 'lying/sleeping', *le*: 'lying prostrate/dead', *angaly*: 'standing'; *mol*: is also used as a marker of habitual aspect. They are also developing into aspect markers.

6.2.4. The interaction of the three types of verbal classifier

Classificatory noun incorporation is a frequent source of verbal classifiers as affixes (also see §13.1.1). According to Mithun (1986: 388), 'all classificatory stems begin life as nouns', being used with a relatively narrow scope, and then being used as generics. Grammaticalization of incorporated nouns may further result in the creation of suppletive classificatory stems.

Unlike verbal classifiers as affixes, classificatory noun incorporation is not used in other classifier environments in multiple classifier languages; it is generally restricted to just this grammatical context. Nouns are incorporated into verbs, and the verbs retain the same argument structure. The incorporated noun is used as a means of categorizing an overtly expressed argument.

More than half of the 100 verbal classifiers in Mundurukú (Tupí: Gonçalves 1987: see examples 6.9 and 6.10 above) coincide in form with nouns. In Terêna (South Arawak: Ekdahl and Butler 1979), some verbal classifiers come from incorporated nouns which underwent phonological shortening; these include the classifier -hi- 'leaf, grass' and the root úhi 'grass' in 6.18.

6.18. moyó-<u>hi</u>-ti-raú   úhi-ti
       dry-CL:LEAF-PROGR-DEM   grass-NPOSS
       'Grass is dry'

Other classifiers bear no resemblance to nouns—such as the classifier -pu'i 'round' in 6.8.

The connection between classificatory noun incorporation, verbal classifiers and nouns can be more complex. One such case is Anindilyakwa (Australian). In this language 'bound forms' of nouns belonging to certain semantic groups (such as body parts) are incorporated into the predicate to signal the S/O argument. 6.19 illustrates an incorporated body part *yakwi* 'chest', which refers to the O argument, *athalyima* 'river' (Leeding 1989: 347), to categorize the river with respect to its extended, flat shape.

6.19. wirra+yakwi+yiwi+rni   ana   athalyima
       2NON.SG+CL:CHEST+follow+TNS   DEM   river
       'Follow the river!'

Classifiers in Anindilyakwa are also used as incorporated nouns. According to Leeding (1996: 201), only a relatively small proportion of the incorporated roots show any similarity with corresponding free form nouns. Similarly, in Tiwi (Australian: Osborne 1974: 48–9) most incorporated verbal classifiers are in a suppletive relationship with a noun they categorize. This is dramatically different from the case of Terêna, where the connection between some classifiers and free nouns is transparent. In these cases it is impossible to decide whether classifiers 'begin their life' as incorporated, or as free nouns.

Many prefixing languages from northern Australia show the incipient reanalysis of incorporated nouns as classifiers. In Emmi (Australian: Ford 1998) incorporated body parts are often used 'almost' as classifiers, referring to a particular shape of the referent of an argument. For instance, *mari* 'belly' is used as a classifier for 'concave-shaped interiors', e.g. dishes and buckets, while *miri* 'eye' is used for circular openings (such as doors or windows).

A complicated system of verbal classifiers (called 'class morphemes') and classificatory verbs in Cherokee (Iroquoian: Blankenship 1996; Mithun 1986) shows an intermediate stage in the process of evolution from incorporated classifiers to suppletive classificatory verbs. Cherokee has at least forty verbs for which the choice of the form is determined by the nature of its S/O argument (Blankenship 1996; 1997; Haas 1978). The classes of referents distinguished are LIVING (or ANIMATE), LIQUID, FLEXIBLE, LONG, and COMPACT. The following examples illustrate the use of classificatory verbs (Blankenship 1997: 92).

6.20. Wèésa   gà-káà-nèè'a
 cat   3SG.A+3SG.O-CL:LIVING-give:PRES
 'She is giving him a cat.'

6.21. Àma   gà-nèèh-néé'a
 water   3SG.A+3SG.O-CL:LIQUID-give:PRES
 'She is giving him water.'

6.22. Àhnàwo   gà-nv́v́-nèè'a
 shirt   3SG.A+3SG.O-CL:FLEXIBLE-give:PRES
 'She is giving him a shirt.'

6.23. Gànsda   àa-d-éé'a
 stick   3SG.A+3SG.O-CL:LONG-give:PRES
 'She is giving him a stick.'

6.24. Kwàna   àa-h-nèè'a
 peach   3SG.A+3SG.O-CL:COMPACT-give:PRES
 'She is giving him a peach.'

Examples 6.20–4 show the presence of classifier-like morphemes which refer to an S/O constituent.[6] Synchronically suppletive classificatory verbs

---

[6] Unlike Terêna, Mundurukú, or Anindilyakwa, different sets of class morphemes are used with different groups of verbs in Cherokee (Blankenship 1997: 97).

in Cherokee have been shown to result from the depletion and fusion of verb-incorporated classifiers (Mithun 1984: 884, 392; Blankenship 1996: 97). Cherokee also has non-productive noun incorporation used with verbs which refer to putting on and changing clothes. Noun incorporation can change the transitivity of a verb (Mithun's type I); or not; this involves the advancement of an oblique argument into the direct object position 'vacated' by the incorporated constituent (Mithun's type II: Blankenship 1996: 68; 1997).

The three types of realization for verbal classifiers can be seen as distinct points on a grammaticalization continuum (see Chapter 13).

6.3. Verbal classifiers and syntactic function of the argument

Verbal classifiers signal the presence of a surface NP. In every language this NP may be in S and in O function, that is, they operate on an 'absolutive' basis (Keenan 1984).[7] In a few languages, verbal classifiers can also refer to peripheral arguments. However, no examples have been found of a classificatory verb stem referring to a peripheral constituent.

In Motuna (Papuan: Southern Bougainville) verbal classifiers can signal the presence of an S argument (as in 6.25), an O (as in 6.26), or a peripheral argument (as in 6.27) (Onishi 1994: 175–6).

6.25. . . . hoo   koto   honna   rii-kui-no-wori
      ART:MASC   up   big   be.3S-IMAG-LINK-CL:ANIMATE
      '. . . the elder one (animate) who would be big'

6.26. ong   topo   inak-i-heeto-no-uru
      DEM:MASC   well   look.after-3o+2A-FUT-LINK-CL:HUMAN
      'This is one (lit. human male) you will look after well.'

---

[7] No exceptions have been found to Keenan's (1984) generalization concerning the absolutive basis of verbal classifiers. In Motuna, a verbal classifier can refer to the A argument of the predicate of the participle clause. Onishi (1994: 176) gives one such example: *hoo-no jii eejee nii minno-wah-no-wori* (ART:M-COMIT and my.opposite.sex.sibling me follow-PART-LINK-CL:ANIMATE) '. . . and with one (animate) of my brother who was following me (age-wise)'. He mentions that such examples are extremely rare in Motuna texts. Here, the A argument of the participle clause ('who was following me') is coreferential with an oblique constituent of the main clause. Thus, it can be argued that examples of this sort in Motuna are not true exceptions to Keenan's generalization.

The sentence *Teni toire' tareuri-ma-Ø-i bau'uri-ma-Ø-i* (The.FEM children care.for-PRES.HAB-DER.SUFF-CL:FEM feed-PRES.PROGR-DER.SUFF-CL:FEM) 'The lady who cares for the children (is) the one who feeds them', from Nasioi (Papuan, Bougainville: Hurd 1977: 144) shows agreement of the predicate in verbal classifier with A function in both main and subordinate clause. This example could qualify as a counterexception to Keenan's generalization unless the predicate 'the one who feeds them' should be analysed as a deverbal nominalization (Masa Onishi, p.c.).

6.27. u'kisa   hoo   kitori   hoo   kongsi'
     long ago ART:MASC children ART:MASC mango
     haaro'-ki-no-<u>mori</u>   hoo   kongsi'
     fall+3S-HAB.PAST-LINK-CL:SEASON ART:MASC   mango
     u'w-a-hee   uwi-ki-ng
     pick.from.ground-3o+3PCL.A-DEF.FUT   go+3PCL.S-HAB.PAST-MASC
     'Long ago, in the season when mangoes fall, the children went to pick mangoes from the ground.'

Verbal classifiers in Tarascan (Southwest Mexico isolate: Friedrich 1970: 390) frequently refer to a locative argument. Tarascan has thirty-two verbal suffixes of 'locative' space, which 'signify the features of a location, often including its dimension and shape'. See 6.28 (Friedrich 1970: 393).

6.28. inčá-hpa-mu-ku-nta-ni
     to.enter-suddenly:ADV-SPATIAL.SUFF:ORIFICE.EDGE-ACTIVE-RECURRENT-NON.FINITE
     '(And then the cantor) suddenly re-entered the building by the door.'

6.4. Combinations of different types of verbal classifier

Languages which have several distinct systems of verbal classifier in complementary distribution are considered in §6.4.1. Languages which have affixed verbal classifiers and classificatory verbs as distinct systems are discussed in §6.4.2.

No example has been found of a language which combines classificatory noun incorporation and affixed verbal classifiers as different systems. An intermediary stage which could be accounted for by grammaticalization of incorporated nouns as verbal classifiers was described in §6.2.4 for Cherokee.

No language is known to combine classificatory noun incorporation and classificatory verb stems.

6.4.1. Different types of verbal classifier in complementary distribution

The only known example of a language with two sets of verbal classifier affixes in complementary distribution is Palikur (North Arawak: Aikhenvald and Green 1998; also see §8.2 below). There are two largely overlapping sets of verbal classifiers. One set is used on stative verbs to refer to the S, or to the head noun if a stative verb is used as a modifier. The other is used on transitive verbs, to refer to the O argument; the same set refers to the derived S of detransitivized passive verbs.[8]

---

[8] Some multiple classifier languages have two sets of classifier morphemes: a closed set of affixes and an open class of repeaters. In Tariana both sets are employed similarly to verbal classifiers. See §9.3.

Classifiers

The assignment of verbal classifiers is semantic, and shape-based; there are no distinctions based on animacy, all animate nouns being treated as 'irregular-shaped'. Verbal classifiers can be used without the overt NP as referent-tracking devices. Similarly to numeral classifiers, an inanimate noun can be used with different classifiers depending on the aspect of the S/O constituent that is involved in the action.

All verbal classifiers are optional. They are used (a) if the corresponding constituent (S or O) is fully involved in the activity, or displays the full degree of a 'property'; or (b) the action/state involves the whole surface of the object.

The forms and semantics of verbal classifiers are given in Diagram 6.1. If a classifier is used with both stative, and transitive verbs, the first form given is the one used with a stative verb and the second is the one used with a transitive verb (surface differences are due to morphophonological processes). Classifiers used with stative verbs only are marked with an asterisk.

Verbal classifiers are used on stative verbs of the following semantic types (following Dixon 1982: 16):

(i) dimension, e.g. *pugum* 'thick', *imu* 'tall';

(ii) physical property, e.g. *mtibdi* 'soft', *ivat* 'hard', *kiki* 'smooth', *kiyaw* 'sharp, abrasive (of cloth)', *miyaw* 'blunt', *barew* 'clean; pretty', *patauh* 'dirty, not pretty', *dax* 'stained';

(iii) colour, e.g. *puhi* 'black', *sey* 'white', *duruweh* 'red', *ayeweye* 'blue, green', *kuwikwiye* 'yellow'.

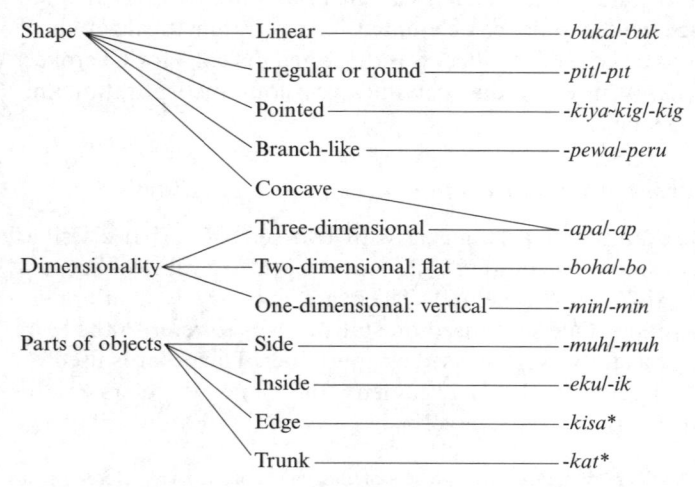

Shape	Linear	-bukal-buk
	Irregular or round	-pitl-pɪt
	Pointed	-kiya-kigl-kig
	Branch-like	-pewal-peru
	Concave	
	Three-dimensional	-apal-ap
Dimensionality	Two-dimensional: flat	-bohal-bo
	One-dimensional: vertical	-minl-min
Parts of objects	Side	-muhl-muh
	Inside	-ekul-ik
	Edge	-kisa*
	Trunk	-kat*

DIAGRAM 6.1. *Verbal classifiers in Palikur*

Stative verbs of other semantic groups—such as speed, age, difficulty, qualification, human propensity, and value—do not cooccur with classifiers. Verbal classifiers are only used if the stative verb describes the complete involvement of the S, or of the head of a head-modifier construction. In 6.29, a classifier is used to indicate the complete blackness of the bird's feathers. (In the examples below, classifiers are underlined.)

6.29. gu-sipri   puhi-pti-ye
      3sGF-feather   black-V.CL:IRREG-DUR.NF
      'Her (bird's) feathers are completely black.'

Verbal classifiers are used with transitive verbs which imply direct physical contact with the object. These are:

(i) physical actions such as 'grab', 'wash', 'dry', 'hit', 'rub'; or
(ii) positional verbs such as 'hang', 'stand', or 'lie'.

Classifiers are employed with telic verbs such as 'look' (as opposed to 'see'). Accordingly, they are not used with verbs denoting mental processes, such as 'think' or 'remember', or with verbs which do not involve direct physical contact with the object, such as 'hear', or 'say'. The restriction on classifier use depending on the semantics of verbs is reminiscent of Athabaskan languages and Ika (see §6.2.3 and §11.2.5).

Verbal classifiers are only used if the object does not have to be, of necessity, completely involved in the action. They are not used with the verb 'kill', since it always involves the whole object—'non-complete' killing is not killing at all. Verbal classifiers may be used to refer to an O, as in 6.30, or to the derived S of a passive, as in 6.31.

6.30. yak-pit-apa-e-gu-kis   nikwe
      sting-V.CL:IRREG-TOTAL-COMPL-3F-PL   therefore
      'So (the killer bees) stung them all over (their bodies).'

6.31. gu-apitiw   wanak-pita-ka   a-kak   mawru
      3F-head   tie-V.CL:IRREG-PASS   3N-with   cotton
      'I see [that] the head [of the rattle] is tied with cotton.'

The origin of most verbal classifiers is unknown. However, at least three come from parts of the body, or parts of a plant: *-kig* 'pointed' is related to *-kig* 'nose'; *-pewa/-peru* 'branch-like' is related to *-peru* 'branch' (cf. *a-peru* 'on a branch'), and *-kat* 'trunk' is related to *akat* 'trunk (of a tree)'. Palikur also has body part incorporation. Note that incorporated body parts cannot cooccur with verbal classifiers since they go in the same slot (see Green and Green 1972, on verb structure in Palikur). Incorporated body parts and verbal classifiers differ in their morphosyntactic behaviour and in their semantics (see Aikhenvald and Green 1998: §5, for details).[9]

Waris (Waris family, Papuan: Foley 1986: 90–1; Brown 1981) has affixed verbal classifiers and also 'stance' classificatory verbs (see (B) in §6.2.3 on Ku Waru) which are used to categorize the argument as to its orientation in space, in combination with its inherent properties.

Prefixed verbal classifiers in Waris are similar to classifiers in Imonda (see example 6.7) both in semantics and in origin: they derive historically from compounded verbs. The choice of verbal classifiers is dictated by such properties of the direct object as consistency, shape, function, arrangement, and measure (Brown 1981: 101–3). There are two 'unique' classifiers: see Table 6.9, and (B) in §11.2.5.

TABLE 6.9. *Verbal classifiers in Waris*

A. Consistency	D. Arrangement
Soft and pliable: *mwan-*	Objects inside a container: *vela-*
Leaf-like with soft stem: *lé-*	Container: *ev-*
Leaf-like with hard stem: *pola-*	Bundle: *selvo-*
Grainy: *ih-*	
	E. Form, nature and measures
B. Shape	Pieces cut from longer lengths: *tuvv-*
Spherical (balls, fruit): *put-*	
	Cut lengths of vine: *kov-*
C. Function and nature	
Cooked food: *ninge-*	F. Unique classifiers
Food removed from the fire ready to eat: *vet-*	For bunch of betelnut: *sengeit-*
Dead game: *vend-*	For pitpit fruit: *si-*

The classificatory verb system for existential verbs is similar to that of Enga (cf. Table 6.7 above, and Kamoro: Table 11.12 below). Classificatory verbs (see Table 6.10) refer to the position of the S argument, and to its shape. The two systems of verbal classification in Waris have a different origin; prefixed classifiers are a later development in the language than classificatory verbs (Brown 1981; cf. §13.1.3).

---

[9] While the use of a classifier is linked, basically, to the completeness of involvement of the O/S in the action, the use of an incorporated body part implies the lack of individuation of the noun which is in the O/S function, and its non-focused status.

Another important difference in behaviour between incorporated body parts and verbal classifiers concerns possibilities of lexicalization of the former. Only incorporated body parts can get lexicalized with certain verbs. That is, they may result in the creation of unique idiomatic expressions in which the meaning of the whole cannot be determined from the meanings of the parts. This happens both with transitive verbs, e.g. *kamax-duka* (grab-CHEST +REFL) 'He had a quick snack' (lit. he grabbed his own chest), and with stative verbs, e.g. *nah barew-wok* (1SG clean-HAND) 'I am poor, destitute' (lit. I am clean-handed)'. Nothing of this sort ever happens with verbal classifiers.

TABLE 6.10. *Classificatory verbs in Waris*

Verb	Semantics	Nouns it occurs with
lohv	be standing	Vertical or standing things: man, tree, garden, dog, pig, fish in water, sugar cane, sun, sky
av	be sitting	Small roundish things: woman, small animal, insect, taro in garden, bunch of betelnut on tree
liv	be lying prone	Water, liquids, yam in garden, snake
dihilv	lie or sit	Axe, road, tractor
nalohv	lie or sit (orderly)	Firewood
diav	lie or sit (disorderly)	Fallen trees in newly-cut garden
endv	be hanging	Fruit, rattan, peanuts on stem underneath the earth
vilv	lie crumpled or folded	Net bag, towel

Unlike Athabaskan languages (see §6.4.2), the two kinds of verbal classifier are in a complementary distribution with respect to the argument they refer to, one set referring to the O argument and the other to the S argument.

6.4.2. *Distinct systems of verbal classifiers*

A few North Athabaskan languages have two kinds of affixed verbal classifier, and they also have classificatory verbs (§6.2.3). A typical system is found in Koyukon[10] (Axelrod forthcoming: 4; Thompson 1993: 315–16); one set of verbal classifiers in Koyukon is shown in Table 6.11. (Note that Athabaskan linguistic tradition calls verbal classifiers 'genders'; the term 'classifier' is, misleadingly, used for voice-like markers.)

TABLE 6.11. *Affixed verbal classifiers in Koyukon*

Classifier	Meaning
ne-	Round things: beads, berries, face, eyes, strings and ropes
de-	Wood, plants, rigid containers, stiff clothing, language
dene-	Round, heavy objects: animal heads, cabbages, apples, rocks; long cylindrical objects: pipe, bridge, pencil
hʉde-	Weather
Ø-	People, animals

[10] The system found in Koyukon is fairly typical of the majority of Athabaskan languages, though the details vary. The two most widespread verbal classifiers are *d* 'long, slender objects' and *n* 'round objects'. Verbal classifiers are highly productive in Koyukon, Dena'ina, Ahtna, Tanana, and Carrier (Thompson 1993), but are also found in others including Navajo and Slave (Keren Rice, p.c.). See Kari (1990: 34) on the semantics of verbal classifiers ('genders') in Ahtna.

168 *Classifiers*

These verbal classifier prefixes are used to refer to the S or O argument of the verb. Another kind of verbal classifier, termed the 'areal' prefix, *hʉ-*, is used to refer to extended objects, places, events or abstractions. The verbal classifier prefixes listed in Table 6.11, and the areal prefix, share a number of morphosyntactic properties. They are used to categorize the S/O argument in terms of its shape.

A verbal classifier is shown to refer to the S argument in 6.32, and to the O argument in 6.33. The areal prefix is used to refer to the S argument in 6.34. Examples are from Thompson (1993: 316–17).

6.32. tɬ'ool   n-aal'onh
     rope   CL-be.there
     'A rope (*ne-* classifier) is there.'

6.33. tɬool   n-aan-s-'onh
     rope   CL-PREF-1SG-arrive.carrying
     'I arrived carrying a rope (*ne-* classifier).'

6.34. yeh   h-ool'onh
     house   AREAL-be.there
     'A house (*hʉ-* areal prefix) is there.'

The areal prefix differs from other verbal classifiers in the following ways (Thompson 1993: 317–18).

(i) Unlike other classifiers, the areal prefix may be used in a further morphosyntactic context: it can cross-reference the argument of a locational postposition, as shown in 6.35.

6.35. Fairbanks   hʉ-ts'e   taalyo
     Fairbanks   AREAL-to   went
     'S/he went to Fairbanks.'

(ii) The areal prefix occupies a slot in the verb different from that of classifiers (Thompson 1993: 319–21);[11] it behaves like prefixes which belong to the pronominal slot; the other classifiers occupy a quite different 'qualifier' slot (see further discussion in Thompson 1993).

(iii) The areal prefix has other functions, e.g. that of impersonal and proximate subject. Verbal classifiers do not have such functions.

(iv) In some Athabaskan languages with verbal classifiers these cannot cooccur with each other, but they can cooccur with the areal prefix; this happens in Carrier (Morice 1932: 141–4; Bill Poser, p.c.).

---

[11] See Kari (1989) on prefix positions in Athabaskan languages.

(v) Some Athabaskan languages do not have verbal classifiers other than the areal prefix, e.g. Gwich'in, Holikachuk (Thompson 1993: 318).[12]

A diachronic study of Athabaskan suggests different origins for verbal classifiers *de-* and *ne-*, and for the areal prefix. According to Thompson (1993: 332), 'the history of the areal prefix suggests that it has always been an inflectional and productive mopheme'. According to Jeff Leer (p.c.), the verbal classifiers *de-* and *ne-* come from incorporated nouns (i.e. the type discussed in §6.2.1) in Proto-Eyak-Athabaskan, and these later grammaticalized as classifiers.

Whatever the whole story is, the two types of verbal classifier in Athabaskan languages have different synchronic functions and different origins.

6.5. Distribution of verbal classifiers

Map 5 shows the distribution of verbal classifiers in the languages of the world.

In North America, verbal classifiers are found in all Eyak-Athabaskan languages and in Haida. Northern Athabaskan languages have suppletive classificatory verbs and verbal classifiers (termed 'genders' in the Athabaskan linguistic tradition: see Thompson 1993). Classificatory verbs are an areal feature of the Southeast (including all the Muskogean languages, cf. Kimball 1991: 452–8 and Haas 1978, on Koasati; Campbell 1997: 342, on Tunica, Natchez, Atakapa, Chitimacha, Yuchi, Biloxi, and Dhegiha). In the Great Basin area Nevome (Piman: Uto-Aztecan) has suppletive verbal classifiers. Among Californian languages, Pomoan languages have verbal classifiers, as do Tarascan (isolate, Southwest Mexico: Costenla Umaña 1991: 116; Friedrich 1971), Wakashan, Hokan, some Salish, Iroquoian, Caddoan languages, and Dakota (Siouan) (Campbell 1997). The existence of classificatory verbs in a few Mesoamerican languages has been suggested by Suárez (1983: 90–1); however, the evidence is not clear and more work is needed (see the criticism of Suárez by Quinn forthcoming and Campbell 1985).

In Australia, verbal classifiers are found in some northern Australian prefixing languages, e.g. Mayali (Gunwinjgu), Nunggubuyu, Ngandi, Tiwi, and Anindilyakwa (Sands 1995: 272 ff.; Dixon 2002: 423–9).

Verbal classifiers are found in Papuan languages of southern and central

---

[12] Verbal classifiers *d* and *n* also occur in some nouns as a kind of derivational marker, e.g. Slave *dechĭ* 'stick' (with *d* marker) (Keren Rice, p.c.); in Ahtna *n* is said to occur 'in compound nouns that are roundish or rope-like', e.g. *c'enluu* 'unripe berries', *-nts'ese'* 'seed, pit' (Kari 1990: 285) (the classifier *n* is in bold type).

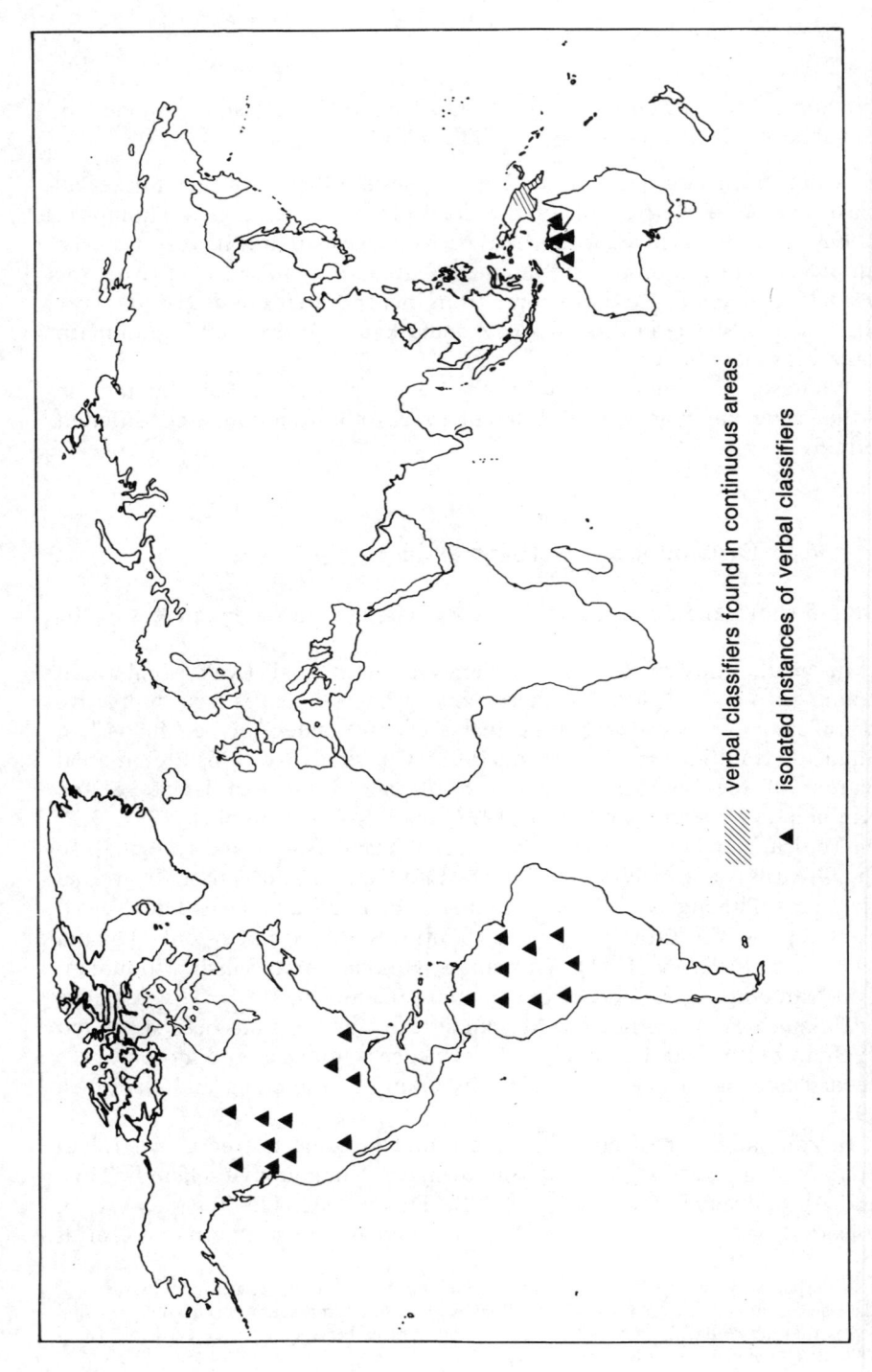

MAP 5. *Distribution of verbal classifiers in the languages of the world*

Bougainville, and in the Waris language family (Brown 1981; Seiler 1983). They may also be found in Reef-Santa Cruzan languages (see Wurm 1992a; 1992b). Classificatory existential verbs are extremely widespread in Papua New Guinea—they are found in Engan, Waris, Asmat, Kiwaian families, in Chimbu, Melpa, and in Huon languages (see Lang 1975: 115–20, for an overview; W. Seiler 1986; 1989; Foley 1986; Lang 1975; Brown 1981; Merlan *et al.* 1997); and also in some Ok languages (Christensen 1995).

Quite a few languages of Lowland Amazonia have verbal classifiers. These include North Arawak, Yagua, Harakmbet, a few Tupí languages (e.g. Mundurukú and Karo), and some isolates, such as Waorani (Derbyshire and Payne 1990). Partly analysable classificatory verbs are found in Ika (Chibchan: Frank 1990).

There are no verbal classifiers in the languages of Africa or Eurasia or in the Austronesian family.

7 Locative and Deictic Classifiers

7.1. The structure of this chapter

This chapter describes two further types of classifier which have a noun phrase as their scope: locative classifiers which occur in locative noun phrases (§7.2) and deictic classifiers which occur on deictic modifiers and/or articles in head-modifier noun phrases (§7.3). More examples of these classifiers in the languages of the world would need to be discovered before their typological profile could be fully established.

7.2. Properties of locative classifiers

Locative classifiers are morphemes which occur in locative noun phrases. Their choice is determined by the semantic character of the noun involved—in all the cases described here, it is the argument of a locative adposition. Classifiers of this type are rare; all the examples discussed here come from South American Indian languages on which information has only recently become available: Palikur and Lokono (North Arawak), in Carib languages and in Dâw (Makú). This is the reason why they have rarely been considered in previous typologies of classifiers.[1]

In all the known cases, locative classifiers are 'fused' with an adposition (preposition or postposition). The choice of adposition then depends on physical properties of the head noun, e.g. shape, or consistency. (Following the analogy of classificatory verbs (§6.2.3), they could be called classificatory adpositions.) The choice of a locative classifier is semantic.

Palikur (North Arawak; Aikhenvald and Green 1998) offers the only clear-cut example of locative classifiers. Palikur has three genders, and also five distinct types of classifier: numeral classifiers, two subsets of verbal classifiers (those occurring on stative verbs, which are frequently used as modifiers in NPs, and those occurring on transitive verbs: see §6.4), as well as possessive classifiers (generic nouns used in possessive constructions with some alienably possessed nouns (§5.5.1) (and discussion in §8.2).

The choice of locative classifiers is based on the shape, dimensionality and boundedness of the head noun (see Diagram 7.1); it does not involve

---

[1] Locative classifiers were first introduced as a distinct subtype by Allan (1977: 286).

animacy distinctions. These morphemes can be used as locative adpositions by themselves meaning 'on' or 'in'. Whether they cross-reference person, number, and gender of the head noun and whether they are used as prepositions or as adpositions depends on the pragmatic status of the head noun (see details in Aikhenvald and Green 1998). Note that the shape and dimension terms are the same as in Diagram 6.1, but one boundedness related term and the specific classifiers are different. Those morphemes in Diagram 7.1 which are the same as verbal classifiers (see Diagram 6.1) are marked with an asterisk (*).

Shape
- Linear — -buhku(-mna)
- Irregular or round — -pit*
- Pointed — -kigsa
- Branch-like — -peru*
- Sharp edge — -kigbi(-mna)
- Concave

Dimensionality
- Three-dimensional — -apa
- Two-dimensional: flat — -madka
- One-dimensional: vertical — -min*

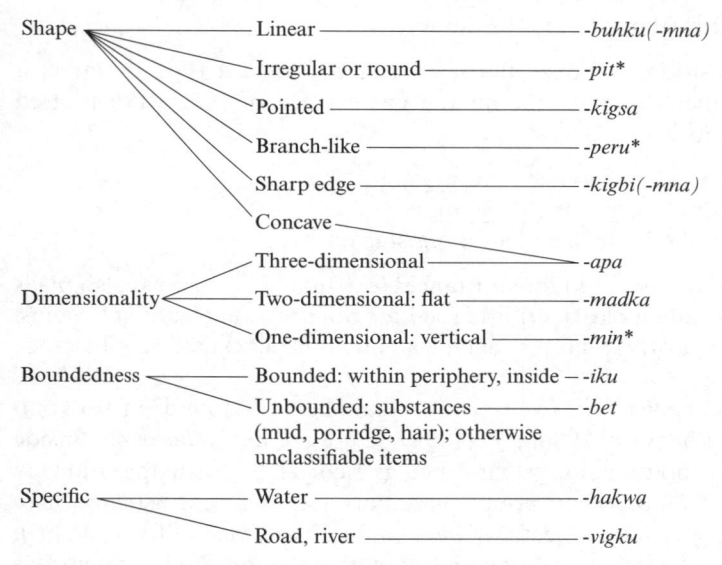

Boundedness
- Bounded: within periphery, inside — -iku
- Unbounded: substances — -bet
  (mud, porridge, hair); otherwise unclassifiable items

Specific
- Water — -hakwa
- Road, river — -vigku

DIAGRAM 7.1. *Locative classifiers in Palikur*

Classificatory locative adpositions cooccur with the locative suffixes to form directionals, elatives, and perlatives: *-t* 'directional: into, to', *-tak* 'elative: from', *-iu* 'perlative: along'. In 7.1 *-min* is used to refer to the vertical location: the arm. In 7.2 *-peru* is used to refer to a branch-like location, a tree.

7.1. pis   keh   paha-t   arab   pi-wan
     2SG   make   one-NUM.CL:VERT   shield   2SG-arm
     min
     on.VERT
     'You make a shield on your arm.'

7.2. ig-kis   ute-e-gi   ig   motye
     3M-PL   find-COMPL-3M   3M   wasp
     ay-h-te   a-peru   ah
     there-INT-DISTAL   3n-on.BRANCH LIKE   tree
     'They found the wasps on the tree.'

Example 7.3 shows a directional marker on locative classifier -*hakwa* 'in.WATER'.

7.3. wis-uh   tarak-e-gu   a-hakwa-t   un
     1PL-EXCL   push-COMPL-3F   3n-in.WATER-DIR   water
     'We push it (the canoe) into the water.'

In an adpositional phrase, the head can be omitted. For example, a locative classifier ('on.flat', i.e. on the flat surface of the rattle) is used headlessly, as in 7.4.

7.4. ka-daha-ni   warukma   gu-madka
     ATT-for-POSS   big.star   3F-on.FLAT
     'It (rattle: feminine, flat) had a big star on it.'

The adposition -*bet* used for substances (e.g. mud, clay, faeces) also plays the role of a residual classifier: it is used for otherwise unclassifiable items. These include abstract nouns, such as thoughts, darkness, coolness or suffering.

A smallish system of five locative classifiers is found in Lokono (Arawak) (Aikhenvald 1996b; Pet 1987: 37–8). One, *koborokon* 'inside of an animate body, among living beings', correlates with the animacy of the referent of the head noun; three correlate with consistency (*loko* 'inside a hollow or solid object'; *rakon* 'in a fluid'; *kolokon* 'in fire or light'), and one with interioricity and dimensionality (*roko* 'on the inside surface of').

Dâw (Makú, Northwest Amazonia: Martins 1994: 53 ff.) has five locative classifiers. Their choice depends on the physical properties of the referent of the head: *kɛd* 'inside a bounded object', *mĩ'* 'inside liquid, or fire', *bɨt* 'underneath an object with an upper boundary', *wə?* 'above an unbounded object', *ʃaʃ* 'inside a mixture'. Locative classifiers are fused with locational markers, just like in Palikur. In 7.5, -*kɛd* 'in:HOLLOW' is used with the noun *canoe*. In 7.6 -*mĩ'* 'in:LIQUID' is used with the noun 'river'. 7.6a is ungrammatical.

7.5. xoo-kɛd
     canoe-IN:HOLLOW
     'in a canoe'

7.6. nââx-pis-mĩ'
    water-small-IN:LIQUID
    'in a small river'

7.6a. *xoo-mĩ'?
    canoe-IN:LIQUID

Locative classifiers are also found in Carib languages (Derbyshire forthcoming) where the choice of a locative classifier depends on the dimensionality and consistency of a referent. See Table 7.1 (Derbyshire 1999) and 7.7, from Hixkaryana.

TABLE 7.1. *Locative classificatory suffixes in three Carib languages*

	Apalaí	Hixkaryana	Macushi
Liquid, in	kua-o	kwa-wo	ka
into	kua-ka	kwa-ka	ka-ta
Flat surface, on	po	ho	po
to	po-na	ho-na	po-na
Open area, on	ta-o	ta-wo/ya-wo	ya
to	ta-ka	ta-ka/ya-ka	ya-pɨh
Enclosed place, in	a-o	ya-wo	ta
to	a-ka	ya-ka	ta-pɨh

7.7. asama   y-ahe-tawo
    trail   GENITIVE-edge-CL:ON.OPEN.AREA
    'at the edge of the trail'

The locative classifiers in Lokono, Dâw, and in Carib languages are not used elsewhere in these languages. In contrast, three of the locative classifiers in Palikur are also used as verbal classifiers (see §8.2). No language with locative classifier affixes has been found so far.[2]

Directionality and location are semantic parameters widely used in verbal classifiers (see §11.2.5). The choice of a classificatory verb may correlate with the type of location referred to. For instance, in Cherokee (Blankenship 1997: 95) 'for materials which can assume the shape of their container, the quality of the container often determines the class. Sugar in a bowl is COMPACT, but sugar in a bag is FLEXIBLE.' One of the four classificatory existential verbs in Qiang (Tibeto-Burman: LaPolla forthcoming: 120–1) is used with referents located within a container of some

---

[2] A possible example of locative classifiers as affixes is Kadiweu (Guaicuruan family: Griffiths and Griffiths 1976: 111), where some classifiers are prefixed to locational adverbs. This issue deserves more in-depth study; for an alternative interpretation of this issue in Kadiweu, see Sândalo (1996).

type (see §6.2.3). Verbal classifiers can be used in locative expressions. The so-called 'areal' prefix in Athabaskan languages can be used on locative prepositions in Koyukon (example 6.35: Thompson 1993). Verbal classifiers appear on locatives in Eyak (Krauss 1968; §9.1, Table 9.2 below).

Distinctions comparable to locative classifiers may be found in other languages. In Archi (Northeast Caucasian: Aleksandr J. Kibrik, p.c.) the choice between the two locative cases (glossed as IN, e.g. inside a container, and INTER, e.g. among) appears to depend on the semantics of the noun. These cases are, by and large, used with different nouns; but there are a few instances of a reclassification of the same item. So, for instance, 'village-in' means 'in a village as a place', 'village-inter' means 'among villagers'. The two locative cases have some similarity with locative classifiers. Similar distinctions are found in other Northeast Caucasian languages, e.g. Tsez (Bernard Comrie, p.c.). These issues deserve further investigation. Locative meanings are often expressed with other noun categorization devices; for example, agreement classes with locative meanings are found in Bantu languages (cf. e.g. Givón 1969; Bresnan and McChombo 1986), in Motuna (Onishi 1994: 76–7), and in Nasioi (Hurd 1977: 137).

In many languages, including English and Tongan (see Broschart 1997), the choice of a preposition or of a locational expression depends, to a varying extent, on the properties of the head noun. For instance, the referent of a noun has to have a surface for the preposition 'on' to be used with it; and have an 'inside' for 'in' to be used. However, this lexical choice is different from locative classifiers—in the same way that the choice of verbs like 'drink' and 'chew' in English (see §6.2.3) is different from the choice of classificatory verbs in Athabaskan languages. In Palikur and other languages with locative classifiers described in this section the obligatory choice of an adposition is made depending strictly on the properties of the referent noun; there are paradigmatic relations between the types of nouns and the choice of an adposition. This is not so in English.

7.3. Properties of deictic classifiers

Deictic classifiers obligatorily occur with deictic elements such as articles and demonstratives. Their choice is semantic, and they categorize the noun in terms of its shape, animacy, and position in space; they do not always appear on the noun itself. Deictic classifiers were first identified by Barron and Serzisko (1982) and then by H. Seiler (1986). Craig (forthcoming: 42–3) also mentions the existence of 'classifying systems' in articles in some

North American Indian languages. In §7.3.1 I consider examples of deictic classifiers, and provide justification for considering them a classifier type. Discussion and conclusions are in §7.3.2.

7.3.1. Examples of deictic classifiers

Deictic classifiers have been described for (A) The North American languages Yuchi and the Siouan family, (B) Guaicuruan languages of South America, and (C) Eskimo, where they are fused with demonstratives (unlike in A and B).

(A) Deictic classifiers in North American languages

Classifiers are obligatorily used with deictics and articles in a number of Siouan languages, especially Mandan and Ponca (Barron and Serzisko 1982, and a resumé in H. Seiler 1986: 87 ff.). The classifier morphemes come from grammaticalized stance verbs 'sit', 'stand', and 'lie' (cf. Rankin 1976). They indicate the stance of the antecedent, as well as the form of the antecedent: one-dimensional (long, vertical, or 'standing'), two-dimensional (horizontal, or 'lying'), or three-dimensional (round, or 'sitting'), e.g. Mandan (Barron and Serzisko 1982: 99; Watkins 1976: 30):

7.8. dɛ-mãk
 this-DEICTIC.CL:LYING
 'this one (lying)'

7.9. dɛ-nãk
 this-DEICTIC.CL:SITTING
 'this one (sitting)'

7.10. dɛ-hãk
 this-DEICTIC.CL:STANDING
 'this one (standing)'

Stance verbs in North American languages with deictic classifiers are also used as classificatory verbs the choice of which correlates with the shape of the intransitive subject: long objects 'stand', round objects 'sit' and flat objects 'lie' (Watkins 1976: 30, for Siouan; H. Seiler 1986: 89).

Ponca (Siouan: Watkins 1976: 33–4; Barron and Serzisko 1982: 86) has two sets of definite articles the choice of which is determined by the animacy of the referent, its position, and, for an animate referent, its number and whether it is at rest or in motion. (If the noun is indefinite it is used without an article or *wĩ* is used irrespectively of the properties of the referent.) See Table 7.2.

178   *Classifiers*

TABLE 7.2. *Article classifiers in Ponca*

Inanimate articles	Animate articles
k'e 'horizontal'	*ak'á* 'sg.subj at rest'
t'e 'standing; collective'	*amá* 'sg.subj in motion; pl.'
¢ã 'rounded'	*t'ã* 'sg.object standing'
ge 'scattered'	*¢ĩ* 'sg.object moving'
	ma 'pl.object' (see *amá*)
	¢iñk'e 'sg.object sitting'
	¢añk'a 'pl.object sitting'

Examples 7.11a–c (Barron and Serzisko 1982: 93) illustrate how the use of different article classifiers results in varying interpretations of a polysemous noun. This is similar to the semantic functions of other classifiers, e.g. numeral classifiers and noun classifiers (cf. §3.2.2).

7.11a. nî   t'e
water ART:STANDING, COLLECTIVE
'the water'

7.11b. nî   ¢ã
water ART:ROUNDED
'the handful of water (cupped)'

7.11c. nî   k'e
water ART:HORIZONTAL
'the (line of) water, the stream'

The same set of morphemes are also used predicatively, as locative expressions (Barron and Serzisko 1982: 94–5).

Yuchi (isolate: Watkins 1976: 35; Barron and Serzisko 1982: 96–7) has a largeish set of morphemes the choice of which is determined by whether the object is one-dimensional (long, vertical), two-dimensional (horizontal), or three-dimensional. There is also a special plural class. These morphemes appear to be obligatorily marked on the demonstrative and on the noun itself and have an article-like meaning, e.g. *ya-fa* (wood-ART:VERTICAL) 'the tree', *ya-'ɛ* (wood-ART:HORIZONTAL) 'the log'; *nɛ-fa ya-fa* (this-ART:VERTICAL wood-ART:VERTICAL) 'this tree'.

(B) Deictic classifiers in Guaicuruan languages

Classifiers which indicate spatial position/location of an object, its absence vs. presence in the visual field and its form (extendedness vs. non-extendedness; horizontal vs. vertical extension) are used in Toba and Pilagá (Guaicuruan family, Argentina).

Toba distinguishes six classifiers (termed 'locative particles' by Klein 1979: 89–91; 1978: 151 ff.); they are obligatory with headless demonstrative pronouns (which distinguish masculine and feminine genders) and optionally cooccur with nouns. The system of classifiers in Toba is shown in Diagram 7.2 (Klein 1979: 91).

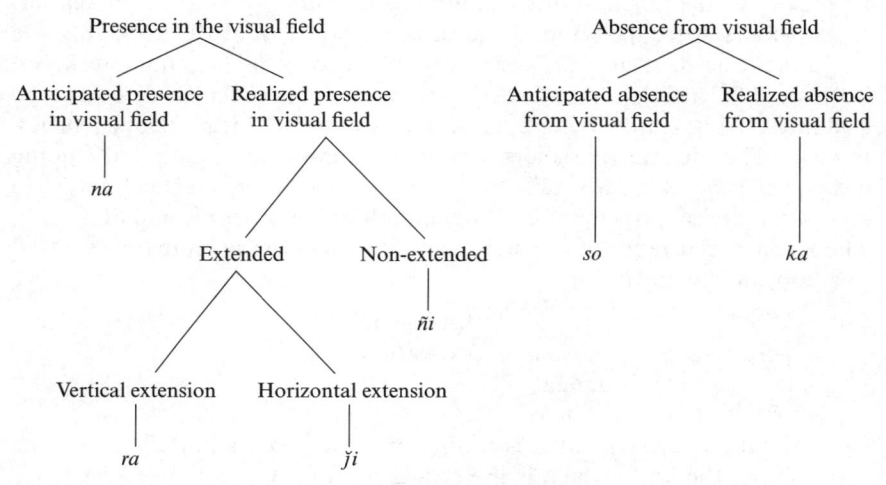

```
              Presence in the visual field                          Absence from visual field
             /              \                                       /              \
Anticipated presence    Realized presence              Anticipated absence    Realized absence
   in visual field       in visual field                from visual field      from visual field
         |                  /      \                           |                     |
         na              Extended  Non-extended                so                    ka
                         /    \         |
                              \        ñi
              Vertical extension  Horizontal extension
                      |                 |
                      ra                ji
```

DIAGRAM 7.2. *Classifiers with spatial semantics in Toba*

Examples of demonstrative and third person pronouns with classifiers and gender markers (ø for masculine and *ha-* for feminine) in Toba are given in 7.12–15 (Klein 1978: 155–7 and p.c.).

7.12. Ø-ra-mari
MASC-VERTICAL.EXTENSION-3RD.PERSON.PRONOMINAL.BASE
'he (standing)'

7.13. ha-ka-mari
FEM-REALIZED.ABSENCE.FROM.VISUAL.FIELD-3RD PERSON.PRONOMINAL.BASE
'she (unseen or unknown to the speaker)'

7.14. Ø-ra-ra
MASC-VERTICAL.EXTENSION-REDUPLICATION
'this (one masculine) standing'

A classifier with a noun is shown in 7.15 (Klein 1978: 151).

7.15. hinakta   Ø-ra-ngoto-lek
is.biting   MASC-VERTICAL.EXTENSION-youth-MASC
Ø-ñi-mpi'oq
MASC-NON.EXTENDED-dog
'A (sitting) dog is biting a (standing) boy.'

Classifiers in Toba do not qualify as locative classifiers, since they do not cooccur with spatial adverbs or adpositions (see Croft 1994). They categorize nouns; and at the same time they obligatorily cooccur with deictics.

Classifiers in Pilagá, another language of the Guaicuruan family (Vidal 1994; 1997), are similar to those in Toba; they are preposed to nouns, and refer both to the position of the noun in space and to its form. Pilagá has six classifiers: three 'positional' and three 'deictic' (Vidal 1997: 75, 78). The positional classifiers are: *da7* 'vertically extended, long' (e.g. humans, trees, horses), *ñi7* 'sitting/non-extended, rounded' (mammals, snakes, insects, buildings, fruits), *di7* 'lying/horizontally extended' (dead people, fishes, towns). The deictic classifiers are *na7* 'coming/proximal', *so7* 'going away/past', *ga7* 'absent/distal'. In 7.16 the classifier *da7* 'vertical' refers to a person (vertical position is considered 'inherent for people and animals'). The second occurrence of the same classifier refers to the knife (in a vertical position) (Vidal 1997: 76).

7.16. da7   siyawa   di-kiyana-a
      DEIC.CL:VERT person   3SG-eat-OBJ.AGR
      da7   ganaat
      DEIC.CL:VERT knife
      'That person (standing) is eating something with a knife.' (i.e. He/she shows the knife which is in vertical position.)

Classifier *ñi7* 'sitting, non-extended' is used with buildings and with mammals, birds and insects, as in 7.17. It can also be extended to humans in a sitting position, as shown in 7.18.

7.17. ñi7   siyaq   netawe   ñi7   emek
      CL:NON.EXT animal   LOC   CL:NON.EXT house
      'The animal is inside the house.'

7.18. ñi7-ca7   weta   di7   noik   sekaet
      CL:NON.EXT-PRO LOC   CL:HORIZ   town   yesterday
      'That one who is sitting (far from me . . .) was in the town yesterday.'

Classifier *di7* is used with objects which are perceived as 'horizontally extended', such as 'town' in 7.18, or 'fire' in 7.19.

7.19. an-toñi-igi   di7-m7e   dole
      2SG-warm-MOD   CL:HORIZ-DEM   fire
      'Warm yourself up by the fire.'

Like Toba, Pilagá also has derivational markers which refer to the sex of human referents, and physical properties of non-human referents (Vidal 1997: 63–5). An optional marker of feminine gender, *ha*, appears attached to demonstratives, pronouns, and deictic classifiers (cf. *ha-* as the feminine marker in Toba in 7.13), e.g. *ha-ñi7-m7e yaw7o* (FEM-CL:NON.EXT-DEM woman) 'that woman' (sitting or non-extended) (Vidal 1997: 68).[3]

Similarly to Siouan languages, the classifiers used with deictics in Guaicuruan languages come from verbs. Some of the positional deictics reconstructed by Céria and Sândalo (1995: 181) for Proto-Guaicuruan, the ancestor language of Toba, Pilagá (and Kadiweu), are given in Table 7.3. According to Filomena Sândalo (p.c.), deictic classifiers in Toba and Pilagá correspond to existential verbs in Kadiweu.

TABLE 7.3. *A sample of demonstratives in Proto-Guaicuruan*

Gender	Presence/absence from the visual field	Position	Demonstrative
Masculine	Absent	General	*k:ae
		Standing	*(e)-d:a
		Sitting	*(e)-n:i
	Present	Lying	*(e)-d:i
		Coming	*(e)-n:a
		Going	*(e)-dyu
Feminine	Absent	General	*a-kae
		Standing	*a-d:a
		Sitting	*a-n:i
	Present	Lying	*a-d:i
		Coming	*a-n:a
		Going	*a-dyu

(C) Deictic classifiers in Eskimo

In Eskimo, classifiers which combine reference to boundedness and visibility of the objects appear fused with demonstratives. Central Yup'ik classifiers fused with deictics (data from the Chevak dialect: Woodbury 1981: 237–8) are shown in Table 7.4.

The use of a classifier is illustrated with a following example from Gagné (1966), cited by Denny (1979a: 103):

7.20. unaaq paŋna aiguk
 harpoon EXTENDED:one.up.there get
 'Get that [visible, extended] harpoon up there.'

7.3.2 *Conclusions and discussion*

We saw in §7.3.1 that in (A) Siouan and Yuchi, and in (B) Toba and Pilagá, deictic classifiers combine reference to the position of the noun categorized

---

[3] This feminine marker can also be used to refer to inanimate referents; the rules of assignment are unclear (Vidal 1997: 68).

TABLE 7.4. *Deictic classifiers in Eskimo*

Restricted	Extended	Obscured
Refer to objects or areas which are bounded in all dimensions: point-like, rounded, stationary, or confined	Refer to objects or areas which are unbounded in one or more directions: a line, long object, or something in linear motion through time or space (one unbounded dimension); an expanse (two unbounded dimensions); or a space or vast object (three unbounded dimensions)	Refer to what is far away or invisible

and to its shape. In Eskimo their choice is determined by extendedness and visibility of the object. In (A) and (B) deictic classifiers have arisen as the result of the grammaticalization of posture verbs. At the same time, different classifiers may be used with the same referent if its position is varied (compare examples 7.16 and 7.18, from Pilagá); they can also be used to distinguish different meanings of a polysemous noun (7.11 from Ponca). The use of deictic classifiers in North American languages is linked to definiteness. H. Seiler (1986: 94) pointed out the 'intermediary' status of 'article classifiers': they have a verbal origin but are 'confined' to a noun phrase and have 'particularly close affinities' with definiteness. We conclude that there is probably enough ground to postulate deictic classifiers as a separate type, whose defining properties are:

(i) the morphosyntactic environment in which they appear: on deictics and/ or articles with scope over a noun phrase;

(ii) categorization of the head noun in terms of shape, extendedness, position, and also animacy.

Deictic classifiers in Eskimo are different. Their choice is conditioned by the shape of the referent noun in terms of 'typical' deictic categories, such as visibility. More studies are needed in order to provide a convincing categorization of Eskimo deictics which are obviously different from the situation described for Siouan and for Guaicuruan.

We have seen in §2.7 that in languages with distinct systems of nominal and pronominal noun classes, demonstratives would pattern with the latter. Demonstratives may be the only modifiers to distinguish genders or noun classes. Waurá (Xinguan Arawak: Richards 1988; Aikhenvald 1996b) provides a dramatic example of this: two genders—masculine and feminine— are distinguished only in deictics and nowhere else. In fact, gender marking is synchronically fused with deictics, e.g. MASC. *eze*, FEM. *izi* 'this'. There are no gender oppositions elsewhere in the system, unlike other Arawak languages. (Waurá also has a largeish set of morphemes used as numeral and as verbal classifiers.) The gender opposition in Waurá which only exists in the system of demonstratives can also be considered analogous to deictic classifiers in other languages. However, if a language has animacy or humanness distinctions marked only on articles or on demonstratives this does not necessarily imply the existence of deictic classifiers, since it may be just a case of noun class agreement on multiple targets (cf. §9.2).[4]

Numeral classifiers are often, but not always, also used with demonstratives, as in Mandarin Chinese or in Hmong. Even if the same set of classifiers is used with numerals and with deictics, they can behave differently (see Chapter 9). We will show in §9.3 that Tariana, a language with classifiers used in multiple environments, employs somewhat distinct sets with various types of deictic, with interrogatives, and with articles, and that this does not mean that every morphosynctactic context involves a distinct type of classifiers. However, the fact that demonstratives and articles can have a distinct agreement system, or employ a distinct subset of classifier forms, may be considered a prerequisite for the emergence of deictic classifiers as a distinct type, as in Siouan, in Yuchi, and in Guaicuruan languages.

[4] Teop (Austronesian, Bougainville: Mosel and Spriggs forthcoming) has three genders marked on articles. This system cannot be considered that of article classifiers because it involves agreement, and thus is better considered a noun class system.

8 Different Classifier Types in One Language

8.1. General observations

Several distinct classifier types may coexist in one language. The cooccurrence of different classifier systems in different morphosyntactic environments constitutes a strong argument in favour of the proposed typology of classifiers based on the morphosyntactic locus of coding of noun categorization devices (together with their scope of categorization, principles of assignment, and the kind of surface realization: see §1.5).

The different sets of morphemes used in distinct classifier environments may partly overlap in their form and/or semantics. Sometimes their semantics is the same, but the form is different; sometimes it is the other way round. The most frequent combination of distinct classifiers within one language is numeral classifiers and noun class systems. Numeral classifiers may also coexist with noun classifiers or with relational classifiers. Verbal, locative, and noun classifiers may coexist with noun classes. Different sets of classifiers interact with other grammatical categories, such as number, in different ways (see Chapter 10).

In Chapters 2–6 I discussed languages with more than one (in most cases, just two) subsets of noun categorization devices of the same type. The most frequent situation is for a language to have two types of noun class system: a 'nominal', and a 'pronominal' one (see §2.7). There is rarely more than one variety of other kinds of classifier (see §4.3 on numeral classifiers, §5.5.2 on classifiers in possessive constructions, and §6.4 on verbal classifiers). No language has been found with two kinds of noun classifiers, or of locative or deictic classifiers.[1]

Two varieties of the same classifier type (e.g. noun classes, numeral or verbal classifiers) can be in a complementary distribution. In §2.7.1 we discussed distinct noun class agreement systems the choice of which depends on the kinds of modifiers (adjectives may have one agreement system, and deictics another). Different kinds of verbal classifier may categorize different arguments: one is used for O and the other is used for S (e.g. Waris, in §6.4.1). Distinct kinds of classifier may cooccur in the same environment. The two noun class systems in Paumarí can be

---

[1] This is to be expected due to the rarity of these types.

marked on the same modifier and on the predicate (§2.7.2); in Athabaskan languages different verbal classifiers coexist in the same environments (§6.4.2).

All these cases are very similar to the ones discussed here. In each instance, every subtype of the 'same' kind of classifier is likely to have its own semantic and functional properties, as well as its own history; or they may correspond to different historical stages of the system. They constitute 'incipient' types of classifiers, grammaticalizing distinct 'focal' points on the continuum of noun categorization.

In other languages the same set of morphemes can be used in more than one classifier environment (see Chapter 9). These morphemes can then have somewhat different grammatical realization, or be more or less obligatory depending on what classifier construction they are in. Then there are more problematic systems—such as Tariana and Baniwa (§9.3), where classifiers in several different environments overlap just slightly. These are fuzzy types, with tendencies towards the grammaticalization of various focal points on the continuum of noun categorization devices. As we will show in §9.3, in most instances—but not always—these focal points correspond to already established classifier types.

We first consider coexisting classifier sets in different contexts (§8.2). In §8.3 we deal with languages where distinct classifier sets cooccur in the same environment. Some conclusions are given in §8.4.

8.2. Coexisting classifier sets in different environments

Two sets of classifiers in one language is by far the most frequent case. Combinations of two classifier systems are discussed in (A). Three or four sets of classifiers are rarer—see (B) and (C) respectively.

(A) Two sets of classifiers

NOUN CLASSES and NUMERAL CLASSIFIERS coexist in a few Indic (Rastorgueva *et al.* 1978), Dravidian (Emeneau 1964), Iranian (Zograf 1976), and some Arawak languages (e.g. Warekena, Yucuna, Achagua). Malto (South Dravidian: Mahapatra 1979) has about thirty numeral classifiers, and two noun classes (genders). Classifiers are used to categorize nouns in terms of animacy, form, shape, and size; there are also a few unique classifiers each used with a single noun. Nouns are divided into two genders: male human vs. the rest in singular; human vs. non-human in plural (see §10.1).

NOUN CLASSIFIERS and NOUN CLASS systems coexist in some prefixing languages of Northern Australia, such as Ngan'gityemerri (Reid 1990; 1997; Sands 1995: 281–2). The systems of noun class markers and classifiers in Ngan'gityemerri are shown in Table 8.1; they overlap semantically. Noun classifiers are optional, while noun class markers are obligatory in noun phrases. Some functions of the noun class markers in Ngan'gityemerri were discussed in §3.5. Examples 3.26 and 3.27 illustrate how noun class markers and noun classifiers are different in their form, and obligatoriness. As Reid (1997) has convincingly shown, historically noun class prefixes developed as the result of grammaticalization and reanalysis of generic noun classifier lexemes (also see §13.8). Ngan'gityemerri also distinguishes masculine and feminine genders in third person singular pronouns.

TABLE 8.1. *Noun classes and noun classifiers in Ngan'gityemerri*

Gloss	Noun class marker	Classifier
Male	wa-	
Female	wur-	
Human group	awa-	
Body parts	da-, Ø-, a-	
Canine	wu-	
Animal	a-	gagu
Plant food, vegetable	mi-	miyi
Trees/things	yerr-	yawurr
Bamboo spears	yeli-	yawul
Strikers		syiri
Fire		yenggi
Liquid		kuru
Digging sticks		kini
Large woomeras		tyin
Canegrass spears		kurum

NUMERAL classifiers and RELATIONAL classifiers coexist in numerous Micronesian languages. Mokilese has four numeral classifier suffixes and around fourteen relational classifiers which are independent nouns (Harrison 1976: 95, 128–31)—see Table 8.2. Relational classifiers are chosen according to the way the possessed noun is 'possessed', or handled by the possessor, and also according to the properties of possessed nouns. Thus, they share the properties of relational and possessed classifiers (see §5.5.1).

Ponapean (Micronesian: Rehg 1981; Carlson and Payne 1989) has around thirty numeral classifiers; there are also relational classifiers. Numeral classifiers are used to categorize objects in term of their form and shape; relational classifiers combine the reference to the way in which items can be possessed, and to their functional properties. Twenty-two

TABLE 8.2. *Classifiers in Mokilese*

Semantics	Numeral classifier	Relational classifier
Animate	-*men*	
Long objects	-*pas*	
Things which have pieces, parts	-*kij*	
General	-*w*	*ah*
valuable, child, pet		*nah*
Food		*kanah*
Drink		*nimah*
Chaw		*ngidah*
Vehicle		*warah*
House		*imwah*
Garland		*mwarah*
Ear decoration		*dapah*
Earring		*siah*
Mat		*kiah*
Land		*japwah*
Sheet		*upah*
Pillow		*wilingah*

relational classifiers are used in the 'common' speech register, while the 'honorific' and the 'humiliative' registers employ fewer classifiers (Keating 1997; see §10.5). No such distinctions are found in numeral classifiers in this language.

Truquese (Micronesian: Benton 1968) has a virtually open class of relational classifiers, which combine properties of possessed classifiers (see examples 5.48, 5.49: §5.5.1). It also has a large inventory of numeral classifiers, some of which are also repeaters (example 4.24).

NOUN CLASSIFIERS coexist with NUMERAL CLASSIFIERS in Akatek (Kanjobal Mayan) and in Minangkabau (Western Austronesian). Akatek has two sets of numeral classifiers: a small closed set of affixed classifiers and a larger set of numeral classifiers as independent lexemes (see examples 4.31–4, and §4.3.2 on the difference between the two types). Akatek also has fourteen noun classifiers (see example 4.31, and also 3.10 and 3.11): see Tables 8.3 and 8.4 (Zavala 1992: 131, 140, 152). The sets of numeral and noun classifiers show a partial semantic overlap. Affixed numeral classifiers characterize the noun in terms of humanness and animacy; independent numeral classifiers characterize the noun with respect to its shape, size, and form. Noun classifiers categorize the nouns in terms of what generic class it belongs to.

Akatek also has a morphological opposition human vs. the rest realized in the plural marker, *eb'*, used to mark human plurals, shown in 8.1 (Zavala 1992: 119). This marker cannot be used with a non-human referent, cf. 8.2.

188 Classifiers

TABLE 8.3. *Numeral classifiers in Akatek*

Semantics of classifiers	Affixed numeral classifiers	Independent numeral classifiers
Human	-wan	
Non-human animate	-k'on	
Inanimate	-eb'	
Long vertical		wa?an
Separate		k'itan
Curved		kupan
Round		šoyan
Big flat		patšan
Extended		xenan
Round three-dimensional		k'olan
Small round three-dimensional		b'ilan
Big round or oval three-dimensional		pilan
Round two- or three-dimensional		šilan
Short three-dimensional		xilan

TABLE 8.4. *Noun classifiers in Akatek*

Semantics	Noun classifier	Noun from which it is derived
Man	nax	winax
Woman	?iš	?iš
Human, known	k'o	?
Human, appreciative	yab'	?
Animal	no?	no?
Wood	te?	te?
Stone	tš'en	tš'een
Maize	(?i)šim	?išim
Kind of rope	tš'an	tš'an
Earth	tš'otš'	tšootš'
Salt	(?a)ts'am	?ats'am
Water	(x)a?	xa?
Plant	?an	?
Fire	q'a?/k'a?	q'a?

8.1. xa?-Ø   eb'   nax   winax
    ACTUALIZER-ABS   PL:HUMAN   NCL:MAN   man
    'There are the men.'

8.2. xa?-Ø   no?   tšee
    ACTUALIZER-ABS   NCL:ANIMAL   horse
    'There are/is horse(s).'

This human vs. non-human distinction in the plural marker in Akatek is reminiscent of noun classes. (It will be shown in §10.1 that it is typologically unusual for a language to have more noun class-like distinctions in non-singular numbers than in the singular; cf. Croft 1990: 214–16.) The distinction between human and non-human nouns in Akatek is reminiscent of languages like Chinantec (see B), which combine numeral classifiers, noun classifiers, and noun classes. Unlike Akatek, Chinantec has a much more regular animacy agreement in adjectives.

Minangkabau (Western Austronesian: Marnita 1996) has noun classifiers and just one set of numeral classifiers. Any noun with generic semantics can be used as a noun classifier to accompany a specific noun (see §3.3). Numeral classifiers are a closed class. Both numeral classifiers and noun classifiers come from independent nouns. The differences between the two types of classifier involve the following:

(i) semantics, especially of the same morphemes used as noun classifiers and as numeral classifiers;

(ii) the use of different noun classifiers and numeral classifiers for nouns of the same semantic group;

(iii) morphosyntactic behaviour;

(iv) obligatoriness.

(A1) Semantics Numeral classifiers have the semantic oppositions shown in Diagram 8.1 with reference to animacy, humanness, and form and shape for inanimate nouns.

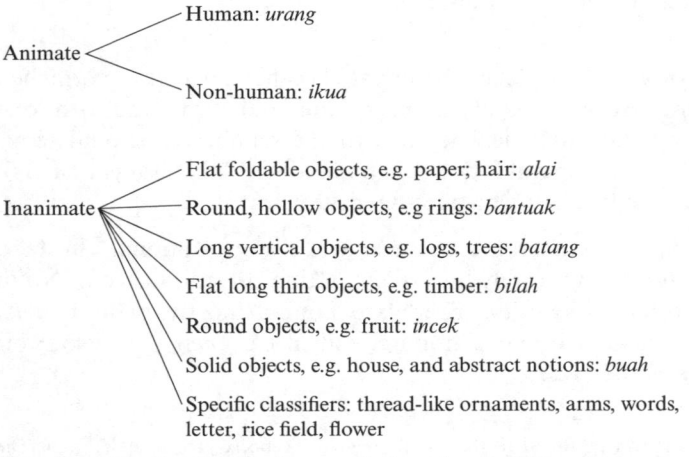

```
                    ┌─ Human: urang
       Animate ─────┤
                    └─ Non-human: ikua


                    ┌─ Flat foldable objects, e.g. paper; hair: alai
                    ├─ Round, hollow objects, e.g rings: bantuak
                    ├─ Long vertical objects, e.g. logs, trees: batang
       Inanimate ───┤─ Flat long thin objects, e.g. timber: bilah
                    ├─ Round objects, e.g. fruit: incek
                    ├─ Solid objects, e.g. house, and abstract notions: buah
                    └─ Specific classifiers: thread-like ornaments, arms, words,
                       letter, rice field, flower
```

DIAGRAM 8.1. *Semantics of numeral classifiers in Minangkabau*

Noun classifiers are generic nouns; unlike numeral classifiers, they signal that the referent of a noun belongs to a certain class of objects, e.g. *buruang* 'bird', *ula* 'snake', *ikan* 'fish', *kayu* 'wood', e.g. *ikan hiu* (NOUN.CL:FISH shark) 'a shark', *kayu candano* (NOUN.CL:WOOD cendana) 'cendana tree'. A few morphemes can be used both as numeral classifiers and as noun classifiers, with a difference in meaning. *Batang*, when used as a noun classifier, means 'trees as a class'. As a numeral classifier, it is used to refer to long vertical objects, e.g. trees. As an independent noun, it means 'tree trunk'. A numeral classifier and a noun classifier can cooccur in one noun phrase, and will have different meanings, as in 8.3 (= 3.16).

8.3. sa-batang   batang   pisang
     one-NUM.CL:LONG.VERT   NOUN.CL:TREE   banana
     'one banana tree'[2]

(A2) The use of different noun classifiers and numeral classifiers for nouns of the same semantic group Nouns of a given semantic group may take different noun classifiers and numeral classifiers. Names of flowers take *bungo* 'flower' as a generic noun classifier. The specific numeral classifier for flowers is *tangkai*, e.g.

8.4. sa-tangkai   bungo
     one-NUM.CL:FLOWER   flower
     'one flower'

A specific name of a flower can be added, as in 8.5.

8.5. sa-tangkai   bungo   ros
     one-NUM.CL:FLOWER   flower   rose
     'one rose'

(A3) Morphosyntactic behaviour Numeral classifiers, which are attached to numerals, are used with small numbers, 'one' and 'two', and form one phonological and morphological word with the number (a special semi-suppletive form *sa* of numeral 'one', *satu*, is used with numeral classifiers). Noun classifiers are independent phonological words.

(A4) Obligatoriness Numeral classifiers are always optional; in fact, young people nowadays rarely use them (Rina Marnita, p.c.). Noun classifiers are often obligatory. There are nouns (mostly plant names) which cannot be used without a noun classifier, e.g. *bungo ros* (NOUN.CL: FLOWER) 'a rose', **ros* 'rose'.

---

[2] Similar examples can be found in the closely related Acehnese (Durie 1985; p.c.). The homophonous noun classifier *boh* 'fruit, egg' and numeral classifier *boh* 'generic' can cooccur within one noun phrase, but their semantics is different, e.g. *dua boh boh mamplam* (two NUM.CL:GENERIC NOUN.CL:FRUIT mango) 'two mangoes'.

RELATIONAL CLASSIFIERS may be distinct from another set of classifiers used in several different environments. This is the case in Kilivila (see §9.1). Relational classifiers in this language are exemplified in 5.36–8.

NOUN CLASSES can be distinct from another set of classifiers which occurs in several environments. Then they can usually cooccur—see the examples from Anindilyakwa (Australian: Sands 1995: 277; Leeding 1989) and Machiguenga (Campa, Peruvian Arawak: Shepard 1997) in §8.3 below.

DEICTIC CLASSIFIERS and POSSESSED CLASSIFIERS coexist in Toba (Guaicuruan). The deictic classifiers (see (B) in §7.3.1) combine information about the shape and the position of a referent noun, and there is one possessed classifier (*lo* 'animal possession') (see (B) in §5.2). Cora combines possessed classifiers ((A) in §5.2) with classificatory verbs (see (A) in §6.2.3).

(B) Three sets of classifiers

Three distinct sets of classifiers are comparatively rare in the languages of the world.

NUMERAL and NOUN CLASSIFIERS coexist in Chinantec languages (Mexico) together with NOUN CLASSES. In Sochiapan Chinantec (Foris 1993: 256 ff.) numeral classifiers and noun classifiers are independent words. There are ten noun classifiers which refer to sex and shape; there are also two diminutive classifiers and one classifier with the meaning 'old, disused'. Some of these derive from independent nouns. There are several dozen numeral classifiers (Foris 1993: 255, 314–21). Numeral and noun classifiers can cooccur in a noun phrase, as in 8.6.

8.6. hñá³   mái̵³   (mi̵³)   jlái̵²
     five   NUM.CL:SPHERE   (NOUN.CL:SPHERICAL)   egg
     'five eggs'³

In examples like 8.6, the noun classifier can be omitted; the numeral classifier is obligatory. Chinantec languages also distinguish animate and inanimate noun classes; this distinction is realized in agreement with modifiers and with predicates. It is illustrated in the following examples (Foris 1993: 280–1). Agreeing adjectives are underlined.

8.7. tiá²   ñí¹-ñí¹tsi̵n²¹   jná¹³   tsa³cuá¹   jli̵nh¹   ni̵²
     not   INT-mount+TA+1sg   I   horse   wet+AN   that
     'I don't want to mount that wet horse.'

8.8. tiá²   ré²   cau³²   cuo¹   jli̵h²¹
     not   well   burn+PRES firewood wet+INAN
     'Wet firewood does not burn well.'

---

[3] Here, and in other examples from Chinantec, numbers stand for tones.

NOUN CLASSES coexist with NOUN CLASSIFIERS and POSSESSED CLASSIFIERS in 'Dongo-ko (Mba, Ubangi branch of Niger-Congo: Pasch 1985). Possessed classifiers in 'Dongo-ko were illustrated in 5.10 and 5.11. Alongside ten possessed classifiers, 'Dongo-ko also has nine noun classes and nine noun classifiers (Pasch 1985: 70 ff.). These have the same semantics, but differ in form and in syntactic conditions of use. A noun can belong to a noun class which is distinct from the noun classifier it takes. In 5.10, $\beta\grave{\imath}$-$g\acute{o}$ 'leopard' has a class 7 noun class; it shows agreement with a possessive marker in noun class 1a: $\emptyset$-$\acute{a}$ 'CL1-poss'. Difference in form between a noun classifier and a noun class marker is illustrated in 8.9.

8.9. ɓì-wó   w-í   rɛ̀
      arm-NCL1   CL1-POSS   1SG
      'my arm'

Dâw (Makú: Martins 1994) has three distinct sets of classifiers: POSSESSOR CLASSIFIERS, LOCATIVE CLASSIFIERS, and NOUN CLASSIFIERS. They differ in form and semantics.

Dâw has two possessor classifiers: -dee' is used for inanimate possessor, and -ēj for animate possessor (see examples 5.45 and 5.46 in §5.4; Martins 1994: 138–41). There are also locative classifiers (Martins 1994: 53ff.) which categorize nouns with respect to their physical properties, and animacy (see examples 7.5 and 7.6 in §7.2). Dâw also has an open class of noun classifiers. They are independent lexemes; apparently, any noun with a generic reference can be used as a noun classifier (Martins 1994: 51; see example 3.5 in §3.2.3).

Possessor and locative classifiers are obligatory. Noun classifiers are optional; they can be omitted if the referent has been established in the previous discourse. Also, unlike possessor and locative classifiers, they are often employed for referent tracking in discourse.

Baniwa (North Arawak; Aikhenvald 1996c) has at least three distinct sets of classifiers. One of them is the 'pronominal' noun class, used in verbal cross-referencing and with deictics (see 2.1; §2.7.1; and (E) in §2.4.2). There are also relational classifiers (see §5.5.2). Yet another set of classifiers is used with numerals, verbs and in possessive constructions; there are also noun class markers some of which are different from all these sets, and some which are not (see Table 9.5). Depending on the interpretation of noun class markers in Baniwa, this language can be said to have three or four sets of classifiers (see §9.3.1).

(C) Four or more sets of classifiers

Palikur (North Arawak: Aikhenvald and Green 1998) has the world's richest system of noun classification devices. Palikur has genders (with two or three agreement forms depending on the construction type), and the following classifier types: numeral classifiers; verbal classifiers with two subtypes—the ones used with stative verbs and the ones used with transitive verbs (discussed in §6.4.1—see Diagram 6.1); locative classifiers (§7.2, Diagram 7.1); and possessive classifiers (which combine properties of relational and of possessed classifiers: see §5.5.1). Only numeral classifiers, the two subtypes of verbal classifier, and locative classifiers show some similarities—i.e. the same forms are used in some instances. There is a significant overlap between the inventories of verbal and locative classifiers, and some overlap with numeral classifiers: see Table 8.5 (further details are in Aikhenvald and Green 1998).

Genders and possessive classifiers are completely independent. The possessive classifiers in Palikur are -*pig* 'pet' used with domesticated animals, -*win* used with animals that are caught to eat, and -*kamkayh* 'child' used with children, e.g. *nu-kamkayh awayg* (1sg-child man) 'my son' (see §5.5.1). Gender in Palikur is realized through agreement of the head-modifier kind, and also of the predicate-argument kind. Typically for an Amazonian language, gender is usually not marked on the head noun itself. Gender agreement is obligatory and every noun has a fixed gender.

TABLE 8.5. *Numeral, verbal and locative classifiers in Palikur*

Semantics	Numeral classifiers	Verbal classifiers		Locative classifiers
		With stative verbs	With transitive verbs	
Animate	-*p*	-*pit*	-*pit*	-*pit*
Round, square	-*ul-so*	-*pit*	-*pit*	-*pit*
Irregular shape	-*al-sa*	-*pit*	-*pit*	-*pit*
Side	-*al-sa*	-*muh*	-*muh*	-*pit*
Vertical objects	-*tl-ta-*	-*min*	-*min*	-*min*
Rigid, thin	-*tl-ta-*	-*ah*	-*min*	-*min*
Flat	-*kl-ka-/-bu*	-*boha*	-*bo*	-*madka*
Concave; numeral classifier: metal	-*mkul-muk*	-*apa*	-*ap*	-*madka*
Edge	-*mkul-muk*	-*kiya*	-*kig*	-*kigbi(-mna)*
Pointed	-*mkul-muk*	-*kisa*	-*kig*	-*kigsa*
Linear; numeral classifier: long and extended	-*tral-tahr-/-bu*	-*buka*	-*buk*	-*buhku(-mna)*
Road, river	-*tral-tahr-/-bu*	-*buka*	-*buk*	-*vigku*
The inside part of; NUM.CL: extended with boundaries	-*ikul-rik*	-*eku*	-*ik*	-*iku*
Tree, plant, trunk	-*ktil-kat*	-*kat*	-*min* 'vertical'	-*pew*
Tree, branch-like	-*ktil-kat*	-*pewa*	-*peru*	-*peru*
Water	—	-*pit*	-*pit*	-*hakwa*

194 Classifiers

Three gender agreement forms (masculine, feminine, and neuter) occur on demonstratives in head-modifier constructions (see Table 8.6); they are also found in predicate-argument constructions on third person cross-referencing affixes, and on independent pronouns.

TABLE 8.6. *Demonstratives in Palikur (singular)*

	In speaker's hand	Near to speaker and to hearer	Far from speaker and near hearer or vice versa	Far from both, visible	Very far from both, not visible
Masc.	ner	ner	nop	netra	nere
Fem.	no	no	nop	notra	nore
Neut.	inin	ini	nop	inetra	inere

Two gender agreement forms (feminine, and masculine-neuter or non-feminine) are found with a number of verbal suffixes in predicate-argument agreement with the subject (A/S) and in head-modifier agreement if a modifier is a stative verb. These 'gender-sensitive' suffixes are shown in Table 8.7. For a few individual lexical items gender agreement is realized via internal vowel change (*o* 'feminine'; *e* or *a* 'masculine/neuter').

TABLE 8.7. *Gender marking on verbs in Palikur*

	Masculine/neuter (NF)	Feminine (F)
Continuative	-ne	-no
Continuative prolonged	-nene	-nano
Non-completed frustrated action	-pa-ri	-pa-ru
Inchoative	-pi-ye	-pi-yo
Durative	-ye	-yo
Individual lexical items	miyap 'he/it dies'	miyop 'she dies'
	nemnik 'approach'	nomnik 'approach'
	nawenewa 'different'	nawenowa 'different'

The coexisting systems of noun categorization devices in Palikur differ on a number of points, but they also have some properties in common. These properties are summarized and contrasted in Table 8.8.

The differences between the classifiers in Palikur are discussed below.

(I) Morphological form

Noun categorization devices in Palikur differ in morphological complexity. Genders have two or three agreement forms depending on the type of construction they are used in. There are also a few morphologically

TABLE 8.8. *Properties of classifiers and genders in Palikur*

		Genders	Numeral classifiers	Verbal classifiers (2 sets)	Locative classifiers	Possessive classifiers
A	Different morphological forms depending on construction type	yes	no	no	no	no
	Different morphological forms depending on classifier	no	yes	no	no	no
	Formal overlap with other noun classification devices	no	partly yes	yes	yes	no
	Irregular forms	yes	yes	no	no	no
	Bound morphemes:	yes	yes	yes	no	no
	Prefixes, suffixes, infixes	prefixes, suffixes, infixes	suffixes, infixes	suffixes	–	–
	Derivational functions	(limited)	no	(limited)	yes	no
B	Every noun 'classified'	yes	yes	yes	yes	no
	Obligatory use	yes	yes	no	yes	yes
C	Cooccurrence with other noun classification devices in one morphological word	yes	no	yes	yes	no

irregular gender forms. Numeral classifiers fall into several subgroups depending on what numbers they are used with. Some are used just with number 'one', e.g. *-imku* 'classifier for wrapped objects'; some with numbers 'one' and 'two', e.g. classifier *-t* 'vertical objects'; and some with other numbers as well, e.g. *-mku/-muk* 'classifier for concave objects'. Unlike gender systems, restrictions on the number of forms a numeral classifier has are idiosyncratic for each particular classifier. Several numeral classifiers have suppletive forms, e.g. the classifier for irregular-shaped objects is *-a* with number 'one', and *-sa* with 'two' (Aikhenvald and Green 1998).

Classifiers of other types do not have variant forms, or show any morphological irregularities.

Classifiers differ in their morphological status. Verbal and numeral classifiers are bound morphemes. Numeral classifiers may be suffixes, or infixes (to number 'two'). Verbal classifiers are suffixes. Gender markers can be suffixes, or prefixes, or infixes. Possessive and locative classifiers are independent morphemes.

Locative classifiers are used as derivational suffixes, while genders and verbal classifiers have limited use as derivational markers. Other classifiers are not used this way.

(II) Function and usage

Not all noun classification devices in Palikur—including gender and possessive classifiers—have to cooccur with an overt NP, that is they can be used anaphorically. All of them allow variable classification of nouns depending on which shape characteristic is in focus. This shows that classifiers are not semantically redundant; they add information to the noun (cf. Denny 1986; Downing 1996: 93).

Every noun in Palikur is assigned a gender, or a numeral, verbal, or locative classifier. Only some nouns are assigned a possessive classifier.

The use of gender, numeral classifiers, possessive classifiers, and locative classifiers are obligatory, while whether verbal classifiers are employed or not depends on whether the S, or the O constituent is completely involved in the action (see §6.4.1).

(III) Cooccurrence with other noun categorization devices

Gender marking can cooccur with verbal classifiers and with locative classifiers, in one morphological word. It does not cooccur with possessive classifiers, or with numeral classifiers (since there is a gender distinction in numeral classifiers—however, this applies only to animate nouns and is more semantically transparent). This is discussed in §8.3.

Table 8.9 summarizes the semantic, pragmatic and functional properties of noun classification devices in Palikur. It also shows their different origins.

TABLE 8.9. *Semantic and functional properties and origin of classifiers in Palikur*

Classifier	Function	Scope	Semantics	Pragmatic effect	Origin
Genders	Head-modifier agreement in NP A/S agreement in clause	NP: three genders with pronouns and demonstratives; two genders with stative verbs as modifiers Outside NP (two genders)	Animacy, physical properties	–	Deictic/3rd person enclitic: Proto-Arawak
Numeral classifiers	Quantification, enumeration	NP	Animacy, physical properties, nature	–	
Verbal classifiers with transitive verbs and verbal classifiers with stative verbs	O/S agreement	Clause	Physical properties, parts of objects	Complete involvement or topicality/contrast of O/S	Some come from nouns, e.g. body parts
Locative classifiers	Location	NP	Physical properties, 'typical' locations	–	
Possessive classifiers	Possession	NP	Function, way of handling	–	Generic nouns

Thus, Palikur can be said to have five distinct sets of classifiers.[4] We have no explanation so far as to why this language has such a uniqely complicated system.[5]

8.3. Different classifier sets in the same environment

If a language has several classifier sets which cooccur in the same environment one of these is always noun classes. This is due to the fact that only noun classes can have scope over a noun phrase, and/or over a whole clause.

In a few languages which have both NOUN CLASSES and NUMERAL CLASSIFIERS both can be marked on numeral modifiers. This is the case in Achagua, a North Arawak language spoken in Venezuela (Wilson 1992: 61–3). Achagua distinguishes two genders—feminine and non-feminine. The gender agreement is obligatory in verb-argument constructions and in head-modifier constructions, e.g. *áuli máanu-i* (dog big-SG.MASC) 'a big dog'. There are also twelve numeral classifiers, used with numbers from one to three (such as 'recipient', 'wide objects', 'long and thin objects', 'round objects', 'humans' etc.), e.g. 8.10.

8.10. áaba-hiza   káasta
     one-CL:LONG.THIN paper
     'one sheet of paper'

If a number is used with an animate noun, it takes both a classifier and a gender marker, as in 8.11. There is no special 'inanimate' classifier; classifier for mammals, -*na*-, is the only one to cooccur with gender markers.

8.11. áaba-na-i   áuli
     one-CL:MAMMAL-SG.MASC   dog
     'one (male) dog'

Palikur also has an obligatory 'double marking'—of animacy and of gender—on the cardinal numbers 'one' and 'two' when they accompany an

---

[4] Diana Green reports that the modern Palikur tell that they have descended from eight groups which came to live together. We may hypothesize that this unusual system could have emerged as the result of different areal influence, and probably language mixing. For instance, locative classifiers and classifiers in possessive constructions are reminiscent of those found in neighbouring Carib languages. Bearing in mind long-term (and none too peaceful) contacts of Palikurs with Carib peoples, one may hypothesize that these classifiers could have been acquired as the result of the Carib influence. Genders are of the Arawak origin (Aikhenvald 1999a).

[5] Kadiweu (Guaicuruan: Griffiths and Griffiths 1976: 111–12) can be said to have distinct sets of noun classes, numeral classifiers, relational classifiers, locative classifiers and deictic classifiers; Sândalo (1996) provides a different interpretation.

animate head noun. Palikur has around eighteen numeral classifiers and three genders (masculine, feminine, and neuter) marked on adjectives and demonstratives as modifiers, and on the verb. The assignment of gender when governing agreement on cardinal numerals is much more semantically transparent than the assignment of gender in other environments: it is predominantly sex-based: males (including 'mythological' males such as heavenly bodies, e.g. sun, moon) belong to the masculine gender, and females belong to the feminine gender. There is no marking for gender on classifiers used with inanimate nouns (gender assignment to inanimates in Palikur is semantically very complex: see Aikhenvald and Green 1998).

The way gender agreement operates on numeral classifiers used with animate masculine and feminine nouns is illustrated in 8.12 and 8.13.

8.12. no   paha-p-ru   tino
      this:F   one-NUM.CL:ANIM-F   woman
      'one woman'

8.13. ner   paha-p-ri   awayg
      this:M   one-NUM.CL:ANIM-M   man
      'one man'

An inanimate head noun cannot trigger gender agreement on numeral classifiers, even though it may agree in gender with a demonstrative or a predicate. The noun 'path' has neuter gender (shown in the form of the demonstrative 'this'). There is no gender agreement on the numeral. That is, there is a generic 'animate' classifier, -p; but there is no generic inanimate form.

8.14. ini   paha-tra   ahin
      this:NEUT one-NUM.CL:EXTENDED   path
      'one path'

The noun *warik* 'river' is feminine. Example 8.15 shows how this noun does not take a gender agreement marker with a numeral because it is inanimate.

8.15. no   paha-tra   warik
      this:F   one-NUM.CL:EXTENDED   river
      'one river'

Machiguenga (Peruvian Arawak: Derbyshire and Payne 1990; Wise 1986; Shepard 1997) distinguishes 'masculine' and 'feminine' genders in verbal cross-referencing. The feminine gender is assigned to females and most inanimate objects, while animates are assigned the masculine gender. In addition, the sun, the moon, lightning, stars, rainbows, and other salient natural phenomena are also treated as 'masculine'. There is also a large system of classifiers used with verbs and with numerals (see §9.1), the choice of which is based on the shape and animacy of the referent noun. Unlike Achagua and Palikur, gender specification on numerals obligatorily cooccurs with a numeral classifier. This is illustrated with 8.16 and 8.17 (Shepard 1997: 35–6). (Note that numeral 'one' is a discontinuous morpheme: the classifiers are infixed.)

8.16. pa-poa-t-iro   sekatsi
      one-CL:CYLINDRICAL.OBJECT-INAN-one   manioc.plant
      'one manioc plant'

8.17. pa-poa-n-iro   parari
      one-CL:CYLINDRICAL.OBJECT-AN-one   river.otter
      'one river otter'

NOUN CLASSES and VERBAL CLASSIFIERS coexist in a number of the Australian languages of Arnhem Land. Nunggubuyu (Heath 1984) and Gunbarlang (Coleman 1982) have five noun classes, and also verbal classifiers. In Gunbarlang, the noun classes have the following semantics:

Class 1: males and items associated with males.

Class 1: females and items associated with females.

Class 3: plants and plant parts, fire, implements not associated with men, prepared or cooked food, some body parts.

Class 4: non-living things associated with the landscape, bodily excretions, places, and abstract nouns.

Class 5: some body parts.

Verbal classifiers categorize the S/O constituent in terms of its shape and function. The following example from Gunbarlang shows a verbal classifier cooccurring with a noun class marker on a verb:

8.18. balangit   na-njambi-buleŋ
      blanket   NCL1-CL:CLOTH-dry
      'The blanket is dry.'

In Anindilyakwa (Australian) A, S, and O are obligatorily cross-referenced for noun class on each verb. The use of verbal classifiers, to characterize the S/O constituent, is optional (Leeding 1989; Sands 1995: 276 ff.).[6] In Tiwi (Australian: Osborne 1974: 38; 46–50) the two genders, masculine and feminine, are cross-referenced on the verb (only subject forms of non-imperative verbs distinguish two genders). There are also verbal classifiers

---

[6] Some languages use noun class prefixes on modifiers, and verbal classifiers with verbs (Evans ms).

which mark agreement with the S or O constituent (6.3 and 6.4). Verbal classifiers (or classificatory noun-incorporation) also coexist with noun class cross-referencing on verbs in Iroquoian and Caddoan languages (Mithun 1984: 864–8). And in Palikur, gender marking on the verb can cooccur with verbal classifiers (see 6.29).

Verbal classifiers and predicate-argument agreement in pronominal noun classes also coexist in a few Lowland Amazonian languages. In Baniwa and Tariana, predicate-argument agreement in pronominal noun classes is found with the A/S_a constituent and—only in Baniwa—with O/S_o; the agreement in verbal classifier is restricted to very few grammatical constructions; it is always with the subject in Tariana, while in Baniwa it may be with either subject or object (see Aikhenvald 1995b). In Baniwa, NOUN CLASSES (obligatorily marked in possessive cross-referencing prefixes) co-occur with RELATIONAL CLASSIFIERS (see ex. 5.51 and 5.52). NOUN CLASSES (cross-referencing the argument of an adposition) can cooccur with LOCATIVE classifiers in Lokono (Arawak: Pet 1987) and Palikur (7.3 and 7.4).

A number of languages employ the same, or almost the same, set of morphemes in different classifier environments, and also possess a small system of 'pronominal' genders marked in verbal cross-referencing and often also on demonstratives (see Chapter 9); they often cooccur. The following example, from Baniwa (Arawak), shows a possessive construction which contains a 3rd person feminine cross-referencing marker and also a classifier suffix, -da 'round objects', used as a possessed classifier:

8.19. tʃinu inaʒu-da   ʒu-dza-da
      dog   woman-ROUND   3SGF-POSS-CL:ROUND
      'A female dog is hers.' (or 'She has a female dog.')

8.4. Conclusions

Several types of classifier—which represent different focal points on the continuum of noun categorization devices—can coexist in one language. In languages with a number of different sets of classifiers in varying morphosyntactic environments, these can differ in their grammatical properties. Thus, noun classifiers are optional in Wardaman and Ngan'gityemerri, but noun class marking is obligatory (cf. Reid 1997). Noun classifiers are optional and numeral classifiers are obligatory in Sochiapan Chinantec. In Palikur, verbal classifiers are optional, but classifiers of other types and noun classes are obligatory.

The attested combinations of different sets of classifiers in different environments are shown in Table 8.10. Table 8.11 shows the attested combinations of different classifiers in the same environment.

TABLE 8.10. *Different classifier sets in different environments in one language*

Noun classes	Numeral	Noun cl	Verbal	Relational	Possessor	Possessed	Locative	Deictic	Examples of languages
x	y	–	–	–	–	–	–	–	Dravidian, Indic, Arawak
x	–	y	–	–	–	–	–	–	Wardaman, Ngan'gityemerri
–	x	–	–	y	–	–	–	–	Ponapean, Mokilese, Truquese
–	x	y	–	–	–	–	–	–	Kanjobal, Minangkabau
–	–	–	x	–	–	y	–	–	Cora
–	–	–	–	–	–	y	–	z	Toba
x	y	z	–	–	–	–	–	–	Chinantec
x	–	y	–	–	y	z	–	–	'Dongo-ko
–	–	x	–	–	–	–	z	–	Dâw
x, y	z	z	z	u	–	z	–	y	Baniwa
x, y	z	–	u	–	–	–	v	y	Palikur

Different letters (x, y, z, u, v) refer to the different classifier sets.

TABLE 8.11. *Different classifier sets in the same environment in one language*

Noun classes	Numeral classifiers	Verbal classifiers	Relational classifiers	Locative classifiers	Examples of languages
x	x				Palikur, Achagua, Machiguenga
x		x			Gunbarlang, Nunggubuyu, Anindilyakwa, Iroquoian, Caddoan
x			x		Baniwa
x				x	Palikur, Lokono

Different Classifiers in One Language   203

No language has been found which has seven distinct sets of classifiers corresponding to all the types of classifiers outlined in Chapters 2–7. The largest number of formally different sets of classifiers is found in Palikur (North Arawak); only some of the functionally different classifiers are identical in their semantics and in their origin.

9 Multiple Classifier Languages

The same, or almost the same, set of morphemes can be used in more than one classifier environment. These morphemes may have different grammatical properties, or be more or less obligatory depending on what classifier environment they are in. We label them 'multiple classifier' systems. Noun categorization in multiple classifier languages is discussed in §9.1. In §9.2 the multiple classifier systems are compared with noun class agreement on different targets. In §9.3 we discuss some borderline cases.

9.1. Noun categorization in multiple classifier languages

The same set of classifier morphemes can be used in up to six different morphosyntactic environments. An example of the same classifier morphemes used with a numeral, with a deictic, and with an adjective is 9.1, from Kilivila (Austronesian, Trobriand Islands: Senft 1996: 18). Classifiers are prefixed to the numeral and to the adjective, and infixed to the demonstrative.

9.1. ke-yu   waga   ma-ke-si-na
     CL:WOODEN-two canoe this-CL:WOODEN-PL-this
     ke-manabweta   (le-kota-si)
     CL:WOODEN-beautiful   (3P.PAST-arrive-PL)
     'These two beautiful canoes (arrived).'

In 9.2, from Tariana (North Arawak), the classifier *-dapana* 'HOUSE', is used with a demonstrative, a numeral, a possessive, an adjective, and the predicate; it also appears as a part of the head noun 'hospital' itself as a derivational suffix.

9.2. ha-dapana   pa-dapana   na-tape-dapana
     DEM:INAN-CL:HOUSE   one-CL:HOUSE   3PL-medicine-CL:HOUSE
     na-ya-dapana   hanu-dapana   heku
     3PL-POSS-CL:HOUSE   big-CL:HOUSE   wood
     na-ni-ni-dapana-mahka
     3pl-make-TOPIC.ADVANCING.VOICE-CL:HOUSE-RECENT.PAST.NON.VISUAL
     'This one big hospital of theirs has been made of wood.'

Systems of this kind are attested in numerous South American languages (e.g. Arawak, Tucano, Guahibo, Tupí, Yagua, Nambiquara), in some

Papuan languages, and in some Austronesian languages, as well as in a number of the languages of East and Southeast Asia such as Chinese, Thai, Vietnamese, or Hmong.

The same classifier morphemes in different environments can differ in their realization and in at least some syntactic properties. In some cases it is possible to decide that one environment is the 'primary' one. If there is no reason to take one classifier environment as primary and the others as secondary, we say that this is just a 'multiple classifier' language.

Languages of agglutinating and isolating profiles tend to use the same morphemes in several classifier environments more often than do fusional languages. There are several restrictions on what classifier environments can be marked with the same morpheme.

(i) If a morpheme is used as a RELATIONAL classifier, it is never used in any other classifier environment (except for the large systems of classifiers which combine the properties of relational and possessed classifiers discussed in §5.5.1).

(ii) If classifiers of any type are fused with the head noun, or with a modifier, they cannot be used in multiple classifier environments. For instance, suppletive classificatory verbs in Athabaskan languages are never used as another type of classifier; in contrast, an affixed verbal classifier (the so-called 'areal prefix') can be used as a locative classifier in some North Athabaskan languages (§6.4.2). Similarly, numeral classifiers which are fused with a numeral in Squamish are not used in other classifier environments. In Nauru (Micronesian) numeral classifiers are fused with demonstratives, and are not employed in any other classifier environment.

(iii) If a language has more than one subtype of a certain type of classifier, it is likely that only one of these may be used in (one or more) other classifier environment(s). Thus, in languages of the Arawak family which have two noun class systems: one for pronouns, and the other for modifiers of other kinds, only the latter is also used in other classifier environments, such as numeral and verbal classifiers. 'Pronominal' genders are never used in other classifier environments (see Table 2.10, §2.7.1).

(iv) There is a correlation between the size of a classifier system, and the likelihood that it will be used in more than one classifier environment. Larger classifier systems tend to be used in more than one environment; such is the case in a few languages of East Asia, such as Chinese, and the Arawak and Tucano families, as well as in such languages as Munduruku and Yagua, of South America. In languages with two noun class systems (§2.7), the larger one tends to be used in other classifier environments; this happens in numerous South American languages.

However, this is by no means true for all languages. Nivkh (Paleosiberian isolate) and Malto (South Dravidian) have largeish systems of numeral classifiers used just in this environment. Hmong has only seven classifiers employed with numerals, and these are also used with demonstratives and in possessive constructions; the same morphemes are also employed as noun classifiers. In Eyak (Eyak-Athabaskan) a small set of classifiers is used as locative and as verbal classifiers.

The maximum number of classifier environments for one set of morphemes established so far is five. Combinations of different classifier environments for one set of morphemes are shown in Table 9.1.

In some of these languages the same classifiers can display differences in their properties when used in different environments. These differences may concern the type of morpheme (e.g. the same morphemes can be infixed in some classifier environments, and suffixed in others), obligatoriness of use, and other characteristics. Examples of different multiple classifier languages are discussed under (A–D). Further functions of classifiers in multiple classifier languages as derivational affixes and nominalizers are discussed in (E). The use of repeaters in multiple classifier languages is discussed in (F). Some conclusions and generalizations are given in (G). The question of whether one classifier environment can be considered 'primary' is dealt with under (H).

(A) One set of morphemes in two environments

The same classifier morphemes are often used with numerals and with demonstratives.[1] This is found in many languages of East and Southeast Asia including Mandarin Chinese (Li and Thompson 1981: 104, 112). 9.3 shows classifier *ge* in a numeral phrase; 9.4 shows the same classifier in a demonstrative phrase.

9.3. sān   ge   rén
     three CL   person
     'three people'

9.4. nèi-ge   cài
     that-CL   course of food
     'that course of food'

A demonstrative can cooccur with a numeral in a classifier construction, and there is then also one occurrence of the classifier, e.g. 9.5.

---

[1] Cf. Craig (forthcoming: 24): 'this type (numeral) of classifiers may also appear on other elements than numerals, i.e. . . . demonstratives.'

TABLE 9.1. *Same set of classifiers in several environments (A–D)*

	Adjectival modifier	Numeral classifier	Noun classifier	Verbal classifier	Possessed classifier	Locative classifier	Deictic classifier	Examples of languages
A	–	x	–	–	–	–	x	Mandarin Chinese
	–	x	–	x	–	–	–	Chayahuita, Anindilyakwa
	–	–	–	x	–	x	–	Eyak, Koyukon
	x	–	–	x	–	–	–	Terêna, Yawalapiti
B	x	x	–	–	–	–	x	Kilivila
	–	x	x	–	–	–	x	Vietnamese, Awará
	–	x	–	–	x	–	x	Nung
	x	x	–	–	–	–	x	Newari
	x	x	–	x	–	–	–	Waurá, Ignaciano, Machiguenga
C	x	x	x	–	–	–	x	Thai
	x	x	–	–	x	–	x	Cantonese, Dulong-Rawang
	–	x	x	–	x	–	x	Hmong
	x	x	–	x	–	–	x	Yagua, Mundurukú, Waorani
	x	x	–	–	x	–	x	Tucano, Tuyuca
D	x	x	–	x	x	–	x	Kubeo, Nasioi, Motuna

9.5. nèi   sān   ge   rén
    that   three CL   person
    'those three people' (Helen Charters, p.c.)

Classifiers show certain differences in behaviour, when used with numerals or other quantifying expressions, and when used with demonstratives. The plural suffix -*men*, which occurs on some nouns with human reference, can occur with the plural classifier *xiē* following a demonstrative but not following a numeral (other than 'one') (Charters 1995). Example 9.6 is grammatical; 9.6a is not.

9.6. nèi   xiē   háizi-men
    that   CL:PLURAL   child-PL
    'those children'

9.6a. *sān   xiē   háizi-men
     three CL:PLURAL   child-PL

Classifiers are optional with demonstratives if the head noun has a human referent while numeral classifiers are always obligatory (Helen Charters, p.c.). It will have been noted that *ge* 'generic classifier' is written as a separate word in 9.3 and in 9.5, where it is used as a numeral classifier; but in 9.4 it is written as a suffix to the demonstrative. This reflects the intuition of speakers; they have a 'feeling' that a classifier forms a closer unit with a demonstrative than it does with a numeral (Helen Charters, p.c.).[2]

The same morphemes may be used as NUMERAL CLASSIFIERS and as VERBAL CLASSIFIERS in a few languages. An example of the same set of morphemes used with numerals and with verbs comes from Chayahuita (Cahuapanan: Derbyshire and Payne 1990: 258–9). Example 9.7 illustrates *rin* 'long, flexible' as a numeral classifier, and 9.8 shows the same morpheme as a verbal classifier.

9.7. cara-rin
    three-CL:LONG.FLEXIBLE
    'three' (e.g. pieces of string, vine)

9.8. i'sho-rin-in
    peel-CL:LONG.FLEXIBLE-3SG
    'He peeled vines'

There is no information concerning any differences in the behaviour of the two types.

The same morphemes are used in the functions of LOCATIVE CLASSIFIER and VERBAL CLASSIFIER in very few languages. The areal prefix in Koyukon is

---

[2] Similar usage was observed in Wei Ning (Wang 1972); see Bisang (1999).

used as a verbal classifier (see example 6.34), and as a locative classifier (see example 6.35).

The same classifiers are used with locational expressions and with verbs in Eyak (Eyak-Athabaskan: Krauss 1968: 195) exemplified in Table 9.2. Classifiers in Eyak are not semantically transparent.

TABLE 9.2. *Locative and verbal classifiers in Eyak*

Classifier	Locative classifier	Verbal classifiers
Residual	ʔuq́ 'on it (stick)'	(dəkịh) ʔu•d sətahl 'it (a stick) lies there'
d-classifier	ʔuda•q́ 'on it' (e.g., a board)	(ciλ) ʔu•d dəsətahl 'it (a board) lies there'
xd-classifier	ʔuxəda•q́ 'on it' (e.g. on a log)	(łe•sǩ) ʔu•d xədəsətahl 'it (a log) lies there'
ti•l-classifier	ʔuti•naʔq́ 'on it' (e.g. a leaf, feather)	(ǩułahł) ʔu•d tị•sətahl 'it (a feather, leaf) lies there'

The same set of morphemes are used with verbs and with adjectival modifiers to mark agreement in Terêna (South Arawak) and Yawalapiti (Xinguan Arawak).

9.9 shows how *pu'i* 'CL:ROUND' is used as a noun class marker on an adjective in Terêna (Ekdahl and Butler 1979; Aikhenvald 1996a). The same classifier used with a verb to characterize the O is given in 9.10 (= 6.8).

9.9. tûti   puru-pu'i
     head   big-CL:ROUND
     'a round head'

9.10. oye-pu'i-co-ti
      cook-CL:ROUND-THEME-PROGR
     'He is cooking (round things).'

9.11, from Yawalapiti, illustrates the use of classifier *-pana* 'CL:LEAF.LIKE' as a noun class marker, with the adjective 'green'. Note that the demonstrative *iʃutiʃa* 'that+FEM' does not take a classifier.

9.11. iʃutiʃa   ata-pana   irula-pana
      that+FEM tree-CL:LEAF.LIKE green-CL:LEAF.LIKE
     'that green leaf'

In 9.12 *-pana* 'CL:LEAF.LIKE' is used on the verb, to refer to the S.

9.12. ata-pana   kuka iʃu   kama-pana
      tree-CL:LEAF.LIKE PAST DEM+FEM die-CL:LEAF.LIKE
     'The leaf which died (i.e. a dry leaf) is there.'

Terêna is one of the few Arawak languages which have lost the gender opposition in the pronominal system. The difference between classifier systems in Terêna and Yawalapiti is that Yawalapiti distinguishes feminine and non-feminine genders in demonstratives and third person pronouns (Mujica 1992; Seki and Aikhenvald forthcoming).

Neither Terêna nor Yawalapiti uses classifiers with numerals. This may be an innovation, since the same morphemes are used as numeral classifiers in other, closely related languages, e.g. Ignaciano (South Arawak) and Waurá (Xinguan Arawak); these are considered under (B) below.

No other combinations of classifiers in just two environments have so far been found.

(B) One set of morphemes in three classifier environments

The same morphemes are used in the function of NOUN CLASS agreement markers with adjectives and with demonstratives, and also with numerals in Kilivila (Austronesian) (Lawton 1993; Senft 1986; 1996).

Kilivila has about 200 classifiers (called 'classificatory particles' by Senft 1986; 1997, following Malinowski 1920). It appears to be difficult to establish the exact number of classifiers in this language, because nouns with inanimate referents can be used as 'repeaters'; which makes classifiers a virtually open class (Gunter Senft, p.c.). In 9.13 (Senft 1986: 77) a classifier is used with a numeral, and in 9.14 (Senft 1986: 64) with a demonstrative. Classifiers used with demonstratives are infixes; they are prefixes in all the other environments.

9.13. te-tala   tau
      CL:MAN-one   man
      'one man'

9.14. mi-na-na   vivila
      this-CL:WOMAN-this   woman
      'this woman'

Adjectives fall into three classes, depending on whether they can be used with classifiers, and whether this is obligatory. 9.15 illustrates an adjective which requires a classifier (Senft 1986: 85).

9.15. valu   kwe-manabweta
      village   CL:THING-beautiful
      'beautiful village'

Classifiers are used with all the numerals; in contrast, not all adjectives take classifiers.[3]

[3] Lawton (1993) reports that classifiers are used with demonstratives more frequently than in other environments; see criticism of this statement by Senft (1996: 179).

The same set of morphemes is used with numerals, with demonstratives and as noun classifiers in Vietnamese (Goral 1978: 11 ff.). This situation is fairly typical for languages of Southeast Asia (Goral 1978). Example 9.16 illustrates a numeral classifier in Vietnamese.

9.16. ba   cúôn   sách
      three CL:BOOK   book
      'three books'

The first occurrence of *cúôn* 'CL:BOOK' in 9.17 is as a noun classifier, and the second is as a deictic classifier.

9.17. anh múôn cúôn   sách nào   cúôn   kia
      you want CL:BOOK book which CL:BOOK that
      'Which book do you want? That one.'

A 'generic' noun classifier is exemplified in 9.18 (Löbel 2000: 271).

9.18. cái   cây
      CL:NON.LIVING.THINGS   tree/plant
      'a tree/plant'

All the classifiers are used for referent tracking and marking definiteness (see §12.1.3, and also Goral 1978: 14, and Löbel 2000). Unlike classifiers with numerals, classifiers are not obligatory with demonstratives (Goral 1978: 15). Generic classifiers are often omitted in general statements, e.g. in proverbs (Goral 1978: 14):

9.19. mèo sợ   chuột
      cat fear mouse
      'Cats are afraid of mice.'

Awará, a Papuan language from the Morobe province in New Guinea, appears to have a somewhat similar system (Susan Quigley, p.c.). Classifiers are prefixed to the numbers 'one' and 'two' and suffixed to demonstratives; they appear to be obligatory with numbers, but not with demonstratives. When used as noun classifiers, they are independent words.

The same morphemes are used with numerals, demonstratives and in possessive constructions in Nung (Tai: Saul and Wilson 1980: 25 ff.). There are four classifiers. The generic classifier *áhn* as a numeral classifier was illustrated in 4.38. The use of *áhn* as a possessed classifier in a predicative construction (the head noun is omitted) is shown in 9.20. Example 9.21 illustrates the 'animate' classifier *tú* in a non-predicative possessive construction. The classifier NP is in square brackets.

9.20. mi su'   [áhn   hau]
     not correct   CL:GEN   myself
     'It's really not mine.'

9.21. hã   [slóng tú   luhc bao]   mu'hn   va
      tell two   CL:ANIM   child boy   he   say
     'Tell his two sons that . . .'

9.22 illustrates *tú* 'animate classifier' with a demonstrative.

9.22. lẽo [tú   tế]   chỉhng ma
      then CL:ANIM   that then   come
     'Then that one came.'

Similarly to Vietnamese, classifiers can occur with nouns, e.g. *tú me* (CL:ANIMATE wife) 'the wife'.

Classifiers with numerals are used somewhat differently from classifiers in other environments. They are optional with powers of ten; no such restrictions are found for other classifier environments (Saul and Wilson 1980: 27).[4]

Newari (Tibeto-Burman: Bhaskararao and Joshi 1985) has 53 classifiers used with numerals and interrogative quantifiers ('how much', 'how many') (9.23), with demonstratives (9.24) and with two adjectival modifiers which refer to dimensions (i.e. 'big' and 'small', as in 9.25). Classifiers tend not to be used with higher numerals (Bhaskakarao and Joshi 1985: 24); in other environments they are obligatory.

9.23. ni-mhA   khica
      two-CL:ANIMATE   dog
     'two dogs'

9.24. thwA:-ma   swã
      this.many-CL:PLANT   plant
     'this many plants'

9.25. tA:-pa-gu   mAri
      big-CL:SWEET.FOOD.ITEMS-CONNECTOR   bread
     'big bread'

The same nouns can require different classifiers when used with a numeral, or with an adjectival modifier. Nouns which normally require a general classifier *-gu* take the classifier *rhÃ* when accompanied by an adjectival modifier 'big' or 'small'. In 9.26, *-gu* is a classifier on a number *ni-gu* (note that in *tA:-rhÃ-gu gu* is a homophonous morpheme, a connector).

[4] Bisang (1999) discusses further morphosyntactic differences between classifiers used with numbers and with demonstratives in Chinese, Vietnamese, Thai, and a number of Miao-Yao languages.

9.26. ni-gu   tA:-rhÃ-gu   sAphu:
      two-CL:GEN   big-CL:GEN-CONNECTOR   book
      'two big books'

One set of morphemes is used as agreement markers on adjectival modifiers, with numbers, and with verbs (similarly to verbal classifiers) in a few South American Indian languages, e.g. Waurá (Xinguan Arawak). 9.27 illustrates a numeral classifier in Waurá (Jackson 1966). Example 9.28 shows a classifier as an agreement marker on an adjective, and 9.29 features a verbal classifier (Richards 1973).

9.27. mepiawa-pa   ita
      two-CL:POINTED   horn
      'two horns'

9.28. atakahi   ityula-pana
      grass   green-CL:LEAF.LIKE
      'green grass'

9.29. i-tsitya-pi-tsa
      CAUS-entwine-CL:LINEAR-CAUS
      'entwine linear objects'

A similar system is found in Ignaciano (South Arawak) and in Machiguenga (Peruvian Arawak: Shepard 1997). The two-way gender distinction in Machiguenga was discussed in §8.3. The difference between Waurá and Ignaciano is that Waurá employs the masculine and feminine distinction only for demonstratives (see §7.3.2); Ignaciano has a three-way masculine, feminine, and inanimate distinction in third person pronouns, cross-referencing affixes and demonstratives (Ott and Ott 1983; Aikhenvald 1996b). There is not enough information on classifiers in Waurá to evaluate the possible differences in behaviour of classifiers of different types. In Machiguenga, classifiers are infixes to numbers and suffixes in other environments.

(C) One set of morphemes in four environments

The same set of morphemes is used with numerals, demonstratives, a limited class of adjectival modifiers and also as noun classifiers in Thai. Example 9.30 illustrates the use of a classifier with a numeral, 9.31 with a demonstrative, and 9.32 with an adjectival modifier (referring to dimension and colour) (Hundius and Kölver 1983).

9.30. rôm   săam khan
      umbrella   three CL:LONG.HANDLED
      'three umbrellas'

9.31. rôm   khan   níi
     umbrella   CL:LONG.HANDLED   this
     'this umbrella'

9.32. nók   tua   jàj
     bird CL:BODY big
     'the big bird'

The order is numeral-classifier, classifier-demonstrative, and classifier-adjective. Further restrictions of ordering in classifier constructions in Thai are considered by Hundius and Kölver (1983: 177–81). When there are several adjectives or demonstrative modifiers, the classifier is repeated with each, as in 9.33 and 9.34.

9.33. nók   tua   sǐi-khǐaw   tua   jàj
     bird CL:BODY green   CL:BODY big
     'the big green bird'

9.34. rôm   khan   sǐi-khǐaw
     umbrella   CL:LONG.HANDLED   green
     khan   jàj   khan   níi
     CL:LONG.HANDLED   big   CL:LONG.HANDLED   this
     'this big green umbrella'

In contrast, the classifier is used only once in a numeral noun phrase, as shown in 9.35.

9.35. rôm   sǎam   khan   níi
     umbrella   three   CL:LONG.HANDLED   this
     'these three umbrellas'

Noun classifiers are optional, and they are used to distinguish different meanings of the same noun, e.g. *bay-phluu* (CL:LEAF-betel) 'betel leaf', *tôn-phluu* (CL:VINE-betel) 'betel vine' (DeLancey 1986: 440). They have been frequently interpreted as 'class nouns', e.g. *bay-máay* (CL:LEAF-wood) 'leaf' (DeLancey 1986: 440–1).

Hundius and Kölver (1983: 169, 172) point out that classifiers are optional with adjectives and with demonstratives; they are obligatory with numerals. They attempt to provide a unified account for classifier uses, arguing for the 'primary' character of classifiers used with numerals. We return to this in (H) below.

In Cantonese classifiers are used with numerals and in quantifying expressions, with demonstratives, with a limited class of 'size' adjectives and in possessive constructions (see Pacioni 1997; forthcoming). While classifiers are obligatory with numerals and in quantifying expressions and with demonstratives, they appear to be optional in other contexts where their presence or absence correlates with the specificity of the referent. Thus, these forms in Cantonese can be said to have two functions: that of numeral classifiers, and that of 'specificity' markers—which span a number of morphosyntactic environments—but are most regularly found as deictic classifiers.[5] Similarly, in Dulong-Rawang (Tibeto-Burman: Randy LaPolla, p.c.) classifiers are obligatory with numerals. They are used with nouns (as noun classifiers) to indicate specificity; they may optionally appear with possessives and with most adjectives in the same function—as specificity markers. Their primary function is that of numeral classifiers, and as deictic classifiers (also see (H) below).

Hmong (Miao-Yao: Bisang 1993; Jaisser 1987) uses the same set of morphemes with numerals (9.36), demonstratives (9.37), in possessive constructions and as noun classifiers.[6] The classifier follows the number in 9.36, and precedes the noun—followed by a demonstrative.

9.36. Lawv muaj rau tus   me nyuam
      they have six CL:LIVING.BEING child
      'They have six children' (Jaisser 1987: 172)

9.37. lub   tsev no
      CL:OBJECT house this
      'this house' (Jaisser 1987: 171)

In 9.38 the classifier is used in a possessive construction to characterize the possessed noun.

9.38. nws rab   riam ntaj
      he CL:MAN.MADE.OBJECT   sword
      'his sword' (Bisang 1993: 29)

Classifiers can be used with nouns by themselves as noun classifiers, as shown in 9.39 (Bisang 1993: 20–2).

9.39. zaj   teev ntuj
      CL:STORY,POEM   pray heaven
      'prayer'

The use of noun classifiers correlates with the definiteness of the referent—cf. 9.40 (Jaisser 1987: 171). The omission of a classifier is ungrammatical if a definite referent is implied (9.40a). (In actual fact, the correlation

---

[5] A similar situation has been reported for Yue dialects, Hakka, and Hokkien: see Pacioni (1997). According to Bisang (1993: 30) a similar system is found in other Miao-Yao languages of China.
[6] Conklin (1981: 187) showed that the numeral classifier morphemes are used with demonstratives, possessives, adjectival modifiers, and as noun classifiers in White Tai and Dioi; their frequency of use varies. While in Dioi classifiers are usually employed in all these environments, in White Tai they appear 'at least sometimes'.

between degrees of definiteness and the use of classifiers in Hmong is not that simple; see Bisang 1993: 26 ff., for details.)

9.40. tus   tsov   tshaib   tshaib   plab
       CL:LIVING.BEING   tiger   be.hungry   be.hungry   stomach
       'The tiger was very hungry.'

9.40a. *tsov tshaib tshaib plab

The same classifier can be used twice in the same noun phrase thus forming several classifier constructions, as in 9.41. The classifier may be used just once, as in 9.42 where the classifier *zaj* is employed with a numeral and as a noun classifier (Bisang 1993: 21).

9.41. ob   zaj   zaj   tshoob
       two   CL:STORY,POEM   CL:STORY,POEM   songs
       'two wedding songs'

9.42. nws   hais   ib   zaj   teev   ntuj
       he   say   one   CL:STORY,POEM   pray   heaven
       'He is praying once (one prayer).'

Unlike classifiers in other environments, possessed classifiers in Hmong are used differently depending on whether the head noun is alienably or inalienably possessed (see 5.22 and 5.23).

The same morphemes are used in the function of agreement marker on adjectives, numeral classifiers, verbal classifiers, and deictic classifiers in a few languages of Lowland Amazonia. One such example is Mundurukú (Tupí: Gonçalves 1987; Crofts 1973; 1985). Mundurukú has over 100 classifiers, at least half of which coincide, or show resemblances with, a corresponding nominal root (see §13.1, on how classifiers could originate from full nouns). Examples 6.9 and 6.10 above illustrate the classifier ba^4 'long rigid object' as a verbal classifier, and as a derivational suffix on a noun itself, in $a^2ko^3\text{-}ba^4$ 'banana'. 9.43 shows ba^4 as a numeral classifier; 9.44 shows the same morpheme as a deictic classifier (Gonçalves 1987: 35). (In the examples below, pa^4 and ba^2 are related by regular phonological processes described in Gonçalves 1987: 64.)

9.43. $xep^3xep^3\text{-}pa^4$ $a^2ko^3\text{-}ba^4$
       two-CL:LONG.RIGID   banana-CL:LONG.RIGID
       'two bananas'

9.44. $i^2ja^3\text{-}ba^2$ $a^2ko^3\text{-}ba^4$
       this-CL:LONG.RIGID   banana-CL:LONG.RIGID
       'this banana'

9.45 illustrates ba^4 as a noun class marker with a descriptive verb in attributive function (example from Crofts 1973: 87).[7]

9.45. a²ko³-ba⁴   i³-ba⁴-dip³
banana-CL:LONG.RIGID   3PRON-CL:LONG.RIGID-beautiful
'a beautiful banana'

The same morphemes in different classifier environments show morphological differences. Classifiers in Mundurukú fall into two groups according to their position in the morphological word. Those used with numerals and demonstratives and as derivational markers on nouns are suffixes; verbal classifiers and markers on adjectival modifiers are prefixes.

In Yagua a single set of classifier morphemes can be used in the same environments as in Mundurukú. Yagua has around forty classifiers (Payne and Payne 1990; Payne 1990). 9.46 illustrates a verbal classifier, 9.47 a deictic classifier.

9.46. súduu-bii-numaa   naváá-bii
be.ripe-CL:SPROUT-now   banana-CL:SPROUT
'The stalk of bananas is now ripe.' (Derbyshire and Payne 1990: 254)

9.47. jiy-see   núúy-see
DEM-CL:STICK   write-CL:STICK
'this pencil' (Payne 1990: 135)

Classifiers used as agreement markers on adjectives, as in 9.48, differ from other classifiers. In this context, classifiers are said to be optional (Payne 1990: 133). Both 9.48 and 9.49 are acceptable.

9.48. rábïï   rúnay-bïï   'its red flower'
its.flower   red-CL:FLOWER

9.49. rábïï   rúnay   'its red flower'
its.flower   red

Classifiers are obligatorily infixed to the numerals 'one' and 'two' (see example 4.21) but suffixed to larger numerals, e.g. *vuyajúúy-nu níínu* (ten-CL:POLE tree) 'ten trees' (Payne and Payne 1990: 349).

Waorani, an isolate from Equador (Derbyshire and Payne 1990: 259; Peeke 1968) has 35 classifier affixes used with numerals, adjectives, demonstratives and verbs. Classifiers are suffixes, when used with demonstratives (9.50), with adjectives (9.51), and with verbs (9.52).

9.50. ĩbæ̃-bõka   'this ear'
this-CL:EAR

---

[7] Mundurukú, apparently, does not have a morphological class of adjectives; descriptive verbs are used as modifiers in noun phrases.

9.51. giyæ̃-ka 'small stone'
       small-CL:STONE

9.52. ko-wa 'to pierce a foot'
       pierce-CL:FOOT

When used with numerals, classifiers are infixes (9.53), similarly to Yagua.

9.53. ado-ba-ke
       one-CL:PALM.LEAF-one
       'one palm leaf'

Thus, in Yagua, Waorani, and Munduruku the same morphemes behave differently in different classifier environments. In Munduruku, noun class markers and verbal classifiers occupy a position in the word different from other classifiers. In Yagua, noun class markers are not obligatory, unlike other classifier types; in Yagua and Waorani, classifiers are infixes with (some) numerals, but suffixes otherwise.

The same set of morphemes is used as agreement markers on adjectives and demonstratives, with numerals and in possessive constructions in numerous East Tucano languages.[8] These languages have a virtually open set of classifiers used with inanimate nouns. A gender-like distinction (masculine vs. feminine) applies to animate nouns. Examples 9.54–7 illustrate the use of classifiers in Tucano as adjectival agreement markers, as numeral classifiers, as possessed classifiers, and as deictic classifiers respectively, as well as use on the noun itself (West 1980; my data). A similar system has been described for Tuyuca by Barnes (1990).

9.54. pinõ   phai-gɨ
       snake   big-CL:ANIM.MASC
       'a big snake'

9.55. ni'cã-wã   wãtĩquẽ'a
       one-CL:EXTENDED.FORM manioc.squeezer
       'one manioc squeezer'

9.56. ati-wi'i   numio-ya-wi'i
       this-CL:HOUSE woman-POSS-CL:HOUSE
       'this house is a woman's; woman's house'

---

[8] Papuan languages of Central Bougainville appear to also use the same classifier morphemes as noun class markers, numeral classifiers, possessed and deictic classifiers, and also as noun classifiers in nominalizations (Kim Blewett, p.c.). At least some of these functions are combined in multiple classifier system of Reef-Santa Cruzan languages spoken in the Solomons (Wurm 1981; 1987; 1992a; 1992b; p.c.). More studies are needed on multiple classifiers in languages of the South Pacific, such as Awará and Wantoat (Morobe province), Angan languages (Angave, Taenae), and the two non-Austronesian languages of East New Britain, Baining and Taulil.

9.57. ati-gɨ̃ (pũ-gɨ̃)
   DEM:INAN-CL:LARGE (hammock-CL:LARGE)
   'this hammock'

In East Tucano languages, classifiers are not used with finite verbs. However, they can be suffixed to nominalized verbs, to mark the predicate of a relative clause. This is illustrated with 3.19, from Tuyuca (Barnes 1990).

(D) One morpheme in five environments

Only rather rarely is the same set of morphemes used as agreement markers on adjectives and demonstratives, with numerals, in possessive constructions and with verbs. One such language is Kubeo (Central Tucano: Gomez-Imbert 1996).

Kubeo has a system of classifiers which is very similar to East Tucano languages, exemplified in 9.54-7. Unlike them, Kubeo also uses classifiers with main clause predicates. The classifier -kɨ is used in 9.58 with a demonstrative and with a verb.[9]

9.58. i-kɨ hoé-kɨ beá-kɨ-bu
   this-CL:CYLINDR axe-CL:CYLINDR good-CL:CYLINDR-INAN
   'This axe is good.'

Nasioi (Papuan of Southern Bougainville: Hurd 1977) has over a hundred classifiers used in the same environments as in Kubeo. A possessed classifier in Nasioi is shown in 5.21, and a verbal classifier in note 7 to Chapter 6. Example 9.59 illustrates classifiers with a numeral and with a demonstrative.

9.59. nto-na-ru' bee-ru'-pi
   water-DER.SUFF-CL:UNIT.OF.LIQUID three-CL:UNIT.OF.LIQUID-PL
   a-ru'-daang
   this-CL:UNIT.OF.LIQUID-inland
   'These three inland lakes.'

In 9.60, a classifier marks the agreement of an adjective with a head noun.

9.60. tamp-a-u'
   good-DER.SUFF-CL:TARO
   'a good (taro)' (Hurd 1977: 132)

Motuna, from the same language family, has 51 classifiers used in the same environments as Nasioi (Onishi 1994). A possessive classifier in

---

[9] The verbal classifiers in Kubeo, unusual from a Tucano perspective, are due to the areal influence of Baniwa (see Gomez-Imbert 1996).

Nasioi is illustrated in 5.21; verbal classifiers are discussed in note 7 to Chapter 6. Example 9.61 (Onishi 1994: 163) illustrates a classifier used with a numeral.

9.61. no-uru
      one-CL:HUMAN
      'one human'

Classifiers are also used with several determiners, such as the demonstrative *o-*, the article *ti-*, *muuko* 'other', and *jee* 'what'. 9.62 (Onishi 1994: 164) illustrates a classifier with a demonstrative.

9.62. o-'ri
      DEM-CL:ROUND
      'this round object' (Malayan apple)

A few adjectives require a classifier in attributive constructions, as in 9.63 (Onishi 1994: 173) (in Motuna, classifiers are only obligatory with some adjectives).

9.63. tii   miru   mohko-muru
      ART:DIM   string   short-CL:PIECE.OF.LONG.OBJECT
      'a/the short piece of string'

It is possible that classifier morphemes in Nasioi and Motuna may also be used as possessor classifiers (see 5.47); this requires further investigation.

(E) Derivational functions of classifiers in multiple classifier systems

Classifiers in multiple classifier languages are often used as derivational affixes and as nominalizers (see Payne 1990, for a discussion of the role of classifiers in Yagua, a multiple classifier language, in inflection and derivation). Examples of classifiers as derivational devices in Tariana (North Arawak) were given in §3.5. In this language several classifiers can cooccur on a head noun; this is a productive derivational process, e.g. *kaɾa-ka-whya* (REL+fly-THEMATIC-CL:CANOE) 'plane', *kaɾa-ka-whya-puna* (REL+fly-THEMATIC-CL:CANOE-CL:STRETCH) 'airstrip'. A similar use of classifiers is attested in Waurá (Xinguan Arawak: (B) above), e.g. *kunuma-tai* (cotton-CL:CURVED) 'thread' (Jackson and Richards 1966), cf. Yagua *ruu-dasiy* (blow-CL:THIN,POLE) 'blow gun' (Payne and Payne 1990: 446); cf. *pũ-gɨ̃* (hammock-CL:LARGE) 'a hammock' in 9.57, from Tucano. In Terêna, the same set of morphemes is used on verbs and as agreement markers on adjectives (see 9.9 and 9.10); they are also used as derivational suffixes, e.g. *opé-pu'i* (bone-CL:ROUND) 'skull'.

Classifiers employed as derivational markers on the head noun can transform mass or collective nouns into countable nouns. This happens in a number of North Amazonian languages, including Guahibo, Bora-Witoto,

Tucano, and North Arawak, e.g. Tariana *heku* 'wood', *heku-na* (wood-CL:VERT) 'tree', *heku-da* (wood-CL:ROUND) 'fruit'. Only a noun which contains a classifier can be pluralized with a suffix *-pe*, e.g. *heku-na-pe* 'trees', *heku-da-pe* 'fruits', but not *heku-pe (see also West 1980, for Tucano; Kerr 1995, for Cuiba (Guahibo); Thiesen 1996, for Bora (Bora-Witoto family)).

Classifiers often mark nominalizations and predicates of relative clauses (cf. 3.19, from Tuyuca, an East Tucano language). In 9.64, from Yagua (Peba-Yagua: Payne 1990: 132), the classifier *-ra*, 'neuter', derives a noun from an inherently verbal root (this example is given in underlying form).

9.64. machǫǫ–ra-numaa   riy-rooriy
      remain-CL:NEUT-now   3PL-house
      'Their house was what remained' (lit. their house was now a remaining thing).

In Waorani classifiers function as deverbal nominalizers, as in 9.65.

9.65. õkĩ-bẽ
      3SG.make-CL:VINE
      'string which he will make'

Example 9.66 demonstrates nominalization with a classifier in Tucano. The verb 'be big' is nominalized with *-ri*, and then the classifier, of a repeater type, is attached (West 1980: 195–6).

9.66. pa-rí-sawero   wáa-yiro
      be.big-SG.NOM-CL:EAR.SHAPED   go-INAN.PAST.EVIDENTIAL
      'An ear-shaped area that was big was left (in the manioc bread after a piece had been torn out)'.

Classifiers can also be used as nominalizers in Motuna (Masa Onishi, p.c.), as shown in 9.67.

9.67. ong   poti kongsi'   haaro'ko-no-mori
      DEM:MASC   time mango   fall+PRES-LINKER-CL:SEASON
      roki manni   tokotokohah
      really   hot
      'The season when mangoes fall is really hot.'

Nambiquara (Nambiquara family: Lowe 1999) has fifteen classifiers used in several distinct environments (their form and semantics are given in Diagram 11.10). They are prefixed to numbers, as in 9.68, but suffixed to adjectives as agreement markers, as in 9.69.

9.68. $a^3lã^3a^2$ $so^1l?i^3$ ki^3-ha^1li^1 hut^3tit^3-ta^1-$hẽ^3$-ra^2
      parrot   only   CL:ROUND-two   shoot-1SG-PAST-PERFECTIVE
      'I shot only two parrots.'

9.69 wã²la²   wi³win³-ka³lo³-a²
      cloth   blue-CL:FLAT.SHEET-definite
      'the blue cloth'

Classifiers are also used as derivational suffixes on nouns, e.g. huk^3-$ẽn^1$-su^2 (shooter-CL:HOLE.LIKE-indefinite) 'shotgun' (the gun barrel being a hole), huk^3-$kɨ^3$-su^2 (shooter-CL:ROUND-indefinite) 'bow' (the arc of the bow is round). They are also used as relativizers, e.g. $sʔi^2ha^2$ $ʔyau^3$ -ain^1-$thĩ^3$ -na^2 (house live-they-CL:HOUSE-definite) 'the house they live in'; $wãn^3ta^2$ e^3e^3-$kʔi^2$-$sain^1$-$jauʔ^3$-ai^2na^2 (word speak-to-they.to.me-CL:WORD-this.definite) 'this word that they spoke to me'.

We saw in §3.5 that classifiers realized as independent words can also be used to mark relative clauses, in a function similar to relative pronouns, e.g. 3.14, from Lao.

(F) Repeaters in multiple classifier environments

Repeaters are used in multiple classifier environments in at least three groups of languages of Lowland Amazonia: (1) the East Tucano subgroup,[10] (2) Tariana (North Arawak), and (3) the Guahibo family. Their choice depends on the morphological structure of the noun; it has pragmatic effect.

(F1) Repeaters in the East Tucano languages The same set of classifier morphemes is used with numbers, with demonstratives, in possessive constructions, and as derivational markers and nominalizers (see (C) and (E) above); there are also three genders in cross-referencing.

Nouns fall into three morpho-semantic classes according to what classifier morphemes are used with each. Examples below are from the Tucano language.

(i) Animate nouns divide into feminine and non-feminine; agreement suffixes are -$gɨ$ 'non-feminine' (including 'sun/moon'), -go 'feminine', e.g. $pinõ$ $phai$-$gɨ$ (snake big-CL:AN.NON.FEM) 'a big snake'.

(ii) Inanimate nouns have one of the following affixes: -kal-ga 'spherical'; -$tɨ$, -$rɨ$ 'containers, e.g. pots'; -$kɨ$/$gɨ$ 'long, large'; -$pɨ$/-$wɨ$ 'transport'; -pal-wa 'extended'; -$poro$ 'banana-like'; -phi 'long, e.g. knife'; -ro 'general object'; -pe 'hole, seed'; -kwi 'plain'; -ra 'plain (water)'; -pa 'plain (land)'; -se 'uncountable' (West 1980: 119; my field data). They use the same affixes as agreement markers, e.g. ati-$gɨ$ $pũ$-$gɨ̃$ (DEM:INAN-CL:LARGE hammock-CL:LARGE) 'this hammock'.

---

[10] This may also apply to West Tucano, but data is lacking. Repeaters are also found in Yagua (Payne and Payne 1990: 448); however, the data and descriptions are not sufficient to analyse them; and possibly in Bora-Witoto languages of Northeastern Peru and adjacent areas of Colombia (Thiesen 1996; Wise 1999).

(iii) To mark agreement with all other nouns with inanimate referents, the whole of the noun is repeated on the modifier, e.g. 9.70 and 9.71.

9.70. ati-wi'i numio-ya-wi'i
this-CL:HOUSE woman-POSS-CL:HOUSE
'this house is a woman's; a woman's house'

9.71. (kahsero) phairi-kahsero
bark big-CL:BARK
'big (piece of) bark'

If a noun is a compound, or contains a derivational suffix, the last two syllables or the suffix is used for agreement, e.g. 9.72.

9.72. (yuhkɨ-gɨ-dɨhpɨ) phairi-dɨhpɨ
tree-CL:LARGE-branch big-CL:BRANCH
'a big branch'

(F2) Tariana Repeaters in Tariana (North Arawak) are used to mark agreement on modifiers (noun classes), demonstratives (deictic classifiers), and verbs (verbal classifiers) as an alternative to non-repeater classifiers (some of which are listed in Table 9.6) under three conditions:

(i) the noun must have an inanimate referent;

(ii) the noun must not contain a derivational suffix;

(iii) the noun must be in contrastive focus in discourse (see Aikhenvald 1994a, for further discussion).[11]

In 9.73, a regular classifier *-dapana* 'CL:HABITAT' is used when the noun 'house' is not in focus. The head noun is omitted, as often happens in Tariana discourse (see §12.1.2).

9.73. nuha hnuta nu-dia nu-a-de du-a-pidana
I 1SG+take 1SG-return 1SG-go-FUT 3SGNF-say-REM.P.INFR
nu-ya-dapana-se du-a-pidana ñamu
1SG-POSS-CL:HABITAT-LOC 3SGF-say-REM.P.INFR evil.spirit
i-sa-du
INDEF-spouse-FEM
'I shall take you back to my house, said the wife of the evil spirit.'

In 9.74 the same noun, 'house', is in contrastive focus, and so the repeater (identical to the noun *panisi*) is used. The head noun is omitted.

---

[11] In Kilivila, repeaters are used as an alternative 'way' of classification, to indicate more emphasis of the 'expressed nominal concept' (Gunter Senft, p.c.).

9.74. kayi du-ni   dhuta   du-dia   du-a-pidana
      so   3SGF-do   3SGF+take   3SGF-return   3SGF-go-REM.P.INFR
      du-ya-panisi-se
      3SGF-POSS-CL:HOUSE-LOC
      'After she did so, she took (them) back to her very house.'

If a noun is derived, its derivational suffix is used as an agreement marker, e.g. *hala-yawa hanu-yawa* (open-DER.AFF:HOLE big-CL:HOLE) 'a big hole'.

(F3) Guahibo languages These languages have large complex systems of classifiers. In Cuiba (Kerr 1995) the set of classifiers is virtually open, due to the existence of repeaters. The same morphemes are used as noun class agreement markers on adjectives, e.g. *peru-nae* (old-CL:WOODEN.THINGS) 'old (canoe)'; with numerals, e.g. *cae-bo* (one-CL:HOUSE) 'one (house)'; with demonstratives, e.g. *barapo-bo* (this-CL:HOUSE) 'this (house)' (Kerr 1995: 143), and in possessive constructions, e.g. *piya-nae jera* (3MASC.SG.POSS-CL:WOODEN.THINGS canoe) 'his canoe' (Kerr 1995: 134).

Unlike Tucano languages and Tariana, the use of repeaters is confined to inalienably possessed nouns (Kerr 1995: 132, 336–7), e.g. *cou* 'track', *pe-cou* (3SG.MASC.POSS-CL:TRACK) 'his track'. More work is needed to describe them fully.

The examples of repeaters discussed above show that:

(i) repeaters are usually only one of the mechanisms of marking agreement; no example has been found so far of a language where this is the only way of marking;

(ii) repeaters always have semantic, morphological, and sometimes discourse constraints; they are often used with inanimates only.

(G) Conclusions and generalizations

We have seen that the same set of classifier morphemes can be used in up to five environments. Classifier morphemes often display differences in their morphological form and in how obligatory they are in different contexts. Differences in the behaviour of the same[12] set of morphemes in different classifier constructions are summarized in Table 9.3.

Classifiers used with numerals are a different morpheme type from other classifiers in Yagua, Waorani, and Nambiquara. In contrast, in Munduruku classifier suffixes are used with numerals, with demonstratives and as derivational markers, and prefixes are used with verbs and adjectives. This may be due to the fact that adjectives are morphologically a subclass

---

[12] The same morphemes in multiple classifier environments can be considered polysemous morphemes.

TABLE 9.3. *Same morphemes in several classifier environments*[13]

Language	Place of morpheme	Obligatoriness
Kilivila (B)	Deictic classifiers are infixes; numeral and adjectival classifiers are prefixes	Deictic classifiers more obligatory than others; classifiers are not used with some classes of adjectives
Yagua, Waorani (C)	Numeral classifiers infixed, others suffixed	–
Munduruku (C)	Verbal classifiers and adjectival markers are prefixes, numeral, deictic classifiers and classifiers in derivational function are suffixes	–
Hmong (C)	–	Possessed classifiers not always obligatory
Nambiquara (E)	Numeral classifiers are prefixes, agreement markers and relativizers are suffixes	–

of verbs in this language, and verbs have a highly prefixing profile. In Kilivila, classifiers are infixes with demonstratives, and prefixes with numerals and adjectives.

The fact that different kinds of behaviour correspond to different kinds of morphosyntactic loci of classifiers may be considered an additional argument in favour of the validity of a morphosyntactically based typology of classifiers.

Some preliminary generalizations can be made as to the use of the same set of classifiers in distinct environments.

(i) Classifiers in multiple environments have derivational, relativizing, and nominalizing functions if also used as noun classifiers (see §3.2.4, for some examples from Jacaltec and from Lao), or if also used as agreement markers on adjectives (as in Tariana, Yagua, Tucano, Munduruku, or Nambiquara). Verbal, relational, possessed, or locative classifiers are not used as derivational markers. For instance, classifiers used in locative expressions and in verbal classifier constructions in Eyak play no role in derivation. Only in Palikur (Aikhenvald and Green 1998) are the distinct sets of verbal and of locative classifiers also used as derivational affixes. Verbal classifiers added to some nouns transform them into colour terms, e.g. *ahamna-bo-ye*

---

[13] Letters in brackets after language names indicate the subsection of §9.1 where classifiers in these languages are considered.

(leaf-V.CL:FLAT-DURNF) 'leaf-coloured', or 'green'. Locative classifiers are sometimes employed as derivational affixes, e.g. *paraw-hakwa* (waves-in.WATER) 'ocean', *pi-duk-madka-ya* (2SG-chest-on.FLAT-PERTAINING) 'the flat part of your chest, your breast plate', *a-kigbimna-ya* (3N-on.EDGE-PERTAINING) 'its frame'. However, these patterns have limited productivity.[14]

(ii) In languages with classifiers as independent words, these are used with a subset of adjectives only if they are also used with demonstratives (as is the case in Cantonese and in Thai). If classifiers are bound morphemes, they may be used with adjectives but not with demonstratives (e.g. the Arawak languages discussed above, such as Waurá, where a small class of pronominal genders is marked on demonstratives).

(iii) In multiple classifier languages classifiers are not used as relational classifiers; however, they can be used in possessive constructions in a function similar to that of possessed classifiers (i.e. categorizing the possessed).

(iv) In all the attested examples, classifiers are used in possessive constructions only if they are also used in head-modifier noun phrases.

(H) Which classifier environment is primary?

The question of which (if any) classifier environment is a 'primary' one, and which one is 'derived', can only be answered on the basis of language internal criteria.

The first question is which morphosyntactic environment is historically primary, and which one is a later development. In the history of Chinese the usage of classifiers with numerals appears to predate usage with demonstratives; the use of classifiers in possessive constructions in some Chinese languages such as Cantonese, Hakka, and Hokkien is historically an even later development (cf. Hashimoto 1977; Pacioni 1997).

The analysis of the patterns of genetic inheritance and areal diffusion in some Arawak languages from Northern Amazonia shows that some morphosyntactic environments for classifier use emerged historically later than others. Tariana and Resígaro 'extended' the use of classifiers to demonstratives under the areal influence of neighbouring languages, Tucano and Bora-Witoto respectively; genetically close Arawak languages use classifiers with adjectival modifiers, numerals, and verbs, but not with demonstratives (see Aikhenvald 1996a; 2001). In Kubeo,

---

[14] Another possible exception to the above claim is Pareci (Xingu-Pareci subgroup of Arawak: Rowan and Burgess 1979; Aikhenvald 1996b: 164). Pareci appears to have verbal classifiers, e.g. *-koa* 'flat' in *aotaka-koa-tya* (burn-VCL:FLAT-VB) 'burn (e.g. a field, a garden)'. Classifier morphemes are also employed as derivational suffixes, e.g. *máre-koa* (field-CL:FLAT) 'platform'. However, we have no information about the productivity of classifiers as derivational devices; the sketchy grammar of Pareci provides little information on the NP structure.

a Central Tucano language, classifiers began to be used with verbs under the influence of Baniwa, a neighbouring Arawak language (Gomez-Imbert 1996). This historical information is obtained as the result of comparison within each language family and with the neighbouring languages; in many cases we do not have access to any information of this sort.[15]

The second question is whether any synchronic functional priority can be given to one morphosyntactic environment. The use of classifiers with demonstratives in Chinese and in Austroasiatic languages is often considered an 'extension' of numeral classifiers (see Hashimoto 1977; Conklin 1981: 186). In Chinese as well as in Austroasiatic languages classifiers are indeed obligatory with numerals, but can be omitted in other noun phrases (see (A) above, for Chinese). In some languages only a subset of classifiers can be used with modifiers other than numerals. In Nung and Black Tai only the general classifiers for animates and inanimates are used with demonstratives, adjectives and possessives (Conklin 1981: 188). This may also be an indication in favour of the primary use of classifiers with numerals. However, in Northern Tai languages, according to Conklin (1981: 190), the numeral phrase usage 'is not the primary usage' of classifiers, since classifiers appear regularly with nouns in any context 'serving as their substitutes'.[16]

The subset of adjectives which require classifiers always includes the dimension type (as in Cantonese and other Chinese languages), and also the colour type (as in Thai). This restriction on the semantics of adjectives which require classifiers in isolating languages could provide an additional argument in favour of quantification as a primary function of classifiers (and thus, possibly, the usage of classifiers with numerals being the 'primary' one). The behaviour of classifiers used with adjectives in isolating languages like Chinese or Thai deserves further in-depth study (which is

---

[15] Derbyshire and Payne (1990: 266) hypothesize that classifiers in Mundurukú and other multiple classifier languages such as Waorani and Chayahuita developed from classificatory noun incorporation; i.e. that verbal classifiers developed first and numeral and adjectival agreement markers developed later. However, there is no language-internal evidence in favour of that. We have seen that languages which use classifiers with numerals and demonstratives are likely also to use them with adjectives; verbal classifiers are a much rarer type, and their existence does not seem to correlate with the use of classifier morphemes in other environments. Until more historical evidence becomes available there is no reason to believe that any one of the classifier environments in Mundurukú, Waorani, Chayahuita, Waurá, or Ignaciano is historically 'primary'.

[16] Hundius and Kölver (1983: 181) make an attempt at providing a functional explanation for the use of classifiers in multiple environments in Thai. They define the function of classifiers as indicating that an 'NP applies to specified or specifiable numbers of individual objects'. Then, the classifier is obligatorily used in quantitative expressions, while it is optional with determiners which do not necessarily relate to quantity (such as adjectives). This hypothesis deserves further justification, especially since the question of priority of each environment is not addressed.

lacking from the existing literature, mainly, because of the presupposition that these are nothing but a 'funny' parasitic extension of numeral classifiers to another environment).[17]

9.2. Multiple classifier languages and noun class agreement on multiple targets

Noun class agreement on multiple targets is functionally similar to multiple classifier systems in that it may include adjectives, numerals, and other modifiers, possessives, the noun itself and the predicate (cf. (D) in §2.4.2, and example 2.13 from Swahili).

Often, different subsets of noun classes are used with different modifiers and with the predicate. We have seen that Palikur distinguishes three gender forms in demonstratives as modifiers (see Table 8.8) and two gender forms in active verbs and stative verbs (the latter can be used as predicates and as modifiers) (see Table 8.9). Genders also differ in their realization depending on the morphosyntactic environment they occur in. More agreement forms are distinguished in demonstratives and personal pronouns than in gender-sensitive verbal affixes, in conformity with an almost universal tendency to distinguish more gender agreement forms with 3rd person pronouns and/or with demonstratives than with modifiers from open classes.

In many languages of the world a gender opposition is found only in personal pronouns (e.g. English; Kaingáng, a Jê language from South Brazil; Rikbaktsa, a Macro-Jê language from Central Brazil; Kakua, a Makú language from Colombia: see Aikhenvald 1999a; numerous languages from Southeast and east-central Australia, e.g. Pittapitta, Yandruwanhtha, Awabakal, and Gadjang: Dixon 2002: 461–3). In other languages, such as Dyirbal, an Australian language from North Queensland, noun classes are restricted to determiners, the demonstrative, and the locational interrogative. Waurá and Yawalapiti, two Xinguan Arawak languages from Brazil (from the same family as Palikur), distinguish masculine and feminine genders only in demonstratives, which are also used in the function of 3rd person pronouns (Aikhenvald 1996b: 165–7).

The use of one form for both masculine and neuter gender agreement with gender-sensitive verbal suffixes reminds us of a phenomenon known as 'concordial superclassing' ((C) in §2.4.4) in Australian linguistics (Sands 1995: 264–5), where fewer agreement forms are used with some modifiers,

---

[17] These restrictions are reminiscent of restrictions on the use of verb types in languages with verbal classifiers, discussed in Chapter 6: there, verbs which require classifiers are mostly posture and location verbs, and also verbs which imply handling objects.

such as demonstratives.[18] Further examples of different subsets of noun classes/genders with different modifiers are given in (G) in §2.4.2.

Noun class agreement on varying targets sometimes involves different morphological realizations (e.g. prefixes in one case and suffixes in another: see (A) in §2.6.2), or the use of the same set of morphemes with different properties. Numeral classifiers sometimes have different realization depending on the choice of a numeral or of a quantifier. For instance, in Bahwana (Ramirez 1992: 55) classifiers are obligatorily suffixed to quantifiers (4.22), and infixed to numbers one and two (4.23). In Palikur, numeral classifiers are suffixes to the numeral 'one' and infixes to the numeral 'two'; and often different forms of classifiers are used with 'one' and with 'two' (see Aikhenvald and Green 1998). In multiple classifier systems it is frequently the case that the same set of classifiers in distinct environments display different properties (see Table 9.3).

The main differences between multiple classifier languages and noun class agreement realized on different targets are the following.

(i) Noun class agreement realized on different targets is a grammaticalized agreement system whose semantic motivation varies. This involves both semantic and non-semantic agreement (see (F) in §2.4.2). In contrast, multiple classifier systems may involve lexical selection rather than agreement; this is especially striking in the case when multiple classifiers are realized through independent lexemes. The choice of a classifier in a multiple classifier language is always semantically based.

(ii) Noun class agreement on different targets retains all the properties of noun class systems (see §2.2); in particular, every noun must be assigned a noun class, and the semantic motivation involves animacy and/or sex. Multiple classifier systems are different in that not all the nouns require a classifier; their semantic motivation is more comparable to that of numeral or verbal classifiers.[19]

(iii) Noun class agreement on different targets obeys the Agreement Hierarchy (see (F) in §2.4.2). The choice of classifier environments in multiple classifier systems does not. It appears to be difficult to establish any hierarchy in motivating the choices for classifier environment in multiple classifier languages; some preliminary generalizations have been suggested in (G) above.

---

[18] Unlike Palikur, however, superclassing in Australian languages often has a discourse function: more general agreement forms are used when the head noun has a general reference, or is backgrounded.

[19] In Karirí (Kipeá-Kariri family: Rodrigues 1997: 69–72) the same morphemes are used with numerals and with adjectives referring to dimension, consistency, and colour. However, our knowledge of this extinct language is not sufficient to decide whether this is noun class agreement or a multiple classifier system.

230 *Classifiers*

(iv) Noun class agreement markers used on different targets have the same origin as other noun class systems, and show the same principles for their interaction with other categories as do noun classes. In contrast, multiple classifier systems pattern in these respects more like other classifier types (see Chapter 10).

9.3. Fuzzy types: overlapping classifiers in multiple environments

Languages can use almost but not quite the same classifier sets in several different environments. In this section we present two case studies, from genetically closely related languages. In §9.3.1 we consider classifiers in Baniwa (Arawak: Aikhenvald 1996c); and in §9.3.2 we deal with classifiers in Tariana. Some conclusions as to the possible analysis of these transitional systems are given in §9.3.3.

Both languages have large sets of classifiers, and also two pronominal genders (feminine and non-feminine). The environments in which classifiers and genders are employed in the two languages are given in Table 9.4. Unlike Tariana, Baniwa has a closed set of 44 classifier morphemes; while Tariana employs 'repeaters' (see (F) in §9.1) alongside a large set of over sixty 'established' classifiers (see Aikhenvald 1994a). Classifiers are not employed on locatives. Also unlike Tariana, Baniwa has relational classifiers (see 5.51 and 5.52).

TABLE 9.4. *Environments in which genders and classifiers are used in Baniwa and Tariana*

Language	Genders	Classifiers
Baniwa	Demonstratives, cross-referencing affixes, personal pronouns	Noun classes, numerals, verbs, head nouns, possessives
Tariana	Cross-referencing affixes, personal pronouns	Noun classes, numerals, verbs, head nouns, possessives, demonstratives

9.3.1. Multiple classifiers in Baniwa

A complete list of classifiers in Baniwa is given in Table 9.5 (arranged semantically, according to the parameters in Chapter 11). The inventories of (a) noun class markers and (b) numeral, noun, verbal and possessed classifiers only partly overlap.

Some adjectival agreement markers on adjectives are 'derived' from a classifier with the help of an adjectivizing morpheme -*y*, or feminine -*ʒu*, or non-feminine -*ri*. These are marked with * in the table. Noun class markers differ from classifiers in the way they interact with plural number (see §10.1). Plural noun class markers which are not used as classifiers are given under (G) in Table 9.5. The two classifiers in (H) are not used as noun class markers.

A possessed classifier in Baniwa was shown in 5.50. Example 9.75 illustrates a classifier with a numeral.

9.75. apa-kha a:pi
   one-CL:CURVED snake
   'one snake'

Classifiers are employed with the predicates of relative clauses,[20] where their use depends on whether the noun is in focus. In 9.76 the classifier -*kha* 'curved' is used to focus the snake. It is not used in 9.77 since the snake is not in focus.

9.76. a:pi nu-inua-ri-kha   awakada-riku
   snake 1SG-kill-REL-CL:CURVED bush-LOC
   'The very snake I killed is in the bush.'

9.77. a:pi nu-inua-ri awakada-riku
   snake 1SG-kill-REL bush-LOC
   'A snake I killed is in the bush.'

A noun class marker which consists of a classifier + adjectivizer -*y* is shown in 9.78. A noun class marker which coincides with a classifier is shown in 9.79.

9.78. a:pi maka-khay
   snake big-NCL.CURVED
   'a big snake'

9.79. pan-ţi   maka-dapana
   house-NON.POSSESSED big-CL:HOUSE
   'a big house'

Examples 9.80 and 9.81 show the derivational use of classifiers.

9.80. i-thi-da
   INDEF-eye-CL:ROUND
   'eye'

9.81. i-thi-maka
   INDEF-eye-CL:PIECE.OF.CLOTH
   'eye lid'

---

[20] And also on verbs in the form of the topic-advancing voice, as in *bulaʃa na-iʒa-nita-mi* (*na-iʒa-ni-ita-mi* (underlying form)) (biscuit 3PL-consume-ARGUMENT.MANIPULATING-CL:ANIM-PAST) 'biscuits have been eaten'.

TABLE 9.5. *Classifiers in Baniwa*

	Classifier	Adjectival agreement marker	Gloss	Examples
A. Animate, feminine				
1.*	-ita	ite < ita-y, -da-ɾi	Non-feminine animate / Animate human attributes	tʃinu 'dog', nukapi 'hand'
2.*	-hipa	same as cl.1	Non-feminine human	waɾi-paɾi 'young man', atʃiãɾi 'man'
3.*	-ma	-da-ʒu	Feminine human	inaʒu 'woman', haddua 'mother'
B. Form and shape				
4.*	-da	-da-ɾi	Round objects; generic	idza 'rain', hnuwida 'my head'
5.	-api	-api	Hollow objects	tʃipaɾa:pi 'pan', ma:wipi 'blow gun'
6.	-aphi	-aphi	Limited space	kiniki 'garden', kaɾita 'lake'
7.	-apu	-apu	Long thin stick-like object	haikwapu 'stick', dzawithyapu 'bow'
8.	-hiku	-hiku	Pointed, long objects	ɾi-api 'his bone', garafa 'bottle'
9.	-hiwi	-hiwi	Thin sharp objects	tʃikuɾe 'a hair', nukapida 'my finger'
10.	-iʃi	-iʃi	Small seed-like objects	pipeʃi 'seed of a palm tree fruit', a:ʈi 'pepper'
11.	-ku	-ku, -ki	Pieces of cloth; hammock	piete 'hammock', enikaɾya 'cobweb'
12.*	-kwa	-kwe < -kway	Flat, round, extended	kanaɾi 'looking glass', kaida 'beach'
13.*	-kha	-khay < kha-y	Curvilinear objects	a:pi 'snake', hinipu 'road'
14.*	-na	-ne, -nay <- na-y	Vertical objects	haiku 'tree', dzawi 'jaguar'
15.	-pi	-pi	Long thin objects	teɾuɾipi 'manioc squeezer'
16.*	-phe	-phe, phay	Thin flat foldable objects	yamakaʈi 'cloth', papeʒa 'paper'
17.	-wa	-wa	Small holes	nu-numa 'my mouth', hipadaphi 'hole in a stone'
18.*	-Ø	-yaɾi	Hollow smallish objects	a:ta 'cup', kuɾeya 'spoon'

	Classifier	Adjectival agreement marker	Gloss	Examples
19.	-yawa	-yawa	Holes, open spaces	panṭinuma 'door', harayawa 'hole'

C. Functional properties

	Classifier	Adjectival agreement marker	Gloss	Examples
20.*	-apa	-apa-ɾi	Non-feminine flying animate; semi-oval objects	pitiʒi 'bat', kepiʒeni 'bird', ainidzu 'mosquito', paɾana 'banana'
21.*	-apa	-apa-ʒu	Feminine flying animate	kaɾaka 'hen'
22.*	-maka	-make < maka-y	Piece of cloth	tsaia 'skirt', dzawiya 'jaguar's skin'
23.	-peku, -peki	-peku, -peki	Extended long stretches	hinipu 'road', u:ni 'river'

D. Structure

	Classifier	Adjectival agreement marker	Gloss	Examples
24.*	-ahna	-anha-y	Liquids	u:ni 'water', kutʃiaka 'drink of manioc flour'

E. Quantification

	Classifier	Adjectival agreement marker	Gloss	Examples
25.	-hipada	-hipada	Piece, half	paɾahnepada makhepada 'piece of banana'
26.	-ida	-ida	Half	apaida mawiʒu 'half a pineapple'
27.*	-ima	-ima-ɾi	One side	nukapi makemaɾi 'one side of my hand'
28.	-naku, -naki	-naku, -naki	Bundle of thin long objects	lapi '(bundle of) pencils'
29.*	-pa	-pa-ɾi	Bundle, box, parcel	apa-pa itsa maka-pa-ɾi 'a box of fishing hooks'
30.	-puku, -puki	-puku, -puki	Bundle of long objects	apa-puki paɾana 'a bundle of bananas'
31.	-tawahɾe	-tawahɾe	Joint	apa-tawahɾe nukaphiwida 'finger-joint'
32.	-waɾi	-waɾi	Time cycle	hamuɾi 'year', hekwapi 'day'
33.*	-wana	-wane < wana-y	Thin slice	apawana kuphe makawane 'a big thin slice of fish'
34.*	-wata	-wate < wata-y	Bundle ready for carrying	paɾana makawate 'a bundle of bananas'

TABLE 9.5. (*contd.*)

Classifier	Adjectival agreement marker	Gloss	Examples
F. *Specific classes (each applying to a single noun)*			
35.* ∅	-a, -aɾi	Canoe	iːta 'canoe'
36. -dapana	-dapana	House	panṭi 'house'
37. -ihwe	-ihwe	Egg, stone (of a fruit)	kaɾakehwe 'hen's egg'
38. -hipani	-hipani	Waterfall	hipa 'waterfall'
39.* -pawa	-pawani	Big river	uːni 'river'
40.* -ʃa	-ʃa-ɾi	Excrement	iʃa 'excrement'
41. -tuhwya	-tuhwya	Room	tuhwya 'room'
42.* -ya	-ya, -yaɾi	Skin	dzawiya 'jaguar's skin'
G. *Morphemes used only as noun class markers*			
1. -peʒi		Inanimate; collectives	ʧikuɾe yapi-peʒi 'long hair'
2. -peni		Animate nouns; their attributes	dzawithipa matʃia-peni 'beautiful footsteps of a jaguar' (an ornament)
H. *Morphemes used only as numeral and verbal classifiers*			
1. -i		Bundle	ape pipiʒi 'a bundle of pupunha' (palm tree fruit)
2. -iʧia		Bundle of small fruit	apeʧia manakhe 'a bundle of açai'

The choice of a classifier in a given environment depends on what aspect of the referent is highlighted (cf. examples 2.18–20). Classifiers with verbs in Baniwa are less obligatory than classifiers in other environments; their use depends on pragmatic factors. Otherwise, classifiers behave in a similar manner. The system of classifiers in Baniwa can be analysed in two distinct ways. One can say that it is a multiple classifier system with the same set of morphemes used with adjectives, numerals, verbs and as derivational suffixes; the formal differences between the 'adjectival' classifiers and the rest are due to the presence of additional attributive markers which appear on adjectives with some classifiers (but not all of them).

Alternatively, Baniwa can be said to have noun classes marked on adjectives as a type of noun categorization device which is distinct from classifiers employed with numerals and with verbs, as well as in a derivational function.

The argument against the second solution is that semantically, noun classes and classifiers coincide; and they are also very similar formally.

The argument in its favour lies in the existence of morphemes which are used only as noun class agreement markers ((G) in Table 9.5), and of morphemes used only as numeral and verbal classifiers ((H) in Table 9.5).

Both analyses are equally acceptable. Baniwa is the case of a language in transition from a system with classifiers in multiple environments to a system with noun classes distinct from other noun categorization devices.

9.3.2. Multiple classifiers in Tariana

Classifiers in Tariana (also from the North Arawak subgroup) are used as noun class agreement markers on adjectives; with numbers (one to four) as possessed classifiers in possessive NPs, where they attach to the possessive marker and characterize the possessed noun (see examples 5.18 and 5.19); with verbs; with demonstratives, articles, and other modifiers from closed classes; and on head nouns, as derivational suffixes. Classifier morphemes fall into three groups: (i) classifiers used in all these environments with a distinct form in each; (ii) classifiers used—with the same form—only in two environments: as noun classes and as derivational markers on the head noun itself; and (iii) classifiers used in all the environments with the same form in each. In the last group, the classifier -*ma* 'feminine' is not used with the article.

The classifier -*dapana* 'HOUSE', from group (iii), was illustrated with a demonstrative, a numeral, a possessive, an adjective and the predicate; and on the head noun 'hospital' itself as a derivational suffix in 9.2 above.

We can now consider the classifiers of group (i). The 'animate' noun class marker is -*ite*; the form -*ita*[21] is used with numerals and verbs: see 9.82. Noun class markers also differ from other classifier types in the ways they correlate with the grammatical category of number (see §10.1), e.g. 9.82 and its plural counterpart, 9.83.

9.82. pa-ita   tʃãɾi   hanu-ite
       one-CL:ANIM   man   big-N.CL:SG.ANIM
       'one big man'

9.83. ãtʃa   hanu-peni
       man:PL   big-N.CL:PL.ANIM
       'big men'

For group (i), the same form is used with numerals, verbs, in possessive constructions and on the noun itself (except for -*ita*/-*ite*). There is also a

---

[21] -*ite* in Tariana comes from -*ita-y*, -*y* being the adjectivizing morpheme used on some noun class markers in Baniwa. The difference between this noun class marker and the corresponding classifier in Tariana is thus reminiscent of the one in Baniwa. It can be considered an archaism, due to the areal influence of Tucano languages on Tariana (Aikhenvald 1994a; 1996b).

TABLE 9.6. *Classifiers in Tariana*
(i) *Classifiers with distinct forms in different environments*

Semantics	Examples	Noun class singular	Noun class plural	Numeral classifier	Noun classifier	Possessed classifier	Verbal classifier	Classifier with deictics
Generic Animate	*tʃãri* 'man', *inaru* 'woman'; *tʃinu* 'dog', *a:pi* 'snake'; human attributes: *siruli* 'trousers'	*-ite*	*-peni*	*-ita*	*-ite*	*-ite*	*-ita*	Animate form of demonstrative
Human	*tʃãri* 'man', *inaru* 'woman'	*-ite*	*-peni*	*-hipa*	*-ite*	*ite*	*-ita*	As above

(ii) *Classifiers used in only two environments*

Semantics	Examples	Noun classes and noun classifiers	
Collective	*pumeni-peri* 'sugar', *u:ni* 'water', *saña-peri* 'sweat'	*-peri*	
Abstract nouns, places	*ehkwapi* 'day, weather, world', *iya* 'rain', *panisi-wani* 'place where home is'	*-wani*	

(iii) *Classifiers with the same forms in all classifier functions*

A. *Gender classifier (not used with specifier article)*

Classifier	Semantics	Examples
-ma	Feminine	*inaru* 'woman', *kabueta-ma* 'female teacher'

B. *Shape and form classifiers (a sample out of about 80)*

-da	Round objects	*mawina* 'pineapple', *dithi* 'eye', *heku-da* 'fruit'
-hiwi	Thin long objects	*itfa* 'hair', *nuthiwi* 'eye-lashes'
-ipu	Long, hollow, bundle-like	*haiku-pu* 'log', *nawiki-pu* 'grave'
-kha	Curvilinear	*kule-kha* 'fishing line', *hewya-pi-kha* 'rainbow'
-khi	Thin curved	*maka-khi* 'rope'
-maka	Extended cloth, cloth-like	*yarumakasi* 'cloth', *hitisi-maka* 'funeral mask' (lit. mask of tears)
-mapha	Completely covered	*disinuma* 'his beard', *itfima* 'mane of hair'
-na	Long vertical	*heku-na* 'tree'
-pa	Largeish and long	*deːri* 'banana', *pesanini-pa* 'ladder'
-peku	Thin stretch	*leka-peku* 'a broken longish piece'
-pi	Long, thin, vertical; cycle of time	*hirina* 'manioc squeezer (tipiti)', *deːri-pi* 'banana tree'; *keːri, keːri-pi* 'month'
-pukwi	Round and hollow	*episi-pukwi* 'metal ring'
-puna	A length, stretch	*hinipu* 'road', *karaka-hwya-puna* 'air-strip'
-phe	Leaf-like	*dina-phe* 'feather', *papera-phe* 'leaf of paper'
-(a)phi	Small, hollow	*surupe-phi* 'clay pot', *episi-aphi* 'metal pot'
-yawa	Holes	*hala-yawa* 'hole', *dithaku-yawa* 'his nostril'

C. *Quantifier-like classifiers*

-apa	Pair of	*diphema* 'wings'
-itfi	Bundle of	*manaketfi* 'bundle of açai', *deritfi* 'bundle of bananas'
-ima	A paired object; one side of two	*iphema* '(insect's)wing', *diaranima* '(bird's)wing'
-iphina	A quarter	*pethe-iphina* 'a quarter of a loaf of a manioc bread'
-pada	Piece of	*maka-pada* 'half'
-piu	Time	*pa-piu* 'once'
-sawa	Group	*mare-sawa* 'a group of birds'
-yami	Piece (of cloth)	*yarumakasi-yami* 'piece of cloth'

TABLE 9.6. (contd.)
D. Function classifiers

Classifier	Semantics	Examples
-ita	Instruments	*marie* 'knife', *kanari* 'mirror', *hekuta* 'paddle'
-dapana	Habitation	*panisi* 'house', *ditape-dapana* 'hospital'
-whya	Canoe, transport	*ita-whya* 'canoe', *ka-koloka-whya* 'car'

E. Specific classifiers (each used a single noun)

Classifier	Semantics	Examples
-dawa	Corner, limited space	*maka-dawa* 'room; still part of a river', *karisana-dawa* 'part of a lake with stagnant water'
-ithi	Seed	*ithi* 'seed', *iwi* 'grain of salt'
-iwai	Trap; wall	*nehpaniwai* 'a made up trap', *panisiwai* 'house-wall'
-kada	A day	*pa-kada* 'one day'
-kawa	Leg, handle, anything leg-like	*sidu-kawa* 'the long part of an arrow', *huni-kawa* 'manioc trunk'
-kena	Branch	*heku-kena* 'tree branch', *dikawana-kena* 'crab's leg'
-kiyere	Island	*kewere* 'island', *maka-kyere* 'a big island'

numeral classifier, *-hipa* 'animate', used in this, and in no other environment. This classifier is interchangeable with *-ita* 'animate'; there is a mild preference to use *-hipa* for human male referents (see further details in Aikhenvald in prep.), cf. 9.84 and 9.85.

9.84   phepa (< pa- + -hipa)   tʃãɾi
        one+NUM.CL.HUMAN   man
        'one man'

or

9.85.   pa-ita   tʃãɾi
        one-NUM.CL:ANIM   man
        'one man'

The animate classifier *-ita* is acceptable with a non-human referent, such as *a:pi* 'snake' (9.86). Example 9.87, with the classifier *-hipa*, is acceptable only if the snake is personified, in a traditional legend.

9.86.   pa-ita   a:pi
        one-NUM.CL:ANIM   snake
        'one snake'

9.87.   ?phepa   a:pi
        one+NUM.CL:HUMAN   snake
        'one snake'

Only noun class markers and the classifier morphemes in the derivational function allow 'stacking', that is, the occurrence of more than one classifier morpheme in one word (see examples in §3.5; Aikhenvald 1999b).

Slightly different subsets of classifiers are used with modifiers from closed classes (proximate and distal demonstratives, the demonstrative 'this big', articles, the interrogative-distributive 'which, every', and the interrogative quantifier 'how many?'). The animate noun class marker (see (i) in Table 9.6) *-ite* is used only with the interrogative-distributive 'which, every'. The articles have a feminine form and do not take the feminine classifier *-ma*. Proximate and distal demonstratives differ in how they mark animacy, and in the classifiers they take. The semantics and form of demonstratives with classifiers are shown in Diagram 9.1.

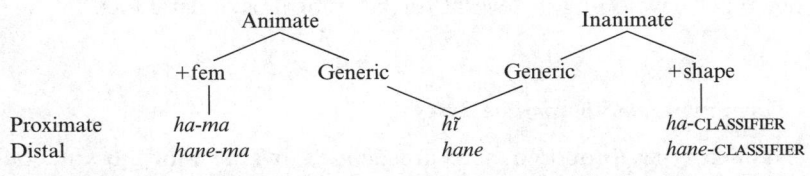

```
                         Animate                    Inanimate
                    ╱─────────────╲              ╱─────────────╲
                 +fem         Generic          Generic       +shape
                  │              │                │             │
Proximate       ha-ma            hĩ                          ha-CLASSIFIER
Distal          hane-ma          hane                        hane-CLASSIFIER
```

DIAGRAM 9.1. *Semantics and form of demonstratives with classifiers in Tariana*

Classifiers

Diagram 9.2 features the semantics and the form of classifiers with articles (Aikhenvald 2000).

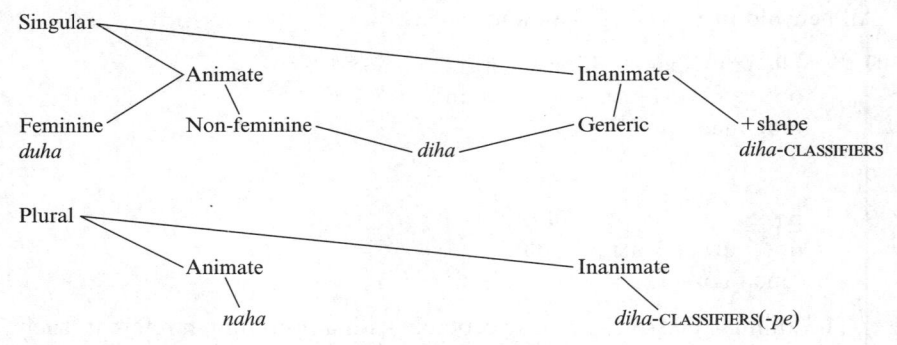

```
Singular
         ╲Animate                    ─ Inanimate
          ╲                           ╱
Feminine   Non-feminine            Generic    +shape
duha                     diha                 diha-CLASSIFIERS


Plural
        ╲Animate                    ─ Inanimate
          ╲                           ╲
           naha                        diha-CLASSIFIERS(-pe)
```

DIAGRAM 9.2. *Semantics and form of articles with classifiers in Tariana*

The agreement forms of the interrogative-distributive *kwa* 'which, every' are given in Table 9.7 (see Aikhenvald forthcoming c for further details).

TABLE 9.7. *Agreement forms of* kwa- *in Tariana*

Animate singular head	Animate singular modifier	Animate plural	Inanimate unmarked non-plural	Inanimate plural	Inanimate form-specific
kwana	*ku-ite*	*ku-ita-peni*	*kwaka*	*kwe-peɾi*	*kwaka-* INANIMATE CL

The question arises: how many classifier sets does Tariana have? If one takes a 'maximalist' approach, every morphosyntactic locus (including every type of modifier from a closed classs) may be considered as representative of a separate type, since each of them (with the possible exception of verbal classifiers) can be shown to employ a slightly different set of forms. Another way of approaching this would be to say that, similarly to Baniwa, Tariana is another, more complicated instance of a language in transition to a system with noun classes and numeral classifiers being distinct from other noun categorization devices, and also of several distinct classifier types developing in several further morphosyntactic loci.

9.3.3. *Fuzzy types and borderline cases*

The classifier types proposed here are defined by the morphosyntactic contexts in which they appear. Each has a set of properties, and there can be variations on them. It is not always an easy matter to assign a particular system of classification unambiguously to just one of the types, as we have seen for Baniwa and Tariana. These languages present examples of fuzzy types, or borderline cases found in systems which can be called transitional in the sense that the classifier types are not as clear-cut as they are in other instances. Systems like Tariana, with distinct subtypes of classifiers for different modifier classes, can develop into further new classifier types (each being used with a variety of closed-class modifiers).

10 Classifiers and Other Grammatical Categories

Noun categorization devices interact with other grammatical and lexical categories in the following ways.

(i) There may be dependencies between noun categorization devices and other categories: the semantics or form of noun categorization devices may correlate with the choice made in another grammatical category. For instance, there may be fewer noun class distinctions in non-singular numbers than in the singular.

(ii) Noun categorization devices may be realized as portmanteau morphemes with other categories, e.g. case or number.

(iii) The meanings encoded through noun categorization devices in some languages can be realized through different categories in others; for instance, the choice of case marking may depend on the animacy or humanness of the referent even if a language does not have an overt classifier system (see Appendix 1).

Distinct classifier types interact in different ways with verbal and nominal grammatical categories; they may also interact with derivational devices. Their presence may influence the structure of the lexicon.

The degree of interaction between classifiers and other categories also depends on the morphological type of the language, and the morphological realization of classifiers. We expect more interactions between categories in a fusional language, because of the higher probability of portmanteau realization of categories (cf. Aikhenvald and Dixon 1998). Consequently, noun classes which are always realized with bound morphemes (see Chapter 2) are likely to display more interdependencies with other categories than numeral classifiers realized as independent words.

We also expect most interactions between noun categorization devices and nominal categories; we have seen in previous chapters that most classifiers have an NP as their scope. Since some do have a clause as their scope, we also expect some interaction between classifiers and predicate categories.[1]

---

[1] We understand predicate categories to be categories typically realized on the predicate, or on the verb, e.g. tense/aspect, or voice. It is sometimes argued that categories such as tense/aspect are clausal rather than just verbal. We will leave this question open here; for further

Interactions between noun categorization devices and the grammatical categories of number, person, marking of grammatical relations, possession, and politeness are considered in §10.1–5. Noun categorization devices also interact with the organization of declensional paradigms—§10.6. In §10.7 we discuss the ways in which classifiers interact with verbal categories; §10.8 deals with the categories characteristic of deictics (e.g. proximal vs. distal) and classifiers. §10.9 describes how classifiers interact with derivational devices and how their existence may affect the lexicon.[2] Conclusions are given in §10.10.

10.1. Classifiers and number

The semantics of number usually depends on the meaning of a noun; this is the reason why classifiers tend to interact with number in many ways. Noun classes display the most complicated interactions and interdependencies with number: §10.1.1. Interdependencies of number with other types of classifier are considered in §10.1.2.

10.1.1. Noun classes and number

Noun classes and number show mutual interdependencies: (a) noun class choice depends on number; or (b) number choice depends on noun class; or (c) there may be different noun class systems in different numbers, or, finally, (d) number and noun class can be expressed with a portmanteau morpheme (see Aikhenvald and Dixon 1998, for further discussion of (a) and (b)).

(A) Noun class depends on number

The choices available for noun classes may depend on the choices made in the number system.[3] In many languages, gender distinctions are made only in the singular and not in the plural—for example, Indo-European languages such as German, Russian, Danish; Manambu (Ndu: Papuan); North Berber languages such as Zemmur and Izayan; and the East Berber language Siwa. Many African languages distinguish fewer noun classes in the plural than in the singular—for example, Ful (Heine 1982a: 207) has twenty-three singular but only five plural classes, and Mba (Ubangi: Heine 1982a: 208) has six singular and three plural classes. Seneca (Iroquoian: Chafe 1967: 13–14)

---

discussion of dependencies between gramamtical systems, see Aikhenvald and Dixon (1998), and references therein.

[2] The ways classifiers which interact with definiteness are linked to their discourse functions are discussed in §12.1.3.

[3] Note that quite a few languages have the same noun class/gender distinctions in all numbers, e.g. Portuguese and Hebrew.

has three genders in the singular and two in the dual and the plural. Polish (West Slavic) distinguishes three genders in singular and two in plural.

Other non-singular numbers often behave differently. There may be more gender distinctions in dual than in plural. In Old Church Slavonic three genders (masculine, feminine, and neuter) were distinguished in the singular, two in the dual (masculine and neuter having fallen together), while no gender distinctions were made in plural. East Slavic languages have lost the dual, and gender is shown just in the singular. In the two languages which do have dual, Upper Sorbian (West Slavic) distinguishes three genders in singular and two in dual and plural (feminine and neuter having fallen together); Slovene (South Slavic) distinguishes three genders in singular and plural, and two genders in dual (masculine and feminine-neuter) (DeBray 1951). In Manambu (Ndu, Papuan) there are two genders in singular but none in dual and plural.

Different choices in different numbers are found in Baining (East New Britain: Parker and Parker 1977: 18), where demonstratives distinguish masculine and feminine genders in singular and dual; in plural, there are distinct forms for human and non-human referents.

Some languages have the same gender distinctions in singular and in dual, but none in plural, e.g. Lavukaleve (Papuan, Solomons: Todd 1975: 813; Angela Terrill, p.c.) and also Angave (Angan: Speece n.d.: 113).

This dependency relates to Greenberg's Universal 37 (1963: 95): 'A language never has more gender categories in non-singular numbers than in the singular', and Universal 45: 'If there are gender distinctions in the plural of the pronoun, there are some gender distinctions in the singular also.' There is, however, a set of counterexamples to these generalizations. A number of Austronesian languages distinguish animate/non-animate forms in the plural only. Biak (South Halmahera, West New Guinea subgroup: Steinhauer 1986) has animate/inanimate forms for 3rd person plural pronouns and demonstratives; there are no such distinctions in the singular, dual, or trial. In a seminal article, Pawley (1973: 100) reconstructs an animate/inanimate opposition for 3rd person plural in Southeast Solomonic languages.[4] Further counterexamples concern the interaction between noun class, number, and person (see (B) in §10.2).

---

[4] A few further counterexamples are given in Plank and Schellinger (1997). Thus, Greenberg's Universals 37 and 45 can be considered tendencies rather than universal statements. It appears true that if there are gender distinctions marked on personal pronouns, there are never more gender distinctions in 2nd person than there are in 3rd person; there is typically the same set of distinctions in all persons in non-singular numbers. It is rare for a language to mark gender on 1st person singular pronouns; more work has to be done to provide an explanation for this.

Greenberg's (1963: 94) Universal 32 claims that 'whenever the verb agrees with a nominal subject or nominal object in gender, it also agrees in number'. There are significant exceptions to this claim, e.g. Caucasian languages (Corbett 1991: 198ff.) and numerous South American languages (e.g. Arawak and Jê) and Papuan languages (e.g. the Ndu family).

Independent personal pronouns in Tamachek (Tuareg Berber: Prasse and ăgg-ălbosṭan ăg-Sidiyăn 1985: 8) distinguish masculine and feminine genders in all three persons in the plural, but only in the 2nd person for singular number. Direct and indirect object pronouns are clitics; they distinguish genders in the 2nd person singular and 2nd and 3rd person plural. (See Table 10.1.)

TABLE 10.1. *Personal pronouns in Tamachek*

	Independent pronouns	Direct object pronouns	Indirect object pronouns
1 SG M, F	năk	-(a)hi	-ahi
2 SG M	kăy	-kăy	-ak
F	kăm	-kăm	-am
3 SG M, F	ənta	-t	-as
1 PL M	năkkăneḍ	} -anăgh	} -anăgh
F	năkkănăteḍ		
2 PL M	kăwăneḍ	-kăwăn	-awăn
F	kămăteḍ	-kămăt	-akmăt
3 PL M	əntăneḍ	-tăn	-asăn
F	əntănăteḍ	-tănăt	-asnăt

Languages may acquire more gender distinctions in non-singular numbers than in the singular for historical reasons. In some Baltic and Slavic languages the dual arose as the result of the grammaticalization of the number 'two' which distinguished genders. Consequently, gender distinctions are found in all persons in dual, and only in 3rd person in singular and plural. This is illustrated from Lithuanian in Table 10.2 (Peterson 1955: 48–9).

TABLE 10.2. *Personal pronouns in Lithuanian*

	SG	DU	PL
1 M	} àš	mùdu (cf. masc. dù 'two')	} mẽs
F		mùdvi (cf. fem. dvì 'two')	
2 M	tù	jùdu	jũ
F		jùdvi	
3 M	jìs	juõdu	jiẽ
F	jì	jiedvi	jõs

In Slovene (Priestly 1993: 406–8) two genders are distinguished in 1st and 2nd person dual and plural, and in 3rd person dual; there are three gender forms in 3rd person singular and two in plural, and none in 1st and

2nd singular (Table 10.3). Thus, there are more gender distinctions in the 1st and 2nd person non-singular than in the singular forms for the same persons.

TABLE 10.3. *Personal pronouns in Slovene*

		SG	DU	PL
1	M	jàz	mîdva	mî
	FEM/NEUT		mệdve, mîdve	mệ
2	M			
		tî	vîdva	vî
	FEM/NEUT		vệdve, vîdve	vệ
	M	òn	ónadva	óne
3	F	óna	} ónidve, onệdve	} óna
	N	óno		

In Bora-Witoto languages (which have two gender distinctions in pronouns and large multiple classifier systems), feminine and masculine are distinguished for all persons only in the dual, but only for 3rd person in singular and none in plural (e.g. Minor and Minor 1971: 10, on Murui Witoto). According to Aschmann (1993: 133), such a system can be reconstructed for Proto-Bora-Witoto. In Bora (Thiesen 1996: 33) masculine and feminine genders are distinguished in all persons in dual (with the exception of dual inclusive) and in 3rd person singular. This system has been calqued into Resígaro (Allin 1975) an Arawak language which underwent drastic restructuring under the Bora influence (see Aikhenvald 2001). Table 10.4 features personal pronouns in Resígaro and in Bora. The morphemes which have been borrowed from Bora into Resígaro are in bold.

In languages with multiple noun class systems, pronominal noun classes tend to develop more interactions with number than nominal ones. In Paumarí (Arawá) pronominal gender depends on number (two genders in the singular are neutralized in the plural); there is no such dependency for the *ka-* noun class (see §2.7.2).

In Tariana and Baniwa, North Arawak languages with two pronominal genders and a large set of noun classes, both depend on number: all pronominal genders and some noun classes are neutralized in plural (see §9.3).

(B) Number depends on noun class

In some languages number marking is used only on nouns with animate or human referents. This is the case in a few Australian languages. Ngandi

TABLE 10.4. *Personal pronouns in Resígaro and in Bora*

	Resígaro	Bora
1SG	ñó	oó
2SG	phú	uú
3SG MASCULINE	tsú	diibye
3SG FEMININE	tsó	diílle
1 INCL DUAL MASCULINE	fa-*musi*	meé
1 INCL DUAL FEMININE	fa-*mupi*	
1 EXCL DUAL MASCULINE	**muu**-*musi*	muhtsi
1 EXCL DUAL FEMININE	**muu**-*mupi*	muhpɨ
2 DU DUAL MASCULINE	ha-*musi*	á-muhtsi
2 DUAL FEMININE	ha-*mupi*	á-muhpɨ
3 DUAL MASCULINE	na-*musi*	diityé-tsi
3 DUAL FEMININE	na-*mupi*	diityé-pɨ
1 INCLUSIVE	fa?a	meé
1 EXCLUSIVE	**muu**-?a	muúha
2PL	ha-?a	ámuúha
3PL	na-?a	diítye, aátyé

(Heath 1978: 35) has seven noun classes; those with non-human referents have the same prefix for all numbers (*ṇi-*, *ṇa-*, *a-*, *gu-*, and *ma-*). Masculine and feminine classes have prefixes (*ṇi-*, *ṇa-*) in the singular. Prefix *bari-* covers masculine dual; prefix *ba-* is used for masculine and feminine plural, feminine dual, and mixed masculine/feminine dual.

Number marking and number agreement follows the Nominal Hierarchy (Dixon 1994: 85; Silverstein 1976): see Diagram 10.1. The arrow points at the direction of likelihood of overt number expression, or number agreement (also see Smith-Stark 1974; Stebbins 1997).

Pronouns   Proper names/Kinship nouns < Common nouns
1<2<3   Humans < Other animates < Inanimates
◄───

DIAGRAM 10.1. *Animacy hierarchy and expression of number*

In Anindilyakwa (Australian: Leeding 1996), number is obligatorily expressed only with personified nouns. In numerous South American languages with non-obligatory expression of number, agreement is more frequently encountered with humans and higher animates than with inanimates (e.g. North Arawak languages Tariana, Warekena, Bare). In Palikur (North Arawak: Aikhenvald and Green 1998), number marking and agreement is restricted to human nouns. Bora (Bora-Witoto: Thiesen 1996: 33–4) uses different forms for animate and inanimate plurals. In

Tamil number marking is obligatory on nouns denoting 'rational' beings (adult humans, gods and demons); irrational beings (which include infants and animals) do not have to be marked for number (Asher 1985: 135). (Further examples are given in Chapter 2; e.g. Table 2.6, for Khinalug.)

The way in which nouns from different noun classes have different number distinctions may involve *superclassing* (see (C) in §2.4.4). For instance, Motuna (Papuan, Bougainville) distinguishes four numbers for nouns with animate and human referents (singular, dual, paucal, plural) and two numbers (singular and non-singular) for nouns with inanimate referents.

(C) There may be different noun class systems in different numbers

If noun classes have a different semantic basis in different numbers, there is no hierarchical dependency of one upon the other. For instance, Malto (South Dravidian) has male vs. the rest in the singular and human vs. non-human in the plural (Mahapatra 1979: 60), as shown in Table 10.5.

Table 10.5. *Gender in Malto*

Singular	Plural
Male referent	Male referent
Female referent	Female referent
Non-human referent	Non-human referent

(D) Noun class is realized as a portmanteau with number marking[5]

This is the case in many fusional languages, e.g. Bantu, Indo-European, and Afroasiatic, and in predominantly agglutinating or polysynthetic languages, e.g. Arawak or Tucano. For instance, portmanteau gender/number endings in Modern Hebrew are:

MASC SG	MASC PL	FEM SG	FEM PL
-Ø	-im	-a, -Vt	-ot

In Kiowa-Tanoan languages nouns are divided into a number of classes on the basis of their number marking. In Kiowa, for one noun class the singular/dual are unmarked and plural is shown by the suffix *-gɔ*; all animate nouns belong to this class; for a second one the singular and plural are unmarked and the singular shown by *-gɔ*; and for a third class dual is unmarked with the singular and plural shown by *-gɔ*.

---

[5] Some typologists, e.g. Serzisko (1982), define the notion of a concordial class through its cooccurrence with number, which is typically the case in Bantu languages (see Chapter 2).

10.1.2. Number and other classifier types

NUMERAL CLASSIFIERS may interact with number in an indirect way. Number is normally not expressed in numeral classifier constructions, being marked elsewhere (e.g. on modifiers within an NP, or on the predicate).[6] The use of numeral classifiers may depend on the countability of a noun; classifiers tend to be employed with countable rather than with mass nouns. In some languages, e.g. Malay, mass nouns may be left unclassified (see Hopper 1986: 313, 316). In numeral classifier languages, the distinction between countable and uncountable nouns is realized through classifiers and quantifiers, instead of overt number marking on nouns (De Leon 1987: 27).

It has been claimed that numeral classifier languages always lack 'compulsory number' (Greenberg 1990: 188; Sanches and Slobin 1973; cf. §4.1 above). This means that number marking is optional or it is restricted to a set of nouns, most frequently humans or animates. There are a number of exceptions to this claim; for instance, Yuki, Nootka, Tlingit, and Dravidian languages have numeral classifiers and obligatory number marking, and so does Ejagham, a Benue-Congo language (see 4.2). De Leon (1987) showed that the number category became more obligatory in Tzotzil, a language with a large system of numeral classifiers, under Spanish influence.

Numeral classifiers and the expression of number share a number of semantic parameters. The distinction between mass and unit, and between countable and uncountable nouns, is important for both. There are sometimes special classifiers for mass nouns; in addition, some classifiers are restricted to countable nouns only. In harmony with this, number systems tend to apply to countable nouns expressing units.

The choice of numeral classifier may occasionally depend on number. Bengali has five numeral classifiers in the singular; in the definite plural all classifiers are replaced by one marker -*gulo* (cf. Greenberg 1990: 188). This can be explained in terms of the origin of classifiers in Bengali. We will see in §13.5 that numeral classifiers in Bengali are thought to have developed as the result of a reanalysis of a noun class system.

VERBAL CLASSIFIERS and CLASSIFICATORY VERBS may interact with number in several distinct ways, reminiscent of how noun classes interact with number.

First, there may be a classificatory verb stem used just to refer to non-singular objects. That is, fewer shape-based semantic distinctions are present in classificatory verbs which refer to plural objects than in those which refer to singular ones. In Hupa and Chipewyan (Haas 1967: 360; Carter 1976: 25, 27) one classificatory verb stem is used to refer to all plural objects, or objects in sets (e.g. stem *la* in Chipewyan: Table 11.11).

---

[6] There are a few cases in which number is marked in numeral phrases in classifier languages. In Tariana and Tucano languages, nouns in phrases with numbers bigger than 3 obligatorily take a plural marker, e.g. Tariana *ñama-da heku-da* (two-CL:ROUND tree-CL:ROUND) 'two fruit', *kehpunipe-da-pe heku-da-pe* (four-CL:ROUND-PL tree-CL:ROUND-PL) 'four fruit'.

Second, the choice of a non-singular classificatory stem may correlate with the shape of objects. Navajo (Hoijer 1945) has a classificatory stem for an aggregate of non-singular objects, and another one for a set of parallel, long objects. In Slave the choice of classificatory verb stem for non-singular referents correlates with number and with shape: there is a classificatory verb stem for plural objects and aggregates[7] (*-tl'ih*, also used for liquids), and for dual objects (*-keh*, also used for rope-like objects) (Rice 1989: 788), and a number of classificatory stems used to refer to masses (e.g. *-tlé* 'to handle an uncontained wet mass, e.g. mud, or dough': Rice 1989: 789; *-déh* 'fall (used of a two dimensional, changing—but maintaining unity—mass': Rice 1989: 788).[8]

Other Athabaskan languages make different choices in their classificatory stems for non-singular objects. In Western Apache there is a stem for pairs of non-animal, non-contained objects. In Chiricahua Apache (Hoijer 1945: 19–21; Carter 1976: 28) there are three stems which refer to non-singular objects: a set of objects, a set of parallel objects, and a set of two objects (also used for rope-like objects). Dogrib distinguishes between plurality of similar, and of disparate objects (Carter 1976: 28). This variation within the Athabaskan family led Carter (1976: 28) to a conclusion that 'notions of non-singularity were not an integral part of the Proto-Athabaskan classificatory verb system, but that non-singularity was handled by semantic extension of the core system, typically by an extension of the rope-like object category'.

Choices of classificatory verb stems may also depend on the animacy or inherent nature of a non-singular referent. Koyukon has a classificatory verb stem for general plural, one for plural objects scattered about and one for plural animate (Chad Thompson, p.c.).

Tewa (Kiowa-Tanoan) has a limited set of classificatory verb stems with the meaning 'to be in a place' (or 'to have') and 'to put or set down' (Speirs 1974). The S or O is characterized in terms of its position in space and shape (like classificatory verbs in Enga, or Waris: Tables 6.7 and 6.10). Six classificatory verbs are used with singular and dual objects, and only five with plural objects—the distinction between 'be sitting' and 'be lying' is neutralized with one classificatory stem being used for both.[9] See Table 10.6.

---

[7] These stems are used for falling objects rather than for location of objects (Keren Rice, p.c.).

[8] The different choices for classificatory verb stems referring to non-singular objects are independent of so-called 'verb themes indicating number' (Rice 1989: 791–2), which are mostly found for semantic groups of verbs which are different from classificatory verbs.

[9] 'Be lying' and 'be sitting' are also neutralized in the plural in Kiowa (Watkins 1984: 154); however, it is not clear whether positional verbs have the same classificatory function in Kiowa as they have in Tewa. Similarly to Kiowa (see §12.5.2), nouns in Tewa belong to six different classes conditioned by their choice of number forms; the interrelation with classificatory verbs which are also number-sensitive provides an unusual cross-classification.

TABLE 10.6. *Classificatory verbs in Tewa and their semantics*

Singular/dual	Plural	Translation	Objects classified
-ʔán ⎫ -k'ó: ⎭ -čą́	-k'wǫ -sa:	'be sitting' 'be lying' 'be attached, be a container (in normal position), be in a container'	Squat bulky objects, e.g. clock Long objects, e.g. pencil Attached or rooted objects, e.g. tree; or container, e.g. dish
-win	-win	'be standing'	Upright objects, e.g. shovel
-yíʔ	-yíʔ	'be walking about'	Moving objects, e.g. dog
-ná	-ná	'existence of time or event'	Phenomena of nature, events, institutions, time

In Creek (Muskogean), suppletive dual and plural verbs are developing into classificatory verbs, and there is a correlation between consistency and the physical nature of the object, and the number form of the verb (see (B) in §6.2.3).[10]

An interaction between number expressed on verbs and animacy of the S (or S/O) is frequently attested in languages with number-sensitive verbs. Jarawara, an Arawá language from Brazil, has two genders (Dixon 1995). The verbs 'sit' and 'stand' distinguish between animate and inanimate S in plural, but not in singular or dual. Jarawara displays a dependency between number and animacy which goes in the opposite direction to Tewa, where fewer classificatory stem choices are available in plural than in singular or dual. In contrast, the Jarawara verbs shown in Table 10.7 have more animacy distinctions in plural than in singular or dual.

TABLE 10.7. *Animacy marking on verbs in Jarawara (Arawá)*

Verb	Singular	Dual	Plural	
			Animate S	Inanimate S
Sit	-ita	joro -na-	-naho-	sii na-
Stand	-wa(a)-			

Verbal classifiers often do not have to make any special reference to the number of objects (cf. Table 6.7 and Table 6.11).

DEICTIC CLASSIFIERS can be fused with number if the number has to be marked in an NP on a modifier, e.g. Pilagá (Guaicuruan: Vidal 1997: 85)

---

[10] Jack Martin (p.c.) informs me that this is a typical phenomenon in many languages of the Southwest of the USA.

da7m7e 'CL:VERTICAL:SINGULAR/COLLECTIVE', *da:m7e* 'CL:VERTICAL:PAUCAL'. However, unlike noun classes, there is no dependency between the choice of a deictic classifier and a choice made in a number system.

NOUN CLASSIFIERS or CLASSIFIERS IN POSSESSIVE CONSTRUCTIONS do not interact with number since number tends to be marked elsewhere in NPs; neither do LOCATIVE CLASSIFIERS.

Classifiers in multiple functions can be employed as derivational markers on the head noun; they may also transform mass or collective nouns into countable nouns—see (E) in §9.1.

10.2. Classifiers and person

The interaction between classifiers and person is limited to pronominal elements—independent personal pronouns and cross-referencing bound pronouns. That is, in many languages noun class and person are realized as portmanteau morphemes.

Correlations between noun categorization and person have been observed mostly for noun classes[11] and for those noun classifiers which tend to be used anaphorically for pronominalization.

(A) Noun class distinctions often depend on person

Most frequently, NOUN CLASS specification is made just in 3rd person. Examples are numerous—Indo-European, Caucasian, and a number of Australian languages, e.g. Yaigin (Australian: Crowley 1979); some languages do not have a 3rd person pronoun, and use demonstratives in this function. Then, gender distinctions are found in demonstratives, e.g. in Paumarí (Arawá) (Chapman and Derbyshire 1991: 267). First and second person are uniquely specified and their sex is presumably known, so gender specification here is communicatively redundant.

Pronominal usage has been reported for NOUN CLASSIFIERS, for instance, in Mayan languages (Mam, Jacaltec, or Akatek), and in Mixtec (De Leon 1987: 175). Since noun classifiers are used as 3rd person pronouns only, it can be said that more classificatory distinctions are made for 3rd person than for 1st and 2nd persons.

A few languages also show gender in 2nd (but not in 1st) person. If gender oppositions are found in 2nd person, they will normally also be there in 3rd, and if they are found in 1st, which is rare, they will normally also be there in 2nd and 3rd. The majority of Afroasiatic languages (Semitic, Berber) distinguish masculine and feminine genders in 2nd and

---

[11] See Chapter 2, on how there tend to be more noun class distinctions with personal and other pronouns than elsewhere.

3rd person singular and plural. Iatmul and Abelam, languages of the Ndu family (East Sepik region of New Guinea), distinguish masculine and feminine genders in 2nd and 3rd persons only, while Manambu and Ngala, from the same family, distinguish feminine and masculine in all persons.[12]

There are a few exceptions. Two genders are distinguished in 1st (but not 2nd or 3rd) person just in possessive pronouns in Kalaw Kawaw Ya, the Western Torres Strait language (Ford and Ober 1991: 138), where a masculine possessor will use *ngaw* and a feminine will use *nguzu* for 'my'. In Maká (Mataguayo: Gerzenstein 1994: 175) feminine gender is marked on the 1st person inclusive personal pronoun only; other personal pronouns have no gender marking. Minangkabau (Western Austronesian) distinguishes two gender forms of 2nd person singular pronouns; there are no gender distinctions for other pronouns—see Table 10.8 (adapted from Marnita 1996: 64).

TABLE 10.8. *Personal pronouns in Minangkabau (singular)*

Person	Masculine	Feminine
1st	(a)den	
2nd	waang/ang	kau
3rd	inyo	

(B) Noun class distinctions often depend on a combination of categories which include person

Noun class distinctions can correlate with person and with number. Berber languages Siwa (Laoust 1931: 108) and Izayan (Laoust 1928: 187) distinguish masculine and feminine genders in 2nd and 3rd person singular but not in the plural.

A few languages distinguish masculine and feminine genders in all persons in plural pronouns, but only in 3rd person for singular number. Examples are Spanish (Table 10.9) and Tariana (North Arawak; Table 10.10). In Spanish, 1st and 2nd person plural pronouns have been derived from a combination of a personal pronoun + indefinite adjective *otro* 'other' (masculine), *otra* (feminine) (Corominas 1954: 523).[13] In Tariana feminine plural pronouns consist of a personal pronoun plus feminine marker *-ma* plus plural *-pe*. In both languages 'masculine' plural pronouns are used if feminine gender does not have to be specified.

---

[12] In Manambu genders are distinguished in 1st person in the remote past, but not in other tense forms.
[13] Spanish also has an old neuter form, *ello*, used in fixed expressions, and as a neutral agreement form (Corbett 1991: 214).

TABLE 10.9. *Personal pronouns in Spanish*

	SG		PL	
	MASC.	FEM.	MASC.	FEM.
1	*io*		*nosotros*	*nosotras*
2	*tu/vos*		*vosotros*	*vosotras*
3	*el*	*ella**	*ellos*	*ellas*

TABLE 10.10. *Personal pronouns in Tariana*

	SG		PL	
	MASC.	FEM.	MASC.	FEM.
1	*nuha*		*waha*	*waha-ma-pe*
2	*piha*		*iha*	*iha-ma-pe*
3	*diha*	*duha*	*naha*	*naha-ma-pe*

Further counterexamples to Greenberg's Universal 45 (see (A) in §10.1.1) concern the mutual dependency between person, noun class and number. In a few North Berber languages, independent pronouns distinguish masculine and feminine genders in 2nd and 3rd person singular and plural, and also in 1st person plural, but not in 1st singular (e.g. Tazerwalt Shilh: Stumme 1899: 85, and closely related Ntifa: Laoust 1918: 211). Tuareg languages (South Berber, e.g. Tamachek: Prasse and ăgg-ălbosṭan ăg-Sidiyăn 1985: 8; Simone Nientao, p.c.; Ahaggar: Prasse 1972) distinguish two gender forms for all persons in plural and in 2nd person singular; there are no distinctions in 1st and 3rd person singular (see Table 10.1). Nama (Khoisan: Hagman 1977) distinguishes three genders (feminine, masculine, and common) in 2nd and 3rd person singular, and in all persons in plural; dual has two gender forms (masculine and feminine-common) for all persons, while 1st person singular has no gender marking.

The choice of noun class distinctions may correlate with tense and person. Non-present tense forms of the verb in Hebrew have distinct masculine and feminine for both 2nd and 3rd person in the singular; in the plural we find: 2nd person masculine, 3rd person masculine, and a single form covering both 2nd and 3rd person feminine. That is, the contrast between 2nd and 3rd persons is neutralized in feminine gender and plural number. See the future paradigm of *katav* 'write' in Table 10.15 (see also example from Tucano languages in §10.7).

10.3. Classifiers and grammatical function

Of all the noun categorization devices, only noun classes and verbal classifiers interact with the marking of the grammatical function of an NP in a clause, since both classifier types have the clause as their scope.

Grammatical functions can be marked with (a) nominal case (in dependent marking languages) or (b) verbal cross-referencing (in head marking languages) (see Nichols 1986). The two types of marking interact with noun classes.

10.3.1. Noun classes and grammatical function

There are mutual dependencies between choices available in noun class systems and those in case systems.

(A) Dependencies between case and noun class

The choices available in case systems may depend on the choice made in noun class system (cf. Aikhenvald and Dixon 1998). In Latin (and many other Indo-European languages), case distinctions depend on gender. All nouns belonging to masculine and feminine genders (whether their reference is human, animate, or inanimate) distinguish nominative and accusative cases, but this distinction is neutralized for all nouns belonging to neuter gender.

Some determiners, e.g. demonstratives, have the same ablative form for masculine and neuter singular, and a different form for feminine singular (cf. Lyons 1968: 293).

Further interactions involve noun classes, case, and number. In Latin, demonstratives do not distinguish any gender forms in dative and ablative plural; and only two forms (masculine-neuter and feminine) are distinguished in genitive plural; all three genders are distinguished in nominative plural.

More complicated interactions can involve noun classes, case, person and number. In Lithuanian, masculine and feminine genders are distinguished in nominative, accusative, and vocative cases in 1st and 2nd person dual; for 3rd person dual, they are distinguished in all cases except for genitive (Peterson 1955: 48–9).

The realization of noun classes in different persons may correlate with grammatical function. In Berber languages there are three series of pronouns: independent subject, direct object, and indirect object (also used with prepositions and as possessive pronouns). Genders are regularly distinguished in 2nd and 3rd persons in all the three series in the singular. The only exception is the 3rd person indirect object pronoun, which employs just one form for both genders.[14] Berber languages show a correlation between noun classes, person, case forms, and number. We have seen above that some Berber languages (e.g. Siwa, Izayan, Zemmur) do not distinguish genders in plural; Kabyle and Tamachek distinguish genders in 2nd and 3rd person in the plural in direct and indirect object pronouns, and in all persons in independent pronouns. Shilh distinguishes two genders in 2nd and 3rd person singular and all persons in plural only in independent subject pronouns. Direct and indirect object pronouns have gender distinctions for all persons and numbers excluding 1st person plural.

(B) Portmanteau realization of noun class and case

This is widespread in fusional languages of the Indo-European type, e.g. Latin, Sanskrit, or Russian, where case forms of all nominals usually convey information about noun class/gender, case, and number. The paradigm of *is* 'this' in Latin is given in Table 10.11.

TABLE 10.11. *Paradigm of Latin is 'this'*

Case	SG			PL		
	MASC.	NEUT.	FEM.	MASC.	NEUT.	FEM.
Nominative	*is*	*id*	*ea*	*iī*	*ea*	*eae*
Accusative	*eum*	*id*	*eam*	*eōs*	*ea*	*eās*
Dative		*eī*			*iīs*	
Ablative	*eō*		*eā*		*iīs*	
Genitive		*ēius*			*eōrum*	*eārum*

(C) Dependencies between cross-referencing and noun class

In head-marking languages, noun classes can be marked on verbs to cross-reference S, A, and O; then cross-referencing affixes combine the reference to noun categorization and syntactic function. Often, the choice of noun class depends on the choice made in the person system. For instance, in Anindilyakwa (Australian) different series of verbal prefixes cross-reference A, S, and O, and four noun class forms are distinguished in bound pronouns, while five noun class forms are distinguished in free forms (Leeding 1989).

The choice of noun class in cross-referencing may depend on person and number. In the majority of Arawak languages feminine/non-feminine pronominal gender distinctions are only made in 3rd person singular

---

[14] For an attempt at a reconstruction of Proto-Berber personal pronouns, see Aikhenvald (1986).

cross-referencing prefixes (typically used for A/S_a) and suffixes (used for O/S_o).

The choice of noun class can depend on the grammatical function realized in cross-referencing. Chinantec languages distinguish animate and inanimate gender realized in agreement with modifiers in NPs; verbs are inflected to agree with S/O depending on whether it is animate or not. There are no animacy distinctions for A (see Westley 1991: 11, 23, for Tepetotutla Chinantec, and Anderson 1989: 6, 18, for Comaltepec Chinantec). In Ungarinjin (Australian) four noun classes are distinguished in S/O bound pronouns, and none is distinguished for A pronouns, while in Alawa and Tiwi two noun classes are distinguished for A/S and none for O (Dixon 2002: 480).

'Oro Nao (Chapacuran: Everett and Kern 1997: 329) always distinguishes masculine, feminine and neuter genders of third person O. At least in some of the verb paradigms gender is not distinguished for A/S. In Lavukaleve (Papuan, Solomon Islands: Angela Terrill p.c.) three genders are distinguished in cross-referencing prefixes which mark O, but not for those which mark S/A. In Emmi (Australian: Ford 1998) gender distinctions are neutralized in 'minimal' transitive subject (A) cross-referencing markers, but not in other numbers or functions.

In a language with two noun class systems these may relate to different case functions. In Paumarí (Arawá: §2.7.2) there are two types of transitive construction. In one of these masculine/feminine gender of the subject (A) is cross-referenced on the verb, and in the other that of the object (O) gets cross-referenced. In both constructions, however, the verb cross-references the shape-based *ka*-noun class of the object (O). In intransitive clauses, both gender and *ka*-noun class cross-reference the subject (S).

10.3.2. Verbal classifiers and grammatical function

Verbal classifiers and classificatory verbs always contain reference to the grammatical function of an argument. This function is usually S/O (see Keenan 1984 and §6.3). In Palikur (Aikhenvald and Green 1998) the classifiers refer to O and derived S of a passive, or to the S of a stative intransitive verb (see §6.4.1).

10.4. Classifiers and types of possession

The way a noun can be possessed may correlate with the intrinsic properties of its referent. The division of nouns into alienably and inalienably possessed may be considered as a kind of noun categorization device (see

Nichols 1992: 134–5, and the discussion in §5.3.2).[15] Of all the noun categorization devices only noun classes and the three types of possessive classifier show an interaction with types of possession (since only these classifier types can have possessive NPs as their scope).

10.4.1. Noun classes and types of possession

Noun class realization and agreement in a possessive NP can depend on the type of possessive construction. Some languages make more noun class distinctions in constructions with INALIENABLE possession than in those with ALIENABLE possession. Jarawara (Arawá) distinguishes alienably and inalienably possessed nouns (see Dixon 1995; Dixon forthcoming). The gender of the possessor is cross-referenced on the inalienably possessed noun, and not on an alienably possessed one. Examples 10.1 and 10.2 show that the gender of the possessor is marked on the inalienably possessed noun 'home'.

10.1. Okomobi   taboro
     Okomobi(masculine) home+MASC
     'Okomobi's home'

10.2. Sasa   tabori
     Sasa(feminine)   home+FEM
     'Sasa's home'

The noun 'house' in 10.3 and 10.4 is alienably possessed, and there is no gender agreement with a possessor.

10.3. Okomobi   kaa   jobe
     Okomobi(masculine) POSS house
     'Okomobi's house'

10.4. Sasa   kaa   jobe
     Sasa(feminine)   POSS house
     'Sasa's house'

Interrelations between possession type and gender and noun class agreement may be more complicated. In 'Oro Nao (Chapacuran: Everett and Kern 1997: 299) gender is marked on possessed forms of inalienably possessed nouns, as in Arawá languages, e.g. *capija-in wao'* (mouth-3neut small.basket:neuter) 'rim of the basket'; *capija-con wom* (mouth-3masc cotton:masculine) 'hem of the skirt'; *capija-cam narima'* (mouth-3fem

---

[15] Possession types may be more complicated than just alienable and inalienable. There may be special type of 'unpossessable' nouns, or 'body part' or 'kinship possession'. For a useful overview, see Chappell and McGregor (1996).

woman: feminine) 'woman's mouth'. Unlike Arawá, Chapacuran languages have three genders: feminine (used for human females, collective nouns, mixed gender groups), masculine (for human males, high animates, and culturally significant objects, and also for nature phenomena, insects, fish, etc.), and neuter (used for most inanimate objects, newly introduced objects/animals/plants, loans, nominalizations). Gender marking is realized on modifiers, possessed forms and in verbal cross-referencing.

In East Tucano languages and in Tariana (North Arawak) more noun class distinctions are found in constructions with ALIENABLE possession than in those with INALIENABLE possession. These languages have a closed set of pronominal noun classes, and a large set of morphemes used as noun class markers and as numeral and noun classifiers (see Chapter 9; Aikhenvald 1994a: 427; 1996a). Possessed classifiers in alienable possessive constructions appear on the possessive morpheme *ya*. Thus:

10.5. Tucano: mɨ'ɨ ya-gɨ̃   pũ-gɨ̃
              2SG   POSS-CL:LARGE   hammock-CL:LARGE
              'your hammock'

10.6. Tariana: pi-ya-ku   ama-ku
              2SG-POSS-CL:EXTENDED   hammock-CL:EXTENDED
              'your hammock'

10.4.2. *Classifiers in possessive constructions and types of possession*

The choice of a RELATIONAL CLASSIFIER usually depends on possession type (see §5.3.2). Relational classifiers which contain information on how an object can be handled, or whether it is consumable or not, are restricted to alienably possessed nouns.

In numerous cases, POSSESSED CLASSIFIERS are also used exclusively with alienably possessed nouns. This is the case in Yuman and Uto-Aztecan languages in North America, and in Carib, Tupí-Guaraní, Macro-Jê, Nadëb (Makú) and a few Arawak languages (Island Carib, Bahwana, Achagua and Palikur) in South America (see §5.2).

Possessed classifiers are used independently of possession type only in a few North Arawak and Tucano languages and in the Mba group (Ubangi, Niger-Congo) (see §5.2).

It is hard to make any generalizations about possessor classifiers. In Dâw (Makú: Martins 1994) discussed in §5.4, possessor classifiers can only be used with alienably possessed nouns. In Nasioi (Papuan: Bougainville), which may feature another example of possessor classifiers, they are also restricted to just one type of possessive constructions (see 5.47; Hurd 1977: 138).

10.5. Classifiers and politeness

There may be a grammatical category indicating politeness or social status marked on nouns, or on verbs. Politeness can be expressed in the same morphosyntactic contexts as classifiers. Consequently, one expects interrelations between classifiers and politeness. The choice of a politeness form often correlates with the animacy or humanness of the referent: polite forms, or forms sensitive to social status, are applicable only to human (or, more rarely, to animate) referents. Social status is frequently expressed in systems of NUMERAL CLASSIFIERS for humans (see Chapter 11).[16] For instance some Austroasiatic languages have elaborate systems of 'honorific' numeral classifiers based on social status. So do some Indo-Aryan languages (e.g. Assamese: see Table 4.1), Korean (Lee 1997), Burmese and Thai (Bisang 1999).

Social status is often expressed in a system of NOUN CLASSIFIERS (see §11.2.2 and Chapter 3; also see the discussion on noun classifiers and social deixis in Mixtec in De Leon 1987: 171–2).

Occasionally, the choice of a possessed classifier can depend on the social status of speakers, or the speech style. Ponapean (Micronesian: Keating 1997) has twenty-two possessed classifiers used in the common speech register. Only objects related to rank in the society are reclassified in the honorific register. This is shown in Table 10.12 (based on Keating 1997: 252–3, 255, 258).

In contrast, in the humiliative register (used to address socially inferior people) there is just one kind of possessive classifier, a combination of general classifier *ah* and a specific humiliative classifier *tungoal* (lit. 'food'); all the semantic distinctions present in honorific and common style classifiers are neutralized (see §12.3, for a socio-cultural explanation). Table 10.13 provides examples of noun categorization in humiliative speech and in the common speech register (Keating 1997: 255).

As in other Micronesian languages, possessive classifiers in Ponapean appear only in constructions with alienably possessed items. This is, however, not true for the possessive classifier used in humiliative speech which is used with any item in humiliative speech, independently of whether it is treated in other speech styles as alienably or inalienably possessed; thus, body parts which are inalienably possessed in common speech, e.g. *moahng-ei* (head-1sg.POSS) 'my head', take the only possessive classifier, *ah tungoal*, in humiliative speech, e.g. *ei tungoal moahng* (POSS.CL:GEN+1sg.POSS POSS.CL.HUMIL:FOOD head) 'my (lower status) head' (Keating 1997: 256).

---

[16] See also Senft (1996: 202, 203 and *passim*) on the interaction between classifiers and sociolinguistic variables in Kilivila.

TABLE 10.12. *Possessed classifiers and speech styles in Ponapean*

Common	Semantics	Honorific	Semantics	Humiliative
ah	General classifier	*sapwellime*	General classifier	
nah	General, dominance of possessor			
kene	Edible	*koanoat*	Possession of food/drink by paramount chief	
		pwenieu	Id. by paramount chieftainess	
nime	Drinkable	*sahk*	Id. by secondary chief	
sapwe	Land	*nillime*	Land	
imwe	Buildings	*tehnpese*	Dwellings	
were	Vehicles	*tehnwere*	Vehicles	
kie	Sleeping pads	*moatoare*	Things to sleep on	*ah tungoal*
ipe	Sleeping covers	Same as in common speech		
ulunge	Pillows			
rie	Siblings			
kiseh	Relatives			
ullepe	Maternal uncles			
wahwah	Nieces, nephews			
sawi	Clan members			
pelie	Peers			
seike	Catch			
pwekidah	Share of feast food			
mware	Name, title, garland			
ede	Names			
tie	Earrings			
dewe	Location			

TABLE 10.13. *Examples of possessed classifiers in common and humiliative speech in Ponapean*

Common	Humiliative	Translation
kene mwahng (POSS.CL:EDIBLE taro)	*ah tungoal mwahng* (POSS.CL:GEN.POSS CL HUMIL:FOOD taro)	'her taro'
nah pwihk (POSS.CL:GEN pig)	*ah tungoal pwihk*	'her pig'
were sidohsa (POSS.CL: VEHICLE car)	*ah tungoal sidohsa*	'her car'

The existence of an elaborate system of politeness in a language does not presuppose classifiers which refer to social status; politeness is important as a grammatical category in Japanese, however, there is just one honorific, unlike Korean—see §12.4.

In some languages the choice between various first and second person pronouns tends to be made according to the social status of the speaker, or of the addressee. Then politeness and gender can be considered portmanteau. In Minangkabau 2nd person pronouns combine information on the sex and social status and age of the referent: *waang*, or *ang*, '2nd person singular masculine' and *kau* '2nd person feminine' are used to refer to people younger than the speaker, while *uda* '2nd person singular masculine' and *uni* '2nd person singular feminine' are used to refer to people older than the speaker and higher on the social hierarchy (Marnita 1996: 64).[17]

Meanings related to politeness, such as social status and respect, can be expressed through NOUN CLASS. In Jarawara, a woman can be referred to with the marked masculine gender instead of the unmarked feminine as a sign of respect (R. M. W. Dixon, p.c.). In Amharic, the marked feminine gender is used for respectful reference to men (Mengistu Amberber, p.c.).

'Respect' vs. 'disdain' can be an extension of positive vs. negative values assigned to genders. In Lokono (Arawak: Pet 1987: 26–7; (C) in §2.4.4; §11.2.1), masculine gender covers (a) all males of the speaker's tribe, except if they are despised; (b) males who are not of the speaker's tribe, if they are friends of the speaker or if a relationship of mutual respect exists with the speaker, and also (c) animals, objects and spirits 'considered to be good and desirable or when they are protagonists in stories'. Feminine gender includes (a) all females and males who are despised; (b) males who are not of the speaker's tribe; and (c) animals, objects, and spirits not included in masculine gender. The 3rd person human plural is used 'for male and female humans who are Arawaks or with whom the speaker is in sympathy' (Pet 1987: 27).

10.6. Classifiers and declensional classes

Declensional classes and the organization of paradigms is usually independent of classifier systems. However, NOUN CLASS and declension correlate in languages with morphological gender assignment, e.g. Indo-European languages such as Latin, Lithuanian, or Russian. For instance, in Latin 2nd declension nouns are usually masculine, and 1st declension nouns are usually feminine. In Modern Irish, some nouns choose 'feminine' or 'masculine' declension forms due to the historical merging of paradigms (Ó Siadhail 1989: 145–6).[18]

---

[17] Some Asian languages, e.g. Thai, Burmese, Vietnamese, and Japanese, have different sets of personal pronouns (for all persons) the choice of which is determined by the sex of the speaker and their status (cf. Cooke 1986). These systems cannot be considered on a par with noun classification devices, but are similar to other elements of men's and women's speech, such as different lexical choices or pitch. Using different kinship terms of address for female and male relatives is not treated here as a gender distinction.

[18] Noun class assignment in Arapesh was analysed as a function of a morphological declensional class by Aronoff (1991). However, Nekitel (1985; 1986; ms) presents convincing arguments in favour of semantic assignment of at least some classes in Abu' Arapesh.

There are no correlations between other classifier types and declensional classes. This may be explained by the fact that only noun classes can be assigned on morphological principles (see §2.3).

A few languages which have lost genders have retained traces of gender-like distinctions in declensions. Lezgian, a Northeast Caucasian language which lost its gender system, has oblique stem suffixes which correlate with the semantics of nouns: *-Adi* is used with nouns which denote a non-discrete mass, *-rA* is used with most nouns which denote animals, or people (Haspelmath 1993: 76–7; see Alexeyev 1985: 27 ff., for other Lezgic languages).

In Armenian, which lost Indo-European gender distinctions, the opposition 'person'/'non-person' is present in inflectional paradigms (Garibian 1976). Further examples of a correlation between the organization of paradigms and categorization are given by Nichols (1992: 134–6), under the heading of 'non-agreeing classification'. This appears to be the property of the organization of paradigms in Indo-European languages, where concordial gender displays a correlation with the organization of declensions. Gender and declensional classes seem to be independent and orthogonal systems in some Daghestanian languages. Chechen and Ingush have genders, declension classes marked by thematic suffixes and declension subclasses marked by different ergative case and/or plural endings. Human and/or animate can be used in the description of the semantic basis of all three, but all these systems are independent (Nichols 1992: 134).

10.7. Classifiers and verbal categories

Of all the classifier types, only NOUN CLASSES and VERBAL CLASSIFIERS interact with verbal categories.

NOUN CLASSES can interact with tense. The choices available in the noun class system may depend on choices made in the tense system. Then noun classes are distinguished in some tenses, but not in others.[19] For example, in Manambu gender is distinguished in 1st person singular in the immediate past tense, but not in the remote past.[20] In Russian the verb in non-past tenses inflects for person and number of subject but not gender; in the past tense the verb marks singular and plural and, within singular, masculine, feminine, and neuter gender, but not person. The person system thus applies only in non-past; three genders are distinguished only in the past singular. The paradigm of *dela-t'* 'do' is shown in Table 10.14.

---

[19] In all these cases, noun class distinctions also depend on person and number, alongside tense. See Aikhenvald and Dixon (1998).
[20] Manambu has complicated correlations between gender marking on verbs, mood, and tense. See Aikhenvald (1998a).

264 *Classifiers*

TABLE 10.14. *Paradigm of* dela-t' *'do' in past tense in Russian*

Present				Past			
1SG	*delaju*	1PL	*delaem*	MASC. SG	*delal*	PL.	*delali*
2SG	*delaesh*	2PL	*delaete*	FEM. SG	*delala*		
3SG	*delaet*	3PL	*delajut*	NEUT. SG	*delalo*		

In Hebrew, with two genders, the verb in present tense is inflected for gender and number (the gender distinction is made in both singular and plural, but not person). In other tenses the verb inflects for number and person, with gender being specified just for 2nd and 3rd person. That is, person is only distinguished in non-present, and gender is restricted to second and third person in non-present. This is illustrated with the paradigm of the verb *katav* 'write' in past and present in Table 10.15.

TABLE 10.15. *Paradigm of* katav *'write' in Modern Hebrew*

Past				Future		Present	
1SG	*katavti*	1PL	*katavnu*	*extov*	*nixtov*	FEM. SG	*kotevet*
2SG F	*katavt*	2PL F	*ktavten*	*tixtəvu*	*tixtovna*	MASC. SG	*kotev*
2SG M	*katavta*	2PL M	*ktavtem*	*tixtov*	*tixtəvu*	FEM. PL	*kotvot*
3SG F	*katva*			*tixtəvi*	*tixtovna*	MASC. PL	*kotvim*
3SG M	*katav*	3PL	*katvu*	*yixtov*	*yixtəvu*		

There are diachronic reasons for this split in grammatical marking. The past in Russian and the present in Hebrew have both developed out of deverbal adjectives, and inflect in a manner typical of nominals.

An interaction between noun class, person, and tense is observed in Tucano (West 1980), which has two systems of noun categorization (similarly to other languages mentioned in §2.7): the 'pronominal' one (a masculine/feminine/inanimate opposition) is used with verbal cross-referencing and personal pronouns; the 'nominal' one, which is much larger, is used with the remaining modifiers—numerals, deictics, adjectives. Pronominal classes are distinguished for all three persons in future tenses; in past and present tenses they are distinguished only for 3rd person.

Noun class distinctions can depend on clausal polarity (see the discussion in Aikhenvald and Dixon 1998). In some languages all specifications of person, number, and gender are neutralized in negative forms, e.g. Tariana, or Manambu. Similarly, in Palikur, two genders are distinguished in certain aspects; but these aspects are not used in negative clauses: there are fewer aspect choices in negative clauses than in positive ones. Consequently, gender is not contrastive under negation. Gender agreement is marked on the durative suffix which is typically used with stative verbs (10.7). In 10.8, the negative counterpart of 10.7, it is suppressed.[21]

10.7. tino   barew-yo
woman be.pretty/clean-DUR.F
'The woman is pretty.'

10.8. tino   ka-barew
woman NEG-be.pretty/clean
'The woman is not pretty.'

The choice of VERBAL CLASSIFIERS may depend on (a) verb class, or (b) other verbal categories, e.g. the choice made in the tense-aspect system, or in the voice system.[22]

(A) The choice of verbal classifiers depends on verb class

For example, in Koyukon (Athabaskan: Axelrod forthcoming) verbal classifiers (traditionally named 'genders' in Athabaskan linguistic tradition) never occur with attributive verbs (e.g. 'be happy'). Suppletive classificatory verbs are never used attributively.

Palikur has two sets of verbal classifiers—one used with transitive verbs, and the other with intransitive stative verbs. Intransitive active verbs do not take classifiers.[23]

(B) Verbal classifiers may be restricted to certain verbal categories

In Tariana and Baniwa (North Arawak) classifiers are used only with relativized verbs, verbs in purposive mood, and in the form of argument manipulating derivation. In Palikur, verbal classifiers can only be used if the O of a transitive verb, or the S of a stative verb are completely involved in action or state; consequently, classifiers are almost always used with verbs marked for completive aspect (see further examples in §6.4.1).

---

[21] However, the gender agreement is obligatory in negative clauses with emphatic contrastive negation (marked by both negative prefix *ka-* and a negative suffix *-ma*), e.g. *tino ka-barew-yo-ma* (woman NEG-be.pretty/clean-DUR.F-NEG) 'The woman is not pretty at all'.
[22] An analogy between numeral classifiers (also used with demonstratives and interrogatives, and with some adjectives) in Newari and morphemes which marks repetitive action with verbs depending on the type of action performed and thus, in a way, 'classifiying' verbal actions, is drawn by Bhaskararao and Joshi (1985) for Newari (Tibeto-Burman). This analogy is radically different from the dependencies considered in this section.
[23] This dependency has to do with semantic restrictions on classes of verbs used with classifiers; see Chapter 11.

10.8. Classifiers and deictic categories

Categories typically found in deictics (e.g. distance from speaker or hearer, or visibility) interact with noun categorization devices expressed in deictics—NOUN CLASSES and DEICTIC CLASSIFIERS.

Noun classes can be portmanteau with deictic categories, e.g. Warekena (North Arawak) *eni* 'this: masculine', *ayupalu* 'this: feminine'. The choice of noun class may depend on degree of distance realized in deictics. Palikur (Table 8.6) has five sets of deictics; three genders are distinguished in all but the series which refers to objects located far from speaker and near hearer. In Bare (North Arawak: Aikhenvald 1995a: 22) masculine and feminine genders are regularly distinguished for the distal deictic only; no distinction has been observed for proximal ('near to speaker') or medium distance ('nearer to hearer').

Deictic classifiers combine reference to visibility, distance, and proximity of the referent, and its shape, directionality, or other nature-based properties (see §11.2.6). In Eskimo deictic classifiers interact with visibility; in Toba and Pilagá they contain additional reference to the presence or absence of an object in a visual field.

10.9. Classifiers, derivation, and lexicon

Classifiers interact with derivational devices; in this way they can enrich the lexicon. Noun classes and genders often combine inflectional (i.e. concordial) and derivational properties (see Payne 1990; §2.4.1).[24] Gender markers are productively used in derivation in Brazilian Portuguese, e.g. *ministr-o* 'minister', *ministr-a* 'she-minister'; *juiz* 'judge', *juiz-a* 'she-judge'. In Bantu languages, e.g. Swahili, most stems usually occur with a prefix of one class. Prefixes can be substituted to mark a characteristic of an object. *M-zee* means 'old person' and normally takes the human class prefix *m-*. It can be replaced by *ki-* (inanimate class) to yield *ki-zee* 'scruffy old person' (Dixon 1982: 166). Classifiers in multiple environments in Amazonian languages are often used as derivational devices (see (E) in §9.1).

In other languages there may be a number of genders expressed by derivational affixes, but only a subset of these operates in an agreement system. Gondi (South Dravidian) has feminine, masculine, and neuter in derivation, but only two genders (masculine and non-masculine) in agreement (Subrahmanyam 1968) (see also Evans ms; 1997, for further differences between head and agreement classes in Mayali).

[24] The distinction between head classes and agreement classes (see §2.6.1; Evans 1997) illustrates the difference between the two functions.

Classifiers of all types provide cross-categorization of nouns, and offer additional information about a noun's referent (see §12.1.2). Noun classifiers are often used to highlight different aspects of the meaning of a polysemous noun (see §3.2.2). This variable classification is a characteristic property of noun classifiers, numeral classifiers, and verbal classifiers (see Table 12.4, for an example of the 'reclassification' of an inanimate noun in Burmese, and discussion in Chapter 12).

Variable noun class marking in Maung (Capell and Hinch 1970: 47–52) has a similar semantic effect. Maung has five noun classes the assignment of which is partially based on semantics. Class 1 consists of names of male beings; Class II of names of female beings; Class III includes objects associated with the ground (except plants); Class IV consists of trees and their parts; and Class V of vegetable foods and plants. Noun classes are overtly marked on nouns, and also realized through subject and object agreement on verbs and/or agreement on adjectives and possessives. Changing the noun class of some nouns may result in a change of meaning. The noun -*nimi* expresses the idea of a 'long bone'. Used with a 'human male' Class 1 prefix, *(j)i-nimi* means 'his backbone'; with a Class II, female human class, *ninj-imi* means 'her backbone'. With a Class IV prefix, *ma-nimi* means 'trunk of a tree', and with a class V prefix *ad-imi* means 'main radicle' of a potato plant or yam vine (Capell and Hinch 1970: 47). Table 10.16 illustrates how noun classes are used with another noun root, *mawur* 'arm, long part of'.

TABLE 10.16. *Variable noun class assignment in Maung*

Class I	*i-mawur*	'man's arm'
Class II	*ninj-mawur*	'woman's arm'
Class III	*u-mawur*	'tributary of a river'
Class IV	*ma-mawur*	'branch of a tree'
Class V	*a-bawur*	'tendril of a vine'

In systems with the same or overlapping sets of classifiers in different functions, classifier morphemes are typically used in the same way. In Baniwa (North Arawak), a noun can be associated with more than one classifier in accordance with which the semantic aspect of the referent the speaker wishes to stress—see 2.18–20.

The taxonomies expressed by classifier systems differ not only from those encoded by nouns; they also differ from one another (see §11.1). As Benton (1968: 142–3) put it, in his analysis of the system of two classifier types in Truquese, an Austronesian language, 'the classifiers . . . thus at the same time provide a means for ordering the universe, and a method for structuring concepts without multiplying vocabulary'.

268   *Classifiers*

This is yet another way in which the presence of classifiers in a language may affect its lexicon. Languages with classifiers, the semantics of which includes reference to shape, dimensionality, and other nature-based properties of entities, tend to have fewer lexical items—adjectives, or functionally related categories—which describe shapes or dimensions. Along with a rich system of shape-based classifiers, Palikur has very few stative verbs corresponding to adjectives in other languages for such semantic groups as dimension. The same lexical item, *pugum-/pugub-/pugu-* can be translated as 'thick', 'broad', 'large', and 'big' with further semantic distinctions being made by classifiers. Thai and Lao have one stative verb meaning 'big' or 'large'; further subtleties referring to shape are expressed with classifiers (Adam Chapman, p.c.). Tariana has just one word for 'big' (covering the same semantic range as in Palikur); unlike Thai and Lao, there is no adjective meaning 'round' since the concept is expressed through a classifier for round objects. (Note that Bare and Warekena—languages from the same North Arawak family without extensive classifier systems—have lexical items for these concepts.)

The ways the presence of classifiers in a language can reduce the actual lexicon by expressing the same concepts through grammar relates to a well-known facet of the interface between grammar and lexicon. Another problem is which concepts tend always to be realized in grammar, and which can 'shift' into the lexicon, or be realized in both. The human and non-human distinction is widespread in classifier systems; however, all languages, including the ones with classifiers, also have other—more lexical—ways of distinguishing humans from non-humans, or persons from non-persons. Thus, grammar and lexicon feed each other in the semantic domains covered by classifiers.

10.10. Conclusions

How classifiers of different types interact with nominal and verbal grammatical categories is summarized in Table 10.17.

NOUN CLASSES interact with all the categories described here, with the exception of politeness (though they also interact with social status in a limited way). They show mutual interdependencies with number, person, marking of grammatical relations, possession, verbal, and deictic categories; they can also be realized as portmanteau morphemes with these categories, and with declension markers and derivational morphemes.

NUMERAL CLASSIFIERS show no correlations with categories other than politeness and, in a limited way, number.

NOUN CLASSIFIERS interact with person and politeness; they can also be used for derivational purposes. POSSESSIVE CLASSIFIERS interact just with

TABLE 10.17. *Classifiers and their interaction with other grammatical categories*

	Noun classes	Numeral classifiers	Noun classifiers	Possessive classifiers	Verbal classifiers	Locative classifiers	Deictic classifiers
Number	yes	limited	no	no	yes	no	(yes)
Person	yes	no	no	no	no	no	no
Grammatical function	yes	no	no	no	yes	no	no
Types of possession	yes	no	no	yes	no	no	no
Politeness	limited	yes	yes	no	no	no	no
Declensions	yes	no	no	no	no	no	no
Verbal/clausal categories	yes	no	no	no	yes	no	no
Deictic categories	yes	no	no	no	no	no	yes
Derivational categories	yes	no	yes	no	no	no	no

Symbols used: 'yes' indicates the existence of a dependency, or of a correlation, 'no' indicates its absence, and (yes) means that further investigation is required.

types of possession. VERBAL CLASSIFIERS show interdependencies with number, with the ways grammatical relations are expressed, and with various verbal categories. DEICTIC CLASSIFIERS interact with deictic categories (such as distance and visibility), and sometimes with number. LOCATIVE CLASSIFIERS show no interdependencies at all.

The ways different classifier types interact with other categories depend on (a) their scope and (b) possibilities of their realization as bound morphemes or as free morphemes. NOUN CLASSES can have an argument NP and a clause as their scope; this accounts for the maximum amount of interactions for this classifier type. They are often realized as portmanteau morphemes with other categories—note that noun class markers are never free morphemes, so they are likely to fuse with other markers.

The scope of VERBAL CLASSIFIERS is the clause; they also categorize the argument, hence interactions with number, with grammatical relations, and with verbal categories (some of which could alternately be considered clausal; see Aikhenvald and Dixon 1998). Again, they are never free morphemes, so one would expect a considerable amount of fusion with other categories. CLASSIFIERS IN POSSESSIVE CONSTRUCTIONS have a possessive NP as their scope; their interaction with possessive categories is expected. NUMERAL and NOUN CLASSIFIERS show fewer correlations with other categories, and so do DEICTIC and LOCATIVE CLASSIFIERS. This can be accounted for by limitations of their scope; they can also be realized as independent morphemes.

In languages with more than one noun class system, different noun classes may interact with different categories. All types of classifier show some interaction with the lexicon—this topic requires further study.

The ways in which classifiers used in different morphosyntactic environments interact with different categories is a direct consequence of their morphosyntactic loci of marking, and their scope. We return to this topic in Chapter 15.

11 Semantics of Noun Categorization Devices

All noun categorization devices have some semantic basis. Different classifier types tend to correlate with different semantic parameters. Many systems allow variable choice of classifiers; then classifiers may specify the meaning of a polysemous noun. The semantic parameters employed in noun categorization are discussed in §11.1. The semantics of each type of classifier is considered in §11.2. The semantic organization of classifier systems and their functions are considered in the next chapter.

11.1. Semantic parameters in noun categorization

All classifier systems employ a number of basic semantic parameters (§11.1.1). There are additional semantic properties of objects which may be relevant for noun categorization (§11.1.2).[1] The semantic relationships between a classifier and a noun are dealt with in §11.1.3.

11.1.1. Basic parameters of categorization

A number of basic semantic parameters tend to be encoded in different types of classifiers.[2] These parameters fall into three large classes: animacy, physical properties, and function.[3]

---

[1] The semantic features discussed here are probably universal, or close to universal (this is a topic for a future study). The semantic parameters used in noun categorization are framed within a typological approach followed by Frawley (1992) and Dixon (1982).

[2] There have been various attempts at identifying cross-linguistic universal semantic properties of noun classifications devices (see Adams and Conklin 1973; Conklin 1981; Denny 1976; Allan 1977; Dixon 1982; Craig 1991; forthcoming; Frawley 1992; Kiyomi 1992; Croft 1994). Croft (1994) made an attempt to establish a number of implicational hierarchies of semantic distinctions associated with different types of classifier. The main problem with this kind of approach appears to be the possibility of using the same morpheme in multiple classifier environments. See §11.2.8.

[3] Further semantic characteristics may be considered concomitant with each of these. Frawley (1992: 68 ff.) considers eight classes of entities which cover different semantic divisions of nouns only some of which are reflected in classifier semantics. In particular, SPECIFICITY (Frawley 1992: 69) is only indirectly connected with classifier systems. BOUNDEDNESS (Frawley 1992: 81) is associated with countability, and is particularly relevant for numeral classifiers (§11.2.3). Other classes discussed by Frawley are ANIMACY, GENDER, KINSHIP, SOCIAL STATUS, PHYSICAL PROPERTIES, and FUNCTION. See discussion in this chapter.

Animate nouns[4] can be further divided into human/non-human, person/ non-person, or relating to sex. Humans can be classified according to their social status and function, age, and kinship relationship. The notion of animacy plays a significant role in the morphology and syntax of many languages (see Comrie 1981; Frawley 1992: 89). Though an animate/ inanimate distinction is found in the lexicon and grammar of most languages, language-internal criteria have to be applied to decide how entities are divided into animates and inanimates. This binary division can be found in Russian (where all living beings, within the masculine gender, belong to the animate declension: see (C) in §2.4.4, and Table 2.7), or in Jarawara (Arawá) (where all animate beings must be referred to with the third person plural pronoun *mee*: R. M. W. Dixon, p.c.). On the other hand, Baniwa (Arawak) has a classifier for humans, while animals are classified by shape, similarly to inanimate nouns; personal pronouns can be used with humans and with higher animals (e.g. mammals) and birds, but not with insects.

Languages also differ in how they treat supernatural beings: benevolent gods and angels are frequently personified, i.e., treated on a par with humans, or at least with animates, while malevolent spirits, e.g. ghosts, may be treated like inanimates, or even be completely outside the system. Thus, some Austroasiatic languages simply have separate classifiers for supernatural beings (see examples of Mon in Adams 1989: 58, Khmuic in Adams 1989: 60). In Minangkabau the human numeral classifier is used with angels; but bad spirits such as ghosts are simply not classified.

Inanimate nouns—and, more rarely, animates—can be classified according to their physical properties and function. The most common properties reflected in classifier systems are listed below. Properties (a–h) relate to the time-stable or inherent properties of an entity. Properties (i) and (j) relate to its temporary state, e.g. configuration or arrangement;[5] they are often encountered in mensural numeral classifiers. The way objects can be handled or used (property (h)) may correlate with their inherent as well as temporary properties. Each property is exemplified in §11.2.

(a) EXTENDEDNESS has two sub-parameters: SHAPE/DIMENSIONALITY and DIRECTION.

DIMENSIONALITY has three values: one-dimensional (or long), two-

---

[4] 'Animate' is defined by Trask (1993: 16) as 'denoting a noun or noun phrase which is perceived as referring to a conscious, volitional entity, a human or higher animal' (cf. also Matthews 1997: 19). In some languages insects and fish are also considered animate. Semantic parameters of animacy and humanness are universal; they are found in most systems of noun categorization, i.e. classifiers of distinct types (Kiyomi 1992), or elsewhere in the grammar (see Frawley 1992: 89 ff. and App. 1). Further discussion of the universality of animacy is given by Frawley (1992: 89–91).

[5] This distinction is similar to the opposition of 'permanent' and 'temporary' characteristics in the classifier system of Tzeltal introduced by Berlin (1968).

dimensional (or flat), and three-dimensional (spherical). Dimensionality and shape often occur together, but they can also be separate. Many languages differentiate more shapes for one- and two-dimensional objects (Hundius and Kölver 1983: 206; Denny 1979a). Three-dimensional objects can also be classified in terms of their different shapes (e.g., round and irregular shape). SHAPE is a cover term for other, form-related properties (e.g. curved, linear, pointed, or blunt).

DIRECTION, or ORIENTATION, refers to a distinction between objects which are vertically extended and those which are horizontally extended.

(b) INTERIORICITY refers to the way an entity 'differentiates its inside from its outside', e.g. the distinction between rings and holes. BOUNDEDNESS is a related parameter, and it indicates whether or not outlined entities have a delimitation (for instance, flat objects can be bounded, e.g. tortillas, or unbounded, e.g. plains).

(c) SIZE has two values, large and small.

(d) CONSISTENCY refers to the plasticity of the object under manipulation. The two most frequent values are flexible and rigid. Other possible values include viscosity of a liquid, or its surface tackiness (Frawley 1992: 128).

(e) CONSTITUTION, or STATE, refers to the physical state of an entity, such as liquid or solid. It is often fused with CONSISTENCY, DIMENSIONALITY, and/or SHAPE. For instance, many classifier systems have a single term for liquids while classifiers for solid objects always include reference to whether the object is long or round.

(f) MATERIAL out of which an object is made may be reflected by classifiers; there may be classifiers for wooden and for metal objects.

(g) Other INHERENT NATURE or TIME-STABLE properties used in noun categorization have to do with the material and function of the items. Often, there are special classifiers for plants, houses, canoes, verses of poetry, books, and so on. Inherent nature properties are often realized through SPECIFIC, or UNIQUE classifiers which combine with just one noun, e.g. the Korean classifier *hwan1* for 'ball-shaped Chinese traditional medicinal pill' (Lee 1997: 55). These classifiers are generally culture-specific (see §12.3).

(h) FUNCTION, or functional interaction[6] classifiers refer to specific uses of objects, or kinds of action which are typically performed on them. Languages tend to encode culture-specific functional properties in classifiers. Objects can be classified depending on whether they can be consumed (eaten, drunk), or whether they can be planted, or domesticated; there are often classifiers for means of transport, clothing, and housing. Actions

---

[6] Functional interaction is, in a sense, parallel to social interaction in classifiers which refer to social status (cf. Denny 1976).

performed on objects and encoded in classifiers may involve cutting, piercing, harvesting, peeling, and so on (see Berlin 1968, for examples of highly idiosyncratic function-based numeral classifiers in Tzeltal).

Objects can be classified by their VALUE, which is ultimately determined by their functional properties. Thus, among relational classifiers there is often a term for 'valuable' possessions.

(i) ARRANGEMENT refers to the configuration of objects, e.g. coil of rope, or objects strung together. Arrangement very often correlates with consistency, and material (e.g., Nivkh has a special classifier for fishes strung on twigs: see Table 4.4).

(j) QUANTA is similar to ARRANGEMENT and refers to number, or quantity of objects, e.g. cluster, set, flock, bunch. Quanta correlate with consistency and material. For instance, a 'cluster' refers to a quantum which is also irregularly shaped and dense (Frawley 1992: 128).

Some nouns in a language may lie outside the scope of existing classifiers. A RESIDUE, or DEFAULT classifier can then be used with otherwise 'unclassifiable' nouns; the functions of a 'default' member of a classifier system are discussed in §12.1.4.

11.1.2. Additional semantic characteristics

A number of other properties of objects are relevant for the semantic organization of different kinds of classifiers. COUNTABILITY involves the distinction between count and mass nouns (this property may also correlate with the distinction of boundedness/unboundedness: Frawley 1992: 84–8). Different classifiers which refer to configurations and quanta of objects can be used with a noun depending on whether it is countable or not.[7] The distinction between count and mass nouns also affects correlations between classifiers and other categories, e.g. number.[8] The mass/unit distinction is important for numeral classifiers. In addition, one of the functions of affixed noun classifiers in some South American languages is to make mass, uncountable, or collective nouns into countable ones.

[7] Countability, and how it is important for distinguishing between classifiers and quantifiers in noun phrases with numerals, was discussed in Chapter 4. Classifiers used with countable nouns which are 'natural units' have an individualizing function, while classifiers with uncountable nouns are mainly used to 'create' units by measuring them (Croft 1994). Classifiers which refer to quanta and configuration can also be used to create 'new' units out of count nouns, e.g. *one bunch of carrots*. Depending on language-internal criteria, measure terms may or may not be considered a subtype of classifiers. In many cases, there can be a continuum between 'true' classifiers and quantifiers.

[8] The count/mass distinction is closely tied to grammatical number; however, the correlation between mass and singularity, and count and plurality, is not straightforward (see Allan 1980; Wierzbicka 1985, for an analysis of an iconic relationship between grammar of plural vs. singular marking in mass nouns and the internal structure of referents; see also Stebbins 1997).

The division of nouns into ABSTRACT and CONCRETE is another property relevant for the structure of classifier systems. Often, abstract nouns are not classified; some may take specific classifiers.

11.1.3. Semantic relationship between a classifier and the referent

The semantic relationship between the referent of a noun and a classifier can be of two kinds.

(i) A classifier is chosen according to the time-stable, or temporary properties of a referent noun.

(ii) A classifier is a superordinate term which indicates a larger class of 'prototypical' referents to which the noun belongs as a subordinate member.

Then, classifier and noun are in a generic-specific relation. The differentiation between the superordinate level of noun categorization (animal, plant, vehicle, etc.) and the subordinate level is basic to this relationship. The generic-specific relationship is basic to the organization of the lexicon. Generic terms usually cover inherent nature properties ((a–g) above) and functional properties, (h).

11.2. Semantics of classifier types

Our next step is to investigate the semantics of different noun categorization devices, to see whether there are any significant correlations or preferences between classifier types and the semantic parameters used. The semantics of different noun categorization devices is considered in §11.2.1–6. The semantics of different classifiers coexisting in one language is dealt with in §11.2.7, and the semantics of multiple classifier systems is discussed in §11.2.8.

11.2.1. Semantics of noun classes

Nouns are assigned to noun classes on a semantic basis, or on a combination of semantic and other—morphological or phonological—properties of nouns. Because of the highly grammatical status of noun classes, their assignment is often at least to some degree semantically opaque (see §2.3.1), and every noun tends to belong to just one class (see §2.4.3 on variability in noun class assignment).[9]

---

[9] However, as we have shown in §2.3.4, even if noun class assignment is based on a combination of different properties, there is always some ultimate semantic basis to it. The

The semantic basis of noun classes involves animate/inanimate, human/non-human, person/non-person, and sex: see (A) below. Additional parameters for noun class assignment of inanimates may include (B) physical and (C) other properties. Semantic complexity and opacity in noun class assignment are discussed under (D), and semantic parameters in split noun class systems are considered in (E).

(A) Animate/inanimate, human/non-human, person/non-person, and sex in noun class systems

These parameters interrelate in different ways depending on the system. Some Dravidian languages divide nouns into human and non-human (or person/non-person). Siouan and Algonquian languages divide nouns into animate and inanimate classes. In many Afroasiatic, Eastern Nilotic, and Central Khoisan languages, nouns are divided into feminine and masculine depending on their sex. 'Rationality' can be an extension of 'humanness'; nouns divide into rational (humans, gods, demons) and non-rational in Tamil and other Dravidian languages. (The term 'neuter' is often used to refer to 'irrational', inanimate gender, or as a residue gender with no clear semantic basis.)

Languages can combine these parameters. Zande and Ma (Ubangi, Niger-Congo) distinguish masculine, feminine, non-human animate, and inanimate. Godoberi (Northeast Caucasian) has feminine, masculine, and non-rational genders (for further examples, see §2.3.1; Corbett 1991; Aikhenvald 1999a).

(B) Physical properties in noun class systems

Inanimate nouns can be assigned genders based on their shape, size, and also position and consistency. Physical properties employed in noun class assignment, summarized in Table 11.1,[10] are iconic and nature-based: women are usually smaller and rounder than men and are perceived to sit more than men, so round shape and squat position tend to be associated with feminine gender.

---

pervasive character of animacy-based distinctions is best illustrated with languages which have phonological noun class assignment. Noun class agreement in Arapesh and Bukiyip, Papuan languages from the East Sepik, is partly phonologically based. A more detailed analysis of the way noun classes are assigned shows its semantic motivation. In Bukiyip, nouns divide into eighteen classes. Four of these classes include animate nouns: males, females, non-human animates and personal names; and all the rest include inanimates classified according to their shape and other physical properties (see also §2.3, for an example of semantic and phonological principles of noun class assignment in Yimas).

[10] The semantics of gender in the languages of the Sepik region is discussed by Bruce (1984), for Alamblak and by Aikhenvald (1998a) for Manambu; for Oromo, see Clamons (1993); for Cushitic, East Nilotic, and Khoisan, see Heine (1982a); for Tiwi, see Osborne (1974) and Lee (1987); see data on Cantabrian Spanish in Table 2.2.

TABLE 11.1. *Examples of physical properties in noun class assignment*

Parameter	Masculine	Feminine	Example
Size	Large (and wide)	Small (and narrow)	Some Afroasiatic languages, e.g. Dasenech, Oromo, Amharic, Turkana, Camus (Eastern Nilotic)
	Narrow (and small)	Wide (and large)	Cantabrian Spanish, Central Khoisan, small in Tiwi (Australian)
Shape	Straight	Round	Alamblak, Manambu, Central Khoisan, Tiwi
Position	Vertical	Horizontal, squat	Manambu, Cantabrian Spanish
Solidity	Solid	Hollow, deep, concave	Katcha (Kadugli-Kongo)

Further examples of shape-based gender assignment to inanimates are found in Papuan languages of New Guinea. In Yonggom, an Ok language spoken in the Western province (Christensen 1995: 9–10), feminine gender assignment to inanimates is associated with large size, with masculine gender assignment being linked with elongated shape; a similar system is found in Olo (Torricelli phylum: Laycock 1975: 770; McGregor and McGregor 1982: 55). In Wära (Fly river; Risto Sarsa, p.c.) long inanimate objects are assigned masculine gender, while round objects and objects consisting of multiple parts are feminine. In Abau (isolate; East Sepik province) feminine gender assignment is associated with flat shape (Arjen Lock, p.c.).

A cluster of physical properties is typically used for gender assignment. Dimensionality is never the only physical property on which gender assignment for inanimates is based; rather, it always correlates with other properties, such as size or position.

If gender assignment to inanimates is SHAPE-based and SIZE is secondary, then masculine gender is associated with narrow, vertical, longish items. In contrast, feminine items get associated with the opposite: wide, horizontal, round items (e.g., Tiwi, Cantabrian Spanish, Central Khoisan).

If gender assignment is SIZE-based, and SHAPE is secondary, masculine items are typically associated with large size, and feminine items are considered small (e.g. Oromo and a few East Nilotic languages).

In some shape-based gender assignments to inanimates it is impossible to decide whether size or shape is primary, since the choice of a semantic parameter depends on the semantic group of the noun. The principles of masculine and feminine gender assignment to animates and to inanimates

278   *Classifiers*

in Manambu (Aikhenvald 1998a) are shown in Diagram 11.1. The gender assignment for humans depends on their sex. Gender assignment to animals is determined by their size, while gender choice for inanimates and lower animates (e.g. mosquitoes or flies) is determined by their size and shape. Gender choice for mass nouns (blood, dirt) is determined by their quantity; for natural phenomena it is determined by their 'extent': for instance, a very dark night or a very strong wind are masculine, while a moonlit night or a light breeze are feminine.

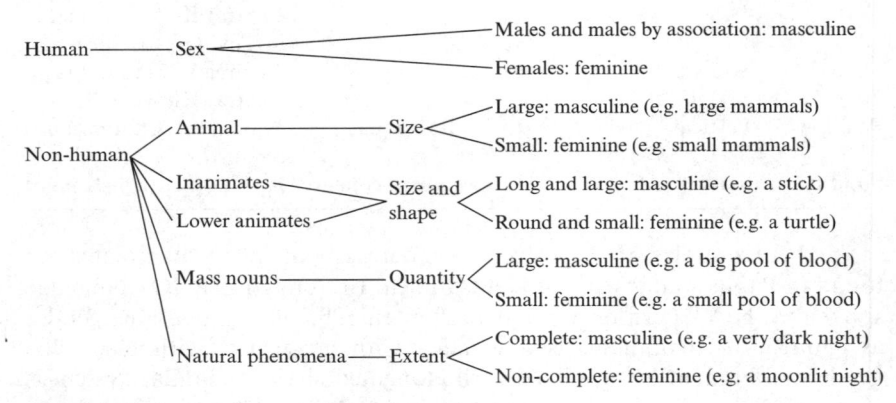

```
Human ─────── Sex ─┬──────────────── Males and males by association: masculine
                   └──────────────── Females: feminine

Non-human ─┬─ Animal ─────── Size ─┬── Large: masculine (e.g. large mammals)
           │                       └── Small: feminine (e.g. small mammals)
           ├─ Inanimates ──┐
           │               ├ Size and ─┬── Long and large: masculine (e.g. a stick)
           ├─ Lower animates┘  shape   └── Round and small: feminine (e.g. a turtle)
           │
           ├─ Mass nouns ─────── Quantity ─┬── Large: masculine (e.g. a big pool of blood)
           │                               └── Small: feminine (e.g. a small pool of blood)
           │
           └─ Natural phenomena ── Extent ─┬── Complete: masculine (e.g. a very dark night)
                                           └── Non-complete: feminine (e.g. a moonlit night)
```

DIAGRAM 11.1. *Gender assignment in Manambu*

This complicated interaction between the semantic group of a noun and the way it is assigned a gender shows that the shape and size in gender assignment to inanimates in this language requires a more complex semantic explanation than just 'stereotypical semantic associations with each sex' (cf. Croft 1994, in his debate with Kiyomi 1992).

Physical properties are only rarely employed to assign genders to animates. In Manambu (Ndu), a man can exceptionally be referred to with feminine gender if used pejoratively to refer to a fat, round, or squat person. In Palikur, if the sex of a person is unknown, gender is assigned by size: an adult is masculine, and a child is feminine. Some non-human animates (fish and birds) are assigned gender depending on their size.

(C) Additional oppositions

Noun class systems can use additional semantic features. Northeast Caucasian languages with four classes often have a special class to include animals (e.g. Lak or Andi: Corbett 1994b).

Function is rarely used in noun classes. A notable exception is Australian languages where one class, that of non-flesh (or vegetable) foods, is based on the function of the referent. A typical Australian noun class system has four classes: masculine (I), feminine (II), vegetable (III), and neuter, or 'residue' (IV) (cf. Evans 1997; ms).

There may be special genders for locative nouns, as in Bantu languages (see Chapter 13), e.g. ChiBemba Class 17 *uku-* 'target of motion or adherence', Class 18 *umu-* 'in ground, in water'. Motuna (Papuan, Bougainville) has distinct noun classes for locational and for manner nouns (Onishi 1994).

Genders often have affective values. In Oromo and Berber languages feminine gender is also used for diminutives, and often implies endearment. This is especially striking in systems which allow variability in gender assignment. In Amharic, close male friends and relatives may address each other in feminine gender; feminine can also be used with reference to males to express admiration, e.g. *təsfaye gobəz nəč* (Tesfaye smart/clever/brave be.PF.3FEM.SG) 'Tesfaye (a man) is smart/clever/brave' (Mengistu Amberber, p.c.). In contrast, in Polish expressive masculine forms of feminine names have endearing value. The masculine gender 'signals an attitude of affectionate jocularity' (Wierzbicka 1996: 398). Secondary value distinctions are often found of Bantu noun classes—see Table 11.3.[11] In Palikur, gender assignment to non-human animates depends on their value and on speakers' attitude. Feminine gender is associated with positive value, while masculine goes together with negative feelings. The rat is a small animal; however, it is assigned masculine gender because it is looked upon as dirty and bad. But a cute little baby rat would be referred to as feminine. Along similar lines, turtles are usually feminine; but a turtle which is a nuisance and has to be got rid of would be referred to as masculine; all insects are masculine in spite of their small size, according to an explanation by a native consultant, 'because none of them are any good for food and all they do is bother people, eat crops and cause sickness' (Aikhenvald and Green 1998).

In Lokono (Arawak: Baarle and Sabajo 1997; cf. §10.5) just male humans belong to the masculine gender, and all the rest are feminine. But there is much more to it: to be assigned masculine gender, a male person must also belong to the Arawak community (all foreign men are treated as feminine). Masculine gender assignment is associated with positive value, while feminine gender goes together with negative feelings. Animals and birds which are thought of as having a 'positive personality' are masculine—they include turtles and hummingbirds. Domestic animals to which speakers have a special attachment, for instance, a dog, are masculine; however, one's neighbour's dog is more likely to be feminine. Attractive animals are masculine, while bigger animals are feminine: the tapir is feminine just because of its big size.

---

[11] And see Aksenova and Toporova (1994: 81) for data on Kuria.

Some semantic parameters appear never to be used in noun class systems, e.g. kin and social status for humans, or material and value for inanimates.[12] Colour is never used as a basis for noun categorization.[13]

(D) Semantic complexity and opacity in noun class assignment

It has been often stated that there is no real semantic basis for gender assignment in some well-known Indo-European languages. In a seminal study, Zubin and Köpcke (1986) provided a semantic rationale for gender assignment of nouns from different semantic groups in German. In agreement with the natural sex principle, masculine and feminine genders mark the terms for male and female adults of each species of domestic and game animals, and neuter is assigned to non-sex-specific generic and juvenile terms. Masculine gender is used for types of cloth, of precipitation and wind, and of minerals. Types of knowledge and discipline have feminine gender, and games and types of metal—with the exception of alloys—have neuter gender.

Almost all nouns with vague generic reference, such as *das Ding* 'thing', *das Gerät* 'implement, apparatus', *das Gut* 'goods' have neuter gender (with one exception: *die Sache* 'thing' is feminine). Superordinate terms usually belong to neuter gender, and items of a more basic level are feminine or masculine, more rarely neuter—see Table 11.2 (Zubin and Köpcke 1986: 147 ff.). There are a few exceptions. Two superordinate terms are feminine: *Pflanze* 'plant, herb' and *Farbe* 'colour'.

TABLE 11.2. *Semantic basis of gender choice in German: an illustration*

Superordinate	Basic level
Instrument (N) 'musical instrument'	*Guitarre* (F) 'guitar', *Trompete* (F) 'trumpet'
Obst (N) 'fruit'	*Apfel* (M) 'apple', *Pflaume* (F) 'plum'
Spielzeug (N) 'vehicle'	*Bauklotz* (M) 'block', *Puppe* (F) 'doll'
Land (N) 'land'	*Wald* (M) 'woods', *Sumpf* (M) 'swamp', *Wiese* (F) 'meadow'

Noun class assignment is usually more opaque for inanimates and for non-human animates. In Mayali (Evans ms: 104–6) masculine class

---

[12] These semantic features are found in correlation with others. Noun classes may contain reference to hierarchically higher, or more powerful, humans: see §12.3.1, on noun classes in Akan.

[13] 'Lustre', or 'visibility', is reported to be one of the classificatory parameters in assigning noun classes in Anindilyakwa (Australian: Leeding 1989; 1996). The use of visibility or lustre as a parameter for noun categorization could be associated with the cultural importance of 'lustre' and 'light' in Northern Australian Aboriginal culture (Mark Harvey, p.c.); however, more study is needed to understand how these parameters are employed.

includes male humans, the names of certain malevolent beings mostly associated with the sky, items associated with painting (a male activity), and also some mammals, some snakes, and some birds and fish. Feminine class includes female humans, and also some reptiles, fish, and birds. Vegetable class includes all terms for non-flesh foods, but also a few bird names. Finally, the 'neuter', or 'residue' class is the most semantically heterogeneous—it includes items which do not 'fit' into other classes, e.g. most body parts, generic terms for plants, and terms for various inanimate objects.

In Dyirbal water, fire and items associated with fighting belong to Class 2. In contrast, in Gurr-goni and Mayali fire and related things are 'neuter'; 'water' belongs to the neuter class in Gurr-goni, and to vegetable class in Mayali. In Gurr-goni (R. Green 1995) males and most animals, fish, and birds belong to the masculine Class I; human females, turtles, and a few other animals belong to feminine Class II; most living plants and non-flesh foods belong to 'vegetable' Class III, together with traditional canoes, corroborees, and songs. Terms which belong to Class IV ('neuter', or 'residue') cover the following semantic domains: the natural environment; water, rain and other liquids; fire and associated things; a few plants; a few body parts; time, structure, and buildings; and language and ceremonies.

In Jingulu (Pensalfini 1997: 254) nouns divide into four classes, only some of which are more or less semantically transparent. The vegetable class includes mostly objects which are long, thin, or pointed; this class happens to include most vegetables, as well as body parts such as colon, penis, and neck, instruments such as spears, fire-drills and barbed wire, natural phenomena such as lightning and rainbows, and also roads and trenches. The feminine class includes female humans and higher animates, and also words for axes, the sun, and most smaller songbirds. The semantic content of the remaining two classes, masculine and neuter, is harder to define: masculine is mostly used for the rest of animates and neuter for the rest of inanimates, except that flat and/or rounded inanimates—such as most trees and eggs, and body parts such as liver and brow—are masculine. The choice of the four genders in Wambaya (Nordlinger 1998: 63–4), which is closely related to Jingulu, is somewhat different: for instance, the 'vegetable' (or 'non-flesh food') class is associated with round shape rather than with being long or thin. There may be culture-specific explanations for these varying classifications.

Noun classes in Bantu languages are another example of a semantically opaque system. Table 11.3 summarizes 'a basic semantic grid common to Bantu noun class systems' (Spitulnik 1989: 207) based on an interaction of shape, size, and humanness. However, these parameters provide only a partial semantic motivation for the Bantu noun classes.

TABLE 11.3. *Noun classes in Bantu*[14]

Class	Semantics
1/2	Humans, a few other animates
3/4	Plants, plant parts, foods, non-paired body parts, miscellaneous
5/6	Fruits, paired body parts, miscellaneous inanimates
7/8	Miscellaneous inanimates
9/10	Animals, miscellaneous inanimates, a few humans
11/10	Long objects, abstract entities, miscellaneous inanimates
12/13	Small objects, birds
6	Masses
14	Abstract qualities, states, masses, collectives
15	Infinitives

Only the Class 1/2 'human' is semantically homogeneous. Shape and size are also employed as semantic parameters of noun categorization. Classes associated with shape in ChiBemba are shown in Table 11.4, and classes associated with size in Table 11.5 (Spitulnik 1989: 210, 212).[15] Diminutive and augmentative classes carry affective overtones (diminutives are endearing and augmentatives are pejorative).

TABLE 11.4. *Shape-based classes in ChiBemba*

Class	Meaning
11 *ulu-*	'long', 'extending over space'
14 *ubu-*	'flat', 'surface'
9 *iN-*	'bounded space', 'orifice-edge', 'round'

TABLE 11.5. *Size-based classes in ChiBemba*

Class	Meanings	Associated affective notions
7/8 *ici-/ifi-*	'large'	'gross', 'despised'
12/13 *aka-/utu-*	'small'	'charming', 'quick', 'cunning'
6 *ama-*	'mass', 'collective'	'exaggerated'

Denny (1979a: 109–10) suggested the following scheme for some Bantu noun classes based on configurations involving extendedness (also cf. Denny 1976 and Denny and Creider 1986).

---

[14] This grid differs somewhat from the semantics reconstructed by Denny and Creider (1986) and Creider (1975): see Table 2.1.
[15] A test of the semantic reality of noun classes in Kikuyu conducted by Burton and Kirk (1976) showed a correlation between the size of animals and birds and their noun class assignment. Class 11 was associated with large size, and class 9 with small size.

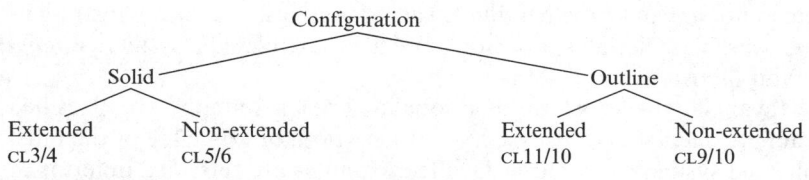

```
                        Configuration
                    ┌───────┴───────┐
              Solid─┘               └─Outline
            ┌───┴───┐             ┌───┴───┐
       Extended  Non-extended  Extended  Non-extended
        CL3/4      CL5/6       CL11/10    CL9/10
```
DIAGRAM 11.2. *Extendedness in Proto-Bantu noun classes*

Class 9/10, 'non-extended outline', includes rings, holes, and also containers (e.g. clay pots and gourd bottles), together with houses and geographical spaces. Class 11/10 involves an outline figure of a different sort: an extended curve with an interior, e.g. hill, rib, palm of the hand. Ropes and cords are also placed into this class due to the fact that the parts joined together by ropes and cords 'must be inside the curve of the cord' (Denny 1979a: 110). The use of the parameters 'extendedness' and 'outline' resembles the way shape is used in numeral classifiers (cf. Table 9.5, for Baniwa). In the Bantu noun class systems, the only semantically transparent and straightforward principle of assignment is animacy and/or sex, unlike Baniwa, where the assignment of almost all the classes is transparent.

(E) Semantic parameters in split noun class systems

In languages with split noun class systems, pronominal noun classes tend to be based on animacy and sex distinctions, while physical (extendedness, shape, and size) parameters are found in the non-pronominal classes: see §2.7.2, for Paumarí, and Table 9.5, for Baniwa. Markers of non-pronominal noun classes are often used in other classifier environments: see Chapter 9.

11.2.2. Semantics of noun classifiers

Noun classifiers as independent lexemes are 'superordinate' terms in a generic-specific relation with a noun (see §11.1.3). The semantics of generic noun classifiers relates to the inherent nature of the object and to its functions. There is usually a classifier for humans, or animates,[16] one or more classifier(s) for non-human animates, and a number of classifiers for inanimates based on their inherent properties or functions.

The content of HUMAN classification differs from system to system. Western Austronesian languages, such as Minangkabau, Acehnese, or Indonesian, have just one general term for person, e.g. Minangkabau *urang padusi* (NOUN.CL:PERSON woman) 'a woman'.

---

[16] The Daly languages of Northern Australia have a human/non-human opposition in noun classes, but not in noun classifiers (Reid 1990). There may be a historical explanation to this: noun class markers in these languages go back to grammaticalized noun classifiers (see §13.4).

Human nouns can be further divided according to SEX. Yidiny (Australian) has a generic classifier *bama* 'person', and also sex-related classifiers *waguja* 'man' and *bunya* 'woman'.

In Mayan languages of the Kanjobalan branch humans are classified according to their SOCIAL STATUS, KINSHIP RELATION, or AGE. One of the most complicated systems is found in Jacaltec. Humans are classified in terms of sex, respect, kin versus non-kin, and age. There are also two classifiers for deities: male and female—see Table 11.6 (Craig 1986c: 266–7).

TABLE 11.6. *Noun classifiers for humans and deities in Jacaltec*

cuman	Male deity
cumi7	Female deity
ya7	Respected human
naj	Male non-kin
ix	Female non-kin
naj ni7an	Young male non-kin
ix ni7an	Young female non-kin
ho7	Male kin
xo7	Young male kin
ho7 ni7an	Young male kin
xo7 ni7an	Young female kin
unin	Infant

Noun classifiers for humans in Akatek distinguish 'known human', 'human, appreciative', and 'man' and 'woman' (see Table 8.4; Zavala 1992: 152). Mam (Table 13.3) has classifiers for men and women; for young and old men and women; for old men and women to whom respect is due, and for someone of the same status as the speaker. There is also a classifier for babies, and just one non-human classifier.

In Australian languages, noun classifiers which refer to social status include such distinctions as 'initiated man' (§3.2.1). Murrinhpatha (Walsh 1997: 256) has a classifier for Aboriginal people (which also covers human spirits) and another one for non-Aboriginal people, which also covers all other animates and their products.[17]

Nouns with non-human, or inanimate, referents are classified in terms of inherent nature-based properties ((g) in §11.1.1). They belong to natural domains of human interaction: animals, birds, fish, plants, water, fire, minerals, and artefacts. Individual systems may vary. There is often

---

[17] A system of honorific classifiers, as documented by DeLancey (1998: 121) for Tibetan, can be considered a subtype of functional categorization of nouns based on humans and the world of their experience.

a general term for birds and fish, as in Minangkabau (Table 13.4); Ngan'gityemerri and Akatek have a noun classifier for animals (see Tables 8.1 and 8.4). Classifiers in Murrinhpatha cover fresh water and associated concepts; flowers and fruits of plants; spears; offensive weapons; fire and things associated with fire; time and space; speech and language; and there is a residue classifier (see §12.1.4).

There is usually a noun classifier for culturally important concepts. Mayan languages have a noun classifier for corn which is important for traditional agriculture, and for domesticated dogs, while Daly languages have classifiers for spears, diggings sticks, and woomeras. Table 11.7 shows the set of classifiers for non-human nouns in Jacaltec (Craig 1986c: 267).

TABLE 11.7. *Noun classifiers for non-humans in Jacaltec*

no7	Animal
metx'	Dog
te7	Plant
ixim	Corn
tx'al	Thread
tx'añ	Twine
k'ap	Cloth
tx'otx'	Soil/dirt
ch'en	Rock
atz'am	Salt
ha7	Water
k'a7	Fire

Noun classifiers can distinguish nouns in terms of their functions, e.g. 'habitable place', or 'drinkable liquid' (cf. Dixon 1977, on Yidiny). A distinction between flesh and non-flesh food is typical for Australian languages with noun classifiers, cf. Yidiny *minja*, Emmi *awa* 'flesh food', Yidiny *mayi*, Emmi *miya* 'non-flesh food' (Dixon 1977: 483; Ford 1998). Functional distinctions may include 'movable', e.g. Yidiny *wirra*.[18]

Physical properties of referents, arrangement, and quanta ((a–f), (h–i) in §11.1.1) are not used for classifying nouns with noun classifiers which are in a generic-specific relation with the accompanying noun.[19]

---

[18] Inherent nature- and function-based classifiers are relatively independent systems. We mentioned in §3.2.1 that function classifiers can cooccur with inherent nature classifiers in Yidiny.

[19] It can be argued, however, that constitution or state, such as liquid, is a concomitant semantic feature used with function-based noun classifiers. However, constitution is never used by itself as a parameter.

11.2.3. Semantics of numeral classifiers

Numeral classifiers divide into SORTAL and MENSURAL types. Sortal numeral classifiers describe inherent properties of referents, and mensural classifiers describe the ways they can be measured (see §4.4). Consequently, sortal classifiers tend to use inherent properties (a–g) more, while mensural classifiers prefer temporary ones (h and i).

The choice of SORTAL classifiers is often based on animacy, humanness, or, more rarely, sex (A). Further classification of humans is often based on social status or age (B). Additional properties employed in numeral classifiers are (C) physical properties, (D) functional properties, and (E) arrangement and quanta. Mensural classifiers (F) combine these.

(A) Animacy, humanness, and sex in numeral classifiers

Numeral classifiers often provide a two-way division of nouns into HUMAN and NON-HUMAN, as in numerous small classifier systems in Dravidian languages, e.g. Telugu and Kannada (Emeneau 1964: 649), and in Ainu.

Alternatively, nouns can be divided into ANIMATE and INANIMATE. This is the case throughout languages of the Tai family (see Conklin 1981: 130–6; DeLancey 1986: 447). There may be a separate class for humans, and a number of classes for non-humans, as in Toba Batak, Makassar, Bugis, Mori, and Gorontalo (Austroasiatic: Conklin 1981: 241). Acehnese (Durie 1985: 139) has a special classifier for humans (*droe*); all the other classifiers are confined to non-humans (which include animals).

A three-way classification may divide nouns into HUMANS, NON-HUMAN ANIMATES, and INANIMATES. Jacaltec (Kanjobalan Mayan) and Squamish have three numeral classifiers: human, animal, inanimate (Craig 1986b: 265; Table 4.6 above). There may be a special classifier for humans, one for animals, and a number for inanimates,[20] as in Malay, Indonesian, Minangkabau, and Balinese (Conklin 1981: 240 ff.; Marnita 1996), and in the Dravidian language Malto (Mahapatra 1979: 126), and in Nivkh (Table 4.4).

Numeral classifiers can involve reference to ANIMACY and SEX.[21] There are several possibilities. There may be a male animate, a female animate, and

---

[20] Animals can be categorized in different ways. Malay and Minangkabau have just one classifier for animals. In Achagua (Arawak: Wilson 1992: 62) the animal classifier is applied only to mammals. Bahwana (Arawak: Ramirez 1992) has several classifiers for different species of mammals and lizards. Different classificatory techniques can be used for animates and for inanimates. Movima (Bolivian isolate: Colette Grinevald, p.c.) uses repeaters as numeral classifiers to classify inanimates; there are special classifiers just for humans and for animates.

[21] The existence of sex- and humanness/animacy-based systems in numeral classifiers goes against predictions formulated by Adams and Conklin (1973) on the basis of Austroasiatic languages, and repeated by Croft (1994).

an inanimate classifier, as in Bora (Bora-Witoto: Thiesen 1996: 43), East Tucano, and Warekena, Baniwa, and Tariana.

There are hardly any examples of numeral classification based just on sex. However, in Kolami (Dravidian) and Marathi (Indo-Aryan) numeral classifiers are used only with animates, and they distinguish masculine and feminine (Emeneau 1964: 648).

Animate/inanimate or human/non-human are distinguished in most systems of numeral classifiers (cf. Croft 1994). There are three groups of exceptions.

(i) Languages with two sets of numeral classifiers may have animacy distinctions in one, but not in the other. Akatek (Zavala 1992: 130–1, 140–1) distinguishes humans, animals and inanimates in the suffixed set of numeral classifiers. 'Independent' numeral classifiers are assigned according to shape, position and size (see Table 8.3 and §4.3.2; for Jacaltec, see Craig 1986b: 265).

(ii) Animacy-based oppositions may be absent from numeral classifier systems if they are found elsewhere in the language. Sochiapan Chinantec distinguishes animate and inanimate forms of numerals and some modifiers (Foris 1993: 305, Table 6.14 therein), but there are no animacy-based distinctions in numeral classifiers (Foris 1993: 317 ff.). A similar system is found in the closely related language, Comaltepec Chinantec (Anderson 1989: 57).

(iii) Some recently developed systems of numeral classifiers do not have any special classifier for animates, or humans. Classification is achieved according to the physical and functional properties of entities. Kana (Kegboid, Cross River: Ikoro 1996a: 90–1) has nineteen numeral classifiers the assignment of which is based predominantly on the shape of a referent. Most animate nouns are classified with the default classifier kà; some do not take any classifier (e.g. nēē 'person'). The word bēē 'child' is classified with bēē 'seed-like small objects'. Unlike Akatek and Chinantec, there are no animacy-based distinctions.[22] Wantoat and Awará, two closely related languages from the Morobe province of Papua New Guinea, also have no special classifier for humans, or for animates (Davis n.d.; Susan Quigley, p.c.). Classifiers are used with numbers one and two, with demonstratives and as derivational markers with nouns. Orientation appears to be one of

---

[22] Nouns with human and with non-human referents differ in some ways (see E in Appendix 1). For instance, only proper nouns with a human referent can be pronominalized; in a topic-comment construction a moved O can be pronominalized only if human; emphatic personal pronouns usually refer to humans (Ikoro 1996b). Similarly, no animacy distinctions have been observed in the numeral classifier system in Ngyembɔɔn, a Grasslands language with numeral classifiers (Viktor Vinogradov, p.c). This is by no means the case in all African languages with numeral classifiers. Manessy (1961: 158) reports human/non-human and animate/inanimate distinctions for some Bwamu dialects.

the important semantic parameters used in classifier assignment; humans are assigned the same classifier as 'upright' objects (e.g. tree, pole) (Davis n.d.: 4).

(B) Further classification of humans

If a language has more than one human classifier,[23] there is further classification of humans according to their social function and status. In Austroasiatic, some Tibeto-Burman languages, and Korean, humans are classified by social rank or according to kinship; the choice is culturally determined. Other variables may include age: children are often classified as 'underhumans'. Age may be associated with social status in a more complicated way, e.g. Dioi uses $paou^1$ for respected males and mai^5 for little-respected groups of younger females (Conklin 1981: 132).

Lisu has different classifiers for female kin one generation away, male kin one generation away, all lateral kin, and all kin two generations away (Adams and Conklin 1973: 4). Pre-revolutionary Khmer had separate classifiers for clergy and monks, high persons, dignitaries, and superior and inferior honourable people (Adams 1989: 63; 1992).

(C) Physical properties

Numeral classifiers used with inanimates, or non-humans, employ many more values for physical properties than do noun classes (see (B) in §11.2.1).

SHAPE and DIMENSIONALITY are widely used in numeral classifier systems. Languages differ in how many dimensions they use and how differentiated the shapes are in each dimension. Languages tend to encode one and two dimensions more often than three dimensions (Frawley 1992: 123). In Thai, flat shapes are less differentiated than long ones and three-dimensional ones hardly at all (Hundius and Kölver 1983: 206). In Japanese (Downing 1984; 1986) the three-dimensional classifier *ko* 'roundish small objects' is less frequent than classifiers for flat, and for long objects (Frawley 1992: 123, 134).

Semantic parameters of EXTENDEDNESS, INTERIORICITY, and BOUNDEDNESS ((a) and (b) in §11.1.1) usually overlap in numeral classifier systems. The interaction between boundedness and dimensionality in Totonac (Totonac-Tepehuan: Levy 1994) is shown in Diagram 11.3.

---

[23] Many languages have just one human numeral classifier, e.g. Achagua (Arawak), Tzeltal and Tzotzil (Mayan), Indonesian, and Japanese (Kiyomi 1992: 20). Japanese has just one classifier for humans, and several classifiers for non-humans. The latter is based on divisions in species, e.g. *hiki* 'animals, insects, fish', *too* 'large animals (horses, cows)', *wa* 'birds', *bi* 'fish', and *hai* 'squids'.

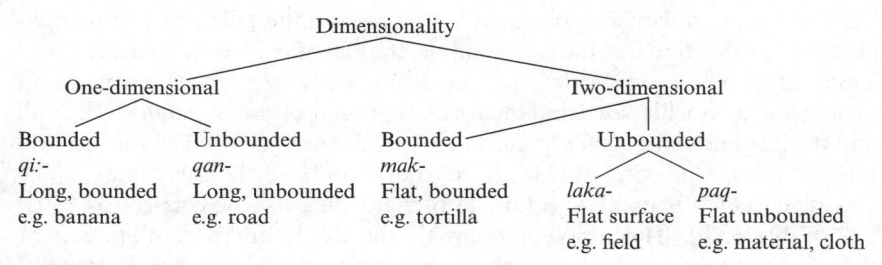

```
                            Dimensionality
              ┌──────────────────┴──────────────────┐
        One-dimensional                       Two-dimensional
       ┌──────┴──────┐                       ┌──────┴──────┐
   Bounded       Unbounded               Bounded        Unbounded
   qi:-          qan-                    mak-          ┌────┴────┐
   Long, bounded Long, unbounded         Flat, bounded laka-     paq-
   e.g. banana   e.g. road               e.g. tortilla Flat surface Flat unbounded
                                                       e.g. field   e.g. material, cloth
```

DIAGRAM 11.3. *Numeral classifiers in Totonac*

DIRECTIONALITY, or ORIENTATION, goes together with dimensionality and shape in numeral classifiers. Unlike verbal and deictic classifiers (§11.2.5, §11.2.6; cf. Croft 1994; Frawley 1992: 124–5), it never appears by itself, but often gets expressed with the same item as dimensionality. Flat objects are often horizontally spread (see also Palikur, in Diagram 11.4), and long objects tend to be vertical (e.g. *batang* 'long vertical objects' in Minangkabau: Diagram 8.1).

INTERIORICITY (Denny 1979a: 108) refers to the distinction between rings and holes. While rings 'focus' on the outside outline, holes 'focus' on the interior of the outline. Tzeltal (Mayan: Berlin 1968: 123; Denny 1979a: 111) has four 'hole' classifiers which differ with respect to complete or non-complete perforation, and with respect to size. The parameter of interioricity in Tzeltal correlates with material makeup, or consistency; the classifiers listed in Table 11.8 are applicable to non-flexible objects alone.

TABLE 11.8. *Hole classifiers in Tzeltal*

	Complete perforation	Incomplete perforation
Large	*hom*, e.g. complete large perforation in a board	*puh*, e.g. incomplete large perforation in a board
Small	*huht*, e.g. complete small perforation in a board	*č'ub'*, e.g. complete small perforation in a board

SIZE is rarely employed as an independent parameter; it usually clusters with dimensionality and shape, as in Minangkabau *alai* 'flat, flexible, sheet-like', *bidang* 'extended surfaces, e.g. field, farm, garden', *petak* 'square objects', or with interioricity, as in Minangkabau *bantuak* 'circular objects, e.g. rings and fishhooks' (Marnita 1996: 107).

All languages where numeral classifiers categorize inanimates with respect to their physical properties employ dimensionality and shape. In contrast, CONSISTENCY (flexible, rigid) and CONSTITUTION (liquid, solid) are physical properties never encoded by themselves in numeral classifiers.

They usually correlate with dimensionality. For instance, flat objects are often classified as thin and flexible (for example, the classifier *ôn* in Acehnese: Durie 1985: 139). These properties may correlate with size, or with form and arrangement. Sochiapan Chinantec has a special classifier *hmáih*[32] for tall and flexible referents, such as maize plants and vines; and *máih*[32] for fine and long objects, e.g. wire, thread, vine (Foris 1993: 322, Table 6.21). The classifier *ziánh*[13] is used for a bundle of rigid stick-like objects (Foris 1993: 322, Table 6.20). The unifying rationale for the frequent combination of these parameters could lie in their 'handling ability'. In other numeral classifier languages, such properties as rigid, flexible, or liquid are not used at all, e.g. Akatek Mayan (Table 8.3), or Achagua (Wilson 1992).

Numeral classifiers for inanimates can be based on a complex combination of DIMENSIONALITY, SHAPE, BOUNDEDNESS, and CONSISTENCY. Diagram 11.4 shows how these parameters interact in the system of Palikur sortal numeral classifiers for inanimates. Inanimates are classified according to their shape, dimensionality, and boundedness; there is also one specific classifier, for plants. Consistency goes together with shape and dimensionality.

Shape
— Linear (+consistency) — Straight, curved, flexible: river, rope (-*tra*/-*tahr*-)
— Equal dimensions (2/3) — Round or square: orange, box (circle) (-*u*/-*so*-)
— Irregular dimensions (2/3) — Other shapes (oval, rectangular) and irregular: egg, basket, house, land (-*al*-*sa*-)
— Concave

Dimensionality
— Three-dimensional — Bowl, canoe, ring (-*mku*/-*muk*-)
— Two-dimensional — Flat, nonextended: hammock, mat (-*k*/-*kal*-*bu*)
— One-dimensional (+consistency) — Rigid, vertical: arrow, cigar (-*t*/-*ta*-)

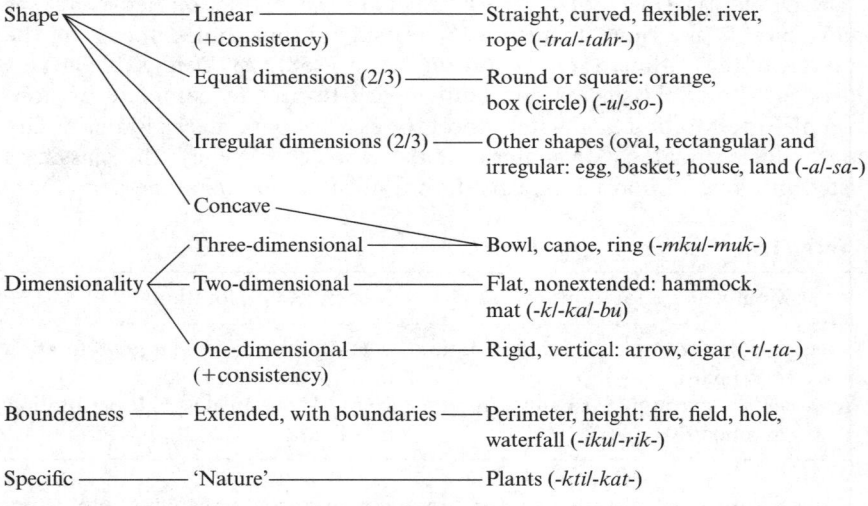

Boundedness — Extended, with boundaries — Perimeter, height: fire, field, hole, waterfall (-*iku*/-*rik*-)

Specific — 'Nature' — Plants (-*kti*/-*kat*-)

DIAGRAM 11.4. *Numeral classifiers for inanimates in Palikur*

Numeral classifier systems often contain a number of semantically highly specific classifiers based on the MATERIAL and other inherent properties of objects. Tai languages have specific classifiers for wooden objects (Conklin 1981: 144). Nivkh has classifiers for sledges and fish-nets (Table 4.4), while Baniwa has a special classifier for excrement (Table 9.5), because of the importance of identifying animal droppings when hunting game. Type of material may correlate with other physical properties, most frequently with shape and dimensionality. Thus, in Minangkabau, *batang* 'long vertical objects' is most often used to categorize wooden things.[24]

(D) Functional properties

Functional properties are not as frequent in numeral classifier systems as shape and dimensionality. A frequently cited example of a function-based classifier in Thai is *khan*, originally used to refer to things with long handles which now includes cars, bicycle, motorcycles, buses, and other vehicles (see §12.3.4). In Hmong (Walter Bisang, p.c.) the classifier *rab* is used for tools and instruments in general, and especially for objects with a handle. In Austroasiatic languages a large number of classifiers have to do with written and oral speech; classifiers used for counting written materials can be organized according to the type of material (books, newspapers, or magazines), or varying literary forms (play versus poem); function as a semantic parameter of noun categorization may interact with shape—units of speech may also be classified as long or flat (Adams and Conklin 1973: 7–8).

Table 11.9 presents a set of function-based numeral classifiers from Burmese (Burling 1965; Denny 1976: 127–8).

TABLE 11.9. *Function-based classifiers in Burmese*[25]

Classifier	Gloss
hte	'clothing for the body (not headgear or footwear)'
sin	'cutting tools'
si	'vehicles'
saun	'written materials (literary pieces, documents)'
le'	'hand implements' (also eyeglasses)
koun	'loop-shaped objects that are worn: garlands, necklaces'
hsaun	'houses, monasteries, royal buildings'

Function-based classifiers are often highly culture-specific. Gilbertese, a Micronesian language (Silverman 1962), has a classifier *kai* for means of subsistence, *wa* for transport (especially canoes), and *kora* for baskets.

---

[24] Large systems of numeral classifiers can have even more complicated interactions of shape, dimensionality, and consistency. Tzeltal has two classifiers for non-flexible objects which correlate with other parameters. One, *lehč*, is unspecified for dimension and is used for thin non-flexible objects of variable shape, e.g. basket, hat, gourd; the other one is used for two-dimensional objects: *pehč* for 'thick, non-flexible flat objects where width is greater than thickness', e.g. bricks, tortillas (Berlin 1968: 99). Classifiers for flexible objects correlate with the way objects are handled, e.g. *lihk/hil* for 'slender, flexible object in natural extended state', *t'im* for slender, flexible objects in stretched position, like a clothes line; and *tim* for slender, flexible objects stretched between two points but not taut like a clothes line (Berlin 1968: 109).

[25] Transcription changed in agreement with the standard one used for transcribing Burmese, supplied by Randy LaPolla.

Function-based classes in Western Austronesian and Austroasiatic languages include weapons, tools, and implements, and also various types of fields relevant for agricultural functions (Adams and Conklin 1973: 8). The degree to which a language uses functional interaction as a semantic basis 'shows how selective classifiers are in underlining a few key concepts to do with cultural ecology' (Denny 1976: 128); see §12.3.

The way objects can be used often depends on their physical properties; this is why functional and physical properties are often expressed with one classifier. For instance, Burmese *koun* describes loop-shaped objects which can be worn (Table 11.9).

The interaction between physical properties (shape, or dimensionality; consistency; and material make-up) and function in numeral classifiers for inanimate referents in Minangkabau is exemplified in Diagram 11.5 (adapted from Marnita 1996: 104). It is impossible to decide whether shape and dimensionality and material or function are primary in this interaction. In the overall structure of numeral classifier systems function can be considered as a secondary semantic feature simply because functional characteristics are not obligatorily present in numeral classifier systems, unlike physical properties (though function can be a primary parameter for some classifiers in some languages, e.g. *rab* 'tools and instruments' in Hmong). No numeral classifier systems are based just on functional properties, and there are some which do not use them at all (e.g. Palikur, Achagua, Chinantec).

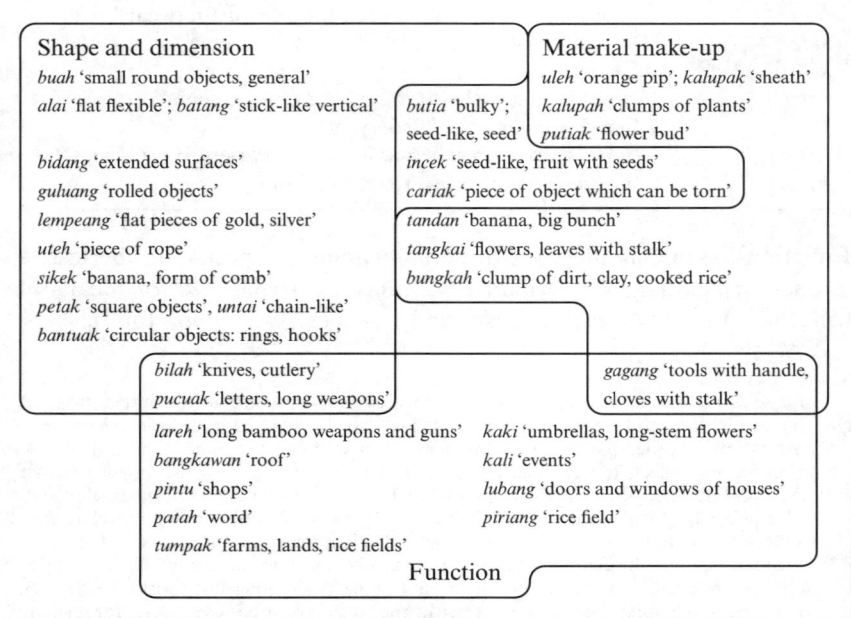

Shape and dimension
buah 'small round objects, general'
alai 'flat flexible'; *batang* 'stick-like vertical'
butia 'bulky'; seed-like, seed'

bidang 'extended surfaces'
guluang 'rolled objects'
lempeang 'flat pieces of gold, silver'
uteh 'piece of rope'
sikek 'banana, form of comb'
petak 'square objects', *untai* 'chain-like'
bantuak 'circular objects: rings, hooks'

Material make-up
uleh 'orange pip'; *kalupak* 'sheath'
kalupah 'clumps of plants'
putiak 'flower bud'

incek 'seed-like, fruit with seeds'
cariak 'piece of object which can be torn'
tandan 'banana, big bunch'
tangkai 'flowers, leaves with stalk'
bungkah 'clump of dirt, clay, cooked rice'

bilah 'knives, cutlery'
pucuak 'letters, long weapons'

gagang 'tools with handle, cloves with stalk'

lareh 'long bamboo weapons and guns'
bangkawan 'roof'
pintu 'shops'
patah 'word'
tumpak 'farms, lands, rice fields'

kaki 'umbrellas, long-stem flowers'
kali 'events'
lubang 'doors and windows of houses'
piriang 'rice field'

Function

DIAGRAM 11.5. *Interaction of semantic domains in numeral classifiers in Minangkabau*

There may be further distinctions made in large classifier systems. Japanese has a few specific classifiers used with abstract nouns *ken* 'incident', *toori* 'method', *han* 'crime', *denwa* 'phone call'. (These classifiers go back to repeaters.) Abstract nouns can also be used with the 'default' classifier *tsu*, or without any classifier (Downing 1996: 73); see §12.1.4.

(E) Arrangement and quanta

Arrangement and quanta are frequently used in sortal and in mensural classifiers. They typically interrelate with physical properties of objects and their material makeup. Korean has special sortal classifiers for counting pairs of chopsticks, and pairs of clothing (gloves, shoes). The ways in which inherent properties correlate with arrangement are often culture specific and unpredictable. Minangkabau has different mensural classifiers for bunches of vegetable and fruit, parts of sugar cane, for pieces of meat on a skewer, or for small objects (fish, fruit) on a skewer.

(F) Semantic properties of mensural classifiers

Mensural classifiers operate with animacy distinctions to a lesser extent than sortal classifiers. In some languages, e.g. Chinantepec Chinantec, mensural classifiers are used with inanimate referents only. In other languages, e.g. Sochiapan Chinantec, Akatek or Tzotzil, there are a few mensural classifiers for animate referents. Tzeltal tends to use 'temporary state' mensural classifiers only with inanimate referents. Physical properties used in mensural classifiers are dimensionality, shape, and consistency, and other nature- or function-related properties (e.g. a number of special mensural classifiers for tobacco in Minangkabau).

11.2.4. Semantics of classifiers in possessive constructions

In this section we will discuss the semantics of relational and possessed classifiers. Possessor classifiers which refer to the properties of the possessor are very rare, so that no generalizations can be made.[26]

(A) Semantics of relational classifiers

RELATIONAL classifiers characterize the relationship between the possessor and the possessed depending on how the possessed object can be handled, or used. Therefore, categorization of the possessive relationship is based on functional interaction.

(i) The primary semantic division of nouns is often into CONSUMABLE and NON-CONSUMABLE, as in Boumaa Fijian (Dixon 1988: 136), or general and alimentary, as in Manam or Kaliai-Kove (Lichtenberk 1983a: 151–2).

---

[26] Possessor classifiers discussed in Chapter 5 are based on the animate/inanimate distinction.

CONSUMABLE objects can be further classified according to the ways in which they can be consumed (i.e. eaten or chewed, or drunk, sucked, or licked), or how they can be prepared. For instance, Kosraean (Micronesian: Lee 1975; Lichtenberk 1983a: 154–5) has classifiers for chewable, drinkable, and uncooked food. In Kipeá, an extinct language from Northeastern Brazil (Rodrigues 1995, 1997), foodstuff was classified depending on whether they were gathered or cultivated, or how they were prepared (by boiling, or roasting).

NON-CONSUMABLE objects can be classified depending on how they were acquired (i.e. found, or received as a gift, as in Kipeá), or transported (as in Kosraean).

(ii) A number of other, culture-specific, functional distinctions can be mapped onto relational classifiers, e.g. clothing, vehicles, dwelling-places, as in Kilivila, or Marshallese.

Tamambo, an Austronesian language from Vanuatu (Jauncey 1997: §7.4.2), has four relational classifiers: *no-* 'personal property, general term for belongings', *ha-* 'edible items', *ma-* 'drinkable items', *bula-* 'plants and animals one owns' (with the exception of pigs which are the main commodity, almost equal to money, and which take *no-*).

VALUE is a semantic parameter associated with function and widely used in relational classifiers. Oceanic languages from Vanuatu have special classifiers for valued possessions, e.g. 11.1, from Raga (Lichtenberk 1983a: 154).

11.1. qoe   pila-ma
     pig   CL:VALUED.POSSESSION-your
     'your (sg) (valued) pig'

(iii) Human classification found in some systems of relational classifiers can be described as relating to social function, i.e. the kinship relationship. In Ponapean, six of the twenty-one relational classifiers refer to kinship. A noun can be 'reclassified' depending on the choice of a relational classifier, e.g. *pwutak* 'boy': in *nah pwutak* 'CL:DOMINANCE.OF.THE.POSSESSOR boy' 'his son', *rie pwutak* 'CL:SIBLING boy' 'his brother', *kiseh pwutak* 'CL:RELATIVE boy' 'his boy relative', *wahwah pwutak* 'CL:NEPHEW boy' 'his nephew', *sawi pwutak* 'CL:CLAN.MEMBER boy' 'his boy clansmember', *pelie pwutak* 'CL:PEER boy' 'his peer-group boy' (Rehg 1981: 183).

Relational classifiers can also reflect the closeness of the relationship between possessor and possessed.[27] In Baniwa (Arawak), two relational classifiers correlate with the degree of closeness of the possessed to the

---

[27] On similarities between classification in possessive constructions, alienable and inalienable distinctions, and other types of noun classifications, see Chappell and McGregor (1989).

possessor: 'my dog which I found' as opposed to 'my dog which I raised' (examples 5.51 and 5.52). In Kilivila (Senft 1986: 49–54) nouns are divided into edible, consumable, and closely or more distantly associated with the possessor.

(B) Semantics of possessed classifiers

Unlike relational classifiers, POSSESSED classifiers characterize the possessed noun in terms of its (a) animacy and (b) physical properties: shape, size, and consistency. Possessed classifiers can also be in a generic-specific relation with the noun they classify (see 5.7, from Apalaí); similarly to relational classifiers, they can categorize the noun in terms of its function.

Generic possessed classifiers describe the possessed noun in terms of animacy and/or humanness. In this, they differ from relational classifiers. Cora (Uto-Aztecan: Casad 1982: 236) has classifiers for human, animate and inanimate (see other examples in Chapter 5). Generic possessed classifiers are often function-based. Luiseño has a classifier *'aač* for pets. Chemehuevi (Southern Numic branch of Uto-Aztecan) has two possessed classifiers: *-puŋku* 'pet' and *-ɨgapɨ* 'domesticated plant' (Press 1979: 60–1). In South American languages function-based possessed classifiers usually include terms for food and pets.

Large systems of possessed classifiers can combine several semantic features. Classifiers in Apalaí (Carib: Koehn 1994) categorize the possessed noun in terms of its function (field produce, drink, killed game); there are a number of other specific classifiers which refer to inherent properties of culturally significant objects (e.g. nut, corn, seed, firewood, manioc cake).

Classifiers which combine the properties of relational and possessed classifiers are based on inherent properties of a noun and its function—for example, relating to the way it can be handled (see Table 5.4 for a sample of classifiers in Puluwat).

11.2.5. Semantics of verbal classifiers

Verbal classifiers show several distinct tendencies in their semantics depending on the type of relationship between a noun and its classifier. (A) There can be a generic-specific relationship between the verbal classifier and the nominal argument, or (B) the classifier can be chosen according to the properties of the referent.

(A) Generic-specific relation in verbal classifiers

Generic verbal classifiers come from incorporated generic nouns. They have the same semantics as generic noun classifiers (§11.2.2). There is usually a classifier for animates, or humans, e.g. *walŋa* 'body', a classifier for humans in Ngandi (Australian: Heath 1978b), or *guk* 'body' as a classifier for animates in Mayali (Evans ms: 269–71). Some languages have a classifier which refers to an aspect of human classification, e.g. Mayali *yaw* 'CL:BABY' (Evans 1996: 77). Nouns can be classified in terms of their inherent properties, such as function or constitution, e.g. Mayali *bo* 'CL:LIQUID', or more specific properties. Mayali has generic classifiers for fruit, meat, or pelt. A generic 'tree' is used to classify species of trees, e.g. 11.2 (= 6.2).

11.2. ga-rrulk-di an-dubang
     3NP-VCL:TREE-stand(NP) NCLIII(vegetable)-ironwood.tree
     'An ironwood tree is there.'

(B) Properties of verbal classifiers and classificatory verbs

Verbal classifiers and classificatory verbs chosen according to the properties of the noun may operate in terms of animacy, physical properties, and sometimes function and arrangement.[28]

(B1) Semantic restrictions on verbal classifiers and classificatory verbs In most languages verbal classifiers can be used with all or almost all verbs. Not all verbs, however, are classificatory.

In North American Indian languages—notably Athabaskan and Iroquoian, and also some languages of Central and South America (e.g. Ika, from Colombia: Frank 1990)—classificatory verbs have to do with handling physical objects ('put', 'carry', 'drop', etc.) or with their position and location, or existence ('lie', 'hang', 'fall', etc.). According to Carter (1976: 24), suppletive classificatory verbs in Athabaskan languages refer to concrete objects, and they describe 'objects at rest, in motion, being handled, being dropped, or falling' (Carter 1976: 24). In Cora (Casad 1996: 246) classificatory verbs comprise a group of stems whose basic meaning is 'carry'. In Papuan languages classificatory verbs are mostly existentials; they may also refer to location, posture, sometimes motion (e.g. 'carry', as in Enga).[29]

In a few languages, the use of verbal classifiers follows similar restrictions. In Palikur, only stative verbs which refer to dimension, physical propensity and colour take classifiers. Among transitive verbs, classifiers are used only with those which imply direct physical contact with the object. Verbal classifiers are used to focus on the shape of an object completely involved

---

[28] Possibly, different semantic parameters are used in verbal classifiers in sign languages, e.g. a classifier for 'shiny substance' in American sign language (Suppalla 1986: 213). This is a topic for a separate study.
[29] See Goddard (1996) on difficulties of distinguishing existential from locational meanings of Enga classificatory verbs, since locative verbs tend to grammaticalize into existentials.

in an activity; apparently properties related to form and dimensionality are important only when the direct physical contact is involved.

(B2) Animacy in verbal classifiers and classificatory verbs Animacy distinctions are only sometimes present in classificatory verbs; they are in the Athabaskan languages Chipewyan (Carter 1976) and Slave (Rice 1989: 779), in Cherokee (Iroquoian: Blankenship 1996), and in Nevome (Uto-Aztecan); Cora has distinct classificatory verbs for domesticated animals and for humans.

Unlike noun classes, numeral and possessed classifiers, verbal classifiers, and classificatory verbs often do not classify nouns in terms of their animacy, or human/non-human distinction (*pace* Croft 1994: 156 ff.). Some languages, e.g. Iroquoian (Mithun 1986: 386), do have a verbal classifier for animals, or for humans. Alternatively, there may be some other strategy for dealing with humans. In Imonda (Papuan: Seiler 1986) human nouns are not classified at all. Imonda does have a few classifiers which refer to animate nouns, e.g. *u(e)-* 'small animals' such as fish and frogs. Athabaskan verbal classifiers—*d* for round things and *n* for long things—do not include any term for people, or for animals: these remain unclassified.

(B3) Physical properties in verbal classifiers and classificatory verbs Verbal classifiers and classificatory verbs categorize nouns with respect to their extendedness, i.e. shape/dimensionality and position; consistency (flexible, rigid); and constitution (liquid or solid). In Palikur, verbal classifiers are based on the form and dimensionality of objects (see Diagram 6.1).

SHAPE/DIMENSIONALITY usually go together with CONSISTENCY. This is illustrated for two Algonquian languages, Ojibway and Cree, in Table 11.10 (Denny 1979a: 99).

TABLE 11.10. *Verbal classifiers in Ojibway and Cree*

Verbal classifier	Translation
kinw-āpēk-an long-one.dimensional.and.flexible-it.is	'it is long' (e.g. rope)
kinw-ēk-an long-two.dimensional-it.is	'it is long' (e.g. cloth)
napak-āpīk-at flat-one.dimensional and flexible-it is	'it is flat' (e.g. ribbon)
napak-(i)minak-isi flat-three dimensional-it.is	'it is a flat "roundish" thing'
wāwī-(y)ēk-an round-two.dimensional-it.is	'it is round' (e.g. cloth)

Dimensionality and orientation can be employed alongside consistency and other inherent nature properties, e.g. 'granular masses'. Table 11.11 features Chipewyan classificatory verbs (Carter 1976: 25, 27).[30]

TABLE 11.11. *Chipewyan (Athabaskan) classificatory verbs*

Verb stem ('be in')	Object the verb classifies	Example
-ʔą	'inanimate solid objects'	Lake, axe, stone, hat, body parts, ball
-łti	'dead beings'	Dead person, bear carcass, dead dog, raw fish
-tį	'people, sleeping beings'	Person, girl, sleeping baby, sleeping bear
-ką	'liquids'	Water, blood, boiling water, milk
-dzáy	'granular masses'	A pile of sand, a pile of sugar, loose tobacco, powdered milk
-la	'rope-like objects; objects in sets, or plurality of objects'	Rope, veins, several arrows, eyeglasses, two or more fish, three dogs, two oranges
-tą	'stick-like objects or empty containers'	Airplane, bow, empty box, canoe, chair, firewood, spear, cigarette, pen
-łtą	'containers with contents'	Box with stuff in it, can of beer, pack of cigarettes, cup of coffee, bottle of whisky
-ltšuθ	'fabric-like objects'	Calendar, parka, pants, sheet of paper, writing pad, book, one glove, a tree's leaf

How the consistency correlates with dimensionality and extendedness can be illustrated in terms of the binary oppositions for classificatory verbs in Western Apache (Denny 1979a: 107). Dimensionality is relatively independent from extendedness.

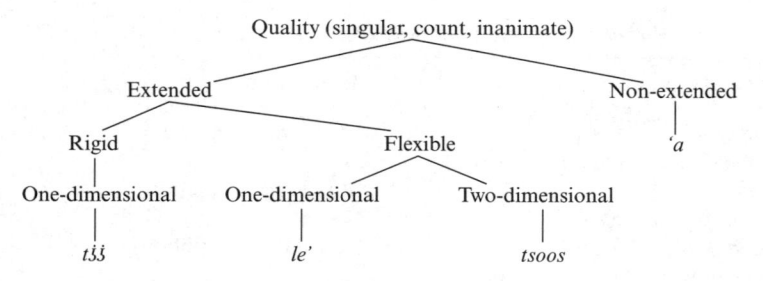

```
              Quality (singular, count, inanimate)
              /                                  \
        Extended                              Non-extended
        /      \                                   |
     Rigid    Flexible                            'a
       |      /      \
  One-dim  One-dim  Two-dim
       |      |        |
      tììì   le'      tsoos
```

DIAGRAM 11.6. *Classificatory verbs in Western Apache*

---

[30] Among verb stems listed by Carter (1976), -*da* 'sit' used for 'awake beings' (frog, spider, sitting bear, sitting person, beaver, sitting baby) is usually not included in the set of classificatory verbs (Chad Thompson, Keren Rice, p.c.).

Classificatory verbs and verbal classifiers often categorize nouns in terms of their orientation in space. Nevome (Uto-Aztecan: Shaul 1986: 12; Table 6.6 above) has different sets of classificatory verbs for animate and inanimate referents depending on their position: horizontal ('lying') or vertical ('standing').

ORIENTATION may correlate with SHAPE/DIMENSIONALITY. Dakota (Siouan: Boas and Deloria 1941: 126) uses positional verbs to classify nouns in terms of their dimensionality, e.g. *nażį* 'stand', for people and animals; *hą* 'stand' for long, upright inanimate objects'; *lipaya* 'lie', for other inanimate objects.

The use of POSTURE verbs as classificatory verbs in Enga (see Table 6.7) and in a number of other Papuan languages correlates with the shape of the object and its position in space. Table 11.12 illustrates classificatory existential verbs in Kamoro, a language from the Asmat family (Drabbe 1955: 39; Lang 1975: 116).[31]

TABLE 11.12. *Classificatory existential verbs in Kamoro (Asmat)*

Classificatory verb	Semantics	Nouns used with
ame	Stand	Vertical, high and tall or slender things, people, houses, trees (alone, singular)
epe	Sit	Pots, dishes, pans, boats on land, plants, mountains, clouds and celestial bodies
kai	Lie	Lands, rivers, lakes, fallen trees or wood
mariki	Float	Fish, people in canoes, anything floating on water
naa	Be there, be above	Hanging objects, small things, big masses such as a heap of rice or a pile of sago, things lying on top of something else

Different semantic parameters may interact to yield semantically complicated systems. DIMENSIONALITY and SHAPE may correlate with CONSISTENCY, FORM, and DIRECTIONALITY. A system of classificatory verbs in Ika

---

[31] Classifcatory existential verbs are also found in Kewa (Franklin 1981), Asmat (Asmat family), Kiwai (Kiwaian family), Huli (Engan), Melpa (Chimbu), Banz, Sinasina (Chimbu), and Kâte (Huon) (see Lang 1975: 115–20, for an overview). A similar system was described for Southeastern Pomo by Moshinsky (1974: 85–7), e.g. *sca-* 'non-long object rests on a surface', 'sit' (for humans); *kto-* 'long object rests on a surface in a vertical position', 'stand'; *mti-* 'long object rests on a surface in a horizontal position', 'lie'; *tla-* 'long object turns on a horizontal axis' (singular forms are given). In many languages positional verbs describe a noun in terms of its position and even shape. Emmi (Australian) uses the verb 'lie' to refer to long and flat objects and to geographically extended localities, while 'stand' is used with reference to trees and mountains (Lys Ford, p.c.). However, this correlation is not systematic, as in Enga and other Papuan languages; this is why these languages cannot be said to have verbal classifiers: see (B) in §6.2.3.

(Frank 1990: 55) combines these properties: see Table 6.3 and 6.16 and 6.17. Classificatory verbs are found only for location and handling.

(B4) Arrangement and quanta The choice of a classificatory verb may depend on the quantity of objects. Hani (Tibeto-Burman: LaPolla 1994: 75) has a classificatory existential verb ky^{31} 'existence within a group' (the full system of classificatory existential verbs in this language is given under (A) in §6.2.3).

(B5) Function Function is also sometimes used as a semantic basis for verbal classifiers. Imonda (Papuan: Seiler 1986: 190–3) has verbal classifiers for 'fruit to be picked' (*põt*), or 'objects which are normally broken', e.g. biscuits (*pui-*) (see Table 13.6).

(B6) Semantics of different systems of verbal classifiers in one language Languages with several different systems of verbal classifiers are important for exploring the semantic possibilities of verbal classifiers. Two systems cooccur in Waris, a language from the same family as Imonda. There is a system of verbal classifiers which refer to the direct object (Brown 1981: 101–3); the categorization is based on consistency, shape, function, arrangement and measures (including two specific classifiers): see Table 6.9. Classificatory verbs (shown in Table 6.10) refer to the orientation of the S argument, and to its shape. The semantic parameters employed in the two systems complement each other. In contrast, the two sets of verbal classifiers in Palikur (Diagram 6.1) overlap; classifiers used with stative verbs distinguish more parts of objects than classifiers employed with transitive verbs. There are also a few further, subtler distinctions: the classifier *-kig* 'pointed objects' is used with transitive verbs for *-kiya* 'sharp edge' (on stative verbs); and the classifier *-min* used with transitive verbs covers one-dimensional thin and rigid objects, e.g. tree trunks (classified with *-kat* on stative verbs).

11.2.6. Semantics of locative and of deictic classifiers

Locative classifiers are rather rare (found only in South American languages: see §7.2). In their semantics, they are similar to non-animacy-based verbal classifier systems. Categorization is based on physical properties, e.g. shape and dimensionality, as in Palikur (Diagram 7.1).

The choice of a locative classifier may correlate with consistency. Dâw (Makú) has different locative adpositions depending on whether the referent of the argument is solid or flexible (see examples 7.5. and 7.6). The choice of a locative classifier in Carib languages depends on dimensionality and consistency of the referent of a noun (see Table 7.1). Animacy as a parameter for locative classifiers has been found only in Lokono (see §7.2).

Deictic classifiers combine reference to shape and position, or to the directionality of the item classified, similarly to non-animacy based verbal classifiers (historically, they often come from grammaticalized posture verbs; see §13.1.3). There is no special classifier for animates or for humans. The deictic classifiers in Siouan languages indicate the orientation of the referent: one-dimensional (long, vertical, or 'standing'), two-dimensional (horizontal, or 'lying'), or three-dimensional (round, or 'sitting') (see §7.3; Barron and Serzisko 1982: 99 ff.). Deictic classifiers fused with demonstratives can combine reference to other properties of the item, such as extendedness, as in Eskimo (Denny 1979a: 101; Table 7.4). Deictic classifiers in the Guaicuruan languages Toba and Pilagá combine reference to visibility, extendedness and position in space of the object (see Diagram 7.2, and (B) in §7.3).

There are not enough examples of locative or deictic classifiers in the languages of the world for anything but very preliminary generalizations concerning their semantics.

11.2.7. *Semantic parameters in languages with several different types of classifier*

In languages with several different types of classifier these may semantically overlap to some extent. However, in languages with noun classes and noun classifiers, the former tend to be animacy, or humanness-based, while the latter tend to be function-based.

In Ngan'gityemerri, noun classes distinguish male, female, groups of humans and a culturally important animal class (canine) (Table 8.1); noun classifiers categorize inanimate objects in terms of their function and nature (strikers, fire, liquid, digging sticks, large woomeras, and canegrass spears). Table 8.1 also shows that the two systems exhibit a semantic overlap (one is historically the source for the other: see Chapter 13).

Numeral classifiers tend to be based on animacy and physical properties, while relational classifiers are based on function, and on the inherent nature of objects. Ponapean (Rehg 1981: 125, 179) has at least twenty-one relational classifiers and twenty-nine numeral classifiers. The choice of a numeral classifier depends on dimensionality, shape and size (round, long), arrangement (bundle, oblong piece of, strip, heap, etc.). There are a few specific classifiers, e.g. for yams and banana. Relational classifiers are function-based. Inanimate nouns are classified into edible and drinkable; there are special classifiers for things to sleep on and for things to cover with, as well as for buildings, vehicles, pillow, and catch (at sea or land); human nouns are classified according to their kin relationship. There are also a few specific classifiers which combine the properties of relational, and of possessed classifiers (e.g. classifiers for names and for earrings: Rehg 1981: 180–1). A similar point is illustrated with Mokilese in Table 8.2.

302 *Classifiers*

Numeral classifiers involve distinctions in terms of physical properties (shape/dimensionality, boundedness, directionality), and noun classifiers are more function and inherent-nature based. An example from Akatek is given in Diagrams 11.7 and 11.8 (see Tables 8.4 and 8.5).

```
                    ┌─ Human
          ┌─ Animate ┤
          │         └─ Non-human
Animacy ──┤
          └─ Inanimate: dimensionality, shape, directionality and size
             (vertical, curved, round, big flat, extended, etc.)
```

DIAGRAM 11.7. *Semantics of fourteen numeral classifiers in Akatek*

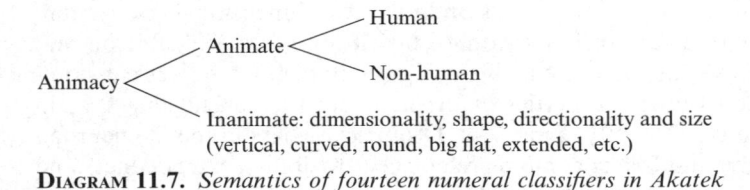

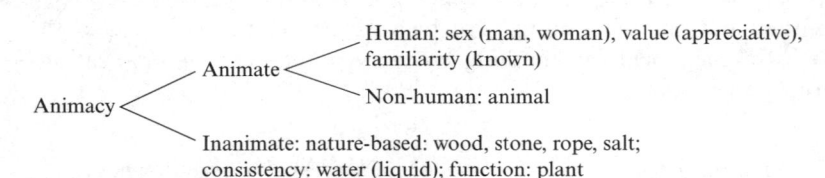

```
                    ┌─ Human: sex (man, woman), value (appreciative),
          ┌─ Animate ┤  familiarity (known)
          │         └─ Non-human: animal
Animacy ──┤
          └─ Inanimate: nature-based: wood, stone, rope, salt;
             consistency: water (liquid); function: plant
```

DIAGRAM 11.8. *Semantics of fourteen noun classifiers in Akatek*

Noun classifiers are usually based on a generic-specific relation, while the choice of a numeral classifier depends on properties of the object. The same noun can be grammaticalized in the function of a generic noun classifier, and in that of a numeral classifier. The polygrammaticalization (for this term, see Craig 1991) within Minangkabau of *batang* 'tree' as a noun classifier, and as a numeral classifier is shown in Diagram 11.9.

```
                       ┌─ Generic noun classifier ── 'Tree as a generic'
batang 'tree' ─────────┤
                       └─ Numeral classifier ──
                              'Vertical long object, often made of wood'
```

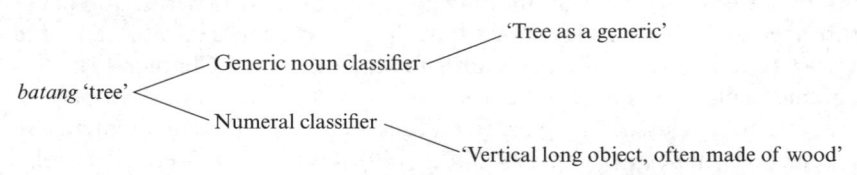

DIAGRAM 11.9. *Polygrammaticalization of* batang *'tree' in Minangkabau*

In Palikur, animacy and humanness is distinguished only in noun classes (genders), and in numeral classifiers. Numeral classifiers, verbal classifiers, locative classifiers and noun classes operate with shape, dimensionality and other physical properties in different ways. Numeral classifiers distinguish three dimensions (with three values for two-dimensional objects, two values for three-dimensional objects, and one value for one-dimensional objects), boundedness and consistency, and a specific nature-based classifier (tree). Verbal classifiers distinguish less values for three-dimensional objects, and more values for one-dimensionals; they distinguish parts of objects (side, edge, inside, parts of trees), and form (pointed). This may be explained by the semantics of the verbs which take classifiers. Transitive verbs which take classifiers imply direct physical contact with the object, and stative verbs refer to dimensions, physical properties of objects, and their colours. Locative classifiers are similar to verbal classifiers; unlike these, they distinguish constitution (liquid), but do not distinguish different cylindrical or flat shapes. Gender assignment is based on animacy, humanness and consistency, which goes with shape and material.

Languages with partly overlapping classifiers in multiple functions show that numeral classifiers tend to have more animacy—or humanness-based—distinctions. Baniwa (Table 9.5) has a human/non-human distinction just in numeral classifiers. Verbal classifiers, noun classifiers, and noun classes distinguish just non-feminine humans, as opposed to non-feminine animates.

11.2.8. Semantic parameters in multiple classifier systems

Multiple classifier systems (discussed in Chapter 9) are always based on animacy, humanness, or sex. Inanimates—and, in some systems, also non-human animates—are classified according to their shape/dimensionality, boundedness, interioricity, consistency, constitution, and other 'inherent nature' properties, as well as function. That is, they combine most semantic parameters found in classifier systems in general, except for directionality.

In Nambiquara (Nambiquara family, Southern Amazonia, Brazil: Lowe 1999) classifiers divide into the semantic groups shown in Diagram 11.10. Nouns are divided into human and the rest. Humans are further classified by sex, and the rest by shape, interioricity, constitution, and other specific (inherent) properties, and by function. There is no classifier for higher animates—these are unclassified (Ivan Lowe, p.c.). Classifiers are prefixed to numbers, as in 9.68; they are suffixed to adjectives as agreement markers, as in 9.69. They are also used as derivational suffixes on nouns, e.g. $huk\text{-}ẽn^1\text{-}su^2$ (shooter-CL:HOLE.LIKE-INDEFINITE) 'shotgun' (see (E) in §9.1).

Motuna (Papuan: Onishi 1994) has fifty-one classifiers which are used with numbers, articles, and demonstratives, possessives, and as derivational affixes on nouns. There are three general classifiers based on ANIMACY and HUMANNESS—-uru 'human', -wori 'animate', -mah 'thing'. Nine classifiers refer to SHAPE and DIMENSIONALITY, e.g. round, concave, slender, stick-like, fine, string-shaped, lengthwise objects. One classifier refers to ARRANGEMENT and SHAPE (-jaa 'object which is wrapped lengthwise'). Five morphemes classify artefacts by FUNCTION. There are also classifiers by QUANTA, and nature-based properties (plants and their parts, human habitation). A few classifiers refer to time (day, month, year/season).

In Kilivila (Austronesian), classifier 'particles' are used with numerals, as

Classifiers

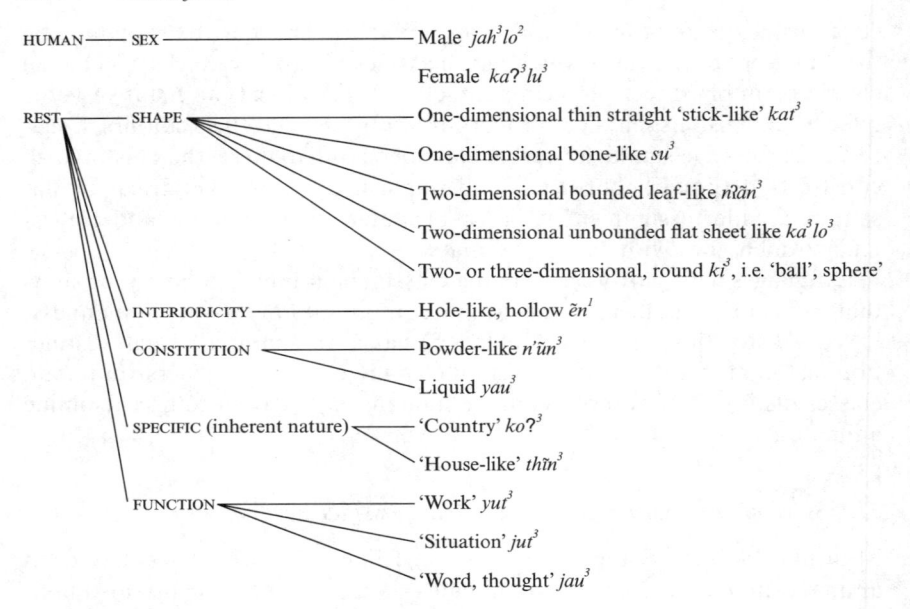

```
HUMAN ──── SEX ──────────────── Male jah³lo²
                                Female ka?³lu³
REST ──┬── SHAPE ──┬──────────── One-dimensional thin straight 'stick-like' kat³
       │           ├──────────── One-dimensional bone-like su³
       │           ├──────────── Two-dimensional bounded leaf-like nũãn³
       │           ├──────────── Two-dimensional unbounded flat sheet like ka³lo³
       │           └──────────── Two- or three-dimensional, round kĩ³, i.e. 'ball', sphere'
       ├── INTERIORICITY ─────── Hole-like, hollow ẽn¹
       ├── CONSTITUTION ──┬───── Powder-like n'ũn³
       │                  └───── Liquid yau³
       ├── SPECIFIC (inherent nature) ──┬── 'Country' ko?³
       │                                └── 'House-like' thĩn³
       └── FUNCTION ──┬───────── 'Work' yut³
                      ├───────── 'Situation' jut³
                      └───────── 'Word, thought' jau³
```

DIAGRAM 11.10. *Classifiers in Nambiquara*

agreement markers on adjectives, and with demonstratives and other deictic type markers (e.g. interrogatives). The three environments of classifiers in Kilivila were illustrated in example 9.1. The classifier *ke* 'wooden objects' is used on a number, and also on a demonstrative and on an adjective (Senft 1996: 18).

The semantic domains covered by Kilvila classifiers are shown in Diagram 11.11 (Senft 1991: 139; 1996: 237–90). Nouns are classified with respect to their animacy. Inanimate nouns can be further classified according to their functional properties, shape, dimensionality, etc. There are also classifiers which refer to the quantity of animate and inanimate referents.

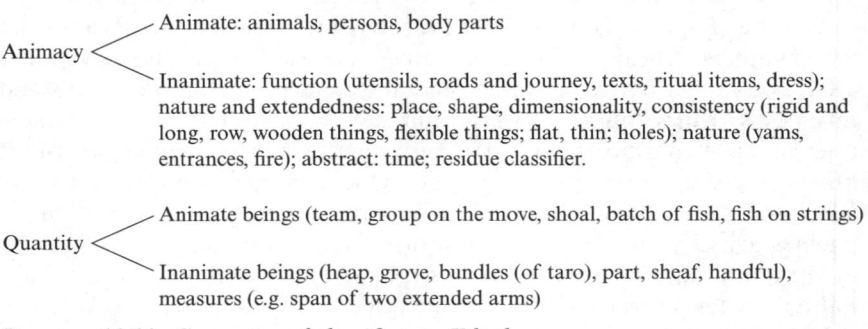

```
Animacy ──┬── Animate: animals, persons, body parts
          │
          └── Inanimate: function (utensils, roads and journey, texts, ritual items, dress);
              nature and extendedness: place, shape, dimensionality, consistency (rigid and
              long, row, wooden things, flexible things; flat, thin; holes); nature (yams,
              entrances, fire); abstract: time; residue classifier.

Quantity ──┬── Animate beings (team, group on the move, shoal, batch of fish, fish on strings)
           │
           └── Inanimate beings (heap, grove, bundles (of taro), part, sheaf, handful),
               measures (e.g. span of two extended arms)
```

DIAGRAM 11.11. *Semantics of classifiers in Kilivila*

11.2.9. Conclusions

The possibility of the same classifier morpheme being used in up to six environments (see Chapter 9) goes against establishing strict correlations between the morphosyntactic environment for a classifier and its semantics. We can only establish a number of tendencies which emerged from the data discussed in this chapter. These are shown in Table 11.13.

ANIMACY or HUMANNESS or SEX are basic for noun classes, numeral classifiers, and possessed classifiers. Verbal, locative, deictic, and relational classifiers do not have to be animacy-based. (See Appendix 1, on how animacy and human/non-human distinctions can be expressed through other categories in languages with neither noun classes nor classifiers.) Further subdivisions of humans, or animates, according to their SOCIAL STATUS and KINSHIP RELATIONSHIP are found only for numeral classifiers and noun classifiers. Physical properties such as SHAPE, FORM, SIZE, BOUNDEDNESS, INTERIORICITY, and CONSISTENCY are less often found in noun classes. They are usually found in all other classifier types except noun classifiers and relational classifiers. Size, boundedness, interioricity, and consistency tend to be concomitant with shape.

DIRECTIONALITY or ORIENTATION is found in numeral classifiers, verbal classifiers (especially classificatory verbs), and deictic classifiers as a feature concomitant to shape. FUNCTION is almost always a semantic dimension of relational and possessed classifiers, and it is often found with numeral, noun and verbal classifiers. It is rare, however, in noun class systems. NATURE-based specific classifiers are found in all the classifier types but only rarely in noun class systems. QUANTA and ARRANGEMENT are found with numeral classifiers and with verbal classifiers. GENERIC-SPECIFIC relations are used only in noun classifiers, possessed classifiers, and verbal classifiers (and rarely in numeral classifiers).

These semantic preferences are universal.[32] However, they are not strict rules. In reality, classifiers of different types show a large degree of semantic overlap, and the same morpheme can be used in several classifier environments.

---

[32] We will see in Chapter 13 how they can be important for semantic extenstions in the course of the historical development of classifiers.

TABLE 11.13. *Preferred semantic parameters in classifiers*

Classifier	Grammatical function	Scope	Typical semantics	Generic-specific relation
Noun classes	Determination, head-modifier agreement	NP	Animacy, physical properties, rarely nature or function	No
	predicate-argument agreement	clause		
Numeral classifiers	Quantification, enumeration	NP	Animacy, social status and kinship relationship, directionality and orientation, physical properties, nature, quanta, arrangement, functional properties	Rare
Noun classifiers	Determination	NP	Social status, functional properties, nature	Yes
Verbal classifiers	O/S agreement spatial location	clause	Physical properties, directionality and orientation, nature, function, quanta, arrangement, rarely animacy	Yes
Relational classifiers	Possession	NP	Functional properties, nature	No
Possessed classifiers	Possession	NP	Physical properties, nature, animacy, functional properties	Yes
Locative classifiers	Spatial location	NP	Physical properties, nature, rarely animacy	No
Deictic classifiers	Spatial location, determination	NP	Directionality and orientation, physical properties, nature	No

12 Semantic Organization and Functions of Noun Categorization

This chapter considers various aspects of the semantics of noun categorization devices and their implications for the study of human cognition and culture.

Semantic features encoded in noun categorization reflect principles of human cognition and world perception. This is why it has often been argued that classifiers offer 'a unique window' into studying how humans construct representations of the world and encode them into their languages (Lakoff 1986; Craig forthcoming). The semantics of classifiers is often conditioned by the socio-cultural and physical environment in which a language is spoken and is often affected by social changes, language planning, and cultural obsolescence.

In §12.1 I discuss the semantic organization and functions of classifiers. Cognitive and perceptual mechanisms which underlie the structuring of the world seen in terms of classifiers are analysed in §12.2. How noun categorization could depend on social and cultural environment—and change if the society changes—will be dealt with in §12.3; conclusions are given in §12.4.

12.1. Semantic organization and functions of classifier systems

The semantic complexity of an individual classifier varies, and so does its scope. Some classes are semantically straightforward, while others are heterogeneous. In this section we consider the principles of overall semantic organization of individual classes, and of systems at large. First, in §12.1.1, we look at semantic complexity in classifier systems, including principles of semantic extensions and opacity in classifier choice.

Classifiers can have different functions. They can be employed to delimit the scope of reference of a noun, or of a modifier within a noun phrase, or of the predicate within a clause. Classifiers are seldom semantically redundant, because they highlight some relevant aspect of the noun referent (e.g. its shape, function, or value). The semantic roles of classifiers are discussed in §12.1.2, and their discourse-pragmantic functions in 12.1.3. The applicability of classifiers, default classes, and residue classes are analysed in §12.1.4.

12.1.1. Semantic complexity in classifier systems

The choice of noun classes and classifiers can be semantically transparent. In Malay and Minangkabau the classifier 'person' is used with all humans; the animal classifier (with a literal meaning 'tail') is used for all animals (Marnita 1996: 106).

On the other hand, the semantic structure of a class can be extremely heterogeneous. The semantic structure of the classifier -*hon* in Japanese (Lakoff 1986: 25–6; Matsumoto 1993: 676–81) is complex. In its most common use it covers saliently one-dimensional objects, e.g. long, thin, rigid objects such as sticks, canes, pencils, candles, trees, dead snakes, and dried fish. It also covers martial arts contests with swords (which are long and rigid), hits in baseball, shots in basketball, Judo matches, rolls of tape, telephone calls, radio and TV programmes, letters, movies, medical injections, bananas, carrots, pants, guitars, and teeth.

This heterogeneity results from various processes of semantic extension. Different classes are heterogeneous in varying ways, because of different extensions and relations within the semantic fields of classifiers. While defining a category by simply listing its members is possible for any classifier, we search for a general characterization which will accord with the idea of internal homogeneity of cognitive and linguistic processes. A prototype model accounts for semantic extensions of classifiers.[1]

Thus, classifiers do not have to be homogeneous lexical categories bounded by a set of features shared by all the members (see Sweetser 1986, for different mechanisms behind polysemy and abstraction).

(A) Prototype approach

Some members of a given class are perceived by native speakers as more salient than others—these members are cognitively more central.[2] Other,

---

[1] Downing (1996: 96–8) obtained four sorts of definition for Japanese numeral classifiers with respect to their membership: specification of kind by means of reference to a roughly equivalent noun (inductive rule); listing of members; citation of a representative member of a category; specification of characteristics of members of the category (e.g. shape for *hon* 'classifier for long, thin things').

[2] Diagnostic criteria for prototypes used in the literature, summarized by Downing (1996: 103–4), include: (i) frequent and/or early appearance on lists of category members; (ii) appearance as the model for an analogical change or as the source for metaphor- or metonymy-based additions to the category; (iii) appearance as the source for the meaning of morphological derivatives of the category label; (iv) high acceptability rating as a category member; (v) consistency with the etymological source of the category label; (vi) loss of category members unrelated to this one; (vii) frequent usage of the category label with respect to this category member (e.g. frequent citation in dictionary entries for the category label); (viii) ability of subjects to quickly judge statements about the category affiliation of this member; (ix) early acquisition as category member by children. One should keep in mind

more peripheral members are associated with a particular class because they share at least one feature with one, or more, prototypical members (on 'prototype effects' see Rosch 1973; 1975a; 1975b; 1987; Barsalou 1987; Lakoff 1987).

For instance, prototypical members covered by the classifier *hon* in Japanese would be sticks, or canes; hits in baseball (see below) or phone calls are more marginal. Idiolectal variation is typical of peripheral membership of classifier category. Matsumoto (1993: 676) points out individual variation as to the use of the Japanese classifier *hon* for non-central members of the 'one-dimensional' class—i.e. one-dimensional objects which are circular (e.g. rubber bands or tubes). With respect to child language acquisition of non-central members of classifier categories, Matsumoto (1985) noted that his five- to seven-year-old Japanese-speaking subjects had no difficulty in applying *hon* to novel objects with a perceptually salient thin, long shape; but it was difficult for them to apply it spontaneously to non-central, conventionalized members of the *hon* category obtained by metonymical extension. His explanation for the acquisition of these conventionalized uses was that children have to 'learn the use of *hon* for atypical cases in an item-by-item fashion, for the acquisition of knowledge of the membership of atypical members of a classifier category seem to depend heavily on the actual exposure to these uses in the input' (Matsumoto 1985: 168).[3] Extensions from central to less central members are discussed in (B).

(B) Extension principles: chaining and metonymy

The prototype and extension model presupposes the existense of more and less central members. Complex categories are structured by chaining, i.e. by common properties.

Classifier categories often contain members which have been taken into this category because of some semantic relationship they bear with its preexisting members. Japanese *hon* used for long, thin things has been 'extended' to hits in baseball, since they refer to 'straight trajectories, formed by the forceful motion of a solid object, associated with a baseball bat, which is long, thin and rigid' (Lakoff 1986: 25; but see criticism in

---

that diachronic semantic extensions (see Chapter 13) have to be distinguished from the synchronic organization of a class.

[3] A recent application of the prototype theory to a selection of classifiers in Mandarin Chinese (Chang-Smith 1996) confirmed the existence of prototype effects in linguistic categorization with classifiers. The prototypical member of the category covered by a classifier proved to be the preferred one, e.g. 'car' for $liang^4$ 'CL:LAND.VEHICLES', 'paper' for $zhang^1$ 'CL:FLAT.THIN.OBJECTS', and 'pen' for zhi^3 'CL:LONG.RIGID.OBJECTS'. There were no 'favoured nouns' for classifier $tiao^2$ 'CL:LONG.FLEXIBLE.OBJECTS' which might play the role of prototypes; this may be due to the wide range of salient perceptual properties associated with this classifier (Chang-Smith 1996: 52).

Matsumoto 1993: 677, and Downing 1996: 100). Then it was 'extended' to shots and serves in other sports, and even to phone calls. This is what Craig (forthcoming: 13) describes as a 'chaining model'.

As a result, classifiers and their semantic representations can differ in complexity, and may be difficult to characterize in terms of a set of abstract features, or of the prototypicality of their referents. For instance, the human non-feminine classifier -*ite* in Baniwa applies to some human attributes; this marker is employed to refer to shirts and other items of clothing, eyeglasses, and musical tunes. Thus, it is only mildly heterogeneous. In contrast, Japanese *hon* is extremely heterogeneous because of various chaining extensions from the prototype. Most of these extensions become conventionalized; those which do not display idiolectal variability.

A new member can be taken into a category either because it shares certain characteristics with most members of the category or because it is judged to have some similarity with only some of them (see the discussion of these cognitive principles by Langacker 1987). In Garo (Adams and Conklin 1973; Conklin 1981) the classifier which refers to round objects (stones, balls, eyes, coins and round fruit, e.g. oranges and mangoes) can be extended to just a few other fruit of a different shape (e.g. bananas).

Extensions can be based on certain rules for transferring class membership. Dyirbal employs the following principle (Dixon 1982: 179):

(i) If some noun has characteristic X (on the basis of which its class membership would be expected to be decided) but is, through belief or myth, connected with characteristic Y, then generally it will belong to the class corresponding to Y and not that corresponding to X. (ii) If a subset of nouns has some particular important property that the rest of the set do not have, then the members of the subset may be assigned to a different class from the rest of the set, to 'mark' this property.

According to these principles 'idealized models of the world'—for instance, myths and beliefs—can account for other chaining links within the structure of a class. In Dyirbal, birds belong to 'feminine' Class II because they are believed to be the spirits of dead human females. In Palikur, heavenly bodies—sun, moon, stars, and also thunder and lightning—are the only inanimate objects with masculine gender; this is because they are human males in myth. Other extensions are linked to similarities in shape, or directionality. 'Image-schema' transformation involves various extensions, e.g. the ones based on analogy between shape and trajectory of an object ('conduit-metaphor': Matsumoto 1993: 677). These extensions for the Japanese classifier *hon* employed for one-dimensional objects and their paths—e.g. hits and home runs in baseball, as well as serial stories, movies and play scripts—are based on 'experiential one-dimensionality' (cf. Lakoff 1986: 26–7).

A further type of extension is the 'Domain of Experience Principle' which links together members considered as associated with the same experience domain. Thus, fish in Dyirbal belong to Class 1 since they are animate, and so do fishing implements because they are associated with the same activity. These domains are often culture-specific, and subject to change with socio-cultural changes. The numeral classifier *tay* in Korean was originally used with reference to traditional vehicles, and then got extended to introduced European artefacts with wheels. There was a further extension, to any electric machinery, and to other kinds of machines or instruments, including even the piano (Lee 1997).

Metonymical models of different sorts are also applied when linking objects together in one class. A metonymical model presupposes that 'a word or expression normally or strictly used of one thing is used of something physically or otherwise associated with it' (Matthews 1997: 224; Lakoff 1986: 33, for their properties). Extensions and metonymic transfers are important for explaining synchronic and diachronic semantic changes in classifiers. In Austroasiatic languages, shape parameters in inanimate categorization can be described as 'geometrical generalizations from naturally occurring forms'. In Tai (Conklin 1981: 136), these generalizations are derived from plants and their component parts. Some typical generalizations are: small and roundish (from seed), round (from fruit), bulky (from tuber), flat and sheet-like (from flower, leaf, fibre), long (from stalk, stick, sprout) (Conklin 1981: 341).

(C) Metaphors in classifier systems

Metaphors and metaphorical transfers (see the definition in Sapir 1977: 6) are important for the semantic organization of classes and the ways in which they get extended. This can be illustrated from the semantic organization of numeral classifiers in Burmese described by Becker (1975; 1986). The structure of underlying Burmese categorization is based on an interpretation of self—see Table 12.1. As Becker (1975: 118) puts it, 'the structure underlying classification starts with the self at the centre, divides the self into head and body, and then ranges objects at four distances from the self, associating them either with the head (metaphorically top, round) or with the body (metaphorically, bottom, straight)'. The system of categorization operates on 'applied metaphors'; thus 'head to the body' is the same as 'cup to saucer', and so on; the relationship above/below is basic for categorization. Moreover, since several of the classifiers are words for parts of a tree, one can say that 'the tree is the metaphor for the person'.

TABLE 12.1. *Burmese numeral classifiers for inanimate objects*

Centre 1st Orbit Self: part of self (inalienable)	2nd Orbit On self (alienable)	3rd Orbit Near self	4th Orbit Far from self
Head *ywɛ'*: hair on head leaf	*pain*: head-dress	*loun*: round, upper things: posts furniture cup script	*sin*: upper things which have circular orbit: sun rivers, sea arrows needles
Body *chaun*: hair on body fingers and toes teeth *pin*: sticks twigs pens	*kwin*: body dress body ornaments *thɛ*: folded clothes	*cha'*: flat, lower things: boards mats saucer palmleaf for writing *le'*: instruments used in the hand; swords; musical instruments; puppets	*si*: lower things which move in straight lines: vehicles hunted animals horses dupes *thwɛ* rivers roads

Understanding metaphorical transfers in classifier systems requires knowledge of historical and cultural background. As Becker (1986: 337) puts it: 'The important thing here is to see that the classifier is selected from a kind of conceptual space which has been historically shaped.' Thus, in Burmese, 'unless one knows that the traditional Burmese pictorial map of the cosmos has man located on an island, from the centre of which flows a river in a spiral course to the sea, one may question why rivers and oceans are classified here along with arrows and needles, which move in circular orbits' (Becker 1975: 118). Rhetorical uses of classifiers are further extensions of metaphors, and 'the use of classifiers in Burmese . . . is in part an art and not just a grammatical convention' (Becker 1975: 113).

Personification is a typical metaphorical extension. It can be realized with different means. In Standard English, personal pronouns tend to be used with humans; but they can also be used with non-human animates—say, pets—to express their particular closeness or dearness to the speaker; then they become almost human-like. The Tasmanian variety of English (described in Pawley 2002) has strict rules which govern the choice of pronouns *he* and *she* with non-human referents. For instance, when the sex of a higher animal is not known, the animal is referred to as 'he'; when referring to an inanimate entity, *he* is used with plants or parts of living plants, and any item of goods or portable property (other than vehicles) that is viewed as trade goods rather than a personal possession.

Gender languages often use gender metaphorically to describe unusual situations (see (C) in §2.4.3). In Manambu, a small, effeminate man can be jokingly referred to as feminine. Gender distinctions can be used metaphorically in languages with no, or almost no, agreement gender. Ilocano (Austronesian: Rubino 1997: 75-6) does not have genders; the natural gender of humans may be distinguished lexically, e.g. *lalaki* 'boy', *babai* 'girl'. These lexemes are also used to distinguish natural gender of hybrid nouns, e.g. *kabsat a lalaki* 'brother', *kabsat a babai* 'sister'. They can also cooccur with inanimates, highlighting semantic features associated with a metaphorical extension of 'masculinity' or 'femininity'. For instance, *basi a lalaki* 'strong sugar cane wine' is associated with masculinity; and *basi a babai* 'sweet sugar cane wine' with femininity.

Gender languages often manipulate gender in legends. Personification of nouns with inanimate or abstract referents follows the gender which is assigned by non-semantic rules. For instance, Russian *smert'* 'death' is feminine and so is personified as a woman in folk tales and cartoons (Rothstein 1973: 464).[4] Similarly, *morte* 'death', a feminine noun in Portuguese, is depicted as *Dona Morte* (Lady Death) in cartoons.

Change of genders can have a stylistic effect. Some nouns of feminine gender, essentially hostile epithets, can be applied to human beings. According to Rothstein (1973: 464), in Russian it is more insulting to call a man *dura* (fool: feminine) than *durak* (fool: masculine) (cf. (C) in §11.2.1; on the use of masculine diminutives of feminine names to express affective jocularity in Polish, see Wierzbicka 1996: 398).

Some systems accept metaphorical extensions more easily than others— this happens because systems differ in their productivity. The productivity, or vitality, of a system is measured by its ability to accept and classify new members, and reanalyse and extend the semantic range of a noun categorization device over time. Thai has an old classifier system which has great vitality and productivity; the more productive a system is, the more metaphorical and other types of extensions it accepts. In contrast, the Jacaltec system of noun classifiers can be looked upon as frozen. New loanwords are simply left unclassified; the system does not accept semantic extensions either (Craig forthcoming). Frozen or non-productive systems do not have to be in decay, though they sometimes are, as is the case of many classifier systems changing due to language obsolescence and contact.[5]

---

[4] In this and similar cases we cannot tell whether 'death' is depicted as a woman 'because' it is feminine, or the other way round.

[5] There are two ways of expanding membership of a noun class: intensional, i.e. based on the characteristics shared by most members, and extensional, i.e. based on chaining analogy

314   *Classifiers*

An instructive example of prototype-and-extension in a multiple classifier system comes from the classifier *tua* in Thai. The structure of the category is schematized in Diagram 12.1 (Carpenter 1987: 46). Lines indicate extensions from a prototypical member to less prototypical ones (Carpenter 1987: 45–6; cf. Downing 1996: 101–2).

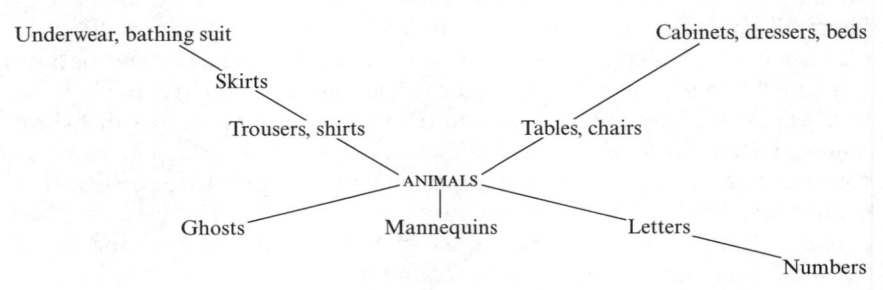

```
Underwear, bathing suit                          Cabinets, dressers, beds
         \                                              /
         Skirts                                        /
             \                                        /
          Trousers, shirts              Tables, chairs
                     \                    /
                     ANIMALS
                        |
        Ghosts       Mannequins         Letters
                                              \
                                              Numbers
```

DIAGRAM 12.1. *Structure of the tua category in Thai*

Carpenter (1987: 45–6) gives the following explanation of the extension and chaining principles which apply to *tua* (semantic features which could have served as basis for the extensions are provided by me in small caps):

> This covers a wide, but not incoherent, range of things. The articles of clothing used with /tua/ are trousers, shirts, jackets, skirts, and, less often, dresses, underwear and bathing suits. The items of furniture most likely to be used with /tua/ are tables and chairs, and less often, dressers and beds. These assignments suggests that it is THE PRESENCE OF LIMBS, giving these objects a body-like shape, that causes speakers to classify them with /tua/. Originally, the classifier was used with animals, and the PROTOTYPE is probably some good QUADRUPEDAL ANIMAL, such as a dog or a water buffalo. Tables and chairs were included on the basis of SHAPE, either because of their general quadrupedal outline or perhaps because of the specific presence of limbs. Other kinds of furniture were then added because of their shared FUNCTION with tables and chairs. Trousers and shirts were also included because of their SHAPE, again either because generally they follow the contours of the body of

with few members. Downing (1996: 117) hypothesizes, for Japanese, that when the classifier is associated with a large referent class, 'the sheer number of members meeting the intensional requirements for membership will work against member-focused expansion. No such obstacle would exist in the case of categories composed of but a single member, or of a few members bearing no obvious intensional relationship to each other, as in the case of *sao* "chests, flags, poles, samisens, stick-shaped sweets" where it is *only* the extension-based assimilation that is possible.' The overall preference for intensional rather than extensional expansion of classifiers is corroborated by a tendency to 'optimization' of prototype-centred categories in achieving structural stability and semantic flexibility and adaptability. Cf. Geeraerts (1988: 223): 'the categorial system can only work efficiently if it can maintain its overall organisation for some time . . . At the same time, however, it should be flexible enough to be easily adaptable to changing circumstances. To prevent it from becoming chaotic, it should have a built-in tendency towards structural stability, but this stability should not become rigidity, lest the system stops being able to adapt itself to new and unforeseen circumstances.'

their wearer, or specifically because they have limbs. Other kinds of clothing were included because of their SHAPES. A letter (of the alphabet) in Thai is a compound, /tua nangseu/ 'body book', so a combination of shape and repetition of the generic compound head caused letters to be classified with /tua/. Numbers were included either on the basis of shape or by their shared function with letters.

Similarly, ghosts were included because of their similarity with the shape of a human body. Carpenter concludes: 'The internal structure of this category, then, clearly, mixes prototypes and chains, with strongest members being those closest to an animate quadruped, but some chaining based on similarities to non-prototypical members.'

Opacity in classifier assignment can be due to semantic extensions that are explainable but unpredictable. Table 12.2 illustrates human classification in Burmese based on social status and age (Becker 1975: 116) and its extensions to human attributes.

TABLE 12.2. *Animate classifiers in Burmese*

hsu	pa	u:	jau'	kaun
Buddha and his attributes: relics, images, the Law	Deities, saints, monks, royalty	People of status, teachers, scholars	Ordinary humans	Animals, ghosts, dead bodies, depraved people, children

The classifier *hsu* used for Buddha got extended to Buddha's words, and thus to Buddhist law. This classifier has undergone further analogical and metaphorical extensions. *Hsu* can apply to the whole field of human existence, and this term was extended to items 'conceptually similar to the system with its centre and measured distances, e.g. concentric networks like mosquito nets and fish nets (both of which in traditional Burma were conical in shape), gardens (which were laid out as a wheel), and staircases' (Becker 1975: 116). These extensions, ultimately based on extendedness and shape, are reminiscent of shape extensions of genders and noun classes (see §11.1.1). They contribute to the increase of opacity in classifier assignment.

Similar metaphorical extensions are found in other languages. In Bugis, *tau* 'human classifier' is usually employed for counting people; however, classifier *lisə* 'small spherical objects' can be used for counting people who died in a war, presumably, because the heads of dead enemies used to be cut off and people were counted by their heads (Sirk 1983: 63).

Thus, the composition of a classifier category and its expansion may be hard to predict. Though it is often possible for an analyst to suggest a rationale for the inclusion of most members of a given category, this may have not been the actual rationale employed by speakers. There is also a certain degree of unpredictability associated with social and cultural conventions.[6]

(D) Semantic structure and hierarchical organization of classifiers

Classifier categories are semantically heterogeneous. There have been a few attempts to present the semantic organization of classifiers in terms of taxonomic trees and binary oppositions (Denny 1979a; 1979b; see criticism by Downing 1996: 125); however a superordinate-subordinate approach has limited applicability to classifier systems. The reason why superordinacy relations are limited and are unlikely to involve all the classifiers lies in the coexistence of different and cross-cutting semantic rationales (kind and quality classifiers), and on different types of extension. Some referents are included in more than one class (see §12.1.2 on variability in classifier assignment and the issue of semantic roles and functions of classifiers). Thus, a sword in Japanese can be referred to by a shape-based classifier *hon* 'long, slender object', by a kind classifier *furi* 'sword', or by a function-based quality classifier *ten* 'items in an inventory, works of art'. It is also impossible to make all shape-based classifiers superordinate to kind classifiers which possess appropriate shape, because kind classifiers may unite referents of different shapes (e.g. the verbal classifier *-pit* used for any irregular shape object in Palikur). Other problems with creating distinct taxonomies result from a generic classifier, such as Japanese *tsu*, which participates in all of them.

There are hardly any hierarchical relations in the assignment of noun classes (genders), deictic or locative classifiers; hence the discrepancies between scientific and folk taxonomies and noun categorization devices. Assignment of relational classifiers implies a functional categorization of objects, with no clear-cut hierarchical relations.

The few Japanese numeral classifiers which have superordinate-subordinate relation are given in Table 12.3. In all these cases 'the more general term [can] be used for all members of the category denoted by a more specific term' (Downing 1996: 126).

---

[6] A problem may arise in how to distinguish metaphors from polysemy. For instance, in Kilivila (Senft 1996: 19) a 'dinghy' can be referred to with a classifier 'child', as well as 'wooden', e.g. *ma-gudi-na waga ke-kekita* (this-CL:CHILD-this canoe CL:WOODEN-small) 'this small dinghy'. This can be interpreted in two ways: either as a metaphorical extension (child > small object), or a polysemy: child, any small creature, or object. We think that a decision should be made in terms of language-internal criteria on what is literal and what is metaphorical meaning, before there is a universally accepted 'serviceable' 'clarification of the distinction . . . between conventional metaphor and systematic polysemy', to 'separate (even provisionally) the literal from the metaphorical . . . we need to accommodate the fact that over time metaphorical expression-systems may lose their metaphorical duality and assume the status of literal meanings, as when body-part terms become locational adpositions' (Goddard 1996: 150). This change is somewhat similar to semantic processes which take place in grammaticalization.

TABLE 12.3. *Verified superordinate–subordinate pairs in Japanese numeral classifiers*

Superordinate	Subordinate
1. *dai* 'vehicles, furniture, machines'	*ki* 'air vehicles', *ryo* 'train cars', *taku* 'tables, desks'
2. *hen* 'literary work'	*shu* 'poems', *ku* 'poems' [7]
3. *hiki* 'animals'	*too* 'large animals'
4. *heya* 'rooms'	*shitsu* 'rooms', *ma* 'Japanese style rooms'
5. *nin* 'human beings'	*mei* 'human beings' (honorific)
6. *hon* 'long, thin objects'	*furi* 'swords'
7. *tsu* 'inanimates'	most kind-classifiers for inanimates

The situation is different with generics. The generic-specific taxonomy can be nature-based, or functionally defined (produce, pets, food, prey). Evidence from Yidiny shows a hierarchical relation between the two (cooccurrence of the two, i.e. 'person' plus 'man', or 'person' plus 'woman'), which is by no means universal (see §3.2.1 and 3.4 above).

Thus, a taxonomic approach to classifiers may be useful, but only in limited circumstances.[8] On the other hand, prototype-extension and chaining models are more applicable in heterogeneous non-hierarchical systems such as noun classes, numeral classifiers, some verbal, and all locative and deictic classifiers. These models do not apply to those instances in which there is a generic-specific relationship between classifier and noun.

12.1.2. *Semantic roles of classifiers*

We saw in §11.1 that classifiers differ as to the degree of 'abstractness' of the features involved. This is particularly relevant for classifiers of inanimates because these involve many more shape- and function-based features. We saw in §11.2 that there are fewer 'specific' classifiers in the domain of animates and especially of humans (though there are examples, e.g. 'guest' in Kana, 'dog' in Cahuilla, or 'canine' in Ngan'gityemerri). Classifiers which centre round a narrow array of representative members are 'inductive' or 'kind classifiers'; also called taxonomy-specific (Downing 1996: 90 ff., 118), and those which are organized on the basis of a feature are 'deductive', or 'quality classifiers'. The two differ in how restricted they are. Kind classifiers are more culture-specific, they are acquired later, and they are more semantically redundant. Quality classifiers lack these properties.

Classifiers can have several semantic functions which are linked together.

---

[7] The classifier *ku* refers to haiku (17-syllable poems) and other short poems, while *shu* refers to other poems (Downing 1996: 20 and 22).

[8] See Löbel (2000) for a convincing application of this model to Vietnamese; a somewhat different analysis is suggested by Goral (1978).

(A) Quantifying and individuating functions

The quantifying function of numeral classifiers is connected to the idea that 'the noun refers to some kind of mass and the classifier gives a unit of this mass' (Denny 1986: 298). A numeral classifier is then viewed as a unit of collectivity (Greenberg 1978).[9] Classifiers are used when reference to particular individuals is required (see (B) below). This function explains the anaphoric use of classifiers. Nouns are more often deleted from numeral phrases than classifiers, since classifiers refer to the type of individual being enumerated, and nouns only specify some of their properties (Denny 1986: 301). In the following example from Minangkabau (Marnita 1996: 93), both the noun and the classifier appear in the question, but only the classifier is retained in the answer:

12.1. bara   lamang   sa-batang
      how.much   lamang[10]   one-NUM.CL:LONG.RIGID
      'How much is one lamang?'

12.2. saribu   sa-batang
      one.thousand   one-NUM.CL:LONG.RIGID
      'One thousand (rupees) for one.'

Once the property, or domain of reference (traditional food 'lamang'), is established, the noun can be omitted; but reference to a general class of long-shaped objects is essential.[11]

Individuation is essential for the use of classifiers with deictics (see also Löbel 2000: 308–9, examples 6.28–30 for an illustration of the singulativizing function of classifiers in Vietnamese). With Thai demonstratives, classifiers are more likely to be used when reference to particular individuals has to be stressed, for instance, in the case of contrastive focus. In 12.3, from Thai (Conklin 1981: 86), the classifier $lang^5$ 'building, roof', cannot be omitted.

12.3. baan³ lang⁵   nii⁴ mii¹   (pra²tuu¹) saam⁵ pra²tuu¹
      this CL:ROOF this have (door)   three CL:DOOR
      suan² lang⁵   nan⁴ mii¹   sɔɔng⁵   pra²tuu¹
      but   CL:ROOF that have two   CL:DOOR
      'This building has three doors, but that building has two doors.'

---

[9] T'sou (1976) gives a different explanation for quantifying functions of numeral classifiers in terms of quantity and entity.

[10] Lamang is traditional Minangkabau food made of glutinous rice which is cooked inside a medium-size piece of bamboo.

[11] A separate question is to what extent numeral classifiers have to express actual counting, enumeration, or just specification. Also, is enumeration universal? Hale (1975) showed that so-called numbers in Australian languages are specifiers which traditionally did not have any counting functions. In some South American languages numbers establish quantity; but contexts of actual counting are almost nonexistent (see §4.1).

(B) Classifying and categorizing functions of classifiers

Classifiers provide information about sorts, or classes, of units. Consequently, one of the functions of classifiers with nouns is to provide expectations about the verb predicates; conversely, a function of classifiers with verbs is to provide information about a nominal argument. For instance, only some predicates are appropriate with human or with inanimate subjects, or objects (Denny 1986: 302–3). Classifiers serve to organize human knowledge into classes according to the principles of human perception and human functioning; they 'have a specialized role separate from that of nouns—they establish expectations about the verb predicate which the speaker will use, and about other verb predicates which are likely to be relevant as thought and conversation continue . . . nouns have the quite different role of helping to identify the thing being referred to' (Denny 1986: 303). Classifiers also represent semantic categorization, i.e. the organization of knowledge encoded in a language. This knowledge correlates with socio-cultural variables, and with universal principles of cognition. It may reflect the cognitive and functional categorization of objects within a particular culture (see §§12.2 and 12.3).

However, classifiers encode different information from that carried by nouns. There are then two possibilitites—both show that classifiers are not semantically redundant.

One is ADDING INFORMATION to the nominal. This is especially salient in cases when different classifiers are used with the same noun. This 'variability' in categorization is attested for almost any classifier type.

The choice of a classifier for humans may depend on their social status. A student can be considered an ordinary person, or else a member of a higher class, as in Korean. When inanimate nouns appear with different classifiers, these highlight different aspects of their meaning.

A well-known example from Burmese (Becker 1975: 113) illustrates this point. 'River' can be spoken of in at least eight contexts, shown in Table 12.4. Note that here numeral classifiers are most certainly not semantically redundant.

TABLE 12.4. *Reclassification of an inanimate noun in Burmese*

Noun	Numeral	Classifier	Translation
myiʔ	tə	yaʔ	'river one place' (e.g. destination for a picnic)
myiʔ	tə	tan	'river one line' (e.g. on a map)
myiʔ	tə	hmwa	'river one section' (e.g. a fishing area)
myiʔ	tə	'sin	'river one distant arc' (e.g. a path to the sea)
myiʔ	tə	thwɛ	'river one connection' (e.g. tying two villages)
myiʔ	tə	'pa	'river one sacred object' (e.g. in mythology)
myiʔ	tə	khu'	'river one conceptual unit' (e.g. in a discussion of rivers in general)
myiʔ	tə	myiʔ	'river one river' (the unmarked case)

Specific classifiers ('kind classifiers' in Downing 1996: 93) can also add information about the referent, since they allow speakers to distinguish one sense of the referent from all the others. The repeater *myi?* in Table 12.4 indicates that a river is looked upon just as a river, and helps discard other senses (see further examples in Downing 1996: 92–3).

Classifiers can add unusual information about the referent. The use of *ten*, a classifier for works of art, with stamps in Japanese may be done to convey the idea that some particular stamps are of artistic value (Downing 1996: 94; ex. (38)). The classifier *dai* 'small countable objects' can be used with nouns normally describing large objects (e.g. houses or boats) to refer to toys.

Examples of variable categorization can be given from other types as well. In Yidiny, different noun classifiers can be used with a word for 'cave' depending on whether it is looked upon as a possible habitation, or as something made of stone. 'Plant', or 'banana' can be either planted or eaten, and these functions require the use of different possessed classifiers, as in Palikur or Apalaí (see Chapter 5).

In closed noun class systems the variability of categorization is often limited. Variable noun class assignment and its semantic effects were discussed in §2.4.3.

Classifiers also SUPPLEMENT the information carried by nominals. They provide speakers with the means of accommodating new referents into the pre-existing system of categorization. In Japanese, for instance, *kokki* 'national flag' can be used with different classifiers depending on its position, e.g. whether it is flying or folded up. If a language has several noun categorization devices, these may supplement the information carried by nouns in varying ways. Taxonomies reflected in two classifier systems differ from one another, and supplement the information contained in nouns in different ways.[12]

12.1.3. Discourse-pragmatic functions of classifiers

Semantic roles of classifiers correlate with discourse. The use of noun categorization devices often depends on the role of the nominal argument

---

[12] Benton (1968: 142–3) illustrates the point about how classifiers supplement the lexical contents of nouns: 'The judicious use of classifiers ... makes possible the extension of meaning of a particular base with a minimum of ambiguity. Nouns thus often have a highly generalised meaning, different segments of which are expressed with the aid of different classifiers. Within the classifier systems themselves different patterns emerge. There are points of overlap, and points of contrast. Where the use of different classifiers within a system reveals different shades of meaning, the juxtaposition of numeral and possessive classifiers may extend the process further. The classifiers in Truquese thus at the same time provide a means for ordering the universe, and a method for structuring concepts without multiplying vocabulary.' Classifiers may have additional functions. In Palikur, verbal classifiers are used depending on the completeness of involvement of a referent (see §6.4.1, and see also Aikhenvald and Green 1998).

in the discourse, its topic continuity, or the specificity of its reference, especially if classifiers are not obligatory in a given morphosyntactic context. Classifiers of different types show certain preferences for different discourse parameters (see (A–C) below). All classifiers can be used anaphorically; they help to track participants in discourse (see (D) below). This is associated with the individuating role of classifiers; they are found with almost any type.

(A) Discourse functions of noun classes

Agreeement in NOUN CLASSES, and overt noun class marking often depends on the definiteness, topicality, and givenness of the referent noun in discourse. This means that noun class agreement or overt noun class marking may depend on whether the noun is newly introduced into the text, or refers to an already known participant. These functions are also known as 'reference management';[13] they are explained in (A1–3) below. The choice of a noun class marker may also correlate with the specificity of the referent (discussed in (A4)). These correlations are typically found in cases where the overt marking of noun class, or noun class agreement, is not grammatically obligatory.

(A1) Agreement in noun class often correlates with definiteness or topicality of the noun Noun class agreement in NPs can depend on the referential properties of the noun, such as its definiteness. Noun class agreement often occurs only if the noun is topical, or definite. In Motuna (Papuan) gender agreement of the predicate-argument type is obligatory only with a topical subject constituent (see (C) in §2.4.2). In 'Oro Nao (Chapacuran: Everett and Kern 1997) the object-marking enclitic which distinguishes three genders is used only if the direct object is definite.

(A2) Overt noun class marking on a noun can signal its definiteness In Gola (West Atlantic: Westermann 1947: 17; Heine 1982a: 193), class-marking prefixes and suffixes act similarly to definite articles; an indefinite noun is unmarked for noun class, e.g. *kul* 'a tree', *ke-kul* 'the tree'; *gbalia* 'a dwarf antelope', *o-gbalia-a* 'the dwarf antelope' (note that here noun class is marked by a combination of a prefix and a suffix).[14]

(A3) Overt noun class marking can correlate with the function of a noun in discourse In the Australian languages Nunggubuyu (Heath 1984: 169–70) and Warray (Harvey 1987: 53) the presence of a noun class prefix on a noun is correlated with definiteness or givenness, and its absence indicates

---

[13] For discussion of general mechanisms of reference management and reference tracking, see Chafe (1994).
[14] The correlation between gender marking and specificity, or individuation, is the basis for tracing gender markers to article-like elements (see Greenberg 1978: 61 ff.).

focus and foregrounding. In Wardaman noun class prefixes are used when introducing a new participant and for maintaining reference to the noun throughout the discourse (Merlan 1983). This is typical for a number of northern Australian prefixing languages with noun classes; see Merlan *et al.* (1997: 85). In Abau, an isolate from the East Sepik of Papua New Guinea, the choice between masculine and feminine gender may be determined by the discourse prominence of a noun: a foregrounded noun is assigned masculine gender and a backgrounded one is assigned feminine (Lock forthcoming). Overt noun class marking can also signal focusing of a particular noun-class-related property. In Alamblak (Papuan) overt gender marking on nouns correlates with focusing a particular shape-related property of the noun. For example, the use of *kuñ-r* 'house' with a masculine rather than the usual feminine suffix indicates that the house is unusually long (Bruce 1984: 97).

(A4) Overt noun class marking can depend on specificity of a referent The presence of an overt marker can correlate with a specific individuated referent, and its absence with a more generic referent. In Turkana (Eastern Nilotic), the overt gender prefix on nouns can be omitted from the names of animals in folk tales when the names are used in a generic sense (Dimmendaal 1983: 221).

(B) Discourse functions of other classifier types

Among other classifier types, the use of NOUN CLASSIFIERS and of NUMERAL CLASSIFIERS—provided they are not obligatory—frequently depends on the definiteness and pragmatic properties of the referent noun: whether it has just been introduced into the discourse; whether it is topically continuous; or whether it is PRAGMATICALLY SALIENT—i.e. either is in focus or is important in the discourse.

NOUN CLASSIFIERS in Minangkabau have to be used with a specific noun when a new referent is being introduced (Marnita 1996: 85–6). After the referent has been introduced in 12.4, it is referred to just with a noun classifier in 12.5.

12.4. Mak   ado   buruang   merpati
     mother   have   NOUN.CL:BIRD   pigeon
     datang   ka   rumah   awak
     come   to   house   1PL
     'Mother, there is a pigeon coming to our house.' (a child speaking)

12.5. Buruang   sia   tu   garan
     NOUN.CL:BIRD   who   that   probably
     'Whose bird is that?' (mother answering)

Noun classifiers are often omitted if the referent has already been established in discourse or is known from the context (Marnita 1996: 84–5).

NOUN CLASSIFIERS in Jacaltec (Craig 1986b) signal thematically salient NPs. Classifiers typically accompany referential nouns, and non-referential nouns in attributive functions may be unclassified. In 12.6a a non-referential noun, a proper name 'Gabriel Mateo', is used as a nominal predicate without a classifier (note that the classifier *naj* is used in a pronominal anaphoric function: see §3.2.4); while in 12.6b the same proper name used as a referential subject noun takes a classifier (Craig 1986b: 267).

12.6a. Kap   Mat   s-b'ih
Gabriel Mateo POSS-name
naj
NOUN.CL:MALE.NON.KIN
'Gabriel Mateo was his name.'

12.6b. caw cañ ye naj   Kap   Mat
very smart is NOUN.CL:MALE.NON.KIN Gabriel Mateo
'Gabriel Mateo is very smart.'

Noun classifiers function similarly to markers of definiteness. A noun is usually introduced with the indefinite marker (homophonous with the numeral 'one'), or without a classifier, and noun classifiers are found with second mentions of it (Craig 1986b: 269–70). In 12.7a, the word 'pigs' is used without a classifier when first mentioned; in 12.7b, at its next mention, the classifier *no7* 'animal' is used.

12.7a. xto   pax   ix   k'opo   a7o7
went again NOUN.CL:FEMALE.NON.KIN girl   give
yet   txitam
food.of   pigs
'The girl went back to feed pigs.'

12.7b. chin tit   pax   a7o7 yet   no7
I   come back give food.of NOUN.CL:ANIMAL
txitam   an
pig   PL
'I will come back to feed the pigs.'

Classifiers are also used as discourse markers of 'importance': there is a clear tendency for an indefinite NP with a classifier to refer to an important participant (Craig 1986b: 272–3). Noun classifiers (which are also used as numeral classifiers) also function as specificity markers in Dulong-Rawang, a Tibeto-Burman language (Randy LaPolla, p.c.).

The use of NUMERAL CLASSIFIERS is often regulated by the status of the noun in discourse. Classifiers often occur with nouns in NPs for initial mentions of referents (Japanese: Downing 1986; Malay: Hopper 1986; Burmese: Becker 1986). Discourse factors which influence the use of classifiers in Malay are shown in Diagram 12.2 (Hopper 1986: 313–14).

← MORE	CONDUCIVE TO USE OF CLASSIFIER	LESS →
(a) Specific		Non-specific
(b) Persistent		Not persistent
(c) Presentative		Anaphoric

DIAGRAM 12.2. *Factors regulating the use of classifiers in Malay*

The parameter specific/non-specific refers to the opposition between a single intended referent as opposed to a generic class of referents. Specific indefinite nouns are new in discourse, and they are usually accompanied by a classifier; indefinite nouns which are not specific refer to a class of entities, a role or a function, and they are left unclassified (Hopper 1986: 314). Persistence in discourse relates to the topical continuity of a noun in discourse, and its importance; unclassified nouns in Malay discourse tend to be mentioned less than those accompanied by classifiers. This is linked to the 'presentative' function of a noun: classifiers are typically used to accompany a newly introduced noun 'which is being presented for deployment' (Hopper 1986: 320) as subjects of predicates such as *datang* 'come, arrive', *kelihatan* 'be seen, be sighted', or the existential particle *ada* 'there is/are'. In contrast, nouns which are not new in discourse are almost never classified. This contrasts with the use of noun classifiers as definiteness markers in Jacaltec.

A similar correlation with definiteness and classifier use has been observed for Mandarin Chinese (Erbaugh 1986: 408); unlike Malay, a distinction is made between specific classifiers and the general classifier *ge*. Specific classifiers typically mark the first mention of a new item; they occur with indefinite nouns rather than definite ones; 'once reference is established, subsequent mentions take the general classifier or constructions where no classifier is required' (Erbaugh 1986: 408). In 12.8 the first mention of 'bicycle' is accompanied by a specific classifier ('vehicle'); after that 'bicycle' is used with the general classifier *ge* (classifiers are underlined).

12.8. cóng   neì.bian   guòlái   yí.ge   xiăo   hái-zi,
      from   there   over come   one.GEN.CL   small   child
      uh, . . . qĭ,   qĭ,   qĭ.zhe   yí-liàng   jiăotāchē uh
      uh   ride   ride ride.PROG one-CL:VEHICLE   bicycle   uh
      shì   yí.ge   hěn kěaì.de   xiăo.de   jiăotāche
      be   one.GEN CL   very cute.MOD little.MOD bicycle
      'From over there comes a child, uh, ride, ride, riding <u>a-vehicle</u> bicycle, uh, (it) is <u>a-general classifier</u> very cute little bicycle.'

The obligatory use of a classifier in Malay, or of a specific classifier in Mandarin, is reminiscent of the role overt noun class markers play in discourse organization in Wardaman and Nunggubuyu (see (A3) above).[15]

MULTIPLE CLASSIFIERS in the classifier languages of East and Southeast Asia are used depending on the discourse prominence of a referent. In White Hmong, classifiers serve two functions: they increase the precision of reference and degree of discourse prominence and they individualize the referent (Daley 1996, Riddle 1989, Bisang 1993). A newly introduced noun has to be used with a classifier, as in 12.9 (Bisang 1993: 25).

12.9. ua   ciav nws pom ib   lub
       suddenly   he   see one CL:HOLLOW, ROUND[16]
       nkau npuas
       pigpen
       'Suddenly, he discovered a pigpen.'

Indefinite nouns with a generic referent typically occur without a classifier.[17] Unlike Malay, a definite NP takes a classifier, as shown in 12.10 (Bisang 1993: 26):

12.10. ces   nyob nyob tus   poj ntsuag txawm yug
       then   one   day   CL:ANIM   widow   then   give.birth
       ta   ib   tug   me tub
       TAM   one   CL:ANIM   son
       'Finally, one day the widow gave birth to a son.' (The widow has been introduced in the preceding sentence.)

Within a narrative discourse, further occurrences of the same participant can be left without a classifier. Classifiers may then be used by speakers to indicate higher salience of one referent relative to the other referents in the local context. In 12.11a, *teb chaws* 'country' (underlined) is used without a classifier; the same item, *teb chaws* 'country', appears with a classifier in 12.11b. Here, the classifier is used to emphasize the fact of the speaker's possible stay in Laos after the war broke out and everyone was leaving for Thailand (Daley 1996: 105–6; Riddle 1989).

---

[15] This also agrees with the Categoriality Hypothesis developed by Hopper and Thompson (1984), according to which the prototypical function of a noun is to 'introduce a significant new participant into the discourse' (Hopper 1986: 323). Since classifiers in Malay come from nouns, and 'classification is as good an example of purely nominal morphology as it is possible to have in Malay', this prototypical property of a noun agrees with the concreteness, individuation, and discourse-persistence of classified nouns.
[16] Gloss provided in accordance with Bisang (1993: 31).
[17] Compare the absence of classifiers in VO constructions such as *nuv ntses* 'to catch fish', or *caij nees* 'to ride a horse' (Bisang 1993: 26).

12.11a.
neeg	kuj	txhua	leej	txhua	tus	tsuas
person	then	all	person	all	CL:ANIM	only
nrhiav	kev	tawm	teb chaws		los tsuas	
look.for	way	leave	country		Laos	
tuaj	mus	rau	sab	thaib teb		
come	go	to	side	Thailand		

'Everyone looked for a way to leave Laos and go to the Thai side.'

12.11b.
Kuv	tau	peb	hnub	tomqab	xav	hais tias
I	get	three	day	after	think	that
yog	tsis	khiav	ces	yuav	nyob	
if	not	run	then	will	stay	
lub			teb chaws	los tsuas	ntawd	
CL:HOLLOW.ROUND			country	Laos	there	

'Three days after that I thought that if I didn't escape, then I would live in Laos . . .'

Thus, classifiers are not just definiteness markers.[18] Along similar lines, classifiers correlate with a definite and singularized interpretation of a referent, and are widely used for referent tracking in Vietnamese (Löbel 2000). In Thai, classifiers in NPs which contain demonstratives serve to foreground the noun, and tend to be used when 'a contrast or emphasis is expressed'. They can substitute for a noun 'where their presence indicates that the nominal has been previously mentioned (or is understood)' (Conklin 1981: 88). In Newari, a numeral classifier can be repeated on the noun itself 'to bring in emphasis', or 'for rhetorical purposes' (Bhaskararao and Joshi 1985: 22).

DEICTIC CLASSIFIERS often function similarly to definite articles, as is the case in the Siouan languages Yuchi and Mandan (Barron and Serzisko 1982). In Pilagá (Guaicuruan) the use of deictic classifiers also correlates with individuation of nouns (Vidal 1997).

Classifiers which combine NUMERAL and DEICTIC uses are often used as specificity markers in other environments (see Chapter 9). This is the case in Cantonese (Pacioni 1997; forthcoming).

CLASSIFIERS IN POSSESSIVE CONSTRUCTIONS and LOCATIVE CLASSIFIERS usually have no discourse functions (see (C) below). VERBAL CLASSIFIERS are often obligatory, and their use does not then depend on discourse parameters

---

[18] As Riddle (1989) put it (quoted in Bisang 1993: 29): 'the classifier is not a marker of definiteness like *le* in French or *the* in English per se, although its use partially overlaps with these articles. In each case, the classifier is used, if needed, to clarify reference, or to emphasise individuation or individual characteristics. In other words, a major function of the use of a classifier is to mark an NP as referentially salient if this would not be obvious from the context. This may occur because of some inherent potential ambiguity in the context or because the speaker wishes to put forward a particular point of view.' Similarly, in Vietnamese classifiers are used to identify thematically significant referents in the narrative (see Daley 1996: 106–7).

(see (D) below for their use as anaphoric markers). However, in some multiple classifier systems in Northern Amazonian languages the use of non-obligatory verbal classifiers may depend on the pragmatic salience and discourse-persistence of the S/O constitutent. In these cases classifiers are not used to relate to newly introduced nouns; rather, they are employed to emphasize an important, or an unusual, participant. For instance, in Baniwa of Içana (Aikhenvald 1996c) classifiers are used on the predicate of a relative clause, or of a purposive clause to refer to the O of the predicate of the main clause if it is definite or focal. The classifier is used to mark agreement with a definite referent in focus in 12.12. In 12.13 the referent of the object constituent is indefinite, and the verbal classifier is not used with the purposive verbal form. (Purposive forms are underlined.)

12.12. wa-tua wa-takha puapua
1PL-go-FUT 1PL-cut arumã
wa-dzekata-kaʒu-pa
1PL-make-PURP-CL:STICK.LIKE
'We shall go and cut arumã (palm tree) to use (it).'

12.13. peʒi ɾi-uhwa ɾi-kapa awakada-ɾiku
hawk 3SGNF-sit 3SGNF-see bush-LOC
ɾi-kapa-kaʒu kwaka i-nu-ɾi i-kahɾe
3SGNF-see-PURP what INDEF-come-REL INDEF-to
'The hawk was sitting in the bush in order to look in the direction of whoever was coming.'[19]

In Palikur verbal classifiers are used to refer to an S/O argument to indicate its complete involvement in the action, or state (see §6.4.1). Classifiers are also used—as a kind of focus marker—if the noun in S/O function is unusual. The verb 'cook' is rarely used with verbal classifiers (because it presumably always implies complete involvement of the object; cooking a little is not cooking). However, the classifier is used in 12.14 in which the serpent is cooking a person which is an unusual object to cook (Aikhenvald and Green 1998).

12.14. eg iw-e-gi ay-ta-re nikwe-ni eg
3F take-COMPL-3M there-DIR-ANA thus-PAUSAL 3F
bat-ha-kis un awah-wa-ye un
seated-VB-CAUS water hot-?-DUR.MASC water
a-daha-ni sakah-pita-e-gi
3N-for-POSS cook-V.CL:IRREG-COMPL-3M
'She (serpent) took him (man) there [and] put hot water on to cook him.'

---

[19] A similar principle operates in relative clauses (Aikhenvald 1996c); similar examples for Tariana are discussed in Aikhenvald (1994a: 427).

(C) Obligatory classifier systems and discourse

Obligatory noun categorization devices show many fewer correlations with discourse properties and the definiteness of nouns than do optional devices. The variability of classifier assignment may be accounted for by the discourse properties of a noun. This variability may involve (i) choice between a specific and a general classifier; (ii) choice between different specific classifiers; (iii) different agreement choices; and (iv) choice between different classificatory techniques.

(C1) Choice between a specific and a general classifier In Mandarin Chinese the choice of a specific or general classifier depends on whether the noun is newly introduced into discourse, or is already established (see 12.8). An in-depth experimental study of general classifiers *tsu* and *ko* in Japanese (Zubin and Shimojo 1993: 496) showed 'a shift away from specific classifiers and toward *tsu* and *ko* as more focus is placed on the numeral itself', and 'a pragmatic substitution of a general for a specific classifier when attention is shifted away from the nature of the referent'.[20]

(C2) Choice between different specific classifiers depending on the focused property In Tariana, a female can be referred to with a numeral, verbal, or possessed classifier *-ita* 'human non-feminine' if her femininity does not have to be focused on, or is clear from the context; otherwise a human feminine classifier, *-ma*, is preferred. This is similar to 'variable categorization' of nouns, where different classifiers are used to highlight different aspects of the same referent, to focus on its particular property; this applies to large classifier systems, and sometimes also to small systems of noun classes. In Oromo (East Cushitic) some nouns can be assigned masculine gender instead of their usual feminine gender, and this indicates an unusually big size of the object, e.g. *ablee tun* (knife this.FEM) 'this knife', *ablee xun* (knife this.MASC) 'this (big) knife' (Table 12.4 shows the possibilities of 'reclassifying' one noun, 'river', in Burmese). Variable noun categorization can have semantic effect, and pragmatic effect.

(C3) Different agreement choices Variable categorization and variable agreement can result in focusing different properties of a referent. In Australian languages, concordial superclassing (which means that one functionally unmarked class is used with modifiers instead of the expected agreement classes) often depends on the function of the noun in discourse. In Warray, masculine agreement appears on modifying adjectives when a comment is being made rather than new information being provided by the

---

[20] For similar phenomena in some multiple classifier systems, see Senft (1996: 239 ff.) and Aikhenvald (1999a).

modifier (Harvey 1987; Sands 1995: 264). New information is associated with functionally marked classes.

(C4) Choice between different classificatory techniques In Tariana, a multiple classifier language, different classifier techniques are used depending on the status of a noun in discourse. If an inanimate noun is not in focus, or does not have to be emphasized, a regular classifier will be used (Aikhenvald 1994a). Otherwise, the noun itself must be used as a 'repeater' classifier—see 9.73 and 9.74.

(D) Classifiers as anaphoric and participant tracking devices

Classifiers of any type can be used as anaphoric and participant-tracking devices. NOUN CLASS markers are used as anaphoric elements for participant tracking in Australian and Papuan languages, e.g. Ungarinjin (Rumsey 1982: 37) (cf. Merlan *et al.* 1997). In Yimas, with its highly elliptical discourse, concordial system (i.e. noun class) marking on verbs, is fundamental in the tracking of referents in discourse (Foley 1986: 88) (see also Dixon 1972: 71–2, for anaphoric uses of noun-class marked determiners in Dyirbal).

NUMERAL CLASSIFIERS are used anaphorically in Japanese, Burmese, Vietnamese, and Malay (see Downing 1986; 1996; Becker 1986; Daley 1996; Hopper 1986), as well as in Vietnamese, Hmong, and Cantonese (see Bisang 1999; Löbel 2000). In Minangkabau numeral classifiers can be used anaphorically[21] without the noun to refer to a previously mentioned object, or if the referent is clear from the context (Marnita 1996: 93). If a person is buying bananas, they can take a bunch and ask for the price (12.15a); 12.15b is the continuation of the dialogue.

12.15a. bara   pisang   sa-sikek   Mak
       how.much   banana   one-NUM.CL:BUNCH   2nd.FEM.HON
       'How much does a bunch of banana cost?'

12.15b. agiah duo   sikek
        give   two   NUM.CL:BUNCH
        'Give (me) two (bunches).'

In Japanese, numeral classifiers can be considered an extremely advantageous mechanism for anaphoric reference, since 'they provide a means of anaphorically representing a group of referents in an evenhanded way, without focusing the reference on one as opposed to others of the individuals involved in the grouping' (Downing 1986: 369). For instance, the

---

[21] A similar usage is frequent in Tzotzil (Mayan), e.g. a question: *jay-p'ej alaxa* (INTER-NUM.CL:ROUND orange) 'How many oranges?', and an answer: *j-p'ej no'ox* (one-NUM.CL:ROUND only) 'One (round) only' (De Leon 1987: 76).

choice of an anaphorically used numeral classifier *hu-tari* (two-CL:PERSON) 'two people' can be preferred to other ways of referring to two people—e.g. with a collective noun—in order to 'avoid their destruction as individuals', or 'avoiding the nuance that the couple is centered round one member or the other' (Downing 1986: 370).

VERBAL CLASSIFIERS can be used anaphorically to maintain reference to participants in discourse. In the following example from Imonda (from Seiler 1985: 220, discussed in Merlan et al. 1997: 96–7), a woman, *agõ*, is an established participant; she is reintroduced in the first line of 12.16 (she has not been mentioned for several lines in the narrative), and then referred to anaphorically with the classificatory prefix *fa-* in the following line (Rushforth 1991 exemplifies the anaphoric uses of classificatory verbs in Mescalero Apache).

12.16. ed-nèi   ne-n-b   agõ-ianè-m
        PX-SOURCE   eat-PAST-DUR   woman-NON.PL-GOAL
        ainam   fa-i-kõhõ   fa-eha   kse
        quickly   CL-LINK-go   V.CL-put   fuck
        'He ate this and then quickly grabbed the woman, laid her down and fucked her.'

Anaphoric functions of classifiers often go together with their deictic uses. 12.17, from Tzotzil (De Leon 1987: 54), illustrates the use of numeral classifiers with anaphoric and deictic functions.[22] This example involves buying candles in a store. The referent, candles, is not overtly mentioned, but it is being pointed at. Both merchant and customer are looking at a collection of multicoloured candles hanging on a line; the classifier *ch'ix* 'longish objects' is used to refer to them.

12.17a. jay   ch'ix   cha-k'an
         INTER   NUM.CL:LONGISH   2p-want
         'How many (longish ones) do you want?'

12.17b. ta   j-kan   ox   ch'ix
         preposition   1ERG-want   NUM.CL:LONGISH   three
         'I want three (longish ones).'

Deictic and anaphoric functions are attested with classifiers of other types.[23] NOUN CLASSIFIERS are used in both functions in a number of Mayan

---

[22] Similar examples are found in Minangkabau (Marnita 1996: 94); cf. a conversation in a tobacconist's shop between a customer and a shopkeeper: *bara (ko) salai Pak* (how.much (DEM) one+NUM.CL:FLAT 2nd.MASC.HON) 'How much does this (tobacco leaf) cost, sir?' A customer uses a classifier without the accompanying noun, pointing at the object. The demonstrative, *ko*, is optional.

[23] Deixis is usually distinguished from anaphora. As Lyons (1977: 673) puts it, 'anaphora presupposes that the referent should already have its place in the universe of discourse. Deixis

languages (Jacaltec: Craig 1986a; 1986b; 1986c; or Mam: England 1983). Example 12.18 shows an anaphoric use of noun classifiers in Jacaltec which is functionally equivalent to pronominalization. A referent mentioned in 12.18 is subsequently referred to just by a classifier in 12.19 (underlined) (Craig 1986c: 264). Anaphoric noun classifiers are extensively used in possessive constructions in Jacaltec; see ex. 3.12 and 3.13, for an illustration of their syntactic roles (Craig 1986c: 275–6).

12.18. xil   naj   xuwan   no7
       saw   NOUN.CL:MALE.NON.KIN   John   NOUN.CL:ANIMAL
       lab'a
       snake
       'John saw the snake.'

12.19. xil   naj   no7
       saw   NOUN.CL:MALE.NON.KIN   NOUN.CL:ANIMAL
       'He saw it.'

DEICTIC CLASSIFIERS may also be used anaphorically (see 7.18, from Pilagá, and the discussion in §7.3).

Anaphoric uses are widespread in multiple classifier languages. They are crucial for 'securing coherence in discourse' in Kilivila (Senft 1996: 21). In 12.20a, a noun, 'tataba-board', is introduced without a classifier; then it is referred to with the classifier *ke* 'CL:WOODEN' in 12.20b, and the overt noun is ellipsed.

12.20a. a-tatai   tataba
        1SG-carve   tataba.board
        'I carve a tataba-board.'

12.20b. tauwau   tabalu   m-to-si-na
        men   Tabalu.subclan   this-CL:MALE-PL-THIS
        ma-ke-na   si   koni
        this-CL:WOODEN-this   their   sign.of.honour
        'These men belonging to the Tabalu-subclan, this wooden one [i.e. tataba-board] is their sign of honour.'

In Tariana, classifiers can be used anaphorically in two discourse situations: (a) a participant is mentioned once, in the beginning of the narrative, and then it is consistently referred to with the help of a classifier; (b) a

---

does not; indeed deixis is one of the principal means open to us of putting entities into the universe of discourse so that we can refer to them subsequently.' It has been claimed that anaphora depends on deixis, and that pronominalization involves both anaphoric and deictic reference (De Leon 1987: 53–4). Frequent combination of both anaphoric and deictic uses of classifiers, and their use for pronominalization, confirms this (see further examples in De Leon 1987: 40).

participant whose identity is clear from the context is only referred to with the help of a classifier.

Example 12.21 illustrates a situation of type (a). It is taken from a story about how two men met an evil spirit on a river where they came to fish; the evil spirit took off his shirt, and then the whole story evolves round this shirt which has all the power of the evil spirit itself. The magic shirt (*yaɾumakasi*) is introduced at the beginning of the narrative (12.21a). The case-marking (*-nuku* 'topical non-subject': see Aikhenvald 1994b) indicates that the shirt is going to be the future topic of discourse. Later on, the shirt is consistently referred to either as *ha-ne-maka* 'that (distant) one made of cloth' (12.21b) or as *diha-maka* 'it-made.of.cloth' (12.21c). Examples 12.21a–c are consecutive in the text they come from.

12.21a. diha <u>yaɾu-maka-si-nuku</u>   di-sõle(. . .)
         he   thing-CL:CLOTH-NONPOSS-TOP.O   3SGNF-take off(. . .)
         'He [the evil spirit] took off the shirt [lit. thing made of cloth].'

12.21b. iɾa-mha   pa-pe-niki
         need-PRES.NON.VIS   IMP-throw-CMPL
         <u>ha-ne-maka-nuku</u>
         DEM:INAN-DIST-CL:CLOTH-TOP.O
         na-pidana   nu-kesini   hau   piha   pi-a
         3pl+say-REM.P.INFR   1SG-friend   yes   2SG   2SG-go
         pi-pe-niki   <u>ha-ne-maka-nuku</u>
         2SG-throw-CMPL   DEM:INAN-DISTAL-CL:CLOTH-TOP.O
         <u>ha-ne-maka-naka</u>   kaɾuna-naka   wa-na
         DEM-DIST-CL:CLOTH-EYEW.PRES   be.afraid-EYEW.PRES 1PL-OBJ
         'It is necessary to throw <u>that</u> [shirt] away, they [the men] said, my friend, yes, you go and throw <u>that</u> [shirt] away. <u>That</u> [shirt] is dangerous for us.'

12.21c. haiku-na   dhita   di-na-tha-pidana
         tree-CL:VERT   3SGNF+take   3SGNF-OBJ-FRUST-REM.P.INFR
         di-ni-thepi   di-pe-niki   di-na-pidana
         3SGNF-make-TO.WATER   3SGNF-throw-CMPL   3SGNF-OBJ-REM.P.INFR
         <u>diha-maka</u>   dhe-kha   di-a-hna
         he-CL:CLOTH   3SGNF+enter-AWAY   3SGNF-go-PAUS
         'He (one of the men) took a tree-trunk and tried to throw it away, in vain. <u>It</u> [shirt] came upon the man.'

A situation of type (b) is illustrated with 12.22. The story is about how a deer and a jaguar decided to live together. It is important that they chose to live in the same house, one in one room, and the other in the other. Neither the house, nor the rooms are introduced with the help of full lexemes, since the meaning is clear from the context. Numeral classifiers are used. The lexical item *panisi* 'house' is used only in the last sentence of the text, 12.22b, to summarize what happened to the house.

12.22a. pa-piu-pidana iʃiri na-siwa-kaka na-ni
one-CL:TIME-REM.P.INFR animals 3PL-self-REC 3pl-do
pa-dapana-pidana na-yã yawi neri
one-CL:HAB-REM.P.INFR 3PL-live jaguar deer
neri pa-dawa-se yawi pa-dawa
deer one-CL:ROOM-LOC jaguar one-CL:ROOM
na-yã-pidana pa-dapana-ya
3PL-live-REM.P.INFR one-CL:HAB-EMPHATIC
'Once the animals decided between themselves to live in one [house], jaguar and deer, deer in one [room], jaguar in another [room], they lived in one [house].'

12.22b. ne-pidana naha panisi-nuku na-peni-kha
SO-REM.P.INFR they house-TOP.O 3PL-leave-AWAY
'So they abandoned the house.'

In East and Central Tucano languages a full noun is almost always omitted from a noun phrase; classifiers are used in anaphoric function (Barnes 1990: 289). Similar functions are attested for classifiers in other languages, e.g. Yagua (Payne 1990; Payne and Payne 1990), Munduruku (Gonçalves 1987), Palikur (Aikhenvald and Green 1998), Resígaro (Allin 1975), Bora (Thiesen 1996: 42), and Nambiquara (Lowe 1999). As a result, classifiers are more frequent in discourse than full nouns (and this may be one of the reasons why Resígaro borrowed classifiers rather than full nouns from Bora: see §13.7.1).

(E) Conclusions

All non-obligatory classifier systems have some discourse-pragmatic functions. The use of classifiers correlates with referentiality, specificity, definiteness, topical continuity, and the salience in discourse of the noun. Generic noun classifiers tend to correlate with definite referents, while numeral classifiers are often used to introduce a new referent.

Obligatory classifier systems tend to display similar properties, but to a lesser extent. All classifier types are used as anaphoric pronouns and as participant tracking devices. Further grammaticalization of classifiers in these functions leads to their syntacticization as relative clause markers. The way classifiers can participate in the organization of discourse relates to their other functions (discussed in §12.2). The discourse-pragmatic and anaphoric functions of classifiers described in this chapter provide a counterargument against the idea of 'redundancy' for noun categorization devices.

12.1.4. Applicability of classifiers and default classes

Noun categorization devices differ in their applicability. Noun class systems usually involve an obligatory choice: every noun in a language must be assigned to a noun class.[24] Classifiers of other types vary from one language to another. In languages with numeral classifiers, every countable noun generally has to be classified; there may be a few abstract nouns which are used without a classifier (Downing 1996). Noun classifiers, verbal classifiers, relational and possessed classifiers are often used only with nouns of particular semantic groups. In Athabaskan languages only nouns with concrete reference are classified using classificatory verbs. Possessed classifiers in South American languages are used only with nouns whose referents can be handled in certain culturally significant ways (consumed, domesticated, planted, etc.).

The applicability of classifiers depends on how productive the system is. In a fully productive system, each newly introduced object must be classified in some way or ways. If the system is frozen, new items may be unclassified. It does not necessarily mean that the system is in decay. Craig (1986a) reports that in Modern Jacaltec nouns which refer to newly introduced artefacts (e.g. made of nylon or plastic) are not used with a classifier.[25] This is a matter in which noun classes behave differently: in a noun class system, every noun has to be assigned to a class.

The applicability of a classifier system correlates with the function and semantics of classifiers. If classifiers are bound morphemes, they tend to form an obligatory system in which every noun in a language has to be assigned a classifier.[26]

The lack of a classifier can be considered a special noun categorization device. Abstract nouns can also be used without a classifier in Japanese (Downing 1996: 73) and Korean (Lee 1997). In Thai, classifiers are also omitted in arithmetical statements (e.g. 'three plus three is six'), and in cases when the numeral does not denote any quantity, e.g. 'page 23', or 'room 23' (Hundius and Kölver 1983: 182–3).

The absence of a classifier may also be due to the lack of salience of a referent; this appears to be the case with nouns left 'unclassified' in Vietnamese (Daley 1996: 136). The use of repeaters instead of classifier affixes in some multiple classifier systems (see (F1) and (F2) in §9.1) is an alternate technique used for classifying otherwise unclassifiable nouns and

---

[24] Occasional exceptions are exemplified in §2.3.

[25] The productivity of a system can change historically. Noun classifiers in Jacaltec must have been more productive at the time of the conquest and colonization than they are now: noun categorization then absorbed the names of new artefacts made of metal and glass introduced by Spaniards into the 'rock' class (Craig forthcoming).

[26] Even then some nouns may be left unclassified; e.g. in Nambiquara (Ivan Lowe, p.c.) large mammals are not classified.

for marking the discourse salience of nouns which do have a 'regular' classifier.

Classifiers in Vietnamese can be omitted if they denote something which is inherent to the meaning of the enumerated noun, as in *máy bay* (airplane) *bốn* (four) *động cỏ* (engine) 'four-engined airplane', as opposed to *máy bay* (airplane) *vối* (with) *bốn* (four) *chiếc* (classifier) *động cỏ* (engine) *lỏn* (big) 'airplane with four big engines', where the classifier has to be used. The omission of classifiers also correlates with the lack of referentiality of a noun: if a classifier is omitted a noun cannot be modified (see further examples in Löbel 2000: 294–8).

If noun categorization is based on universal parameters which can be assigned to any object—e.g. animacy or physical properties—every noun will be classified. In contrast, if noun categorization is based on culture-specific features which cannot be assigned to every entity—e.g. function, or social hierarchy—some nouns will be left unclassified.

The multiple classifier system in Palikur is such an example. The semantics of genders, and of numeral, verbal, and locative classifiers are based on animacy and/or physical properties (the choice depends on the type of classifier), and every noun has to be assigned a classifier. In contrast, possessed classifiers classify objects depending on their function and use (e.g. plants can be cultivated or eaten); so nouns get classified only if they refer to objects for which these particular functional uses are appropriate. Human nouns (except for 'child') do not take any possessed classifier (see §5.5.1).

If every noun in a language has to be classified, some nouns may turn out to be semantically incompatible with the categories used for classifier assignment. To give the inventory of classifiers its systemic structure, a 'general', or 'residue' or 'default' member is employed to encompass otherwise unclassifiable nouns. This is how neuter gender is used in German, or the classifier *ge* is used in Mandarin.

However, the notion of a 'general' classifier appears to be semantically and functionally complex. At least three distinct phenomena can be distinguished under the rubric of 'general', or 'default' classifier (Zubin and Shimojo 1993: 491). A general classifier can be in a 'RESIDUE' (or 'complement': Zubin and Shimojo 1993) function if it is a remainder category for referents outside the domains covered by other classifiers. It is in DEFAULT function if it can be substituted for other classifiers under specialized pragmatic conditions. The third function is UNSPECIFIED REFERENT FUNCTION; then a classifier is used to refer to an unknown entity. In addition, general classifiers often have a core meaning of their own.

Japanese has a few specific classifiers used with abstract nouns—*ken* 'incident', *toori* 'method', *han* 'crime', *denwa* 'phone call'. (These classifiers go back to repeaters.) Abstract nouns can also be used with the 'default' classifier *tsu*, or without any classifier (Downing 1996: 73). Similar tendencies have been observed for many languages with large classifier systems. In Vietnamese and Burmese, abstract nouns appear without a classifier (Nguyen 1957: 131–2; Pe 1965: 181), and in Tai languages they tend to take a classifier of the repeater type, or appear without any classifier (Conklin 1981: 364). In Palikur, they take the 'vertical' numeral classifier -*t* (as a default, or residue term).

Residue classifiers are found in noun categorization systems of most kinds. 'Neuter' gender often plays this role in gender systems (e.g. in Latin, or Palikur). In Diyari (Austin 1981) it is masculine gender, and in Kalau Lagaw Ya (Bani 1987) it is feminine (both languages have just two genders, masculine and feminine). Most numeral classifier systems have a residue classifier, e.g. Mandarin *ge*, Korean *kay*. In Athabaskan languages a verb stem which refers to three-dimensional objects is used for reference to objects to which no other classifier can be applied (e.g. Koyukon, as described by Landar 1967; Henry and Henry 1965; see Denny 1979a: 99). A residue member is also found in systems of relational or possessed classifiers, e.g. *ah* in Ponapean (Rehg 1981: 180), and Apalaí -*kyry*- 'thing' (Koehn 1994: 42). Pilagá has a residue deictic classifier *hen* used with mass nouns with no specific reference, and with otherwise 'unclassifiable nouns' (e.g. sky, land/earth, moon or sun) (Vidal 1997: 82).

Residue classifiers may also be used in default function. In Baniwa, the classifier 'round' is used for otherwise unclassifiable items; it can also substitute for other classifiers if no particular shape property of the item is focused on. The same residue classifier can be used to refer to unspecified objects.

Some languages use different classifiers in residue function, and to refer to an unspecified referent. In Navajo a classificatory verb for three-dimensional objects is used for otherwise unclassifiable things; and a verb for flat flexible objects is employed for unspecified referents (Carter 1976).

Residue classifiers can have a core meaning of their own. The residue numeral classifiers in Ponapean and in Burmese are associated with roundness (cf. Denny 1979a: 100). The residue and default classifier *ge* in Mandarin derives from a noun meaning 'bamboo stalk'; later it came to be used with humans and as a general classifier. In Korean, the residue and default classifier *kay* means 'small countable inanimates'.[27] Japanese has two residue classifiers, *tsu*, of Japanese origin, and *ko*, a Sino-Japanese term. It was shown by Zubin and Shimojo (1993) that *tsu* does not have any meaning of its own, and is used only as a residue and default classifier

---

[27] It can also be used as an alternative classifier for most small countable items (Lee 1997), e.g. *yenphil twu kay* (pencil two CL:RESIDUE) 'two pencils'. If it is used with large items, e.g. boats (instead of classifier *chek*), or houses (instead of classifier *chay*), the noun is automatically understood as referring to a toy boat, or a toy house.

for non-animate concepts. In contrast, *ko* seems to have a core meaning of its own: it refers to smallish concrete inanimates.[28]

A residue category may be more complex. In German, all three genders are used as residue terms depending on the semantic domain. In the 'beverage' domain, the residue category is masculine, within the 'ship' domain it is feminine, and within the 'building' domain it is neuter (Zubin and Shimojo 1993: 492). Neuter gender is also used for unspecified referents.

Languages with multiple classifier systems can have several residue classifiers, one for each function. In Palikur, neuter gender is an 'everything else' category for inanimate nouns; the numeral classifier for vertical objects is used as a residue term in this system. And for verbal and locative classifiers the default classifier is the one which refers to 'irregular shape'.

12.2. Human cognition and classifiers

Languages use noun categorization devices in different ways to map basic cognitive categories onto their systems. This section discusses how categories reflected in classifiers correlate with what we know of mechanisms in terms of which human cognition operates. As Allan (1977: 308) put it: 'That languages should classify entities along similar lines is not surprising if one takes the view that human perceptions are generally similar, and that they stimulate a cognitive categorization of the world which is reflected by linguistic categories and classes.'

In §12.2.1 we consider the perceptual correlates of semantic parameters used in classifiers. §12.2.2 surveys the cognitive mechanisms at work in noun categorization.

12.2.1. Perceptual correlates of noun categorization

Noun categorization devices in all languages reflect the same physical world. We have seen that all languages use a number of properties of referent nouns for their categorization; these properties are based on their nature, and function. Nature-based properties relate to animacy and humanness; for inanimates they are based first and foremost on shape. Reasons for the importance of vision related parameters in noun categorization have been suggested by Adams and Conklin (1973: 8): 'One of the most fascinating facts of numeral classification is its dependence on the visual feature of form. There are no metaphors based on sound, feel, taste, or smell'; these might be 'less useful because the impressions gained from

---

[28] These classifiers possibly differ in other functions, too. The classifier *tsu* can serve as a dummy inanimate slot filler if no particular referent is being denoted (rather like *it* in English).

them are more time based and transitory'. Note also Allan (1977: 308): 'To say that a classifier has meaning is to say that it indicates the perceived characteristics of the entities which it classifies; in other words, classifiers are the linguistic correlates to perception.'

The evidence for the universality of parameters such as animacy and dimensionality comes from child language acquisition. In a seminal paper, Clark (1977) showed that the patterns of overextensions of lexical items by English-speaking children are based on parameters very similar to the ones used in classifier systems. These universal natural categories include animacy, shape, size, texture (or material), and function. The most frequent categories of overextension are ROUND and LONG. (Thus, for instance, the children's lexical item *mooi* 'moon' is overextended to such round objects as cakes, round marks on windows, round shapes in books, round postmarks, letter 'O'; and the children's item *tee* 'stick' was used for canes, umbrellas, rulers, and other stick-like objects.) Relative size tends to be less important than shape. Other properties, like colour, are never used as the basis for overextensions; neither is this property used in classifier systems. She then arrives at the conclusion that

> both classifier systems and children's over-extensions reflect a basic categorisation process that goes on *first* at the non-linguistic level . . . One way that people seem to organize entities is to group them on the basis of their perceptible properties, with shape playing a very important role . . . The data from children suggest that some properties of shape may be more salient than others and thus more likely to be used in categorisation . . . Within classifier systems, then, one might expect to see a progression from systems that only distinguish animates from inanimates, to systems with more and more complex subdivisions using several dimensions at once to produce a large number of classifier-categories. (Clark 1977: 460–1)[29]

Children prefer to group basic level objects by perceptual features rather than by functional features because perceptual features are readily available; this explains the predominance of perceptual features over functional ones in categorization via classifiers (Tversky 1986: 72).

Other studies confirm the 'anchoring' of categories encoded in classifiers in the mentally projected world (Frawley 1992: 134). More specific connections between various parameters of perception have been established by the current theory of vision (Marr 1982; Baron 1987; Frawley 1992: 134–5). Visual processes involve the following sequence of computations: one dimension > two dimensions (flat surfaces) > two dimensions (curved surfaces) > three dimensions (normal objects). This explains why more shape distinctions tend to be made in classifiers which apply to one- and two-dimensional objects than to three-dimensional ones. One- and two-

---

[29] Also see Rosch (1975a; 1975b), on the importance of shape in human perception. For some criticism of Clark (1977), see Senft (1996: 13).

dimensionality are perceived first, before three-dimensionality. The prominence of curvature in visual perception also explains why curved shape appears to be important in classifier semantics.

Salient physical properties encoded in classifiers are integrated into the domain of physical interaction of humans with their environment, and this is where functional properties come in. Functional properties reflected in classifier systems correlate with social interaction and socio-cultural environment (§12.3.2).[30]

12.2.2. Cognitive mechanisms and noun categorization

What cognitive mechanisms underlie human categorization of the world encoded in classifiers of different morphosyntactic types? The mechanism of human cognition reflected in noun categorization devices is from basic level to subordinate level of categorization.

Classic work by Rosch and other psychologists has confirmed the existence of a basic level of categorization: 'In taxonomies of concrete objects, there is one level of abstraction at which the most basic category cuts are made. Basic categories are those which carry the most information, possess the highest category cue validity, and are, thus, the most differentiated from one another' (Rosch *et al.* 1976). The cognitive importance of basic level categories lies in their predictive power, due to clustering of mutually independent properties of entities. Lee (1988: 232) exemplifies this with the following:

It is a fact about the world that animals which have wings are almost invariably birds and have other properties of birds (feathers, two short legs, beak, etc.). In this sense, the property 'has wings' has a high 'cue validity', that is, it is a good predictor of other properties. . . . Because of these . . . correlations, we need only identify one of these properties when we want to know what kind of animal we are dealing with. *Bird*, for the urban English speaker, is therefore a basic level category.

Basic-level categories also show a high degree of internal coherence, and their members share many more properties with each other than with members of other categories. Generic-specific relations in noun categorization systems are the result of setting up classes of objects, or persons, on the principle of basic-level categorization. Generic classifiers (like the ones found in Mayan, Austronesian, or Australian languages) are the direct correlates of the basic-specific (or subordinate) categorization level.

The basic level of categorization is associated with salient properties of objects, such as shape and other physical properties (e.g. consistency) via extension of classes to new nouns. Since 'cognitively salient properties tend

---

[30] For further issues concerning the psycholinguistic reality of noun categorization in cognition, see Carroll and Casagrande (1958) and the discussion in Lucy (1992b: 201–7).

to be those with high cue validity' (Lee 1988: 236), it is natural to suggest that initial members of classes serve as prototypes for further extensions based on these properties. 'Shape' is generally considered the most important of these properties, since 'the function of an object may be unknown, or variable over time' (Erbaugh 1984).[31] However, function extensions may have higher cue validity than shape extensions, and this is what happens with respect to such domains as human categorization where social status is a kind of functional categorization. One expects more functional extensions in the realm of possessive constructions which are more directly linked to handling of objects and to the ways objects relate to their possessor. This is indeed the case. What functional categories have most validity in a system is necessarily linked to the ways categories are conventionalized and formed through socio-cultural environment.[32]

12.3. Social and cultural issues in noun categorization

Universal semantic features encoded in noun categorization devices are the reflection of perceptual and cognitive mechanisms shared by humans. Different parameters are exploited to different extents; and the specific choice of parameters is related to cultural, environmental, and social variables. These variables are employed to different extents in different noun categorization devices. They often play a role in the way semantic extensions operate in languages; and they are frequently used to explain the choice of semantically opaque classifiers.

At first sight, the semantic organization of noun categorization devices is a confirmation of a version of the Sapir–Whorf hypothesis—that 'through the analysis of a language one can show the viewpoint of a people' (Denny 1979a: 117, n. 1). Indeed, of all nominal and verbal grammatical categories, classifiers are the easiest to immediately connect with extralinguistic phenomena—either of physical environment, or of culture.[33] For instance,

---

[31] According to Rosch (1975a), colour is not predictive of other attributes, and is thus a relatively useless attribute for categorization of objects.

[32] Cf. Rosch (1975a: 28): '[when] we speak of the formation of categories we mean their formation in the culture.'

[33] Attempts have been made to provide extralinguistic motivation for other categories. For example, numerous failed attempts have been made to relate ergativity to the psychology of people (Dixon 1994: 214–15). Spatial distinctions may obviously connect to physical environment: a language is likely to distinguish 'up hill' and 'down hill' in a deictic system only if it is spoken in mountaneous regions, as are Caucasian languages. If a language distinguishes alienable and inalienable possession, the attribution of an object to the inalienable class may depend on how valuable it is, e.g. houses in North Arawak culture. However, even if there are correlations between these grammatical categories and some extralinguistic parameters, more studies are needed to investigate whether they will change in the case of cultural change.

if a language has a classifier for 'domesticated animals', people must be familiar with domestication of animals, and, consequently, are unlikely to be nomadic hunters and gatherers; and one would not expect people in a desert to have a classifier for 'canoes'. Moreover, it will be shown that a cultural change (e.g. introduction of new artefacts, or rapid social changes) often results in a change—or in restructuring—of a classifier system.

We saw in §2.4.3 that variable noun class, or gender assignment may reflect metaphorical extensions which create a jocular effect. In Machiguenga (Peruvian Arawak: Shepard 1997), a language with masculine and non-masculine noun classes and a large set of numeral and verbal classifiers, non-masculine noun class (which covers females and inanimates) can be used by men in jocular reference to a 'third man', as a 'part of typical male joking behaviour in which men feminise one another with sexual, and especially homosexual, comments and jokes' (Shepard 1997: 53).

In establishing correlations between linguistic and non-linguistic parameters one should avoid circularity. Does Palikur have an elaborate system of numeral classifiers based on shape and dimensionality because it has an elaborate system of ethnogeometrical distinctions, or is the explanation the other way round? The danger of circular explanation has been pointed out by Craig (1986c: 290):

> It is difficult to avoid a certain amount of circularity when trying to argue that the set of classifiers of social interaction reflects the social and religious organization of the Jacaltec culture. Although one may find ethnographic evidence based on observation of the social organization which is relatively independent of language, whatever is known of the organization of the Jacaltec pantheon is based on language data . . . The existence of ample language-independent ethnographic evidence of the material culture will greatly lessen the problem of circularity encountered here.[34]

In §12.3.1 we show how sex (also known as 'gender') roles and social structure can be reflected in noun categorization devices relating to humans. The relevance of physical environment and of various cultural parameters for noun categorization of inanimates is discussed in §12.3.2. The culture-specific character of metaphorical extensions is dealt with in §12.3.3. Evidence from language planning and language change, especially in the context of language obsolescence, provides further support for a close link between noun categorization and extralinguistic parameters (§12.3.4). Not all semantic parameters employed in noun categorization depend equally on extralinguistic parameters. This, and the problem of the predictability of social and cultural parameters employed in noun categorization, are considered in §12.4.

---

[34] An interesting discussion of the importance of sex (or natural gender) distinctions in Turkish—which has no gender or classifiers—can be found in Braun (forthcoming a and b).

12.3.1. Social structure in noun categorization

Hierarchical social structure and kinship relations are frequently reflected in a system of numeral and noun classifiers relating to humans (see §11.2.2, 11.2.3). Austroasiatic languages typically have numeral classifiers for deities, humans of high status (e.g. governors), and monks (Adams 1989: 59–61).

Noun classifiers used with humans in Mayan languages reflect 'the organization of the powers that be . . . in the midst of, and beyond the world of humans' (Craig 1986b: 272). Social and kinship status can be encoded in relational classifiers, as is the case for Ponapean (see (A) in §11.2.4).

In a recent study on possessive classifiers in Ponapean, Keating (1997) showed how social status of the speaker and of the addressee is reflected in the choice of a possessive classifier in Ponapean. Possessive classifiers used in honorific speech register differ semantically from those used in the common register. For instance, the common register distinguishes the classifiers *kene* 'edible things' and *nime* 'drinkable things'; in the honorific register (used when addressing a chief or speaking in the chief's presence) three classifiers—*koanoat*, *pwenieu*, and *sak*—refer to all comestibles (food and drink); they distinguish the rank of possessor: paramount chief, the paramount chieftess, and the secondary chief, respectively (Keating 1997: 262). Thus, if one is invited to share a chief's food, this share would be referred to with a classifier corresponding to the status of the owner. Keating (1997: 262) illustrates this in the following way: 'a plate of food sent to me by the paramount chieftess, as I stood by the video camera filming a feast, was announced to the gathering as *Elizabet, kepin pwenieu*!' (lit. portion POSS.CL:paramount chieftess). In contrast, 'humiliative' or status lowering speech is characterized by neutralization of all the semantic oppositions found in common speech (see §10.5). One would not expect to find classifiers related to social hierarchies in egalitarian societies, e.g. in Australian languages; and indeed, they are absent there.

Social status and the power associated with it may be encoded in different ways. Various attempts have been made to establish a link between the semantics of noun classes and its cultural motivation in Niger-Congo languages. Osam (1994: 127–32) showed how Akan ontology is reflected in the semantic organization of its noun class system. The hierarchical ordering of the Akan structure of being reflects a 'decreasing order of power where one entity is of higher power than the one below' (Osam 1994: 127). The issue of power is central to Akan ontology; and the Proto-Akan noun categorization system of animates apparently also involves a hierarchy of social interaction, from the physical sphere to spiritual. Class 1 contains nouns which refer to powerful beings. These beings may have spiritual power, e.g. 'devil', 'god', or more culturally specific persons, e.g. 'master drummer' (because of his ability to play and invoke the spirits). Some also have social power, e.g. 'priest', 'elder', and a number of names for professions. Animals which are in Class 1 can also be considered powerful, e.g. 'elephant', or 'eagle' (who is 'the king of the air': Osam 1994: 131). Class 2 contains humans, animals, instruments, and other miscellaneous items. Humans which belong to this class have no power, either physical or social (e.g. 'child', 'slave', 'servant', 'orphan'). Animals in this class are less dangerous, or less powerful.

Palmer and Arin (1995a; 1995b) investigated the semantic basis of Shona noun classes from the point of view of correlations with Shona culture. Classes 1/2, 5/6, and 9/10 consist of participants, instruments, and distinctions which are intrinsically linked to scenarios of possession by ancestral spirits and associated rituals. Thus, persons and ancestors belong to Class 1/2; at least some central participants which fit into the schema of ritual danger, and mediums of ancestral chiefs, belong to 5/6. The central participants of Class 9/10 can be described as governed by a scenario of ritual protection, dominance and fertility. There is an abstract semantic opposition of Class 5/6 to Class 9/10: 'danger and evil versus protective dominance' (Palmer and Arin 1995a: 25). All the elements in these classes relate to central participants and instruments by similarity, metaphor, or metonymy (see §12.3.3).

12.3.2. Environment and culture in noun categorization

Functional parameters encoded in noun categorization devices are directly related to the culture of the speakers of a language. Consequently, an elaborate system of relational classifiers presupposes certain kinds of activities. Speakers of languages which have relational classifiers for vehicles are bound to have vehicles; speakers of languages which have classifiers for 'fruit to be picked', as does Cahuilla, must undertake this sort of activity.

In Cahuilla, 'temporary' classifiers describe the way in which an item can be handled, e.g. the ways in which food can be cooked. These classifiers also correlate with the semantics of the possessed nouns. For instance, only certain fruits or blossoms can be picked from trees; they are classifed with *ʔáyʔa* 'classifier: picked items'. This classifier cannot be used with such objects as the acorn (which is employed with another classifier, *číʔa*, used for edible items after they have fallen off the tree (or plant) and when they are dry and picked from the ground—Seiler 1977: 302). One classifier, roughly translated as 'partner', is used with a limited subclass of animals (which refer to a totemic moiety) (Seiler 1977: 305–6). The use of relational classifiers depends on socio-cultural conventions. In Cahuilla, certain animals, e.g. 'feral cat', cannot be pets, due to socio-cultural restrictions (Seiler 1977: 306).

344   Classifiers

Typical functions appear important in the choice of unique or specific classifiers which relate to the function or nature of objects. It is no wonder North Amazonian languages spoken by people who live along big rivers have a special classifier for 'canoes'. That longhouses are divided into culturally important compartments, or 'rooms', also gets expressed through the classifier system; see, for instance, the classifiers in Baniwa in Table 9.5. The existence of a special class used to refer to cows in Fulfulde (see Breedveld 1995: 69) can be considered a direct consequence of the importance of cattle in the culture.

Typical functions and objects which relate to them can be found in numeral classifier systems. Japanese and Korean have classifiers for books and written documents, while vernacular Amazonian languages do not have such classifiers, since they lacked these artefacts.

An overall study of classifiers in Jacaltec, and Jacaltec culture, by Craig (1986c: 287) showed that this 'linguistic system overtly marked the main features of the culture at some point back in time', and that it 'encompasses all aspects of traditional Jacaltec life'. The classifiers are 'few enough to isolate very selectively certain objects of the Jacaltec culture (corn but not beans, weaving but not carpentry), and at the same time, they are in enough number to produce together a very realistic picture of the Jacaltec culture as a whole (human beings and powers of nature, men's work, women's work, and how basic subsistence needs are met)' (p. 287).

Some semantic oppositions in classificatory verbs in Athabaskan languages relate to culturally important notions. Classificatory verbs in Slave distinguish two manners in which different objects can be handled: one is 'careful, controlled, respectful, polite, humble, reserved, gentle, concerned with human behavior', and the other implies 'lack of care, reservation and control', but 'not negative in connotation'. As Rice (1989: 784) points out, this distinction in manner of handling between the two sets of verbs is 'relevant throughout the entire culture'.

Possessive classifiers in Ponapean show an interesting correlation with traditional beliefs and with the kinship system, more precisely, with a culturally important notion of *mana* which describes 'the sacred and dangerous power which flows from the deities through the chiefs to the people'; '*mana* flows matrilineally to descendants within chiefly clans', and consequently the 'belief that *mana* extends to possessions makes possessive constructions a meaningful category' in distinguishing honorific, status-lowering, and common speech registers (Keating 1997: 249).[35] Consequently, in Ponapean *maternal* and not paternal relatives have specific classifiers (e.g. *ullap* 'paternal uncle', *wahwah* 'man's sister's child')

---

[35] We have seen in §10.5 how Ponapean employs different systems of possessive classifiers depending on the speech style.

(Keating 1997: 253). That the honorific general classifier, *sapwellime*, is composed of *sapwe* 'land' and *lime* 'hand, arm' can be explained by a strong cultural link between high status and land ownership; in contrast, the all-purpose possessive classifier in humiliative speech, *tungoal*, means 'food, eating and this correlates with the link between low status and food, or nourishment as the product of the land' (Keating 1997: 264–5).

Function is rarely encoded in noun class systems (see (C) in §11.2.1). This is why one hardly ever finds correlations between functional aspects of material and spiritual culture and the semantics of noun classes assigned to inanimates. Australian languages, with a noun class of 'non-flesh food', are a notable exception to this.[36]

The predictive power of these correlations is, however, rather limited. It is quite understandable that classifier languages spoken in hunter-and-gatherer societies (like in Aboriginal Australia) with their heavy reliance on vegetable food growing in the bush, would have a special classifier for non-flesh food. However, classifier languages such as Dâw or Nambiquara spoken within other hunter-and-gatherer societies in other parts of the world do not have such a class (see Dixon and Aikhenvald 1999).

Correlations between physical properties encoded in classifier systems and physical environment or other cultural parameters are much more diffucult to establish. An attempt to establish such correlations was undertaken by Denny (1979a: 108, 112–15). He explains the existence of deictic classifiers in Eskimo and Toba which are portmanteau with visible and non-visible members—he calls this a 'distal' style—by the fact that they 'hunt in open treeless environment';[37] and 'the Athabaskans and Algonquins who hunt in closed forest environment, employ a proximal style in which classification is embedded in verbs of handling, proximal variables such as hardness and flexibility occur, and the extendedness variable has proximal values' (p. 108). The presence of interioricity (holes vs. rings) as a variable in noun categorization is said to relate to the way land used to be settled, the presence of fixed domicile, and the division of landscape into privately owned areas. The distinction between rigid and flexible gets encoded in classifier systems due to technology systems. Thus, because of different cultures and dwelling types of societies, the physical properties— equally accessible to all—get encoded in one system but not in the other. Attractive and convincing as this may seem, there is a danger of circularity (especially since not all peoples who live in similar environments have exactly the same classifier systems).

---

[36] We will see in Chapter 13 that this noun class developed as the result of grammaticalization of noun classifiers, where 'function' is a frequently employed semantic parameter.

[37] However, this hypothesis can easily be falsified. Dyirbal, traditionally spoken in a thick rainforest, distinguishes visible and invisible deictics, while coastal Yidiny does not (see Dixon 1977: 181).

12.3.3. Culture-specific metaphorical extensions

Metaphoric extensions of sex- and animacy-based noun classes and classifiers to inanimates are often linked to the socio-cultural stereotypes associated with sex. In a fascinating study of sex roles as revealed through gender reference, Mathiot (1979) showed how role images of males and females are realized in the use of personal pronouns. The use of the pronouns *he* and *she* observed with inanimate referents in American English was found to correlate with a number of stereotyped features—part of the inherent image and role image American men and women have of themselves, and of each other. The semantic opposition BEAUTIFUL/UGLY manifests men's conception of women's vs. men's appearance; and the semantic opposition manifesting men's conception of women's and men's achievement potential is INCOMPETENT/COMPETENT. Thus a beautiful flower is referred to as 'she', and an ugly cactus as 'he' (Mathiot 1979: 18–19). In contrast, the inherent image and role image American women have of themselves and of men can be formulated in one semantic opposition: MATURE/INFANTILE (Mathiot 1979: 25).

Regular polysemy of feminine and diminutive in Afroasiatic languages is often accounted for by the low and subdued status of women in traditional Afroasiatic speaking societies (Diakonoff 1988). This is another example of a correlation between gender and social status.

In a few New Guinea languages with masculine and feminine genders, masculine is associated with culturally important roles, and feminine with insignificant things. This is the case in Angave, an Angan language (Speece n.d.: 111), and in Abu' Arapesh (Otto Nekitel, p.c.). Robert Conrad (p.c.) reports that in Felefita, an Arapesh language (Torricelli phylum), masculine can replace any other gender provided the object is sufficiently important. In coastal Arapesh languages, this results in the massive expansion of masculine gender, which has become the unmarked one.

We saw under (B) in §12.1.2 how metaphorical extensions based on the linguistic map of the world in Burmese culture explain why rivers and oceans are put into the same class as arrows and needles. Along similar lines, the complicated semantic structure of the *nge*-class—the specific class for cows—in the Maasina dialect of Fulfulde can be explained by Diagram 12.3, based on two metaphorical extensions: from cows to sources of light, and from cows to ceremonies (Breedveld 1995: 70–1).

Sources of light (fire, light, sun)   Ceremony

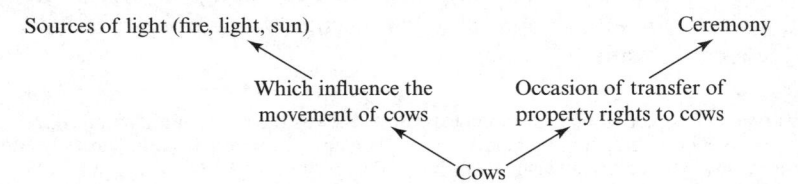

Which influence the   Occasion of transfer of
movement of cows   property rights to cows

Cows

DIAGRAM 12.3. *Semantic network of the nge-class in Maasina Fulfulde*

Semantic extension principles, such as the Myth-and-Belief principle and Important Property principles in Dyirbal (see Dixon 1982), are based on cultural intricacies. Once they become obsolescent, the classifier assignment becomes opaque.

12.3.4. Socio-cultural motivations for change in noun categorization

Further evidence for the socio-cultural motivation of noun categorization devices comes from language change, language obsolescence, and language planning. Noun categorization devices are probably the only grammatical category which directly reflects these social phenomena and shifts; they are freely reflected in the lexicon.

These processes affect classifiers which relate to the function of objects, and also classifier assignment based on cultural knowledge.

(A) Change in noun categorization can be motivated by social changes

Social changes which affect the social organization of a society may affect the set of classifiers related to human categorization. Pre-revolutionary Khmer had a complicated system of classifiers for humans and deities, typical for an Austroasiatic language. This system had terms for monks, the royalty, the image of Buddha; people were divided into 'high persons', 'dignitaries', 'superior persons', and 'inferior persons' (Adams 1989: 63). The Khmer Rouge revolution affected the social order, terms of address, and honorific classifiers.[38] (Note that after the defeat of the Khmer Rouge the classifier system was at least partly restored: Tony Diller, p.c.) This is very similar to the way the lexicon can get affected by social changes (e.g. Comrie and Stone 1977; Selischev 1928).

Social changes may affect principles of assignment of noun class, or gender—at least to some extent. Russian has a number of hybrid nouns for which gender agreement is determined by the sex of the referent, and not by their form (see §2.3.2). Rothstein (1973: 464) reports that the number of 'hybrid' nouns referring to professions in Russian increased with the liberation of women after the 1917 revolution. More professions became open to women, and consequently, nouns like *vrač* 'doctor (masculine)', or *sudja* 'judge', began to allow variable agreement according to sex.

Noun class assignment can change with a shift in social attitudes. Lak (Northeast Caucasian) has four noun classes. Class 1 consists of human males, Class 2 of human females, Class 3 of other animates and some inanimates, and Class 4 of inanimates only. According to Khaidakov

---

[38] As Shawcross (1979: 376) puts it, in post-revolutionary Cambodia, 'all forms of address that betoken social or family relationships were abolished and names were simplified. Father, mother, doctor were all replaced by comrade.'

(1963: 49–50), modern etiquette requires that in addressing women outside one's own family the markers of Class 3 be employed (no further details are given).

Changes and variation in noun categorization can be motivated by socio-cultural factors. Wolof (West Atlantic: Irvine 1978) has eight singular and two plural classes. Noun class assignment is based partly on semantics and partly on phonological principles. The society is highly stratified. Verbal fluency, correctness, and elaboration are associated with low social rank, for high ranks 'incorrect' speech is the norm. Deliberate 'errors' in noun classs assignment are associated with high rank of the speaker (Irvine 1978: 41–3). One class (*bi-* class) is expanding at the expense of other classes among middle-aged noblemen for whom 'incorrect' speech is an indicator of their social status, and this change in a prestige group is now being imitated by lower classes (Irvine 1978: 60–1; also see discussion in McLaughlin 1997).

The composition of a classifier can change due to technological innovations. In Thai, *khan*, a classifier for objects with handles, once applied to bicycles, was later extended to all vehicles, according to their similarity of function (see §13.9.2).

(B) Set of classifiers, or classifier assignment, can be affected by language obsolescence

Numerous examples show how cultural obsolescence leads to the reduction of largeish classifier systems, e.g. numeral or relational classifiers.

Cahuilla (Uto-Aztecan: Seiler 1977: 306) had a special possessive classifier for 'moiety animals'. In the early days Cahuilla society was divided into two moieties, one associated with the Coyote, and the other with the Wildcat. The two moieties were in an exogamic relationship. However, the obsolescence of the moiety system led to the loss of appropriate classifiers.

A drastic reduction in the system of numeral classifiers has been observed for Minangkabau (Marnita 1996: 163–5). This reduction goes together with a narrowing of the spheres in which the language is used, under the pressure of Indonesian, the national language. The increase in use of loan measure terms (metre, litre, and kilogram) contributed to the loss of traditional mensural classifiers. Young people appear to be unfamiliar with some culture specific classifiers, e.g. *sumpik* 'blowing bamboo weapon', simply because they do not use the object. Obsolescence of traditional practices among young city-dwellers has resulted in the loss of appropriate classifiers, e.g. *cabiek* 'piece of betel leaf'. Younger speakers of Korean and Japanese, especially those born overseas and not exposed to traditional culture, tend to know relatively few specific classifiers (Lee 1997; Sanches 1977; Masa Onishi, p.c.). This is comparable to the loss of lexical knowledge.

The principles of noun class assignment can be affected by cultural obsolescence.[39] Schmidt (1985: 156–7) describes a series of changes in rules for noun class assignment in Young People's Dyirbal. Mythological association as a basis for class membership is lost. In traditional times birds were believed to be spirits of dead human females, and consequently assigned to Class II, 'feminine'. With the loss of this belief, speakers of Young People's Dyirbal treat birds as members of the 'animate' Class 1.[40]

(C) Language planning can affect the use of classifiers

Thai has a number of rules concerning the use of classifiers in the 'royal linguistic register'.[41] Juntanamalaga (1988: 319) gives an example of an order of King Mongkut issued in 1854 whereby 'noble' animals such as elephants and horses should be counted without any classifier; the classifier *tua* could only be used for animals of a 'lower' status. Royal vocabulary replaced the classifier *kha* 'egg'—which developed associations with testes—with *fo':ng* 'water bubbles' (Juntanamalaga 1988: 320–1).

In Setswana (Bantu) all human beings and many names of tribes and peoples belong to the human Class 1/2. A number of ethnonyms which refer to strange and unusual groups such as Chinese or Bushmen belong to Class 5/6, together with substances, e.g. dirt or clay, and abstract nouns, e.g. foreign institutions (Anderson and Janson 1997: 34–5; Joe Tsonope, p.c.). In modern prescriptive Setswana it is, however, not recommended to use this class to refer to Bushmen (human class should be used then), since it is felt that they are being treated 'like dirt' when referred to with a non-human class (Joe Tsonope, p.c.).

Until recently, the masculine pronoun *he* in English was used as a generic term for human reference and also as one subordinate term, for male reference (see the discussion in Alpher 1987). During recent years, it has become the norm that the generic unmarked pronoun 'they' be used (to avoid linguistic chauvinism). This is illustrated in Diagram 12.4.

---

[39] Though the number of closed noun classes does not necessarily get reduced; see §13.7.3 on language obsolescence and reduction of noun class and gender systems.

[40] Other changes may be due to overall simplification of the system to make it more similar to gender in English. This may explain why concept association is also abandoned (Schmidt 1985: 157). Traditional Dyirbal assigned *yarra* 'fishing line' and *barrban* 'fish spear' to Class I, by association with *jabu* 'fish'; speakers of Young People's Dyirbal place these two words into Class IV, with other inanimates.

[41] The use of classifiers in Thai is regulated by stylistic rules. Omission of classifiers is characteristic for informal Thai (Juntanamalaga 1988: 316). The choice of a particular classifier can depend on speech register. Classifiers *an* (a general inanimate classifier) and *bay* (small leaf-like or roundish objects) are replaced by repeater constructions (Juntanamalaga 1988: 320). The use of classifiers in Thai is also directly linked to speech styles. Classifiers are widely used anaphorically by common people, and also as a sign of familiarity with each other; but not in 'royal' speech styles. Some classifiers, such as *tua*, are totally unacceptable when speaking to members of the royal family (Tony Diller, p.c.).

350 *Classifiers*

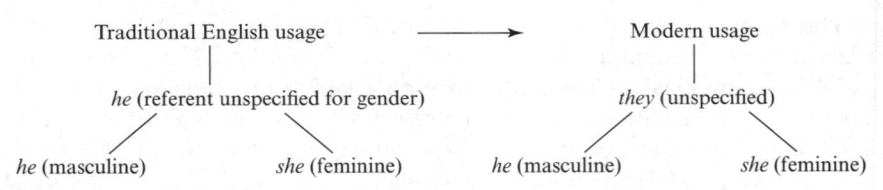

```
        Traditional English usage            ─────▶            Modern usage
                    │                                                │
        he (referent unspecified for gender)              they (unspecified)
              ╱           ╲                                    ╱           ╲
   he (masculine)      she (feminine)              he (masculine)      she (feminine)
```

DIAGRAM 12.4. *Gender pronouns in former and contemporary prescribed English usage*

12.4. Conclusions

We have seen that, semantically, classifiers are heterogeneous, non-hierarchically organized systems which employ both universal and culture-specific parameters. The ways these parameters work are conditioned and restricted by cognitive mechanisms and the socio-cultural environment. Among the universal parameters are animacy, humanness, and physical properties, e.g. shape, dimensionality, consistency. Culture-specific parameters can cover certain functional properties and social organization.

Classifiers are the grammatical means languages use for structuring and organizing concepts without multiplying lexical vocabulary. This organization is founded on basic-level categorization which involves perceptually salient parameters also important for physical, functional, and social interaction of human beings with their environment. Not all noun categorization systems, and not all semantic parameters, correlate equally with non-linguistic factors. Large systems of classifiers show more dependency on non-linguistic parameters than do grammaticalized noun classes.

Classificatory parameters associated with function rather than physical properties are more sensitive to cultural and other non-linguistic factors. Human categorization, as a sort of 'social' function, depends entirely on social structure. Functional categorization of inanimate and non-human objects is directly related to cultural notions. Animacy and sex, when extended metaphorically, are influenced by social stereotypes and beliefs.

Correlations between the choice of physical properties encoded in classifiers and non-linguistic parameters are much less obvious. They may relate to the cultural salience of certain shapes or forms; and they may be ultimately based on typical metaphorical extensions.

A further problem with finding cultural correlates for noun categorization is their inductive character. In quite a few cases we can explain what social, cultural, or even environmental parameter a classifier correlates with in a given society. But we will never be able to predict the ways in which non-linguistic parameters would be reflected in the grammar of a language. The example of the lack of vegetable food class outside Australia was mentioned above. Another example along similar lines is human categorization in Japanese (Downing 1996: 157). One would expect Japanese, a language with a well-developed system of honorifics, to have a well-developed system of classifiers reflecting different social statuses—just like Korean. However, unlike Korean, Japanese has just one honorific classifier (*mei*).

13 Origin and Development of Noun Categorization Devices

This chapter deals with the origin, evolution, and decay of classifiers of different kinds which may have different language-internal—lexical or grammatical—sources and may involve different grammaticalization paths. I also discuss the paths of evolution and restructuring of noun categorization devices, and the development and loss of agreement on different targets. Language-internal and language-external motivation for the emergence, restructuring and decay of classifiers are considered next. Further on, I analyse the semantic changes within classifier systems which take place in the course of grammaticalization—from a lexical source to a classifier—as well as within an already established classifier system. Appendix 2 provides further examples of semantic changes in classifiers.

Different kinds of classifiers tend to have different language-internal sources—some have lexical sources (see §13.1), while others come from closed grammatical classes; for instance, a demonstrative can become a gender agreement affix, or an adposition can become a locative classifier (see §13.2).

The problem of the relative 'age' of classifier systems in a given language, with a special focus on languages with several classifier types and on the relative age of noun categorization devices, is discussed in §13.3.

In the course of the history of a language, one noun categorization device can develop into another; the principles underlying this internal evolution of noun categorization devices are discussed in §13.4. Grammaticalization and reanalysis in the evolution of noun categorization devices are considered in §13.5. Processes of reduction and loss of noun categorization are analysed in §13.6. Language-external motivations for the emergence, restructuring, and decay of noun categorization are considered in §13.7. The genesis, evolution, and decay of agreement are dealt with in §13.8. The development and internal evolution of noun categorization devices go together with semantic changes which occur in the passage from lexical sources to classifiers or within an already established system; these issues are considered in §13.9. Finally, §13.10 presents a set of conclusions.[1]

---

[1] I am fully aware that prehistories of many of the language families considered here—especially of those without a documented history and a fully reconstructed prehistory—are far from clear.

13.1. Lexical sources for classifiers

Classifiers often come directly from open classes of lexical items, or from a subclass of an open class (Craig forthcoming: 61). This involves grammaticalization—from a lexical item to a grammatical marker—or polygrammaticalization, whereby one lexical item gives rise to more than one grammatical marker. The development of nouns into classifiers also involves the evolution of a classifier construction out of syntactic constructions of other types.

The most common lexical source for classifiers are nouns; verbs are used less frequently. In languages which have adjectives or adverbs as open lexical classes these tend not to develop into classifiers. Different semantic groups of nouns and verbs give rise to different classifier types. In §13.1.1, I show which semantically defined subgroups of nouns tend to become classifiers. The difference between nouns and verbs as potential sources for classifiers is that verbs which grammaticalize to classifiers usually come from a semantically defined subgroup. In contrast, there are cases where almost any noun can be used as a classifier of the 'repeater' variety: see §13.1.2. Classifiers can come from verbs (§13.1.3) or from deverbal nominalizations (§13.1.4). All classifiers of a given type in a language may have one kind of source (either nouns or verbs); classifier systems of mixed origins—some from nouns, and some from verbs—are discussed in §13.1.5.

13.1.1. From a noun to a classifier

The choice of which set of nouns becomes classifiers is typically language-, family-, or area-specific (why certain nouns become grammaticalized as classifiers in some languages but not in others can to some extent be accounted for by socio-cultural conventions and traditions: see §12.3). Australian languages typically use generic nouns such as 'vegetable food', 'meat' (or 'edible animal'), and various human divisions (e.g. 'man', 'woman', 'person') as generic classifiers. Mayan languages typically have a number of classifiers which refer to the domain of social interaction, culture and beliefs (e.g. 'male kin', 'respected male', 'deity'). Classifiers can come from words for 'animal', 'dog', 'corn', 'rock', 'water'. Words referring to food, drink, or pets may become relational classifiers, or possessed classifiers.

Semantic subgroups of nouns which frequently grammaticalize as classifiers are: (A) body parts; (B) kinship nouns, and nouns denoting humans (man, woman) and higher animates; (C) generic (or superordinate) nouns; (D) unit counters.[2] This list is by no means exhaustive. Nouns of other

---

[2] Greenberg (1990: 189) mentions the following semantic groups: '(a) superordinate terms such as a "person" as a classifier for humans, and "tree" for individual species; (b) items in

semantic groups which refer to culturally important objects, or notions—such as a house or a canoe—can also become classifiers (E).

Many of these nouns—notably, body parts, kinship nouns and generic nouns—can give rise to more than one classifier type, both cross-linguistically and within a single language; then they are said to undergo polygrammaticalization. The kinds of semantic changes which typically occur when nouns from these semantic groups become classifiers are discussed in §13.9.

Table 13.1 shows the lexical groups of nouns which tend to grammaticalize and the different types of noun categorization devices that they develop into.

TABLE 13.1. *Groups of nouns which tend to develop to classifiers*

Lexical groups of nouns	Types of classifier	Examples of languages
A. Body parts	Verbal classifiers	Mundurukú, Yanomami, Australian (e.g. Mayali), Palikur, Southeast Asian languages (Thai, Chinese)
	Numeral classifiers	Totonac, Mayan, Minangkabau, Hmong, Palikur, Kana, Southeast Asian languages
	Locative classifiers	Palikur
B. Nouns referring to kinship, humans and higher animates	Noun classifiers	Mayan, Australian, Austroasiatic, Austronesian, Dâw (Makú)
	Noun classes	Eastern Nilotic, Zande
	Possessed classifiers	Ponapean
C. Generic nouns	Noun classifiers	Minangkabau, Mayan, Mixtec, Australian
	Verbal classifiers	Australian
	Possessed classifiers	Carib languages, Nadëb (Makú), Yuman languages; Palikur, Island Carib, Bahwana (Arawak), Tariana, Tupí-Guaraní
	Numeral classifiers	Viet-Muong, Thai, Lao
D. Unit counters	Numeral classifiers	Kana, Minangkabau
E. Culturally important items: e.g. house, canoe	Any type	Arawak languages, Ngan'gityemerri, Ponapean

one-to-one relation to the objects being counted, among the most common of which are "head" for animates and "trunk" or "stalk" for trees; (c) words which themselves designate arbitrary or insignificant units like "piece" and "grain", etc.'

(A) Body parts as a source for classifiers

Of the groups mentioned in Table 13.1, body parts are the most frequent source of VERBAL classifiers—see the examples in Chapter 6. For instance, in Mundurukú (Tupí), of about 120 classifiers, at least 96 originate from body parts (Gonçalves 1987: 24–9).

The connection between the lexical source and verbal classifier is often transparent, as in Baniwa (Table 9.5). Some Australian languages use special semi-suppletive forms of body parts as classifiers (e.g. Tiwi: §6.2.4); the connection between an incorporated body part and a classifier can sometimes only be reconstructed (see §6.4.2 on the origin of shape-related classifiers in Athabaskan languages).

Verbal classifiers often originate in grammaticalized constructions with body part incorporation. Incorporated body parts can be syntactically and semantically distinct from the same items grammaticalized as verbal classifiers (see §6.2.1, for these distinctions in Mayali based on Evans 1996: 76–8; also see §6.4.1, and Aikhenvald and Green 1998, for criteria distinguishing incorporated body parts and verbal classifiers in Palikur). Sometimes, if the same morpheme functions as a verbal classifier and as an incorporated noun, ambiguities may arise, as in 13.1 from Xamatauteri (Yanomami: Ramirez 1994: 131). The use of verbal classifiers in Yanomami is obligatory for nouns in S/O function, and in copula clauses. The morpheme *ko* has two meanings and two functions: it means 'heart' as a body part, and 'round object' as a verb-incorporated classifier.

13.1. korekoremɨ-ko
type.of.parrot-heart/VCL:ROUND
'This is a parrot's heart', or 'This is one parrot.'

Body parts and parts of plants often become NUMERAL classifiers. They often tend to become mensural classifiers; more rarely, they may become sortal classifiers. This development is typical for Mesoamerican languages. In Totonac (Totonacan-Tepehuan family: Levy 1993), many numeral classifiers, SORTAL as well as MENSURAL, come from body parts—see examples in Table 13.2.

Numeral classifiers derived from body parts can combine 'sortal' and 'mensural' functions. Two of the eleven numeral classifiers in Palikur are derived from body parts, *uku/wok* 'hand' and *biyu/biy* 'mouth' (Aikhenvald and Green 1998). They can be used to classify the noun they come from, as in 13.2.

13.2. pi-wok-na   i-wak-ti
TWO-NUM.CL:HAND-TWO   INDEFINITE.PERSON-hand-NON.POSSESSED
'two hands, or fingers'

TABLE 13.2. *Numeral classifers from body parts in Totonac*

	Gloss	Meaning as body part
Sortal classifier		
cha':-	Human	*cha':n* 'leg'
tan-	Animal	*tan* 'buttocks'
laka-	Flat, surface	*lakán* 'face'
paq-	Flat, unbounded	*paqán* 'arm, wing'
Mensural classifier		
ak-	Units of length, e.g. 'metres'	*akán* 'head'
qalh-	Sips, bites of food	*qalh* 'mouth'

Unlike all other numeral classifiers they can be also used as measure terms, as shown in 13.3.

13.3. paha-uku-wa kumat
one-NUM.CL:HAND-EMPHATIC beans
'one handful of beans'

Body part terms are widely used as MENSURAL classifiers in Tzotzil (De Leon 1987: 93). The most frequently used mensural classifiers are associated with the hand and its parts, e.g. *k'et* 'handful', used to refer to a pile of grains such as corn, beans and coffee, *tom* 'two hands (hank) of thatch'; *poch:* 'palm', and *ch'utub:* 'span between thumb and forefinger'. In Minangkabau (Marnita 1996: 131) and in Hmong (Bisang 1993: 35), body parts tend to become mensural classifiers, e.g. Hmong *jan* 'finger', and also 'a term used for measuring cloth'.[3]

Less frequently, body parts become just SORTAL classifiers; then they categorize nouns in terms of their shape. There are typically just a few body parts which get grammaticalized that way. In Kana, a Cross River Benue-Congo language with a system of numeral classifiers (see Chapter 4), only two classifiers out of nineteen are derived from body parts: *ákpá* 'flatly shaped objects', is derived from 'skin', and *dɛ̄ɛ̄* 'spot-like objects' is derived from 'eye' (Ikoro 1996a: 90–6). Of over twenty numeral classifiers in Ngyembɔɔn, a Niger-Congo language from Cameroon, only two come from body parts ('head' and 'hand': Viktor Vinogradov, p.c.). Body parts used as superordinate class nouns are a source for sortal numeral classifiers in languages from east and mainland Southeast Asian languages (Bisang 1996). They are used in classification of animates, and more rarely of inanimates. In Bahnar (Central Bahnaric) *kŏ˙l* 'head' is used for living beings, people and bonded souls (i.e. slaves), as well as to count animals, boats and valuables, and as a

---

[3] This is reminiscent of systems with incipient numeral classifiers (§4.4); these often come from body parts such as 'head' and 'horn'.

denigrating term for humans; *măt* 'eye, pupil of the eye' is one of the honorific classifiers for humans (Adams 1989: 71). In Chrau, Mnong Gar, and Ro'lo'm (South Bahnaric) *vôq* 'head' is used as a generic classifier for animals (Adams 1989: 77) (see Appendix 2 for further examples).

Body parts and parts of plants may grammaticalize as LOCATIVE CLASSI-FIERS. Three of the twelve locative classifiers in Palikur originated from body parts: *-kigsa* 'on.POINTED' is related to *-kig* 'nose'; *-vigku* 'on.ROAD, RIVER' derives from *-vigik* 'bone, marrow'; *peru* 'on.BRANCH.LIKE' comes from *pew* 'branch' (see Diagram 7.1).

(B) Nouns referring to kinship, humans, and higher animates as a source for classifiers

Some members from the large category of animates, humans and kinship terms frequently develop into NOUN CLASSIFIERS. This is typical for Mayan languages (Kanjobalan branch), Australian, Austroasiatic, Austronesian, and a few South American languages, e.g. Dâw (Makú).

In Jacaltec (Kanjobal subgroup of Mayan: Craig 1986c: 266–7), twelve noun classifiers which belong to the subsystem of social interaction are derived from nouns with human referents, and from kinship nouns (noun classifiers for humans are derived from nouns meaning 'man' and 'woman' in Akatek, a language from the same subgroup—see Table 8.4; Zavala 1992: 152). The majority of noun classifiers in Mam, another language of the same family, are derived from nouns denoting humans and kinship terms (the only exception is a classifier for 'non-human') (England 1983: 158–9). Table 13.3 (England 1983: 158) shows noun classifiers in Mam; those derived from kinship terms and nouns referring to humans are in bold. In some cases, the grammaticalization of nouns as classifiers involves phonological reduction and semantic changes (see §13.5.1).

TABLE 13.3. *Noun classifiers derived from common nouns in Mam*

Classifers	Semantics	Common nouns	Semantics
jal	Non-human	*jiil*	Wild animal
nu7xh	**Baby**	nu7xh	Child
b'ixh	Person of the same status, fondly	?	?
q'a	**Young man**	q'aa	Young man
txin	**Young woman**	txiin	Young woman
ma	Man	*matiij*	Big
xu7j	**Woman**	xu7j	Woman
swe7j	**Old man**	swe7j	Old man
xhyaa7	**Old woman**	yaab'aj	Old woman
xnuq	**Old man, respectfully**	xiinaq	Man
xuj	**Old woman, respectfully**	xu7j	Woman

Animate or human nouns are frequently grammaticalized as DERIVATIONAL devices which overtly mark the gender of a noun on the noun itself. Many languages use words for 'man' or 'male', and 'woman' or 'female', with a classifier-like function as a technique to distinguish genders of hybrid nouns, e.g. English *female crocodile, male crocodile*.[4] In other languages, these terms have taken on the formal status of noun class markers. The development of nouns with a human referent and kinship nouns to overt NOUN CLASS markers on nouns, which then got extended to be agreement markers within noun and verb phrases, was suggested for Eastern Nilotic by Heine and Vossen (1983) (cf. Heine and Reh 1984: 219–20). Two gender markers can be reconstructed for Proto-Eastern Nilotic—masculine *lo and feminine *na—which are 'likely to be derived from the relational nouns, *lV 'member/person of' and **nyaa-* 'girl, daughter'. These new gender markers emerged as the result of the reanalysis of lexical items, initially used as heads of genitive constructions. Later, they got grammaticalized as prenominal modifiers, combining with the existing demonstrative roots, and then replacing them. Along similar lines, Mupun, a West Chadic language, inherited the Proto-Chadic system of two genders realized through agreement on nominal modifiers (Frajzyngier 1993); this language is also developing an overt gender marking on proper names, some common nouns, and even pronominal elements, via grammaticalization of *naa* 'woman' which has given rise to the prefix *nà-*, and *daa* 'man', which has given rise to the prefix *dà-*, e.g. *nà-kómtàk* 'such and such a female', *dà-kómtàk* 'such and such a male'.[5]

Lexical nouns can develop into personal pronouns, and subsequently get reanalysed as NOUN CLASS markers. Such a scenario was reconstructed for Zande (East Adamawa, or Ubangian: Claudi 1985; Heine and Reh 1984: 220–5). Synchronically, Zande has four genders in the singular (masculine, feminine, animal, and inanimate), and three in the plural (human, animal, and inanimate). Gender is distinguished in personal, possessive, and reflexive pronouns, and also realized in agreement between the subject and adjectival predicates. It is not marked on head nouns. Diachronic evidence shows the following lexical origins for the gender system in Zande (Heine

---

[4] In Tucano, a language with three genders and a large number of classifiers-repeaters, the lexemes 'man' and 'woman' are used to differentiate the sexes of animals, e.g. *semê imi* 'male paca (a large rodent)' (lit. paca man), *semê numiô* 'female paca' (lit. paca woman) (Ramirez 1997: 208). In Manambu, where masculine and feminine gender are usually not marked on the noun, the lexemes *takw* 'woman' and *du* 'man' are sometimes used as parts of compounded structures to provide disambiguation, e.g. *yanan* 'grandchild', *yanan-takw* 'granddaughter', *yanan-du* 'grandson'. Lexical expression of gender distinction sometimes cooccurs with overt gender marking on nouns, e.g. colloquial Portuguese *filho homem* 'son man', for 'son', and *filha mulher* 'daughter woman', for 'daughter'.

[5] The forms themselves may be loans into Chadic, cf. Proto-Benue-Congo *na 'mother' and *da 'father': Frajzyngier (1993: 44).

and Reh 1984: 224; Claudi 1985: 127–35): 'man, male' > masculine gender marker; 'person' > human; 'thing, prey' > animal (sg); 'animal, meat' > animal (pl); 'thing' > inanimate. See §13.5.1 on the grammaticalization of nouns to pronouns, and then to agreement markers.

Grammaticalization of lexical nouns may account for just a few noun classes out of a system. For instance, the diminutive gender marker *pi* in the Bantu languages of Cameroon comes from Niger-Congo *bi 'child'; the locative gender marker *ku* comes from the noun *ku 'the outside' (Heine 1982a: 214). The augmentative marker *kà-* (a vestigial noun class prefix) appears to be derived from *kà* 'mother' in Kana (Ikoro 1996a: 60). See §13.3, on how this may correlate with the relative age of classifier systems.

Kinship nouns can also get grammaticalized as POSSESSED classifiers. Ponapean (Rehg 1981; Keating 1997: 253) has twenty-two possessed classifiers, three of which developed out of kinship nouns, e.g. *kiseh* 'POSS.CL:RELATIVE', lit. 'relative'; *ullepe* 'POSS.CL:MATERNAL.UNCLE', *ullap* 'maternal uncle'; *wahwah* 'POSS.CL:NIECE,NEPHEW', lit. 'man's sister's child'. This is not attested outside Micronesia.

(C) Generic nouns as classifiers

Generic nouns which develop into different classifier types usually include a term for humans (see B), for non-human animates, and for plants and various types of food. Generic or superordinate nouns often develop into NOUN CLASSIFIERS. A sample of generic classifiers in Minangkabau (Marnita 1996: 82) is given in Table 13.4. Each of these is also used as an independent noun. (This is often not the case; for example, not all classifiers in Mam have an identifiable corresponding independent noun; and many of those which do underwent considerable phonological changes: see Table 13.3.)

TABLE 13.4. *Generic classifiers in Minangkabau*

Classifier	Semantics
urang	Person, human
ikan	Fish
buruang	Bird
batang	Tree, species of plants
kayu	Wood, tree
daun	Leaf
incek	Seed
anak	Seedling (lit. child)
aia	Water, drink

Noun classifiers in Mixtec developed via grammaticalization of syntactic compounds which contained generic nouns, e.g. 'man', 'woman', 'animal', 'tree' as their first component (De Leon 1987: 148–50). Examples of noun classifiers from generic nouns in Australian languages were discussed in Chapter 3.

Incorporated generic nouns can develop into VERBAL classifiers. This is a typical development for some northern Australian languages. In Mayali (§6.2; Evans 1996: 76–8) incorporated generic noun classifiers are a closed class of about forty items, which include 'tree', 'baby', 'ground', 'grass', 'fire', 'liquid'.

Generic nouns frequently develop into POSSESSED classifiers. These often include various types of food, firewood, and pets (see examples in (A) of §5.2). Systems vary as to what proportion of possessed classifiers maintain their connection with the lexical nouns. In Apalaí, a Carib language (Koehn 1994), the connection between possessed classifiers and their lexical sources is transparent. So is it in a number of Arawak languages (Palikur, Island Carib, and Bahwana). These languages have a small number of possessed classifiers (e.g. 'food', 'pet', 'catch', 'plantation') apparently acquired recently under the possible influence of Carib. In other Carib languages, such as Panare (Carlson and Payne 1989; see also Table 5.1 above), the origin of some items can only be recovered if compared to lexical items in other languages (cf. the comparison in Koehn 1994: 42–3); not all possessed classifiers originate in generic nouns.

POSSESSED classifiers, NOUN classifiers, and NUMERAL classifiers often come from a word meaning 'thing'. In Tariana *yarupe* 'thing' is a generic possessed classifier for non-human nouns (Aikhenvald 1994a). In a number of Tupí-Guaraní languages of South America, *mba'e* 'thing' tends to develop into a kind of noun classifier for non-humans. In Apalaí (Carib), *kyry* 'thing' is developing into an unmarked generic possessed classifier, alongside other generics. In some Viet-Muong languages *cái* 'thing' is used as a generic NUMERAL classifier (Adams 1989: 182–3). In Thai and Lao *ʔan* 'thing' can be used as a numeral classifier for any inanimate, or abstract noun (Adam Chapman, p.c.).

(D) Unit counters as a source for classifiers

Unit counters and measure words often give rise to NUMERAL CLASSIFIERS of the mensural type (I have found no examples of unit counters becoming sortal classifiers). They may include abstract words, such as Kana *ákpó*, a classifier used to count 'inanimate objects with a trunk', e.g. tree, which comes from *ákpó* 'length'; and *àkpò* (note different tones), a classifier 'used to count objects which have either irregular or heap-like shapes', from *kpò* 'heap' (Ikoro 1996a: 90, 94–5). They are often anthropomorphic measure terms, as in Minangkabau *kapa*, a classifier used for 'objects that can be held in the palm of one's hand', e.g. cooked rice, sand, dirt from *kapa* 'handful', or *ujuang jari*, a classifier used for 'things which one can take with a tip of one's finger', lit. 'finger tip' (Marnita 1996: 134).

(E) Nouns from other semantic groups as sources for classifiers

Specific classifiers used in any function often arise from culturally important lexical items, e.g. a canoe, or a house, as in Arawak languages of South America; or large woomeras, canegrass spears, or digging sticks, as in Ngan'gityemerri (Australian). In Ponapean (Rehg 1981, Keating 1997: 253), a number of possessed classifiers for items of personal use come from names for these items, e.g. *mware* 'POSS.CL:TITLE/GARLAND' from *mwar* 'title', or *ede* 'POSS.CL:NAME', from *ahd* 'name'. A noun which grammaticalizes as a classifier may undergo some semantic changes, e.g. *were* 'POSS.CL:CANOE,VEHICLES', from *wahr* 'canoe', or *pelie* 'POSS.CL:SIBLING', from *pelie* 'member of a matched pair' (see §13.9).

13.1.2. Repeater phenomena and the origin of classifier constructions

In some languages any—or almost any—noun can be used in the classifier slot, to classify the same noun, or semantically related nouns. This 'repeater' phenomenon is widespread in Southeast Asian languages, in some Micronesian languages, and in some South American languages (see §9.1). Repeaters and partial repeaters as numeral classifiers are reported in Thai, Lao, Burmese, and Lahu (Goral 1978: 33–4; see Chapter 4 above). In Truquese repeaters are used both as numeral classifiers and as possessive classifiers (Chapter 8; Benton 1968). Repeaters are developing into ad hoc classifiers for various inanimate objects in Tariana (Aikhenvald 1994a: 447–8); the repeater technique in this language is the result of areal diffusion from East Tucano. For instance, the form *ehkwapi* 'day, daylight, weather' is used as a repeater to 'classify' itself, and can occasionally be employed as a classifier for any natural phenomenon.

Repeaters can be shown to be the source for more grammaticalized classifier systems. Classifier constructions in Chinese and other Sino-Tibetan languages originated from constructions with 'repeaters'. Hashimoto (1977) suggests the following structure for the erstwhile classifier construction:

$NOUN_1 + NUMERAL + NOUN_1$

The 'repeated' part (i.e. the second occurrence of the noun) then underwent 'certain generalization of meaning', and a number of classifiers appeared (Hashimoto 1977). For instance, a general term for man, jen^2, is used for humans, instead of repeating their specific names. If the head noun is a compound, or a disyllabic word, only part of it may be repeated.

In Nakhi (Sino-Tibetan: Hashimoto 1977) it is usually the 'categorial noun stem', as in 13.4.

13.4. ʐər-ndzər   tṣ'ɨ   ndzər
      willow-tree this   tree
      'this tree'

In Tariana and East Tucano languages, it is usually the last derivational suffix; 13.5 is from Tariana (also see (F) in §9.1).

13.5. diha-kema   pasole-kema
      this-SIDE   left.hand-SIDE
      'this left hand side'

Repeater constructions can be the source for large systems of noun categorization devices which typically include numeral, deictic, possessed, and relational classifiers. Verb-incorporated classifiers and noun classes can originate in repeaters if the same set of classifier morphemes is used in different morphosyntactic environments (as in Tariana, or East Tucano languages). There is no evidence that closed grammaticalized noun class systems can be created in this way.

13.1.3. From a verb to a classifier

Verbs become classifiers more rarely than nouns. Table 13.5 shows the semantic subgroups of verbs which can become classifiers.

TABLE 13.5. *Semantic groups of verbs which develop into classifiers*

Lexical groups of verbs	Classifiers	Examples
Posture and motion verbs	Classificatory verbs	Engan, Ku Waru
	Deictic classifiers	Guaicuruan, Siouan
Verbs of handling (involving typical activities)	Verbal classifiers	Imonda
	Possessed classifiers	Ponapean
	Relational classifiers	Mam
	Numeral classifiers	Tzeltal

POSTURE and MOTION verbs tend to become CLASSIFICATORY verbs. Posture verbs are used as classificatory existential verbs in Ku Waru (Papuan: Table 6.8). In Engan and Waris classificatory verbs include posture verbs ('stand', 'sit', 'hang', 'lie inside', 'lie'), one motion verb ('come') and one transitive verb ('carry') (Tables 6.7 and 6.10 respectively). A tendency for POSTURE verbs to develop classificatory overtones, i.e. to be used to classify their S argument in terms of its form, is found in a number of Indo-

European languages. The use of posture verbs in Russian correlates with the position and physical form of its subject (Rakhilina 1998); the same tendency has been described for German by Borneto (1996).

POSTURE verbs also develop into DEICTIC classifiers, as in Siouan and in Guaicuruan languages. Deictic classifiers in Guaicuruan languages go back to combinations of deictic elements plus posture verbs, e.g. Proto-Guaicuruan 'singular masculine absent vertical' *(e)-d:a, from Proto-Guaicuruan *d:a 'stand' (Ceria and Sândalo 1995: 181). In Siouan languages, such as Mandan, deictic classifiers which refer to the position of animate objects, and to the form of inanimate objects, often function as main or auxiliary verbs (Barron and Serzisko 1982: 100). Thus, classifiers retain a synchronic link with the source verb. In 7.8 and 13.6 -mãk 'lie' is used as a deictic classifier for long horizontal objects (e.g., a river):

13.6. ma:ta   mãk-omakoc
      river   lie-NARRATIVE.PAST
      'The river was there (lying).'

This semantic development is due to the fact that deixis by its nature is connected to position and location in space. Systems of spatial deixis often include reference to parameters such as visibility, dimensions such as height, and reference to up and down: see Anderson and Keenan (1985: 290–2; Himmelmann 1997).[6]

VERBS OF HANDLING—as a part of serial verb constructions—gave rise to verbal classifiers in Imonda (W. Seiler 1983; 1986), and a number of other languages from the Waris family (W. Seiler 1986: 194; Foley 1986: 91; see §6.2.2 above); a sample of these verbs is given in Table 13.6 (W. Seiler 1986: 190–3; see also §13.5.2 below). These classifiers refer to an O or S argument.

TABLE 13.6. *A sample of verbal classifiers in Imonda*

Classifier	Semantics	Source verb	Semantics
põt-	'fruit to be picked'	põt	'pick fruit'
pui-	'objects which are normally broken'	puiual	'break in two'
i-	'scooping water out of an area dammed up for the purpose of collecting fish'	i	'scoop water out'

Many objects in Imonda are classified depending on how they can be handled; hence multiple class membership: for instance, a fish, tõbtõ, is

---

[6] Posture verbs in Siouan languages undergo polygrammaticalization (Barron and Serzisko 1982: 102): besides becoming classifiers, they grammaticalize as auxiliary verbs; they also grammaticalize as demonstratives.

typically referred to with different classifiers depending on the state it is in—still to be caught and killed, or already cooked and ready to be eaten (W. Seiler 1986: 202–3). An example like 13.7 (repeated from 6.7) could have meant at an earlier stage 'pick (up) and give me coconut'. The first verb was just specifying a way of manipulating an object in this state, and it gradually lost its verbal meaning in this context (but not in others, in the case of *pot-* 'pick fruit') becoming reanalysed as a classifier (cf. Foley 1986: 91).[7]

13.7. sa   ka-m   põt-ai-h-u
coconut 1SG-GOAL CL:FRUIT-give-RECIPIENT-IMPERATIVE
'Give me the coconut.'

POSSESSED classifiers can be derived from verbs of handling which involve typical activities. A number of possessed classifiers for specific inanimate objects in Ponapean (Keating 1997: 253) are derived from verbs, e.g. *tie* 'POSS.CL:EARRINGS', from *tie* 'to wear earrings', *ullunge* 'POSS.CL:PILLOWS', from *ulung* 'to use a pillow'. A number of relational classifiers which describe the way the possessed noun can be handled by the possessor in Mam (Mayan: Craig forthcoming; Roberto Zavala, p.c.) could derive from verbs of manipulation which describe typical activities involving the object to be classified; the relational classifier *chi'* 'cooked food' could have come from the verb *chi'* 'to eat cooked food', and the relational classifier *lo'* 'fruit' could have come from the verb *lo'* 'to eat fruit' (e.g. *n-chi'-ye' kyix* (1sg-POSS.CL:COOKED-POSS fish) 'my (cooked) fish').[8]

Verbs and verbal roots are never the only source for RELATIONAL, POSSESSED, or NUMERAL classifiers. If a numeral classifier system is of mixed origins (discussed in §13.1.5) some classifiers can come from verbs. These verbal roots refer to handling done with body parts (e.g. in Tzeltal, 'strike with an open hand', or 'take large mouthfuls', or 'break between fingers': Berlin 1968: 213). They can also include other verbs such as 'sleep', 'press', 'break', or 'trap' (Berlin 1968: 214). Hopkins (1970) provides further examples of numeral classifiers derived from transitive and positional verbs in Tzeltal, Jacaltec, and Chuj (Mayan). Usually, all these verbs contain information about the shape, size, material, or position of the O or S argument. Verbs which describe mental processes, or perception, or modal verbs, do not become classifiers. This is reminiscent of two phenomena.

---

[7] Which verbs will become classifiers in Imonda is scarcely predictable. Many of them seem to describe typical activities and ultimately relate to cultural and social issues (cf. §12.3). The etymological link between the source verb and a classifier can be easily established in some cases; in other cases, however, the process of grammaticalization of a verb to a classifier has resulted in phonological reduction and semantic bleaching; further examples are given by W. Seiler (1986: 202–3).

[8] According to Lyle Campbell (p.c.), they may alternatively have derived from nouns.

First, classificatory verbs (see §6.2) always describe manipulations which imply contact with the S or O (not the A). Second, in many languages verbal classifiers can only be used with verbs which presuppose physical contact and manipulation of the S or O argument.

13.1.4. Classifiers from deverbal nominalizations

Deverbal nominalizations are often the source for RELATIONAL and POSSESSED classifiers. In Cahuilla (Uto-Aztecan: H. Seiler 1983: 36–8; 1977: 299–305; §5.5.2 above) the classifiers in possessive constructions are derived from nominalized verbs. These verbs describe the ways in which objects can be handled, e.g. *ʔáyʔa*, the classifier used for 'fresh fruit or blossoms plucked from the tree', from the transitive verb stem *ʔáy* 'pluck' (ex. 5.53); *čí'a*, the classifier used for edible items fallen off the tree and picked from the ground, from *čí-* 'pick from the ground'; *wés'a*, the classifier used for planted trees and fruits, from *wés* 'plant'; and *ʔaš*, the classifier for pets, from the transitive verb stem *-áš* 'own' (Seiler 1977: 305). The generic classifier used for inanimates, *-éxan*, is derived from the verb *-éxan* 'do' (p. 300).

In these examples the semantic connection between the source verb, and the classifier is transparent. A more opaque connection may only be explainable by reference to the cultural background. Thus, *kíʔiwʔa* (Seiler 1977: 300), a classifier used for trees, plants and fruits in a group, growing wild, comes from the transitive verb stem 'wait'. Trees and their fruits were not privately owned; the places where they grew were instead assigned to a lineage. The members of a lineage were allowed to harvest these places when the appropriate time came. So, 'waiting' used to be essential for the appropriate handling of these objects (see §12.3).

RELATIONAL classifiers in Micronesian languages go back to deverbal nominalizations, as suggested by Harrison (1988: 74–5). The classifier for edible things is 'obviously related to an extant, or reconstructable verb "to eat"' (Harrison 1988: 67); see also Manam *'ana-* 'edible possessive classifier', from *'ani* 'eat' (Harrison 1988: 77); and see Lichtenberk (1985: 119) for a possible connection between the Proto-Oceanic classifier **ma* 'drinkable items', and the verb **inum* 'drink'.

In Apalaí (Carib: Koehn 1994: 42–3) just a few POSSESSED classifiers can also be shown to come from deverbal nouns, e.g. *-napy* 'vegetable/fruit', *-enapy* 'eat vegetable or fruit'. Other classifiers derive from nouns. Similarly, in a number of Austroasiatic languages, some deverbal nominalizations are used as NUMERAL classifiers. The form *vanông*, derived from a verb stem *vông* 'fall down' with the nominalizing infix *-an-*, is used as a classifier for animals in general in Chrau (Mon-Khmer; Adams 1989: 77).

13.1.5. Classifiers of mixed origin

In many cases the whole system of classifiers comes from just one source. For instance, in Kilivila (Senft 1993; 1996) all classifiers derive from nouns. In some languages, however, classifiers of one type can have mixed origins: some may come from nouns, and some from verbs.

Dixon (2002: 492–7) suggests a mixed origin for most noun class systems in Australian languages. The 'vegetable', or non-flesh-food class typically comes from a generic noun classifier (see §13.4), while markers for masculine and feminine class tend to come from masculine and feminine forms of third person singular free pronoun.

NUMERAL classifiers come from verbs as well as from nouns in numerous Austronesian and Austroasiatic languages; but statistically, more classifiers appear to come from nouns. Objects are classified according to the ways they can be handled, or consumed; or in agreement with their inherent properties ('drink' can be used as a classifier for liquids). About one-fifth of the numeral classifiers in Minangkabau are derived from verbs. Most of these are mensural classifiers, and they derive from verbs which imply physical manipulation, such as *atua* 'to pierce' (for fish and small fruits on a skewer), *balah* 'to cut in two parts' (for objects cut in halves), *kapiang* 'cut with an axe' (for big pieces of wood). A number of classifiers come from ingestive verbs, e.g. *taguak* 'swallow', for drinks; *suok* 'feed', for food eaten with a hand; and from verbs which refer to an action performed with a body part, e.g. *pikua* 'to carry on the shoulder', for objects carried on the shoulder (Marnita 1996: 121 ff.). Only a few sortal shape-based classifiers are derived from verbs, and they have a very specific meaning, e.g. *guluang* 'to roll' for a rolled object, such as a roll of paper; *lempeang* 'to slice', a classifier for 'flat piece of silver, gold and bronze'.

In Austroasiatic languages the majority of numeral classifiers come from nouns; but there are a few instances of numeral classifiers for inanimate nouns derived from verbs, e.g. Gold Palaung *kạr-vyāng* 'the classifier for circles or coils', from *vyāng* 'go round' (Adams 1989: 103).

Ponapean (Micronesian: Rehg 1981; Keating 1997: 253) is an example of a system of POSSESSED classifiers of mixed origins. Of twenty-two classifiers used in the common speech register (see §10.5), five classifiers referring to humans come from nouns; and four classifiers for food, drink, catch (e.g. of fish) and a share (e.g. of food) come from verbs; of ten classifiers for specific items (titles, names, buildings, etc.) and locations three come from verbs, and six from nouns (the etymology of two generic classifiers and the classifier *kie* 'sleeping pads' is unknown). One classifier, *rie* 'siblings', comes from the word for 'two'. Classifiers used in humiliative and honorific registers come from nouns, e.g. *tungoal*, a humiliative possessed classifier (used for all possessions), comes from the word for food, or eating; *moatoare*, a possessed classifier in honorific register used for sleeping gear, comes from the word for mat, or sleeping, used in the honorific speech. A few classifiers in the honorific register appear to be derived from compounds, e.g. *sapwellime* 'possessed classifier in honorific register for general possession' comes from *sahpw* 'land' and *lime* 'hand' (honorific); Keating (1997: 263-4) provides socio-cultural reasons for this—high status is linked with ownership of land.

Classifiers can be derived from roots which belong to more than one class. In Mayan languages NUMERAL classifiers are typically related to a class of roots called 'positionals' which indicate position or shape; they may be nouns in one language and verbs in another. In Tzotzil, classifiers typically derive from positional roots, or transitive roots which encode semantic dimensions of shape, size, material, position, etc. (De Leon 1987: 60-1), e.g. *jav* 'cut, sever' (positional), *jav-* 'to be cut' (intransitive verb), *-jav* 'to cut' (transitive verb) > *jov* 'piece' (numeral classifier); *vA`*: 'standing up in bipedal position' (positional root), *va`i-* 'to stand up' (intransitive verb), *-va`an* 'to stand something' (transitive verb) > *-vo`* 'numeral classifier for persons'. In Tzeltal (Berlin 1968: 20-2) numeral classifiers form a subclass of nouns derived from transitive verb roots, positional verb roots, and from a few noun roots.

13.2. From a closed class to a noun categorization system

Items from closed grammatical classes, such as demonstratives or locatives, usually give rise to a relatively small closed system of noun classes, and not to large systems of classifiers. Only in Loven (West Bahnaric) is there a form *yur* used for classifying animals in general which comes from a demonstrative, or interrogative 'that' or 'what' (Adams 1989: 77), and is one term in a large system of numeral classifiers.

Greenberg (1978) suggested the following chain for the evolution of overt gender marking from a demonstrative, or from an anaphoric element:

Stage 0 ⟶ Stage 1 ⟶ Stage 2 ⟶ Stage 3
(1) Demonstrative (2) Definite article (3) Non-generic marker on (4) Marker of nominality
nouns, or specific article

DIAGRAM 13.1. *Evolution of gender markers (1)*

This development was reconstructed by Greenberg (1978: 61 ff.) for Voltaic languages. His scheme involves semantic change from demonstrative to definite article, and from definite article to specific article, plus a passage from article to noun marker. It also involves formal changes, e.g. a shift from free word to clitic (such as demonstrative to article) and from clitic to affix.

A similar development for overt gender markers on nouns can be suggested for Berber languages. In Berber, masculine gender is usually marked with the prefix *a-*, and feminine with *t-a-*; these can be shown to go back to fossilized and desemanticized definite articles (see Vycichl 1957; Aikhenvald 1984). Turkana (Eastern Nilotic: Dimmendaal 1983) is a particularly instructive example of how overt gender markers on nouns are used as markers of nominality (Stage 3), and at the same time sometimes maintain their function as specific 'articles' (see §12.1.3, on how Turkana gender prefixes correlate with discourse organization: Dimmendaal 1983: 222); also see Childs (1983), on the application of Greenberg's schema to the development of noun classes in the Southern branch of West Atlantic languages.

Another path of evolution, suggested by Heine (1997b) for Khoe languages, implies that, besides demonstratives, erstwhile 3rd person pronouns can trigger the spread of gender marking. In Hiechware, person, gender, and number are marked on personal pronouns only; in Kxoe there is optional gender marking on demonstratives (and in one language, Naro, it has also spread to adjectives in a noun phrase). Heine hypothesizes that personal pronouns were used as specifiers and markers of emphasis; later they combined with demonstratives and other modifiers and lost their pragmatic overtones in some languages. The structure of personal pronouns in Kxoe shows that person/number/gender markers in this language have to do with emphasis: the demonstrative stem is used to emphasize personal pronouns. Third person pronouns which distinguish two genders consist of a demonstrative stem *xà-* and the appropriate person, number, and gender marker, e.g. *xà-má* '3rd person singular masculine', *xà-hé* '3rd person singular feminine' (Heine 1997b). Emphatic 1st and 2nd person pronouns can also be formed by adding the same demonstrative stem onto the personal pronoun, e.g. *tí* '1st person singular non-emphatic'; *xà-tí* '1st person singular emphatic'. In the 3rd person, non-emphatic pronouns are no longer used.[9]

These considerations allow us to suggest the alternative scenario—see Diagram 13.2.

Stage 1 ⟶ Stage 2 ⟶ Stage 3
3rd person pronoun (also used as a specificity marker)   Article-like marker   Marker of nominality

DIAGRAM 13.2. *Evolution of gender markers (2)*

---

[9] A similar scenario can be reconstructed for the Arawak languages of South America. There, gender markers (masc. or non-feminine *-ri*, feminine *-ru*) on nouns go back to 3rd person pronouns and cross-referencing affixes.

The chains represented in Diagram 13.1 and in Diagram 13.2 are not so different: cross-linguistically, demonstratives and 3rd person pronouns often overlap in their functions.

The development of gender, animacy, and a human/non-human distinction in pronouns may have to do with their reference. Personal pronouns are often restricted to humans, while demonstratives can be used for non-human referents. This may give rise to a new animate/inanimate, or personal/non-personal, distinction. In formal Finnish, the 3rd person pronoun *hän* is used for human referents only, while the erstwhile proximate demonstrative *se* is used for non-humans (Tiit-Rein Viitso, Liisa Järvinen p.c.; also see Appendix 1). In Bengali, an Indo-Aryan language with numeral classifiers but no grammatical genders, 3rd person pronouns refer only to humans, and demonstratives refer to non-humans (Masa Onishi, p.c.).[10] In languages which already have noun classes this may lead to creation of a different system of classes (or genders) for different word classes and targets. Warray (Australian: Harvey 1987) has four noun classes, generic noun classifiers, and a feminine/non-feminine distinction in 3rd person singular pronouns. Independent pronouns can have only human referents, and this may result in the creation of an additional, human/non-human distinction (see (C) under §2.4.4). Genders, or noun classes can also develop via reanalysis of other closed grammatical systems (e.g. Kiowa-Tanoan languages: §13.5.2).[11]

A closed class of locative adpositions can be a source for NOUN CLASSES. The rise of new 'locative' genders then relates to the reanalysis of locative expressions. These may contain a relational noun which refers to a place; for instance, the neuter gender prefix *i-* in Turkana arose from a grammaticalized anaphoric noun meaning 'place just referred to'. Locative adpositions can be clitics which ultimately go back to a subclass of nouns with locative meanings. Locative genders in languages of the Congo branch of Bantu go back to locative and adverbial expressions (Greenberg 1990: 260; also see Givón 1976: 173–5). According to Heine (1982a: 214), at least some of these derive from locational nouns (e.g. **ku-* 'the outside', which is still used as a preposition in a number of Bantu languages). Classifiers of other types can also come from locational adpositions which are used as derivational suffixes (some of these probably go back to independent locational nouns).

The morpheme *-(V)ku* is used as a classifier 'inside of; cavity; extended' in many Arawak languages (Payne 1991a: 384). In Palikur (Aikhenvald and

---

[10] See also Corbett (1991: 311) for how such a distinction is developing into a new gender system in Persian, and for a similar phenomenon in Latvian.
[11] According to Nichols (1992: 141), 'all that is needed in order for noun classes to arise is a covert animacy system, a potentially recruitable formal distinction, and pre-existent agreement patterns'.

Green 1998) it is used as a numeral classifier, as a verbal classifier, and as a locative classifier. Synchronically, however, there are three independent morphemes, since they display different allomorphy. This form can also be used in multiple classifier systems—in Tariana and Baniwa it appears as an adjectival agreement marker, as a numeral, and as a verbal classifier. In other languages of the family the same morpheme is used as a locative case marker (e.g. Machiguenga *-ku*, Bare *-uku* 'locative'); or as a derivational affix marking location (Tariana *-iku* 'place of'). Palikur also has a locative classifier *-hakwa* 'on.LIQUID' which is used as a derivational formative in locational nouns such as *paraw-hakwa* (water-on.LIQUID) 'ocean'.

13.3. Languages with several classifier types, and the relative age of noun categorization devices

Multiple classifier systems which use different morphemes in different functions often come from different lexical sources. The emergence of such systems from different and sometimes from the same lexical source can be considered as the result of polygrammaticalization processes (see Craig 1991; Heine 1992; §13.5.1 below). The basic assumption is that if a system is semantically transparent, and connects easily with lexical sources, it is relatively new. The old noun classes in Bantu are difficult to trace back to lexical sources (Traugott and Heine 1991b: 10). In Palikur, different nouns from the same semantic group—e.g. body and plant parts—give rise to different classifier types: 'hand' and 'mouth' become numeral classifiers, while 'branch' and 'nose' became verbal classifiers and locative classifiers, and 'trunk' gave rise to both numeral and verbal classifiers.

In Truquese repeaters which become classifiers have the same meaning independently of whether they are used as numeral or as possessed classifiers (Benton 1968). Example 8.3 illustrates the same item *batang* 'tree' as a numeral classifier, and as a noun classifier in Minangkabau; as a numeral classifier it describes the noun in terms of its shape (long and vertical), and as a noun classifier it is a superordinate item.

The same items used as numeral classifiers and as noun classifiers can also be said to undergo polygrammaticalization (cf. DeLancey 1986: 440–1, on the categorization of nouns with numeral classifiers and with noun classifiers in Tai languages). Classifier morphemes of more than one type in a language can correspond to different stages of grammaticalization of the same set (see the discussion of Ngan'gityemerri in §13.5.1 and in §13.8.1).

Sometimes, of a large classifier system only a few specific classifiers can be shown to have a lexical origin. Motuna, a Papuan language, has fifty-one classifiers; of these, only a few specific classifiers—those which refer to time spans—can be related to nouns, e.g. *-ru* 'day' from *ruu* 'day', *-mu* 'day (in the past)' from *muu* 'night', *-mori* 'year' from *moi* 'canarium almond season/year' (Onishi 1994: 169), with all the rest having no known etymology. This system must be old. In contrast, of nineteen numeral classifiers in Kana (Kegboid: Ikoro 1996a), only two have no etymology. We conclude that this system must be relatively new; this is confirmed by other historical and comparative considerations of the origin of numeral classifiers in Kegboid languages (Suanu Ikoro and Gerrit Dimmendaal, p.c.).

In Dâw (Makú) noun classifiers come from superordinate generic nouns which are still used in the language in a non-classifier function (e.g. *dâw* 'CLASSIFIER:PEOPLE', 'person', also used as a 3rd person pronoun: Martins 1994). Some locative classifiers can be shown to be historically derived from nouns; however, a lexical source can only be reconstituted by comparison with a genetically related language. For instance, the locative classifier *-mĩ'* LOC.CL:LIQUID' is cognate to the noun *mi* 'water' in Nadëb, a language from the same family. This term for water is not used in Dâw. Thus, since locative classifiers lost their lexical source in Dâw, and noun classifiers did not, one may assume that locative classifiers are older than noun classifiers.

Another indication of the age of a system is the degree of phonological reduction of a morpheme. Chinantec (Foris 1993: 257, 302–3) has nine noun classifiers, and several dozen numeral classifiers. In just one case the same lexeme is used in two classifier functions, i.e. undergoes polygrammaticalization. *Máɨ³* 'sphere' gave rise to a numeral classifier for round objects (*máɨ³*), and a noun classifier *mɨ³* also used with round objects and spheres (example 8.6). The noun classifier underwent phonological reduction while the numeral classifier did not. The different degree of phonological depletion shows the difference in the relative age of the two systems.

In languages with a small closed system of two or three genders and a large system of classifiers in several functions these two may have different origins. In North Arawak languages with multiple classifier systems, classifiers have lexical origins, and gender markers come from a closed class of cross-referencing markers. Gender markers go back to Proto-Arawak. Given the areal distribution of classifiers in the Amazon, we may hypothesize that the classifiers were acquired more recently, at the level of individual subgroups (Aikhenvald 1996c; further evidence is given in Aikhenvald 2001).

In other cases the relative age of different noun categorization systems just cannot be established. In some Arawá languages of Southern Amazonia, both gender and the *ka-* noun class (see §2.7.2) are semantically non-transparent and do not easily connect to any lexical sources. Consequently, it is impossible to determine their relative ages.

13.4. Internal evolution of noun categorization

The internal evolution of noun categorization devices often involves a passage from one type of noun categorization to another. A lexical noun categorization device can develop into a closed grammaticalized system; then this system may become less semantically transparent. Noun classifiers grammaticalize in this way, and become noun class or 'gender' markers (the hypothesis that noun classifiers, or class terms, could have been reinterpreted as numeral classifiers in Thai has been put forward by DeLancey 1986: 444–5; see also Bisang 1993; 1999). This development is also linked to the emergence of agreement (see §13.8). Following the general principle of unidirectionality in grammaticalization, the reverse development never occurs.

This scenario has been suggested for Proto-Australian (Dixon 1982: 171; Sands 1995: 253, 285–6). Australian languages show a continuum of grammaticalization: from generic nouns in noun classifier function to noun class agreement markers on modifiers and verbs. Thus, some noun class markers are less advanced on the grammaticalization continuum from semi-lexical noun classifiers to noun classes than others (I return to this issue in Chapter 15).

The most instructive example is the behaviour of the class of 'vegetable food' which ranges from a generic noun to a grammaticalized noun class marker (Sands 1995: 285–6). This passage from an optional generic in a noun phrase to an obligatory and sometimes semantically opaque prefix or suffix can be shown as a grammaticalization chain with three stages. Grammaticalization chains of this sort can be recovered if related languages are compared (cf. Heine 1992; 1997b).

Stage 1. Generic-specific pairings as a discourse device. In Guugu Yimidhirr and many other languages generic *mayi* may be used in generic-specific constructions for vegetable foods (Haviland 1979).

Stage 2. The generic noun comes to be used as an obligatory component of noun phrases as a noun classifier omissible under specific conditions. For instance, in Yidiny (Dixon 1977; 1982) *mayi* is one of the set of noun classifiers used with specific terms; it can be omitted under certain conditions (see Chapter 3).

Stage 3. The noun classifier is grammaticalized as a noun class affix; then it undergoes phonological reduction. There are two possibilities.

(a) In Dyirbal the suffix *-m* 'vegetable food' attaches to deictics and determiners as an agreement marker.

(b) In north Australian languages of the prefixing type, a prefix *ma-* (or *mi-*, or *m-*) 'vegetable food class' is attached to the head noun, and is also used as an agreement marker, e.g. Ngandi (Heath 1978b). The semantics of this noun class may be widened, as in Yanyuwa, where it covers non-flesh food, firesticks, articles made of fibrous materials, etc. In Wardaman the *ma-* class includes all flora (Merlan 1994: 60; see (B) in §13.9.2). In Olgolo phonologically reduced generic noun classifiers are being transformed into overt prefixed markers on nouns. They are optional, e.g. *y-* is based on *úyu-* 'fish' and *ṇ-* on *iṇa-* animal'. This evolution of noun-class prefixes from free classifier forms has a phonological motivation: the language is eliminating vowel-initial words (which appeared as the result of consonant-initial dropping) (Dixon 1982: 207–10). There are no indications that noun classes tend to develop first as derivational markers (head classes), or as agreement markers (see §13.8). In Zande (§13.1.1) and Dyirbal gender markers never developed a derivational function; they did in Ngandi and in Wardaman.

Changes in noun categorization can involve evolution from covert to overt noun class marking. In African languages an additional noun class marking affix is sometimes added to the noun to 'strengthen' the overt class marking (see Greenberg 1978). This results in a renewal of overtly marked head classes.[12] In the Southern branch of West Atlantic languages noun class marking suffixes on the head nouns are used to reinforce the prefixes of the old noun classes. In these languages (Childs 1983: 25–6) the 'prefix erosion' was followed by introduction of noun class-marking suffixes which, at least in some languages, develop from pronouns (following the scenario outlined in §13.2 above; see also Greenberg 1978).

The development of a new agreement target can result in the creation of a new classifier type, through extension of existing classifier morphemes to another function. This can be triggered by areal diffusion (§13.7). The development of a new agreement class may be achieved by substitution of independent pronominal forms for the affixed pronominal forms. If new 3rd person pronouns have an animacy distinction this is a way of setting up a gender agreement system (cf. Nichols 1992: 141). A noun categorization system can undergo expansion via grammaticalization of repeaters (see §13.5.1) or reanalysis of other nominal grammatical categories (§13.5.2) (further changes in noun categorization systems are discussed in §13.9.2).

---

[12] This phenomenon is also attested in Bantu languages with pre-prefixes (Greenberg 1978: 66–7). In many Bantu languages, the nasal prefix of the human noun class became fused with the stem, and another prefix was added, e.g. *ba-n-tu* (NCL2:PL-NCL-person) 'people'.

13.5. Grammaticalization[13] and reanalysis in noun categorization systems

The development and reanalysis of noun categorization devices involves grammaticalization, and often polygrammaticalization, of lexical and grammatical items. Grammatical closed classes such as demonstratives or anaphoric specificity markers tend to grammaticalize into markers of closed agreement classes. Lexical classes tend to grammaticalize into larger classes of classifiers. These paths conform to the principle of unidirectionality of grammaticalization. Grammaticalization in the development of noun categorization is discussed in §13.5.1, and in §13.5.2 I deal with reanalysis in noun categorization.

13.5.1. Grammaticalization in the development of noun categorization

Grammaticalization focuses on how grammatical forms and constructions arise, how they are used, and what the most probable paths for their development are (cf. Hopper and Traugott 1993: 1–2). The development of noun categorization involves grammaticalization of members of open lexical classes (nouns and verbs, discussed in §13.1), and of closed classes, e.g. demonstratives or locative adpositions (§13.2). Grammaticalization follows the principle of unidirectionality (Bybee *et al.* 1994: 17; Heine *et al.* 1991): once an item gets grammaticalized the process usually cannot be reversed.

Grammaticalization of members of open classes as classifiers often involves a grammaticalization chain (Heine 1992; 1997b), from a lexical item to an element of a closed class, and then to a grammatical marker. When lexical nouns get grammaticalized as markers of noun class they assume a pronominal (anaphoric) or a deictic function. In Zande (East Adamawa: Claudi 1985; Heine and Reh 1984: 222–4; §13.1 above) full gender markers arose via pronominalization of nouns. The masculine pronoun *kɔ́* in Zande comes from a noun **ko* 'man, male' (which is still used as an independent noun in related languages, e.g. Banda *kɔ*, Ngala *kwā*). Zande is developing gender agreement on adjectives in predicative use, as shown in 13.8.

13.8. kɔ́-ní bakɛ́rɛ́-kɔ́
he-be big-he
'He is big.'

---

[13] I use the term 'grammaticalization' with the sense of 'the attribution of a grammatical character to a formerly independent word' following Meillet (1912: 132). See also the definition by Heine (1997a: 76), who considers grammaticalization as a process 'whereby a linguistic expression E, in addition to its conventional meaning M_1, receives a more abstract and more grammatical meaning M_2'.

In Zande, the same items are used as pronouns, and as gender markers. In some Mayan languages noun classifiers derived from nouns are also used anaphorically as pronouns (see §3.2.4; and see England 1983: 155, for Mam; Craig 1977: 177, for Jacaltec). Gender markers *lo 'masculine' and *na 'feminine', reconstructable for Proto-Eastern Nilotic 'are likely to be derived from relational nouns (*lV 'member/person of', and *nyaa- 'girl, daughter' which formed the head of genitive constructions before they developed into pre-nominal modifiers *lo and *na' (Heine and Reh 1984: 219)); they became agreement markers on adjectives in some languages, e.g. Ongamo. When a noun class system is established, additional genders can be acquired through grammaticalization of other anaphoric elements. Maasai has an incipient third gender which originates in a reanalyzed locative phrase (Tucker and Mpaayei 1955: 15–33; Heine and Claudi 1986: 43–51; Corbett 1991: 313–14).

Different stages of grammaticalization processes may (but do not have to) coexist in a single language. We have seen in §13.4 that in some Australian languages noun classes derived from noun classifiers—used as anaphoric pronouns—coexist with them, but in others it is not the case.

If a set of lexical items becomes classifiers of different kinds, this will involve polygrammaticalization (Craig 1993; Heine 1992).[14] Body parts can undergo polygrammaticalization in two ways. They can be used simultaneously as numeral classifiers (both sortal and mensural), and as quantifiers. Mensural classifiers are often derived from body parts in Minangkabau (see (A) under §13.1.1), e.g. *jari* 'finger', a mensural classifier used for measuring cloth (Marnita 1996: 131). There is also a sortal classifier derived from a body part: *ikua* 'tail' is a numeral classifier used for all animals (Marnita 1996: 107). A few other body parts are used as specific sortal classifiers, e.g. *kaki* 'leg', for umbrellas; *tangkai* 'stem, stalk' for flowers with a stalk. The development of sortal classifiers out of body parts involves metonymy in most cases. In languages with multiple classifier systems different body parts can get grammaticalized in different functions. For instance, in Palikur 'hand' and 'mouth' are used as numeral classifiers (see examples 13.2 and 13.3 and discussion of their ambiguous status as sortal and mensural classifiers). *Kig* 'nose' is grammaticalized as a verbal classifier, and as a locative classifier. One item, *kat* 'vertical', is derived from a word for 'trunk, stem of a plant', and is used in two functions: as a numeral classifier and as a verbal classifier (with stative verbs only). See §13.3, on the polygrammaticalization of *máɨ³* 'sphere' in Chinantec (Foris 1993).

---

[14] Polygrammaticalization implies the passage of lexical item 1 to grammatical functions A and B; e.g. in Rama (Chibchan; Craig 1991: 487), the verb 'go' gets grammaticalized as a purposive marker and as a marker for a tense-aspect choice.

GENERIC NOUNS can undergo polygrammaticalization; in this case they give rise to noun classifiers and to noun class markers. A generic noun which undergoes polygrammaticalization can become a bound morpheme and at the same time can still be used as a noun classifier. In Ngan'gityemerri *miyi* is used as a noun classifier; there is also a prefix *mi-* used for vegetable food (see further discussion in §13.8 on how this correlates with the development of agreement).

Another grammaticalization path in the development of classifiers is from repeaters, as an almost open class, to a more closed class of classifiers. In Tariana (North Arawak: Aikhenvald 1994a) repeaters become extended to items other than themselves; for instance, *tuɾapa* 'cone' can be used to classifiy not only the same noun, but also any other object which is cone-like in shape, e.g. *tuɾapa hanu-tuɾapa* (cone big-NCL.REPEATER:CONE) 'a big cone'; *yeɾi hanu-tuɾapa* (basket big-NCL:CONE) 'a big cone-shaped basket'. In Kilivila (Senft 1993a; 1996: 353) some repeaters undergo phonological depletion and are extended to items other than themselves.

Grammaticalization of nouns as classifiers often goes together with their phonological reduction (in harmony with the Parallel Path hypothesis, according to which semantic change in grammaticalization goes together with phonological change: Bybee *et al.* 1994: 19). The development of noun classifiers from independent generic nouns in Mixtec involved 'abbreviation' of generic nouns (Pike 1949: 129–31; De Leon 1987: 148–50), in the course of change from a syntactic compound to procliticized classifier-plus-nouns. This is shown in Diagram 13.3.

Syntactic compound ⟶	Proclitic classifier + noun ⟶	Meaning
kiti-kwaa	*ti-kwaa*	
ANIMAL, ROUND.OBJECT-yellow	NOUN.CL:ANIMAL, ROUND.OBJECT-yellow	'orange'
zito-tichi	*to-tichi*	
TREE-avocado	NOUN.CL:TREE-avocado	'avocado tree'

DIAGRAM 13.3. *Phonological reduction in the development of noun classifiers in Mixtec*

In Dâw a generic classifier plus specific noun constitute one phonological word, with the classifier losing its independent tone (a similar phenomenon is attested in Tucano: Ramirez 1997, and Tariana: Aikhenvald in prep., spoken in the same linguistic area). Different noun classifiers can show different degrees of phonological depletion. In Mam (Kanjobalan Mayan: England 1983; Table 13.3 above) some noun classifiers preserve the same form as nouns (e.g. *nu7xh* 'NOUN.CL:BABY', *nu7xh* 'baby'); and some undergo reduction (e.g. *xnuq* 'NOUN.CL:OLD.MAN:RESPECTFULLY', *xiinaq* 'old man'). The tendency appears for noun classifiers to become monosyllabic. In Chinantec (Foris 1993) phonological reduction is obligatory for some noun classifiers, but not for others: the derivation of $mɨ^3$ 'NOUN.CL:SPHERICAL.OBJECTS' from $mái^3$ 'sphere' involves vowel elision; while vowel and tone change in $mu^{21}/mĩ^1$ 'NOUN.CL:FLAT' from mu^{21} 'leaf' is optional. In contrast, numeral classifiers do not undergo phonological depletion, e.g. $mái^3$ 'NUM.CL:SPHERICAL.OBJECTS', from $mái^3$ 'sphere'. These examples show that phonological depletion is a tendency rather than the rule in grammaticalization.

13.5.2. Reanalysis in noun categorization

New noun classes often arise as the result of reanalysis of another grammatical category of the noun. These categories are typically the ones with which noun classes tend to interact (see Chapter 10). Noun classes often interrelate with number; the choice of number frequently depends on the animacy of the noun. In the Kiowa-Tanoan languages nouns have an inherent number which conditions the assignment of noun classes (Watkins 1984: 78, p.c.; §10.1; this is called 'spontaneous generation of categories' by Nichols 1992: 141). And see Corbett (1991: 198–9) on how new singular–plural pairings gave rise to new genders in Andi dialects (Northeast Caucasian).

The creation of a new agreement noun class via reinterpretation of number may go together with the reduction of a proto-system. Grebo, a Kru language from Africa, underwent a drastic reduction of the Proto-Kru system. Of four original singular classes, only two remain. The proto-human class *ɔ now also includes humans and important and valuable items, while proto-non-human *ɛ is restricted to small, unimportant, or worthless things (Marchese 1988: 329). In the plural there is an opposition of human (*o-*) and non-humans (*e-*). The disintegration of the Proto-Kru class system resulted in the creation of a 'new' singular–plural pairing and, consequently, of a new set of agreement classes—see Diagram 13.4.

	Singular	Plural
Humans }	ɔ	o
Important valuable non-humans }	}	e
Small worthless things	ɛ }	

DIAGRAM 13.4. *Singular and plural noun classes in Grebo*

CASE forms can be reanalysed so that new noun classes emerge. Slavic languages innovated a new subgender based on animacy. The development of a new declension pattern was due to the necessity to distinguish subject from object in those languages where constituent order was not used for marking grammatical relations (Comrie 1978). For most masculine nouns, the distinction between nominative and accusative was lost in the singular, and then the extension of genitive to accusative function allowed the distinction to be reintroduced. This happened first with masculine human nouns, and was then extended to all animate nouns (see Corbett 1991: 99). Other devices used for marking grammatical relations can be reinterpreted as gender markers. In Pre-Proto-Northern Iroquoian cross-referencing prefixes developed a human/non-human opposition (Chafe 1977: 505).

New gender oppositions can be created as the result of the reanalysis of DERIVATIONAL morphology. Indo-European languages originally had two genders: animate and inanimate (as preserved in Hittite). The feminine gender appeared later within animate through reanalysis of feminine derivational affixes -*a:* and *-*i:* (Meillet 1964; Brosman 1979, Melchert 1994).

There may be an expansion of already existing derivational suffixes. The South Dravidian subgroup of Proto-Dravidian (Krishnamurti forthcoming) innovated a gender distinction in personal pronouns by extending the feminine derivation suffix *-*al̲* which already existed in nominal morphology to the underlying pronominal root *aw; then the originally non-masculine human and non-human *atu was restricted just to non-human. Diagram 13.5 shows the Proto-Dravidian gender system (in singular number), and Diagram 13.6 shows the modified system in Proto-South-Dravidian.

Proto-form	**awan̲tu*	*atu
Meaning	masculine human	non-masculine human, non-human

DIAGRAM 13.5. *Gender in Proto-Dravidian (singular)*

Proto-form	**awan̲tu*	**awal̲*	*atu
Meaning	masculine human	feminine human	non-human

DIAGRAM 13.6. *Gender in Proto-South-Dravidian (singular)*

In Spanish, the reanalysis of a dialectal masculine form of the article *lo* may have given rise to the new neuter gender which is used for abstract nouns, e.g. *lo hermoso* 'the beautiful' (Posner 1966: 134). Reanalysis and subsequent grammaticalization can follow more complicated routes. In Yanyuwa (Australian), a noun classifier for edible vegetable class became a noun class prefix, as in other Australian languages. However, it involved an unusual case of reanalysis and subsequent grammaticalization. Yanyuwa is an ergative language; nouns in the function of the transitive subject take an ergative case suffix -*ŋgu*. When the 'food' class prefix *ma*- is added to a noun in ergative form it has the form *muŋgu*- (with vowel assimilation). We can hypothesize that originally a transitive subject NP consisted of generic *mayi* 'vegetable food' (the source for class prefix *ma*-) + ergative case *ŋgu*, and a specific noun + ergative case, and then *mayi+-ŋgu* was reinterpreted as a class marker, and underwent phonological reduction (Dixon 2002: 499–502).

Verbal classifiers emerged as the result of reanalysis in Imonda (Papuan: W. Seiler 1983; 1986). This language developed verbal classifiers out of desemanticized and often phonologically depleted first components of serial verb constructions (see §13.1.3). The classifier *fa* which is used as a generic classifier, arose as the result of reanalysis of the first syllable of the verb *fa-ka* 'give', and then became generalized as a classifier (W. Seiler 1986: 194–5).

When one kind of noun categorization device is lost in the evolution of a language it may be replaced by another, via reanalysis. Bengali lost its grammatical gender and number marking due to phonological coalescence of paradigms (Kölver 1982b; §13.6) and acquired numeral classifiers using, in part, the same morphological 'material'. The feminine gender marker *-i* in Old Indo-Aryan and New Indo-Aryan (see Chatterji 1926: 672 ff.; Kölver 1982b) became reanalysed as a diminutive used with numeral classifiers.[15]

13.6. Reduction and loss of noun categorization devices

Reduction and loss of noun categorization can be due to language-internal reasons. Noun classes can get reduced, and even lost—due to the coalescence of paradigms—for morphological and/or phonological reasons. This is typically found in fusional languages. Loss of noun classes is often accompanied by loss of number or case distinctions with which noun classes interacted.

In Indic and Iranian languages the masculine and feminine declensional paradigms merged. This resulted in a complete loss of gender oppositions in Assamese, Bengali, Nepali, Oriya, Persian, Beludzhi, and Ossete (see Kölver 1982b, for the history of Bengali). In the history of French, masculine and neuter endings merged in the period between the end of the fifth century and the end of the eleventh (Pope 1952); as the result, neuter gender was lost.[16]

---

[15] In other instances, the material used may be completely different, but the traces of the original system could still be felt. Kana (Kegboid, Cross River) lost a Proto-Cross-River noun class system, but acquired a typologically unusual set of numeral classifiers (see §4.2.3). We are not aware of a whole system of genders, or noun classes, developing into a classifier system. We predict that this is not likely to happen, since such a development would contradict the principle of unidirectionality in grammaticalization.

[16] The majority of neuter nouns became masculine (Posner 1966: 134–5). Certain Latin neuter nouns became masculine in some Romance languages and feminine in others. So, *mare* 'sea' became feminine in French *la mer* but masculine in Italian *il mare*, and Portuguese *o mar* (Posner 1966: 135). Even in Latin these nouns are sometimes treated as neuter, and sometimes

Morphological causes may contribute to the restructuring and loss of gender classes. Old English lost gender classes partly due to the convergence of inflections (genitive singular -*es*, originally only masculine and neuter, spread to feminine; and nominative-accusative plural -*as*, originally only masculine, spread to feminine and neuter) (see Dixon 1982: 171, and references therein). The loss of noun classes in Jukun (Central Jukunoid branch of Platoid; Benue-Congo, Niger-Congo: Storch 1997) was conditioned by word stem apocope and morphological reduction.

Coalescence of paradigms and the ensuing collapse of genders in Indo-European languages could be speeded up by the semantic opacity of gender. In most cases, the first gender to be lost appears to be neuter. The Sele Fara dialect of Slovene completely lost its third gender, neuter, in favour of masculine (Priestly 1983). The main mechanisms were phonological and analogical. The reduction of final unstressed -*o*, a nominative singular marker on neuter nouns, to ə followed by the regular loss of this short vowel accelerated their reinterpretation as masculine singular, e.g. *město > məstə > məst* 'town'. The nominative-accusative plural neuter ending in -*a* was reinterpreted as belonging to the feminine gender; later it was 'masculinized', too, by analogy with the masculine accusative plural. The neuter gender disappeared completely within three decades (Priestly 1983: 353–4).

Loss of genders can be due to the loss of formal markers. A number of North Arawak languages lost gender-sensitive pronominal cross-referencing suffixes, and this must have contributed to the overall loss of gender distinctions in Bare and Bahwana (Aikhenvald 1995a; Ramirez 1992).

Gender reduction may go together with the expansion of a functionally unmarked gender. In Kore, an Eastern Nilotic language, feminine is the unmarked gender. The feminine demonstrative has been generalized to refer to both masculine and feminine nouns (Gerrit Dimmendaal, p.c.). A similar expansion of the functionally unmarked masculine class in Mayali (Evans 1997 and ms) has led to the loss of agreement in one dialect of this language.

In languages with a distinction between noun classes on nouns and on pronouns, pronominal noun classes tend to be more conservative (Heine

---

as masculine. In Spanish 'sea' can be either masculine or feminine, with a subtle change in meaning: *el mar* means 'the sea as something difficult or foreboding', and *la mar* describes the sea as something pleasant and peaceful (Lyle Campbell, p.c.). In the history of Old French the neuter gender merged with masculine very early; some nouns became feminine (e.g. some plural neuter forms ending in -*a* were 'mistaken' for feminine, e.g. Latin *arma* 'arms' which became feminine in all Romance languages: Posner 1966: 134). Most changes occurred as the result of morphological and semantic analogy; thus, abstract nouns in -*orem* became feminine under the influence of other abstract nouns. Tree names in -*us* became masculine following masculine gender assignment of the ending -*us*; later *arbor* 'tree' also became masculine (Pope 1952: 304).

1982a: 214). Animere, a Togo Remnant language from Eastern Ghana, distinguishes two genders in personal pronouns; nominal genders have been lost (Heine 1982a: 207–8). Some Arawá languages of Southern Amazonia have lost the shape-based *ka-* noun class (see §2.7.2, for the discussion of Paumarí); but all of them still distinguish masculine and feminine genders. Pronominal genders tend to be more semantically transparent (see Chapter 2), possibly because pronouns frequently refer only to humans (this may be one of the factors which favour the retention of gender distinctions). (See §13.8.2, on the different ways in which noun class and gender agreement undergo loss depending on the target.)

Traces of old gender distinctions may 'survive' somewhere else in the grammar. Bengali reinterpreted the old feminine form in terms of its system of numeral classifiers (also see Barz and Diller 1985; Masa Onishi, p.c.). Kegboid languages, a subgroup of the Benue-Congo family spoken in Nigeria, lost Proto-Benue-Congo noun classes but acquired a peculiar system of numeral classifiers, an unusual phenomenon for African languages (Ikoro 1996a). A gender system can survive in the form of derivational-type affixes, as in the Australian languages Gunbarlang, Limilngan, Rembarrnga, and Nungali (Sands 1995: 269 ff.).

When classifier systems other than noun classes get reduced, classifiers for animates and humans appear to be more stable than others. Oceanic languages have a tendency to lose numeral classifiers. Fijian has only one remainder of a former system of numeral classifiers: *lewe*, used for counting humans (Churchward 1941: 44; Dixon 1988: 148). A comparison of traditional Malay classifiers and classifiers in Bahasa Indonesia (Conklin 1981: 211) shows that the human classifier (*orang*) and the animal classifier (*ekor*) are the most stable. Specific classifiers tend to disappear first. Classifiers for inanimates based on shape, function, and material tend to be replaced by the generic classifier *buah* previously used for round objects (Marnita 1996: 148–55; 165–6); specific classifiers, such as *lempeang* 'flat piece, traditionally used for pieces of tobacco, gold and dirt', are replaced by shape-based classifiers, such as *alai* 'flat'.

The system of noun classifiers became reduced in Acehnese (Durie 1985: 134–5) (especially if compared to the closely related Minangkabau: Marnita 1996); however, classifiers for person, plants and plant parts, birds and fishes are retained. (This is reminiscent of some recently acquired systems of noun classifiers, as in the case of Dâw, or Awa Pit. Noun classifiers are obligatory with persons and plants, and optional with other semantic groups.)

Loss of classifiers of other types has also been observed. However, it is not clear whether any of these were lost for phonological or morphological reasons. Many Athabaskan languages lost the verbal classifiers (traditionally referred to as 'genders') *d* 'round objects' and *n* 'long objects'. Only

Koyukon, Dena'ina, Tanana, Ahtna and Carrier retain productive verbal classifiers (Thompson 1993; Kari 1990; Bill Poser, p.c.; see above n. 10 to Chapter 6).

Many Oceanic languages have reduced the sphere of use of relational classifiers; some have eventually lost them. In Longgu, an Oceanic language spoken in the Solomon islands (Hill 1992), the relational classifiers, 'edible' and 'drinkable', are used only for predicative possession; even in this context they are frequently omitted (for an overview of systems of relational classifiers, see Lichtenberk 1983a). Many Oceanic languages lost *ma 'classifier for drinks', with *ka 'the classifier for food' replacing it. In some languages it happened the other way round: *ma replaced *ka as a marker of alimentary possession in general, as in Tabar, an Oceanic language spoken off New Ireland (Lichtenberk 1985: 118). These processes resulted in restructuring the composition of classes; some relational classifiers got lost as a result (Lynch 1992: 19–20).

According to Lynch (1992; 1993), one of the factors favouring simplification and, ultimately, even loss of relational classifiers could have been contacts with Papuan languages, especially in the case of the Austronesian languages spoken in the Solomons and in New Ireland (see (A) under §13.7.1). Takia (Karkar island: Bruce Waters, p.c.) has two sets of possessive affixes which are used interchangeably, thus having lost a distinction between relational classifiers.

13.7. Language-external motivations for the development and decay of noun categorization

Language-external motivations for the emergence of noun categorization devices include language contact, pidginization, creolization, and language obsolescence. The creation and restructuring of noun categorization often result from language contact (§13.7.1), while creolization and language obsolescence more often lead to their loss and reduction (§13.7.2 and §13.7.3). The impact different language external motivations can have on noun categorization is considered in §13.7.4.

Areal diffusion—in addition to direct borrowing—is often explicable by language contact in a bi- or multi-lingual situation. Borrowing usually takes place from a prestige language into languages with lesser prestige. This is an explanation offered for the penetration of Spanish into Quechua; Tucano into Tariana, or Malinke (Mande) loans into the minority language, Badyaranké (Northern subgroup of West Atlantic, spoken in Guinea Bissau: Ducos 1979). Or the linguistic group which provides the source of borrowing may just be more numerous, without having more prestige; this is the case of Baniwa and Kubeo discussed under A2 in (A),

§13.7.1. Direct diffusion is often limited because of prohibitions against lexical loans, as in the Vaupes region (see Aikhenvald 1996a). This is not the case in Australian languages.

Areal diffusion in Australian languages (as described by Heath 1978a; Evans ms, 1997; Harvey 1997; Dixon 1997; 2002: 25–6) could be of an entirely different nature. There, the linguistic systems have been in close contact for a long time, in a situation of equilibrium, with no special prestige or other social pressures. A different kind of reason for the borrowing of Bantu class prefixes into Ndunga-le—their phonological salience—was suggested by Pasch (1988: 59).[17]

13.7.1. Language contact and noun categorization

Structural changes induced by language contact may result in indirect diffusion of patterns and categories. Another possibility is straight borrowing of forms (see the notion of indirect diffusion vs. direct diffusion, or borrowing, in Heath 1978a; and the distinction between contact as a situation, and borrowing as a process in Harris and Campbell 1995: 122). Direct diffusion is more rarely the principal reason for the emergence of new noun categorization devices—or for the restructuring of the already existing ones—than is indirect diffusion. Indirect diffusion will be considered under (A), and direct diffusion, or borrowing, under (B) below.

(A) Indirect diffusion and noun categorization

Noun categorization devices can emerge under areal influence. Or an already existing system of noun categorization devices can change in a certain way, i.e., undergo reduction, augmentation, or restructuring under areal influence (cf. Nichols 1992: 139; Bisang 1996).

(A1) Creation of noun categorization systems The more lexico-syntactic the noun categorization is, the easier it is to diffuse. That is, the most frequently diffused new patterns involve syntactic constructions with classifiers which have a clear lexical source rather than with more grammaticalized noun class agreement systems. Possessed classifier constructions of the type generic noun plus possessed noun were borrowed from Carib languages into a number of North Arawak languages, e.g. Palikur, Island Carib, and Bahwana (see Aikhenvald and Green 1998). In the South Asian

---

[17] Recently a number of universal claims have been proposed concerning grammatical borrowing (see the exposition and criticism in Campbell 1993; Harris and Campbell 1995: 120–41). The data on language external sources for noun categorization systems confirm some of these principles, e.g. the structural compatibility requirement. However, some data discussed below provide a counterexample to these universal tendencies, e.g. the example from Ayacucho Quechua where gender agreement has been borrowed goes against the statement that 'free-standing grammatical forms are more easily borrowed than bound morphemes'.

linguistic area numeral classifiers have been shown to have spread from the Indo-Aryan languages of the region to Dravidian languages (Emeneau 1964: 644–50).

Indirect diffusion of closed grammatical systems is rarer. Kakua, a Makú language spoken in the Vaupes region, is the only language in the family to have a feminine/non-feminine gender distinction in 3rd person independent pronouns and subject prefixes. This language underwent strong areal influence from neighbouring East Tucano languages; it is likely that Kakua acquired gender under areal influence from East Tucano (Martins and Martins 1999). The Oceanic languages spoken in Southwest New Britain are likely to have acquired incipient gender distinctions under the influence of surrounding Papuan languages (Malcolm Ross, p.c.).[18]

Noun categorization devices are often so much a feature of a linguistic area that it is difficult to establish the direction of diffusion—i.e. which languages got them first. This is the case in Mesoamerica (Campbell et al. 1986: 550), in the Caribbean area (Costenla Umaña 1991), and in the linguistic area of East and Mainland Southeast Asia (Bisang 1996). Shape-based genders in particular, and other kinds of gender marking, are likely to be an areal feature of the Sepik river basin in New Guinea (Foley 1986: 265); however, the source of diffusion is impossible to establish.[19]

(A2) Restructuring of noun categorization Indirect areal diffusion may result in the partial restructuring of classifier systems. This involves introducing new classifier types into a system which already has classifiers. Kubeo, a Central Tucano language spoken in a community bilingual in an Arawak language, Baniwa, uses classifiers with verbs following the pattern found in Baniwa (Gomez-Imbert 1996: 451).

Tariana extended the use of classifiers to demonstratives under the areal influence of East Tucano languages in the context of obligatory multilingualism in the Vaupes river basin. In Arawak languages (for example, the closely related Baniwa) spoken outside the Vaupes area, demonstratives distinguish only feminine and non-feminine forms. Example 13.9 is from Tariana. A classifier of a repeater type *panisi* 'house' is attached to the demonstrative. The same technique can be observed in 13.10, from Tucano.

---

[18] It is possible that Eastern Nilotic languages (Turkana, Teso, Lotuko, Maa) acquired their gender structures due to areal influence of neighbouring Niger-Congo languages (Heine 1982a: 215).

[19] In these cases it is hard to decide whether shared classifiers or genders are due to areal diffusion or are inherited. This throws doubt on the suggestion by Nichols and Peterson (1998: 612) that 'the presence of numeral classifiers is among the genetically most stable of features' (cf. also Nichols 1997).

13.9. ha-panisi
DEM:INAN-HOUSE
'this (house)'

13.10. ati-wi'i
DEM:INAN-HOUSE
'this (house)'

In contrast, Baniwa uses a non-feminine form of a demonstrative, as in *hliehẽ panṭi* (DEM:NF house) 'this house.' A similar expansion of classifiers onto demonstratives took place in Resígaro, another North Arawak language, which is in close contact with Bora and Ocaina (Bora-Witoto family). Like Tucano languages, but unlike Arawak, Bora also has classifiers used with demonstratives (Thiesen 1996; Allin 1975; Aikhenvald 2001).

Reduction and augmentation of gender and noun class systems often happen through diffusion in Australian languages. In Mayali (Arnhem Land, Australia) the southwestern dialect has become more like its neighbour Jawoyn, with only three instead of four agreement classes, and the easternmost dialect has become more like their neighbours Rembarrnga and Dangbon, both of which lack noun class agreement (Evans 1997; cf. Harvey 1997).

Changes in the composition of noun classes, or in classifier assignment can be accounted for by areal diffusion. In Tariana all animals are classified as 'animate non-feminine', under the influence of the Tucano languages. In Baniwa, Tariana's close relative, animals are classified according to their shape (e.g. a jaguar is classified as vertical, and a bird is classified as concave, or banana-shaped). Kubeo is a Tucano language which has been in close contact with Baniwa for a long time; in this language animals have come to be classified according to their shape, just like in Baniwa (Gomez-Imbert 1996).

Language contact can affect principles of gender assignment, without changing the number of genders or their composition. For example, in Western Oromo dialects the system of gender assignment became semantically transparent (with feminine as the gender for diminutives and masculine as the unmarked one) under the influence of other Lowland East Cushitic languages, and of Arabic (Clamons 1995).

A language can acquire a system of noun classes via grammaticalization of classifiers under areal pressure. Yanyuwa (Australian) is spoken on the edge of the region whose languages have prefixes and noun classes; both features have recently diffused into Yanyuwa (Dixon 2002: 499–502, 663–4). It has acquired a system of seven noun classes marked by prefixes (Kirton 1971: 20, 38). At least some of these are the result of typical

Australian grammaticalization of noun classifiers into noun class markers, e.g. *ma-* 'food', from *mayi* 'edible vegetable' (see §13.4).

(A3) Reduction of noun categorization Language contact can result in the reduction of noun categorization. The Minangkabau spoken by the younger generation tends to reduce the system of numeral classifiers to make it similar to Bahasa Indonesia in which virtually all Minangkabau speakers are bilingual. The number of numeral classifiers commonly used in Bahasa Indonesia (as compared to traditional Malay) has been drastically reduced during the course of this century, after it became the national language, possibly, due to the influence of Javanese and English (Conklin 1981: 201; also see §12.3).

It has also been observed that mensural classifiers tend to undergo more dramatic reduction in the speech of younger people than sortal classifiers. This is due to the fact that mensural classifiers often refer to culture-specific arrangements and measures, and the obsolescence of cultural knowledge inevitably leads to their loss (Marnita 1996, for Minangkabau; Lee 1997, for Korean; also see Sanches 1977, for Japanese).

An example of the loss of a multiple classifier system as the result of areal diffusion comes from Retuarã, a Central Tucano language which is in contact with Yucuna, a North Arawak language. Yucuna has the typical Arawak opposition of two genders, and a small system of numeral classifiers. Under pressure from Yucuna, Retuarã lost the typical Tucano multiple classifier system, preserving just a gender system (inanimate, masculine and feminine) (Strom 1992: 45–50; Gomez-Imbert 1996: 445).[20]

(B) Direct diffusion and noun categorization

We have no example of a complete system of noun categorization being borrowed. However, parts of a system have been borrowed in different parts of the world.

According to Heath (1978a: 88), 'the spread of noun-class systems over much of north-central and north-western Australia may well have been largely accomplished through direct diffusion of the actual affixes, rather than by independent development in each language group'. This is especially conspicuous in the cases where there is no internal etymology available for noun class affixes in a language; but these are available in a neighbouring language. As Heath (1978a: 88) puts it, 'while in some languages a correlation can be made between some noun-class affixes and particular noun stems (for example, *ma-* as a non-human noun-class prefix and a stem like *mayi* meaning "vegetable food"), this is not possible

---

[20] Reduction of large classifier sets as the result of language attrition has been reported by Wurm (1992a, for Reef-Santa Cruzan languages). These languages are in the process of losing verbal classifiers but not classifiers in other contexts (Stephen Wurm, p.c.).

in Nunggubuyu, Ngandi and Warndarang. There is consequently a strong probability that the noun-class systems in these languages were borrowed from languages to the west.' Furthermore, Warndarang borrowed non-human prefixes for three classes from Ngandi or from pre-Nunggubuyu (Heath 1978a: 90–1).

Another example of a massive borrowing of noun class markers which resulted in the restructuring of a system comes from Africa (Pasch 1988). Ndunga-le, a Mba language from Ubangi, an Eastern subgroup of Niger-Congo, has an original system of six singular and three plural noun classes. There are over fifty non-borrowed nouns which also contain singular and plural noun class prefixes borrowed from the neighbouring Bantu languages; in some cases the first syllable of a borrowed noun was reanalysed as a noun class prefix (Pasch 1988: 58).

Resígaro, a North Arawak language which underwent drastic restructuring under the influence of the genetically unrelated Bora, borrowed a large number of grammatical morphemes (Aikhenvald 2001). Bora influence on the Resígaro classifiers involves borrowing of bound morphemes, and grammaticalization of borrowed free morphemes as classifiers. Resígaro has around fifty-six classifiers (Allin 1975: 154 ff.), of which thirty-six have been borrowed from Bora. Some classifiers which correspond to bound morphemes in Bora, e.g. Resígaro *-gú* 'long and flat', Bora *-k^waá* (classifier which appears in words for 'finger', 'toe'); Proto-Bora-Muinane *-gai* (Aschmann 1993: 131). Other classifiers in Resígaro correspond to bound morphemes and to free morphemes in Bora. In Resígaro, a classifier of a Bora origin may be attached to the noun of Arawak origin, e.g. Resígaro classifier *-mi* 'canoe' in *hiítá-mi*[21] 'canoe' (also used as a classifier in Bora: *-mɨ* 'canoe; other transport'— Thiesen 1996: 102—and as a root in Bora *mɨɨ-ne* 'canoe', cf. Proto-Bora-Muinane **mɨɨ-ne*—Aschmann 1993: 136). Classifiers which correspond to free morphemes in Bora include some for body parts, e.g. Resígaro *-ʔosí* 'cl: hand', singulative *-ké-ʔosí* 'hand' (Resígaro *-ké* from Proto-Arawak **kapi*: Payne 1991a); Bora *hojtsɨɨ* 'hand', Proto-Bora-Muinane *-ʔóxtsɨɨ* 'hand'. The extensive borrowing of classifiers in almost all the semantic fields can be explained by the important role classifiers play in discourse: once the referent is established it is referred to with a classifier, so that classifiers appear to be more frequent in discourse than nouns themselves.[22]

---

[21] Cf. the cognates of Resígaro *hiitu/hiita* in Arawak languages: Bare *isa*, Achagua *iida*, Tariana *ita(-whya)*, Baniwa *ita*, Piapoco *ída*, Yucuna *hiita*.

[22] Languages with no gender or noun class distinction may acquire a gender-marking derivational suffix via borrowing and reanalysis. Finnish and Estonian acquired a feminine derivational suffix, Finnish *-ttare/-ttäre*, Estonian *-tar* from the reanalysis of the word for 'daughter' (*tytär*), itself reportedly borrowed from Baltic (Lithuanian/Latvian); this grammaticalization may have been motivated by matching the feminine suffix in German (Lyle

Borrowing of an agreement system is extremely rare. One such example comes from Ayacucho Quechua (see §2.4.4). A similar example comes from Ilocano (Austronesian: Rubino 1997: 138–9). Similarly to many other Austronesian languages, Ilocano does not have grammatical gender; however, a large number of loan adjectives from Spanish resulted in the creation of masculine and feminine distinctions in loan adjectives, e.g. *tsismoso* 'gossipy' (masc.), *tsismosa* 'gossipy' (fem.), from Spanish *chismoso, chismosa* 'a gossip, gossipy'. Nouns borrowed from Spanish often have two gender forms to distinguish the sexes, e.g. *kosinero* 'cook (masc.)', *kosinera* 'cook (fem.)', *sugalero* 'gambler (masc.)', *sugalera* 'gambler (fem.)' (Rubino 1997: 75).

Reduction of an agreement system and of noun class marking may be due to massive borrowing. Ducos (1979) describes the loss of the Proto-Gur noun class system in Badyaranké. This loss may be due to massive lexical borrowing from Malinke, a Mande language which has been the language of prestige among Badyaranké for 500 or 600 years. Lexical borrowing of prefixless nouns led to the loss of derivational—and then of agreement—functions of noun classes.

13.7.2. Creolization and noun categorization

The REDUCTION and LOSS of class/gender distinctions is a universal feature of the pidginization and creolization of languages (Heine and Reh 1984: 42). Indo-European-based creole languages do not have any gender distinctions; and there are no genders in the Nubi language of Kibera, an Arabic-based creole (Heine 1982b). In pidginized Hausa the loss of gender led to the replacement of feminine gender markers by masculine ones (which are functionally unmarked). Similar examples have been observed in Kenya Pidgin Swahili (Heine and Reh 1984: 42; see also Alexandre 1968: 280). Noun class systems in Lingala and Zairian Swahili were simplified due to the influence of non-Bantu languages and creolization processes (see Bokamba 1977; Helma Pasch, p.c.); this simplification has to do with the reduction of agreement domains (see §13.8.2). Kinshasa Lingala, which originally developed as a trade language, is moving towards a unified plural marking, whereby the plural marked with *ba-* (Class 1a) is extended to all nouns, even those that belong to other classes. Kituba, a creole spoken in

Campbell, p.c.). Limited borrowing of gender-marking derivational morphemes is also found in languages with agreement gender systems (see Pasch 1988: 60 for more examples of borrowing noun class affixes whereby they usually lose their primary meaning). The Berber languages of Central Morocco have gender-differentiated compounds with the first component borrowed from Arabic; the second component does not have to be borrowed, e.g. *bu* (from Arabic *bu* 'father, man of . . .') in *bu uḥam* 'master of the house' (Laoust 1928: 14–15). All gender-indicating suffixes in Turkish are borrowed from languages with grammatical gender, such as Arabic (*-e*) and Slavic (*-içe*) (Braun forthcoming b).

southern Zaire and derived from Kikongo, is evolving just one plural marking thus eliminating the traditional one-to-one singular-plural noun class correspondence and contributing to the overall disintegration of the noun class system (Stucky 1978). A similar situation is found in Fanagalo, a Bantu-based creole spoken in Botswana (Anderson and Janson 1997: 183).

Most creoles and pidgins have no numeral classifiers (even if they are surrounded by classifier languages).[23] The Russian-Chinese pidgin spoken in Harbin (northeastern China) in the early twentieth century had no numeral classifiers (Johanna Nichols, p.c.).

An instructive example of language change in the context of partial creolization and language shift comes from Modern Tiwi spoken by about 1500 people on Melville and Bathurst Islands in the far north of Australia. The Tiwi community has undergone rapid changes during the last few decades through contact with European-Australian culture (Lee 1987: 9). Traditional Tiwi, which is still one of the four language codes used in the community, underwent a restructuring which is described as 'creolization' as it became Modern Tiwi, or 'anglicised' Tiwi (Lee 1987: 10).[24] Traditional Tiwi distinguishes two genders, masculine and feminine. Gender is assigned on the basis of sex and physical size (masculine referents are considered narrow and small, feminine ones wide and large: see Table 11.1; gender assignment is, however, not transparent, e.g. all trees are feminine whatever their size) (Osborne 1974: 51). Young people and children tend to assign gender on the basis of natural sex, and are inconsistent in gender assignment to nouns other than those denoting humans and dogs (Lee 1987: 84). The feminine form of an adjective and of possessive pronouns is used with any referent, as the unmarked choice in a noun phrase (Lee 1987: 92–3, 109, 243).[25] Modern Tiwi also tends to systematically distinguish just human/non-human, instead of the erstwhile masculine/feminine.

13.7.3. Language obsolescence and noun categorization

LOSS or REDUCTION of noun classes is often observed in language obsolescence. These processes are often accelerated by patterns which exist in a dominant language, due to bilingualism.

---

[23] The only example of a creole language with numeral classifiers appears to be Chacabano Zamboangueño, a Spanish-based creole spoken in the Philippines (Carl Rubino, p.c.).

[24] Whether Modern Tiwi is an example of a creole or not is still an open question—see the excellent analysis of this problem in Lee (1987: 355–7). She arrives at a preliminary conclusion that Modern Tiwi appears to be 'a creolised form of an anglicised Baby (Talk) Tiwi'. 'In the development of M(odern) T(iwi), children (and adults to a certain extent) have drawn upon Tiwi, English, and Pidgin English, to produce a hybrid or amalgam' (Lee 1987: 357).

[25] Another factor which might have contributed to some loss of gender agreement in Tiwi could have been phonological reduction, as compared to traditional Tiwi (see Lee 1987: 118, 145).

Traditional Dyirbal had four semantically assigned noun classes (§2.4.1). Young People's Dyirbal has gradually simplified its noun class system so that it became similar to the way *he, she, it* are used in English. The noun class referring to 'non-flesh food' was lost. The scope of noun Class 2 was reduced and came to be reserved only for females (it used to include water, fire, and things associated with fighting). Gender assignment by mythical association was lost; exceptions became regularized; and the use of the residue class was expanded (Schmidt 1985). Dahalo (Cushitic) is losing ground to Swahili, and is accordingly losing the common Cushitic distinction of masculine and feminine gender (Dimmendaal p.c.).

Loss and restructuring of gender distinctions among semi-speakers in a situation of language attrition has been observed for Scottish Gaelic (Dorian 1981: 124–9, 147–8). Gaelic has masculine and feminine genders marked by initial mutation of the noun after the definite article by agreement of an attributive adjective (by initial mutation), by the form of the definite article, and by the form of pronouns; there is also a gender-marked diminutive suffix. In personal pronouns, there is a tendency to extend the masculine pronoun *a* to all inanimate nouns (Dorian 1981: 125). Adjective agreement via consonantal lenition shows considerable variation. Gender marking on nouns remains very strong. However, since only a subclass of nouns can be diminutivized, and there are phonological limitations of head-marking gender lenition, it appears that even for fluent speakers the gender system has become more limited in its application (Dorian 1981: 129).

Dorian (1981: 148) predicts that if Eastern Sutherland Gaelic had 'future generations of fluent speakers', gender marking in pronouns and agreement on adjectives 'would surely disappear', but head-marking gender on nouns would survive, 'producing a kind of lexicalization of gender specification linked to specific nouns'. That head-marking noun classes appear to be more persistent than noun class agreement, may be related to the differences in 'speed' of obsolescence of grammar and of the lexicon; see §13.8.2.

Language attrition does not necessarily result in loss of noun class. Rather, an endangered language may try and assimilate its gender patterns to the dominant language. In Arvanitika, an endangered dialect spoken by Albanians who immigrated to Greece in the eleventh and fifteenth centuries, the three genders remain distinct. This may be due to the fact that the three-way gender distinctions in Arvanitika and Greek are structurally similar (Trudgill 1977: 35; Sasse 1985). In contrast, the gender systems of Gaelic and English, or Dyirbal and English, are quite different; the result is a drastic reduction of the system in the obsolescent language.

Language obsolescence often results in the obsolescence of numeral classifiers if the dominant language does not have them. Warekena (North Arawak: Aikhenvald 1998b) is in the process of being replaced by Língua

Geral (Tupí-Guaraní) and by Portuguese; it has almost lost its numeral classifiers. Some northern Australian languages display loss and obsolescence of verb-incorporated and numeral classifiers due to language contact. Modern Tiwi, as compared to Traditional Tiwi (Lee 1987: 318), has lost 'virtually all incorporated forms', and, consequently, verbal classifiers, as the result of an overall simplification of the verbal structure.

Partial language obsolescence may result in the restructuring of a classifier system (see §13.7.1, on the reduction of classifier inventory in Minangkabau to make it more similar to the dominant Indonesian language).

13.7.4. Language-external motivations and their impact on noun categorization

Language contact, creolization, and language obsolescence show a few notable differences in their impact on noun categorization. Creolization typically leads to the LOSS or drastic REDUCTION of noun categorization. Language contact may lead to the CREATION of a new system, or to its RESTRUCTURING. Language obsolescence results in LOSS or RESTRUCTURING of noun categorization according to the pattern present in the dominant language. While 'dying languages . . . show much the same sorts of change we are familiar with from perfectly ordinary change in "healthy languages"' (Dorian 1981: 151), they tend to restructure their noun categorization devices according to the patterns found in the dominant language.[26] Another distinguishing feature of change in language obsolescence and creolization is its speed: drastic grammatical restructuring sometimes happens within a short timespan (see Schmidt 1985: 213, on Young People's Dyirbal); areal diffusion within linguistic areas is usually slower (Aikhenvald 1996a).[27]

13.8. Development and loss of agreement

13.8.1. The genesis and development of agreement

The two types of agreement considered in §2.4, (a) agreement of the predicate with its arguments, and (b) head-modifier agreement within an NP, develop in different ways.

---

[26] Development in language obsolescence also differs from normal historical development for a 'healthy' language in that it is modelled on a dominant pattern while normal diachronic change is not (cf. Campbell and Muntzel 1989; Sasse 1992).
[27] In all the examples so far, the dominant language has had a smaller system of classifiers. We have no clear examples in which it is the other way round; see discussion in Aikhenvald (2001).

(A) Predicate-argument agreement

VERBAL agreement usually arises from an anaphorically-used independent pronoun which is subsequently cliticized to the verb; it then becomes incorporated as an agreement marker. The mechanism is basically pragmatic, and it involves reanalysis and grammaticalization of independent members of a closed class. This happened in Manambu (Ndu); see also the examples in Lehmann (1982) and Corbett (1991: 137–9).[28]

Properties associated with discourse-topic NPs have also played an important role in the development of subject–verb agreement in Arabic (Russell 1984). There is no regular etymological relationship between the verb agreement affixes and anaphoric pronouns in Semitic languages. Person-, number-, and gender-sensitive agreement suffixes (used in the perfect) seem to have originated from nominal and adjectival inflections. Verb-argument agreement emerged as the result of the expansion of agreement markers from head-modifier type constructions to other construction types.[29]

(B) Head-modifier agreement within a noun phrase

For the development of gender agreement within a noun phrase two mechanisms have been proposed by Heine and Reh (1984: 230–1). Agreement may arise if demonstratives develop into subordination markers, e.g. relative clause markers, as the result of their grammaticalization. Given that relative constructions are an important strategy for forming nominal qualifiers, they may become the main source for gender agreement. Example 13.11, from Maasai, an Eastern Nilotic language, shows how relative clause markers are used to 'introduce nominal qualifiers' (Heine and Reh 1984: 231).

13.11. in-kíshú   na-á-pishana   na-á-íbɔr
       PL-cattle   REL-PL-seven   REL-PL-be.white
       'seven white cows'

In Eastern Nilotic languages gender marking did not affect personal

---

[28] Grammaticalization of agreement goes together with a conflation of topic marking and of grammatical marking of a constituent. Givón (1976: 151) remarks: 'when a language reanalyses the topic constituent as the normal subject or object of the neutral, non-topicalised sentence pattern, it perforce also has reanalyzed subject-topic agreement as subject agreement and object-topic agreement as object agreement.' Bresnan and McChombo (1986) offer a theoretical discussion of the relation between anaphora and agreement and suggest possible steps by which such a historical sequence might take place.

[29] Lehmann (1988: 59–60) suggests that agreement of the verb-argument type (external agreement), and agreement of the head-modifier type (internal agreement) originate in different sorts of pronoun: the former comes from anaphoric pronouns, and the latter from personal pronouns. In §13.2, we have seen that noun class agreement markers can originate in classifiers or pronouns which were also used anaphorically.

pronouns, and did not lead to the emergence of verbal agreement. However, it is important to note that, since there is a widely used grammaticalization mechanism involving development from demonstratives to 3rd person pronouns, the demonstrative gender distinction may well spread to personal pronouns as well, and subsequently give rise to gender agreement by the mechanism referred to above (Givón 1976).[30]

Another path for creating gender agreement involves the pragmatic use of 3rd person pronouns[31] as a kind of 'afterthought' to specify additional information. This development is described for Khoe, a Central Khoisan language, by Heine and Reh (1984: 232–4; see also Heine 1997b). The original 3rd person pronouns which distinguish three genders (masculine, feminine, and common) and three numbers (singular, dual, and plural) gave rise to gender and number agreement. The interrogative mã/mà- may be used on its own, e.g. mã hĩ-nyè-tã (who do-JUNCTURE-ASPECT) 'Who has done it?'. However, it is frequently followed by gender-sensitive personal pronouns to narrow the range of possible referents, e.g. mà-má (who-3sg.masc) 'who?' (male referent), mà-hè (who-3sg.fem) 'who?' (female referent). This kind of structure, in which a gender sensitive pronoun is used to emphasize the gender of the referent, is used with other word classes, too. This has resulted in the creation of agreement constructions, illustrated in 13.12.

13.12. xá-mà   mà-má   á-mà
       DEM-3SG.MASC   who-3SG.MASC   DEM-3SG.MASC
       'Who (male) is this?'

(C) Further evidence in favour of the independent development of predicate-argument and head-modifier agreement

The thesis of independent development of agreement on verbs and within noun phrases is corroborated by the existence of 'split' agreement systems (see §2.7). In these systems an argument agrees with its predicate, and the head noun agrees with its modifiers, for different categories. Since verbal agreement markers often originate in anaphorically used demonstratives or 3rd person pronouns, and these are more prone to have a small number of animacy-related gender categories, it is then understandable why in split systems the gender agreement is preferred on verbs, and largeish noun classes and classifiers are used to mark agreement with other targets (see Table 2.10 above). In addition, predicate-argument and head-modifier agreement markers behave differently in language evolution and

---

[30] This process seems to have just started in some Eastern Nilotic languages, e.g. Bari and Toposa—see Heine and Reh (1984: 231, n. 1).
[31] Note that the noun class agreement markers can also develop from lexical sources, e.g. nouns, or noun classifiers via their pronominalization (see §13.1).

in obsolescence. In Warekena and Bare, two endangered North Arawak languages from the North Amazon, gender agreement is maintained in predicate-argument contexts but lost from adjectival modifiers and from some demonstratives.[32]

(D) Head-class or agreement class?

A generic noun classifier can first develop to be an overt noun class marker on the head noun, via cliticization and phonological reduction, and then to be an agreement marker. An alternative scenario would involve cliticization of a generic noun to a modifier which immediately results in the creation of an agreement system. This scenario has been suggested for the development of the Ngan'gityemerri noun class system by Reid (1997: 215–17).

Stage 1: The precursor to the development of agreement: generic-specific 'pairing' of nouns as a common construction type, as in 13.13.

13.13. gagu   wamanggal kerre   ngeben-da
       animal   wallaby   big   1sGS+AUX-shoot
       'I shot a big wallaby.'

Stage 2: the generics are independent words, often favoured over specifics especially to maintain reference; as a result, one can get a noun phrase made up of a generic noun plus a modifier, as in 13.14.

13.14. gagu   kerre   ngeben-da
       animal   big   1sGS+AUX-shoot
       'I shot a big [wallaby].'

Stage 3: where specific nouns are included, both the specific noun and modifiers tend to 'attract' generics. This 'repetition' of generics is the predecessor of agreement, as in 13.15.

13.15. gagu   wamanggal gagu   kerre   ngeben-da
       animal   wallaby   animal   big   1sGS+AUX-shoot
       'I shot a big wallaby.'

Stage 4: Repeated generic nouns cliticize to the following specific nouns, and undergo phonological reduction. They are reduced to proclitics and develop into agreement noun class markers, as in 13.16.

13.16. wa=ngurmumba   wa=ngayi   darany-fipal-nyine
       male=youth   male=big   3sGS+AUX-return-FOCUS
       'My initiand son has just returned.'

---

[32] The genesis of 'agreement'-type phenomena in verb-incorporated classifiers has been explained by Mithun (1986: 384). Incorporation resulted in lexicalization of compounds, and then external arguments were added to specify the meaning.

Stage 5: Noun class marking proclitics become obligatory prefixes in head class and agreement class functions. They become more fused with the stem (e.g. a series of morphological processes start applying on the boundaries). At this stage, they become fully grammaticalized (note that - stands for an affix boundary, and = for a clitic boundary).

13.17. wú-pidìrri   wu=mákarri
       CANINE-dingo   CANINE-bad
       'a bad dog'

Stage 6: There is now 'prefix absorption' which implies the lexicalization of head class prefixes. Some noun class prefixed roots may be interpreted as stems which can take further noun class marking (Reid 1997). This may lead to double class marking, e.g. *wa-mumu* (male-police) 'policeman'; *wur-wa-mumu* (female-male-police) 'policewoman'. (Historically, this may lead to loss of head-class marking prefixes once they become fused with the stem. This may, or may not affect agreement; see below.)

This scenario is not applicable to other prefixing Australian languages with noun classes, where class markers have typically come from a variety of sources—such as generics and 3rd singular pronouns (see Dixon 2002: 497–506). The typical developmental scenario in Australian languages is for pronominal prefixes to first develop on verbs, and then, at a slightly later stage (and in just some languages) for the prefixing profile to be extended to nouns through development of noun class prefixes. Indirectly, this confirms the idea of relatively independent development of agreement on verbs, and within a noun phrase.

A different scenario applies to Dyirbal, an Australian language with no prefixes, where some noun classes developed out of generics. Generic nouns have become suffixes to modifiers, i.e. deictics and determiners.[33] The following stages in the development can be suggested:

Stage 1: Generic-specific pairings.

Stage 2: Constituent order being 'Demonstrative Generic Specific' generics become cliticized to prehead modifiers (they cannot become prefixes because there is no prefix slot available).

Stage 3: Cliticized generics become suffixes to prehead demonstratives, and undergo phonological reduction. This is how agreement arises.

In this case, the development of agreement classes does not presuppose previous existence of head classes. This is corroborated by further observations.

Firstly, there is often a certain mismatch between 'head' classes and

---

[33] A similar scenario could apply to Bandjalang (Crowley 1978; Dixon 2002: 464–6).

'agreement' classes in Australian languages (e.g. examples in §2.4.3). This may indicate their different relative age. In Mayali, nouns with animate reference trigger agreement according to the sex of the referent, and it may be different from the noun class prefix which appears on the noun itself (see §2.4.3). !Xóõ, a Southern Khoisan language, has five noun classes (Traill 1994: 20–2). They are marked by suffixes on nouns and also realized in agreement on various targets (adjectives, relativizers, object markers). Noun suffixes bear a strong phonological similarity to agreement markers; an example of such an 'alliterative' concord is given in 13.18 (= 2.14). Noun class markers are underlined (only nouns from classes one to four may be head-marked; if they are not, the concord is not alliterative).

13.18. ñ à |nà-i̱ |à-i̱   !xà-i̱   t-i̱
       I past   see-NCL1:O   lion-NCL1   big-NCL1   which-NCL1
       |'âa |ìi   k-i̱
       dead   is   which-NCL1
       'I saw a large dead lion'

Second, some languages have no head classes, just agreement classes. This is the case with gender marking in many Papuan and Amazonian languages, especially those with multiple classifier systems, and in some Australian languages (e.g. Gaagudju and Ungarinjin). We saw in §9.1 that in some languages of northwest Amazonia which mark noun class on the head noun, this marking has a different semantic effect than agreement class marking: it is associated with the countability and individuation of the noun, e.g. Tariana *deri* 'banana: collective', *deri-pi* (banana-CL:LONG) 'banana tree', *deritfi* (banana+CL:BUNDLE) 'banana bundle'. Head classes and agreement classes are acquired by children at different rates (see Tsonope 1988, and Chapter 14 below).

The loss of overt gender marking on nouns does not necessarily precede the loss of gender agreement. It can be argued that coalescence of nominal paradigms with their overt gender marking triggered the overall gender loss in some Indo-European languages. However, in Old Iranian the overt marking of masculine and neuter gender on nouns was lost, but agreement on modifiers remained intact.

Lower Cross languages largely lost head-class marking, but there are remnants of agreement on adjectives and verbs (Faraclas 1989: 390–1). In Albanian neuter gender seems to have been lost from adjectives, and not from nouns (Priestly 1983; Hamp 1958).

We conclude that there is not enough general evidence in favour of the primacy of development either of head classes or of agreement classes. At least in some cases, the two could have developed independently.

(E) Expansion of agreement

Once an agreement system has been established, it can be expanded to other targets. The expansion can occur under areal influence.[34] A dialect of German, spoken in Canton Wallis in Switzerland, close to French-speaking regions, acquired agreement between nouns and predicative adjectives, under French influence (Edgar Suter, p.c.).

A possible source for the expansion of agreement could be alliterative agreement, or repetition. Repeaters are a frequently-used source for ad hoc classifiers which then get grammaticalized and restricted to usage with a particular group of nouns. In Tariana, *ehkwapi* 'day; something that appears during the day', was first used as a repeater, to classify the same noun, e.g. *ehkwapi matʃa-ehkwapi* (day nice-NCL:REPEATER:DAY) 'a nice day'. Then it was extended to mark agreement with several nouns referring to natural phenomena, e.g. *enukwa matʃa-ehkwapi* (sky nice-NCL:DAY) 'nice, clear sky', *de:pi matʃa-ehkwapi* (night nice-NCL:DAY) 'nice, clear night'.[35]

Noun class agreement on different targets may have different origins. In some Mindi languages (Australian: Nordlinger 1998: 262–3; I. Green 1995) noun class is marked on case suffixes, while in another Mindi language noun class is marked on case prefixes; demonstratives have noun class prefixes in all the languages. Dixon (2002: 503–4) reconstructs the following scenario for the development of noun class agreement in these languages.

(i) There would have first evolved markers—separate words or clitics attached to some word in a noun phrase—that combined information about noun class and about case (possibly, from an earlier classifier-plus-case).

(ii) These markers then attached to demonstratives as prefixes; this is why all the Mindi languages have noun class prefixes on demonstratives.

(iii) At a later stage, in the Eastern Mindi branch the case-class markers became enclitics to a noun phrase and then suffixes; after that they became obligatory suffixes to both nouns and adjectives. In one West Mindi language, Nungali, the case-class markers became proclitics to a noun phrase

---

[34] In multiple classifier systems, it is often hard to show which target developed first. In some cases development of new agreement targets was triggered by areal diffusional patterns. This is the case for classifiers used on demonstratives in Resígaro (under Bora and Ocaina influence), and in Tariana (under Tucano influence), mentioned in §13.7.

[35] In many languages of the world repetition of a constituent is a syntactic and pragmatic device for emphasis, e.g. English *this table is a big table*. The difference between these syntactic constructions, and 'repetition' as an agreement device in Tariana is that repeaters used as classifiers in Tariana form a part of a corresponding grammatical word; also, unlike the syntactic constructions in English repeater phenomena represent obligatory agreement. Repetition as an agreement device may come from grammaticalization of constructions like the English one above (see §13.1.2, on repeaters and the origin of noun categorization).

and then prefixes to nominal modifiers such as adjectives (being later generalized to also apply to some, but not all, nouns).

13.8.2. Decline and loss of agreement

The decline and loss of agreement is in no way the mirror image of its rise and evolution since it happens for different reasons. As with the loss of noun categorization devices, (A) it can take place due to language-internal reasons, and (B) it may happen differently on different targets. Agreement can be affected by language-external phenomena—language contact, creolization and language obsolescence (C).

(A) Decline and loss of agreement for language-internal reasons

Agreeement may be lost due to a merger of paradigms because of a sound change. For instance, in Lower Cross languages (Benue-Congo: Faraclas 1989: 390–1) overt marking of noun classes was lost due to the assimilation of prefix vowels, and the loss of CV prefixes; this contributed to the loss of agreement classes.

It can also happen via morphological analogy, as in many Indo-European languages (Priestly 1983). Loss of concord is one of the reasons for—or concomitant effects of—gender loss. The loss of gender in Old English is partly due to the loss of agreement with adjectives and demonstratives (Dixon 1982: 171 and references therein).

(B) Decline and loss of agreement on different targets

Gender and gender agreement are most persistent in personal pronouns (see Demuth *et al.* 1986: 459, for Cross River and Kru languages; Priestly 1983, for Indo-European; Heine 1982a: 212, for Daju dialects (Eastern Sudanic), Aikhenvald 1995a, for Bare). Reconstruction of the development of gender and number in Dravidian languages (Krishnamurti 1975) shows that neutralization in gender takes place in verbs before it spreads into pronouns; hence pronominal gender is more stable.

Similar evidence comes from Akan, a Kwa language of Ghana. Akan is in the process of losing a noun class system which it inherited from the proto-language (see Williamson 1989: 11–12, on noun classes in Kwa languages). There are six classes with a partial semantic basis and vestiges of singular–plural pairings of the Bantu type (Osam 1994: 120–1; see also §12.3.1 above on semantics of noun classes in Akan). Noun class agreement in noun phrases has been completely lost. A few nominalized adjectives contain Class 1 (human) class prefixes (Osam 1994: 123); they are used headlessly and reflect a 'derivational' use of noun class prefixes, e.g. ɔ-kɛseɛ (CL1-fat) 'a fat person, a fat one'. Subject–verb agreement has been lost in the majority of dialects. Only Twi dialects preserve an animate/

inanimate distinction in cross-referencing subject prefixes (Osam 1994: 124–5, 132, 138), e.g. ɔ-bɛ-yera (3sg.Subj:Animate-FUT-be.lost) 'S/he will get lost', and ɛ-bɛ-yera (3sgSubj:Inanimate-FUT-be.lost) 'It will get lost'.[36]

In Kru languages overt noun class marking has been largely reanalysed as a part of the noun stem (Marchese 1988: 332), but the agreement system is still active. Class agreement is often lost from adjectives; agreement in demonstratives tends to be more resistant (Marchese 1988: 335).[37]

The loss of agreement often involves lexicalization and fossilization of gender markers, as is the case in the Australian languages of Arnhem Land (Sands 1995: 255–6). For instance, in Warray (Harvey 1987: 55 ff.) noun class prefixes become lexicalized with nouns; the pronominal agreement is regular, but the system of adjective agreement with nouns is being lost.

This agrees with the hierarchy of retention of gender oppositions put forward by Priestly (1983: 340): NOUN > ADJECTIVE > PRONOUN. For instance, many Indo-European languages lose neuter gender and neuter agreement; but there are sometimes remainders of neuter in anaphoric pronouns, e.g. French *ce*, Italian *ciò* < *ecce hoc*. Thus, agreement appears to be more stable on pronouns and demonstratives than on other targets. But note that this is at odds with the data on the obsolescence of gender in Scottish Gaelic (see §13.7.3); this shows that language change in obsolescence may be distinct from language-internally motivated change.

(C) Decline and loss of agreement in language contact, creolization, and obsolescence

Agreement patterns can undergo changes as the result of indirect areal diffusion (some examples were given in §13.7.1). In creolization and language obsolescence, agreement undergoes more changes than head-marking of noun classes or genders.

Noun class agreement is being gradually lost from creolized Bantu languages. In the Mankandza dialect of Lingala, a trade language (Bokamba 1977), noun class agreement with the subject is obligatory; in other dialects, such as Kinshasa Lingala, agreement still exists, but is reduced to a notional opposition animate/inanimate. Thus, the reduction of agreement involves semantic change in the composition of classes, into just animate and inanimate. It can be seen from the following examples that noun Class 7 has been reinterpreted as a general 'inanimate' marker.

---

[36] There is no singular/plural distinction in these old noun class prefixes.
[37] There may be some semantic hierarchy of the adjectives involved; 'good' and 'big' seem most resistant; but this deserves a special analysis (Marchese 1988: 355). Further study is needed to provide a hierarchy of agreement in terms of reduction and loss of agreement. Evidence from Lower Cross languages suggests that agreement on numerals is the first to disappear (Faraclas 1989). (Note that Kru languages do not have agreement on verbs.)

Example 13.19 comes from Mankandza Lingala, and 13.20 from Kinshasa Lingala.

13.19. mu-nkanda   mu-ko-kweya
       NCL3-book/letter   NCL3-TA-fall
       'A/the book will fall down.'

13.20. mu-nkanda   e-ko-kweya
       NCL3-book/letter   NCL7-TA-fall
       'A/the book will fall down.'

The same phenomenon is discussed for Swahili by Bokamba (1977; see also Alexandre 1968; Polomé 1968). In various Lingala dialects, and in some varieties of Swahili, adjectival agreement is lost, e.g. Mankandza Lingala *mo-sɔni mu-ye* (NCL3-pencil NCL3-this) and Kinshasa Lingala *mo-sɔni oyo* (NCL3-pencil this) 'this pencil'. The process of agreement loss in a creolized language can go even further. In Kituba (a creole based on Kikongo: Stucky 1978: 227–8) agreement has been lost with all targets.

Reduction of agreement in language contact and creolization can go together with a tendency towards the semantic restructuring of classes. In modern 'anglicized' Tiwi, agreement with demonstratives is regular with humans, or high animate head nouns (Lee 1987: 118). This is part of the tendency to restructure the Traditional Tiwi masculine and feminine opposition into human and non-human (see §13.7.2).

Different agreement types can be lost at different speeds in language obsolescence. Such evidence comes from Bare and Warekena, obsolescent Arawak languages from Brazil. Both have almost lost gender agreement on adjectives; however, gender marking is still obligatory in cross-referencing on verbs (Aikhenvald 1995a; 1998b).

Similar processes occur in the obsolescence of languages with multiple noun class systems. In Paumarí (Arawá) the shape-based *ka-* noun class is being lost by younger speakers whose main language is Portuguese (Aikhenvald MS). The feminine/masculine gender distinction is more persistent. This may be due to the influence of Portuguese, with its two genders.

13.9. Semantic changes in noun categorization devices

When lexical items become grammaticalized as noun categorization devices, they undergo semantic changes. The general principles underlying these changes are outlined in §13.9.1. I show in §13.9.2 how the changes affect the composition of classes and their semantic opacity.

13.9.1. From lexical item to classifier: principles of semantic change

Grammaticalization of noun categorization devices involves semantic changes. These semantic changes fit in well with the general tendencies of semantic change discussed in grammaticalization theory. They involve 'bleaching', 'abstraction', and metaphorical extensions (cf. Heine et al. 1991: 39–45), or a meaning change from a more concrete notion (e.g. a word for 'fruit') to a more abstract notion (e.g. a classifier for 'round objects').

Lexical items which get grammaticalized as classifiers can have generic meanings, e.g. 'person', or 'thing'. They can also have more specific meanings, and belong to a 'subordinate' level of categorization. Semantic extensions and principles of semantic changes[38] depend on the type of classifier, its preferred semantics, and the type of lexical source. In (A) we consider semantic change from a noun to a classifier. Changes which take place in the passage from a verb to a classifier are analysed in (B).

(A) From a noun to a classifier: semantic changes

When nouns become classifiers they may undergo a number of semantic changes: (A1) a noun with generic reference may become a generic classifier; (A2) a noun with generic reference may become a classifier restricted to a specific class of referents; (A3) a noun with specific reference may become a classifier for a more general class of referents; or there can be semantic changes by extension, which may be due to metaphor and metonymy (cf. §12.1.1).[39] Little or no semantic change is involved in the creation of highly specific classifiers; for instance, in Baniwa specific classifiers for a room in the house, and for excrement come from the words for room and for excrement respectively. These terms may be then extended to further items, by metaphor, metonymy, or just salient properties (A4).

It is generally accepted that 'the source concepts' in grammaticalization are of frequent and general use, and their frequent use is due to their being

---

[38] Natural tendencies of semantic change in lexical items are still a largely unexplored field. Semantic change between lexical items may be conceived as the addition of an element of meaning to the semantic system, or the loss of an element of meaning 'while the form remains constant' (e.g. Wilkins 1981; 1996: 269). Semantic changes 'within a speech community involve polysemy at their beginning point or at their endpoint' (Wilkins 1996: 269). For the semantic change from a lexical item to classifier there is often no evidence of synchronic polysemy at the endpoint; that at the beginning can only be reconstructed. The form itself often does not remain constant; the more grammaticalized the classifier, the likelier it is to undergo phonological reduction.

[39] A noun which comes to be used as a classifier can shift its meaning as a free noun. In Northern Iroquoian languages, the liquid classifier -hnek- assumed a specialized meaning of 'whisky, liquor' when used as a free noun (Mithun 1986: 391). Thus, classifiers and free nouns of the same origin can undergo independent semantic change (which may have corresponded to polysemy at an earlier stage). Synonyms, when used as classifiers, can have slightly different meanings which are often unpredictable. Minangkabau *butia* 'seed' is used for inorganic seed-like and bulky objects; and *incek* 'seed' is used for organic seed-like objects (Marnita 1996).

'fundamental' elements. They can often be defined as belonging to the basic level of categorization, like basic-level verbs of physical state such as 'sit', 'stand', and 'lie' (Heine *et al.* 1991: 33). Another generalization is that 'categories of the subordinate level are unlikely to serve as source concepts' (Heine *et al.* 1991: 33; Sweetser 1988: 402). Exceptions to these generalizations can be found with classifiers, since there are frequent examples of changes from a subordinate (more specific) level of categorization to a superordinate (more 'abstract') level (A3). However, these changes reflect universal cognitive mechanisms which underlie the structure of noun categorization (see §12.2.2).

(A1) Noun with generic reference becomes a generic classifier Superordinate nouns meaning 'man' or 'woman' often give rise to NOUN CLASSES; a noun meaning 'man' becomes a marker for masculine, and one meaning 'woman' is used for feminine (see the examples from Mupun, Zande, and some Australian languages in §13.1.1). A generic term for 'person' may develop into a gender marker if there is a gender/sex-based distinction already in the system. 'Person' developed into the non-feminine marker in Eastern Nilotic, after feminine had already evolved (Heine and Reh 1984: 219).

Generic nouns used as NOUN CLASSIFIERS preserve their generic meaning. The generic term 'person' is often used as a source for noun classifiers, e.g. in Australian, and as a source for numeral classifiers meaning 'human in general'. In Minangkabau, *batang* 'tree, trunk' (a reflex of Austronesian 'trunk; tree; timber; platform': Conklin 1981: 259) is used as a generic classifier for all trees, and the generic 'flower' is used as a generic for flowers (cf. Minangabau *bungo*, Acehnese *bungöng*: Durie 1985: 135).

The same can be observed for VERBAL classifiers. A generic noun, 'domestic animal', covers all animals, including pigs, in Cayuga (Iroquoian); 'water' becomes a classifier for all drinkable liquids in Ngandi (Mithun 1986: 387, 389; Heath 1978b).

In the languages of Southeast Asia, default classifiers are often based on a generic term for 'body', or 'person'. Default human numeral classifier *pui* in the Southern Lawa group of the Palaungic branch of Mon-Khmer derives from Proto-Waic **bɤu* 'person' (Adams 1992: 110). 'Fruit' is another frequent source of a default classifier, e.g. Indonesian and Minangkabau *buah* 'fruit, generic classifier'; White Tai *xang³* 'fruit', 'classifier for objects in general' (Conklin 1981: 150). A classifier for 'round things' is frequently used as a default classifier (§12.1.4), the semantic change being then fruit > round > generic. A similar change is found in Totonac *aq* 'a default classifier' which comes from *aq* ~ *akán* 'head' (Levy 1994). General classifiers may also come from an item meaning 'thing', e.g. the possessive classifier in Tariana *yarupe* 'thing'.

This semantic change fully agrees with current ideas on lexical sources for grammaticalization. When a noun meaning 'man' or 'woman' becomes a noun classifier, very little, if any semantic change is involved, e.g. Akatek (Zavala 1993) woman > woman; man > man; Jacaltec woman > female non-kin classifier.

(A2) Noun with generic reference becomes a classifier for a specific class of referents A change from a generic to a more specific referent takes place with noun classifiers. In Mam (Table 13.3) a generic noun 'man' acquired the more specialized meaning of 'old man, respectfully', and 'woman' that of 'old woman, respectfully'. In Kana, a generic noun came to be used as a specific classifier: the numeral classifier *nēē* derived from the word for 'person', is used with only one noun 'guest' (Ikoro 1996a: 93).

(A3) Noun with specific reference becomes a classifier for a more general class of referents In Eastern Nilotic, kinship terms at a more subordinate level of categorization became gender markers (e.g. a noun meaning 'daughter, girl' became a feminine gender marker: Heine and Reh 1984: 219). Kinship terms can be used to classify humans according to their age and social status. *Bà* 'grandmother' in Vietnamese is used as a numeral classifier to classify women over 40; *ông* 'grandfather' is used to classify 'personified or deified animals', e.g. tigers, elephants, and whales in proverbs (Adams 1989: 86–90). It is unusual to derive generic classifiers from kinship terms. This is, however, the case in Kana. The 'default' numeral classifier comes from the word *kà* 'mother' (Ikoro 1996a: 90–1).

In Khmu (Austroasiatic), *tà* 'grandfather' is used as a masculine class term with names of boys (as opposed to *i*, with unknown etymology, used with names of girls) (Adams 1989: 57). In West Bahnaric **raaʔ*, the 'numeral classifier for humans', comes from a more specific noun 'adult human' (Adams 1992: 110). A noun meaning 'child' often appears as a source for noun classifiers, and numeral classifiers for any young animate. In Kana, *ŋwíí* 'child', or 'offspring' is the source for a classifier for young beings, human or non-human. In the noun classifier system in Mam, it is used as a classifier for babies. In noun class systems, 'child' can get grammaticalized as a diminutive gender marker (as in Bantu languages: Heine 1982a: 214).

The way in which a noun with specific reference can become a generic classifier for the whole species is similar to the development from a prototype to its extensions. In Cayuga, the stem for 'car' is used as a classifier for all vehicles. In Mohawk the classifier for fruit *(-ahy-)* is also the word for 'berry' (Mithun 1986: 391).[40]

---

[40] Synchronically, this does not mean that the source-noun retains its prototypicality. For instance, modern speakers of Mohawk do not consider 'berries' such as strawberries and blackberries as prototypical 'fruit' any more (Mithun 1986: 391).

(A4) Semantic extensions The preferred semantics of different classifier types can explain different patterns of semantic change. Shape is more important as a semantic basis in numeral classifier systems than for noun classifiers. In contrast, material make-up and function are more important in noun classifier systems (see Chapter 11).

Thus, for noun classifiers with inanimate reference, the most common semantic changes from noun to noun classifier are as now listed.

(a) Extension by material makeup

The specific noun *kuru* 'water' in Ngan'gityemerri (Reid 1997) and *bana* 'fresh water' in Yidiny (Dixon 1982: 199) are used to classify all drinkable liquids. In the languages of the Kanjobalan branch of Mayan the classifier for corn is used for corn, and also for products made of corn. Similarly, the classifier for 'stone' is used with objects made of stone (Zavala 1992: 158–9).

Material makeup can involve different extensions by common properties, e.g. in Ngan'gityemerri *yenggi* 'fire' is used to classify all things associated with fire, such as firewood, charcoal, smoke, firestick.

(b) Extension by function

In Ngan'gityemerri *syiri* 'weapon' became extended to all things which involve striking, e.g. lightning; and *yawurr* 'tree' was extended to all wooden artefacts, and then to all modern manufactured products, even if they are not made of wood (Reid 1997).

The most common extensions from noun to numeral classifiers are the following.

Extension by shape, e.g. *batang* 'tree, trunk' used to classify vertical things in Minangkabau (Conklin 1981: 259; Marnita 1996; see also Appendix 2 below);

Extension by material makeup, e.g. *batang* 'tree, trunk' used for categorization of wooden things and long parts of plants in Bugis and Banggais (Conklin 1981: 259);

Extension by shape and material, e.g. *batang* 'tree, trunk' used to classify vertical things fabricated from wood and other long inflexible objects in Indonesian (Conklin 1981: 259); *tôn* 'tree' is used to classify both plants and vertical things in Thai (Carpenter 1992);

More rarely, extension by material makeup and function, e.g. in Kana *té* 'tree' is used to classify wooden objects used as means of transport (Ikoro 1996a: 91–2). In Thai, the classifier for objects with handles, initially used only for bicycles, was extended to all other vehicles (with the exception of carts) (Carpenter 1986). In Tariana the classifier for 'canoe', *-whya*, is used for any vehicle. 'Leaf' is often used as classifier for containers in Austroasiatic languages, e.g. Siamese *bai¹* 'leaf'. Interestingly, fruits are also covered by this classifier—they are then conceived as 'flesh-covered, meat-holding vessels' (Conklin 1981: 152). In Ponapean (Micronesian), *wahr* 'canoe' was grammaticalized as *were* 'POSS.CL:CANOE,VEHICLES' (§13.1.1).

These extensions are typical for nouns with inanimate referents. 'Child', unlike other nouns with a human referent, can be extended to small and round things. In Vietnamese, *con* 'child, be small' is used to classify people 'less than humans' (i.e. of low social status), monsters, animals in general, some inanimate items such as kites, and images of animate beings. This classifier also covers body parts which are considered more 'lively' (eye, pupil of the eye, heart, penis), and by semantic extension, a number of other things (figure, number, cards which may be related to the images of human beings) (Adams 1989: 89–91). In Siamese *luuk³* 'child' is used as a classifier for round things (Conklin 1981: 152).

In each case the semantic extensions may be language-specific and almost unpredictable (cf. Matisoff 1991, on the unpredictability of semantic change in grammaticalization). One lexical item, 'leaf', gets extended to various semantic domains in a number of Tai languages (Conklin 1981: 159); in each case it involves different shape properties. In Wu-Ming, Nung, and White Tai 'leaf' is used to cover FLAT EXPANDED objects (paper, fabric, board), CONTAINERS (plates, hats, baskets, pails, bottles, fruits), ROUND FLAT objects such as rice cakes and paper, FLAT surfaces, such as paper and documents, and also blades. In Dioi, the same classifier is used only with paper, fabric, and board, and is not extended to either containers or blades. In Black Tai, it has the same meanings as in Nung but for the 'container' extension. In Western Austronesian languages, seed-based classifier meanings extend from small round objects to teeth, eggs, fruits, and even to mid-sized spherical objects and bulky objects (Conklin 1981: 246–8). 'Fruit/stone'-based classifiers—as generic classifiers—range from fruit and stones to medium range objects, bulky objects, lumps/loaves, inanimates and even animals (Conklin 1981: 261–2).

Numeral classifiers frequently come from body parts. Semantic changes often involve extensions by shape and size (e.g. 'eye' becomes a classifier for small round objects); however, extensions are often fairly idiosyncratic. Semantic changes from a lexical noun to a classifier for a noun with an inanimate referent often involve metonymy (description of the whole by its part). This happens with nouns which refer to parts of plants, or of inanimate objects. 'Bay of a house' became a classifier for houses in Khmer; and 'roof' is used to classify houses in Waic languages (Adams 1989: 120). Handles are often used to classify objects with handles (see (C) in §13.9.2, on classifier *khan* in Thai).

(B) From a verb to a classifier: semantic changes

When a verb becomes a classifier it will specify some of the properties of its original argument in S or O function, but never in the function of an A (this agrees with the predominantly absolutive basis on which verbal classifiers operate: cf. Keenan 1984). Typical semantic changes in verbs are:

(i) Posture verbs become deictic classifiers and verbal classifiers which refer to the SHAPE and ORIENTATION of their S arguments. For instance, the verb 'stand' becomes a classifier for vertical or one-dimensional referents which may also be large and strong. 'Lie' becomes a classifier for two-dimensional or horizontal objects, which can be associated with the ground, e.g. locations or crawling animals in Enga. 'Sit' tends to be associated with three-dimensionality, or roundness (see Table 6.7 above).

(ii) Stance and posture verbs become deictic and verbal classifiers referring to POSITION. 'Hang' is used to refer to objects which have this functional property—i.e. hanging, or protruding, as in Enga (Table 6.7).

(iii) Verbs of handling become classifiers which refer to the FUNCTION of the object or the way it has to be handled. In Imonda, 'pick fruit' became a verbal classifier for 'fruit to be picked', and 'break in two' for 'objects which are normally broken' (Table 13.6). (Examples from Cahuilla were given in §13.1.4.)

(iv) Verbs from other semantic groups may become specific numeral classifiers for their typical S or O arguments, e.g. the development of 'spread out' to 'clothing' in Tai (Conklin 1981: 167), and to 'mats' in Makassar (Conklin 1981: 442). Other examples include 'rinse, bath' to 'storms' in Dioi (Conklin 1981: 380); 'be long and straight as bamboo' to 'flutes and guns' as in Shan, a Tai language (Adams 1989: 127); note also 'hang down' as a classifier for clothing; 'pluck' for 'flowers', and 'slice' for slices as of bread in Bugis (Conklin 1981: 435), 'tie together, bind' for bundles in Shan (Conklin 1981: 406); and 'roll up' for cigars, rolled leaves, and other sorts of rolls in Siamese (Conklin 1981: 426).

Mensural classifiers often come from body-oriented verbs. The classifier will then refer to the result of the action, e.g. Minangkabau *gigik* 'bite', for a bite of food, or *(h)isok* 'inhale', for traditional cigarettes, and *palik* 'to take with a tip of a finger', for creamy things in a small amount (see also examples in De Leon 1987).

(v) Verbs can also become verbal classifiers which describe the location or instruments typical of the activity, e.g. 'carry' in Enga used for referents of sexual activities, such as vagina or penis (see Table 6.7).

13.9.2. Further changes in noun categorization devices

The composition of an established system of noun categorization may change as the result of losing or acquiring new members. Semantic changes may result in the increasing semantic opacity of assignment of a noun class, or of a classifier, or lead to a more semantically transparent system.

(A) Change in composition of a noun class

In numerous Bantu languages, the human class (1/2) tends to absorb non-human animates. This semantic extension results in the change of the composition of the class. For instance, in Kuria this class includes personified animals (Aksenova and Toporova 1994: 76), and in Pogoro and Tonga all animals are included in this class (Aksenova and Toporova 1990: 28). Consequently, in these languages, the 'human' noun class became simply animate. (Note that here noun class assignment does not become more opaque.) In Shona, semantic changes in the composition of classes affected the class assignment of humans and animates which became distributed between several different classes. Class 1/2 is the main class for ordinary and public persons; it also includes chiefs, evil spirits, and thunder. Class 5/6 is organized around the notion of ritual danger; it includes persons who inspire fear (e.g. ancestors, wild persons, foreigners). Class 9/10 centres around 'protection' against the potential danger; it includes protective spirits and medicine men. Palmer and Arin (1995a) hypothesize that the reason for this restructuring lies in the social organization of the Shona (see §12.3.1 above).

Semantic changes within a classifier system can occur as the result of introducing a new member into a system of noun categorization devices. This happens most often in languages with classifiers as independent lexical items. In Thai, the influx of new items of material culture resulted in the creation of new classifiers (Carpenter 1986: 18–19). Some of these new classifiers are loanwords themselves, e.g. *chut* (from English *suit*), which is used to refer to dresses and Western style suits, as well as to pyjamas and bathing suits. Others are of Thai origin. For instance, *lawt* 'tube' came to be used as a classifier for test tubes, light bulbs, and drinking-straws, and *rian* 'coin' is used colloquially for counting dollars.

(B) Increasing opacity in noun class assignment

In Australian languages the class which originally referred to 'edible vegetables' (typically marked with initial *ma-*, *mi-*, or *m-*) often underwent changes in its composition. As a result, its assignment can become extremely opaque. In Ngan'gityemerri, it includes exclusively edible plants (the only exception being *ngikin* 'dried faeces'; this extension is explained by Reid (1997) in terms of the vegetable appearance of dried faeces of herbivores). In Dyirbal, the corresponding class includes all vegetable foods and honey. In Wardaman (Merlan 1994: 61) this class underwent a number of extensions: it includes all flora, especially vegetables and vegetable parts. The 'vegetable food' class assignment is very opaque in Gurr-goni (R. Green 1995: 58–9): its central meaning is still 'edible vegetables', covering most living plants and vegetable foods and most items made from plant materials, most body parts, dead bodies, and faeces; and also corroborees and songs, traditional canoes, paper, bombs, and directions. Some of these changes in the composition of noun classes are explainable by (i) semantic extension by important property, for instance, from edible vegetables to all flora, as in Wardaman; (ii) metaphorical extensions; for instance, the inclusion of traditional canoes and other means of transport into the vegetable class in Gurr-goni may be accounted for by the fact they used to be made out of wood; then canoes were extended as a means of transport, and this is how a loanword, *erriplen* 'plane', got assigned to the vegetable class (R. Green 1995: 58), and (iii) metonymy: from edible vegetables, or flora to parts of plants (cf. §13.4).[41]

Loss of formal gender markers can make gender assignment rules more complicated. In Colloquial French, the loss of final *-e*, the feminine marker, has led to the creation of complicated phonological and morphological rules of assignment (cf. Corbett 1991).

(C) Increasing opacity in classifier choice

Changes in composition may affect numeral classifiers. A few classes in Thai have been reorganized under the pressure of new concepts, or new items from Western culture (Carpenter 1986: 19). The classifier *khan*, with its lexical meaning 'long handle' or 'dyke between rice paddies', was originally used to refer to things with long handles. Nowadays it includes cars, bicycles, motorcycles, buses, and names for other vehicles (with the exception of ox-cart), and words like spoon, fork, and umbrella, as well as traditional musical instruments and other utensils. This semantic extension appears to have started from bicycles, an object with handlebars, that are like handles, which was the first foreign vehicle to be introduced to Thailand. Subsequently, automobiles and other vehicles were assigned the same classifier, as a 'class extension based on the functional category of vehicle'.

---

[41] Mayali (Evans 1997) provides another example of increasing semantic opacity of the 'vegetable food' class. Besides all non-meat foods, it includes a variety of other nouns, such as (a) anatomical terms pertaining to genitalia, sexually produced fluids or excretion, (b) some geographical terms, (c) a few bird names, (d) some wooden implements, e.g. weapons, (e) words for rain and rain-water, and (f) manner adverbials.

(D) Increasing semanticity of noun class assignment

Gender systems can shift from more grammatical to more semantic, as in Cantabrian Spanish (§2.3.4). If a language loses gender agreement and preserves the gender distinctions in personal pronouns only, the assignment tends to become predominantly semantic even if it was not so before; this is the case in English with its three genders just in third person pronouns, *he/she/it*. Along the similar lines, Chechen speakers 'sometimes point out that words of the B-gender refer to round objects, as some of them in fact do, although many do not . . . If there is a speaker expectation that gender classes will be shape-based, then analogical reclassifications over time will probably lead to just such a situation' (Nichols 1992: 140).[42]

(E) Semantic changes due to introduction of new semantic features

Classes 7/8 and 12/13 in ChiBemba (Bantu) acquired additional values of 'large' and 'small' respectively which got extended to affective notions ('despised' and 'endeared') (Spitulnik 1989: 212); for instance, in Kuria, Classes 5/6 and 20 have augmentative and pejorative values (Aksenova and Toporova 1994: 81, 102).

(F) Historically attested semantic changes

Languages with a long-standing written tradition provide evidence for the development of classifier systems over time. In Chinese, classifiers were used sporadically with culturally salient objects during the classical period (500–206 BC); the use of classifiers increased from about 100 AD (Bisang 1996: 540). Semantic development of Chinese classifiers from highly specific to generalized reference is discussed by Erbaugh (1986: 428–31). Table 13.7 illustrates the historically attested semantic changes from individual to general reference of three Mandarin Chinese classifiers.

Semantic extensions are usually made by shape, which is the preferred semantic property of numeral classifiers (see Chapter 11; and note the development from 'small branch' to 'long things in general' in the history of the classifier *tiáo*, in Table 13.7). Extralinguistic factors, such as the cultural importance of an object, may influence the rate of change. In Mandarin, culturally important classifiers, e.g. *pǐ* 'horses' and *běn* 'books' have retained their exclusive reference. Other classifiers underwent semantic changes, e.g. *gēn* 'threads, hairs, strings' first referred to stalks of grass;

---

[42] This tendency often appears in poetry and metaphors. A famous example of direct association between masculine gender and masculinity and feminine gender and femininity in German comes from Goethe's poem 'Der Tannenbaum' (DEF.ART:MASC pine.tree), 'the pine tree' who is dreaming of encountering a she-palm tree (*die Palme*) (H. Seiler 1987). This effect was lost in Lermontov's translation of the poem into Russian, since both tree-names are feminine.

410   *Classifiers*

TABLE 13.7. *Historical changes in Mandarin Chinese classifiers*

Dynasty, time	Classifier *tiáo*	Classifier *méi*	Classifier *gè*
Shang, c.1400 BC	Small branch	Trunk of bamboo tree	Bamboo
Zhou, 1100 BC		Trees	
Qin, 255 BC	Sticks	Wooden objects	
Han, 200 BC			Lengths of bamboo
Post-Han, 25 AD	Snakes, lengths of cloth, strings of gold ingots	Flutes, swords, birds, fish, jewels, dishes	Arrows
Tang, 600–900 AD	String, clothing	General classifier	Arrows, candles, dogs, chickens, horses
Song, 960–1117 AD	Long things in general		Fruit, birds, people
Ming, 1368–1643 AD			General
Qing, 1644–1912 AD			General classifier for people, and unclassified objects
Modern, 1912–		Virtually dies out except for needles, badges	

kē was first used to classify peaches, then all fruits, then all small, round objects in general (Erbaugh 1986: 430).

An overview of the historical development of Japanese numeral classifiers is given by Downing (1996: 39–46). She notes the importance of animacy distinctions in the eighth-century Japanese system; round objects lacked their own classifier, and the gap was filled by the use of the general classifier *tsu*. There were a number of classifiers used for small functionally-defined culturally-salient categories, e.g. *hata* for counting looms, or *hashira* for counting gods and exalted persons (these items do not appear in the classifier inventories of Modern Japanese: Downing 1996: 19–22). The default, or general, classifier *tsu* was used to refer to any entity except human beings and, probably, gods (Downing 1996: 46). In the early documents in Thai, *tua* was used to refer exclusively to four-legged animals; later it became extended to articles of clothing, ghosts, and letters (cf. Diagram 12.1).

The analysis of classifier production by representatives of varying social groups and generations in Kilivila, a multiple classifier language, by Senft (1996: 202–27) shows several tendencies illustrating the language change in progress. Speakers tend to replace specific classifiers with shape-based classifiers. The greatest number of innovations have been observed among school children aged from 8 to 14 'because of their readiness for a playful exploration of the possibilities the C(lassifier) P(articles) system offers and because of their increased linguistic awareness' (Senft 1996: 235). Innovations and language change patterns in classifier usage have also been observed among adults between 21 and 35. This tendency has a sociolinguistic explanation: it appears that consultants with low social status try to overcome language barriers that mark intrasocietal status by changing patterns of classifier use.

13.10. Sources of noun categorization devices: a summary

Noun categorization devices of different kinds tend to develop from different lexical sources—open classes of nouns or verbs, or closed classes of pronouns or adpositions. Only numeral, relational, and possessed classifiers develop from deverbal nominalizations; these classifiers can also have mixed origins in some language groups: see Table 13.8.

The internal evolution of highly grammaticalized noun categorization devices is often based on the reanalysis of other categories, and internally motivated by phonological and morphological factors. The evolution of noun categorization devices is often due to language external reasons, e.g. areal diffusion, creolization, and language obsolescence. If a noun categorization system tends to be lost, animate and human classes are more stable than others.

The general principles of semantic change in noun categorization systems correspond to the main parameters of cognitive extension—metaphor and metonymy, conditioned and bounded by cultural and social constraints. There is a great deal of similarity between the diachronic semantic change from lexical nouns to classifiers, and the synchronic semantic extensions which correlate with preferred semantic parameters for each classifier type. Thus, numeral and verbal classifiers tend to get extended according to the physical properties of their referent, such as shape or dimensionality.

Table 13.8 summarizes the information contained in Tables 13.1 and

412   Classifiers

13.5, and the accompanying discussion. We have also seen that culturally important items can give rise to most classifier types (see Table 13.1); they are especially well represented in large multiple classifier systems.

TABLE 13.8. *Typical sources for noun categorization devices*

Noun categorization devices	Sources
Noun classes	Nouns (kinship, humans and higher animates)
	Demonstratives
	Locatives
	Derivational suffixes
	Mixed origin
Numeral classifiers	Nouns (unit counters, body parts, generics, etc.)
	Generic nouns
	Deverbal nominalizations
	Verbs of handling (involving typical activities)
	Mixed origin
Noun classifiers	Generic nouns
	Nouns referring to kinship, humans and higher animates
Locative classifiers	Nouns referring to body parts
Deictic classifiers	Posture verbs
Possessed classifiers	Nouns referring to kinship and humans
	Generic nouns
	Verbs of handling (involving typical activities)
	Deverbal nominalizations
	Mixed origin
Relational classifiers	Verbs of handling (involving typical activities)
	Deverbal nominalizations
	Mixed origin
Verbal classifiers	Incorporated nouns—body parts and generics
	Reanalysed serial verbs
Classificatory verbs	Incorporated nouns (body parts)
	Posture and motion verbs

14 Noun Categorization Devices in Language Acquisition and Dissolution

The behaviour of noun categorization devices in child language acquisition and language development, as well as in language dissolution, provides important clues as to how such devices are assigned, what the categorical interrelations between them are, and which of them is the most stable. It also provides us with information on the psycholinguistic reality of the assignment of noun categorization devices.

In this chapter, we consider language acquisition, development, and dissolution of two kinds of noun categorization device, noun classes and numeral classifiers. We have to restrict ourselves to the discussion of just these two because of the limitations of actual psycholinguistic research undertaken thus far. No experiments have been undertaken on language acquisition or dissolution of other classifier types, or of how these processes take place in multiple classifier systems. These are topics for future study.

In §14.1 we look at child language acquisition of gender and noun classes, and agreement patterns. Section 14.2 considers the acquisition of numeral classifiers. Processes of language dissolution in noun class and classifier systems are described in §14.3. Conclusions are given in §14.4.

14.1. Acquisition and development of noun classes

Acquisition and development of noun classes (which include genders) have been studied for Indo-European, Bantu, and Semitic languages. Studies of gender acquisition overlap with acquisition of agreement since noun classes are realized through agreement. In mixed (i.e. morphologically, semantically, and phonologically determined) systems of gender assignment, the formal characteristics of genders and noun classes are mastered first.

For instance, in Hebrew, every noun is assigned to masculine or feminine gender; and the two genders are distinguished in the singular and in the plural. The assignment is mixed; as was shown in §2.3.4, most feminine nouns have their plural in *-ot*, and masculine in *-im*; but there are exceptions.

A longitudinal and cross-sectional study by Levy (1983a; 1983b) showed the importance of phonological features for acquisition of portmanteau gender and number marking, and the comparative irrelevance of semantics or syntax. In particular, sex-gender correspondence proved irrelevant to the acquisition of inflected animate nouns. In the acquisition of Hebrew, young children make most errors in assigning correct gender to nouns whose gender cannot be predicted by their form (Berman 1985: 299–301). Working out formal correspondences between nouns to assign genders and to mark agreement appears to be important in morphologically complex languages, especially in the cases where gender-sensitive morphemes are portmanteau with number (see §10.1). Similar results have been achieved for Russian (Popova 1973), German, and French (Karmiloff-Smith 1979).

Children can also operate with a number of different intralinguistic cues at a time. The study of the acquisition of genders in Spanish by Pérez-Pereira (1991) showed that the greater the number of converging cues the more easily the children acquire the gender assignment. In his experiment, children aged from four to eleven pay far more attention to morphophonological and syntactic than to extralinguistic clues. The feature animacy/inanimacy did not produce any substantial difference in the way Spanish children handled nouns. In assigning genders, children rely on intralinguistic regularities. The relative markedness of genders is another important clue which follows from the dominance of formal, rather than semantic, principles of gender assignment in early gender acquisition. Spanish children tended to attribute masculine gender to nouns most often because it is unmarked, and therefore easier to acquire (Pérez-Pereira 1991: 584). The same tendency was observed for French (Karmiloff-Smith 1979), and Hebrew (Levy 1983a; 1983b; Berman 1985). A different result was achieved for German where the feminine forms of the definite article *die* and of the indefinite *eine* get overgeneralized at first.[1] This can be explained by their frequency of use, and greater salience than other forms.

Salience of actual forms appears to be an important factor in the acquisition of genders in Spanish and French (Pérez-Pereira 1991: 587). Neutralization of gender forms and syncretism can be an obstacle in gender acquisition. Smoczynska (1985) noted that Polish children master gender much earlier than Russian children in spite of considerable similarities between the two languages. The suggested reasons have to do with Russian phonology. One reason is reduction of both *a* (typical feminine singular ending) and *o* (typical neuter singular ending) in post-tonic syllables to [ʌ] or [ə], so that the actual forms are neutralized.[2] This is not the case in

---

[1] The article *die* could have overgeneralized also due to the fact that it is identical to the plural definite article (with no gender distinction).
[2] A study of child acquisition of genders in Russian dialects where there is no vowel reduction in post-tonic syllables would be helpful to prove this point.

Polish. Another reason for delayed gender acquisition by Russian children is the existence of numerous hypocoristic forms which refer to boys, or men, but end in -*a* and have a feminine declension, e.g. *Kolja* 'diminutive for Nicholas'. There is also a number of frequently used common nouns with masculine reference which end in -*a* and belong to a 'feminine' declension; for these, however, agreement is masculine, e.g. *djadja* 'uncle'. In children's speech, these nouns often take feminine agreement, e.g. *djadja sidel-a* 'uncle sit+PAST-FEM', instead of *djadja sidel* 'uncle was sitting' (Popova 1958: 109).

Morphological complexity may slow down the process of gender acquisition. Children have more difficulties in mastering gender systems of languages with three genders where gender markers interact with other categories, such as number and case, and where genders are 'ambiguous, barely transparent and scarcely predictable morphophonological markings' (Pérez-Pereira 1991: 587). This is the case in German, Czech, Serbo-Croatian, and Russian (see Pérez-Pereira 1991: 585, 587, and references therein). In contrast, children learning languages with clearly differentiated and regular marking of just two genders—e.g. Egyptian Arabic, Hebrew, French, or Spanish—master these systems more easily and more quickly (Levy 1983b; Pérez-Pereira 1991: 588).

Another important feature in gender acquisition is its formal opacity and regularity. It has been shown that children rely more on formal than on semantic cues when identifying antecedents of gender-marked genitive pronouns in German (Böhme and Levelt 1979). Slightly different results were achieved for Icelandic (Mulford 1983). To determine reference based on pronominal gender Icelandic children needed semantic as well as formal information. These differences may be due to different degrees of 'opacity' in gender marking in these two closely related languages. In German, formal correlates of grammatical gender are relatively stable and are easier to 'discover', while in Icelandic the formal gender correlates are more opaque, and so children have to rely much more on natural gender distinctions (Mulford 1983: 89).

It has been noticed that English children acquire the right use of gender-sensitive 3rd person pronouns later than, say, German children. This result shows that 'the more extensive and productive the system of gender marking in a language, the easier is its learning' (Pérez-Pereira 1991: 588). Note also Mills (1986: 107): 'It would rather appear that the extensive system of grammatical gender marked on many different parts of speech gives the German child more opportunity to seek regularities in the system and to learn to produce these forms accurately.' (See Corbett 1991: 82–8, for further examples of acquisition of genders in Indo-European languages.)[3]

---

[3] Another aspect of language acquisition is how children assign gender, or gender and number portmanteau markers, to nonce words. Levy (1983a: 119) reports that children did

Considerable work has been done on child language acquisition of noun class systems in a number of Bantu languages (Demuth 1988; Demuth et al. 1986; Kunene 1986; Suzman 1980; Herbert 1991; Tsonope 1988). As we saw in Chapters 2 and 10, noun class prefixes are portmanteau with number. Noun class assignment is semantically opaque (though a certain semantic core is associated with almost every class: see Chapter 2 and Spitulnik 1989). Agreement is heavily linked to phonology, i.e. there is a large amount of alliterative agreement.

The data on Sesotho child acquisition of noun classes described by Demuth (1988) showed that the system of gender agreement was established before nouns were divided into gender classes. In Sesotho, a noun and its modifier are attributed a class feature specification and are treated as 'some kind of prosodic, cognitive, or grammatical unit' (Demuth 1988: 316). Young language learners then start using agreement productively, gradually working out the appropriate phonological marking for nouns. Sesotho nouns are learned in conjunction with their inherent noun class features realized in agreement; and the head-marked noun class appears later. Similar results have been documented by Tsonope (1988) for Setswana. That noun class is first acquired as a feature of a phrase, rather than a feature of an individual noun, is accounted for by the fact that the Bantu noun class agreement system is phonologically transparent and pervasive.[4] As we saw above for Indo-European gender acquisition, formal regularity helps acquisition of gender agreement systems. The fact that there are very few examples of 'overgeneralization' of a particular set of noun class prefixes in the studies of Bantu noun class acquisition indicates that the noun prefix is first learned as a part of the noun, and it is not segmented till later (Tsonope 1988: 148; Herbert 1991: 11).

The semantics of noun classes does not seem to play any important role in noun class acquisition for Bantu languages: the acquisition of formal regularities precedes the acquisition of semantics. Tsonope (1988) showed that children begin to consolidate semantically based noun classes, such as human nouns, only later, after the agreement system has been acquired. In some cases semantic clues may have played a limited role. For instance, the acquisition of demonstratives by Setswana children seemed to suggest that they are able to make a distinction between human and non-human nouns very early. However, other factors

better in inflecting nonce words denoting animates than in inflecting nonce words denoting inanimates; however, younger children had difficulties with inflecting nonce words. Kunene (1986), who worked on getting children to recognize and assign class to novel words, arrived at slightly different conclusions as to noun class assignment with SiSwati-speaking children from those reached by Demuth (1988).

[4] Lehmann (1982) also argues that noun class is prototypically realized through agreement within a phrase.

could have contributed to this (e.g. the frequency of human nouns in discussions, or phonological restrictions).[5]

In the acquisition of the semantics of the Bantu noun class system, there is a tendency to acquire the human/non-human distinction before other underlying semantic contrasts. This explains the tendency for all nouns denoting humans to be occasionally treated as members of Class 1/2 (predominantly human) (cf. Suzman 1980, for Zulu). Overgeneralization of human classes took place in experiments of noun class assignment to novel nouns. When given a choice of uncontextualized noun class assignment, children tended to classify plural nouns into just human/non-human. However, in spontaneous speech production no overgeneralization occurred (Demuth *et al*. 1986: 466).

The main conclusion, for child acquisition of the Bantu noun class system, is that agreement principles are acquired before the actual marking of nouns. This may also be linked to the phonological reduction of nouns in children's speech (Herbert 1991: 111). Demonstratives and possessives have been shown to be the first targets which show agreement (Demuth 1988: 319; Herbert 1991: 111). In Zulu the first concordial subsystem consistently employed was for subject marking on verbs (Suzman 1982: 57).

The primacy in acquisition of concordial noun classes over head marking agrees with certain developments in the history of Bantu languages. In Grebo (Kru: see Diagram 13.4 above; also Demuth *et al*. 1986: 467) the overt noun class marking is lost, but the concord system remains. The fact that the first signs of subject/verb agreement to appear in children's speech are anaphoric (Suzman 1982; Herbert 1991: 111) confirms the hypothesis of an anaphoric origin for the genesis of agreement (see §13.5 and §13.8).

14.2. Acquisition of numeral classifiers

Similar to the studies of gender and noun class acquisition, existing studies on the acquisition of numeral classifiers are limited to a few languages—Chinese (Erbaugh 1986), Thai (Carpenter 1991; 1992; Gandour *et al.* 1984), Japanese (Sanches 1977; Matsumoto 1985), Garo (Burling 1973), and Kilivila (Senft 1996).[6]

Classifier acquisition is reported as much slower than acquisition of noun classes. For instance, even ten-year old Thai children got only 89

---

[5] The acquisition of noun classes can be influenced by sociolinguistic parameters: subjects with urban backgrounds may acquire these noun classes which include the most borrowings faster (Suzman 1980: 52).

[6] Both Chinese and Thai use classifiers with deictics and with numerals; however, there are no data on how classifiers are acquired with deictics. Kilivila (Senft 1996) also employs classifiers in several different environments; there are no data on which environment is acquired first.

per cent of their classifiers right (Carpenter 1991: 98). Classifier production in Kilivila starts at the age of about four; the frequency of classifier production increases dramatically at the age of nine (Senft 1996: 180). In contrast, the noun class agreement system is acquired by Sesotho children at three years of age (Demuth 1988).[7]

Studies on the acquisition of numeral classifiers shows that, unlike noun classes, extralinguistic regularities and semantics are very important at the first stages of classifier acquisition. In the acquisition of Garo classifiers, the animacy distinction was acquired before other categories (Burling 1973). The same results were obtained for Thai classifiers (Gandour *et al.* 1984). Overuse of the general classifier was reported for Japanese children (Sanches 1977; Matsumoto 1985). Children tend to overextend the use of classifiers based on shape and function. At age seven, the general classifier is still overused.

In her seminal study on how children acquire classifiers in Mandarin Chinese, Erbaugh (1986: 431) established the order in which classifiers of different types are acquired. In principle, classifier use by children was similar to that by adults. Children, however, used classifiers more rarely, and showed a tendency to overuse the general classifier *gè*, especially at an early age, starting from two years (Erbaugh 1986: 415). Specific classifiers developed slowly and were rarely used between the age of one year and ten months and three years and ten months. They started being used lexically, specific to a single referent, and were then extended to mark a prototypical member of a class, and so on to further extensions.[8] The most frequently generalized feature used for semantic extensions was shape (predominantly vertical extension and small size, similar to some patterns of historical development of classifiers considered in §13.9).

The following scheme shows the relative order of acquisition of Chinese classifiers (< stands for 'acquired earlier': Erbaugh 1986: 431):

classifiers for discrete, countable, portable concrete objects < classifiers for large immovable ones < classifiers for actions < classifiers for abstractions and honorifics;

measures < special classifiers;

valued items < common ones < conventionalized sets.

Items with unique reference were acquired before the prototypical members. Abstraction by extension, and small size, occurred before shape.

---

[7] Susan Quigley (p.c.) also reports that young Awará-speaking children in New Guinea do not use some specific classifiers.

[8] This order of acquisition may also relate to the order of development of conversation about different objects, in which case it could be an artefact of communication strategies with children.

This last statement is also confirmed by results of child acquisition of Japanese numeral classifiers. Sanches (1977: 61) arrives at the conclusion that most numeral classifiers in Japanese 'are learned in relation to the items they classify, in lists, rather than as representative of categories of criterial attributes that are potentially generalizable to an infinite variety of items'.

Animate classifiers are acquired first in Kilivila. They are followed by general classifiers for inanimates, and the classifiers which are acquired next denote concrete, specific objects, and salient features of objects (Senft 1996: 192). These conclusions have also been corroborated by investigations on Hokkien (Ng 1989: 123), and Cantonese (Luke and Harrison 1986).

A recent study of acquisition of classifiers by young Mandarin-speaking children showed the dependency between frequency of a classifier and its order of acquisition (Hu 1993). This study showed that the classifier *zhī* 'animate' is acquired very early, due to its frequency. Other classifiers which are acquired early are those which relate closely to the child's life. In contrast, the honorific classifier *wèi* and the classifier *tái* used for machines do not occur in children's speech until the age of six. This may be due to the irrelevance of such distinctions in the children's life (Hu 1993: 125).

As we saw in Chapter 9, Chinese uses classifier morphemes in two environments: with numerals and with deictics. These uses were acquired differently; classifiers with numbers were acquired before those with demonstratives. Classifiers with near-demonstratives were acquired before the far ones.

Errors in the acquisition of Thai classifiers showed the early overuse of general classifier *ʔan*, and repetition of the head noun in the classifier slot instead of making reference to its semantic content. In learning correspondences between perceptual properties of nouns and classifiers children have to figure out which perceptible characteristics are relevant to semantic categorization, since historical changes in classifier systems sometimes make the classifier assignment opaque. The first semantic opposition to be acquired is animate vs. inanimate (Juntanamalaga 1988: 322). Children then start making semantic overextensions based on extralinguistic resemblances among category members (shape, consistency, and function being frequent bases for extensions), to compensate for semantic limitations of classifier assignment (Gandour *et al.* 1984: 471–2). One strategy is overextension of more 'comprehensive', or 'general' classifiers and their overuse in place of more specific classifiers (e.g. general classifier *ʔan*). The opposite strategy consists in the overuse of 'repeaters', i.e. overspecialization—the use of every noun as its own classifier. Both strategies make the choice of classifiers less dependent on the inherent, or conventionalized semantic features of an object. This 'lightens' the semantic load of a classifier, and makes it easier to use classifiers without having access to the full range of extralinguistic information.

Language-specific properties of the semantic organization of classifier systems play a role in the order of their acquisition.

The shape-based classifiers appear to be acquired relatively early by speakers of Mandarin Chinese; classifiers which refer to non-extended round objects are acquired earlier than classifiers which refer to extended objects.

The results obtained by Ng (1991) concerning classifier use by Hokkien speakers of different ages, showed the overuse of the general classifier among children aged five to eight, indicating that 'Hokkien children learn the conventional use of classifiers after going through a long period of only producing the general classifiers' (p. 81). There was a certain number of overextensions based on perceptual clues (shape and form) and on animacy. In contrast, Gandour *et al.* (1984) demonstrated that in Thai, classifiers which refer to arrangement and quanta are acquired before the shape-based classifiers. Ng (1991: 81) hypothesizes that Hokkien children acquire the shape classifiers more easily than Thai children due to a larger degree of semantic complexity encoded in Thai classifiers, and also to the fact that Thai has more classifiers referring to shape than does Hokkien; Thai has at least six classifiers for one-dimensional objects, four classifiers for two-dimensional objects, and four more classifiers for three-dimensional objects, while Hokkien only has five shape-based classifiers.

Thus, the rate of acquisition of classifiers may be determined by their semantic complexity, that is, the number of contrasts encoded in them. The one-dimensional classifier *hon* and the two-dimensional classifier *mai* in Japanese do not encode concomitant features of flexibility or rigidity unlike their Hokkien counterparts; according to the results obtained by Matsumoto (1985), they are acquired earlier than the corresponding classifiers in Hokkien because they are semantically 'simpler'.

Stages in the acquisition of classifiers are best characterized as 'stages of organizing knowledge' (Carpenter 1991: 108–9). Children make almost no word order mistakes with classifiers. Once they have learnt that something 'belongs in the post-numeral position, they figure out its identity bit by bit, starting with the information that it must come from a closed set of words that conventionally appear in the post-numeral position' (Carpenter 1991: 109). This also explains why children tend not to be innovative with classifiers (Carpenter 1992).

These results agree with the results on acquisition of genders and noun classes—namely that children are sensitive to formal regularities and syntagmatic patterns. The relationship between a classifier and a number is acquired before the relationship between the classifier and the head noun.

However, to learn the full system of numeral classifiers, syntagmatic intralinguistic patterns are not sufficient. Children must then learn the correspondences between extralinguistic and intralinguistic categories, and this is why acquisition of classifiers is slow. The acquisition of classifiers by children consists in learning a conventional, pre-existing system which involves a large amount of cultural extralinguistic knowledge.

The order of development of classifiers in Mandarin Chinese parallels the historic processes of changes in classifier systems (Erbaugh 1986: 426–30). The results of Thai classifier acquisition as compared to the history of Thai classifiers are not as clear-cut (Carpenter 1992). The main difference between the two is that child language development is teleological, i.e. the end-product is the acquisition of a pre-existing system, while historical change does not have to be this way. We have seen in Chapter 13 that classifier choice can change in response to external factors, e.g. cultural change. Conventionality is more important in child language acquisition. This is why there are differences between the kinds of semantic primes important for classifying objects, for adults and for children. For instance, children seem to use material as an organizing feature much more than adults do. Carpenter (1992: 142) explains this as a consequence of the world of children being a special subculture in which the importance of material features (e.g. breakability) can override other perceptual features, e.g. shape, or size, before the children actually have the linguistic and the extralinguistic experience to know what are the 'right', i.e. the conventionalized attributes of linguistic categories.

In spite of these differences, both developmental and diachronic patterns reveal certain tendencies in common. Among such tendencies are the similarity between shape classifiers and containers, and an historical and a developmental relation between these. Another tendency is for the classifiers which are first learned to be predominantly nouns. We have seen above (Chapter 13), that, in the history of different types of classifier system, classifiers may come from verbs; however, these instances are much rarer, and they are, presumably, acquired later.

The acquisition of classifiers parallels the general tendencies of cognitive categorization, e.g. unique reference before prototypic members and extensions, and more concrete items and categories before more abstract ones (Erbaugh 1986; Lee 1988).

Clark (1977: 460) showed that cognitive paths of categorization in children's acquisition of word meaning resemble categorization patterns in classifier patterns. Both in child language acquisition and in classifiers, shape is the primary basis for categorization. 'Both classifier systems and children's overextensions reflect a basic categorization process that goes on first at the non-linguistic level' (see §12.2).

14.3. Dissolution of noun classes and of numeral classifiers

The expectation that patterns of dissolution in aphasia might be the mirror image of acquisition by children comes from the seminal work by Jakobson (1941). Earlier acquired features are expected to be most resistant to loss in aphasia, and in other situations of language dissolution (Herbert 1991: 125). However, acquisition and dissolution of noun classes show some striking differences.

Herbert's study (1991) is a pioneering one in showing how noun class prefixes and agreement behave in language dissolution in Bantu, namely, Broca-type aphasia, and how this is different from child language acquisition. While children start with acquiring agreement and end up with acquiring overt noun class marking for nouns, the production of nouns with an overt prefix is regular in aphasic speech. There is also no systematic reduction in the inventory of prefixes, and the agreement system is preserved. The most common errors are errors when the noun prefix on the noun is correct but the generated concords are not, i.e. nouns are assigned to 'wrong' agreement classes in subject-verb agreement. Wrong concords appear more rarely in head-modifier Noun Phrases.

Semantically, what child language acquisition shares with the aphasic data is the prominence of a human/non-human distinction. In aphasics, many concord errors involved transfer of nouns with human referents to Class 1/2 (Herbert 1991: 126).

The data on language dissolution agree with data on child language acquisition in that both show the primacy of concord, singular and plural distinctions, and the feature human/non-human. The difference lies in the head-marking of nouns which is stable with aphasics but appears to be acquired later by children (Herbert 1991: 128).

Recent work on dissolution of numeral classifiers in Thai (Gandour *et al.* 1985) agrees with the mirror image hypothesis for language acquisition and language dissolution. Classifiers based on inherent perceptual characteristics of objects are less resistant to aphasic disruption than those which are not. Errors in animate classifiers typically involved substitution of honorifics by classifiers referring to ordinary persons, or by generic *tua* 'animal, thing'. Classifiers based on configuration and quanta, e.g. groups, appeared to be the least stable in language dissolution. Errors made by adult aphasics are here similar to errors made by young children. Aphasics tended to overuse the general classifier *ʔan*, and to use repeaters instead of appropriate classifiers (Gandour *et al.* 1985: 552).[9]

---

[9] Other factors could have contributed to these errors. In informal spontaneous conversation in Thai, the general classifier is an appropriate substitute for almost any special classifier. This is not true for other styles and registers. The overuse of the general classifier could have

Tseng *et al.* (1991) compared two types of aphasic speaker of Mandarin Chinese and Taiwanese: those with Broca's aphasia, resulting in agrammatism (defined as 'dropping out of connective words, auxiliaries, and general loss of obligatory grammar') and those with Wernicke's aphasia, resulting in paragrammatism (defined as 'the substitution of an inappropriate grammatical form for the correct target': p. 185). The general tendency in both types was to substitute a more specific classifier with a general ('neutral') one. It has also been observed that Broca's aphasics tended to avoid classifier constructions, while the Wernicke's patients showed more instances of substitution of a 'correct' classifier with an incorrect one, more often the general one, and even more often the neutral one.[10]

That is, like children, aphasics were trying to 'lighten' the semantic load of each classifier, making the classifier assignment less conventionalized and less dependent on extralinguistic information they did not possess to the same extent as before.

14.4. Conclusions

Children's acquisition of noun classes, and of numeral classifiers, shows a number of fundamental differences. In both cases syntagmatic rules (and agreement, in the case of genders and noun classes) are acquired first. Overt marking of gender and noun class is acquired later. The first semantic division to be acquired relates to human/non-human. The tendency to overgeneralize a particular noun class over others is slight. Children have been shown to rely much more on intralinguistic information than on extralinguistic (Pérez-Pereira 1991).

In contrast, extralinguistic information is more important for lexical-like systems of classifiers. Animacy and shape, material and function, and knowledge of socio-cultural categories are among the most important factors in classifier acquisition. The tendency to 'lighten' the semantic load of classifiers goes in two directions—overgeneralization, i.e. reliance on the general classifier, or overspecialization, i.e. overuse of the repeater technique. In mastering a classifier system, children have to rely on extralinguistic

---

also been due to the fact that aphasics lost their capacity of adequately understanding and manipulating varying styles and registers of discourse (Gandour *et al.* 1985: 552). The overuse of repeaters could have been partly due to echolalia (i.e. mere repetition as a part of the disease). Differences found in classifier responses could have been partly due to frequency of use of the associated noun.

[10] However, according to Ahrens (1994), Tseng *et al.* (1991) underestimated the role of code-switching from Mandarin to Taiwanese among their speakers. Her experimental studies showed that the use of the general classifier ('classifier neutralization') followed the same lines in aphasics and in normal speakers. More studies are needed.

information rather than on intralinguistic. This is why they acquire classifier systems later than agreement noun classes.

Existing studies of language dissolution—however few—also point in the same direction. Language dissolution of numeral classifiers in Thai mirrors the acquisition of classifiers by children. Disintegration of extralinguistic knowledge in aphasics results in overgeneralization (overuse of the general classifier) or overspecialization (overuse of repeaters). However, dissolution of noun classes differs from child language acquisition in that head-marked noun classes which are acquired late by children are not lost in aphasia. The principles of concord also persist; and the main errors in language dissolution concern wrong assignment of agreement classes, and sometimes overgeneralization of classes.

Acquisition of classifiers has much in common with acquisition of the lexicon, unlike the acquisition of noun classes and genders. Acquisition of classifiers has many features in common with principles of their historical development; the same would be arguable for noun classes and genders.

In sum, as Carpenter (1991: 111) put it, 'it is possible that numeral classifiers are acquired differently from other, previously described kinds of noun classes largely because they are organized and represented in speakers' minds in a fundamentally different way'.

More investigation on acquisition and dissolution of other classifier types, especially for multiple classifier systems, is needed, before we can fully understand the underlying cognitive and acquisitional principles.

15 Conclusions

This concluding chapter recapitulates and summarizes the general themes which have emerged from a cross-linguistic study of noun categorization devices. An overview of established classifier types used in different morphosyntactic environments and of their synchronic and diachronic properties—which cover their morphological realization and role in agreement, principles of assignment, interaction with other grammatical categories, semantics, and functions, as well as their origin and role in language acquisition and dissolution—are summarized in §15.1. The co-occurrence of different classifiers in one language, multiple classifier languages, and the problem of prototypes and continua in noun categorization are discussed in §15.2. The last section, §15.3, considers further prospects for the study of noun categorization devices.

15.1. Properties of classifier types

In this section I present an overview of the established types of classifiers. First, I discuss the morphosyntactic environments (loci) in which classifiers appear and constituents which they characterize—(A) morphosyntactic locus of coding and (B) scope, or domain of categorization (as introduced in §1.5). For each type, I outline its prototypical characteristics. Classifiers are then characterized with respect to their other properties outlined in §1.5: (C) principles of assignment; (D) kinds of surface realization; (E) role in agreement; (F) markedness relations; (G) degree of grammaticalization and lexicalization; (H) interaction with other grammatical categories; (I) semantic organization of the system; (J) evolution and decay; and (K) language acquisition and dissolution. Classifier systems also differ as to how obligatory they are, and in their size. Smallish sets of noun classes are more likely to be obligatory than large sets of classifiers of other types. Possessor classifiers are a very rare kind, and as a consequence no generalizations can be made concerning them. Locative and deictic classifiers are quite rare, and the generalizations which can be made concerning them are limited.

(A) Morphosyntactic locus of coding; (B) Scope, or domain of categorization

NOUN CLASS SYSTEMS and GENDERS are closed, highly grammaticalized, obligatory systems, realized through obligatory affixal agreement within and sometimes outside a noun phrase. Their inventory is often smallish (from two to ten). Different subtypes of noun class system can cooccur in one language. Noun classes can have an NP or a clause as their scope. If noun classes have a clause as their scope this signifies 'noun class' agreement of an argument with a predicate. This argument may be A or S, O or S, or an oblique. Noun classes can be marked on the noun itself.

NOUN CLASSIFIERS characterize the head noun itself; they appear independently of any other element in an NP. They can be realized as independent lexical items (cf. traditional terms such as 'generics', or 'sortal classifiers'), or as affixes to the noun. Noun classifiers may develop into noun classes by first fusing with the noun they refer to, and later developing into agreement markers.

NUMERAL CLASSIFIERS characterize nouns in numerical noun phrases and expressions of quantity. They can be realized as independent lexical items, affixes to numbers, or quantifying terms; or they may, very rarely, form one constituent with a noun. Their inventory is often large.

Classifiers in possessive NPs fall into three groups. RELATIONAL CLASSIFIERS characterize the nature of the possessive relation; they are usually independent lexemes, but may be affixed to the possessed noun or possessor pronoun. POSSESSED CLASSIFIERS characterize the possessed noun; they are usually affixed to it, but may alternatively be expressed through an independent word. Some 'borderline' systems combine the properties of the possessed and of the relational type. A rather rare type, POSSESSOR CLASSIFIERS, characterizes the possessor.

VERBAL CLASSIFIERS mark agreement in the verb with an extra-predicate NP argument, almost always in S or O function, but sometimes in an oblique function. Verbal classifiers come in three subtypes: incorporated classifiers, affixes, and suppletive classificatory stems. Different subtypes of verbal classifiers can cooccur in one language.

Two further, rather rare classifier types operate within an NP. LOCATIVE CLASSIFIERS occur in locative expressions, marking agreement with the head noun. They can be affixed to a locative, or fused with it. DEICTIC CLASSIFIERS occur with deictic elements (articles and demonstratives). They can be affixed to or fused with a deictic.

Table 15.1 summarizes the scope of classifier types, their grammatical function and constituents they refer to.

(C) Principles of assignment

When compared to other types of classifiers, noun class systems differ in the principles of assignment. Noun class assignment can be governed by the semantic, morphological, or phonological properties of a noun, or a combination of these. In a sense all systems of noun class assignment are mixed, since there is always a semantic core which involves universal

TABLE 15.1. *Scope of classifier types*

Classifier type	Scope	Grammatical function	Constituent referred to
1. Noun class/gender	Inside a head-modifier NP	Determination	Head noun
	Outside NP	Head-modifier agreement	
2. Noun classifiers	Noun	Predicate-argument agreement	A/S or S/O oblique
3. Numeral classifiers	Numeral/quantifier NP	Determination	Head noun
4. Relational classifiers	Possessive NP	Quantification, enumeration	Head noun
5. Possessed classifiers	Possessive NP	Possession	Possessive relation
6. Possessor classifiers	Possessive NP	Possession	Possessed noun
7. Verbal classifiers	Clause	Possession	Possessor
8. Locative classifiers	Adpositional NP	S/O agreement	S/O or oblique
9. Deictic classifiers	Attributive NP	Spatial location	Argument of adposition
		Spatial location, determination	Head noun

semantic parameters, such as sex, humanness, animacy (see Chapter 2). The assignment of all other classifier types is always semantic, even though it may sometimes be a little opaque; it is never based on the morphological or phonological properties of the noun. This characteristic of noun class systems follows from their higher degree of grammaticalization in comparison to other classifier types. See Table 15.2.

(D) Surface realization; (E) Role in agreement

Noun classes and verbal classifiers can never be expressed with free lexemes, unlike classifiers of other types. Verbal classifiers, locative and deictic classifiers never appear attached to nouns. Classifiers of any type can appear attached to an item in or outside an NP, as a suffix or a clitic. Further details on the morphological devices used for marking each of the classifier types are summarized in Table 15.3. Noun classes, deictic classifiers, possessor classifiers, and verbal classifiers participate in agreement; numeral and possessed classifiers participate in agreement only if expressed with bound morphemes. Relational and noun classifiers belong to non-agreeing noun categorization devices; and so do numeral and possessed classifiers expressed with free morphemes.

(F) Markedness relations

Classifier types differ as to the relations of markedness. There may be a functionally and/or formally unmarked member of a noun class system; markedness relations can seldom be established in other types. However, default classifiers present in some systems may be considered analogous to functionally unmarked noun classes.

(G) Degree of grammaticalization and lexicalization

Noun classes are the most grammaticalized noun categorization devices. Noun classifiers, which are more lexical, may be grammaticalized into noun classes. The choice of other classifier types involves a quasi-lexical selection.

(H) Interaction with other grammatical categories

The ways in which different classifier types show interactions with other categories are shown in Table 10.17. Noun classes tend to interact with noun categories (e.g. number) and verbal categories (e.g. tense), while verbal classifiers show interdependencies with clausal categories (such as grammatical relations) and with verbal categories. Classifiers in possessive constructions may be restricted to one type of possession (e.g. alienable or inalienable). Interaction of any type of classifier with other grammatical categories depends on the scope of the classifier (Table 15.1) and their realization as free or as bound morphemes.

TABLE 15.2. *Assignment of classifiers*

	Noun class	Numeral classifiers	Relational classifiers	Possessed classifiers	Locative classifiers	Deictic classifiers	Noun classifiers	Verbal classifiers
1. Semantic assignment	May be only partially				Fully			
2. Every noun is associated with one class(ifier) or belongs to a class	Yes				Not necessary			

TABLE 15.3. *Morphological realization of classifiers*

	Prefix/proclitic	Suffix/enclitic	Apophony	Suppletion	Stress	Reduplication	Noun incorporation	Repeaters
Noun classes	+	+	+	−	+ (only for classes marked on the noun itself, or head classes)	−	−	yes
Numeral classifiers	+	+	−	+	−	+	−	yes
Noun classifiers	+	+	−	−	−	−	−	(only in multiple classifier systems)
Relational classifiers	rare	+	−	−	−	−	−	−
Possessed classifiers	+	+	−	−	−	−	−	yes
Verbal classifiers	+	+	−	+	−	−	+	−
Locative classifiers	−	+	−	+	−	−	−	−
Deictic classifiers	+	+	−	+	−	−	−	(only in multiple classifier systems)

Conclusions 431

(I) Semantic organization of the system

Classifiers of established types differ in their preferred semantics (Table 11.13); however, preferences for different semantic parameters represent only tendencies. Animacy and physical properties—and, rarely, functional properties—tend to be encoded into noun classes and numeral classifiers. Noun classifiers tend to encode functional properties and social status, and more rarely properties referring to inherent nature. Verbal classifiers tend to encode physical properties, other inherent nature characteristics, and directionality, but not necessarily animacy. Relational classifiers encode functional properties, while possessed classifiers encode physical properties, nature, animacy, and sometimes functional properties. Locative and deictic classifiers tend to encode physical properties; deictic classifiers tend to encode directionality as well. Generic-specific relations are characteristic of noun classifiers, verbal classifiers and sometimes possessed classifiers, but not of other types (they are rare in numeral classifiers).

Classifiers may also differ in the organization of the system. In noun class systems, every noun has to be assigned to a class; this is not necessarily so with other types.

Noun classes in general tend to be obligatory, while the realization of other types may be optional. All classifier types are used anaphorically and as participant tracking devices. The use of optional noun categorization devices correlates more with referentiality, specificity, definiteness, topical continuity, and the discourse salience of a noun than that of the obligatory ones (see Chapter 12).

(J) Evolution and decay

Noun categorization devices differ in their etymological source, and, consequently, in the grammaticalization processes which apply to them. In particular, closed word classes give rise only to noun classes, not to other categorization devices. Nouns are a typical source for all classifier types; however, different lexical groups of nouns tend to grammaticalize as different categorization devices (see Table 13.1). Verbs can give rise only to numeral classifiers, deictic classifiers, relational classifiers, and some kinds of verbal classifier (Table 13.5). A less grammaticalized and less obligatory device may develop into a more obligatory one (e.g. development of noun classifiers into noun classes in Australian languages: see §13.4). Classifiers can get reanalysed and drift into a different type within the same scope (e.g. reinterpretation of an old noun class system as numeral classifiers in Bengali). The development and structure of a classifier system is often affected by sociolinguistic parameters, language planning, and language obsolescence factors; these changes tend to affect large classifier systems more than closed, grammaticalized noun classes.

(K) Language acquisition and dissolution

Acquisition of noun classes and of numeral classifiers show a number of fundamental differences. In mastering a numeral classifier system, children appear to rely more on extralinguistic information than they do in acquiring a more closed and more grammaticalised system of noun classes. Studies in language dissolution appear to be a mirror-image of their acquisition (Chapter 14). More work is needed to substantiate these preliminary generalizations.

In spite of the morphosyntactic differences between classifiers of distinct types, they represent a unitary phenomenon of noun categorization. This was corroborated by the fact that different varieties of classifiers share the same semantic features (see §11.1), and most of the same functions (§12.1); they share etymological sources and paths of grammaticalization, evolution and decay. In addition, one kind of noun categorization device can be reanalysed as another. Languages can have more than one kind of noun categorization device; and one noun categorization device can be realized in multiple environments. But how discrete are the types of noun categorizations, and are there any possibilities of having more types of classifier than those described in this book? This issue is dealt with in the following section.

15.2. Cooccurrence of classifier types and multiple classifier languages; prototypes and continua

We have seen that a number of languages have more than one system of classifiers; in most cases one of these systems is noun classes, while the other one can be of almost any other kind. Typical combinations are: noun classes and numeral classifiers; noun classes and noun classifiers; noun classes and verbal classifiers; numeral classifiers and relational classifiers; and numeral classifiers and noun classifiers.

The possibility of the coexistence of several classifier types within one language discussed in Chapter 8 is a strong argument in favour of the proposed typology, alongside the varying properties of the classifiers as summarized in §15.1. Languages can have up to six formally distinct sets of classifiers, which differ both in function and in semantics.

It is unusual for languages to distinguish all the three kinds of classifier in possessive constructions; however, there are examples of languages with relational and possessed classifiers. The reason for the rarity of deictic classifiers as a separate type may be due to their overlap with noun classes in scope and in the constituent referred to. Locative classifiers may be relatively rare because adpositional NPs are problematic as a separate type of NP (they often overlap with possessive NPs). The extreme rarity of possessor classifiers may be due to the fact that the nature of the possessor allows little variation in languages, a prototypical possessor being human, or animate; there is thus hardly any need to categorize the possessor (see Chapter 5).

Some languages—mostly from Southeast Asia and South America, together with a few Austronesian and Papuan languages—have multiple classifier systems, i.e. morphemes which appear in all the environments listed in Table 15.1 but generally have some behaviourial differences. Multiple classifier languages employ the same—or almost the same—set of morphemes in up to six different environments; see Chapter 9. Multiple classifier systems are distinct from noun classes realized on different targets (see §9.2).

Besides combining several classifier types in one language, languages can have several subtypes of one type of noun categorization. The most widespread instance is the possession of different noun class systems (see §2.7), usually, a larger system of 'nominal', and a smaller system of 'pronominal' noun classes (§2.7.1), which may be in complementary distribution with respect to morphosyntactic environments. I have also described rarer instances of languages with more than one morphological type of numeral classifier (see §4.3), and of languages with two coexisting kinds of verbal classifiers (see §6.4). No languages have been found with several distinct subtypes of noun classifiers, or of any of the classifiers in possessive constructions, or of locative or deictic classifiers.

The existence of different subtypes of established types suggests the possibility of an 'open-endedness' for the proposed typology. I have mentioned several times throughout this book how the established types are better seen as referring to 'focal points' on a continuum of noun categorization devices rather than to discrete types (cf. also Craig forthcoming: 43).

These continuum phenomena are of the following kinds. First, classifiers could be just emerging, having not yet acquired the full status of grammatical morphemes: they may be employed with only a minority of nouns and be easily omissible (cf. the discussion of incipient numeral classifiers in §4.4.2). Second, classifiers may be difficult to distinguish from other morphological mechanisms; for instance, there are often difficulties in distinguishing noun incorporation and verbal classifiers (see Chapter 6, and especially n. 2 there). Third, there are borderline cases where it is far from clear how many classifier types a language has: see the discussion in §9.3.

Continua can also be established within particular types. For instance, in many cases the distinction between mensural and sortal numeral classifiers can be seen as that of a continuum (see Chapter 4, and the examples from

434   *Classifiers*

Palikur body parts in Chapter 13 which show that the same morpheme can be used in both ways). It may be difficult to distinguish one type of classifier from another; for instance, if a language has classifiers used on demonstratives, it may be unclear whether this implies the presence of deictic classifiers, or just noun classes which are realized on this target (cf. §7.3). In the case of poorly known languages (such as Kipeá, an extinct Macro-Jê language from Brazil: Rodrigues 1997) it is almost impossible to tell a multiple classifier system from a system with agreement on multiple targets (cf. §9.2).

Thus, the classifier types outlined here correspond to 'focal points' on the cline of possibilities for grammaticalized noun categorization devices realized in distinct morphosyntactic environments. The 'focal' points at the edge of the continuum have more prototypical properties than the points along the continuum. Further morphosyntactic contexts may develop into new contexts in which classifiers may be used—indeed, in some cases it seems to be almost impossible to tell whether we are dealing with new emergent classifier types or extensions of already existing ones; see the discussion in §9.3. In particular, subtypes within certain types—noun classes, numeral, and verbal classifiers—are the most likely candidates to give rise to new kinds of noun categorization devices.

The whole typology of noun categorization devices might be thus best presented in terms of focal points (with their prototypical properties) along a continuum of noun categorization. This conclusion is significant for a descriptive approach to noun categorization devices; instead of trying to fit noun categorization devices in a particular language into a certain type, the important thing is to place them onto a continuum, and then decide which prototypes they most resemble.

15.3. Prospects for future studies

A number of areas require further work in order to refine our understanding of noun categorization systems. In spite of growing interest in noun categorization devices all over the world (see §1.4), there is an urgent need to provide more good descriptive studies of individual systems, especially in areas of little-known 'exotic' and highly endangered languages, such as Amazonia and New Guinea. In many cases, for languages with some documentation the analysis of noun categorization devices requires further work. For instance, gender systems in languages such as Dení and Kulina (Arawá) and Chapacuran, and animacy systems in Baining languages (East New Britain), require urgent further investigation. More studies are required on numeral classifier languages in West Africa, in particular Cross River languages and Grasslands languages. 'Repeater' phenomena as agreement devices are in an urgent need of a systematic study, in particular in West Atlantic languages such as Baïnouk and Landuma.

Multiple classifier languages are most in need of detailed study. These include numerous South Arawak languages (e.g. Pareci, Waurá, Yawalapiti, and various Campa languages), Tupí, Bora-Witoto, Tucano and Makú languages from the Amazon, and Southeast Asian languages such as Miao-Yao. Multiple classifier systems in languages of the South Pacific are in need of urgent systematic study; these include Reef-Santa Cruzan languages from the Solomons, Papuan languages from Central and South Bougainville, and multiple classifier languages from New Guinea, such as Awará and Wantoat, from Morobe province, and languages of the Angan family. Even for well-described languages there is often a need for more detailed study, especially a text-based one, in order to establish relationships between discourse and noun categorization devices.

The acquisition and dissolution of classifiers of different types, especially in multiple classifier systems, is also in urgent need of study—this is probably the most notable gap in classifier studies.

Noun categorization devices offer a rich ground for collaborative research by descriptive linguists, typologists, sociolinguists, and psycholinguists, together with sociologists, philosophers, and psychologists. Noun categorization devices offer numerous possibilities for important projects, in core areas of linguistics, as well as in a wide range of cross-disciplinary fields. The most important task, however, is first to pursue descriptive studies, in order to collect additional materials which may then assist us in rethinking the whole framework.

It is also important to note that in spite of differences along many parameters all classifiers reflect (in different ways) a single phenomenon—the categorization of nominals by humans, through human language. They reflect common cognitive mechanisms, and common semantic features, such as humanness and animacy.

This book includes material from about 500 languages, but these cover no more than one-tenth of the world's languages; further studies of noun categorization devices in previously undocumented or scarcely documented languages will help deepen our understanding of the mechanisms of human cognition.

Appendix 1
Noun Categorization by Means Other than Classifiers

Languages without any noun categorization devices—noun classes or classifiers of other types—tend to express some of the meanings characteristic of classifiers through other categories, e.g. number, case, declensions or derivational affixes. Typically, these categories are then sensitive to animacy and humanness distinctions. In languages with noun classification the choice made in these categories may also depend on animacy or humanness of the referent, alongside with—but independently of—noun classification devices. How these categories can be employed to categorize nouns is discussed here.

(A) In many languages with no noun classification, NUMBER depends on the animacy, or humanness, of the noun. Typically, there are more number distinctions made for animate or human nouns than for inanimates or non-humans. For instance, in Comanche (Uto-Aztecan) dual and plural marking is obligatory for human nouns, optional for animate nouns, and seldom used for inanimates (Charney 1993: 49–50). In Koasati (Muskogean: Kimball 1991: 447) human nouns may be optionally marked with a suffix *-ha*; other nouns have no plural marker. The distinction of animate/inanimate is combined with number marking in Basque (Iturrioz *et al.* 1986a). In Epena Pedee, a Choco language from Colombia (Harms 1994: 55), plural marking is obligatory on nouns with human referents. In Kobon (Papuan), when a generic noun with an inherently plural referent functions as subject, singular or plural marking on the verb depends on the animacy of the noun—plural is marked only if the noun has a human referent (Onishi 1997b: 18; Davies 1981).

This tendency also holds in languages with classifiers but no agreement noun classes. In Ainu, which has two numeral classifiers (*-n/-iw* 'human' and *-pe/-p* 'non-human'), the plural suffix *-utar* is used just with human and animate nouns (Onishi 1996a). In Japanese, number choices correlate with humanness and animacy on the one hand and politeness on the other: polite plural suffixes *-tati* (neutral), *-ra* (intimate), or *-domo* (humble, derogatory) may be attached to a noun with an animate referent; -*gata* 'plural: polite' can only be attached to a noun with a human referent (Onishi 1996b). In Slave and other Athabaskan languages (Rice 1989) the expression of number is obligatory only with human referents.

If a language has optional number marking and/or agreement, fewer choices are available for inanimates and non-humans. In Motuna, a Papuan language from Bougainville with an elaborate multiple classifier system and five noun classes, inanimate nouns do not distinguish dual and paucal, but animate nouns do (Onishi 1994). See also Smith-Stark (1974).

(B) Animate/inanimate and human/non-human distinctions can be realized in the way a language marks GRAMMATICAL RELATIONS. The choice of case marker often depends on animacy, or humanness. In Awa Pit (or Cuaiquer, Barbacoan: Curnow 1997: 66), accusative marking is obligatory only for referential human NPs (Awa Pit has no other noun classification devices, except, possibly, for a small set of noun classifiers: Curnow 1997: 121). In Amele (Papuan) indirect objects (cross-referenced with an enclitic on the verb) must have a human referent; and one class of verbs takes an optional O clitic when a 3rd person singular O has a human or an animate referent (Roberts 1987).

The number of case distinctions—indicating the grammatical function of a noun—correlates with its animacy in agreement with the Nominal Hierarchy proposed by Silverstein (1976); see also Dixon (1994); Frawley (1992: 93–4) (and see Diagram 10.1 above). The choice between ergative and nominative/accusative marking in languages where split ergativity is conditioned by the semantics of nouns is controlled by the degree of animacy of the subject: the more animate it is, the likelier it is to receive nominative/accusative marking. The likelihood of ergative marking is inversely proportional to the degree of animacy of the subject (Dixon 1994: 85).

One often gets more case distinctions for nouns with human or animate reference than for those with non-human or inanimate reference, independently of whether a language has agreement noun classes or not. In Spanish, the preposition *a* is used to mark just human objects. In Yessan-Mayo, a language with two genders from the East Sepik region of New Guinea, the dative case marker -*ni* can also be used to mark O function just with animate nouns (Foley 1986: 101); inanimate transitive objects are unmarked.

Similarly, in Central Pomo a formal distinction between S_a and S_o is made only if they refer to human referents (Mithun 1991: 521–3): *mú·ṭu* is the form for 3rd person human S_o, while another form, *mu·l*, is used to cover human S_a and non-human S_a and S_o. In Wära (Risto Sarsa, p.c.) and Wipi (Dondorp and Shim 1997: 25), languages of the Fly River of New

Guinea, masculine and feminine genders are distinguished for absolutive cross-referencing markers on the verb, but not for the ergative.

In Manambu, only proper nouns and personal pronouns are obligatorily marked for accusative when used as direct objects. In Bengali accusative noun phrases are obligatorily marked by the suffix -*ke* when they have definite human reference (Onishi 1996c). In both Dyirbal, Australian (Dixon 1972: 43), and Dogon, from the Niger-Congo family (Plungian 1995: 12), there is an accusative marker, used for O function only with proper names of people and some nouns with human reference such as the kin terms 'mother' and 'father'.

Some Mayan languages—which have numeral classifiers, but not noun classes—show an interesting dependency between the relative placement of transitive subject and object on the nominal hierarchy and their constituent order. When A and O are equal on the animacy hierarchy (e.g. both are human, or animate), the order is VAO; when the A is higher on the hierarchy than the O, the order is VOA (Campbell 2000; England 1991).

The existence of non-animacy-based classifier systems does not go against the universality of animacy as a parameter for human categorization. Even if animacy or humanness is not found in a classifier system, it is likely to be present somewhere else in the language. Waris has animacy in classificatory verbs, and verbal classifiers have no animacy distinctions; there are also complicated dependencies between humanness or animacy of the referent and the choice of markers for locative and allative cases (Brown 1981: 3). In Ika the verbal prefix *an-* is used with transitive verbs to indicate a non-human object (Frank 1990: 73); however, humanness or animacy are not distinguished in classificatory verbs in this language.

(C) Animacy may be realized through the ways in which POSSESSION is marked. The scope of *-komo* 'collective' in Hixkaryana (Carib) depends on whether the possessor or the possessed are human: it refers to the possessor, if it is human (*ki-kanawa-ri-komo* '1INCL-canoe-POSS-COLL' 'our canoe'); and to the possessed if it is human (*i-ha-ri-komo* '3p-grandchild-POSS-COLL' 'his grandchildren'). If both possessor and possessed are human there is a potential ambiguity: *ki-kuku-ru-komo* can mean both 'our relatives', or 'our (collective) relative' (Derbyshire 1985: 200). In many languages possessors must be animate, or human, as in Hua (Haiman 1980; Onishi 1997a).

(D) The division of nouns into DECLENSIONAL PARADIGMS can reflect animacy or humanness distinctions in languages with no other noun classification devices. These can be remnants of a lost noun class system—see the example of Lezgian in §10.6. Chukchee also has no genders, or classifiers; but nouns are divided into declensional paradigms according to the animacy of the referent (Michael Dunn, p.c.).

In languages with an independent system of noun classes or classifiers, animacy reflected in the organization of paradigms may provide a basis for an additional classification of nouns. So-called subgenders in Slavic languages are based on animacy distinctions; the choice of accusative or genitive case for O function and the choice of agreement forms depends on the animacy of the head noun: see Corbett (1991: 165–7) and (C) in §2.4.4, for an analysis of subgenders in Russian. For just a few words, animate/ inanimate declensions are used to distinguish homonyms. *Koshki*, plural of 'cat', belongs to the animate declension if it refers to the animals; *koshki* in the inanimate declension refers to boots used by alpinists for climbing mountains. The two words are obviously connected historically. Sometimes shifting a noun from inanimate to animate declension type can be used to achieve the stylistic effect of personifying an important referent. In the famous poem by Gumilëv, 'Captains', ships are personified through the use of an animate accusative form (which is the same as genitive) instead of the normal inanimate accusative (the same as nominative) (Rothstein 1973: 465).

(E) There are other ways in which animacy and humanness can be encoded in grammatical systems outside noun classification devices. Personal pronouns tend to be restricted to human referents. Kana (Kegboid: Ikoro 1996a) has almost no animacy distinctions in numeral classifiers; humans are distinguished from non-humans in the ways they can be pronominalized (Ikoro 1996b). In Hua (Papuan: Haiman 1980), a language without any classifiers, personal pronouns must have human referents, and deictics always have inanimate referents. Similarly, in Bengali 3rd person 'ordinary' pronouns are used to refer to humans, and the demonstrative is used with non-humans (Onishi 1996c). In Korafe (Binanderre family, New Guinea: Cindi Farr, p.c.) personal pronouns are used only to refer to human beings and personified non-human animates. In Jarawara, only animates (including the personified sun, moon, and stars) can be referred to by the 3rd person plural pronoun *mee*. In Lao, 3rd person pronoun *man* is normally used for non-human referents, animate or inanimate; with human referents, it is only used for small children (Chapman 1996). In Chinese, the personal pronoun *ta* can only be used with human referents (Walter Bisang, p.c.). Imonda (Papuan) has no verbal classifiers based on animacy or humanness; there are different coordinating clitics for non-humans (*-na*), and for humans (*-i*) (Seiler 1985: 68–9). See also see the discussion of Finnish in §13.2.

Japanese has two existential verbs: *aru* requires an S with an inanimate referent; *iru* requires an S with an animate referent (LaPolla 1994). In

Hua, there are two copulas: one, *bai-*, is used with animate subjects, and the other, *no-*, is used with inanimate subjects (Haiman 1980; Onishi 1997a).

Another technique languages use to distinguish animates from inanimates, or humans from non-humans, is through different interrogative words. Uralic languages typically have no noun classes, or classifiers of other types,[1] the distinction between the human interrogative 'who' (**ki*) and the non-human 'what' (**mikä, *mi*) goes back to Proto-Uralic (Collinder 1965: 138).

Animacy distinctions[2] in interrogatives appear to be independent of whether there are any other animacy-based noun classification devices. For instance, Igbo has different forms for 'who' and 'what'; there are no other animacy distinctions (but see above for derivation); and Tamazight Berber languages (e.g. Zemmur, Seghrouchen, Izayan: Laoust 1928: 197), which distinguish two genders, have just one form, *mai*, for both 'who' and 'what'.

(F) Animacy, humanness, and gender distinctions are often expressed through derivation (see §10.9). Balto-Finnic languages have no noun classes, or other classifiers; however, there are a few feminine derivational suffixes, e.g. in Estonian: *kuningas* 'king', *kuninganna* 'queen', *õpilane* 'student (masculine or feminine)', *õpilanna* 'female student'; *laulaja* 'singer (masculine or feminine)', *laula-tar* 'female singer' (further examples are given in n. 22 to Chapter 13).

Igbo has an animate/inanimate distinction in the way nouns are derived from verbs. If the derived noun is inanimate the prefix is a homorganic nasal; but if it is animate, the derivational prefix is a harmonizing vowel, *ò-* or *ɔ-*, e.g. ŋ̀gwúu dʒí 'yam digger' (an instrument), *ògwuu dʒí* 'yam digger' (a person) (from *gwu dʒí* 'dig up yams') (Ikoro 1997).

Gender distinctions can also be realized in different discourse techniques, proverbs, and terms of verbal abuse (see Braun forthcoming a, for a case study of Turkish). Gender differences can also be reflected in the ways different terms relating to professions are used; in Turkish, 'goldsmith' or 'taxi driver' most often has a male referent, while 'secretary' or 'cleaning person' typically implies a female.

Thus, distinctions between animate/inanimate or human/non-human are made on a grammatical level in the great majority of languages. There are very few languages in which similar distinctions are made on the lexical level only. One such example is Ewe (Kwa: Felix Ameka 1991, and p.c.).

---

[1] However, Hungarian does have numeral classifiers, according to Beckwith (1992).
[2] The semantics of 'who' and 'what' may differ in terms of scope even between related languages; for example, 'who' refers to humans and higher animates in Russian, but only to humans in Polish (Anna Wierzbicka, p.c.).

Ewe lacks a human/non-human or animate/inanimate distinction anywhere in its grammar, even in interrogatives. A question marker *ka* can cooccur with any noun, e.g. *nú ka* (thing INTERROGATIVE) 'which thing, what', *ame ka* (person INTERROGATIVE) 'which person, who', *afi ka* (place INTERROGATIVE) 'which place, where'.

Appendix 2
From Nouns to Classifiers: Further Examples of Semantic Change

(A) Body parts as sources for classifiers: semantic extensions

Body and body part terms can be used as classifiers for humans and/or non-human animates, and for inanimates. In the two cases they undergo different semantic changes.

Only the generic 'body' is used to classify humans and animates as a verbal classifier, e.g. in Ngandi, or Mayali (Chapter 6). Both 'body' and various body parts occur as numeral classifiers to classify humans and animates. 'Body' may be used as a general classifier for 'person', cf. Katu (Katuic, Mon-Khmer: Adams 1992: 109) *chanak* 'general human classifier', from Proto-East Katuic *cak 'body'. Proto-Waic (Mon-Khmer) *kɨʔ 'man, body' is found as a human classifier in Northern Palaungic languages (Adams 1992: 109).

'Body' is a numeral classifier for animals and sometimes for all animates in Tai languages (with the form based on *tua*: Conklin 1981: 135–6). In Thai, *tua* 'body' is becoming a generic classifier (Carpenter 1986). In Burmese, *kauŋ* 'body' is used to classify animals, ghosts, dead bodies, depraved people and children (Becker 1975).

Body parts may be used as classifiers for humans, and animates in general. The use of body parts involves metonymy (a human, or an animate in general is defined by its salient body part). Semantic change is from a more specific to a more general referent. The body parts most frequently used for classifying humans are 'head' and 'eye'.[1] Some examples are given below.

---

[1] This semantic change corresponds to the following natural tendencies of semantic change discovered by Wilkins (1981; 1996: 273): 'It is a natural tendency for a term for a visible person-part to shift to refer to the visible whole of which it is a part . . . e.g. "navel" > "belly" > "trunk" > "body" > "person"', and also 'it is natural tendency for a person-part term to shift to refer to a spatially contiguous person part within the same whole (e.g. "belly" <-> "chest"; "skull" <-> "brain")'.

(A1) 'Top, head'[2] > classifier for humans
This is widespread in Southeast Asian languages. In Nicobarese, *kōi* 'head' is used to classify humans (Adams 1989: 93). In Burmese, the body part noun *'u* 'head', which also has a more abstract meaning 'beginning, origin, top', is used for people of status, scholars, and teachers (Becker 1975).

(A2) Head > classifier for animals
Khmer (Mon-Khmer) uses *kba:l* 'head' for animals, and also—pejoratively— for humans (Adams 1989: 67); the same usage was observed for Bahnar (Central Bahnaric) *ko·l* (Adams 1989: 71). In various South Bahnaric languages, 'head' is also used for animals, e.g. Chrau *vôq* (Adams 1989: 77) (note also English *head of cattle* (Lehrer 1986); and see §4.4.2 on incipient classifier systems using 'head' for animal classification in Omani Arabic).

(A3) 'Eye' > classifier for humans
This is widely attested in Austroasiatic languages. The word for 'pupil of the eye'—probably the most salient part of the eye—can be used as a human classifier (in agreement with the part-to-whole tendency formulated by Wilkins). In North Bahnaric **ngaay* 'human classifier' comes from an item with the reconstructed meaning 'pupil of the eye' (Adams 1992: 110). Vietnamese *ngu·o·i* 'person; human classifier' also comes from this lexeme (Adams 1989: 84). Items meaning 'eye, pupil of the eye' may acquire a more restricted reference. They can become classifiers which refer to the social status of a person (honorifics), e.g. Bahnar (Central Bahnaric) *măt* 'eye, pupil of the eye' used as an honorific (the same morpheme means 'precious stone' in Mon) (Adams 1989: 71).

Rarer possibilities include:

(A4) Tail > classifier for humans
This is found in Aslian languages (Austroasiatic: Adams 1989: 94).

(A5) Tail > classifier for animals
Indonesian and Minangkabau use 'tail' as a classifier for non-human animates (*ekor* and *ikua* respectively). Some Aslian languages also use 'tail' for classifying animals (Adams 1989: 94). Body parts may be used to refer to subclasses of animals. In Khmer, *kɔntúy* 'tail' is used as a classifier for fish (Adams 1989: 67).

(A6) Leg > classifier for humans
Totonac (Totonac-Tepehuan: Levy 1994) has a numeral classifier *cha':* 'human', from *cha':n* 'leg'.

---

[2] I will not discuss the semantic change top <-> head, and the possibility of polysemy for corresponding items; cf. however Wilkins (1981: 172): 'it is a natural tendency for a word for "top" to take on the meaning of "head" and vice versa.'

A function-based semantic extension of a body part can yield classifiers for humans. The word for hand or arm may become a classifier for an artist, or artisan, i.e. a 'handy' person, e.g. Vietnamese *tay* (Adams 1989: 89).

(A7) Skin > non-human animates
This has been suggested as a source for Mal *'nang* 'non-human animates', cf. Tai *nang* 'skin' (Adams 1989: 61).

Names of specific body parts can be used as classifiers for species, or genuses. The changes shell, skin, bark > crabs, and breasts and wings > birds are attested in Sedang (North Bahnaric) (Adams 1989: 79).

When used to classify inanimates, body parts become shape- and size-based classifiers, both when employed as numeral classifiers, and as verbal classifiers (round head, or eye; long arm; short flexible finger). In a few cases, the extension is achieved by function. The selection of an appropriate body part as a shape- or size-based classifier depends on the choice a language makes. The shape and size parameters involved are ROUND, SMALL, FLAT, VERTICAL, LONG FLEXIBLE, and THIN.

'Head' often becomes a classifier for ROUND objects. In Mundurukú a^2 'head' is a classifier for round objects (Gonçalves 1987: 24). Athabaskan verbal classifier *d* which refers to roundish objects (see Chapter 6) is etymologically related to **də* 'head' in Proto-Eyak-Athabaskan (Jeff Leer, p.c.).

Another kind of extension, also found in numeral classifiers, concerns extension by SHAPE and ARRANGEMENT, e.g. Thai *hŭa* 'head', also used as a classifier for clustered and root vegetables (Carpenter 1986).

'Eye' is a frequent source for classifiers for ROUND and SMALL objects. In Kana, *dẹ̄ẹ̄* 'numeral classifier for spot-like objects' derives from 'eye'. In Caddo (Caddoan) the verbal classifier for small round objects, *ič'ah-*, is also the noun stem for 'eye' (Mithun 1986: 390).

Other body parts can be used with a similar meaning, e.g. Yanomami *ko* 'heart, kidney', employed as a classifier for round things (Ramirez 1994: 131). In Tarascan, the classifier for roundish objects comes from 'buttocks'.

A frequent source for a classifier for FLAT objects or objects with extended surface is the word for skin. In Totonac *mak-*, a classifier for flat and bounded objects, comes from *makni* 'body, skin'. In Baniwa and Tariana *-ya*, a classifier for spread out, flat objects—such as skins—comes from *-ya* 'skin', and in Kana *ákpá*, a classifier for flat objects, also comes from the word for skin (Ikoro 1996a: 96). Yanomami (Ramirez 1994: 131) *si* 'skin, bark' is a classifier for objects with an extended surface.

Another source for the classification of FLAT objects is the word for 'arm, or wing'. In Totonac *paq-* 'flat, unbounded' comes from *paqán* 'arm, wing'. Another classifier for flat surfaces comes from 'face': Totonac *laka-* 'flat, surface' and *lakán* 'face'. In Tarascan, the classifier for flat surfaces comes from 'back'.

Classifiers for VERTICAL objects may come from the word for 'arm', e.g. Munduruků *ba^4* 'arm; classifier for long, roundish and rigid objects' (Gonçalves 1987: 25). In Tarascan 'neck' is the classifier for longish objects.

'Finger' is a frequent source for classifiers for LONG FLEXIBLE or THIN objects, e.g. Munduruků *bu^2* 'hand, finger' used as a classifier for long flexible objects. Baniwa and Tariana *-whi* 'needle, thin thing' became a classifier for thin longish objects.

Body parts may be used as sources for shape- and size-based classifiers of particular species. In Yanomami *ũ* is a classifier for long larvae and fruits; and is also the word for bone (Ramirez 1994). In Wu-Ming, *klaau^2* 'head' is used to classify particular round objects, e.g. onions or scallions.

There are also FUNCTIONAL extensions; for instance, Burmese *lɛʔ* 'hand' is used to classify handtools (Adams 1989: 139). Other functional extensions may be less semantically transparent. According to Conklin (1981: 239, 437), *mata* 'eye' is the source of a classifier which refers to the working parts of various instruments, such as knives, and other bladed things, in Toba Batak. This classifier got extended to fishhooks, shovels, and brooms in Gorontalo.

Body parts can be used as specific classifiers for inanimate objects as the result of metaphoric extensions. These extensions often involve metonymy: an object is classified after its salient part. In Vietnamese, *khâu* 'mouth' is used to classify firearms which have an opening similar to a mouth (Adams 1989: 144). In Minangkabau, *kaki* 'leg' is a specific classifier for umbrellas, with their long bodies (Marnita 1996: 115).

Body parts can be used to classify more abstract items, via metonymy, e.g. 'eye' > 'visible aspect, trait, feature', for example, in Dioi (Conklin 1981: 380).

Unexpected semantic extensions may be due to pre-existing polysemy. A polysemous body part 'head, front, beginning' became the classifier for 'roots, tubers', as well as for round vegetables in Lɨɨ (Conklin 1981: 165). Otherwise, 'head' is never used as a classifier for non-round objects.

Body parts which are associated with handling things (mouth for eating or drinking, or hand/arm for grabbing or measuring) often give rise to MENSURAL classifiers. The word for 'mouth' may become a mensural classifier meaning 'bite, sip, mouthful', as in Totonac (Table 13.2). In Hmong linear measures are associated with the hands, or their parts (Bisang 1993: 35), e.g. *ntiv* 'finger' used for a linear measure, a finger-length, or *xib* 'the palm of the hand' used for an equivalent measure; cf. Kilivila *yuma, yam, yuma* 'hand; measure: the span of two extended arms' (Senft 1993a); Palikur *-uku-/-wok-* 'hand', classifier for hands or handfuls. See §13.1, for more examples. The semantics of mensural classifiers can be quite idiosyncratic. In Minangkabau, *jari* 'finger' is used only for measuring cloth, and *kapalo* 'head' is used just for measuring the distance between horses in a race (Marnita 1996: 131–2).

Mensural classifiers are only rarely derived from other body parts. Two examples are Totonac *ak* 'units of length, e.g. meters' which comes from *akán* 'head', and *pa:-* 'units of volume, e.g. pails' which comes from *pa:n* 'belly' (Levy 1994).

(B) Sources for shape-based numeral classifiers

A typical source for a classifier for ROUND objects is the word for 'fruit', as in Kam-Muang and White Tai (Conklin 1981: 154), and Western Austronesian (Conklin 1981: 234–5; Marnita 1996). Another frequent source is 'stone', e.g. Gorontalo *botu* 'stone' and 'classifier for spheres and fruits-like objects' (Conklin 1981: 233); reflexes of the same stem are used to classify round things in a number of Micronesian languages (Conklin 1981: 301); note also Khmer *krɔəp* 'stone, kernel', 'classifier for round things' (Adams 1989: 108).

'Seed' and 'grain' are typical sources for SMALL ROUND things (Adams 1989: 104–5). Some examples are Thai *méd* 'grain', used as a classifier for small things like jewels and buttons (Carpenter 1986); Mon-Khmer *mè?* 'seed, kernel' used as classifier for round things (Adams 1989: 104); and Minangkabau *incek* 'seed', used as a classifier for seeds, grains, and small round objects, e.g. eyes (Marnita 1996: 111). Another source for a classifier for small and round things is 'egg', cf. Baniwa (Table 9.5).

For LONG and VERTICAL things, typical sources are 'tree' or 'tree trunk', or 'stick', e.g. Indonesian and Minangkabau *batang* 'tree, trunk', used as a classifier for long vertical things, e.g. a stick, and Palikur *ah* 'tree trunk' used as a verbal classifier for vertical things.

An additional semantic feature may be FLEXIBILITY and LENGTH; in Gorontalo *agu* 'wood' is used to classify trees, and also flexible objects, such as snakes, and 'anything that has the quality of length, physical or metaphorical' (Conklin 1981: 260, 438).

'Leaf' is a typical source for a classifier for FLAT FLEXIBLE objects, e.g. Proto-Arawak **pana* 'leaf', *-pana* 'classifier: leaf-like, flat'; this is also found in numerous Mon-Khmer languages (Adams 1989: 155), and in Dioi and numerous Tai languages (Conklin 1981: 158–60).

'Threads', 'strings', and 'veins' can be used to classify LONG FLEXIBLE items (examples from Mon-Khmer languages are given in Adams 1989: 143).

The choice of item to be used as the source for a shape classifier is often associated with material culture. Thus, Proto-Arawak *-maka* is the noun for 'hammock', and also a classifier for 'extended cloth like objects'; it is well known that the hammock is a central item in Amazonian culture (see §12.3).

Appendix 3
Fieldworker's Guide to Classifier Languages

The aim of this guide is to provide field linguists working on a previously undescribed language with orientation as to the questions which should be asked in order to establish a complete picture of how noun categorization operates in a language; and, if the language has no classifiers, what other categories can be used to express such universal categories as human/non-human and animate/inanimate.[1]

PRELIMINARY INFORMATION is needed as a starting-point. After that, questions relevant for establishing classifier systems and noun categorization devices are divided into seven broad areas. After each question, a brief explanation is given; relevant chapters of this book are indicated in parentheses.

Preliminary information on the language includes:

(i) morphological type: e.g. isolating, agglutinating, fusional; synthetic, analytic, polysynthetic; head-marking or dependent-marking;

(ii) word classes: open classes (e.g. nouns, verbs, adjectives) and closed classes;

(iii) grammatical categories for open classes (e.g. number for nouns, tense for verbs);

(iv) transitivity classes of verbs;

(v) marking of grammatical relations;

Nature of sources:

(vi) mostly based on texts with corroborative grammatical elicitation and extensive lexical elicitation; or mostly based on elicitation.

One should concentrate on gathering and analysing texts in a language near the beginning of any linguistic fieldwork. The classifier patterns found in texts should then be confirmed and systematically studied through

---

[1] It is based on the author's own field experience in different parts of the world, student supervision in Brazil and Australia, reading of grammars, and talking to other linguists about their field experiences.

carefully directed elicitation. Lexical elicitation is essential to work out the semantics of classifiers and their assignment principles. If at all possible, the researcher should take into account—but not entirely rely on—the intuitions of native speakers when trying to account for seemingly opaque semantics of genders or classifiers. Extensive work with texts is recommended to understand the discourse use of classifiers and agreement variation.

(A) Establishing types of classifier and their inventories in given morphosyntactic contexts (Chapters 2–9)

(A1) Are any noun categorization devices used within an NP? Test the appearance of classifier-like markers (i) on adjectival modifiers within a noun phrase; (ii) on demonstratives, articles, interrogatives (test for noun classes: Chapter 2, and/or deictic classifiers: Chapter 7); (iii) within an NP to characterize a noun by itself, generic-specific type (test for noun classifiers: Chapter 3); (iv) on numerals and quantifiers (test for numeral classifiers: Chapter 4).

(A2) If there is agreement in noun class in NP or clause, is it obligatory? If not, does it depend on (a) discourse saliency of a noun; (b) its topicality or topical continuity; (c) contrastive focus; (d) first mention of a noun in discourse; (e) definiteness of a noun? If it is, are there any variations in the choice of agreement form depending on (a–e) or other factors?

In a language with classifiers, can two or more nouns belonging to different classes be coordinated? What classifier is then chosen (test for classifier resolution)? Are there any formal or functional markedness relations in the classifier system? Is there any zero-agreement, or neutral/default agreement? (See §2.5.1.)

(A3) Is there any overt noun class marking (§2.6 in Chapter 2)? If there are classifiers, are they bound or free morphemes (suffixes, prefixes, etc.)?

(A4) Are there any noun categorization devices used within a possessive NP referring to (i) the ways a referent of the noun can be possessed, or handled, e.g. eaten, or drunk, or sold; (ii) intrinsic properties of the referent of the possessed or of the possessor (e.g. shape, animacy)? (Tests for relational, possessed and possessor classifiers respectively: Chapter 5.)

(A5) Are there any noun categorization devices marked on adpositions (if there are any)? (Test for locative classifiers: Chapter 7.)

(A6) On the verb: does the form of a verb (transitive or intransitive) change depending on (i) the physical orientation of its argument; (ii) other properties—animacy, shape, etc.—of its argument? (Test for verbal classifiers and classificatory verbs: Chapter 6.)

(A7) If a classifier can appear on the head noun and on a modifier, are there any differences in its (i) form; (ii) meaning; (iii) syntactic behaviour?

(A8) How many classifiers are there?

(A9) Are there different choices of classifiers available associated with different types of modifier? For instance, different classifier choices may be made for demonstratives and for adjectives in head-modifier NPs ('split agreement' system). Is there any double marking?

(A10) If there is more than one set of classifier morphemes, used in different morphosyntactic contexts, do they overlap? How are they different? (Chapter 8.)

(A11) If the single set of classifier morphemes is used in several different morphosyntactic environments, are there any differences in form or in meaning? (Test for a multiple classifier language: Chapter 9.)

(B) Correlations with other categories (Chapter 10)

(B1) Do classifier distinctions differ depending on number?

(B2) Do they differ depending on grammatical relations (e.g. genders may be distinguished for O, but not for the subject (A/S))?

(B3) Does the choice of possessive classifier depend on an alienable/inalienable distinction?

(B4) Are any classifier distinctions neutralized in certain verbal tenses, or voices?

(B5) Are there fewer classifier distinctions in some deictic categories?

(B6) Can the use of different classifiers distinguish different meanings of a word?

(B7) Does the presence of classifiers affect the structure of the lexicon? That is, in languages with large systems of classifiers the assignment of which is based on shape, there may be fewer lexical items which refer to the size of the object (e.g. big, large, round). Is this true for your language?

(C) Semantics of noun categorization devices (Chapter 11)

(C1) How are classifiers assigned to humans; non-human animates; inanimate concrete objects? How are higher animates (mammals) distinguished from lower animates?

(C2) How are classifiers assigned to body parts?

(C3) How are classifiers assigned to abstract nouns and natural phenomena? How are classifiers assigned to loans?

(C4) Is there any default or general classifier? If so, how is it used: (i) for otherwise unclassifiable items ('residue' classifier), (ii) for unspecified or unknown referent ('unspecified referent' classifier); (iii) can it be substituted for other classifiers under special pragmatic conditions ('default' classifier)?

(C5) Are there any semantic extensions to classifiers (e.g. 'male/female' to 'big/little'; 'female' to 'cute and small')?

(D) Functions of classifiers (Chapter 12)

(D1) Are classifiers obligatory?

(D2) If not, does their use correlate with any of the parameters in (A2)? Can a classifier be 'dropped', or can a noun be 'dropped', and what is the effect of this?

(D3) If yes, does the choice of a classifier depend on any of (a–c) in (A2)? Are any noun categorization devices marked on the noun itself? If there are numeral or other classifiers are they also used as derivational morphemes (cf. (E) in §9.1)?

(D4) Can a classifier be used without a head noun (i.e. anaphorically)?

(D5) What are the functions of classifiers in narratives? Does the use of classifiers depend on textual genre?

(D6) Does the semantic organization of classifiers correlate with extra-linguistic factors, e.g. the world-view and/or mythological concepts of the speakers? Do social factors affect the composition of each class? Is there any correlation between classifiers and culture, or language planning?

(E) Origin and acquisition of classifiers (Chapters 13 and 14)

(E1) Is there any information about the origin of classifiers (e.g. developed from nouns, or from verbs)?

(E2) Is there any information on the semantic evolution of classifiers?

(E3) Are there any data on the behaviour of classifiers in (i) language obsolescence; (ii) the speech of bilinguals and semilinguals; (iii) language diffusion; (iv) language reduction or expansion?

(E4) Is there any information on generational differences in the use and production of classifiers? Are there any data on how children employ classifiers? (Chapter 14)

(F) Animacy and humanness outside noun categorization devices (Appendix 1)

(F1) Does number marking or number agreement depend on whether the referent of a noun is human, or animate?

(F2) Does the way in which grammatical relations are marked (by case or cross-referencing) depend on the animacy or humanness of the argument (A, S, or O)?

(F3) Are there any derivational devices used for animate or for human nouns?

(F4) Are there any differences in the ways personal pronouns are used with nouns with human and with non-human referents?

(F5) Are there any humanness or animacy distinctions in interrogatives?

References

Abbott, M. (1991). 'Macushi', in Derbyshire and Pullum (1991: 23–160).
Adams, K. L. (1989). *Systems of Numeral Classification in the Mon-Khmer, Nicobarese and Aslian Subfamilies of Austroasiatic*. Canberra: Pacific Linguistics.
—— (1992). 'A Comparison of the Numeral Classification of Humans in Mon-Khmer', *Mon-Khmer Studies* 21: 107–29.
—— and Conklin, N. F. (1973). 'Towards a Theory of Natural Classification', *Papers from the Annual Regional Meeting of the Chicago Linguistic Society* 9: 1–10.
Ahrens, K. (1994). 'Classifier Production in Normals and Aphasics', *Journal of Chinese Linguistics* 22: 203–46.
Aikhenvald, A. Y. (1984). 'A Structural and Typological Classification of Berber Languages'. PhD thesis, Institute of Oriental Studies, Moscow.
—— (1986). 'On the reconstruction of syntactic system in Berber-Lybic', *Zeitschrift fur Phonetik, Sprachwissenschaft und Kommunikationsforschung* 39: 527–39.
—— (1990). *Sovremennyj ivrit* [Modern Hebrew]. Moscow: Nauka.
—— (1994a). 'Classifiers in Tariana', *Anthropological Linguistics* 34: 407–65.
—— (1994b). 'Grammatical Relations in Tariana', *Nordic Journal of Linguistics* 7: 201–18.
—— (1995a). *Bare*. Languages of the World/Materials 100. Munich: Lincom Europa Materials 100.
—— (1995b). 'Person-marking and Discourse in North-Arawak Languages', *Studia Linguistica* 49: 152–95.
—— (1996a). 'Areal Diffusion in Northwest Amazonia: The Case of Tariana', *Anthropological Linguistics* 38: 73–116.
—— (1996b). 'Classe nominal e gênero nas línguas Aruák', *Boletim do museu Goeldi* 10: 137–259.
—— (1996c). 'Classifiers in Baniwa', *Moscow Linguistic Journal* 3: 7–33.
—— (1998a). 'Physical Properties in a Gender System: An Example from Manambu, a Ndu Language of New Guinea', *Language and Linguistics in Melanesia* 27: 175–87.
—— (1998b). 'Warekena', in Derbyshire and Pullum (1998: 215–439).
—— (1999a). 'Arawak Languages', in Dixon and Aikhenvald (1999: 65–106).
—— (1999b). 'Double Marking of Syntactic Function in Tariana', in E. Rakhilina and Y. Testelets (eds.), *Typology and Linguistic Theory: From Description to Explanation. For the 60th Birthday of Aleksandr E. Kibrik*. Moscow: Languages of Russian Culture, 114–22.
—— (2000). 'Unusual classifiers in Tariana', in G. Senft (ed.), *Systems of nominal classification*. Cambridge: Cambridge University Press, 93–113.
—— (2001). 'Areal Diffusion, Genetic Inheritance and Problems of Subgrouping: A North Arawak Case Study', in A. Y. Aikhenvald and R. M. W. Dixon (eds.),

Areal Diffusion and Genetic Inheritance: Problems in Comparative Linguistics. Oxford: Oxford University Press, 167–94.
—— (forthcoming a). 'Gender', in C. Lehmann and J. Mugdan (eds.), *Handbuch der Morfologie.* Berlin: Mouton de Gruyter, article 98.
—— (forthcoming b). 'Typological Distinctions in Word Formation', in T. Shopen (ed.), *Language Typology and Syntactic Description.* Cambridge: Cambridge University Press.
—— (forthcoming c). *The Tariana language of Northwest Amazonia.* Cambridge: Cambridge University Press.
—— MS. 'Noun Phrase Structure in Paumarí: An Interaction of Gender and Noun Class'.
—— and Dixon, R. M. W. (1998). 'Dependencies between Grammatical Systems', *Language* 74: 56–80.
—— —— (1999). 'Other Small Families and Isolates', in Dixon and Aikhenvald (1999: 341–83).
—— and Green, D. (1998). 'Palikur and the Typology of Classifiers', *Anthropological Linguistics* 40: 429–80.
Aksenova, I., and Toporova, I. (1990). *Vvedenije v Bantuistiku* [Introduction to Bantu Linguistics]. Moscow: Nauka.
—— —— (1994). *Jazyk Kuria* [The Kuria Language]. Moscow: Nauka.
Alexandre, P. (1968). 'Note sur la réduction du système des classes dans les languues véhiculaires à fonds bantu', *La Classification nominale*, 277–90.
Alexeyev, M. (1985). *Voprosy sravniteljno-istoricheskoj grammatiki lezginskih jazykov. Morfologija. Sintaksis.* [Problems of comparative and historical grammar of Lezghic languages. Morphology. Syntax]. Moscow: Nauka.
Allan, K. (1977). 'Classifiers', *Language* 53: 284–310.
—— (1980). 'Nouns and Countability', *Language* 56: 341–567.
Allin, T. (1975). 'A Grammar of Resígaro'. PhD thesis, University of St Andrews.
Alpher, B. (1987). 'Feminine as the Unmarked Grammatical Gender: Buffalo Girls Are No Fools', *Australian Journal of Linguistics* 7: 169–87.
Amaya, M. T. (1997). *Categorías gramaticales del ette taara. Lengua de los chimilas.* Bogotá: Centro Ediciones CCELA, Uniandes.
Ameka, F. (1991). 'Ewe: Its Grammatical Constructions and Illocutionary Devices'. PhD thesis, Australian National University.
Anderson, J. L. (1989). *Comaltepec Chinantec Syntax.* Dallas: Summer Institute of Linguistics and University of Texas at Arlington.
Anderson, L.-G., and Janson, T. (1997). *Languages in Botswana: Language Ecology in Southern Africa.* Botswana: Longman.
Anderson, M., and Anderson, T. (1991). *Sudest Grammar Essentials.* Ukarumpa: Summer Institute of Linguistics.
Anderson, N., and Anderson, C. (1976). *Podopa Grammar Essentials.* Ukarumpa: Summer Institute of Linguistics.
Anderson, S. R. (1992). *A-Morphous Morphology.* Cambridge: Cambridge University Press.
—— and Keenan, E. (1985). 'Deixis', in T. Shopen (ed.), *Language Typology and*

Syntactic Description, iii: *Grammatical Categories and the Lexicon*. Cambridge: Cambridge University Press, 259–308.
Andrews, E. (1990). *Markedness Theory: The Union of Asymmetry and Semiosis in Language*. Durham, NC: Duke University Press.
Aronoff, M. (1991). 'Noun Classes in Arapesh', *Yearbook of Morphology*. Dordrecht: Foris, 21–30.
—— (1994). *Morphology by Itself*. Cambridge: MIT Press.
Aschmann, R. P. (1993). *Proto-Witotoan*. Summer Institute of Linguistics and University of Texas at Arlington Publications in Linguistics. Dallas: Summer Institute of Linguistics and University of Texas at Arlington.
Asher, R. E. (1985). *Tamil*. London: Croom Helm.
Austin, P. (1981). *A Grammar of Diyari, South Australia*. Cambridge: Cambridge University Press.
Axelrod, M. (forthcoming). 'Gender and Aspect in Koyukon'.
Baarle, P. van, and Sabajo, M. (1997). *Manuel de la langue Arawak*. Paris: Éditions du Saule.
Bani, E. (1987). 'Masculine and Feminine Grammatical Gender in Kala Lagaw Ya', *Australian Journal of Linguistics* 7: 189–201.
Bantia, T. K. (1993). *Punjabi*. London: Routledge.
Barlow, M. (1992). *A Situated Theory of Agreement*. New York: Garland.
—— and Ferguson, C. A. (1988a). 'Introduction', in Barlow and Ferguson (1988b: 1–22).
—— —— (eds.) (1988b). *Agreement in Natural Language: Approaches, Theories, Descriptions*. Stanford: Center for the Study of Language and Literature.
Barnes, J. (1990). 'Classifiers in Tuyuca', in Payne (1990: 273–92).
Baron, N. S. (1971). 'A Reanalysis of English Grammatical Gender', *Lingua* 27: 113–40.
Baron, R. (1987). *The Cerebral Computer*. Hillsdale, NJ: Lawrence Erlbaum.
Barron, R. (1982). 'Das Phänomen klassifikatorischer Verben', in Seiler and Lehmann (1982: 133–46).
—— and Serzisko, F. (1982). 'Noun Classifiers in the Siouan Languages', in Seiler and Stachowiak (1982: 85–105).
Barsalou, L. W. (1987). 'The instability of graded structure: implications for the nature of concepts', in U. Neisser (ed.), *Concepts and Conceptual Development*. Cambridge: Cambridge University Press, 101–40.
Barz, R. K., and Diller, A. V. N. (1985). 'Classifiers and Standardisation: Some South and South-East Asian Comparisons', in D. Bradley (ed.), *Language Policy, Language Planning and Sociolinguistics in South-East Asia*. Canberra: Pacific Linguistics, 155–84.
Bascom, B. (1982). 'Northern Tepehuan', in R. W. Langacker (ed.), *Studies in Uto-Aztecan Grammar*, iii: *Uto-Aztecan Grammatical Sketches*. Dallas: Summer Institute of Linguistics and University of Texas at Arlington, 267–315.
Basso, K. H. (1968). 'The Western Apache Classificatory Verb System: A Formal Analysis', *Southwestern Journal of Anthropology* 24: 252–66.
Bechert, J. (1982). 'Grammatical Gender in Europe: An Areal Study of a Linguistic Category', *Papiere zur Linguistik* 26: 23–34.

Becker, A. J. (1975). 'A Linguistic Image of Nature: The Burmese numerative classifier system', *Linguistics* 165: 109–21.
—— (1986). 'The Figure a Classifier Makes: Describing a Particular Burmese Classifier', in Craig (1986a: 327–43).
Beckwith, C. I. (1992). 'Classifiers in Hungarian', in I. Kenesei and Cs. Pléh (eds.), *Approaches to Hungarian*, iv: *The Structure of Hungarian*. Szeged: JATE, 197–206.
—— (1998). 'Noun Specification and Classification in Uzbek', *Anthropological Linguistics* 40: 124–40.
Benton, R. A. (1968). 'Numeral and Attributive Classifiers in Truquese', *Oceanic Linguistics* 7: 104–46.
Berlin, B. (1968). *Tzeltal Numeral Classifiers: A Study in Ethnographic Semantics*. The Hague: Mouton.
Berman, R. (1978). *Modern Hebrew Structure*. Tel Aviv: University Publishing Projects.
—— (1985). 'The Acquisition of Hebrew', in D. I. Slobin (ed.), *The Crosslinguistic Study of Language Acquisition*. Hillsdale, NJ: Lawrence Erlbaum, 255–371.
Bhaskararao, P., and Joshi, S. K. (1985). 'A Study of Newari Classifiers', *Bulletin of the Deccan College Research Institute* 44: 17–31.
Birk, D. B. W. (1976). *The Malak Malak Language, Daly River, Western Arnhem Land*. Canberra: Pacific Linguistics.
Bisang, W. (1993). 'Classifiers, Quantifiers and Class Nouns in Hmong', *Studies in Language* 17: 1–51.
—— (1996). 'Areal Typology and Grammaticalization: Processes of Grammaticalization Based on Nouns and Verbs in East and Mainland South East Asian Languages', *Studies in Language* 20: 519–98.
—— (1999). 'Classifiers in East and Southeast Asian languages: Counting and Beyond', in J. Gvozdanovic (ed.), *Numeral types and changes worldwide*. Berlin: Mouton de Gruyter, 113–85.
Blankenship, B. (1996). 'Classificatory Verbs in Cherokee', in P. Munroe (ed.), *Cherokee Papers from UCLA*. California: UCLA, 61–74.
—— (1997). 'Classificatory Verbs in Cherokee', *Anthropological Linguistics* 39: 92–110.
Blewett, K. (forthcoming). *Kunua Grammar Essentials*. Ukarumpa: Summer Institute of Linguistics.
Bloomfield, L. (1933). *Language*. New York: Holt, Rinehart & Winston.
Boas, F., and Deloria, E. (1941). *Dakota Grammar*. Washington: US Government Printing Office.
Böhme, R., and Levelt, W. J. M. (1979). 'Children's Use and Awareness of Natural and Syntactic Gender in Possessive Pronouns', paper presented to the Conference on Linguistic Awareness and Learning to Read, Victoria.
Bokamba, E. G. (1977). 'The Impact of Multilingualism on Language Structures: The Case of Central Africa', *Anthropological Linguistics* 19: 181–202.
—— (1985). 'Verbal Agreement as a Noncyclic rule in Bantu', in D. L. Goyvaerts (ed.), *African Linguistics: Essays in Memory of M. W. K. Semikenke*. Amsterdam: John Benjamins, 9–54.
Bolt, J. E., Hoddinott, W. G., and Kofod, F. M. (1971). *An Elementary Grammar of the Nungali Language of the Northern Territory*. Armidale: Mimeo.

Borgman, D. M. (1990). 'Sanuma', in Derbyshire and Pullum (1990: 15–248).
Borneto, S. C. (1996). 'Liegen and stehen in German: A Study in Horizontality and Verticality', in E. Casad (ed.), *Cognitive Linguistics in the Redwoods: The Expansion of a New Paradigm in Linguistics*. Berlin: Mouton de Gruyter, 459–506.
Braun, F. (forthcoming a). 'Genderless = Gender-neutral? Empirical evidence from Turkish'.
—— (forthcoming b). 'The Communication of Gender in Turkish'.
Breedveld, J. O. (1995). 'The Semantic Basis of Noun Class Systems: The Case of the KE and NGE Classes in Fulfulde', *Journal of West African Languages* 25: 63–74.
Breen, G. (1976a). 'Wangkumara', in R. M. W. Dixon (ed.), *Grammatical Categories in Australian Languages*. Canberra: Australian Institute of Aboriginal Studies, 336–9.
—— (1976b). 'Wagaya', in R. M. W. Dixon (ed.), *Grammatical Categories in Australian Languages*. Canberra: Australian Institute of Aboriginal Studies, 340–2, 590–4.
Bresnan, J., and McChombo, S. A. (1986). 'Grammatical and Anaphoric Agreement', *Papers from the Annual Regional Meeting of the Chicago Linguistic Society* 22: 278–97.
Broschart, J. (1997). 'Locative classifiers in Tongan', in G. Senft (ed.), *Referring to Space: Studies in Austronesian and Papuan Languages*. Oxford: Clarendon Press, 287–315.
Brosman, P. W. Jr. (1979). 'The Semantics of the Hittite Gender System', *Journal of Indo-European Studies* 7: 227–36.
Brown, R. (1981). 'Semantic Aspects of some Waris Predications', in K. J. Franklin (ed.), *Syntax and Semantics in Papua New Guinea Languages*. Ukarumpa: Summer Institute of Linguistics, 93–123.
Bruce, L. (1984). *The Alamblak Language of Papua New Guinea East Sepik*. Canberra: Pacific Linguistics.
Bulygina, T. V., and Shmelev, A. D. (1996). 'Nespecifirovannyj pol i soglasovanie pri anafore' ['Unspecified Gender and Anaphoric Agreement'], *Moscow Linguistic Journal* 2: 98–103.
Burling, R. (1965). 'How to Choose a Burmese Numeral Classifier', in M. E. Spiro (ed.), *Context and Meaning in Cultural Anthropology, in Honor of A. Irving Hallowell*. New York: Free Press, 243–64.
—— (1973). 'Language Development of a Garo and English-speaking Child', in C. F. Ferguson and D. I. Slobin (eds.), *Studies of Child Language Development*. San Francisco: Holt, Rinehart & Winston, 69–90.
Burton, M., and Kirk, L. (1976). 'Semantic Reality of Bantu Noun Classes: The Kikuyu Case', *African Linguistics* 7: 157–74.
Bybee J., Perkins, R., and Pagliuca, W. (1994). *The Evolution of Grammar*. Chicago: University of Chicago Press.
Campbell, L. (1985). 'Review of J. A. Suárez, *The Mesoamerican Indian Languages*'. *Journal of Linguistics* 21: 216–21.
—— (1993). 'On Proposed Universals of Grammatical Borrowing', in H. Aertsen and

R. J. Jeffers (eds.), *Historical Linguistics (1989): Papers from the 9th International Conference on Historical Linguistics*. Amsterdam: John Benjamins, 91–109.
—— (1997). *American Indian Languages*. New York: Oxford University Press.
—— (2000). 'Valency Changing Derivations in K'iche', in R. M. W. Dixon and A. Y. Aikhenvald (eds.), *Changing Valency: Case Studies in Transitivity*. Cambridge: Cambridge University Press, 236–81.
—— Kaufman, T., and Smith-Stark, T. (1986). 'Meso-America as a Linguistic Area', *Language* 62: 530–70.
—— and Muntzel, M. (1989). 'The Structural Consequences of Language Death', in Dorian (1988: 181–96).
Capell, A., and Hinch, H. E. (1970). *Maung Grammar, Texts and Vocabulary*. The Hague: Mouton.
Carlson, R., and Payne, D. (1989). 'Genitive Classifiers', in *Proceedings of the 4th Annual Pacific Linguistics Conference*. Eugene: University of Oregon, 89–119.
Carlson, T. (1991). *Taenae Grammar Essentials*. Ukarumpa: Summer Institute of Linguistics.
Carpenter, K. (1986). 'Productivity and Pragmatics of Thai Classifiers', *Berkeley Linguistics Society: Proceedings of the Annual Meeting* 12: 14–25.
—— (1987). 'How Children Learn to Classify Nouns in Thai'. PhD thesis, Stanford University.
—— (1991). 'Later rather than Sooner: Children's Use of Extralinguistic Information in the Acquisition of Thai Classifiers', *Journal of Child Language* 18: 93–113.
—— (1992). 'Two Dynamic Views of Classifier Systems: Diachronic Change and Individual Development', *Cognitive Linguistics* 3: 129–50.
Carroll, J. B., and Casagrande, J. B. (1958). 'The Function of Language Classification in Behavior', in E. Maccoby, T. Newcomb, and E. L. Hartley (eds.), *Readings in Social Psychology*. New York: Holt, Rinehart & Winston, 8–31.
Carter, R. M. (1976). 'Chipewyan Classificatory Verbs', *International Journal of American Linguistics* 42: 24–30.
Casad, E. (1982). 'Cora', in R. W. Langacker (ed.), *Studies in Uto-Aztecan Grammar*, iv: *Southern Uto-Aztecan Grammatical Sketches*. Dallas: Summer Institute of Linguistics and University of Texas at Arlington, 151–459.
—— (1996). 'What Good Are Locationals, Anyway?' in M. Pütz and R. Dirven (eds.), *The Construal of Space in Language and Thought*. Berlin: Mouton de Gruyter, 239–67.
Céria, V. G., and Sândalo, F. (1995). 'A Preliminary Reconstruction of Proto-Waikurúan with Special Reference to Pronominals and Demonstratives', *Anthropological Linguistics* 37: 169–91.
Chafe, W. L. (1967). *Seneca Morphology and Dictionary*. Washington, DC: Smithsonian Press.
—— (1977). 'The Evolution of Third Person Verb Agreement in the Iroquoian Languages', in C. N. Li (ed.), *Mechanisms of Syntactic Change*. Austin: University of Texas Press, 493–524.
—— (1994). *Discourse, Consciousness, and Time: The Flow and Displacement of*

Conscious Experience in Speaking and Writing. Chicago: University of Chicago Press.

Chang-Smith, M. (1996). 'Chinese Noun Classification in Relation to Prototype Theory'. MA thesis, University of Queensland.

Chapman, A. (1996). 'A Grammatical Summary of Lao', materials for the research project 'Universals of Human Languages', Research Centre for Linguistic Typology, Australian National University.

Chapman, S. MS. *Dicionário Paumarí.* Summer Institute of Linguistics, Porto Velho, Brazil.

—— and Derbyshire, D. (1991). 'Paumari', in Derbyshire and Pullum (1991: 161–354).

Chappell, H., and McGregor, W. (1989). 'Alienability, Inalienability and Nominal Classification', *Proceedings of the Berkeley Linguistic Society* 15: 24–36.

—— —— (eds.). (1996). *The Grammar of Inalienability: A Typological Perspective on Body Part Terms and the Part–Whole Relation.* Berlin: Mouton de Gruyter.

Charney, J. O. (1993). *A Grammar of Comanche.* Lincoln: University of Nebraska Press.

Charters, H. (1995). 'What Are the Consequences of Classifier Languages for Semantic Theory?' MS, Department of Linguistics, Australian National University.

Chatterji, S. K. (1926/1970–2). *The Origin and the Development of the Bengali Language.* 2 vols., London: Allen & Unwin.

Childs, T. (1983). 'Noun Class Affix Renewal in Southern West Atlantic', in J. Kaye, H. Koopman, D. Sportiche, and A. Dugas (eds.), *Current Approaches to African Linguistics,* ii. Dordrecht: Foris, 17–30.

—— (1993). *Grammar of Kisi.* Berlin: Mouton de Gruyter.

Christensen, S. (1995). *Yonggom Grammar Essentials.* Ukarumpa: Summer Institute of Linguistics.

Churchward, C. M. (1941). *A New Fijian Grammar.* Australasian Medical Publishing Company.

—— (1953). *A Grammar of Tongan.* Oxford: Oxford University Press.

Clamons, C. R. (1993). 'Gender Assignment in Oromo', in M. Eid and G. Iverson (eds.), *Principles and Prediction: The Analysis of Natural Language.* Amsterdam: John Benjamins, 269–84.

—— (1995). 'How Recent Contact Erased Ancient Traces in the Gender Systems of the Oromo Dialects', *Berkeley Linguistic Society: Parasession*: 389–400.

Clark, E. V. (1977). 'Universal Categories: on the Semantics of Classifiers and Children's Early Word Meaning', in A. Juilland (ed.), *Linguistic Studies Offered to Joseph Greenberg.* Saratoga: Alma Libri, 449–62.

Classification nominale (1967). *La Classification nominale dans les langues négro-africaines.* Paris: CNRS.

Claudi, U. (1985). *Zur Entstehung von Genussystemen.* Hamburg: Buske.

Codrington, R. (1885). *The Melanesian Languages.* Oxford: Clarendon Press; repr. 1974, Amsterdam, Philo Press.

Cohen, P. (1976). 'The Noun Phrase in Jeh', *Mon-Khmer Studies* 5: 139–52.

Coleman, C. (1982). 'A Grammar of Gunbarlang with Special Reference to Grammatical Relations'. Honours subthesis, Australian National University.
Collinder, B. (1965). *An Introduction to the Uralic Languages.* Berkeley: University of California Press.
Comrie, B. (1978). 'Genitive-Accusatives in Slavic: The Rules and Their Motivation', *International Review of Slavic Linguistics* 3: 27–42.
—— (1981). *The Languages of the Soviet Union.* Cambridge: Cambridge University Press.
—— and Stone, G. (1977). *The Russian Language since the Revolution.* Oxford: Clarendon Press.
Conklin, N. F. (1981). 'The Semantics and Syntax in Numeral Classification in Tai and Austronesian'. PhD thesis, University of Michigan.
Connelly, M. J. (1984). 'Basotho Children's Acquisition of Noun Morphology'. PhD thesis, University of Essex.
Conrad, R. (1978). 'Some Muhiang Grammatical Notes', in *Miscellaneous Papers on Dobu and Arapesh. Workpapers in Papua New Guinea Languages* 25: 89–130. Ukarumpa: Summer Institute of Linguistics.
—— (1996). 'More on Arapesh Noun Classes', MS.
—— and Conrad, J. (n.d.). *Iwam Essentials for Translation.* Ukarumpa: Summer Institute of Linguistics.
Conrad, R. J., with Wogiga, K. (1991). *An Outline of Bukiyip Grammar.* Canberra: Pacific Linguistics.
Cooke, J. R. (1986). *Pronominal Reference in Thai, Burmese, and Vietnamese.* Los Angeles: University of California Press.
Corbett, G. (1979). 'The Agreement Hierarchy', *Journal of Linguistics* 15: 203–24.
—— (1983a). 'Resolution Rules: Agreement in Person, Number, and Gender', in G. Gazdar, E. Klein, and G. K. Pullum (eds.), *Order, Concord, and Constituency.* Dordrecht: Foris, 176–206.
—— (1983b). *Hierarchies, Targets and Controllers: Agreement Patterns in Slavic.* London: Croom Helm.
—— (1988). 'Agreement: A Partial Specification Based on Slavonic Data', in Barlow and Ferguson (1988b: 23–54).
—— (1991). *Gender.* Cambridge: Cambridge University Press.
—— (1994a). 'Agreement', in R. E. Asher (ed.), *The Encyclopedia of Language and Linguistics,* i. Oxford: Pergamon Press, 54–60.
—— (1994b). 'Types of Typology, Illustrated from Gender Systems', in *Agreement, gender, number, genitive. Eurotyp Working Papers: Team 7: Noun Phrase Structure.* Working Paper 23: 1–38. Konstanz: Eurotyp Programme in Language Typology, European Science Foundation.
Corominas, J. (1954). *Diccionario crítico etimológico de la lengua castellana,* iii. Berna: Francke.
Costenla Umaña, A. (1991). *Las lenguas del área intermedia: introdución a su estudio areal.* San José: Editorial de la Universidad de Costa Rica.
Counts, D. L. (1969). *A Grammar of Kaliai-Kove.* Honolulu: University of Hawaii Press.
Craig, C. G. (1977). *The Structure of Jacaltec.* Austin: University of Texas Press.

Craig, C. G. (ed.) (1986a). *Noun Classes and Categorization: Proceedings of a Symposium on Categorization and Noun Classification, Eugene, Oregon, October 1983*. Amsterdam: John Benjamins.
—— (1986b). 'Jacaltec Noun Classifiers', *Lingua* 70: 241–84.
—— (1986c). 'Jacaltec Noun Classifiers: A Study in Language and Culture', in Craig (1986a: 263–94).
—— (1991). 'Ways to Go in Rama: A Case Study in Polygrammaticalization', in Traugott and Heine (1991a: ii, 455–92).
—— (1992). 'Classifiers in a Functional Perspective', in M. Fortescue, P. Harder, and L. Kristoffersen (eds.), *Layered Structure and Reference in a Functional Perspective*. Amsterdam: John Benjamins, 277–301.
—— (1993). 'A Morphosyntactic Typology of Classifiers', contribution to the workshop 'Back to Basic Issues in Nominal Classification', Cognitive Anthropology Research Group, Max-Planck Institute for Psycholinguistics, Nijmegen.
—— (1996). 'Nominal Classification', plenary talk at the 3rd Australian Linguistic Institute, Canberra.
—— (forthcoming). 'Classifiers', in C. Lehmann and J. Mugdan (eds.), *Handbuch der Morfologie*, Berlin: Mouton de Gruyter, article 97.
Creider, C. A. (1975). 'The Semantic System of Noun Classes in Proto-Bantu', *Anthropological Linguistics* 17: 127–38.
Croft, W. (1990). *Typology and Universals*. Cambridge: Cambridge University Press.
—— (1994). 'Semantic Universals in Classifier Systems', *Word* 45: 145–71.
—— (1995). 'Autonomy and Functionalist Linguistics', *Language* 71: 490–532.
—— (1996). '"Markedness" and "Universals": From the Prague School to Typology', in K. R. Jankowsky (ed.), *Multiple Perspectives on the Historical Dimensions of Language*. Münster: Nodus, 15–21.
Crofts, M. (1973). *Gramática Munduruku*. Brasília: Summer Institute of Linguistics.
—— (1985). *Aspectos da língua Munduruku*. Brasília: Summer Institute of Linguistics.
Crowley, T. (1978). *The Middle Clarence Dialects of Banjalang*. Canberra: Australian Institute of Aboriginal Studies.
—— (1979). 'Yaigin', in R. M. W. Dixon and B. J. Blake (eds.), *Handbook of Australian Languages*, i. Canberra: Australian National University Press, 363–84.
Curnow, T. (1997). 'A Grammar of Awa Pit'. PhD thesis, Australian National University.
Daley, K. A. C. (1996). 'The Use of Classifiers in Vietnamese Narrative Texts'. MA thesis, University of Texas at Arlington.
Davidson, W., Elford, L. W., and Hoijer, H. (1963). 'Athabascan Classificatory Verbs', in H. Hoijer (ed.), *Studies in the Athabaskan Languages*. Berkeley: University of California Press.
Davies, J. (1981). *Kobon*. Amsterdam: North-Holland.
Davis, D. R. (n.d.). 'Noun Class Markers in Wantoat'. Ukarumpa: Summer Institute of Linguistics.
De Leon, M. de L. P. (1987). 'Noun and Numeral Classifiers in Mixtec and Tzotzil: A Referential View'. PhD thesis, University of Sussex.
DeBray, R. G. A. (1951). *Guide to the Slavonic Languages*. London: J. M. Dent.

DeLancey, S. (1986). 'Towards a history of Thai classifier system', in Craig (1986a: 437–52).
—— (1998). 'Semantic Categorization in Tibetan Honorific Nouns', *Anthropological Linguistics* 40: 109–23.
Demuth, K. A. (1988). 'Noun Classes and Agreement in Sesotho Acquisition', in Barlow and Ferguson (1988b: 305–22).
—— Faraclas, N., and Marchese, L. (1986). 'Niger-Congo Noun Class and Agreement Systems in Language Acquisition and Historical Change', in Craig (1986a: 453–71).
Denny, J. P. (1976). 'What Are Noun Classifiers Good For?' *Papers from the Annual Regional Meeting of the Chicago Linguistic Society* 12: 122–32.
—— (1979a). 'The "Extendedness" Variable in Classifier Semantics: Universal Semantic Features and Cultural Variation', in Mathiot (1979: 97–119).
—— (1979b). 'Semantic Analysis of Selected Japanese Numeral Classifiers for Units', *Linguistics* 17: 317–35.
—— (1986). 'The Semantic Role of Classifiers', in Craig (1986a: 297–308).
—— and Creider, C. A. (1986). 'The semantics of noun classes in Proto-Bantu', in Craig (1986a: 217–40).
Derbyshire, D. C. (1985). *Hixkaryana and Linguistic Typology*. Dallas: Summer Institute of Linguistics and the University of Texas at Arlington.
—— (1999). 'Carib Languages', in Dixon and Aikhenvald (1999: 23–64).
—— and Payne, D. L. (1990). 'Noun Classification Systems of Amazonian Languages', in Payne (1990: 243–72).
—— and Pullum, G. K. (eds.) (1986). *Handbook of Amazonian Languages*, i. Berlin: Mouton de Gruyter.
—— —— (eds.) (1990). *Handbook of Amazonian Languages*, ii. Berlin: Mouton de Gruyter.
—— —— (eds.) (1991). *Handbook of Amazonian Languages*, iii. Berlin: Mouton de Gruyter.
—— —— (eds.) (1998). *Handbook of Amazonian Languages*, iv. Berlin: Mouton de Gruyter.
Diakonoff, I. M. (1988). *Afrasian Languages*. Moscow: Nauka.
Dimmendaal, G. I. (1983). *The Turkana Language*. Dordrecht: Foris.
—— (2000). 'Noun Classification in Baale', in R. Vossen et al. (eds.), *Mehr als nur Worte.... Afrikanistische Beiträge zum 65. Geburtstag von Franz Rottland*. Cologne: Rüdiger Köppe, 183–203.
Dixon, R. M. W. (1968). 'Noun Classes', *Lingua* 21: 104–25.
—— (1972). *The Dyirbal Language of North Queensland*. Cambridge: Cambridge University Press.
—— (ed.) (1976). *Grammatical Categories in Australian Languages*. Canberra: Australian Institute of Aboriginal Studies.
—— (1977). *A Grammar of Yidiɲ*. Cambridge: Cambridge University Press.
—— (1980). *The Languages of Australia*. Cambridge University Press: Cambridge.
—— (1982). *Where Have All the Adjectives Gone? and other essays in semantics and syntax*. Berlin: Mouton.
—— (1986). 'Noun Classes and Noun Classification in Typological Perspective', in Craig (1986a: 105–12).

Dixon, R. M. W. (1988). *A Grammar of Boumaa Fijian*. Chicago: University of Chicago Press.
—— (1994). *Ergativity*. Cambridge: Cambridge University Press.
—— (1995). 'Fusional Development of Gender Marking in Jarawara Possessed Nouns', *International Journal of American Linguistics* 61: 263–94.
—— (1997). *The Rise and Fall of Languages*. Cambridge: Cambridge University Press.
—— (2002). *Australian Languages: Their Nature and Development*. Cambridge: Cambridge University Press.
—— and Aikhenvald, A. Y. (eds.) (1999). *The Amazonian Languages*. Cambridge: Cambridge University Press.
—— (forthcoming). *The Jarawara Language of Southern Amazonia*.
Dobrin, L. 1999. 'Phonological form, morphological class and syntactic gender: the noun class systems of Papua New Guinea Arapeshan'. PhD dissertation. University of Chicago.
Donaldson, T. (1980). *Ngiyambaa: The Language of the Wangaaybuwan*. Cambridge: Cambridge University Press.
Dondorp, A., and Shim, J.-W. (1997). *Wipi*. Ukarumpa: Summer Institute of Linguistics.
Doneux, J. (1967). 'Discussion for S. Sauvageot 1967', in *La Classification nominale*, 234–5.
Dorian, N. (1978). 'The Fate of Morphological Complexity in Language Death', *Language* 54: 590–609.
—— (1981). *Language Death: The Life Cycle of a Scottish Gaelic Dialect*. Philadelphia: University of Pennsylvania Press.
—— (ed.) (1989). *Investigating Obsolescence: Studies in Language Contraction and Death*. Cambridge: Cambridge University Press.
Downing, P. (1984). 'Japanese Numeral Classifiers: A Semantic, Syntactic, and Functional Profile'. PhD thesis, University of California (Berkeley).
—— (1986). 'The Anaphoric Use of Classifiers in Japanese', in Craig (1986a: 345–75).
—— (1996). *Numeral Classifier Systems: The Case of Japanese*. Amsterdam: John Benjamins.
Drabbe, P. (1955). *Spraakkunst van het Marind zuidkust Nederlands Nieuw-Guinea*. Vienna: Missiehuis St. Gabriel.
Drossard, W. (1982). 'Nominalklassifikation in ostkaukasischen Sprachen', in Seiler and Stachowiak (1982: 155–78).
Dryer, M. S. (1992). 'The Greenbergian Word Order Correlations', *Language* 68: 81–138.
Ducos, G. (1979). 'Évolution d'une langue à classes nominales', *La Linguistique* 15: 43–54.
Dul'son, A. P. (1968). *Ketskij jazyk* [The Ket Language]. Tomsk: Izdateljstvo Tomskogo Universiteta.
Durie, M. (1985). *A Grammar of Acehnese: On the Basis of a Dialect of North Aceh*. Dordrecht: Foris.
—— (1986). 'The Grammaticization of Number as a Verbal Category', *Berkeley Linguistics Society: Proceedings of the Annual Meeting* 12: 355–70.

Eades, D. (1979). 'Gumbaynggir', in R. M. W. Dixon and B. Blake (eds.), *Handbook of Australian Languages*, i. Canberra: Australian National University Press and Amsterdam: John Benjamins, 245–361.
Eather, A. (1990). 'A Grammar of Nakkara (Central Arnhem Land Coast)'. PhD thesis, Australian National University, Canberra.
Edel'man, J. (1980). 'K substratnomu nasledijü centraljnoasiatskogo jazykovogo sojuza' ['Towards the Substatum Inheritance of the Central Asian Linguistic Area'], *Voprosy Jazykoznania* 5: 21–32.
Ekdahl, M., and Butler, N. (1979). *Aprenda Terêna*. Brasília: Summer Institute of Linguistics.
Elbert, S. H. (1974). *Puluwat Grammar*. Canberra: Pacific Linguistics.
Emeneau, M. B. (1964). 'India as a Linguistic Area', in Hymes (1966: 642–53).
England, N. (1983). *A Grammar of Mam, a Mayan Language*. Austin: University of Texas Press.
—— (1991). 'Changes in Basic Word Order in Mayan Languages', *International Journal of American Linguistics* 57: 446–86.
Erbaugh, M. (1984). 'Scissors, Paper, Stone: Perceptual Foundations for Noun Classifier Systems', *Papers and Reports on Child Language Development* 23: 41–9.
—— (1986). 'Taking Stock: The Development of Chinese Noun Classifiers Historically and in Young Children', in Craig (1986a: 399–436).
Evans, N. (1994). 'The Problem of Body Parts and Noun Class Membership in Australian Languages', *University of Melbourne Working Papers in Linguistics* 14: 1–8.
—— (1996). 'The Syntax and Semantics of Body Part Incorporation in Mayali', in Chappell and McGregor (1996: 65–109).
—— (1997). 'Head Classes and Agreement Classes in the Mayali Dialect Chain', in Harvey and Reid (1997: 105–46).
—— (ms). *A Draft Grammar of Mayali*. University of Melbourne.
Everett, D. L., and Kern, B. (1997). *A Grammar of 'Oro Nao*. London: Croom Helm.
Facundes, S. (1994). 'Noun Categorization in Apurinã'. MA thesis, University of Oregon.
Faraclas, N. G. (1989). 'Cross River', in J. Bendor-Samuel (ed.), *The Niger-Congo Languages*. New York and Lanham: University Press of America, 377–99.
Fleischmann, L., and Turpeinen, S. (1975). *Bine Grammar Essentials*. Ukarumpa: Summer Institute of Linguistics.
Foley, W. A. (1986). *The Papuan Languages of New Guinea*. Cambridge: Cambridge University Press.
—— (1991). *The Yimas Language of New Guinea*. Stanford: Stanford University Press.
Ford, K., and Ober, D. (1991). 'A Sketch of Kalaw Kawaw Ya', in S. Romaine (ed.), *Language in Australia*. Cambridge: Cambridge University Press, 118–42.
Ford, L. J. (1990). 'The Phonology and Morphology of Bachamal Wogait'. MA thesis, Australian National University.
—— (1998). 'A Grammar of Emmi'. PhD thesis, Australian National University.
Foreman, V. (1974). *Grammar of Yessan-Mayo*. Summer Institute of Linguistics, Santa Ana, California.

Foris, D. (1993). *A Grammar of Sochiapan Chinantec*. PhD thesis, University of Auckland.
—— (2000). *A Grammar of Sochiapan Chinantec*. Studies in Chinantec languages 6. Dallas: Summer Institute of Linguistics and the University of Texas at Arlington.
Fortune, R. (1942). *Arapesh*. New York: J. J. Augustin.
Frajzyngier, Z. (1993). *A Grammar of Mupun*. Berlin: Dietrich Reimer.
Frank, P. (1990). *Ika Syntax*. Dallas: Summer Institute of Linguistics and the University of Texas at Arlington.
Franklin, K. (1981). 'Existential and Pro-verbs in Kewa', in K. J. Franklin (ed.), *Syntax and Semantics in Papua New Guinea Languages*. Ukarumpa: Summer Institute of Linguistics, 151–72.
Fraser, N. M., and Corbett, G. G. (1997). 'Defaults in Arapesh', *Lingua* 103: 25–57.
Frawley, W. (1992). *Linguistic Semantics*. London: Lawrence Erlbaum.
Friedrich, P. (1970). 'Shape in Grammar', *Language* 46: 379–407.
—— (1971). *The Tarascan Suffixes of Locative Space: Meaning and Morphotactics*. Bloomington: Indiana University.
Gagné, R. C. (1966). *Eskimo Language Course*. Ottawa: Department of Indian Affairs and Northern Development.
Gandour, J., Buckingham, H., and Dardarananda, R. (1985). 'The Dissolution of Numeral Classifiers in Thai', *Linguistics* 23: 547–66.
—— Petty, S. H., Dardarananda, R., Dechongkit, S., and Mukngoen, S. (1984). 'The Acquisition of Numeral Classifiers in Thai', *Linguistics* 22: 455–79.
Garibian, A. S. (1976). 'Armjanskij Jazyk' [Armenian Language], in *Jazyki Azii i Afriki: Indo-evropejskie jazyki*. Moscow: Nauka, 94–109.
Geeraerts, D. (1988). 'Where Does Prototypicality Come From?', in B. Rudzka-Ostyn (ed.), *Topics in Cognitive Linguistics*. Amsterdam: John Benjamins, 207–29.
Gerzenstein, A. (1994). *Lengua maká: Estudio descriptivo*. Instituto de Lingüística, Universidad de Buenos Aires.
Givón, T. (1969). *Studies in Chibemba and Bantu Grammar*. Department of Linguistics, University of California, Los Angeles.
—— (1970). 'The Resolution of Gender Conflicts in Bantu Conjunction: When Syntax and Semantics Clash', *Papers from the Sixth Regional Meeting, Chicago Linguistic Society, April 16–18, 1970*. Chicago: Chicago Linguistic Society, 250–61.
—— (1971). 'Some Historical Changes in the Noun Class System of Bantu, Their Possible Causes and Wider Implications', in C.-W. Kim and H. Stahlke (eds.), *Papers in African Linguistics*. Edmonton: Linguistic Research, 33–54.
—— (1976). 'Topic, Pronoun and Grammatical Agreement', in Li (1976: 149–89).
—— (1981). 'On the Development of Numeral "one" as an Indefinite Marker', *Folia Linguistica Historica* 2: 35–53.
—— (1991). 'Some Substantive Issues Concerning Verb Serialization: Grammatical vs Cognitive Packaging', in C. Lefèbre (ed.), *Serial Verbs: Grammatical, Comparative and Cognitive Approaches*. Amsterdam: John Benjamins, 137–84.
Goddard, C. (1985). *A Grammar of Yankunytjatjara*. Alice Springs: Institute for Aboriginal Development.
—— (1996). 'Cross-linguistic Research on Metaphor', *Language and Communication* 16: 145–51.

Gomez-Imbert, E. (1986). 'De la forme et du sens dans la classification nominale en Tatuyo, Langue Tukano orientale d'Amazonie colombienne', Université Paris IV.
—— (1996). 'When Animals Become "Rounded" and "Feminine": Conceptual Categories and Linguistic Classification in a Multilingual Setting', in J. J. Gumpertz and S. C. Levinson (eds.), *Rethinking Linguistic Relativity*. Cambridge: Cambridge University Press, 438–69.
Gonçalves, C. H. R. C. (1987). *Concordância em Munduruku*. Campinas: Editora da Unicamp.
Gonzalez Ñañez, O. (1985). 'Los numerales en un dialecto curripaco', *Boletín de Lingüística* 5: 15–28.
Goral, D. R. (1978). 'Numeral Classifier Systems: A Southeast Asian Cross Linguistic Analysis', *Linguistics of the Tibeto-Burman Area* 4: 1–72.
Gordon, L. (1986). *Maricopa Morphology and Syntax*. Berkeley: University of California Press.
Gralow, F. L. (1993). *Un bosquejo del idioma Koreguaje*. Bogotá: Asociación Instituto Lingüístico de Verano, Bogotá.
Green, D. (1996). 'O sistema numérico na língua Palikur', *Boletim do museu Goeldi* 10: 261–303.
—— and Green, H. (1972). *Surface Grammar of Palikur*. Brasília: Summer Institute of Linguistics.
Green, I. (1989). 'Marrithiyel'. PhD thesis, Australian National University.
—— (1995). 'The Death of "Prefixing": Contact Induced Typological Change in Northern Australia', *Proceedings of the Annual Meeting, Berkeley Linguistics Society* 21: 414–25.
—— (1997). 'Nominal Classification in Marrithiyel', in Harvey and Reid (1997: 229–53).
Green, M., and Igwe, G. E. (1963). *A Descriptive Grammar of Igbo*. Berlin: Akademie.
Green, R. (1987). 'A Sketch Grammar of Burarra'. Fourth year honours thesis, Australian National University, Canberra.
—— (1995). 'A Grammar of Gurr-goni'. PhD thesis, Australian National University.
Greenberg, J. H. (1963). 'Some Universals of Grammar with Particular Reference to the Order of Meaningful Elements', in J. H. Greenberg (ed.), *Universals of Language*. Cambridge, Mass.: MIT Press, 58–90.
—— (1966). *Language Universals, with Special Reference to Feature Hierarchies*. The Hague: Mouton.
—— (1972). 'Numeral Classifiers and Substantival Number: Problems in the Genesis Type', *Working Papers in Language Universals*, reprinted in Greenberg (1990: 16–93).
—— (1978). 'How Does Language Acquire Gender Markers?' in J. H. Greenberg, C. A. Ferguson, and E. A. Moravcsik (eds.), *Universals of Human Languages*, iii: *Word Structure*. Stanford: Stanford University Press, 241–70.
—— (1990). *On Language: Selected Writings of Joseph H. Greenberg*, K. Denning and S. Kemmer (eds.). Stanford, Stanford University Press.
Griffiths, G., and Griffiths, C. (1976). *Aspectos da língua Kadiwéu*. Brasília: Summer Institute of Linguistics.

Haas, M. R. (1942). 'The Use of Numeral Classifiers in Thai', *Language* 18: 201–5.
—— (1978). 'Classificatory verbs in Muskogee', *International Journal of American Linguistics* 14: 244–6; repr. in A. S. Dil (ed.) *Language, Culture, and History: Essays by Mary R. Haas*. Stanford University Press: Stanford, 302–7.
Haas, M. R. (1967). 'Language and Taxonomy in Northwestern California', *American Anthropologist* 69: 358–62.
Hagman, R. S. (1977). *Nama Hottentot Grammar*. Bloomington: Indiana University.
Haiman, J. (1980). *Hua: A Papuan Language of the Eastern Highlands of New Guinea*. Amsterdam: John Benjamins.
Hale, K. L. (1975). 'Gaps in Grammar and Culture', in M. D. Kinkade *et al.* (eds.), *Linguistics and Anthropology: In Honor of C. F. Voegelin*. Lisse: Peter de Ridder, 295–315.
Hamel, P. J. (1994). *A Grammar and Lexicon of Loniu, Papua New Guinea*. Department of Linguistics, Research School of Pacific and Asian Studies, Australian National University, Canberra.
Hamp, E. (1958). 'Gender Shift in Albanian Plurals', *Romance Philology* 12: 147–55.
Harms, P. L. (1994). *Epena Pedee Syntax*. Dallas: Summer Institute of Linguistics and the University of Texas at Arlington.
Harris, A., and Campbell, L. (1995). *Historical Syntax in Cross-linguistic Perspective*. Cambridge: Cambridge University Press.
Harrison, S. P. (1976). *Mokilese Reference Grammar*. Honolulu: Hawaii University Press.
—— (1988). 'A Plausible History for Micronesian Possessive Classifiers', *Oceanic Linguistics* 27: 63–78.
Harvey, M. (1987). 'The Warray Language from Adelaide River'. MA thesis, Australian National University.
—— (1992). 'The Gaagudju People and Their Language'. PhD thesis, University of Sydney.
—— (1997). 'Nominal Classification and Gender in Aboriginal Australia', in Harvey and Reid (1997: 17–62).
—— (forthcoming). 'Limilngan'.
—— and Reid, N. (eds.) (1997). *Nominal Classification in Aboriginal Australia*. Amsterdam: John Benjamins.
Hasada, R. (1995). 'Number System in Japanese', paper presented at the Workshop on Grammatical Categories, Australian National University, Canberra.
Hashimoto, M. J. (1977). 'The Genealogy of the Classifier in Sino-Tibetan', *Computational Analysis of Asian and African Languages* 7: 69–78.
Haspelmath, M. (1993). *A Grammar of Lezgian*. Berlin: Mouton de Gruyter.
—— (1997). *Indefinite Pronouns*. Oxford: Oxford University Press.
Haviland, J. (1979). 'Guugu Yimidhirr', in R. M. W. Dixon and B. Blake (eds.), *Handbook of Australian Languages*, i. Canberra: Australian National University Press, 27–180.
Hayward, R. J. (1989). 'The Notion of "Default Gender": A Key to Interpreting the Evolution of Certain Verb Paradigms in East Ometo, and Its Implications for Omotic', *Afrika und Übersee* 72: 17–32.

—— and Corbett, G. G. (1988). 'Resolution Rules in Qafar', *Linguistics* 26: 259–79.
Heath, J. (1978a). *Linguistic Diffusion in Arnhem Land*. Canberra: Australian Institute of Aboriginal Studies.
—— (1978b). *Ngandi Grammar, Texts and Dictionary*. Canberra: Australian Institute of Aboriginal Studies.
—— (1983). 'Referential tracking in Nunggubuyu', in P. Munro and J. Haiman (eds.), *Switch-Reference and Universal Grammar*, Amsterdam/Philadelphia: John Benjamins, 129–49.
—— (1984). *Functional Grammar of Nunggubuyu*. Canberra: Australian Institute of Aboriginal Studies.
Heine, B. (1982a). 'African Noun Class Systems', in Seiler and Lehmann (1982: 189–216).
—— (1982b). *The Nubi Language of Kibera: An Arabic Creole*. Berlin: Dietrich Reimer.
—— (1992). 'Grammaticalization Chains', *Studies in Language* 16: 335–68.
—— (1997a). *Possession: Cognitive Sources, Forces, and Grammaticalization*. Cambridge: Cambridge University Press.
—— (1997b). 'Grammaticalization Chains Across Languages: An Example from Khoisan', paper presented at the Symposium on Grammaticalization, Houston, March 1997.
—— and Claudi, U. (1986). *On the Rise of Grammatical Categories: Some Examples from Maa*. Berlin: Reimer.
—— —— and Hünnemeyer, F. (1991). *Grammaticalization: A Conceptual Framework*. Chicago: University of Chicago Press.
—— and Reh, M. (1984). *Grammaticalization and Reanalysis in African Languages*. Hamburg: Helmut Buske.
—— and Vossen, R. (1983). 'On the Origin of Gender in Eastern Nilotic', in R. Vossen and M. Bechchaus-Gerst (eds.), *Nilotic Studies: Proceedings of the International Symposium on Languages and History of the Nilotic Peoples*. Berlin: Reimer, 255–68.
Henry, D., and Henry, K. (1965). 'Koyukon Classificatory Verbs', *Anthropological Linguistics* 7: 110–16.
Herbert, R. K. (1991). 'Patterns in Language Change, Acquisition and Dissolution: Noun Prefixes and Concords in Bantu', *Anthropological Linguistics* 33: 103–34.
Hewitt, G. (1979). *Abkhaz*. Amsterdam: North-Holland.
Hill, D. (1992). 'Longgu Grammar'. PhD thesis, Australian National University.
Himmelmann, N. P. (1997). *Deiktikon, Artikel, Nominalphrase: zur Emergenz syntaktischer Struktur*. Tübingen: Niemeyer.
Hiranburana, S. (1979). 'A Classification of Thai Classifiers', in N. D. Liem (ed.), *Southeast Asian Linguistic Studies*, iv. Canberra: Pacific Linguistics, 39–54.
Ho, J. (1997). 'Socio-semantic Aspects of Human Measure Words in Cantonese', in M. Clark (ed.), *Papers in Southeast Asian Linguistics* 16. Canberra: Pacific Linguistics, 67–77.
Hock, H. H. (1991). *Principles of Historical Linguistics*. Berlin: Mouton de Gruyter.

Hoijer, H. (1945). 'Classificatory Verb Stems in the Apachean Languages', *International Journal of American Linguistics* 11: 13–23.
Holmquist, J. C. (1991). 'Semantic Features and Gender Dynamics in Cantabrian Spanish', *Anthropological Linguistics* 33: 57–81.
Hopkins, N. A. (1970). 'Numeral Classifiers in Tzeltal, Jacaltec and Chuj (Mayan)', *Papers from the Annual Regional Meeting of the Chicago Linguistic Society* 6: 23–35.
Hopper, P. J. (1986). 'Some Discourse Functions of Classifiers in Malay', in Craig (1986a: 309–25).
—— and Thompson, S. (1984). 'The Discourse Basis for Lexical Categories in Universal Grammar', *Language* 60: 703–52.
Hopper, P. J., and Traugott, E. C. (1993). *Grammaticalization*. Cambridge: Cambridge University Press.
Hu, Q. (1993). 'The Acquisition of Chinese Classifiers by Young Mandarin Speaking Children'. PhD thesis, Boston University.
Huffman, F. E. (1970). *Modern Spoken Cambodian*. New Haven: Yale University Press.
Hundius, H., and Kölver, U. (1983). 'Syntax and Semantics of Numeral Classifiers in Thai', *Studies in Language* 7: 165–214.
Hurd, C. (1977). 'Nasioi Projectives', *Oceanic Linguistics* 16: 111–78.
Hyde, V. (1971). *An Introduction to the Luizeño Language*. Banning, Calif.: Malki Museum Press.
Hyman, L. M. (ed.) (1980). *Noun Classes in the Grassfields Bantu Borderland*. Los Angeles: University of Southern California, Department of Linguistics.
Hymes, D. (ed.) (1964). *Language in Culture and Society: A Reader in Linguistics and Anthropology*. New York: Harper & Row.
Ikoro, S. M. (1994). 'Numeral Classifiers in Kana', *Journal of African Language and Linguistics* 15: 7–28.
—— (1996a). *The Kana Language*. Leiden: University of Leiden.
—— (1996b). 'A Grammatical Summary of Kana', Materials for the Research Project 'Universals of Human Languages', Australian National University.
—— (1997). 'A Grammatical Summary of Igbo', Materials for the Research Project 'Universals of Human Languages', Australian National University.
Irvine, J. (1978). 'Wolof Noun Classification: The Social Setting of Divergent Change', *Language in Society* 7: 37–64.
Iturrioz Leza, J. L., Gómez López, P., Leal Carretero, S., and Ramirez de la Cruz, R. (1986). 'Individuación en huichol. II: Aspectos morfológicos y sintácticos de las clases nominales. III: Las séries sufijales', *Función* 1: 422–62; 2: 154–63.
Jackson, E. (1966). *Waurá: formulário dos vocabulários padrões do Museu Nacional*. Brasília: Summer Institute of Linguistics.
—— and Richards, J. (1966). *Tentative Phonemics Statement of Waurá*. Brasília: Summer Institute of Linguistics.
Jaisser, A. (1987). 'Hmong Classifiers', *Linguistics of the Tibeto-Burman Area* 10: 169–75.
Jakobson, R. O. (1941). *Kindersprache, Aphasie und allgemeine Lautgesetze*. Uppsala: Almquist & Wiksell.

—— (1984). 'The Gender Pattern of Russian', in L. R. Waugh and M. Halle (eds.), *Russian and Slavic Grammar: Studies 1931–1981*. Berlin: Mouton, 141–3.
Jauncey, D. (1997). 'A Grammar of Tamambo'. PhD thesis, Australian National University.
Jensen, J. T. (1977). *Yapese Reference Grammar*. Honolulu: University Press of Hawaii.
Jones, R. B. Jr. (1970). 'Classifier Constructions in Southeast Asia', *Journal of American Oriental Society* 90: 1–12.
Jones, W., and Jones, P. (1991). *Barasano Syntax*. Dallas: Summer Institute of Linguistics and the University of Texas at Arlington.
Jun, W., and Guoqiao, Z. (1993). *An Outline Grammar of Mulao*. National Thai Studies Centre, Australian National University, Canberra.
Juntanamalaga, P. (1988). 'Social Issues in Thai Classifier Usage', *Language Sciences* 10: 313–30.
Kakumasu, J. (1986). 'Urubu-Kaapor', in Derbyshire and Pullum (1986: 326–406).
Kari, J. (1989). 'Affix Positions and Zones in the Athabaskan Verb Complex: Ahtna and Navajo', *International Journal of American Linguistics* 55: 424–54.
—— (1990). *Ahtna Athabaskan Dictionary*. Alaska Native Language Center, University of Alaska, Fairbanks.
Karmiloff-Smith, A. (1979). *A Functional Approach to Child Language: A Study of Determiners and Reference*. Cambridge: Cambridge University Press.
Kayser, A. (ed. K. H. Rensch) (1993). *Nauru Grammar*. Yarralumla, Canberra: Embassy of the Federal Republic of Germany.
Keating, E. (1997). 'Honorific Possession: Power and Language in Pohnpei, Micronesia', *Language and Society* 26: 247–68.
Keenan, E. L. (1978). 'On Surface Form and Logical Form', in B. B. Kachru (ed.), *Linguistics in the Seventies: Directions and Prospects*. Urbana: University of Illinois, 163–203.
—— (1984). 'Semantic Correlates of the Ergative/Absolutive Distinction', *Linguistics* 22: 197–223.
Kerr, I. (1995). *Gramática pedagógica del cuiba-wáimonae*. Bogotá: Asociación Instituto Lingüístico de Verano.
Key, M. R. (1972). 'Linguistic Behavior of Male and Female', *Linguistics* 88: 15–31.
—— (1979). *The Grouping of South American Indian Languages*. Tübingen: Gunter Narr.
Khaidakov, S. M. (1963). 'The Principles of Non-class Division in Lak' (in Russian, with a summary in English), *Studia Caucasica* 1: 48–55.
—— (1980). *Principy imennoj klassifikacii v dagestanskih jazykah* [The Principles of Nominal Classification in Daghestanian Languages]. Moscow: Nauka.
Kibrik, A. E., Kodzasov, S. V., and Olovjannikova, I. P. (1972). *Fragmenty grammatiki hinalugskogo jazyka* [Fragments of a Grammar of Khinalug]. Moscow: Izdateljstvo Moskovskogo Universiteta.
Kimball, G. D. (1991). *Koasati Grammari*. Lincoln: University of Nebraska Press.
Kirton, J. F. (1971). *Papers in Australian Linguistics*. Australian National University, Canberra: Pacific Linguistics.
Kiyomi, S. (1992). 'Animateness and Shape in Classifiers', *Word* 43: 15–36.

Klein, H. E. M. (1978). *Una gramática de la lengua Toba: morfologia verbal y nominal*. Montevideo: Universidad de la Republica.
—— (1979). 'Noun Classifiers in Toba', in Mathiot (1979: 85–95).
Koehn, E., and Koehn, S. (1986). 'Apalai', in Derbyshire and Pullum (1986: 33–127).
Koehn, S. (1994). 'The Use of Generic Terms in Apalaí Genitive Constructions', *Revista Latinoamericana de estudios etnolingüisticos* 8: 39–48.
Köhler, O. (1962). 'Studien zur Genussystem und Verbalbau der zentral Khoisan-Sprachen', *Anthropos* 57: 529–46.
—— (1971). 'Noun Classes and Grammatical Agreement in !Xũ (ʒù-/hoà dialect)', *Actes du Huitième Congrès International de Linguistique Africaine, Abidjan 24–28 Mars 1969*. Abidjan, 489–522.
Kölver, U. (1982a). 'Klassifikatorkonstruktionen in Thai, Vietnamesisch und Chinesisch', in Seiler and Lehmann (1982: 160–85).
—— (1982b). 'Interaktion von nominalen Kategorien am Beispiel der Entwicklung des modernen Bengali', in Seiler and Lehmann (1982: 244–51).
Kooyers, O. (n.d.). *Washkuk Grammar Sketch*. Ukarumpa: Summer Institute of Linguistics.
Köpcke, K. M., and Zubin, D. A. (1984). 'Sechs Prinzipien für die Genuszuweisung im Deutschen: Ein Beitrag zur natürlichen Klassifikation', *Linguistische Berichte* 93: 26–50.
Krauss, M. (1968). 'Noun Classification Systems in Athabaskan, Eyak, Tlingit and Haida Verbs', *International Journal of American Linguistics* 34: 194–203.
Krejnovič, E. A. (1961). 'Imennye klassy i sredstva ih vyrazhenija v ketskom jazyke' ['Noun Classes and Means of Their Expression in Ket']', *Voprosy jazykoznanija* 2: 106–16.
Krishnamurti, Bh. (1975). 'Gender and Number in Proto-Dravidian', *International Journal of Dravidian Linguistics* 4: 328–50.
—— (forthcoming). 'Gender and Number in Dravidian'.
—— and Gwynn, J. P.L. (1985). *A Grammar of Modern Telugu*. Delhi: Oxford University Press.
Kuipers, A. H. (1967). *The Squamish Language*. The Hague: Mouton.
—— (1974). *The Shuswap Language*. The Hague: Mouton.
Kunene, E. (1986). 'Acquisition of SiSwati noun classes', *South African Journal of African Languages* 6: 34–7.
Lakoff, G. (1986). 'Classifiers as a Reflection of Mind', in Craig (1986a: 13–52).
—— (1987). *Women, Fire and Other Dangerous Things: What Categories Reveal about the Mind*. Chicago: University of Chicago Press.
Landar, H. (1967). 'Ten'a Classificatory Verbs', *International Journal of American Linguistics* 33: 263–8.
Lang, A. (1975). *The Semantics of Classificatory Verbs in Enga and Other Papua New Guinea Languages*. Canberra: Pacific Linguistics.
Langacker, R. W. (1977). *Studies in Uto-Aztecan Grammar*, i: *An Overview of Uto-Aztecan Grammar*. Dallas: Summer Institute of Linguistics and the University of Texas at Arlington.
—— (1987). *Foundations of Cognitive Grammar*, i: *Theoretical Prerequisites*. Stanford: Stanford University Press.

Langdon, M. (1970). *A Grammar of Diegueño*. Berkeley: University of California Press.
Laoust, E. (1918). *Ntifa: son parler*. Paris: Hachette.
—— (1928). *Cours de berbère marocain*. Paris: Hachette.
— (1931). *Siwa*. v. 1. *Son parler*. Paris: Hachette.
Lapointe, S. (1985). *A Theory of Grammatical Agreement*. New York: Garland.
LaPolla, R. J. (1994). 'Parallel Grammaticalizations in Tibeto-Burman Languages: Evidence of Sapir's "Drift"', *Linguistics of the Tibeto-Burman Area* 17: 61–80.
—— (forthcoming). *Grammar of Qiang with annotated texts and glossary*. Berlin: Mouton de Gruyter.
Laskowski, R. (1988). 'The Systemic Prerequisites of the Development of the Declensional Patterns of the Slavic Languages: The Category of Gender', *Scando-Slavica* 34: 111–25.
Lawton, R. S. (1980). 'The Kiriwinan Classifiers'. MA thesis, Australian National University.
—— (1993). *Topics in the Description of Kiriwina*. Canberra: Pacific Linguistics.
Laycock, D. C. (1969). 'Three LamaLamic Languages of North Queensland', *Papers in Australian Linguistics* 4: 71–97.
—— (1975). 'The Torricelli Phylum', in S. Wurm (ed.), *New Guinea Area Languages and Language Study*, i: *Papuan Languages and the New Guinea Linguistic Scene*. Canberra: Pacific Linguistics, 767–80.
—— and Z'graggen, J. (1975). 'The Sepik-Ramu Phylum', in S. Wurm (ed.), *New Guinea Area Languages and Language Study*, i: *Papuan Languages and the New Guinea Linguistic Scene*, Canberra: Pacific Linguistics, 731–63.
Lee, J. (1987). *Tiwi Today. A Study of Language Change in a Contact Situation*. Canberra: Pacific Linguistics.
Lee, K.-D. (1975). *Kusaiean Reference Grammar*. Honolulu: University Press of Hawaii.
Lee, M. (1988). 'Language, Perception and the World', in J. Hawkins (ed.), *Explaining Language Universals*. Oxford: Blackwell, 211–46.
Lee, Y. (1997). 'Classifiers in Korean'. Honours thesis, Australian National University, Canberra.
Lee Kwok Loong, J. (1997). 'Nominal Classification in Yapese'. Honours thesis, University of Western Australia.
Leeding, V. (1989). 'Anindilyakwa Phonology and Morphology'. PhD thesis, University of Sydney.
—— (1996). 'Body Parts and Possession in Anindilyakwa', in Chappell and McGregor (1996: 193–250).
Lehmann, C. (1982). 'Universal and Typological Aspects of Agreement', in Seiler and Stachowiak (1982: 201–67).
—— (1988). 'On the Function of Agreement', in Barlow and Ferguson (1986b: 55–66).
Lehrer, A. (1986). 'English Classifier Constructions', *Lingua* 68: 109–48.
Levy, P. (1993). 'Totonac Body-parts: Are They Classifiers?', paper presented at the workshop 'Back to Basic Issues in Classification', Nijmegen, May 1993.

Levy, P. (1994). *How Shape Becomes Grammar: On the Semantics of Part Morphemes in Totonac.* Cognitive Anthropology Research Group. Max-Planck Institute for Psycholinguistics, Nijmegen.

Levy, Y. (1983a). 'The Acquisition of Hebrew Plurals: The Case of the Missing Gender Category', *Journal of Child Language* 10: 107–21.

Levy, Y. (1983b). 'It's Frogs All the Way Down', *Cognition* 15: 75–93.

—— (1988). 'On the Early Learning of Formal Grammatical Systems: Evidence from Studies of the Acquisition of Gender and Countability', *Journal of Child Language* 15: 179–87.

Li, C. N. (ed.) (1976). *Subject and Topic.* New York: Academic Press.

—— and Thompson, S. A. (1981). *Mandarin Chinese: A Functional Reference Grammar.* Berkeley: University of California Press.

Lichtenberk, F. (1983a). 'Relational Classifiers', *Lingua* 60: 147–76.

—— (1983b). *A grammar of Manam.* Honolulu: University of Hawaii Press.

—— (1985). 'Possessive Constructions in Oceanic Languages and in Proto-Oceanic', in A. Pawley and L. Carrington (eds.), *Austronesian Linguistics at the 15th Pacific Science Congress.* Canberra: Pacific Linguistics, 93–140.

—— (1995). 'Number Marking in To'aba'ita', paper presented at the workshop on 'Grammatical Categories', Australian National University, Canberra.

Lindrud, S., and Nicholson, R. (n.d.) 'Notes on the Taulil language of East New Britain'. Ukarumpa: Summer Institute of Linguistics.

Lock, A. (forthcoming). *Abau Grammar Essentials.* London: Longmans.

Löbel. E. (2000). 'Classifiers vs. Genders and Noun Classes: A Case Study in Vietnamese', in B. Unterbeck et al. (ed.), *Gender in Grammar and Cognition.* Berlin: Mouton de Gruyter, 259–319.

Lowe, I. (1999). 'Nambiquara family', in Dixon and Aikhenvald (1999: 269–92).

Lucy, J. A. (1992a). *Grammatical Categories and Cognition. A Study of the Linguistic Relativity Hypothesis.* Cambridge: Cambridge University Press.

—— (1992b). *Language Diversity and Thought: A Reformulation of the Linguistic Relativity Hypothesis.* Cambridge: Cambridge University Press.

Luke, K. K., and Harrison, G. (1986). 'Young Children's Use of Chinese (Cantonese and Mandarin) Sortal Classifiers', in S. R. Henry Kao and R. Hoosain (eds.), *Linguistics, Psychology and the Chinese Language.* Hong Kong: University of Hong Kong, 125–47.

Lynch, J. (1992). '"For My Part . . .": The Grammar and Semantics of Part Possession in the Languages of Tanna', *Australian Journal of Linguistics* 12: 249–70.

—— (1993). 'Proto-Oceanic Possessive Marking', paper presented at the 1st International Conference on Oceanic Linguistics, 4–9 July 1993, Port Vila, Vanuatu.

—— Ross, M., and Crowley, T. (forthcoming). *The Oceanic Languages.* London: Curzon Press.

Lyons, J. (1968). *Introduction to Theoretical Linguistics.* Cambridge: Cambridge University Press.

—— (1975). 'Deixis and Anaphora', in T. Myers (ed.), *The Development of Conversation and Discourse.* Edinburgh: Edinburgh University Press, 88–103.

—— (1977). *Semantics.* 2 vols. Cambridge: Cambridge University Press.

Magomedbekova, Z. M. (1967). 'Chamalinskij jazyk' ['Chamalal language'], in E. A. Bokarev and K. V. Lomtatidze (eds.) *Jazyki narodov SSSR*, IV: *Iberijsko-kavkazskie jazyki*. Moscow: Nauka, 384–99.
Mahapatra, B. P. (1979). *Malto: An Ethnosemantic Study*. Manasagangotro, Mysore: Central Institute of Indian Languages.
Malinowski, B. (1920). 'Classificatory Particles in the Language of Kiriwina', *Bulletin of the School of Oriental Studies* 1: 33–78.
Manessy, G. (1961). *Le bwamu et ses dialectes*. Dakar.
Marchese, L. (1988). 'Noun Classes and Agreement Systems in Kru: A Historical Approach', in Barlow and Ferguson (1988b: 323–42).
Marnita, R. (1996). 'Classifiers in Minangkabau'. MA thesis, Australian National University, Canberra.
Marr, D. (1982). *Vision*. San Francisco: Freeman.
Martin, S. E. (1975). *A Reference Grammar of Japanese*. New Haven: Yale University Press.
Martins, S. A. (1994). 'Análise da morfosintaxe da língua Dâw (Maku-Kamã) e sua classificação tipológica'. MA thesis, Universidade Federal de Santa Catarina, Florianópolis, Brazil.
—— and Martins, V. (1999). 'The Makú language family', in Dixon and Aikhenvald (1999: 251–67).
Mathiot, M. (ed.) (1979). *Ethnology: Boas, Sapir and Whorf Revisited*. The Hague: Mouton.
—— and Roberts, M. (1979). 'Sex Roles as Revealed through Referential Gender in American English', in Mathiot (1979: 1–47).
Matthews, P. H. (1997). *The Concise Oxford Dictionary of Linguistics*. Oxford: Oxford University Press.
Matisoff, J. A. (1991). 'Areal and Universal Dimensions of Grammatization in Lahu', in Traugott and Heine (1991a: ii. 383–453).
Matsumoto, Y. (1985). 'Acquisition of Some Japanese Numeral Classifiers: The Search for Convention', *Stanford Papers and Reports in Child Language Development* 24: 79–86.
—— (1993). 'Japanese Numeral Classifiers: A Study on Semantic Categories and Lexical Organization', *Linguistics* 31: 667–713.
Mattéi-Müller, M.-C. (1974). 'El sistema de posesión en la lengua panare', *Antropologica* 38: 3–14.
McGregor, D. E., and McGregor, A. R. F. (1982). *Olo Language Materials*. Canberra: Pacific Linguistics.
McKay, G. R. (1975). 'Rembarrnga, a Language of Central Arnhem Land'. PhD thesis, Australian National University, Canberra.
McLendon, S. (1975). *A Grammar of Eastern Pomo*. Berkerley: University of California Publications in Linguistics 74.
McLaughlin, F. (1997). 'Noun Classification in Wolof: When Affixes Are Not Renewed', *Studies in African Linguistics* 26: 1–28.
Meillet, A. (1912). 'L'Évolution des formes grammaticales', *Scientia* 12/26 (Milan); repr. 1951, in *Linguistique historique et linguistique générale*. Paris: Klincksieck, 130–48.

Meillet, A. (1964). 'The Feminine Gender in the Indo-European Languages', in Hymes (1964: 124).
Melchert, H. C. (1994). 'The Feminine Gender in Anatolian', *Früh-, Mittel-, Spätindogermanisch: Akten der IX Fachtagung der indogermanischen Gesellschaft*. Wiesbaden: Ludwig Reichert, 231–44.
Merlan, F. (1983). *Ngalakan Grammar, Texts and Vocabulary*. Canberra: Pacific Linguistics.
—— (1994). *A Grammar of Wardaman: A Language of the Northern Territory of Australia*. Berlin: Mouton de Gruyter.
—— and Rumsey, A. (1991). *Ku Waru: Language and Segmentary Politics in the Western Nebilyer Valley. Papua New Guinea*. Cambridge: Cambridge University Press.
—— Roberts, S. P., and Rumsey, A. (1997). 'New Guinea "Classificatory Verbs" and Australian Noun Classification: A Typological Comparison', in Harvey and Reid (1997: 63–103).
Mills, A. E. (1986). *The Acquisition of Gender: A Study of English and German*. Berlin: Springer.
Minor, E., and Minor, L. (1971). *Resumen de la gramática* [*Huitoto*]. Lomalinda: Instituto Lingüístico de Verano.
Mithun, M. (1984). 'The Evolution of Noun Incorporation', *Language* 60: 847–94.
—— (1986). 'The Convergence of Noun Classification Systems', in Craig (1986a: 379–98).
—— (1991). 'Active/Agentive Case-marking and Its Motivations', *Language* 67: 510–46.
Moore, B., and Franklin, G. (1979). *Breves notícias da língua Makú-Hupda*. Brasília: Summer Institute of Linguistics.
Moore, D. L. (1984). 'Syntax of the Language of the Gavião Indians of Rondônia'. PhD thesis, City University of New York.
Moravcsik, E. A. (1971). 'Agreement', in J. H. Greenberg (ed.), *Universals of Human Language*, iv: *Syntax*. Stanford: Stanford University Press, 331–74.
Morice, A. G. (1932). *The Carrier Language (Déné family): A Grammar and Dictionary Combined*. 2 vols. Vienna: Collection Internationale de Monographies Linguistiques. Anthropos, vol. 9.
Mosel, U. (1982). 'Number, Collection and Mass in Tolai', in Seiler and Stachowiak (1982: 123–54).
—— (1983). *Adnominal and Predicative Possessive Constructions in Melanesian Languages*. Arbeiten des Kölner Universalien-Projekts, No. 50. Cologne: University of Cologne.
—— and Spriggs, R. (forthcoming). 'A Grammar of Teop'.
Moshinsky, J. (1974). *A Grammar of Southeastern Pomo*. Berkeley: University of California Press.
Moussay, G. (1981). *La Langue Minangkabau*. Paris: Association Archipel.
Mufwene, S. S. (1980). 'Bantu Class Prefixes: Inflectional or Derivational?', *Papers from the Annual Regional Meeting of the Chicago Linguistic Society* 16: 246–58.
Mujica, M. I. O. (1992). 'Aspectos fonológicos e gramaticais da língua Yawalapiti (Aruak)'. MA thesis, Universidade de Campinas.

Mulford, R. (1983). 'Semantic and Formal Factors in the Comprehension of Icelandic Pronoun Gender', *Papers and Reports on Child Language Development* 22: 83–91.
Munroe, P. MS. 'The Garifuna Gender System'.
Nekitel, O. (1985). 'Sociolinguistic Aspects of Abu', a Papuan Language of the Sepik Area, Papua New Guinea'. PhD thesis, Australian National University.
—— (1986). 'A Sketch of Nominal Concord in Abu' (an Arapesh language)', in D. C. Laycock et al. (eds.), *Papers in New Guinea Linguistics* 24. Canberra: Pacific Linguistics, 177–205.
—— (ms). 'Gender in Abu' Arapesh'. University of Papua New Guinea.
Ng, B. C. (1989). 'The Acquisition of Numeral Classifiers in Hokkien, a Southern Min Language'. PhD, La Trobe University.
—— (1991). 'Word Meaning Acquisition and Numeral Classifiers', *La Trobe Working Papers in Linguistics* 4: 73–83.
Nguyen, D. H. (1957). 'Classifiers in Vietnamese', *Word* 13: 124–52.
Nichols, J. (1986). 'Head-marking and Dependent-marking Grammar', *Language* 62: 56–119.
—— (1989a). 'The Nakh Evidence for the History of Gender in Nakh-Daghestanian', in H. I. Aronson (ed.), *The Non-Slavic Languages of the USSR: Linguistic Studies*. Chicago: Chicago Linguistic Society, 158–75.
—— (1989b). 'The Origin of Nominal Classification', in K. Hall, M. Meacham, and R. Shapiro (eds.), *Proceedings of the Fifteenth Annual Meeting of the Berkeley Linguistics Society, February 18–20 1989*: 409–20.
—— (1992). *Linguistic Diversity in Space and Time*. Chicago: University of Chicago Press.
—— (1997). 'Modelling Ancient Population Structures and Movement in Linguistics', *Annual Review of Anthropology* 26: 359–84.
—— and Peterson, D. A. (1998). 'A Reply to Campbell', *Language* 74: 605–14.
Nordlinger, R. (1998). *A Grammar of Wambaya, Northern Territory (Australia)*. Canberra: Pacific Linguistics.
Ó Siadhail, M. (1989). *Modern Irish: Grammatical Structure and Dialectal Variation*. Cambridge: Cambridge University Press.
Onishi, M. (1994). 'A Grammar of Motuna (Bougainville, Papua New Guinea)'. PhD thesis, Australian National University.
—— (1996a). 'A Grammatical Summary of Ainu', materials for the research project 'Universals of Human Languages', Australian National University.
—— (1996b). 'A Grammatical Summary of Japanese', materials for the research project 'Universals of Human Languages', Australian National University.
—— (1996c). 'A Grammatical Summary of Bengali', materials for the research project 'Universals of Human Languages', Australian National University.
—— (1997a). 'A Grammatical Summary of Kobon', materials for the research project 'Universals of Human Languages', Australian National University.
—— (1997b). 'A Grammatical Summary of Amele', materials for the research project 'Universals of Human Languages', Australian National University.
Osam, E. K. A. (1994). 'Aspects of Akan Grammar: A Functional Perspective'. PhD thesis, University of Oregon, Eugene.

Osumi, M. (1996). 'Body Parts in Tinrin', in Chappell and McGregor (1996: 344–462).
Osborne, C. R. (1974). *The Tiwi Language: Grammar, Myths and Dictionary of the Tiwi Language Spoken on Melville and Bathurst Islands, Northern Australia.* Canberra: Australian Institute of Aboriginal Studies.
Ott, W., and Ott, R. (1983). *Diccionario ignaciano y castellano con apuntes gramaticales.* Cochabamba: Summer Institute of Linguistics.
Pacioni, P. (1997). 'Possessive Constructions, Classifiers and Plurality in Cantonese and Some Other Chinese Dialects', in T. Hayasi and P. Bhaskararao (eds.), *A Report of the Joint Research Project: Analysis and Description of Individual Languages and Linguistic Typology.* Tokyo: Institute for the Study of Languages and Cultures of Asia and Africa, 199–222.
—— (forthcoming). 'Classifiers, Specificity and Typology in Asian Languages'.
Palmer, G., and Arin, D. N. (1995a). 'Ancestral Spirit Scenarios in Bantu Noun Classification: The Shape of a Heuristic System', paper presented to the 9th Annual Meeting of the AAA, Washington DC, 15–19 November 1995.
—— —— (1995b). 'The Domain of Ancestral Spirits in Bantu Noun Classification', paper presented at the 4th International Cognitive Linguistics Conference, Albuquerque, New Mexico, 16–21 July 1995.
Panfilov, V. Z. (1968). *Nivxskij Jazyk* [*The Nivkh Language*]. Moscow: Nauka.
Parker, G. J. (1969). *Ayacucho Quechua Grammar and Dictionary.* The Hague: Mouton.
Parker, J., and Parker, D. (1977). *Baining Grammar Essentials.* Ukarumpa: Summer Institute of Linguistics.
Pasch, H. (1985). 'Possession and possessive Classifiers in 'Dongo-ko', *Afrika und Übersee* 68: 69–85.
—— (1986). *Die Mba-Sprachen. Die Nominalklassensysteme und die genetische Gliederung einer Gruppe von Ubangi Sprachen.* Hamburg: Helmut Buske.
—— (1988). 'Die Entlehnung von Bantu-Präfixen in eine Nichtbantu-Sprache', *Zeitschrift für Phonetik, Sprachwissenschaft und Kommunikationsforschung* 41: 48–63.
Paul, P. (1972). 'How Do Loan Words from English Get Their German Gender?' *Queensland Studies in German Language and Literature*, 1: 47–60.
Pawley, A. (1973). 'Some Problems in Proto-Oceanic Grammar', *Oceanic Linguistics* 12: 103–88.
—— (2002). 'Using "He" and "She" for Inanimate Referents in English: Questions of Grammar and World View', in N. Enfield (ed.), *Ethnosyntax: Explorations in grammar and culture.* Oxford: Oxford University Press, 110–37.
—— and Sayaba, T. (1990). 'Possessive-marking in Wayan, a Western Fijian Language: Noun Class or Relational System', in J. H. C. S. Davidson (ed.), *Pacific Island Languages: Essays in Honour of G. B. Milner.* Honolulu: University of London and University of Hawaii Press, 147–71.
Payne, David. L. (1991a). 'A Classification of Maipuran Arawakan Languages Based on Shared Lexical Retentions', in Derbyshire and Pullum (1991: 355–500).

—— (1991b). 'La interacción de la fonologia, la gramática y el léxico en la investigación comparativa del maipuran', *Revista latinoamericana de estudios etnolingüísticos. Lingüística Arawaka* 6: 241–58.
Payne, Doris L. (1986). 'Noun classification in Yagua', in Craig (1986a: 113–31).
—— (1987). 'Noun Classification in the Western Amazon', *Linguistic Sciences* 9: 21–44.
—— (1990). *The Pragmatics of Word Order: Typological Dimensions of Verb Initial Languages*. Berlin: Mouton de Gruyter.
—— (ed.) (1990). *Amazonian Linguistics: Studies in Lowland South American Indian Languages*. Austin: University of Texas Press.
—— and Payne, T. E. (1990). 'Yagua', in Derbyshire and Pullum (1990: 249–474).
Payne, John (1989). 'Pāmir languages', in R. Schmitt (ed.), *Compendium Linguarum Iranicarum*. Wiesbaden: Reichert, 417–44.
Payne, Judith (1989). *Lecciones para el aprendizaje del idioma Asheninca*. Pucallpa: Instituto Lingúístico de Verano.
Pe, H. (1965). 'A Re-examination of Burmese Classifiers', *Lingua* 15: 163–86.
Peeke, M. C. (1968). 'Preliminary Grammar of Auca Ecuador'. PhD thesis, Indiana University, Bloomington.
Pensalfini, R. (1997). 'Jingulu Grammar, Dictionary, and Texts'. PhD thesis, Massachusetts Institute of Technology.
Pérez-Pereira, M. (1991). 'The Acquisition of Gender: What Spanish Children Tell Us', *Journal of Child Language* 18: 571–90.
Pet, W. J. A. (1987). 'Lokono Dian, the Arawak Language of Suriname: A Grammatical Sketch of Its Grammatical Structure and Lexicon'. PhD thesis, Cornell University.
Peterson, M. N. (1955). *Ocherk litovskogo jazyka* [*An Outline of Lithuanian*]. Moscow: Izdateljstvo Akademii Nauk SSSR.
Pike, K. (1949). 'A Problem in Morphology–Syntax Division', *Acta Linguistica* 5: 125–38.
Plank, F. (1986). 'Das Genus der deutschen Ge-Substantive und Verwandtes (Beiträge zur Vererbungslehre 1)', *Zeitschrift für Phonetik, Sprachwissenschaft und Kommunikationsforschung* 39: 44–60.
—— and Schellinger, W. (1997). 'The Uneven Distribution of Genders over Numbers: Greenberg Nos. 37 and 45', *Linguistic Typology* 1: 53–101.
Plungian, V. A. (1995) *Dogon*. Munich: Lincom Europa.
—— and Romanova, O. I. (1990). 'Imennaja klassifikacija: Grammaticheskij aspekt' [Nominal Classification: Grammatical Aspect], *Izvestija Akademii Nauk, Serija literatury i jazyka* 493: 231–6.
Polomé, E. (1968). 'Lumumbashi Swahili', *Journal of African Languages* 7: 15–25.
Pope, M. K. (1952). *From Latin to Modern French with Especial Consideration of Anglo-Norman: Phonology and Morphology*. Manchester: Manchester University Press.
Popova, M. I. (1958). 'Grammatičeskie èlementy jazyka v reči detej preddoš-kol'nogo vozrasta', *Voprosy psixologii* 4: 106–17. (Russian version of Popova 1973.)
—— (1973). 'Grammatical Elements of Language in the Speech of Pre-school

Children', in C. A. Ferguson and D. I. Slobin (eds.), *Studies of Child Language Development.* New York: Holt, Rinehart and Winston, 269–80.
Posner, R. (1966). *The Romance Languages.* Cambridge: Cambridge University Press.
Pozdniakov, K. I. (1995). *Sravniteljnaja grammatika atlanticheskih jazykov* [A Comparative Grammar of Atlantic Languages]. Moscow: Nauka.
Prado, M. (1979). 'Markedness and the Gender Feature in Spanish', in D. L. Malsch *et al.* (eds.), *Proceedings of the Eighth Annual Meeting of the Western Conference on Linguistics.* Carbondale, Edmonton: Linguistic Research Current Inquiry into Language and Linguistics 26: 113–22.
Prasse, K.-G. (1972). *Manuel de gramaire touaregue (Tahaggart).* 3 vols., Copenhagen: Akademisk Forlag.
—— and ăgg-ălbosṭan ăg-Sidiyăn, E. (1985). *Tableaux morphologiques: dialecte Touareg de l'Adrar du Mali berbère.* Copenhagen: Akademisk Forlag.
Press, M. L. (1979). *Chemehuevi: A Grammar and Lexicon.* Berkeley: University of California Press.
Priestly, T. M. S. (1983). 'On "Drift" in Indo-European Gender Systems', *Journal of Indo-European Studies* 11: 339–63.
—— (1993). 'Slovene', in B. Comrie and G. G. Corbett (eds.), *The Slavonic Languages.* London: Routledge, 388–451.
Pullum, G. K. and Zwicky, A. M. (1986). 'Phonological Resolution of Syntactic Feature Conflict', *Language* 62: 751–73.
Pym, N., and Larrimore, B. M. (1979). 'The Iwaidja Verb System: A Description', *Papers on Iwaidja Phonology and Grammar.* Darwin: Summer Institute of Linguistics. Australian Aborigines Branch, 65–151.
Quigley, S. (forthcoming). *Awará Grammar Essentials.* Ukarumpa: Summer Institute of Linguistics.
Quinn, H. (forthcoming). *Systems of Verbal Classification*, iv: *Agent and Patient Oriented Differentiations.*
Rakhilina, E. V. (1998). 'Semantika russkih 'posicionnyh' predikatov *stoatj, lezhatj, sidetj* i *visetj*'. [The semantics of Russian 'positional' predicates *stand, lie, sit* and *hang*]. *Voprosy jazykoznanija* 6: 69–80.
Ramirez, H. (1992). *Bahuana: une nouvelle langue de la famille Arawak.* Paris: Amerindia.
—— (1994). *Le parler Yanomamɨ des Xamatauteri.* Paris.
—— (1997). *A fala Tukano dos Yepâ-masa,* i: *Gramática.* Manaus: Inspetoria Salesiana.
Rankin, R. L. (1976). 'From Verb to Auxiliary to Noun Classifier and Definite Article: Grammaticalization of the Siouan Verbs "sit", "stand", "lie"', in R. L. Brown, K. Houlihan, and A. MacLeish (eds.), *Proceedings of the 1976 Mid-America Linguistics Conference.* Minnesota: University of Minnesota, 273–83.
Rastorgueva, V. S., Efimov, V. A., and Kerimova, A. A. (1978). 'Iranskie jazyki' [Iranian languages], in N. I. Konrad (ed.), *Jazyki Azii i Afriki,* ii: *Indoevropejskie jazyki.* Moscow: Nauka, 7–253.
Rehg, K. (with D. C. Sohl) (1981). *Ponapean Reference Grammar.* Honolulu: University of Hawaii Press.

Reid, N. (1990). 'Ngan'gityemerri: A Language of the Daly River Region, Northern Territory of Australia'. PhD thesis, Australian National University, Canberra.
—— (1997). 'Class and Classifier in Ngan'gityemerri', in Harvey and Reid (1997: 165–228).
Rice, K. (1989). *A Grammar of Slave*. Berlin: Mouton de Gruyter.
Richards, J. (1973). 'Dificuldades na análise de possessão nominal em Waurá', *Série Lingüística* 1: 11–29.
—— (1988). 'A estrutura verbal Waurá', *Série Lingüística* 9: 197–218.
Riddle, R. (1989). 'White Hmong Noun Classifiers and Referential Salience', paper given at the 22nd International Conference on Sino-Tibetan Languages and Linguistics. University of Hawaii, Manoa.
Rigsby, B., and Rude, N. (1996). 'Sketch of Sahaptin, a Sahaptian Language', in *Handbook of North American Indians. Languages*, xvii. Washington, DC: Smithsonian Institution, 666–92.
Rijkhoff, J. (1990). 'Toward a Unified Analysis of Terms and Predications', in J. Nuyts and A. M. Bolkenstein (eds.), *Layers and Levels of Representation in Language Theory: A Functional View*. Amsterdam: John Benjamins, 165–92.
Roberts, J. R. (1987). *Amele*. London: Croom Helm.
Rodrigues, A. D. (1986). *Línguas brasileiras: para o conhecimento das línguas indígenas*. São Paulo: Loyola.
—— (1995). 'Some Morphological and Syntactic Aspects of Kariri', paper presented at the SSILA meeting, Albuquerque, NM.
—— (1997). 'Nominal Classification in Kariri', *Opción* 13: 65–79.
—— (1999). 'Macro-Jê Languages', in Dixon and Aikhenvald (1999: 164–206).
Rosch, E. (1973). 'On the Internal Structure of Perceptual and Semantic Categories, in T. E. Moore (ed.), *Cognitive Development and the Acquisition of Language*. New York: Academic Press, 111–44.
—— (1975a). 'Cognitive Reference Points', *Cognitive Psychology* 7: 532–47.
—— (1975b). 'Cognitive Representations of Semantic Categories', *Journal of Experimental Psychology* 104: 192–233.
—— (1987). 'Principles of Categorization', in E. Rosch and B. B. Lloyd (eds.), *Cognition and Categorization*. Hillsdale, NJ: Erlbaum, 27–48.
—— Mervis, C. B., Gray, W. D., Johnson, D. M., and Boyes-Braem, P. (1976). 'Basic Objects in Natural Categories', *Cognitive Psychology* 8: 382–439.
Rothstein, R. A. (1973). 'Sex, Gender, and the October Revolution', in S. R. Anderson and P. Kiparsky (eds.), *A Festschrift for Morris Halle*. New York: Holt, Rinehart and Winston, 460–6.
Rowan, O., and Burgess, E. (1979). 'Parecis Grammar', *Arquivo Lingüístico* 149. Brasilia: SIL.
Royen, G. (1929). *Die nominalen Klassifikations-Systeme in den Sprachen der Erde: Historisch-kritische Studie, mit besonderer Berücksichtigung des Indogermanischen*. Vienna: Anthropos.
Rubino, C. R. G. (1997). 'A Reference Grammar of Ilocano'. PhD thesis, University of California, Santa Barbara.
Rude, N. (1986). 'Graphemic Classifiers in Egyptian Hieroglyphics and Mesopotamian Cuneiform', in Craig (1986a: 133–8).

Rumsey, A. (1982). *An Intrasentence Grammar of Ungarinjin, North-Western Australia*. Canberra: Pacific Linguistics.
Rushforth, S. (1991). 'Uses of Bearlake and Mescalero (Athapaskan) Classificatory Verbs', *International Journal of American Linguistics* 57: 251–66.
Russell, R. A. (1984). 'Historical Aspects of Subject–Verb Agreement in Arabic', in G. Alvarez, B. Brodie, and T. McCoy (eds.), *Proceedings of the First Eastern States Conference on Linguistics*. Columbus: Ohio State University, 116–27.
Sanches, M. (1977). 'Language Acquisition and Language Change: Japanese Numeral Classifiers', in B. G. Blount and M. Sanches (eds.), *Sociocultural Dimensions of Language Change*. New York: Academic Press, 51–62.
—— and Slobin, L. (1973). 'Numeral Classifiers and Plural Marking: an Implicational Universal', *Working Papers in Language Universals* 11: 1–22.
Sândalo, F. (1996). 'A Grammar of Kadiwéu'. PhD thesis, University of Pittsburgh.
Sands, A. K. (1995). 'Nominal Classification in Australia', *Anthropological Linguistics* 37: 247–346.
Sapir, D. (1977). 'The Anatomy of Metaphor', in J. D. Sapir and J. C. Crocker (eds.), *The Social Use of Metaphor: Essays on the Anthropology of Rhetoric*. Philadelphia: University of Pennsylvania Press, 3–32.
Sapir, E. (1932). 'Two Navajo Puns', *Language* 8: 217–19.
Sasse, H.-J. (1985). 'Sprachkontakt und Sprachwandel: die Gräzisierung der albanischen Mundarten Griechenlands', *Papiere zur Linguistik* 32: 37–95.
—— (1992). 'Language Decay and Contact-induced Change: Similarities and Differences', in M. Brenzinger (ed.), *Language Death: Factual and Theoretical Explorations with Special Reference to East Africa*. Berlin: Mouton de Gruyter, 59–80.
Saul, J. E., and Wilson, N. F. (1980). *Nung Grammar*. Dallas: Summer Institute of Linguistics and the University of Texas at Arlington.
Sauvageot, S. (1967). 'Note sur la classification nominale en baïnouk', in *La Classification nominale*, 225–36.
Saxton, D. (1982). 'Papago', in R. W. Langacker (ed.), *Studies in Uto-Aztecan Grammar*, iii: *Uto-Aztecan Grammatical Sketches*. Dallas: Summer Institute of Linguistics and the University of Texas at Arlington, 93–266.
Schane, S. A. (1970). 'Phonological and Morphological Markedness', in M. Bierwisch and K. E. Heidolph (eds.), *Progress in Linguistics*. The Hague: Mouton, 286–94.
Schaub, W. (1985). *Babungo*. London: Croom Helm.
Schauer, S., and Schauer, J. (1978). 'Una gramática del Yucuna', *Artigos en lingüística e campos afines* 5: 1–52.
Scherbak, A. M. (1977). *Ocherki po sravniteljnoy morfologii tyurkskih jazykov: imya* [Essays on comparative morphology of Turkic languages: noun]. Leningrad: Nauka.
Schmidt, A. (1985). *Young People's Dyirbal: An Example of Language Death from Australia*. Cambridge: Cambridge University Press.
Schwartz, L., Newman, P., and Sani, S. (1988). 'Agreement and Scope of Modification in Hausa Coordinate Structures', *Papers from the Annual Regional Meeting of the Chicago Linguistic Society* 24: 278–90.
Seiler, H. (1977). *Cahuilla Grammar*. Banning, Calif.: Malki Museum Press.

—— (1983). *Possession as an Operational Dimension of Language*. Tübingen: Gunter Narr.
—— (1985). 'Zum Verhältnis von Genus und Numerus', in H. M. Ölberg, G. Schmidt, and H. Bothien (eds.), *Sprachwissenschaftliche Forschungen: Festschrift für Johann Knobloch. Zum 65. Geburtstag am 5. Januar 1984 dargebracht von Freunden und Kollegen*. Innsbruck: Institut für Sprachwissenschaft Innsbrucker Beiträge zur Kulturwissenschaft, 453–7.
—— (1986). *Apprehension: Language, Object and Order*, iii: *The Universal Dimension of Apprehension*. Tübingen: Gunter Narr.
—— (1987). 'Genus und Pragmatizität', *Cahiers Ferdinand de Saussure* 41: 205–18.
—— and Lehmann, C. (eds.). (1982). *Apprehension: Das sprachliche Erfassen von Gegenständen*, i: *Bereich und Ordnung der Phänomene*. Tübingen: Narr.
—— and Stachowiak, F. J. (eds.). (1982). *Apprehension: Das sprachliche Erfassen von Gegenständen*, iii: *Die Techniken und ihr Zusammenhang in Einzelsprachen*. Tübingen: Narr.
Seiler, W. (1985). *Imonda, a Papuan Language*. Canberra: Pacific Linguistics.
—— (1986). 'From Verb Serialisation to Noun Classification', in *Papers in Pidgin and Creole Linguistics* 24. Canberra: Pacific Linguistics, 11–19.
—— (1989). 'Noun-classificatory Verbal Prefixes as Reanalysed Serial Verbs', *Lingua* 68: 189–206.
Seki, L., and Aikhenvald, A. Y. (forthcoming). 'A Reconstruction of the Proto-Xinguan Arawak'.
Selischev, A. M. (1928). *Jazyk revoliutsionnoi epokhi: iz nabliudenij nad russkim iazykom poslednikh let (1917–1926)* [The Language of the Revolutionary Age: From Notes on Russian of the Recent Years]. Moscow: Rabotnik prosveshcheniya.
Senft, G. (1985). 'Klassifikationspartikel im Kilivila: Glosses zu ihrer morphologischen Rolle, ihrem Inventar und ihrer Funktion in Satz und Diskurs', *Linguistische Berichte* 99: 373–93.
—— (1986). *Kilivila: The Language of Trobriand Islanders*. Berlin: Mouton de Gruyter.
——(1987). 'The System of Classificatory Particles in Kilivila Reconsidered: First Results on Its Inventory, Its Acquisition, and Its Usage', *Language and Linguistics in Melanesia* 16: 100–25.
—— (1991). 'Network Models to Describe the Kilivila Classifier System', *Oceanic Linguistics* 30: 131–55.
—— (1993). 'What Do We Really Know about Nominal Classification Systems?', contribution to workshop 'Back to Basic Issues in Nominal Classification', Cognitive Anthropology Research Group, Max-Planck Institute for Psycholinguistics.
—— (1994). 'Grammaticalization of Body-parts Terms in Kilivila', *Language and Linguistics in Melanesia* 25: 98–9.
—— (1996). *Classificatory Particles in Kilivila*. New York: Oxford University Press.
—— (ed.) (1997). *Referring to Space: Studies in Austronesian and Papuan Languages*. Oxford: Clarendon Press.

Serzisko, F. (1982). 'Gender, Noun Class and Numeral Classification: A Scale of Classificatory Techniques', in R. Dirven and G. Radden (eds.), *Issues in the Theory of Universal Grammar*. Tübingen: Gunter Narr, 95–123.
Shaul, D. L. (1986). *Topics in Nevome Syntax*. Berkeley: University of California Press.
Shawcross, W. (1979). *Sideshow: Kissinger, Nixon and the Destruction of Cambodia*. New York: Simon & Schuster.
Shepard, G. Jr. (1997). 'Noun Classification and Ethnozoological Classification in Machiguenga, an Arawakan Language of the Peruvian Amazon', *Journal of Amazonian Languages* 1: 29–57.
Shepardson, K. W. (1982). 'An Integrated Analysis of Swahili Augmentative-Diminutives', *Studies in African Linguistics* 13: 53–76.
Sherzer, J. (1976). *An Areal-Typological Study of American Indian Languages North of Mexico*. Amsterdam: North-Holland.
Shields, K. Jr. (1978). 'English Gender: Some New Approaches to an Old Problem', *Linguistics*, special issue: 205–25.
Silverman, M. G. (1962). 'Numeral Classifiers in the Gilbertese Language', *Anthropology Tomorrow* 8: 41–56.
Silverstein, M. (1976). 'Hierarchy of Features and Ergativity', in Dixon (1976: 112–71).
—— (1986). 'Classifiers, Verb Classifiers, and Verbal Categories', *Berkeley Linguistics Society: Proceedings of the Annual Meeting* 12: 497–514.
Sirk, Ü. (1983). *The Buginese Language*. Moscow: Nauka.
Slobin, Dan I. (1977). 'Language Change in Childhood and in History', in J. Macnamara (ed.), *Language Learning and Thought*. New York: Academic Press, 185–214.
Smith, I., and Johnson, S. (1999). 'Kugu-Nganhcara', in R. M. W. Dixon and B. Blake (eds.), *Handbook of Australian Languages*, v. Melbourne: Cambridge University Press.
Smith-Stark, S. (1974). 'The Plurality Split', *Papers from the Annual Regional Meeting of the Chicago Linguistic Society* 10: 657–71.
Smoczyńska, M. (1985). 'The Acquisition of Polish', in D. I. Slobin (ed.), *The Crosslinguistic Study of Language Acquisition*, i: *The Data*. Hillsdale, NJ: Erlbaum, 595–686.
Sohn, H.-M. (1994). *Korean*. London: Routledge.
Sokolova, V. S. (1966). 'Shugnano-rushanskaya gruppa' [Shugnan-Rushan Group], in V. V. Vinogradov (ed.), *Jazyki narodov SSSP*, i: *Indoevropejskie jazyki*. Moscow: Nauka, 362–97.
Speece, R. (n.d.). *Angave Grammar*. Ukarumpa: Summer Institute of Linguistics.
Speirs, A. (1974). 'Classificatory Verb Stems in Tewa', *Studies in Linguistics* 24: 45–74.
Spitulnik, D. (1989). 'Levels of Semantic Restructuring in Bantu Noun Classification', in P. Newman and R. D. Botne (eds.), *Current Approaches to African Linguistics*, v. Dordrecht: Foris Publications, 207–20.
Sridhar, S. N. (1990). *Kannada*. London: Routledge.
Stebbins, T. (1997). 'Asymmetrical Nominal Number Marking: a Functional Account', *Sprachtypologie und Universalienforschung* 50: 5–47.

Steele, S. (1978). 'Word Order Variation: A Typology Study', in J. H. Greenberg, C. A. Ferguson, and E. A. Moravcsik (eds.), *Universals of Human Language*, iv: *Syntax*. Stanford: Stanford University Press, 585–623.
Steinberg, E., and Caskey, A. F. (1988). 'The Syntax and Semantics of Gender Disagreement: An Autolexical Approach', *Papers from the Annual Regional Meeting of the Chicago Linguistic Society* 24: 291–303.
Steinhauer, H. (1986). 'Number in Biak: Counterevidence to Two Alleged Language Universals: A Summary', in P. Geraghty, L. Carrington, and S. A. Wurm (eds.), *FOCAL I: Papers from the Fourth International Conference on Austronesian Linguistics*. Canberra: Pacific Linguistics, 171–3.
Storch, A. (1997). 'Where Have All the Noun Classes Gone? A Case Study in Jukun', *Journal of African Languages and Linguistics* 18: 157–70.
Strom, C. (1992). *Retuarã Syntax*. Dallas: Summer Institute of Linguistics and the University of Texas at Arlington.
Stucky. S. U. (1978). 'How a Noun Class System May Be Lost: Evidence from Kituba Lingua Franca Kikongo', *Studies in the Linguistic Sciences* 8: 217–33.
Stumme, H. 1899. *Handbuch des Schilhischen von Tazerwalt*. Leipzig: J. C. Hinrichs'sche Buchhandlung.
Stump, G. T. (1993). 'Reconstituting Morphology: The Case of Bantu Preprefixation', *Linguistic Analysis* 23: 169–204.
Subrahmanyam, P. S. (1968). *A Descriptive Grammar of Gondi*. Annamalainagar: Annamalai University.
Suárez, J. A. (1983). *The Mesoamerican Indian Languages*. Cambridge: Cambridge University Press.
Suppalla, T. (1986). 'The Classifier System in American Sign Language', in Craig (1986a: 181–214).
Suzman, S. M. (1980). 'Acquisition of the Noun Class System in Zulu', *Papers and Reports on Child Language Development* 19: 45–52.
—— (1982). 'Strategies of Acquiring Zulu Concord', *South African Journal of African Languages* 2: 53–67.
Sweetser, E. (1986). 'Polysemy vs. Abstraction: Mutually Exclusive or Complementary?', *Berkeley Linguistics Society: Proceedings of the Annual Meeting* 12: 528–38.
—— (1988). 'Grammaticalization and Semantic Bleaching', *Berkeley Linguistics Society: Proceedings of the Annual Meeting* 14: 389–405.
T'sou, B. K. (1976). 'The Structure of Numeral Classifier Systems', in P. N. Jenner, L. C. Thompson, and S. Starosta (eds.), *Austroasiatic Studies*, ii. Honolulu: University of Hawaii Press, 1215–47.
Tai, J. H.-Y. (1992). 'Variation in Classifier Systems Across Chinese Dialects: Towards a Cognition-Based Semantic Approach', in *Symposium Series of the Institute of History and Philology. Academia Sinica. Number 2. Chinese Languages and Linguistics. Chinese Dialects*. Taipei, Republic of China, 587–608.
Talmy, L. (1985). 'Lexicalization Patterns: Semantic Structure in Lexical Forms', in T. Shopen (ed.) *Language Typology and Syntactic Description*, iii: *Grammatical Categories and the Lexicon*. Cambridge: Cambridge University Press, 57–149.
Taylor, D. M. (1952). 'Sameness and Difference in Two Island Carib Dialects', *International Journal of American Linguistics* 18: 223–30.

Taylor, J. R. (1989). 'Possessive Genitives in English', *Linguistics* 27: 663–86.
—— (1995). *Linguistic Categorization: Prototypes in Linguistic Theory*. 2nd edn. Oxford: Clarendon Press.
Thiesen, W. (1996). *Gramática del idioma Bora*. Pucallpa: Instituto Lingüístico de Verano.
Thomason, S. G., and Kaufman, T. (1988). *Language Contact, Creolization and Genetic Linguistics*. Berkeley: University of California Press.
Thompson, C. (1993). 'The Areal Prefix *Hu-* in Koyukon Athabaskan', *International Journal of American Linguistics* 59: 315–33.
Tiersma, P. M. (1982). 'Local and General Markedness', *Language* 58: 832–49.
Todd, E. (1975). 'The Solomon Language Family', in S. Wurm (ed.), *New Guinea Area Languages and Language Study*, i: *Papuan Languages and the New Guinea Linguistic Scene*. Canberra: Pacific Linguistics, 805–46.
Traill, A. (1994). *A Xóõ! Dictionary*. Cologne: Rüdiger Köppe.
Trask, L. (1993). *A Dictionary of Grammatical Terms in Linguistics*. London: Routledge.
Traugott, E. C. (1988). 'Pragmatic Strengthening and Grammaticalization', *Proceedings of the Fourteenth Annual Meeting of the Berkeley Linguistics Society. General Session and Parasession on Grammaticalization*, 406–16.
—— and Heine, B. (eds.) (1991a). *Approaches to Grammaticalization*. 2 vols. Amsterdam: John Benjamins.
—— —— (1991b). Introduction to Traugott and Heine (1991a: 1–14).
Trudgill, P. (1977). 'Creolization in Reverse: Reduction and Simplification in the Albanian Dialects of Greece', *Transactions of the Philological Society* 77: 32–50.
Tseng, O., Chen, S., and Hung, D. (1991). 'The Classifier Problem in Chinese Aphasia', *Brain and Language* 41: 184–202.
Tsonope, J. (1988). 'The Acquisition of Setswana Noun Class and Agreement Morphology—with Special Reference to Demonstratives and Possessives'. PhD thesis, State University of New York at Buffalo.
Tucker, A. N., and Mpaayei, J. T. O. (1955). *A Maasai Grammar with Vocabulary*. London: Longmans.
Tversky, B. (1986). 'Components and Categorization', in Craig (1986a: 63–76).
Vail, L. (1974). 'The Noun Classes in Ndali', *Journal of African Languages* 11: 21–47.
Vapnarsky, V. (1993). *De quelques procédés de classification en Maya Itza: les classificateurs numéraux*. Chantiers Amerindia, 11.2. Paris: Association d'Ethnolinguistique Amerindienne.
Vasmer, M. (1953). *Russisches etymologisches Wörterbuch*, i. Heidelberg: Carl Winter.
Vidal, A. (1994). 'Noun Classifiers in Pilagá: A Study on Grammaticalization and Deixis', paper presented at the SSILA/CAIL conference at the 96th AAA Meeting, Atlanta, Nov.–Dec. 1994.
—— (1995). 'Noun Classification in Pilagá (Guaykuruan)'. MA thesis, University of Oregon, Eugene.
—— (1997). 'Noun Classification in Pilagá: Guaykuruan', *Journal of Amazonian Languages* 1: 60–111.

Vietze, H. P (1979). 'Nominalklassen in altaischen Sprachen', *Zeitschrift zur Phonetik, Sprachwissenschaft und Kommunikationsforschung* 32: 745–51.
Vincennes, L., and Dallet, J. (1960). *Initiation à la langue berbère. Kabylie.* Fort National: Fichier de Documentation Berbère.
Vinogradov, V. A. (1996). 'Coexistent Classificative Systems in Ngyembɔɔn', paper presented at the Department of African Linguistics, Leiden.
Voeltz, E. (1971). 'Surface Constraints and Agreement Resolution: Some Evidence from Xhosa', *Studies in African Linguistics* 2: 37–60.
Vycichl, W. (1957). 'L'Article défini du berbère', in *Mémorial André Basset*, Paris, pp. 139–46.
Wajanarat, S. (1979). 'Classifiers in Mal (Thin)', *Mon-Khmer Studies* 8: 295–303.
Wald, B. (1975). 'Animate Concord in Northeast Coastal Bantu: Its Linguistic and Social Implications as a Case of Grammatical Convergence', *African Linguistics* 6: 267–314.
Walsh, M. (1976). 'The Murinypata Language of North-west Australia'. PhD thesis, Australian National University, Canberra.
—— (1997). 'Nominal Classification and Generics in Murrihnpatha', in Harvey and Reid (1997: 255–92).
Wang, Fu-shih (1972). 'The Classifier in the Wei Ning Dialect of the Miaio Language in Kweichou', in H. C. Purnell (ed.), *Miao and Yao Linguistic Studies: Selected Articles in Chinese, Translated by Chang Yü-Hung and Cho Kwo-ray.* Southeast Asia Program, Cornell University, 111–85.
Waterson, N. (1966). 'Numeratives in Uzbek: A Study in Colligation and Collocation', in C. E. Bazell (ed.), *In Memory of J. R. Firth.* London: Longmans, 454–74.
Watkins, L. (1976). 'Position in Grammar: Sit, Stand, Lie'. Graduate Student Association, University of Kansas..
—— (1984). *A Grammar of Kiowa.* Lincoln: University of Nebraska Press.
—— (1995). 'Noun Classes in Kiowa-Tanoan Languages', paper presented at the Annual Meeting of the SSILA, Albuquerque, NM, 7–9 July.
Watters, J. (1981). 'A Phonology and Morphology of Ejagham—With Notes on Dialect Variation'. PhD thesis, University of California, Los Angeles.
Welmers, W. E. (1973). *African Language Structures.* Berkeley: University of California Press.
West, B. (1980). *Gramática popular del Tucano.* Colombia: Instituto Lingüístico de Verano.
Westermann, D. (1947). 'Pluralbildung und Nominalklassen in einigen afrikanischen Sprachen'. *Abhandlungen der Deutschen Akademie der Wissenschaften zu Berlin* 1945/6. Phil.-hist. Klasse No. 1. Berlin.
Westley, D. O. (1991). *Tepetotutla Chinantec Syntax.* Dallas: Summer Institute of Linguistics and the University of Texas at Arlington.
Whitney, H. (n.d.). *Akoye Grammar Essentials.* Ukarumpa: Summer Institute of Linguistics.
Wierzbicka, A. (1985). 'Oats and Wheat: The Fallacy of Arbitrariness', in J. Haiman (ed.), *Iconicity in Syntax.* Amsterdam: John Benjamins, 311–42.
—— (1996). *Semantics: Primes and Universals.* Oxford: Oxford University Press.

Wiesemann, U. (1972). *Die phonologische und grammatische Struktur der Kaingáng-Sprache*. The Hague: Mouton.
—— (ed.) (1986). *Pronominal Systems*. Tübingen: G. Narr.
Wilkins, D. (1981). 'Towards a Theory of Semantic Change'. Honours thesis, Australian National University, Canberra.
—— (1989). 'Mparntwe Arrernte (Aranda). Studies in the Structure and Semantics of Grammar'. PhD thesis, Australian National University, Canberra.
Wilkins, D. (1996). 'Natural Tendencies of Semantic Change and the Search for Cognates', in M. Durie and M. Ross (eds.), *The Comparative Method Reviewed*. Oxford: Oxford University Press, 264–304.
Williamson, K. (1989). 'Niger-Congo Overview', in J. Bendor-Samuel (ed.), *The Niger-Congo Languages*. Lanham, MD: University Press of America, 3–45.
Wilson, P. J. (1992). *Una descripción preliminar de la gramática del Achagua (Arawak)*. Bogotá: Summer Institute of Linguistics.
Wilson, W. H. (1982). *Proto-Polynesian Possessive Marking*. Canberra: Pacific Linguistics.
Wise, M. R. (1986). 'Grammatical Characteristics of Preandine Languages: Arawakan Languages of Peru', in Derbyshire and Pullum (1986: 567–642).
—— (1999). 'Small Language Families and Isolates in Peru', in Dixon and Aikhenvald (1999: 307–40).
Witherspoon, G. (1972). *Language and Art in the Navajo Universe*. Ann Arbor: University of Michigan Press.
Woodbury, A. C. (1981). 'Study of the Chevak Dialect of Central Yupi'k Eskimo'. PhD thesis, University of California, Berkeley.
Worsley, P. M. (1954). 'Noun-classification in Australian and Bantu: Formal or Semantic?', *Oceania* 24: 275–88.
Wurm, S. A. (1981). 'Notes on Nominal Classification Systems in Äŷiwo, Reef Island, Solomon Islands', in A. Gonzales and D. Thomas (eds.), *Linguistics across Continents: Studies in Honor of Richard S. Pittman*. Manila: Summer Institute of Linguistics and The Linguistic Society of the Philippines, 123–42.
—— (1987). 'Semantics and World View in Languages of the Santa Cruz Archipelago, Solomon Islands', in R. Steel and T. Threadgold (eds.), *Language Topics: Essays in Honor of Michael Halliday*. Amsterdam: John Benjamins, 439–51.
—— (1992a). 'Change of Language Structure and Typology in a Pacific Language as a Result of Culture Change', in T. Dutton (ed.), *Culture Change, Language Change: Case Studies from Melanesia*. Canberra: Pacific Linguistics, 149–65.
—— (1992b). 'Some Features of the Verb Complex in Northern Santa Cruzan, Solomon Islands', in T. Dutton, M. Ross, and D. Tryon (eds.), *The Language Game: Papers in Memory of Donald C. Laycock*. Canberra: Pacific Linguistics, 527–51.
Yu, E. O. (1988). 'Agreement in Left Dislocation of Coordinate Structures', *Papers from the Annual Regional Meeting of the Chicago Linguistic Society* 24: 322–37.
Zalizniak, A. A. (1967). *Russkoje Imennoje Slovoizmenenie* [Russian Nominal Inflection]. Moscow: Russkij Jazyk.
—— and Paducheva, E. V. (1976). 'K tipologii otnositeljnogo predlozhenija' [Towards a Typology of Relative Clauses], *Semiotika i informatika* 6: 51–101.

Zavala, R. (1992). *El Kanjobal de San Miguel Acatán*. Mexico: Universidad Autónoma de México.
—— (1993). 'Multiple Classifier Systems in Akatek Mayan', contribution to the workshop 'Back to Basic Issues in Nominal Classification', Cognitive Anthropology Research Group, Max-Planck Institute for Psycholinguistics, Nijmegen.
—— (2000). 'Multiple Classifier Systems in Akatek Mayan', in G. Senft (ed.), *Systems of Noun Classification*. Cambridge: Cambridge University Press, 114–46.
Zograf, G. A. (1976). 'Indoarijskije jazyki' [Indoaryan Languages], in N. I. Konrad et al. (eds.), *Jazyki Azii i Afriki*, i: *Indoevropejskie jazyki*. Moscow: Nauka, 110–271.
Zubin, D. A., and Köpcke, K. M. (1981). 'Gender: A Less than Arbitrary Grammatical Category', *Papers from the Annual Regional Meeting of the Chicago Linguistic Society* 17: 439–49.
—— —— (1986). 'Gender and Folk Taxonomy: The Indexical Relation between Grammatical and Lexical Categorization', in Craig (1986a: 139–80).
—— and Shimojo, M. (1993). 'How "General" Are General Classifiers? With Special Reference to *Ko* and *Tsu* in Japanese', in J. S. Guenter, B. A. Kaiser, and C. C. Zoll (eds.), *Proceedings of the Berkeley Linguistics Society: Proceedings of the Annual Meeting* 19: 490–502.
Zwicky, A. M. (1977). 'Hierarchies of person', in W. A. Beach, S. A. Fox, and S. Philosoph (eds.), *Papers from the Thirteenth Regional Meeting, Chicago Linguistic Society*, 714–33. Chicago: Chicago Linguistic Society.

List of Languages

Abau (isolate: East Sepik Province, Papua New Guinea)
Abaza (Northwest Caucasian)
Abelam (Papuan)
Abkhaz (Northwest Caucasian)
Abu' (Arapesh)
Acehnese (Western Austronesian)
Achagua (North Arawak, Arawak)
Ahaggar (Tuareg, Berber, Afroasiatic)
Ahtna (Athabaskan)
Aikana (isolate)
Ainu (isolate)
Akan (Kwa)
Akatek (Kanjobalan branch of Mayan)
Akhvakh (Northeast Caucasian)
Akoye (Angan, Papuan)
Alamblak (Sepik, Papuan)
Alawa (Australian)
Albanian (Indo-European)
Amele (Papuan)
Amharic (Semitic)
Amuesha (Arawak)
Ancient Egyptian (Afroasiatic)
Andi (Northeast Caucasian)
Angave (Angan, Papuan)
Animere (Togo Remnant)
Anindilyakwa (Australian)
Apalaí (Carib)
Apurinã (Arawak)
Arabic (Semitic, Afroasiatic)
Arapesh (Torricelli, Papuan)
Archi (Northeast Caucasian)
Armenian (Indo-European)
Arvanitika (dialect of Albanian, Indo-European)
Asmat (Asmat, Papuan)
Assamese (Indo-Aryan, Indo-European)
Atakapa (isolate)
Awa Pit (or Cuaiquier; Barbacoan)

Awabakal (Australian)
Awara (Wantoat family, Morobe province, Papuan)
Ayacucho Quechua (Quechuan)
Aymara (Aymara)
Aztec (Uto-Aztecan), see Nahuatl
Babungo (Bantu)
Badyaranké (Gur)
Bagval (Northeast Caucasian)
Bahnar (Central Bahnaric, Mon-Khmer)
Bahwana (North Arawak, Arawak)
Baining (Papuan, East New Britain)
Baïnouk (West Atlantic)
Balinese (Western Austronesian)
Banda (Eastern Nilotic-Adamawa, Nilo-Saharan)
Banggais (Loinang-Banggai; Central and South Celebes, Austronesian)
Baniwa (of Içana) (North Arawak, Arawak)
Banjalang (Australian)
Banz (Chimbu, Papuan)
Barasano (East Tucano, Tucano)
Bare (North Arawak, Arawak)
Bari (Eastern Nilotic, Nilo-Saharan)
Basque (isolate)
Beludzhi (Indo-Iranian)
Bengali (Indic)
Biak (South Halmahera-West New Guinea subgroup; Austronesian)
Bihari (Indo-Aryan, Indo-European)
Biloxi (isolate)
Bilua (Papuan, Solomon Islands)
Bine (Fly River, Papuan)
Black Tai (Tai)
Blackfoot (Algonquian)
Bodo (Sino-Tibetan)
Bora (Bora-Witoto)
Bororo (Macro-Jê)
Boumaa Fijian (Oceanic, Austronesian)
Bowili (Togo Remnant)
Brazilian Portuguese (Romance, Indo-European)
Budukh (Lezgian, Daghestanian)
Bugis (South Celebes)
Bukiyip (Arapesh, Torricelli, Papuan)
Burmese (Tibeto-Burman)
Burushaski (isolate)
Bwamu (Gur)

Caddo (Caddoan)
Cahuilla (Uto-Aztecan)
Camus (Eastern Nilotic, Nilo-Saharan)
Canela (Jê)
Cantabrian Spanish (Romance, Indo-European)
Carrier (Athabaskan)
Cayuga (Iroquoian)
Central Khoisan (Khoe)
Central Pomo (Pomoan)
Central Yup'ik Eskimo (Eskimo-Aleut)
Chacabano Zamboangueño (creole)
Chamalal (Northeast Caucasian)
Chambri (Lower Sepik, Papuan)
Chamicuro (Arawak)
Chayahuita (Cahuapanan)
Chechen (Nakh-Daghestanian)
Chemehuevi (Uto-Aztecan)
Chenapian (Papuan)
Cherokee (Iroquoian)
Chevak (Central Yup'ik Eskimo)
ChiBemba (Bantu)
Chimila (Chibchan)
Chinese (Mandarin, Cantonese: Sino-Tibetan)
Chinantepec Chinantec (Chinantec, Otomanguean)
Chipewyan (Athabaskan)
Chiricahua Apache (Athabaskan)
Chitimacha (isolate)
Chrau (Mon-Khmer)
Chuj (Mayan)
Chukchee (Chukotka-Kamchatkan)
Classical Arabic, see Arabic
Colville (Salishan)
Comaltepec Chinantec (Chinantec, Otomanguean)
Comanche (Uto-Aztecan)
Cora (Uto-Aztecan)
Cree (Algonquian)
Creek (Muskogean)
Cuaiquer (Barbacoan)
Cuiba (Guahibo)
Czech (Slavic, Indo-European)
Dahalo (East Cushitic, Afroasiatic)
Daju (East Sudanic)
Dakota (Siouan)

492 *Classifiers*

Dangbon (Australian)
Danish (Germanic, Indo-European)
Dasenech (East Cushitic)
Dâw (Makú)
Dena'ina (Athabaskan)
Dení (Arawá)
Dhegiha (isolate)
Dioi (Austroasiatic)
Diyari (Australian)
Dogon (Gur)
Dogrib (Athabaskan)
'Dongo-ko (Mba, Benue Congo)
Dulong-Rawang (Tibeto-Burman)
Dutch (Germanic, Indo-European)
Dyirbal (Australian)
Eastern Sutherland Gaelic (Celtic, Indo-European)
Egyptian Arabic (Semitic, Afroasiatic)
Ejagham (Cross River, Benue-Congo)
Emmi (Australian)
Enga (Engan, Papuan)
English, American English (Germanic, Indo-European)
Epena Pedee (Choco)
Eskimo, Chevak dialect of (Eskimo-Aleut)
Estonian (Balto-Finnic, Uralic)
Ewe (Kwa)
Eyak (Eyak-Athabaskan)
Eywo (Papuan, Central Bougainville)
Fanagalo (Bantu-based creole)
Felefita (Arapesh, Papuan)
Fijian (Oceanic, Austronesian)
Finnish (Balto-Finnic, Uralic)
Folopa, or Podopa (Teberan)
French (Romance, Indo-European)
Ful (West Atlantic)
Fulfulde, see Ful
Gaagudju (Australian)
Gadjang (Australian)
Gaelic (Celtic, Indo-European)
Gapapaiwa (Oceanic, Austronesian)
Garifuna, or Black Carib (North Arawak, Arawak)
Garo (Austroasiatic)
Gavião (Tupí)
German (Germanic, Indo-European)

Gilbertese (Micronesian, Austronesian)
Godoberi (Northeast Caucasian)
Gola (West Atlantic, Niger-Congo)
Gold Palaung (Austroasiatic)
Gondi (Dravidian)
Gorontalo (Austroasiatic)
Grebo (Kru)
Greek (Indo-European)
Guahibo (Guahibo)
Guajiro (North Arawak, Arawak)
Gunbarlang (Australian)
Gunwinjgu (Australian)
Gur (Voltaic)
Gurr-goni (Australian)
Guugu Yimidhirr (Australian)
Gwich'in (Athabaskan)
Haida (isolate?)
Hakka (Sinitic, Sino-Tibetan)
Halia (Oceanic, Austronesian)
Hani (Tibeto-Burman)
Harar (Oromo, East Cushitic, Afroasiatic)
Hausa (Chadic, Afroasiatic)
Hawaiian (Polynesian, Austronesian)
Hebrew (Semitic, Afroasiatic)
Hiechware (Khoisan)
Hindi (Indo-Aryan, Indo-European)
Hittite (Anatolian, Indo-European)
Hixkaryana (Carib)
Hmong (Miao-Yao)
Hohôdene (dialect of Baniwa of Içana, North Arawak, Arawak)
Hokkien (Sinitic, Sino-Tibetan)
Holikachuk (Athabaskan)
Hopi (Uto-Aztecan)
Hua (Papuan)
Hualapai (Uto-Aztecan)
Huave (isolate)
Huli (Engan, Papuan)
Hungarian (Ugric, Uralic)
Hupa (Athabaskan)
Hupda (Makú)
Iatmul (Ndu, Papuan)
Ibibio (Niger-Congo)
Icelandic (Germanic, Indo-European)

Idu (Tibeto-Burman)
Igbo (Kwa, Niger-Congo)
Ignaciano (South Arawak, Arawak)
Ika (Chibchan)
Ilocano (Western Austronesian)
Imonda (Waris, Papuan)
Indonesian, Bahasa Indonesia (Western Austronesian)
Ingush (Nakh-Daghestanian)
Iraqw (South Cushitic, Afroasiatic)
Irish (Celtic, Indo-European)
Island Carib (North Arawak, Arawak)
Italian (Romance, Indo-European)
Itonama (isolate)
Iwaidja (Australian)
Iwam (isolate: Sepik Province, Papua New Guinea)
Izayan (North Berber, Afroasiatic)
Jabutí (isolate)
Jacaltec (Kanjobalan branch of Mayan)
Japanese (isolate)
Jarawara (Arawá)
Javanese (Western Austronesian)
Jawoyn (Australian)
Jeh (Mon-Khmer)
Jingulu (Australian)
Jukun (Jukunoid, Niger-Congo)
Kabyle (North Berber, Afroasiatic)
Kadiweu (Guaicuruan)
Kaingáng (Jê)
Kakua (Makú)
Kalau Lagaw Ya, Kalaw Kawaw Ya, Western Torres Strait (Australian)
Kaliai-Kove (Oceanic, Austronesian)
Kam-Muang (Austroasiatic)
Kamoro (Asmat, Papuan)
Kana (Cross River, Benue-Congo)
Kannada (Dravidian)
Karirí (Kipeá-Karirí, Macro-Jê)
Karo (Tupí)
Karok (isolate)
Katcha (Kordofanian)
Kâte (Huon, Papuan)
Katu (Katuic, Austroasiatic)
Kayapó (Jê)
Kenya Pidgin Swahili (creole)

Keriaka (Non-Austronesian, Central Bougaineville)
Ket (isolate)
Kewa (Engan)
Khinalug (Northeast Caucasian)
Khmer (Mon-Khmer)
Khmu (Khmuic, Austroasiatic)
Khoe (Khoisan)
Kikongo (Bantu)
Kikuyu (Bantu)
Kilivila (Austronesian, Trobriand Islands)
Kiowa (Kiowa-Tanoan)
Kipeá (Kipeá-Karirí, Macro-Jê)
Kituba (Bantu)
Kiwai (Kiwaian, Papuan)
Koaia (isolate)
Koasati (Muskogean)
Kobon (Kalam)
Kolami (Dravidian)
Korafe (Binanderre, Papuan)
Kore (Eastern Nilotic, Nilo-Saharan)
Korean (isolate)
Kosraean (Micronesian, Austronesian)
Koyukon (Athabaskan)
Krahô (Jê)
Ku Waru (Waris, Papuan)
Kubeo (Central Tucano, Tucano)
Kugu-Ngancara (Australian)
Kulina (Arawá)
Kuot (Papuan, New Ireland)
Kuria (Bantu)
Kurripaco (dialect of Baniwa of Içana, North Arawak, Arawak)
Kusaiean (Micronesian, Austronesian)
Kwoma, or Washkuk (distantly related to Ndu family, Papuan)
Kxoe (Khoisan)
Lahu (Tibeto-Burman)
Lak (Northeast Caucasian)
Lama (Gur, Niger-Congo)
Lama Lama (Australian)
Landuma (West Atlantic)
Lao (Tai)
Latin (Italic, Indo-European)
Latvian (Baltic, Indo-European)
Lavukaleve (Papuan, Solomon Islands)

Lezgian (Northeast Caucasian)
Lii (Austroasiatic)
Limilngan (Australian)
Lingala, Mankandza Lingala, Kinshasa Lingala (Bantu)
Língua Geral, or Tupinambá, Tupí-Guaraní
Lisu (Tibeto-Burman)
Lithuanian (Baltic, Indo-European)
Lokono (North Arawak, Arawak)
Longgu (Oceanic, Austronesian)
Loniu (Oceanic, Austronesian)
Lotuko (Eastern Nilotic, Nilo-Saharan)
Loven (West Bahnaric, Mon-Khmer)
Lower Chinook (Chinookan)
Luganda (Bantu)
Luiseño (Uto-Aztecan)
Ma (Ubangi, Niger-Congo)
Maa (Eastern Nilotic, Nilo-Saharan)
Maasai (Eastern Nilotic, Nilo-Saharan)
Maasina (Fulfulde, West Atlantic, Niger-Congo)
Machiguenga (Campa, Peruvian Arawak, Arawak)
Macushi (Carib)
Maká (Mataguayo)
Makassar (South Celebes)
Mal (or Thin) (Mon-Khmer)
Malak-Malak (Australian)
Malay (Western Austronesian)
Malinke (Mande)
Malto (Dravidian)
Mam (Mayan)
Manam (Oceanic, Austronesian)
Manambu (Ndu, Papuan)
Mandan (Siouan)
Marathi (Indo-Aryan, Indo-European)
Maricopa (Yuman)
Marind (Marind, Papuan)
Marrithiyel (Australian)
Marshallese (Micronesian, Austronesian)
Maung (Australian)
Mayali (Gunwinjgu) (Australian)
Mba (Ubangi, Niger-Congo)
Melpa (Chimbu, Papuan)
Menomini (Algonquian)
Mescalero Apache (Athabaskan)

Miao of Wei Ning (Miao Yao, Austroasiatic)
Minangkabau (Western Austronesian)
Missima (Oceanic, Austronesian)
Miwok (Miwok-Costanoan)
Mixtec (Mixtecan, Otomanguean)
Mnong Gar (Austroasiatic)
Mocovi (Guaicuruan)
Mohawk (Iroquoian)
Mokilese (Micronesian, Austronesian)
Mon (Mon-Khmer)
Monumbo (Torrichelli phylum, Papuan)
Mori (Chapacuran)
Motuna (Papuan of Bougainville)
Movima (isolate)
Mparntwe Arrente (Australian)
Mufian (Arapesh, Papuan)
Muhiang (Arapesh)
Mulao (Tai)
Mundurukú (Tupí)
Mupun (West Chadic, Afroasiatic)
Murrinhpatha (Australian)
Murui Witoto (Bora-Witoto)
Nadëb (Makú)
Nahuatl (Uto-Aztecan)
Naiki (Dravidian)
Nakhi (Sino-Tibetan)
Nama (Khoisan)
Nambiquara (Nambiquara)
Napues, or Kunua (Non-Austronesian, Central Bougainville)
Naro (Khoisan)
Nasioi (Papuan of Bougainville)
Natchez (isolate)
Nauru (Micronesian, Austronesian)
Navajo (Athabaskan)
Ndali (Bantu, Niger-Congo)
Ndunga-le (Mba, Ubangi, Niger-Congo)
Nepali (Indo-Aryan, Indo-European)
Nevome (Uto-Aztecan)
Newari (Tibeto-Burman)
Nez Perce (Sahaptian)
Ngala (Eastern Nilotic-Adamawa, Nilo-Saharan)
Ngala (Ndu, Papuan)
Ngalakan (Australian)

498 *Classifiers*

Ngandi (Australian)
Ngan'gityemerri (Australian)
Ngiyambaa (Australian)
Ngyembɔɔn (Grasslands, Niger-Congo)
Nias (Western Austronesian)
Nicobarese (Austroasiatic)
Nivkh, or Gilyak (isolate)
Nootka (Wakashan)
Northern Tepehuan (Uto-Aztecan)
Ntifa (North Berber, Afroasiatic)
Nubi (Arabic-based creole)
Nung (Tai)
Nungali (Australian)
Nunggubuyu (Australian)
Nyanja (Bantu)
Ocaina (Bora-Witoto)
Ojibway (Algonquian)
Old Church Slavonic (Slavic, Indo-European)
Old English (Germanic, Indo-European)
Olgolo (Australian)
Ollari (Dravidian)
Olo (Torricelli, Papuan)
Omani Arabic (Semitic, Afroasiatic)
Omani-Zanzibar dialect of Arabic (Semitic, Afroasiatic)
Ongamo (Eastern Nilotic, Nilo-Saharan)
Oriya (Indo-Aryan, Indo-European)
'Oro Nao (Chapacuran)
Oromo (East Cushitic, Afroasiatic)
Ossete (Iranian, Indo-European)
Palaungic (Austroasiatic)
Palikur (North Arawak, Arawak)
Panará (Jê)
Panare (Carib)
Papago (Uto-Aztecan)
Pareci (South Arawak, Arawak)
Parji (Dravidian)
Patjtjamalh, or Bachamal (Australian)
Paumarí (Arawá)
Persian (Iranian, Indo-European)
Petats (Oceanic, Austronesian)
Piapoco (North Arawak, Arawak)
Pilagá (Guaicuruan)
Pirahã (Mura-Pirahã)

Piratapuya (East Tucano, Tucano)
Pittapitta (Australian)
Pogoro (Bantu)
Polish (Slavic, Indo-European)
Pomoan (Pomo)
Ponapean (Micronesian, Austronesian)
Ponca (Siouan)
Portuguese, Brazilian (Romance, Indo-European)
Potawatomi (Algonquian)
Puluwat (Micronesian, Austronesian)
Punjabi (Indo-Aryan, Indo-European)
Qafar (Cushitic, Afroasiatic)
Qiang (Tibeto-Burman)
Queyu (Tibeto-Burman)
Raga (Oceanic, Austronesian)
Rama (Chibchan)
Rembarrnga (Australian)
Rendille (East-Cushitic, Afroasiatic)
Resígaro (North Arawak, Arawak)
Retuarã (Central Tucano, Tucano)
Rikbaktsa (Macro-Jê)
Ro·lo·m (South Bahnaric, Austroasiatic)
Romansch (Romance, Indo-European)
Roshani (Pamir, Indo-European)
Rotokas (Papuan, Central Bougainville)
Rumanian (Romance, Indo-European)
Russian (Slavic, Indo-European)
Sahaptin (Sahaptian)
Sáliba (Sáliba-Piaroa)
Sanskrit (Indo-Aryan, Indo-European)
Savosavo (isolate)
Scottish Gaelic (Celtic, Indo-European)
Sedang (North Bahnaric, Mon-Khmer)
Seghrouchen (North Berber, Afroasiatic)
Sele Fara, dialect of Slovene (Slavic, Indo-European)
Seneca (Iroquoian)
Serbo-Croatian (Slavic, Indo-European)
Sesotho (Bantu)
Setswana (Bantu)
Shan (Tai, Austroasiatic)
Shilh (North Berber, Afroasiatic)
Shona (Bantu)
Siamese (Austroasiatic)

Sierra Popoluca (Mixe-Zoquean)
Sinasina (Chimbu, Papuan)
SiSwati (Bantu)
Siuci (dialect of Baniwa of Içana, North Arawak, Arawak)
Siwa (East Berber, Afroasiatic)
Slave (Athabaskan)
Slovene (Slavic, Indo-European)
Sochiapan Chinantec (Chinantec, Otomanguean)
Southeastern Pomo (Pomoan)
Southern Paiute (Uto-Aztecan)
Spanish (Romance, Indo-European)
Squamish (Salishan)
Standard Fijian (Oceanic, Austronesian)
Swahili (Bantu)
Swedish (Germanic, Indo-European)
Tabar (Oceanic, Austronesian)
Tacana (Pano-Tacana)
Taenae (Angan, Papuan)
Tagalog (Western Austronesian)
Takia (Oceanic, Austronesian)
Tamachek (Tuareg, Berber, Afroasiatic)
Tamambo (Oceanic, Austronesian)
Tamazight (North-Berber, Afroasiatic)
Tamil (Dravidian)
Tanaina, Dena'ina (Athabaskan)
Tanana (Athabaskan)
Tarascan (isolate)
Tariana (North Arawak, Arawak)
Taulil (Papuan language of East New Britain)
Tazerwalt Shilh (North Berber, Afroasiatic)
Telugu (Dravidian)
Teop (Austronesian of Bougainville)
Tepetotutla Chinantec (Chinantec, Otomanguean)
Tequislatec (Tequislatecan)
Terêna (South Arawak, Arawak)
Teso (Eastern Nilotic, Nilo-Saharan)
Tewa (Kiowa-Tanoan)
Thai (Tai)
Tibetan (Tibeto-Burman)
Timbira (Jê)
Tinrin (New Caledonia, Austronesian)
Tiwi (Australian)
Tlingit (Eyak-Athabaskan)

To'aba'ita (Oceanic, Austronesian)
Toba (Guaicuruan)
Toba Batak (Austroasiatic)
Tolai (West New Britain, Austronesian)
Tonga (Bantu)
Tongan (Polynesian, Austronesian)
Toposa (Eastern Nilotic, Nilo-Saharan)
Totonac (Totonacan)
Trumai (isolate)
Truquese (Micronesian, Austronesian)
Tsafiki (Barbacoan)
Tsez (Northeast Caucasian)
Tsimshian (Penutian)
Tsova-Tush (Nakh, Northeast Caucasian)
Tucano (East Tucano, Tucano)
Tunica (isolate)
Turkana (Eastern Nilotic, Nilo-Saharan)
Turkish (Turkic)
Tuyuca (Central Tucano, Tucano)
Twi (dialects of Akan)
Tzeltal (Mayan)
Tzotzil (Mayan)
Ungarinjin (Australian)
Upper Chinook (Chinookan)
Upper Sorbian (Slavic, Indo-European)
Urubu-Kaapor (Tupí-Guaraní, Tupí)
Uzbek (Turkic)
Vietnamese (Viet-Mường, Austroasiatic)
Wagaya (Australian)
Wambaya (Australian)
Wangkumara (Australian)
Wantoat (Wantoat family, Morobe province, Papuan)
Waorani (isolate)
Wära (Fly river, Papuan)
Warao (isolate)
Wardaman (Australian)
Warekena (North Arawak, Arawak)
Wari' (Chapacura)
Waris (Waris, Papuan)
Warndarang (Australian)
Warray (Australian)
Washo (isolate)
Waurá (Xinguan Arawak, Arawak)

Wayan (Western Fijian, Oceanic)
Wei Ning (Miao Yao, Austroasiatic)
West Flemish (Germanic, Indo-European)
Western Apache (Athabaskan)
Western Oromo (East Cushitic, Afroasiatic)
Western Torres Strait (see Kalau Lagaw Ya)
White Hmong (Miao-Yao)
White Tai (Tai)
Wipi (Fly river, Papuan)
Wiyot (Ritwan, Algic)
Wogamusin (Papuan)
Wolof (West Atlantic)
Worrorra (Australian)
Wu-Ming (Austroasiatic)
Wunambal (Australian)
Xamatauteri (Yanomami)
Xhosa (Bantu)
!Xóõ (Khoisan)
!Xu (Khoisan)
Yagua (Peba-Yagua)
Yaigin (Australian)
Yana (isolate)
Yandruwanhtha (Australian)
Yankuntjatjara (Australian)
Yanomami (Yanomami)
Yanyuwa (Australian)
Yapese (Oceanic, Austronesian)
Yaruro (isolate)
Yavapai (Yuman)
Yawalapiti (Xinguan Arawak)
Yessan-Mayo (Papuan)
Yidiny (Australian)
Yimas (Lower Sepik, Papuan)
Yonggom (Ok)
Yoruba (Kwa)
Young People's Dyirbal (Australian)
Yuchi (isolate)
Yucuna (North Arawak, Arawak)
Yue dialects (Sinitic, Sino-Tibetan)
Yuki (Yukian)
Yurok (Ritwan, Algic)
Zaïrean Swahili, see Swahili
Zande (Eastern Nilotic-Adamawa)

Zapotec (Zapotecan, Otomangean)
Zayse (Omotic, Afroasiatic)
Zemmur (North Berber, Afroasiatic)
Zezuru (dialects of Shona, Bantu)
Zulu (Bantu)

List of Language Families, Linguistic Areas, and Proto-languages

African
Afroasiatic
Algonquian
Amazonian
Anatolian
Angan
Arapesh
Arawá
Arawak
Aslian
Asmat
Athabaskan
Australian
Austroasiatic
Austronesian
Aymara
Baltic
Balto-Finnic
Bantu
Barbacoan
Benue-Congo (Cross River)
Berber
Binanderre
Bolivian
Bora-Witoto
Caddoan
Cahuapanan
Campa
Carib
Caucasian
Celtic
Central American
Central Bahnaric
Central Bougainville

Central Celebes
Central Jukunoid
Central Khoisan
Central Tucano
Chadic
Chapacuran
Chapahuan
Chemakuan
Chibchan
Chimbu
Chinantec (Otomanguean)
Chinookan
Choco
Chukotka-Kamchatkan
Costanoan
Cross River
Cushitic
Daghestanian
Daly
Dravidian
East Bahnaric
East Berber
East Cushitic
East New Britain
East Sepik
East Slavic
East Tucano
Eastern Adamawa
Eastern Mindi
Eastern Nilotic
Eastern Nilotic-Adamawa
Eastern Sudanic
Engan
Eskimo-Aleut

Eyak-Athabaskan
Finno-Ugric
Fly River
Germanic
Gran Choco
Grassfields Bantu
Grasslands Bantu
Great Basin
Guahibo
Guaicuruan
Gulf
Gur
Harakmbet
Hokan
Huon
Indic
Indo-Aryan
Indo-European
Indo-Iranian
Iranian
Iroquoian
Italic
Jê
Jivaro
Kadugli-Kongo
Kalam
Kanjobalan Mayan
Katuic
Kegboid
Khmuic
Khoe
Khoisan
Kiowa-Tanoan
Kipeá-Karirí
Kiwaian
Kordofanian
Kru
Kwa
Lezgian
Loinang-Banggai
Lower Cross
Lower Sepik
Lowland Amazonia

Lowland East Cushitic
Macro-Jê
Magadhan
Makú
Malayo-Polynesian
Mande
Marind
Mataguayo
Mayan
Mba
Melanesian
Mesoamerican
Miao
Miao-Yao
Micronesian
Milne Bay Province
Mindi
Miwok-Costanoan (or Utian)
Mixe-Zoquean
Mixtecan (Otomanguean)
Mon-Khmer
Morobe Province
Munda
Mura-Pirahã
Muskogean
Nakh-Daghestanian
Nambiquara
Ndu
New Caledonia
New Indo-Aryan
Niger-Congo
Nilo-Saharan
Non-Austronesian (or Papuan)
North Arawak
North Bahnaric
North Berber
North Khoisan
North Kimberley
Northeast Caucasian
Northern Athabaskan
Northern Australian
Northern Iroquoian
Northern Jê

506 Classifiers

Northern Palaungic
Northern Tai
Northwest Caucasian
Northwest Coast
Numic (Uto-Aztecan)
Oceanic
Ok
Old Indo-Aryan
Old Iranian
Omotic
Otomanguean
Pacific Coast Athabaskan
Palaungic
Paleosiberian
Pamir
Pano
Pano-Tacana
Papuan
Papuan of Bougainville
Peba-Yagua
Penutian
Peruvian Arawak
Piman
Platoid
Polynesian
Pre-Andine Arawak
Pre-Proto-Northern-Iroquoian
Proto-Afroasiatic
Proto-Akan
Proto-Arawá
Proto-Arawak
Proto-Athabaskan
Proto-Australian
Proto-Bantu
Proto-Benue-Congo
Proto-Berber
Proto-Bora-Muinane
Proto-Bora-Witoto
Proto-Chadic
Proto-Cross-River
Proto-Dravidian
Proto-East-Katuic
Proto-Eastern Nilotic

Proto-Eyak-Athabaskan
Proto-Guaicuruan
Proto-Gur
Proto-Kru
Proto-Oceanic
Proto-South Dravidian
Proto-Uralic
Proto-Waic
Pueblo
Quechua
Reef-Santa Cruzan
Ritwan (Algic)
Romance
Sahaptian
Saho-Afar
Sáliba-Piaroa
Salish
Samoyed
Semitic
Sepik
Sepik Hill
Shugnan-Rushan
Sino-Japanese
Sino-Tibetan
Siouan
Slavic
Solomon Islands
South Amazon
South American Indian
South Arawak
South Bahnaric
South Berber
South Celebes
South Cushitic
South Dravidian
South Halmahera-West New
    Guinea
South Slavic
South Slavonic
Southeast Asian
Southeast Solominic
Southeastern Iranian
Southern Khoisan

Southern Lawa
Southern Numic (Uto-Aztecan)
Southern West Atlantic
Tacana
Tai
Takic (Uto-Aztecan)
Teberan
Tequislatecan
Tibeto-Burman
Ticuna
Togo Remnant
Torricelli
Totonacan
Trobriand Islands
Tuareg, Berber
Tucano
Tungus-Manchurian
Tupí
Tupí-Guaraní
Turkic
Ubangi
Ugric
Uralic
Uto-Aztecan
Viet-Muong

Voltaic
Waic
Wakashan
Wantoat
Waris
West Atlantic
West Bahnaric
West Chadic
West Mindi
West New Britain
West Slavonic
West Tucano
Western Austronesian
Western Fijian
Witoto
Xingu-Pareci
Xinguan Arawak
Yanomami
Yuchian
Yukian
Yuman
Zaparoan
Zapotecan (Otomanguean)
Zoquean (Mixe-Zoquean)

Index of Languages, Linguistic Areas, and Language Families

Abau 67, 77, 123, 277, 322
Abaza 40, 48
Abelam 253
Abkhaz 32–3, 40, 48
Abu' Arapesh 23, 26, 262, 346
Acehnese 84, 91, 97, 190, 283, 286, 290, 381, 402
Achagua 185, 198, 200, 202, 259, 286, 288, 290, 292, 387
African 10, 19, 67–8, 70, 76–7, 101, 243, 287, 373, 381
Afroasiatic 19, 54, 59, 77, 92, 121, 248, 252, 276–7, 288, 346
Ahaggar 254
Ahtna 167, 169, 382
Aikana 80
Ainu 121, 286, 436
Akan 280, 342, 398
Akatek 88, 90–1, 98, 113–14, 117–19, 187–9, 252, 284–5, 287, 290, 293, 302, 357, 403
Akhvakh 23
Akoye 79
Alamblak 27, 42, 56, 58, 276–7, 322
Alawa 257
Albanian 396
Algonquian 79–80, 100, 121, 123, 154, 276, 297
Algonquian-Ritwan 123
Amazonian 7, 10, 51, 82, 95, 193, 266, 396
Amele 437
American Indian 79, 125
American sign language 296
Amharic 262, 277, 279
Amuesha 80
Ancient Egyptian 82
Andi 278, 377
Angan 79, 123, 218, 244, 346, 435
Angave 79, 123, 218, 244, 346
Animere 381
Anindilyakwa 5, 12, 35, 43, 57, 66, 101, 151, 160–1, 169, 191, 200, 202, 207, 247, 256, 280
Apalaí 128–9, 142, 175, 295, 320, 336, 360, 365
Apurinã 57, 143
Arabic 40, 121, 385, 388, 392
Arapesh 26, 59, 62, 79, 262, 276, 346

Arawá 4, 32, 34, 54, 58–9, 70–1, 76, 80, 100, 138, 246, 251–2, 257–9, 272, 371, 381, 400, 434
Arawak 2–4, 12, 14, 39, 50, 54, 57, 69, 76, 80, 93, 100, 106, 123, 143, 150, 174, 183, 198, 201–2, 204–5, 210, 226–7, 230, 244, 246, 248, 256, 259, 262, 272, 279, 286, 288, 294, 360–1, 368–9, 384–7, 400
Archi 43, 47, 176
Armenian 77, 263
Arvanitika 390
Aslian 443
Asmat 171, 299
Assamese 102, 105, 117, 260, 379
Atakapa 169
Athabaskan 9, 11, 123, 152–4, 156, 165, 167–9, 176, 185, 205, 250, 265, 296, 334, 336, 344, 355, 381, 437, 444
Australian 2, 9–10, 12, 23, 25, 31, 33–5, 37–8, 41, 43, 49, 53–7, 59, 65–7, 70, 76, 79, 81–4, 86, 88–92, 95, 97, 99–101, 147, 150–1, 160–1, 191, 200, 228–9, 246–7, 252, 256–7, 277–8, 280, 284–5, 296–9, 318, 321, 328–9, 339, 342, 345, 353–5, 357, 360–1, 366, 369, 372, 275, 378, 381, 383, 385, 391, 395–7, 399, 402, 407, 431, 438
Austroasiatic 97, 116, 121, 227, 260, 272, 286, 291–2, 311, 342, 347, 354, 357, 365–6, 403–4, 443
Austronesian 28, 85, 100, 110, 113, 124–5, 133, 142, 147, 171, 183, 204–5, 210, 244, 267, 294, 303, 313, 339, 354, 357, 366, 382, 388, 402, 433
Awa Pit 86, 97, 381, 437
Awabakal 228
Awará 124, 207, 211, 218, 287, 418, 435
Ayacucho Quechua 48, 383, 388
Aymara 80
Aztec 123

Babungo 24, 57
Badyaranké 61, 382, 388
Bagval 23
Bahnar 356, 443
Bahwana 80, 107, 229, 259, 286, 354, 360, 380, 383

Index of Languages, Linguistic Areas, and Language Families

Baining 33, 79, 218, 244, 434
Baïnouk 59, 61–2, 435
Balinese 286
Baltic 245, 387
Balto-Finnic 440
Banda 374
Banggais 404
Baniwa (of Içana) vii, 4, 10, 31, 37, 39, 58, 69, 77, 100, 116, 131, 133–4, 136, 142–3, 145, 147, 185, 192, 201–2, 219, 227, 230–2, 234–5, 240–1, 246, 265, 272, 283, 287, 290, 294, 303, 310, 327, 336, 344, 355, 370, 382, 384–5, 387, 401, 444–6
Banjalang 79, 395
Bantu 2, 5, 9, 22, 24, 30–3, 35–6, 38, 44, 50, 53, 57, 63, 65–6, 95, 100, 176, 24,8, 266, 279, 281–3, 349, 359, 369–70, 373, 383, 387–9, 398–9, 403, 407, 409, 413, 416–17, 422
Banz 299
Barasano 70
Barbacoan 86, 97, 123, 437
Bare 4, 247, 266, 268, 370, 380, 387, 394, 400
Bari 393
Basque 436
Beludzhi 379
Bengali 77, 102, 105, 249, 369, 379, 381, 431, 438–9
Benue-Congo 24, 57, 59, 99, 101, 110, 124, 249, 356, 380–1, 398
Berber 41, 51, 59, 92, 252–3, 255–6, 279, 368, 388
Biak 244
Bihari 102
Biloxi 169
Bilua 79
Binanderre 439
Bine 33, 79
Black Tai 227, 405
Blackfoot 123
Bodo 105
Bolivian 286
Bora 221, 246–7, 287, 333, 385, 387, 397
Bora-Witoto 69, 80, 123, 220–2, 226, 246–7, 287, 385, 435
Bororo 129
Boumaa Fijian 133–4, 136, 138, 140, 293
Bowili 27
Brazilian Portuguese 42, 266
Budukh 68
Bugis 286, 315, 404, 406
Bukiyip 62, 276
Burmese 100, 103, 260, 262, 267, 291–2, 311–12, 315, 319, 324, 328–9, 336, 346, 361, 442–3, 445
Burushaski 35, 77
Bwamu 287

Caddo 444
Caddoan 169, 201–2, 444
Cahuapanan 208
Cahuilla 143–4, 317, 343, 348, 365, 406
Campa 191, 435
Camus 277
Canela 129
Cantabrian Spanish 27, 45, 276–7, 409
Cantonese 207, 214–15, 226–7, 326, 329, 419
Carib 11–12, 80, 127–9, 147, 172, 198, 259, 295, 300, 354, 360, 365, 383, 438
Carrier 167–8, 382
Caucasian 244, 252, 340
Cayuga 402–3
Central American 80, 123
Central Bahnaric 356, 443
Central Bougainville 79
Central Jukunoid 380
Central Khoisan 246–7, 393
Central Pomo 437
Central Tucano 93, 219, 227, 333, 384, 386
Central Yup'ik Eskimo 181
Chacabano Zamboangueño 389
Chadic 358
Chamalal 32
Chambri 123
Chamicuro 80
Chapacuran 257–9, 321, 434
Chapahuan 123
Chayahuita 207–8, 227
Chechen 27, 41, 49, 57, 263, 409
Chemakuan 79, 121
Chemehuevi 127, 295
Chenapian 67, 123
Cherokee 11, 80, 161–3, 175, 297
Chevak (Eskimo) 181
Chibchan 97, 123, 154, 156, 375
ChiBemba 52, 279, 282, 409
Chimbu 171, 299
Chimila 123
Chinantec 189, 191, 202, 257, 287, 292, 371, 376
Chinantepec Chinantec 293
Chinese 104, 118, 121, 205, 212, 226–7, 273, 354, 361, 389, 409, 417–18, 439
Chipewyan 154, 249, 297–8
Chiricahua Apache 154, 250
Chitimacha 169
Choco 436
Chrau 357, 365, 443
Chuj 364
Chukchee 438
Classical Arabic 120
Colville 123
Comaltepec Chinantec 117–18, 257, 287
Comanche 80, 436
Cora 127, 154, 191, 202, 295–7

Index of Languages, Linguistic Areas, and Language Families 511

Costanoan 80
Cree 297
Creek 158, 251
Cross River 101, 110, 124, 287, 356, 379, 398, 434
Cuaiquer 437
Cuiba 50, 221, 224
Cushitic 28, 92, 276, 390
Czech 415

Daghestanian 60, 263
Dahalo 390
Daju 398
Dakota 158, 169, 299
Daly 97, 283, 285
Dangbon 385
Danish 243
Dasenech 277
Dâw 12, 85, 139, 147, 172, 174–5, 192, 202, 259, 300, 345, 354, 357, 371, 376, 381
Dena'ina, or Tanaina 167, 382
Dení 70, 434
Dhegiha 169
Dioi 215, 288, 405–6, 445–6
Diyari 23, 336
Dogon 438
Dogrib 250
'Dongo-ko 129–30, 147, 192, 202
Dravidian 19, 22–3, 41, 46, 77, 99, 103, 121, 185, 202, 249, 276, 286–7, 384, 398
Dulong-Rawang 207, 215, 323
Dutch 26
Dyirbal 23, 35–6, 41, 43, 45, 56, 79, 228, 281, 310–11, 329, 345, 347, 372–3, 390, 395, 408, 438
  Traditional 349, 390
  Young People's 349, 390–1

East Adamawa 358, 374
East Asian 11, 82, 99, 101, 103, 121, 205–6, 325
East Berber 243
East Cushitic 25, 51, 60, 328
East New Britain 33, 79, 244, 434
East Sepik 4, 24, 42, 54, 58, 62, 123, 253, 276–7, 322, 437
East Slavic 244
East Tucano 4, 50, 70, 110, 131, 218–19, 221–2, 259, 287, 333, 361–2, 384
Eastern Mindi 397
Eastern Nilotic 42, 58, 59, 77, 276–7, 354, 358, 368, 380, 392–3, 402, 403
Eastern Sudanic 21, 398
Eastern Sutherland Gaelic 390
Egyptian Arabic 120, 415
Ejagham 99–100, 105, 111, 124, 249
Emmi 84, 86, 97, 161, 257, 285, 299

Enga 158–9, 166, 250, 296, 299, 406
Engan 158–9, 171, 299, 362
English 21, 24, 26, 29, 36, 54, 86–7, 100, 115–16, 140, 153, 176, 228, 326, 337–9, 349–50, 358, 386, 389–90, 397, 407, 409, 415, 443
  American English 346
  Old 380, 398
  Pidgin 389
  Standard 312
  Tasmanian 312
Epena Pedee 436
Eskimo 177, 181–2, 266, 301, 345
Estonian 387, 440
Ewe 440
Eyak 176, 206–7, 209, 225
Eyak-Athabaskan 121, 169, 206, 209
Eywo 79

Fanagalo 389
Felefita 346
Fijian 2, 11,113, 141, 381
  Old 113
  Standard 133
Finnish 369, 387, 439
Finno-Ugric 102
Fly River 33, 79, 277. 437
Folopa, or Podopa 123
French 19–20. 40, 53–4, 62, 326, 379, 399, 414–15
  Colloquial 408
  Old 380
Ful or Fulfulde 59, 243, 344, 346
Fulfulde or Ful 59, 243, 344, 346

Gaagudju 49, 70, 396
Gadjang 228
Gaelic 390
Gapapaiwa 147
Garifuna, or Black Carib 34, 40, 44
Garo 310, 417–18
Gavião 86
German 24–5, 27, 39, 153, 243, 280, 335, 337, 363, 387, 397, 409, 414–15
Gilbertese 291
Godoberi 23, 276
Gola 58, 321
Gold Palaung 366
Gondi 266
Gorontalo 286, 445–6
Gran Choco 80
Grassfields Bantu 24, 57, 124
Grasslands Bantu 10, 287, 434
Great Basin 123, 169
Grebo 377, 417
Greek 19, 390
Guahibo 36, 50, 80, 94, 123, 204, 220–2, 224

Index of Languages, Linguistic Areas, and Language Families

Guaicuruan 12, 80, 130, 147, 175, 177–8, 180–3, 191, 198, 251, 301, 326, 362–3
Guajiro 54
Gulf 80, 123
Gunbarlang 200, 202, 381
Gunwinjgu 44, 169
Gur 53, 59
Gurr-goni 33, 38, 53–5, 66, 70, 100, 281, 408
Guugu Yimidhirr 372
Gwich'in 169

Haida 121, 169
Hakka 215, 226
Halia 124
Hani 156, 300
Harakmbet 69, 80, 123, 171
Harar 25
Hausa 25, 388
Hawaiian 136
Hebrew 44, 52, 92, 138, 243, 254, 264, 413–15
Hiechware 368
Hindi 53, 102, 121
Hittite 82, 378
Hixkaryana 175, 438
Hmong 12, 104, 131–2, 144–5, 147, 183, 205–7, 215–16, 225, 291–2, 329, 354, 356, 445
Hohôdene 143
Hokan 169
Hokkien 215, 226, 419–20
Holikachuk 169
Hopi 80
Hua 438–40
Hualapai 127
Huave 123
Huli 299
Hungarian 102–4, 115–16, 121, 440
Huon 171, 299
Hupa 123, 249
Hupda 139, 147

Iatmul 253
Ibibio 104
Icelandic 415
Idu 155
Igbo 77, 440
Ignaciano 69, 207, 210, 213, 227
Ika 154, 156, 165, 171, 296, 299, 438
Ilocano 313, 388
Imonda 152, 166, 297, 300, 330, 362–3, 379, 406, 439
Indic 77, 99, 103, 105, 121, 185, 202, 379
Indo-Aryan 27, 102, 260, 287, 369, 384
  Old 379
Indo-European 3, 19, 24, 31, 54, 59, 77, 86, 121, 243, 248, 252, 255–6, 262–3, 280, 363, 378, 380, 388, 396, 398–9, 413, 415–16
Indonesian, Bahasa Indonesia 283, 286, 288, 381, 386, 402, 404, 443, 46
Ingush 27, 41, 49, 57, 263
Iranian 77, 121, 185, 379
  Old 396
Iraqw 26, 70
Irish, Modern 262
Iroquoian 161, 169, 201–2, 243, 296–7, 402
Island Carib 259, 354, 360, 383
Italian 19, 379, 399
Itonama 80
Iwaidja 37
Iwam 123
Izayan 243, 253, 256, 440

Jabutí 80
Jacaltec 82–3, 88, 225, 252, 284–7, 313, 323, 331, 334, 341, 344, 357, 364, 375, 403
  Modern 334
Japanese 2, 8, 21, 99, 106, 113, 121, 155, 261–2, 288, 293, 308–10, 314, 316–17, 320, 324, 328–9, 334–6, 344, 348, 351, 410, 417–20, 436, 439
  Modern 410
Jarawara 54, 59, 100, 251, 258, 262, 272, 439
Javanese 386
Jawoyn 385
Jê 11, 23, 36, 80, 97, 147, 228, 244
Jeh 104
Jingulu 34, 281
Jivaro 80
Jukun 380

Kabyle 39, 256
Kadiweu 130, 175, 181, 198
Kadugli-Kongo 277
Kaingáng 23, 36, 228
Kakua 80, 228, 384
Kalau Lagaw Ya, Kalaw Kawaw Ya 253, 336
Kaliai-Kove 134, 293
Kam-Muang 446
Kamoro 166, 299
Kana 99, 101, 110–11, 287, 317, 354, 356, 359–60, 371, 379, 403–4, 439, 444
Kanjobal of San Miguel Acatán 113
Kanjobalan Mayan 82, 88, 90–1, 97–8, 123, 187, 202, 284, 286, 357, 376,404
Kannada 286
Kariri 11, 229
Karo 171
Karok 80, 123
Katcha 25, 277
Káte 299
Katu 442
Katuic 442

Index of Languages, Linguistic Areas, and Language Families 513

Kayapó 129
Kegboid 101, 110–11, 124, 287, 371, 379, 381, 439
Kenya Pidgin Swahili 388
Keriaka 79
Ket 23, 42, 77
Kewa 299
Khinalug 47, 248
Khmer 104, 117, 288, 347, 405, 443, 446
Khmu 403
Khmuic 272
Khoe 368, 393
Khoisan 42, 59, 77, 254, 276
Kibera 388
Kikongo 30, 389, 400
Kikuyu 57, 63–4, 282
Kilivila 8, 104, 110, 136–7, 141, 191, 204, 207, 210, 223, 225, 260, 294–5, 303–4, 316, 331, 366, 376, 411, 417–19, 445
Kiowa 80, 248, 250
Kiowa-Tanoan 11, 80, 248, 250, 369, 377
Kipeá 11, 133, 136, 147, 294, 434
Kipeá-Kariri 133, 135, 147, 229
Kituba 388, 400
Kiwai 299
Kiwaian 171, 299
Koaia 80
Koasati 158, 169, 436
Kobon 436
Kolami 23, 41, 67, 287
Korafe 439
Kordofanian 25
Kore 380
Korean 106–7, 113, 115, 120–1, 260–1, 273, 288, 293, 311, 319, 334, 336, 348, 351, 386
Kosraean 294
Koyukon 157, 167, 176, 209, 250, 265, 336, 382
Krahô 129
Kru 377, 398–9, 417
Kulina 434
Ku Waru 159, 166, 362
Kubeo 207, 219, 226, 382, 384–5
Kugu-Ngancara 90
Kuot 32–3, 79
Kuria 279, 407, 409
Kurripaco 143
Kusaiean 108
Kwa 398, 440
Kwoma/Washkuk 77
Kxoe 42, 368

Lahu 361
Lak 34, 278, 347
Lama 53
Lama Lama 92

Landuma 61, 435
Lao 89, 103, 222, 225, 268, 354, 360–1, 439
Latin 19, 40, 47, 53, 255–6, 262, 336, 379–80
Latvian 369, 387
Lavukaleve 79, 244, 257ã
Lezgian 60, 263, 438
Lezgic 263
Lɨɨ 445
Limilngan 25, 59, 381
Lingala 388, 400
  Kinshasa 388, 399–400
  Mankandza 399–400
Língua Geral 390
Lisu 288
Lithuanian 245, 255, 262, 387
Lokono 50, 54, 172, 174–5, 201–2, 262, 279, 300
Longgu 382
Loniu 124
Lotuko 384
Loven 367
Lower Chinook 79
Lower Cross 396, 398–9
Lower Sepik 27, 58, 79, 123
Lowland Amazonia 123, 171, 216, 222
Lowland Amazonian 7, 36, 93, 99, 201
Lowland East Cushitic 385
Luganda 52
Luiseño 127, 295

Ma 276
Maa 384
Maasai 375
Maasina 346, 392
Machiguenga 12, 191, 199, 202, 207, 213, 341, 370
Macro-Jê 11, 36, 129, 228, 259, 434
Macushi 128–9, 140, 142, 175
Magadhan 102
Maká 80, 253
Makassar 286, 406
Makú 12, 80, 85, 97, 139, 147, 172, 174, 192, 228, 259, 300, 354, 357, 371, 384, 435
Mal 101, 104, 444
Malak-Malak 70
Malay 249, 286, 308, 324–5, 329, 381, 386
Malinke 382, 388
Malto 23, 102, 104, 112, 185, 206, 248, 286
Mam 87, 140, 252, 284, 331, 357, 362, 364, 375–6, 403
Manam 134, 137, 293, 365
Manambu 4, 32, 37, 42, 45, 54, 58, 243–4, 253, 263–4, 276–8, 313, 358, 392, 438
Mandan 3, 177, 326, 363
Mandarin (Chinese) 98–9, 183, 206–7, 309, 324–5, 328, 335–6, 409–10, 418–23
Mande 77, 382, 388

514 *Index of Languages, Linguistic Areas, and Language Families*

Marathi 102, 106, 121, 287
Maricopa 127
Marind 60, 77
Marrithiyel 37, 97
Marshallese 294
Mataguayo 253
Maung 65, 267
Mayali 31, 38, 41, 53, 55, 92, 150–1, 169, 266, 281–1, 296, 354–5, 360, 380, 385, 396, 408, 442
Mayan 84, 87, 90–1, 97, 103, 113, 115, 123, 140, 252, 285, 288–9, 329–30, 339, 342, 353–4, 357, 364, 367, 375, 438
Mba 33, 67, 75–6, 129–30, 147, 192, 243, 259, 387
Melanesian 110
Melpa 171, 299
Menomini 123
Mescalero Apache 154–5, 157, 330
Mesoamerican 12, 81–2, 97, 101, 153, 169, 335
Mexican 123
Miao 132, 144
Miao of Wei Ning 104
Miao-Yao 12, 131, 147, 212, 215, 435
Micronesian 108, 110, 125, 136, 140–1, 147, 186–7, 205, 260, 291, 294, 361, 365–6, 405, 446
Minangkabau 10, 84–5, 90, 97–8, 100, 117, 120, 187, 189, 202, 253, 262, 272, 283, 285–6, 289, 291–3, 302, 308, 318, 322, 329–30, 348, 354, 356, 359–60, 366, 370, 375, 381, 386, 391, 401–2, 404, 406, 443, 445–6
Mindi 397
Missima 147
Miwok 80
Mixtec 252, 260, 354, 359, 376
Mnong Gar 357
Mocovi 130
Modern Hebrew 22, 28, 53, 248, 264
Modern Irish 262
Mohawk 403
Mokilese 11, 133, 186–7, 202, 301
Mon 272, 443
Mon-Khmer 101, 104, 365, 402, 442–3, 446
Monumbo 59
Mori 286
Morobe Province 79, 124, 211, 287
Motuna 12, 34, 40, 69, 79, 131–2, 162, 176, 207, 219–21, 248, 279, 303, 321, 370, 437
Movima 80, 110, 286
Mparntwe Arrente 82, 84, 88
Mufian 62
Muhiang Arapesh 26
Mulao 9
Munda 77

Mundurukú 12, 123, 152, 160–1, 171, 205, 207, 216–18, 224–5, 227, 333, 354–5, 444–5
Mupun 358, 402
Murrinhpatha 37, 84, 86, 89–90, 97, 284–5
Murui Witoto 246
Muskogean 158, 169, 251, 436

Nadëb 147, 259, 354, 371
Nahuatl 123
Naiki 41, 67
Nakh 41, 47
Nakh-Daghestanian 27
Nakhi 362
Nama 254
Nambiquara 93, 123, 204, 221, 224–5, 303–4, 333–4, 345
Napues, or Kunua 79
Naro 368
Nasioi 12, 79, 131–2, 139, 162, 176, 207, 219–20, 259
Natchez 169
Nauru 99, 110, 205
Navajo 167, 250, 336
Ndali 63–5
Ndu 4, 24, 32, 42, 54, 58, 77, 243–4, 253, 278, 392
Ndunga-le 383, 387
Nepali 102, 379
Nevome 158, 169, 297, 299
New Caledonia 142
New Guinea Highlands 158
New Indo-Aryan 379
Newari 9, 207, 212, 265, 326
Nez Perce 123
Ngala (Nilo-Saharan) 374
Ngala (Papuan) 253
Ngalakan 33, 49, 56
Ngan'gityemerri 84, 89, 92–3, 95, 97, 185–6, 201–2, 285, 301, 317, 354, 361, 370, 376, 394, 404, 407
Ngandi 169, 246, 296, 373, 387, 402, 442
Ngiyambaa 9
Ngyembɔɔn 124, 287, 356
Nias 112
Nicobarese 443
Niger-Congo 33, 58–9, 67, 75–7, 99, 104, 129, 147, 192, 259, 276, 342, 356, 359, 380, 384, 387, 438
Nilo-Saharan 51, 77
Nivkh, or Gilyak 100, 108–9, 121, 206, 274, 286, 290
Non-Austronesian, also see Papuan 32–4, 79, 218
Non-Bantu 38
Nootka 249
North Amazonian 77, 220, 226, 327, 344

Index of Languages, Linguistic Areas, and Language Families 515

North American Indian 11, 97, 105, 147, 154, 158, 177, 182, 296
North Arawak vii, 10, 23, 27, 31, 33–4, 36, 39–40, 44, 50, 58, 60, 69, 92–3, 100, 106–7, 109–10, 116, 131, 133, 142–3, 147, 152, 163, 171–2, 192, 198, 203–4, 220–3, 235, 246–7, 253, 259, 265–8, 340, 371, 376, 380, 383, 385–7, 390, 394
North Bahnaric 443–4
North Berber 39, 243, 254
North Khoisan 58
North Kimberley 34–5
Northeast Caucasian 23, 32, 34, 40, 43, 47, 60, 77, 176, 263, 276, 278, 347, 377
Northern Athabaskan 157, 167, 169, 205
Northern Australian 44, 53–4, 95, 161, 169, 185, 280, 283, 322, 372
Northern Iroquoian 401
Northern Jê 129
Northern Palaungic 442
Northern Tai 227
Northern Tepehuan 127
Northwest Caucasian 32–3, 48, 77
Northwest Coast 79, 121
Ntifa 254
Nubi 388
Numic (Uto-Aztecan) 80
Nung 100, 103–4, 118, 207, 211, 227, 405
Nungali 65–6, 381, 397
Nunggubuyu 33, 59, 66, 92, 150, 169, 200, 202, 321, 325, 387
Nyanja 65

Ocaina 385, 397
Oceanic 6, 11, 97, 121, 124, 133–7, 143, 145, 147, 294, 381–2, 384
Ojibway 121, 154–5, 297
Ok 77, 171, 277
Old Church Slavonic 244
Olgolo 91, 373
Ollari 23
Olo 59, 277
Omani Arabic 120, 443
Omani-Zanzibar dialect of Arabic 120
Omotic 52
Ongamo 375
Oriya 102, 379
Oromo 25, 28, 92, 276–7, 279, 328
'Oro Nao 257–8, 321
Ossete 379
Otomanguean 80, 117–18, 123

Pacific Coast Athabaskan 80
Palaungic 82, 402
Paleosiberian 77, 100, 108, 121, 206
Palikur 3, 8, 12, 27, 39, 69, 100, 112, 142, 163–5, 172–6, 192–203, 225–6, 228–9, 247, 257, 259, 264–5, 268, 278–9, 289–90, 292, 296–7, 300, 302, 310, 316, 320, 327, 333, 335–7, 341, 354–5, 357, 360, 369–70, 375, 383, 434, 445–6
Pamir 60
Panará 129
Panare 127–8, 360
Pano 80
Papago 127
Papuan 3, 10–12, 23, 38, 59, 67, 69, 77, 79, 97, 123, 131–2, 139, 144, 147, 149, 152, 158–9, 162, 166, 169, 205, 211, 218–19, 243–4, 248, 257, 259, 276–7, 279, 296–300, 303, 321–2, 329, 362, 370, 379, 382, 384, 396, 433, 435–7, 439
Pareci 226, 435
Parji 23, 41, 67
Patjtjamalh 84, 97
Paumarí 4, 32, 34, 70–6, 100, 138, 146, 184, 246, 252, 257, 283, 381, 400
Peba-Yagua 80, 123, 221
Persian 77, 121, 369, 379
Peruvian Arawak 191, 199, 213, 341
Petats 124
Piapoco 387
Pilagá 12, 86, 178, 180–2, 251, 266, 301, 326, 331, 336
Piman 169
Pirahã 80
Piratapuya 4
Pittapitta 228
Platoid 380
Pogoro 407
Polish 244, 279, 313, 414–15, 440
Polynesian 135–6
Pomoan 79, 169
Ponapean 11, 186, 202, 260–1, 294, 301, 336, 342, 344, 354, 359, 361–2, 364, 366, 405
Ponca 177–8, 182
Portuguese 2, 25, 28, 31, 30, 43, 45, 47, 52–3, 57, 62, 75, 100, 109, 243, 313, 358, 379, 391, 400
Potawatomi 123
Pre-Andine Arawak 143
Pre-Proto-Northern-Iroquoian 378
Proto-Afroasiatic 92
Proto-Akan 342
Proto-Arawá 60
Proto-Arawak 70, 143, 371, 387, 446
Proto-Athabaskan 250
Proto-Australian 372
Proto-Bantu 24, 283
Proto-Benue-Congo 111, 358, 381
Proto-Berber 256
Proto-Bora-Muinane 387
Proto-Bora-Witoto 246

Index of Languages, Linguistic Areas, and Language Families

Proto-Chadic 358
Proto-Cross-River 379
Proto-Dravidian 378
Proto-East-Katuic 442
Proto-Eastern Nilotic 358, 375
Proto-Eyak-Athabaskan 154, 169, 444
Proto-Guaicuruan 181, 363
Proto-Gur 388
Proto-Kru 377
Proto-Oceanic 124, 134, 365
Proto-South-Dravidian 378
Proto-Uralic 440
Proto-Waic 402, 442
Pueblo 80, 123
Puluwat 140–1, 145, 295
Punjabi 27

Qafar 25, 51
Qiang 155, 175
Quechua 80, 382
Queyu 155

Raga 135, 294
Rama 375
Reef-Santa Cruzan 79, 147, 171, 218, 386, 435
Rembarrnga 381, 385
Rendille 60
Resígaro 50, 69, 226, 246–7, 333, 385, 387, 397
Retuarã 386
Rikbaktsa 36, 228
Ritwan 123
Ro·lo·m 357
Romance 57, 379–80
Romansch 47
Roshani 60
Rotokas 79
Rumanian 45–6
Russian 22, 25–6, 28, 38, 41, 43–4, 48, 51, 54, 57, 115, 120, 138, 140, 153, 243, 256, 262–4, 272, 313, 347, 363, 389, 409, 414–15, 439–40

Sahaptin 123
Saho-Afar 25
Sáliba 80, 123
Salish 79, 109, 114, 212, 123, 169
Sanskrit 256
Savosavo 79
Scottish Gaelic 390, 399
Sedang 444
Seghrouchen 440
Sele Fara, dialect of Slovene 380
Semitic 51, 252, 392, 413
Seneca 243
Sepik 26, 384

Sepik Hill 77
Serbo-Croatian 415
Sesotho 57, 416, 418
Setswana 50, 349, 416
Shan 406
Shilh 256
Shona 32, 65, 343, 407
Siamese 404–6
Sierra Popoluca 123
Sinasina 299
Sino-Japanese 113, 336
Sino-Korean 113
Sino-Tibetan 105, 361–2
Siouan 3, 7, 12, 80, 158, 169, 177, 181–3, 276, 299, 301, 326, 362–3
SiSwati 416
Siuci 143
Siwa 243, 253
Slave 154, 167, 169, 250, 297, 437
Slavic 48, 56, 245, 377, 388, 439
Slovene 244–6, 380
Sochiapan Chinantec 12, 191, 201, 287, 290, 293
Solomon Islands 79, 257
South Amazon 58
South American vii, 2, 10–12, 67, 76, 100, 123, 129, 144–5, 147, 204–5, 244, 247, 274, 295, 300, 318, 334, 357, 361, 433
South American Indian 6, 11–12, 59, 99, 105, 133, 147, 149, 172, 213
South Arawak 152, 160, 209–10, 213, 435
South Bahnaric 357, 443
South Berber 254
South Cushitic 26, 70
South Dravidian 67, 99–100, 102, 104, 112, 185, 206, 248, 266, 378
South Halmahera 244
South Slavic 244
Southeast Asian 11, 82, 90, 99, 101, 103, 121, 205–6, 211, 325, 354, 356, 361, 402, 433, 435, 443
Southeast Solomonic 244
Southeastern Iranian 60
Southeastern Pomo 299
Southern Khoisan 35, 396
Southern Lawa 402
Southern Numic (Uto-Aztecan) 127, 295
Southern Paiute 80
Southern West Atlantic 368
Southwest Mexico 163, 169
Spanish 27, 45, 47–8, 52–3, 110, 249, 253–4, 378, 380, 382, 388–9, 414–15, 437
Squamish 109, 114, 205, 286
Swahili 19, 31, 34–5, 38, 44, 53, 63, 228, 266, 390, 400
   Zairian 388
Swedish 40

Index of Languages, Linguistic Areas, and Language Families 517

Tabar 382
Tacana 80
Taenae 79, 123, 218
Tagalog 48
Tai 9, 97, 100, 103–4, 211, 286, 290, 311, 336, 370, 405–6, 442, 444, 446
Taiwanese 423
Takia 147, 382
Takic (Uto-Aztecan) 143
Tamachek 245, 254, 256
Tamambo 294
Tamazight 39, 440
Tamil 22, 56, 248
Tanana 167, 382
Tarascan 163, 169, 444–5
Tariana vii, 2, 4, 8, 33, 36, 50, 58, 69, 77, 92–4, 100, 110, 1310, 138, 142, 163, 183, 185, 201, 204, 220–6, 230, 235–6, 239–41, 246–7, 249, 253–4, 259, 264–5, 268, 287, 327–9, 331, 354, 360–2, 370, 376, 382, 384–5, 387, 396–7, 402, 404, 444–5
Tashkent Uzbek 102
Taulil 79, 218
Tazerwalt Shilh 254
Teberan 123
Telugu 46, 100, 108, 112, 286
Teop 124, 183
Tepetotutla Chinantec 257
Tequislatec 80
Terêna 80, 152, 160–1, 207, 209–10, 220
Teso 384
Tewa 250–1
Thai 100, 103–5, 118, 205, 207, 212, 214, 226–7, 260, 262, 268, 313–15, 318, 326, 334, 348–9, 354, 360–1, 372, 404–5, 407–8, 411, 417–22, 442, 444, 446
Tibetan 82, 97, 284
Tibeto-Burman 9, 121, 154–6, 175, 212, 215, 265, 288, 300, 323
Ticuna 80
Timbira 129
Tinrin 142
Tiwi 33, 56, 59, 150, 160, 169, 200, 257, 276–7, 355, 389, 400
 Modern 389, 391
 Traditional 389, 391, 400
Tlingit 121, 249
To'aba'ita 113
Toba 130, 178–81, 191, 202, 266, 301, 345
Toba Batak 286, 445
Togo Remnant 27, 59, 381
Tolai 136
Tonga 407
Tongan 136, 176
Toposa 393
Torricelli 26, 59, 79, 277, 346
Totonac 123, 288–9, 354–6, 402, 443–6
Totonacan-Tepehuan 288, 355, 443
Trobriand Islands 204
Trumai 80
Truquese 110, 136, 141, 145, 187, 202, 267, 320, 361, 370
Tsafiki 123
Tsez 40, 176
Tsimshian 121
Tsova-Tush 41, 47
Tuareg 245, 254
Tucano 4, 58, 69., 80, 93, 100, 110, 123, 204–5, 207, 218–22, 224–6, 235, 248–9, 255, 259, 264, 358, 376, 382, 384–6, 397, 435
Tunica 80, 169
Tupí 12, 80, 86, 123, 152, 160, 171, 204, 216, 355, 435
Tupí-Guaraní 11, 129, 147, 259, 360, 391
Turkana 42–3, 58, 277, 322, 368–9, 384
Turkic 99, 102–3, 121
Turkish 341, 388, 440
Tuyuca 93, 207, 218–19, 221
Twi 398
Tzeltal 103, 115, 272, 274, 288–9, 291, 293, 362, 364, 367
Tzotzil 249, 288, 293, 329–30, 356, 367

Ubangi 33, 75–6, 129, 147, 192, 243, 259, 276, 387
Ubangian 358
Ungarinjin 9, 34–5, 56, 257, 329, 396
Upper Chinook 79, 123
Upper Sorbian 244
Uralic 121, 440
Urubu-Kaapor 129
Uto-Aztecan 11, 80, 123, 126–7, 129, 143–4, 147, 154, 158, 169, 259, 295, 297, 299, 348, 365, 436
Uzbek 102, 104

Viet-Mương 354, 360
Vietnamese 103–4, 117–18, 120, 205, 207, 211–12, 262, 317–18, 326, 329, 334–6, 403, 405, 443–5
Voltaic 59, 367

Wagaya 54
Waic 405
Wakashan 121, 169
Wambaya 281
Wangkumara 54
Wantoat 124, 218, 287, 435
Waorani 80, 123, 171, 207, 217–18, 221, 224–5, 227
Wära 79, 277, 437
Warao 80

Wardaman 57, 92, 201–2, 322, 325, 373, 408
Warekena 4, 60, 100, 109, 143, 185, 247, 266, 268, 287, 390, 394, 400
Wari' 32
Waris 3, 149, 152, 159, 166–7, 171, 184, 250, 300, 362–3, 438
Warndarang 387
Warray 70, 92, 321, 328, 369, 399
Washo 123
Waurá 76, 182–3, 207, 210, 213, 220, 226–8, 435
Wayan 11, 133
Wei Ning 104, 208
West Atlantic 35, 58–9, 61, 321, 348, 373, 382, 435
West Bahnaric 367, 403
West Chadic 358
West Flemish 34
West Mindi 397
West New Guinea 244
West Slavic 244
West Tucano 222
Western Apache 250, 298
Western Austronesian 82, 84–5, 91, 97, 112, 124, 187, 189, 253, 283, 292, 405, 446
Western Fijian 11, 133
Western Oromo 385
Western Torres Strait 23, 56, 253
White Hmong 325
White Tai 215, 402, 405, 446
Wipi 79, 437
Witoto 94
Wiyot 123
Wogamusin 67, 123
Wolof 62, 348
Worrorra 34–5
Wu-Ming 405, 445
Wunambal 34–5

Xamatauteri 355
Xhosa 53

Xingu-Pareci 226
Xinguan Arawak 76, 182, 209–10, 213, 220, 228
!Xóõ 35, 396
!Xu 58

Yagua 69, 80, 107, 171, 204–5, 207, 217–18, 220–2, 224–5, 333
Yaigin 252
Yana 80
Yandruwanhtha 228
Yankuntjatjara 82, 88
Yanomami 80, 354–5, 444–5
Yanyuwa 33, 65–6, 373, 378, 385
Yaruro 80
Yavapai 127
Yawalapiti 207, 209–10, 228, 435
Yessan-Mayo 437
Yidiny 2, 83–5, 87, 89, 91, 93, 97, 150, 284–5, 317, 320, 345, 372, 404
Yimas 26, 59, 62, 79, 276, 329
Yonggom 77, 277
Yoruba 77
Yuchi 169, 177–8, 181, 183, 326
Yuchian 80
Yucuna 106, 185, 386–7
Yue 215
Yuki 80, 249
Yukian 80
Yuman 11, 126, 129, 147, 259, 354
Yurok 123

Zande 58, 276, 354, 358, 373–5, 402
Zaparoan 80
Zapotec 123
Zayse 52
Zemmur 243, 256, 440
Zezuru 65
Zoquean 123
Zulu 36, 417

Index of Authors

Abbott, M. 129
Adams, K. L. 6, 11, 82, 97–9, 101, 103, 116–18, 120, 271–2, 286, 288, 291–2, 310, 337, 342, 347, 357, 360, 365–7, 402–3, 405–6, 442–6
ăgg-ălboṣṭan ăg-Sidiyăn, E. 245, 254
Ahrens, K. 115, 423
Aikhenvald, A. Y. 8, 11–12, 22, 27–8, 30, 32, 34, 37, 39–40, 50, 54, 60, 67, 69–70, 74, 76–7, 80, 92–4, 109, 112, 116, 123, 131, 138, 142–3, 150, 163, 166, 172–4, 182, 192–3, 196, 198–9, 201, 209–10, 213, 225–6, 228–30, 235, 239–40, 242–3, 246–7, 255–7, 259, 263–4, 266, 270, 276, 278–9, 320, 327–9, 332–3, 345, 355, 360–1, 368–9, 371, 376, 380, 383, 385, 387, 390–1, 398, 400
Aksenova, I. 279, 407
Alexandre, P. 388, 400
Alexeyev, M. 263
Allan, K. 6, 12–13, 117, 172, 271, 274, 337–8
Allin, T. 246, 333, 385, 387
Alpher, B. 54, 349
Amaya, M. T. 123
Amberber, M. 262, 279
Ameka, F. 440
Anderson, C. 123
Anderson, J. L. 117–18, 257, 287
Anderson, L. G. 349, 389
Anderson, N. 123
Anderson, S. R. 29–30, 363
Andrews, E. 50
Arin, D. N. 343, 407
Aronoff, M. 26, 62, 262
Aschmann, R. P. 246, 387
Asher, R. E. 22, 248
Austin, P. 336
Axelrod, M. 157, 167, 265

Baarle, P. van 279
Bani, E. 23, 56, 336
Bantia, T. K. 27
Barlow, M. 29, 39
Barnes, J. 11, 93, 218–19, 333
Baron, R. 338
Barron, R. 3, 7, 12, 176–8, 301, 326, 363
Barsalou, L. W. 309
Barz, R. K. 11, 102, 117, 381

Bascom, B. 127
Basso, K. H. 11
Becker, A. J. 117, 120, 311–12, 315, 319, 324, 329, 442–3
Beckwith, C. I. 102, 116, 121, 440
Benton, R. A. 103, 110, 141, 187, 267, 320, 361, 370
Berlin, B. 103, 115, 272, 274, 289, 291, 364, 367
Berman, R. 138, 414
Bhaskararao, P. 9, 212, 265, 326
Birk, D. B. W. 70
Bisang, W. 11–12, 21, 101, 103–4, 106, 116–17, 120, 131–2, 144, 208, 212, 215–16, 260, 291, 325–6, 356, 372, 383–4, 409, 439, 445
Blankenship, B. 11, 161–2, 175, 297
Blewett, K. 79, 147, 218
Bloomfield, L. 4
Boas, F. 158, 299
Böhme, R. 415
Bokamba, E. G. 53, 388, 399–400
Boley, P. 70
Bolt, J. E. 66
Borneto, S. C. 153, 363
Boxall, E. 124
Braun, F. 341, 388
Breedveld, J. O. 344, 346
Breen, G. 54
Bresnan, J. 29, 34, 176, 392
Broschart, J. 176
Brosman, Jr., P. W. 378
Brown, L. 112
Brown, R. 3, 11, 166, 171, 300, 438
Bruce, L. 27, 42, 56, 276, 322
Bulygina, T. V. 51, 54
Burgess, E. 226
Burling, R. 103, 116, 291, 417–18
Burton, M. 282
Butler, N. 152, 160, 209
Bybee, J. 374, 376

Callister, B. 147
Campbell, L. 79, 121, 123, 169, 364, 383–4, 388, 391, 438
Capell, A. 267
Carlson, R. 11, 86, 125, 127, 133, 140, 186, 360
Carlson, T. 79, 123

Index of Authors

Carpenter, K. 103, 314, 404, 407–8, 417–18, 420–1, 424, 442, 444, 446
Carroll, J. B. 339
Carter, R. M. 11, 154, 249–50, 296–8, 336
Casad, E. 127, 154, 295–6
Casagrande, J. B. 339
Caskey, A. F. 53
Céria, V. G. 12, 130, 181, 363
Chafe, W. L. 243, 321, 378
Chang-Smith, M. 309
Chapman, A. 89, 268, 360, 439
Chapman, S. 34, 71–2, 138, 252
Chappell, H. 125, 258, 294
Charney, J. O. 436
Charters, H. 208
Chatterji, S. K. 379
Childs, T. 368, 373
Christensen, S. 77, 171, 277
Churchward, C. M. 113, 136, 381
Clamons, C. R. 25, 28, 92, 276, 385
Clark, E. V. 338, 421
Claudi, U. 358–9, 374–5
Codrington, R. 11, 133
Cohen, P. 104
Coleman, C. 200
Collinder, B. 440
Comrie, B. 40, 77, 176, 272, 347, 377
Conklin, N. F. 6, 11, 97, 99, 120, 215, 227, 271, 286, 288, 290–2, 310–11, 318, 326, 336–7, 381, 386, 402, 404–6, 442, 445–6
Connelly, M. J. 22
Conrad, J. 123
Conrad, R. J. 10, 26, 62, 79, 123, 346
Cooke, J. R. 262
Corbett, G. 6, 8, 10, 20, 22–3, 25, 28–9, 32–5, 37, 39–41, 45–8, 51–4, 56, 67, 244, 253, 278, 369, 375, 377–8, 392, 408, 415, 439
Corominas, J. 253
Costenla Umaña, A. 80, 123, 169, 384
Counts, D. L. 134
Craig, C. G. vii, 6–8, 10–14, 67, 81–4, 87–91, 97, 103, 110, 116, 125–6, 176, 206, 271, 284–7, 302, 307, 310, 313, 323, 331, 334, 341–2, 344, 357, 364, 370, 375, 433
Creider, C. A. 24, 57, 282
Croft, W. 7–8, 12, 24, 50–1, 125, 158, 180, 189, 271, 274, 278, 286–7, 289, 297
Crofts, M. 216
Crowley, T. 252, 395
Curnow, T. 86, 97, 437

Daley, K. A. C. 325–6, 329, 334
Dallet, J. 39
Davidson, W. 11
Davies, J. 436
Davis, D. R. 124, 287–8

De Leon, M. de L. P. 249, 252, 260, 329–31, 356, 360, 367, 376, 406
DeBray, R. G. A. 244
DeLancey, S. 82, 86, 97, 214, 284, 286, 370, 372
Deloria, E. 158, 299
Demuth, K. A. 57, 398, 416–18
Denny, J. P. 6, 24, 57, 100, 106, 121, 154, 181, 196, 271, 273, 282–3, 289, 291–2, 297–8, 301, 316, 318–19, 336, 340, 345
Derbyshire, D. C. vii, 6–7, 11, 34, 71, 80, 99, 107, 123, 171, 175, 199, 208, 217, 227, 252, 438
Diakonoff, I. M. 92, 346
Dickinson, C. 123
Diller, A. V. N. 11, 102, 117, 347, 349, 381
Dimmendaal, G. I. 22, 42, 58, 77, 100, 111, 322, 368, 371, 380, 390
Dixon, R. M. W. 2, 4, 6, 9–12, 23, 33–4, 43–4, 50, 54, 56, 59–60, 67, 79–81, 83–5, 87, 91, 97, 99–100, 113, 116, 123, 133–4, 136, 140, 150, 164, 169, 228, 242–3, 247, 251, 255, 258, 262–4, 266, 270–2, 285, 293, 310, 329, 340, 345, 347, 366, 372–3, 379–1, 383, 385, 395, 397–8, 404, 437–8
Donaldson, T. 9
Dondorp, A. 79, 437
Doneux, J. 62
Dorian, N. 390–1
Downing, P. 8, 11, 106, 113, 120, 196, 288, 293, 308, 310, 314, 316–17, 320, 324, 329–30, 334, 336, 351, 410–11
Drabbe, P. 60, 299
Dryer, M. S. 104
Ducos, G. 77, 382, 388
Dul'son, A. P. 23, 42
Dunn, M. 439
Durie, M. 29, 91, 97, 190, 286, 290, 381, 402

Ekdahl, M. 152, 160, 209
Elbert, S. H. 140–1
Emeneau, M. B. 100, 102, 106, 112, 121, 185, 286–7, 384
England, N. 87, 140, 331, 357, 375–6, 438
Erbaugh, M. 324, 340, 409–10, 417–18, 421
Evans, N. 8, 30–1, 33, 38, 41, 44, 49, 53, 55, 65–6, 92, 150–1, 200, 266, 279–80, 296, 355, 360, 380, 383, 385, 408
Everett, D. L. 32, 80, 257–8, 321

Facundes, S. 57, 143
Faraclas, N. G. 396, 398–9
Farr, C. 439
Ferguson, C. A. 29
Fleischmann, L. 33, 79
Foley, W. A. 10, 26, 59–60, 62, 79, 158, 166, 171, 329, 363–4, 384, 437

Ford, K. 253
Ford, L. J. 83–4, 86, 90, 97, 161, 257, 285, 299
Foris, D. 12, 191, 287, 290, 371, 375
Fortune, E. F. 26, 62, 79
Frajzyngier, Z. 358
Frank, P. 154, 156, 171, 296, 300, 438
Franklin, G. 139
Franklin, K. 299
Fraser, N. M. 52
Frawley, W. 14, 271–4, 288–9, 338, 437
Friedrich, P. 163, 169

Gagné, R. C. 181
Gandour, J. 417, 419–20, 422–3
Garibian, A. S. 263
Geeraerts, D. 316
Gerzenstein, A. 253
Givón, T. 29, 52–3, 176, 369, 392–3
Goddard, C. 82, 88, 296, 316
Goethe, J. W. 409
Gomez-Imbert, E. 219, 227, 384–6
Gonçalves, C. H. R. C. 12, 152, 160, 216, 333, 355, 444–5
Goral, D. R. 11, 118, 211, 317, 361
Green, D. 8, 27, 39, 69, 112, 142, 150, 163, 165–6, 172–3, 192–4, 196, 198–9, 225, 229, 247, 257, 320, 327, 333, 355, 370, 383
Green, H. 165
Green, I. 37, 97, 397
Green, R. 33, 38–9, 53–4, 56, 70, 100, 281, 408
Greenberg, J. H. 6, 37, 50–1, 54, 100, 104–5, 120, 244, 249, 254, 318, 321, 353, 367–9, 373
Griffiths, C. 130, 175, 198
Grinevald, C., also see Craig, C. G. 286
Gumilëv, N. S. 439
Guoqiao, Z. 9
Gwynn, J. P. L. 46, 108

Haas, M. R. 9, 158, 161, 169, 249
Hagman, R. S. 254
Haig, G. 28
Haiman, J. 438–40
Hale, K. L. 100, 318
Hamel, P. J. 124
Hamp, E. 396
Harms, P. L. 436
Harris, A. 383
Harrison, G. 419
Harrison, S. P. 11, 133, 186, 365
Harvey, M. vii, 11, 23, 25, 49, 59, 70, 81, 92, 280, 321, 329, 369, 383, 385, 399
Hasada, R. 2
Hashimoto, M. J. 226–7, 361–2
Haspelmath, M. 21, 263

Haviland, J. 372
Hayward, R. J. 51–2
Heath, J. 59, 92, 150, 200, 247, 296, 321, 373, 383, 386–7, 402
Heine, B. 10, 25–7, 37–8, 42, 58–60, 68, 70, 75, 77, 125, 134, 146, 243, 276, 321, 358–9, 368–70, 372, 374–5, 381, 384, 388, 392–3, 398, 401–3
Henry, D. 336
Henry, K. 336
Herbert, R. K. 36, 416–17, 422
Hewitt, G. 32–3, 48
Hill, D. 382
Himmelmann, N. P. 363
Hinch, H. E. 267
Hoijer, H. 11, 154, 250
Holmquist, J. C. 27, 45
Hopkins, N. A. 123, 364
Hopper, P. J. 249, 324–5, 329, 374
Hu, Q. 419
Huffman, F. E. 116
Hundius, H. 103, 213–14, 227, 288, 334
Hurd, C. 12, 132, 139, 162, 176, 219, 259
Hyman, L. M. 10

Ikoro, S. M. 101, 110–11, 124, 287, 356, 359–60, 371, 381, 403–4, 439–40
Irvine, J. 348
Iturrioz Leza, J. L. 436

Jackson, E. 213, 220
Jaisser, A. 215
Jakobson, R. O. 51, 422
Janson, T. 349, 389
Järvinen, L. 369
Jauncey, D. 294
Jensen, J. T. 97
Johnson, S. 90
Jones, P. 70
Jones, Jr., R. B. 104
Jones, W. 70
Joshi, S. K. 9, 212, 265, 326
Jun, W. 9
Juntanamalaga, P. 349, 419

Kakumasu, J. 129
Kari, J. 167–9, 382
Karmiloff-Smith, A. 414
Kayser, A. 110
Keating, E. 11, 187, 260, 342, 344–5, 359, 361, 364, 366–7
Keenan, E. L. 29, 162, 257, 363, 406
Kern, B. 32, 80, 257–8, 321
Kerr, I. 50, 224
Key, M. R. 110
Khaidakov, S. M. 34, 347
Kibrik, A. E. 47, 176

Index of Authors

Kimball, G. D. 158, 169, 436
Kirk, L. 282
Kirton, J. F. 33, 66, 385
Kiyomi, S. 7, 271–2, 278, 288
Klein, H. E. M. 12, 179
Koehn, E. 128
Koehn, S. 128, 295, 336, 360, 365
Köhler, O. 77
Kölver, U. 103–4, 213–14, 227, 273, 288, 334, 379
Kooyers, O. 77
Köpcke, K. M. 24–5, 280
Koval', A. I. 61
Krauss, M. 11, 154, 176, 209
Krejnovič, E. A. 23, 42
Krishnamurti, B. 46, 77, 108, 378, 398
Kuipers, A. H. 109, 114
Kunene, E. 416

Lakoff, G. 307–9, 311
Landar, H. 336
Lang, A. 11, 158, 171, 299
Langacker, R. W. 127, 144, 310
Laoust, E. 39, 253–4, 388, 440
Lapointe, S. 29
LaPolla, R. 48, 155–6, 175, 215, 291, 300, 323, 439
Larrimore, B. M. 37
Laskowski, R. 48
Lawton, R. S. 210
Laycock, D. C. 67, 92, 123, 277
Lee, J. 150, 276, 389, 391, 400
Lee, K.-D. 108, 294
Lee, M. 339–40, 421
Lee, Y.-S. 106–7, 115, 260, 273, 311, 334, 336, 348, 386
Leeding, V. 35, 58, 66, 151, 160, 191, 200, 247, 280
Leer, J. 169, 444
Lehmann, C. 7, 15, 21, 29, 392, 416
Lehrer, A. 116, 443
Lermontov, M. Y. 409
Levelt, W. J. M. 415
Levy, P. 288, 355, 502, 443, 446
Levy, Y. 414–15
Li, C. N. 98–9, 206
Lichtenberk, F. 3, 11–12, 90, 113, 125–6, 133–7, 293–4, 365, 382
Lindrud, S. 79
Lindström, E. 32–3, 79
Löbel, E. 117, 119–20, 211, 317–18, 326, 329
Lock, A. 67, 77, 123, 277, 322
Lowe, I. 93, 221, 303, 333–4
Lucy, J. A. 339
Luke, K. K. 419
Lynch, J. 134, 382
Lyons, J. vii, 115–6, 255, 330

McChombo, S. A. 29, 34, 176, 392
McGregor, A. R. F. 277
McGregor, D. E. 277
McGregor, W. 125, 258, 294
McGuckin, C. 147
McLaughlin, F. 62, 348
Magomedbekova, Z. M. 32
Mahapatra, B. P. 104, 112, 185, 248, 286
Malinowski, B. 210
Manessy, G. 287
Marchese, L. 377, 399
Marnita, R. 85, 97–8, 100, 117, 120, 189–90, 253, 262, 286, 289, 308, 318, 322–3, 329–30, 348, 356, 359, 361, 366, 375, 381, 386, 401, 404, 445–6
Marr, D. 338
Martin, J. 158, 251
Martin, S. E. 106
Martins, S. A. 11, 80, 85, 139, 174, 192, 259, 384
Martins, V. 80, 384
Mathiot, M. 346
Matisoff, J. A. 405
Matsumoto, Y. 308–10, 417–18, 420
Mattéi-Müller 34, M.-C. 127
Matthews, P. H. 28–9, 272, 311
Meillet, A. 374, 378
Melchert, H. C. 378
Merlan, F. 11, 49, 56–7, 92, 149, 159, 171, 322, 329–30, 373, 408
Mills, A. E. 22, 415
Minor, E. 246
Minor, L. 246
Mithun, M. 11–12, 150–1, 160–2, 201, 297, 394, 401–3, 437, 444
Moore, B. 139
Moore, D. L. 86
Morice, A. G. 168
Mosel, U. 124, 136, 183
Moshinsky, J. 299
Moussay, G. 9
Mpaayei, J. T. O. 375
Mufwene, S. S. 31
Mujica, M. I. O. 210
Mulford, R. 415
Munroe, P. 34, 40
Muntzel, M. 391

Nedjalkov, V. P. 109
Nekitel, O. 10, 23, 26, 79, 262, 346
Ng, Bee Chin 419–20
Nguyen, D. H. 336
Nichols, J. 7, 27, 31, 49, 57, 60, 137, 255, 258, 263, 369, 373, 377, 383–4, 389, 409
Nicholson, R. 79
Nientao, S. 254
Nordlinger, R. 281, 397

Ó Siadhail, M. 262
Obata, K. 79
Ober, D. 253
Onishi, M. 12, 34–5, 69, 79, 105–6, 132, 162, 176, 219–21, 279, 303, 348, 369, 371, 381, 436–40
Osam, E. K. A. 342–3, 398–9
Osborne, C. R. 33, 56, 59, 160, 200, 276, 389
Osumi, M. 142
Ott, R. 213
Ott, W. 213

Pacioni, P. 214–15, 226, 326
Paducheva, E. V. 88
Palmer, G. 343, 407
Panfilov, V. Z. 100, 108
Parker, D. 33, 79, 244
Parker, G. J. 48
Parker, J. 33, 79, 244
Pasch, H. 28, 33, 63, 75, 129–30, 192, 383, 387–8
Paul, P. 24
Pawley, A. 11, 124, 133, 244, 312
Payne, David L. 143, 369, 387
Payne, Doris L. vii, 6–7, 11, 30, 69, 80, 86, 99, 107, 123, 125, 127, 133, 140, 171, 186, 199, 208, 217, 220–2, 227, 266, 333, 360
Payne, T. E. 107, 217, 220, 222, 333
Pe, H. 11, 103, 116
Peeke, M. C. 217
Pensalfini, R. 281
Pérez-Pereira, M. 414–15, 423
Pet, W. J. A. 50, 174, 201, 262
Peterson, M. N. 245, 255, 384
Pike, K. 376
Plank, F. 25, 244
Plungian, V. A. 61, 438
Polomé, E. 400
Pope, M. K. 379–80
Popova, M. I. 414–15
Poser, W. 168, 382
Posner, R. 378–80
Pozdniakov, K. I. 77
Prasse, K.-G. 245, 254
Press, M. L. 127, 295
Priestly, T. M. S. 245, 380, 396, 398–9
Pullum, G. K. 53
Pym, N. 37

Quigley, S. 124, 211, 287, 418
Quinn, H. 169

Rakhilina, E. 153–363
Ramirez, H. 107, 229, 286, 355, 358, 376, 380, 444–5
Rankin, R. L. 177

Rastorgueva, V. S. 60, 185
Reh, M. 358–9, 374–5, 388, 392–3, 402–3
Rehg, K. 11, 186, 294, 301, 336, 359, 361, 366
Reid, N. vii, 9, 11, 81, 84, 89, 92–3, 95, 97, 185–6, 201, 283, 394–5, 404, 407
Rice, K. 154, 167, 169, 250, 297–8, 344, 437
Richards, J. 76, 182, 213, 220
Riddle, R. 325–6
Rigsby, B. 123
Roberts, J. R. 437
Rodrigues, A. D. 11, 129, 133, 135, 229, 294, 434
Rosch, E. 14, 309, 338–40
Ross, M. 384
Rothstein, R. A. 313, 347, 439
Rowan, O. 226
Royen, G. 5
Rubino, C. R. G. 313, 388–9
Rude, N. 82, 123
Rumsey, A. 9, 56, 329
Rushforth, S. 149, 154, 157–8, 330
Russell, R. A. 40, 392

Sabajo, M. 279
Sanches, M. 100, 249, 348, 386, 417–19
Sândalo, F. 12, 130, 175, 181, 198, 363
Sands, A. K. 11, 49, 55, 58, 79, 81, 86, 91–2, 95, 97, 150, 169, 185, 191, 200, 228, 329, 372, 381, 399
Sapir, D. 311
Sapir, E. 158
Sarsa, R. 277, 437
Sasse, H.-J. 390–1
Saul, J. E. 100, 103–4, 118, 211–12
Sauvageot, S. 61–2
Saxton, D. 127
Sayaba, T. 11, 133
Schane, S. A. 54
Schaub, W. 24, 57
Schauer, J. 106
Schauer, S. 106
Schellinger, W. 244
Scherbak, A. M. 102
Schmidt, A. 349, 390–1
Schwartz, L. 53
Seiler, H. 7, 11, 125, 136, 143, 146, 171, 176–7, 182, 343, 348, 365, 409
Seiler, W. 11, 152, 171, 297, 300, 330, 363–4, 379, 439
Seki, L. 210
Selischev, A. M. 347
Senft, G. 8, 104, 136–7, 204, 210,223, 260, 295, 304, 316, 328, 331, 338, 366, 376, 411, 417–19, 445
Serzisko, F. 3, 6–7, 12, 28, 75, 176–8, 248, 301, 326, 363
Shaul, D. L. 158, 299

524 Index of Authors

Shawcross, W. 347
Shepard Jr., G. 12, 191, 199–200, 213, 341
Shepardson, K. W. 44, 63
Sherzer, J. 79, 121
Shim, J.-W. 79, 437
Shimojo, M. 328, 335–7
Shmelev, A. D. 51, 54
Silverman, M. G. 291
Silverstein, M. 247, 437
Sirk, Ü. 315
Slobin, L. 100, 249
Smith, I. 90
Smith-Stark, S. 247, 437
Smoczynska, M. 414
Sohn, Ho-Min 107, 113
Sokolova, V. S. 60
Speece, R. 79, 123, 244, 346
Speirs, A. 11, 250
Spitulnik, D. 281–2, 409, 416
Spriggs, R. 124, 183
Stachowiak, F. J. 7
Stebbins, T. 247, 274
Steele, S. 15, 29
Steinberg, E. 53
Steinhauer, H. 244
Stone, G. 347
Storch, A. 380
Strom, C. 386
Stucky, S. U. 389, 400
Stumme, H. 254
Stump, G. T. 63–5
Suárez, J. A. 12, 153, 169
Subrahmanyam, P. S. 266
Suppalla, T. 296
Suter, E. 397
Suzman, S. M. 416–17
Sweetser, E. 308, 402

Talmy, L. 156
Taylor, D. M. 44
Taylor, J. R. 146
Terrill, A. 79, 244, 257
Thiesen, W. 221–2, 246–7, 287, 333, 385, 387
Thompson, C. 9, 11, 167–9, 176, 250, 298, 382
Thompson, S. A. 98–9, 206, 325
Todd, E. 244
Toporova, I. 279, 407
Traill, A. 35, 396
Trask, L. 272
Traugott, E. C. 370, 374
Trudgill, P. 390
Tseng, O. 423

Tsonope, J. 22, 50, 349, 396, 416
T'sou, B. K. 11, 116, 318
Tucker, A. N. 375
Turpeinen, S. 33, 79
Tversky, B. 338

Vail, L. 63
Vasmer, M. 26
Vidal, A. 12, 86, 180–1, 251, 326, 336
Vietze, H. P. 102, 121
Viitso, T.-R. 369
Vincennes, L. 39
Vinogradov, V. A. 61, 124, 287, 356
Voeltz, E. 53
Vogel, A. 59, 258
Vossen, R. 358
Vycichl, W. 368

Waddy, J. 43
Wajanarat, S. 101, 104
Walsh, M. 37, 84, 86, 89–90, 97, 284
Wang, Fu-shih 208
Waters, B. 147, 382
Watkins, L. 80, 177–8, 250
Watters, J. 99, 124
Welmers, W. E. 31–2, 35, 77
West, B. 218, 221–2, 264
Westermann, D. 321
Westley, D. O. 257
Whitney, H. 79
Wierzbicka, A. 274, 279, 313, 440
Wiesemann, U. 36
Wilkins, D. 81–2, 84, 401, 442–3
Williamson, K. 398
Wilson, N. F. 100, 103–4, 118, 211–12
Wilson, P. J. 198, 286, 290
Wilson, W. H. 136
Wise, M. R. 199, 222
Wogiga, K. 62
Woodbury, A. C. 181
Worsley, P. M. 5, 12
Wurm, S. A. 79, 147, 171, 218, 386

Ye, E. O. 53

Zabolocky, N. A. 86
Zalizniak, A. A. 88
Zavala, R. 11, 88, 90–1, 98, 113–14, 118–19, 187, 284, 287, 357, 364, 403–4
Z'graggen, J. 67, 123
Zograf, G. A. 185
Zubin, D. A. 24–5, 280, 328, 335–7
Zwicky, A. M. 52–3

Subject Index

A (transitive subject) 15, 33–4, 37, 60, 73–4, 162, 194, 197, 200–1, 256, 365, 378, 426–7, 438, 449, 451
ablaut 60
asolutive 49, 406
abstract nouns 47, 63, 72, 157, 159, 174, 200, 236, 275, 293, 304, 334–6, 349, 360, 378, 450
acquisition 1, 16, 18, 22, 309, 338, 413–25, 432, 435, 450
  of multiple classifier systems 413, 424
  of noun classes 413–17, 420, 423–4, 432
  of numeral classifiers 417–21, 423–4
adjectival modifiers 15, 35, 69, 207, 209, 212–13, 215, 217, 226, 448
  see also adjective
adjective 17, 19–20, 31, 35, 37–40, 47, 49, 53, 56, 59–61, 70, 94–5, 100, 104, 112, 204, 209–10, 213–21, 224–30, 234–5, 253, 265, 304, 353, 388, 396–400, 447
adpositions 18, 33, 172–4, 176, 180, 352, 369, 427
adverbs 17, 19–20, 34, 180, 353
agglutinating languages 6, 10, 20, 205, 248, 447
  and numeral classifiers 99, 102–3, 109
agreement 5, 15, 20–1, 27, 31–45, 94, 193, 229, 247, 265, 328–9, 358, 425, 428, 436, 439, 448
  anaphoric 21, 29, 47
  constraints on 39-41
  default or neutral 51–2
  double 32, 38
  genesis of 372, 374–5, 391–8, 417
  hierarchy 39, 229
  lack of 88, 125–6
  loss in language dissolution 422
  loss and reduction of 388–9, 398–400
  neutralization of 40
  and numeral classifiers 110, 118, 199
  quirky 38
  semantic 31, 37, 75
  syntactic 31, 37, 75
  target of 36
  variability in 28, 37, 41–4
agreement class 1–2, 95
  see also noun class, agreement
alienable possession, see possession type
alliterative concord 35–6, 396–7

  see also repeaters
alternative ordering of morphemes 94
anaphoric function 21, 50, 70, 329–30, 374, 392, 417
  of classifiers in multiple classifier languages 331–3
  of classifiers in possessive constructions 127, 131
  of deictic classifiers 173, 331
  of noun classifiers 81, 87–9, 252, 329–30
  of numeral classifiers 98, 118, 329
  of verbal classifiers 150, 157, 327, 330
animacy 1–3, 8, 17, 354, 357–9, 363, 366, 369, 373, 377–8, 381, 389–90, 393, 396, 410, 428, 435, 442–3, 448–50
  in classifiers in possessive construction 125–7, 130–1, 139, 143, 146
  in deictic classifiers 173–4
  hierarchy 247
  in language acquisition and dissolution 414, 418–19, 423
  in languages with more than one classifier type 185, 187, 189, 191, 197, 199–200
  in locative classifiers 177, 181
  in multiple classifier systems 213, 218, 222, 227, 239–40
  in noun class systems 21–2, 25–29, 34, 38, 41–2, 44, 47–9, 51, 55, 57, 62, 69–70, 75–7, 79–80
  in numeral classifiers 98, 101–2, 106, 113–15, 117, 121, 123
  and other categories 242, 244, 246, 248, 250–1, 256, 260, 263, 436–40
  as a semantic parameter in noun categorization 271–2, 275, 279–80, 282–3, 286–8, 293, 295, 297, 300–6, 312–13, 315, 317, 319, 329, 335–8, 342, 349–50
  in verbal classifiers 149, 152, 155–6, 158, 161
animate referent, see animacy
aphasia 16, 422–4
apophony 58–9, 430
areal diffusion 198, 219, 226–7, 313, 353, 371, 450, 383–8, 391, 397–8, 399–400
  direct diffusion 382–6, 388, 391
    see also loans

Subject Index

areal diffusion (*cont.*):
  numeral classifiers, as areal feature 101, 121, 123–4
areal prefix:
  in locative expressions 176
  as verbal classifier 168–9
arrangement as a semantic parameter, or configuration 274, 285, 293, 296, 299–300, 304, 422
article 2–3, 7–8, 12, 20, 31, 69, 76, 235, 367, 369
article classifier systems 7, 12, 172, 176–82
  see also classifier, deictic
aspect 242, 264–5
assignment of gender, *see* gender assignment
Athabaskan linguistic tradition 9, 167, 169, 265
attributive noun phrase, *see* head-modifier noun phrase
augmentative 63–4, 359
Australianist linguistic tradition 9
autoclassifiers, *see* repeaters

Bantuist linguistic tradition 9
basic linguistic theory vii, 4
batang, classifier in Minangkabau 90, 189–90, 289, 291–2, 302, 318, 359, 370, 402, 404, 446
body parts 353–7, 405
  body part possession 130–1
  and noun classes 66, 72
  as numerals 100
  polygrammaticalization of 375
  as sources for classifiers 442–6
borrowing, *see* loans
boundedness as a semantic parameter 181

case 21, 57, 242, 377, 379, 397, 436–7
case-marking, *see* case
categorization, linguistic of a noun (referent) vii
chaining model 309–11, 315
child-language acquisition, *see* acquisition
class morphemes 161
  see also classifier, verbal
class nouns 87
classificatory adpositions, *see* classifier, locative
classificatory noun incorporation, *see* noun incorporation
classificatory technique 7
classificatory verb 11, 153–62, 336, 344, 363, 412, 448
  correlations with number 153, 158, 249–52
  existential 155–6, 158–9, 166, 171, 175, 299
  origins of 160–1, 163, 165, 166, 169
  see also classifier, verbal, origin of

partly analysable 156–7, 171
posture verbs 159
stance verbs 166
suppletive 153–6, 161, 169
classifier, deictic 3, 8, 12, 18, 172, 176–83, 306, 425, 448
  and definiteness 177
  and deictic categories 266
  discourse functions of 326
  emergence as a dictinct type 183
  fused with demonstratives 177, 181
  and gender 179–81
  in languages with more than one classifier type 191, 197, 202
  lexical sources for 362–3, 412
  in locative expressions 178
  in multiple classifier systems, *see* multiple classifier systems
  and number 251–2
  obligatoriness of 179
  origin of 177, 182
  and other categories 269–70
  plural class in 178
  reclassification in 178, 180, 182
  semantics of 300–1
classifier, locative 2–3, 8, 12, 18, 172–6, 302, 448
  discourse functions of 326
  distinctions comparable to 176
  in languages with more than one classifier type 192–3, 196–7, 201–2
  lexical sources for 357, 412
  and number 252
  origin of 370, 375
  and other categories 269–70
  residual classifier 174
  semantics of 300–1, 306, 335, 425
  and verbal classifier 175
classifier, noun 2, 5, 8, 11, 285, 306, 425–35, 448
  anaphoric function of 81, 87–9
  cooccurrence of 83–4
  deletion of 89
  discourse functions of 322–3
  distinguishing from compounds 85–7
  distinguishing from free noun 85–7
  grammaticalization of 81, 84–8, 90–1, 93, 95
  in languages with more than one classifier type 184, 186, 191–2, 202
  lexical sources for 357, 359–60, 412
  loss of 381
  in multiple classifier systems 230
    see also multiple classifier systems
  and noun class 92–5, 97
  and number 252
  and numeral classifiers 90

obligatoriness 81, 89, 186
omission of 90, 95
origin of 191, 371–3, 376
and other categories 268–70
properties and realization of 91
as relative clause markers 88–9, 92–3
semantic change in 402–4
size of inventory 81, 84–7
syntactic function of 87
classifier, numeral 2–3, 8, 11, 17, 105, 227–30, 265, 272, 283, 302, 305–6, 426, 435—6, 438, 448
  absence of 100
  applicability of 334
  as areal feature 101, 121, 123–4
  change in 120, 348, 402–6, 408, 409–12
  constituency of 99, 105, 110–11
  dependence on size of number 100, 107, 109, 112, 114, 117–29, 190, 212
  functions of 98, 118, 318–20, 324, 326
  genitive or attributive with 106–7, 121
  incipient system of 101, 120–1
  in languages with more than one classifier type 186–7, 189, 193, 196–8, 202
  lexical sources for 355–7, 360, 362, 364, 366–7, 411–12
  loss of 381, 390–1
  mensural 114–15, 293, 355–6, 366, 386, 406, 445–6
  more than one kind of in one language 101, 112–14
  in multiple classifier languages, *see* multiple classifier systems
  and noun class 98, 109, 184
  and noun classifiers 113–14, 123
  and number category 100–1, 249–52
  obligatoriness of 100, 106, 114, 117, 190
  and obligatory plural marking 100
  origin of 109, 111, 113, 121, 370–2, 375, 379, 384, 386, 443–6
  and other categories 268–70
  pragmatic functions, (uses) of 117
  properties and realization of 98, 102–12
  and quantifier 101, 115–20
  semantics of 186–93, 311–12, 316, 335, 342, 344
  sortal 114–15, 286–93, 355–6, 366, 386
classifier, possessed 2–3, 11, 17, 125, 132–62, 230
  and alienably possessed nouns 126–9, 131–2
  and inalienably possessed nouns 128
  in languages with more than one classifier type 191–2, 202
  lexical sources for 358, 360, 362, 364–7, 411–12

in multiple classifier systems, *see* multiple classifier systems
  and noun classifiers 130
  and numeral classifiers 147
  origin of 383
  and possession types 259
  realization of 126, 145
  used independently of possession type 129–33
  see also classifiers in possessive constructions
classifier, possessor 2–3, 17, 125, 139–40, 306, 425–7, 448
  categorization of possessor in 140
  in languages with more than one classifier type 192, 202
  in multiple classifier systems, *see* multiple classifier systems
  and possession type 259
  rarity of 146
  realization of 139
  see also classifiers in possessive constructions
classifier, relational 2, 11, 17, 125, 133–9, 306, 343, 426–35, 448
  and alienable possession 133–8
  in languages with more than one classifier type 184, 191–2, 197, 201–2
  lexical sources for 364–5
  loss of 382
  in multiple classifier systems, *see* multiple classifier systems
  and possessed classifiers 137–8, 140–2, 144–6
  and possession type 259
  realization of 136, 145
  see also classifiers in possessive constructions
classifier, verb-incorporated, *see* classifier, verbal
classifier, verbal 3, 6, 8, 11–13, 16–17, 227, 302, 305–6, 394, 426–35, 435, 439
  anaphoric functions of 150, 157, 330
  applicability of 334
  difference from lexical selection of verbs 153, 355, 362–5
  discourse functions of 149, 326–7
  generic noun as 150, 403
  and grammatical function 257
  grammaticalization of 160–3
  in languages with more than one classifier type 184, 193, 197, 200–2
  lexical sources for 355, 360, 362–5, 411–2
  limitation to some semantic groups of verbs 149, 153, 165, 296–7
  loss of 382–4

528 Subject Index

classifier, verbal (cont.):
  in multiple classifier systems, see multiple classifer systems
  obligatoriness of 149
  origin of 149, 160–1, 163, 165–6, 169, 370, 375, 379
    see also classificatory verb, origin of
  and other categories 265–6, 268–70
  properties and realization of 149–58
  reclassification 157, 164
  semantic change in 402
  semantics of 295–300, 335
  size of inventory 150, 152
  and verb classes 265
  verbal classifiers:
    in Athabaskan tradition 9, 167, 169, 265
    in Australianist tradition 9
    in South and Southeast Asian tradition 9
classifiers:
  article systems of, see article classifier systems
  coexistence of more than one type in one language 14
  construction 13
  contingent properties of 15–16
  definitional properties of 13, 14–16
  interaction with other categories 15, 21, 41, 57, 425, 428
  marginal types of 8
  in possessive constructions:
    anaphoric function of 127, 131
    change in 348
    discourse functions of 326, 426–35
    generic 126
    in languages with more than one classifier type 193, 196–7
    in multiple classifier systems, see multiple classifier systems
    and number 252
    obligatoriness 126, 142
    omission of 132
    origin of 140
    and other categories 268–70
    and possession types 259
    semantics of 293–5, 301, 305–6, 343–5
    size of inventory 145
    specific 126
    and speech register 342
    syntactic function 127
  size of inventory 6
  specific, see unique classifiers
  typology of 5–12
closed class 19, 36–7, 103, 241, 367, 374, 392, 411, 447
closed systems 17
cognitive mechanisms 13
  see also human cognition
cognitive process 308
colour 338, 340
complementizer 34
complete involvement as a semantic parameter 165–6, 196–7
compounds and numeral classifiers 103, 120
concord, see agreement
concord, alliterative, see alliterative concord
concordial class 10, 19
  see also noun class
concordial systems, see noun class
concrete 275
conjunction of nouns, see coordination
consistency as a semantic parameter 3, 251, 273, 289–91, 293, 295, 297–8, 300, 302, 305–6, 339, 350
  in classifiers in possessive constructions 127
  in locative classifiers 172, 174–5
  in numeral classifiers 115
  in verbal classifiers 149, 156
consonant-initial dropping 91
constituent order 34, 40, 214–15, 378, 395, 420
  and numeral classifier constructions 104, 106–7, 120
constituent:
  peripheral 34, 37
  topical, 34, 197
contact 313
  see also language contact; areal diffusion
continuum 3, 7–8, 13–14, 57, 425, 432–3,
  grammaticalization as a continuum 93, 95, 185
  noun categorization as a continuum 3, 201, 425, 432–3
  quantifier and numeral classifier as continuum 120
  see also prototype and continuum approach
contrast 197
controllers 51
  non-prototypical controllers 51
coordination 52, 56
corpus, see sample
correlations between classifiers and other categories 7
countability 249, 274, 396
  see also countable nouns
countable nouns, or count nouns 24, 115–20, 220–1, 249, 274
creolization of languages 382, 388–9, 391, 398–400
  see also pidginization
cross-classification, see reclassification

cross-referencing 14, 35, 48, 60, 68, 70, 80, 110, 192, 194, 200–1, 213, 252, 255–6, 259, 264, 399, 438

decay of classifiers 16, 18, 352, 425, 431
declension 13, 25, 263, 377, 436, 438
  interaction with classifiers 243, 262–3, 268–9
declension classes, *see* declension
default:
  classifier 141, 274, 279, 281, 293, 304, 307, 335–7, 423, 450
    see also residue classifier
  or neutral agreement forms 53
definiteness 39, 40, 117, 211, 215–16, 243, 249, 321, 323–4, 326–7, 333
deictic classifier, *see* classifier, deictic
deictic modifiers, *see* demonstratives
deictics, *see* demonstratives
demonstratives 8, 14, 17, 19–20, 31, 36, 39, 47, 49, 56, 59, 61, 65, 68–70, 76, 172, 192, 194, 197, 199, 210, 213, 226, 228, 235, 239, 255, 265, 318, 326, 352, 367, 380, 392, 394, 398, 416–18, 439, 448
  distinct classifiers and agreement class for 182–3
  gender on 183, 213
  numeral classifiers with 183, 208
dependencies between derivation and other categories 242–3, 249, 252–7, 268–70
dependent-marking languages 82
derivation 5, 28, 30, 92, 220, 269, 358, 440
derivational functions:
  of classifiers 220–2, 225, 235, 252, 266, 287, 303
  of noun class 84, 358, 388
    see also noun class, overt
determiner 35
  see also demonstratives
development of classifiers 4–5, 16
dimensionality as a semantic parameter 180, 268, 272, 288–93, 297–306, 338, 350, 363, 411
diminutive 25, 63, 69, 105, 111, 279, 358, 379
direct object, *see* O; object, direct
directionality as a semantic parameter 266, 272, 289, 305–6
disambiguating polysemous referent 43
discourse-pragmatic properties 30, 37, 39, 62
discourse conditions for generic nouns 86
dissolution:
  of classifiers 16, 18, 422–423, 425, 432, 435
  of noun classes 422
dual 244–7, 251, 254–5, 393, 437

epicenes 41
ergative 263, 378, 437–8
evolution of classifiers 16, 18, 352, 367–70, 425, 431, 450
existential verbs 155–6, 158–9, 166, 171, 175, 299, 439
extendedness as a semantic parameter 178, 420
extension, semantic 83, 307, 309, 311, 338, 346, 403–4, 408–11, 421, 445

female, *see* feminine 23–4, 26–7
feminine 2, 14, 244–7, 252–6, 259, 262–3, 266, 277–81, 286, 310, 313, 322, 336–7, 346, 350, 358, 368, 378–81, 384, 386, 388–9, 393, 400, 408, 413–15
  in languages with more than one classifier type 186, 194, 197, 199, 200
  in multiple classifier languages 210, 213, 218, 228, 230, 240
  in noun classes 19–27, 32, 35, 37–42, 44–5, 47–8, 50, 54, 56–60, 66–7, 69–72, 75–80, 180, 182
  in numeral classifiers 106
focal instances 14
  see also prototype
focusing 40, 58, 107, 223, 318, 327, 328
form:
  in classifiers in possessive constructions 125–6, 146
  in noun classifiers 82
  in numeral classifiers 102, 106, 113, 123
  as a semantic parameter 185, 187, 297
  in verbal classifiers 152–3
frequency of classifier types 4–5
function:
  in a clause (A, S, O) 3
  as a semantic parameter 83, 87, 186, 271–3, 278, 287, 292–3, 295–6, 300, 305–7, 317, 320–35, 339–40, 344–5, 387, 404, 406, 418, 423
fusional languages 6, 10, 20, 205, 248, 256, 447
  numeral classifier in 99, 105, 108, 121
fuzzy boundaries between types 12
fuzzy types 230–41

gender 2, 8, 10, 19–80, 350, 440
  controller 45–6
  in languages with more than one classifier type 192, 196
  loss of 379–81, 388–9, 390–1, 396
  in multiple classifier languages, 213, 228
    see also multiple classifier systems
  origin of 367–71, 395–6
  residual 47–8
  target 45–6
    see also noun class

Subject Index

gender assignment 10, 15, 21, 22–8, 275–7, 413, 425
  mixed 10, 15, 21, 25–8, 275, 348
  morphological 15, 22–5, 263, 275, 408
  phonological 10, 25, 62, 275, 348, 408
  semantic 15, 56, 275, 348, 390
gender:
  in Athabaskan linguistic tradition 9, 167, 169, 265
  and noun class in Bantuist linguistic tradition 9
  and noun classes, interchangeable use of 8, 9
gender systems, see noun class
gender-sensitive affixes 194, 228
generic:
  classifier 130, 328, 426
  term in agreement 54, 55
generic classifier, or general classifier 212, 442
  see also default classifier
generic noun classifier, see generics
generic-specific:
  pairings 86, 395
  relations 275, 295, 302, 305, 372, 395
generics, or generic nouns 85–6, 128–9, 186, 190, 197, 211, 275, 317, 349, 394–5, 353–4, 358–9
  polygrammaticalization of 376, 402–3
genitive classifier, see classifiers in possessive constructions
grammatical relations 3, 18, 243, 255–7, 268–9, 437, 449
grammaticalization 1, 15,21, 185, 283, 316, 333, 352, 355–9, 361, 370, 372–7, 385, 392, 395, 397, 400–1, 405, 411, 426, 428, 432
  of noun classifiers 81, 84–8, 90–1, 93, 95, 186, 345
  unidirectionality in 372, 374
  of verbal classifiers 160–3
grammaticalized system 19
grammaticization, see grammaticalization
graphic noun classifiers 82

head 29, 63
  in a noun-classifier construction 90
  in numeral classifier construction 105
  in possessive constructions 146
head classes 30, 61, 63, 394–6
head of a noun phrase 13, 39, 165
head-marking languages 82
head-modifier:
  agreement 29, 37, 59, 61, 70, 76, 193–4, 198, 226, 306, 391–4, 422
  noun phrase 17, 29, 31
hon, classifier in Japanese 308–11, 316, 420

honorifics 63, 284, 317, 422, 443
human cognition vii, 2, 3, 13, 18, 307, 319, 337, 339, 424, 435
human noun vii, 19
  see also human referents; humanness
human referents vii, 21
  see also human noun; humanness
humanness 1, 16, 275, 281–8, 295–7, 301–6, 308, 310, 313, 315, 317, 337, 342, 349–51, 354, 357, 359, 369, 373, 378, 381, 388–9, 400, 403, 428, 442–3, 449–50
  and interaction of classifiers with other categories 242, 244, 246, 248, 259–60, 262–3, 268, 435–40
  and language acquisition and dissolution 411–12, 417
  in multiple classifier languages 208
  see also multiple classifier systems
  as a semantic parameter in classifiers in possessive constructions 127, 146
  as a semantic parameter in languages with more than one classifier type 185, 187, 189, 197
  as a semantic parameter in locative classifiers 180
  as a semantic parameter in noun classes 21–6, 39–40, 42–3, 48–50, 53–4, 56–8, 60, 67–8, 72, 77, 79
  as a semantic parameter in noun classifiers 82–3
  as a semantic parameter in numeral classifiers 105, 109, 112–14, 123, 192
hybrid nouns 41, 313, 347, 358

inalienable possession, see possession type
inalienably possessed nouns 33, 65, 71
  see also Chapter 5; possession type
inanimate 312–13, 329, 336
  in classifiers in possessive construction 125–7, 130–1, 139, 146
  in deictic classifiers 173–4
  in languages with more than one classifier type 185, 189
  in locative classifiers 177, 181
  in multiple classifier languages 222–3
  in noun classes 21, 23, 25, 27, 34, 41–3, 47–9, 51, 55, 58, 61, 70, 75, 77, 79–80
  in numeral classifiers 109, 113, 119, 123
  in verbal classifiers 149, 152, 155–6, 158, 161
  see also animacy
incipient types of classifiers 185
incorporation, see noun incorporation
indefinites 21, 55
  see also indefinite pronouns
indefinite pronouns 54–5, 85

indefinite reference 51, 54
individualizing functions of classifier
    morphemes 93
individuation 51, 58, 166
inductive approach 4
inflection 5, 15, 28, 30, 220, 266
inflectional languages, *see* fusional languages
inflectional properties of nouns 81
inherent properties in noun categorization 2,
    17, 272, 303
  classifiers in possessive constructions 125,
      144–5
  numeral classifiers 115
  verbal classifiers 153, 158–9
interioricity as a semantic parameter 273,
    288–9, 302, 305, 345
interrogatives 19, 21, 33, 35–6, 54–5, 59, 61,
    85, 212, 228, 240, 367, 440–1, 448, 451
intralocative classifiers 7, 12
  see also classifier, locative
isolating languages 6, 10, 20, 82, 205, 447
  noun classifiers in 82
  numeral classifiers in 99, 101, 103, 105

khan classifier in Thai 291, 348, 405, 408
kinship:
  possession 146
  as a semantic parameter in noun
      categorization 82, 131, 141, 271–2,
      280, 284, 305–6, 342, 353–4, 357–9
  terms 41, 64, 66, 131, 357

language:
  change 347, 389, 399, 411
  contact 383–8, 398–40
    see also areal diffusion
  obsolescence 5, 307, 313, 347, 348, 382,
      386, 389–91, 398–400, 450
  planning 307, 347
lexicalization 15, 399, 426, 428
lexicon, structure of 242, 243, 347
loans 246, 333, 358, 383, 386–8, 450
  noun class 57, 62
  numeral classifiers 105, 109–10
  see also diffusion, direct
locative classifier, *see* classifier, locative
loss of classifiers 1, 16
lustre, *see* visibility as a semantic parameter

macroclass 49
markedness 15, 50–6, 71, 425, 428
  formal 15, 109
  functional 15, 38, 49, 71, 262
  reversal 51
masculine gender 2, 14, 277–81, 286, 313,
    322, 328, 336–7, 346, 350, 358, 368,
    377, 379–80, 386, 388–9, 393, 400

in multiple classifier languages 208, 210,
    213, 218, 228
  see also multiple classifier systems
and language acquisition and
    dissolution 413–15
as a semantic parameter in languages with
    more than one classifier type 180,
    185–6, 194, 197, 199–200
  in noun classes 19–27, 32, 35, 37–42,
    44–50, 52–4, 56–60, 66, 69–72, 75–80
  in numeral classifiers 106
male, *see* masculine gender
mass nouns 115–20, 220–1, 249, 278, 282
material, *or* material make up 273, 289–90,
    292, 302, 305–6, 404, 423
measure words 115–20, 418
metaphor 311–13, 316, 341, 343, 346, 401,
    408
  and polysemy 316
metaphoric extension 21, 315
  see also metaphor
metonymy 308–11, 315, 343, 401, 405
modifiers 17, 19, 29, 31, 39
morphological loci 13–14, 20, 31, 36–7, 68,
    211, 218–19, 240, 425–6
motion verbs 362–4
multiple classifier systems 12, 16, 36, 77, 118,
    124, 131, 133, 139, 142, 144, 160, 183,
    204–41, 266, 271, 396–7, 425, 432–5,
    437
  adjectives with classifiers in 204, 209–11,
      213, 216–18, 220, 222–3, 225, 227,
      230, 235
  classifiers with deictics/demonstratives
      in 204, 206, 208–10, 212–13, 215–18,
      220, 222–3, 225–7, 235, 265
  classifiers in possessive constructions
      in 222, 225–7
  constituent order in 214
  default classifier in 337
  derivational functions of classifiers in 252
  discourse functions of classifiers in 325–7
  locative classifiers in 206–7, 225
  noun classifiers in 206, 211, 215–16, 370
  numeral classifiers in 370
  numerals with classifiers in 204, 206, 208,
      210–12, 215–19, 222–7, 235, 265
  origin of 370, 386
  possessed classifiers in 370
  relational classifiers in 225–6
  semantics of 303–4
  verbs with classifiers in 206, 208–9, 213,
      216, 219, 225

natural gender, *see* sex as a semantic
    parameter
negation 264–5

Subject Index

neuter 19, 23–5, 40–2, 44–5, 47, 65–6, 199, 222, 244, 255, 263, 266, 276, 279, 281, 335, 337
neutralization of noun class distinctions 51
nominalizations 218–19, 221, 225
nominative–accusative 437
non-feminine 222, 230, 240, 256, 310, 384–5
non-human 16, 244, 247, 268
   in languages with more than one classifier type 185, 189
   as a semantic parameter in classifiers in possessive constructions 127
   in noun classes 41, 43, 48–9, 53, 75, 77
   in numeral classifiers 105, 113, 123
   see also humanness
non-sex differentiable 23, 25
noun class 2, 5, 8, 10, 17, 92, 184, 229, 231, 234–5, 239, 252, 306, 425–35, 436, 438, 440, 448
   agreement, decline of 398–400
      development of 392–8
      on multiple targets 228
   applicability of 21, 334
   changes in 407–9
   covert 56, 57–8, 193, 358, 373
   and deictic cagegories 266
   discourse functions of 321–2
   distinct systems in one language 45
   double marking of 63–6, 95
   and gender, coexistence of 10
   and grammatical function 255–7
   in languages with more than one classifier type 189, 191–2, 198, 200–2
   lexical sources for 358–9, 362, 366, 411–12
   loss of 210, 379–81, 388–9, 390–1, 396
   marked on noun 2, 17
   see also noun class, overt
   markedness relations 50–2, 54–6
   marking of 11, 19–78
   in multiple classifier systems, *see* multiple classifier systems
   nominal 67–77, 184, 380–1
   and noun classifiers 185
   and number 243–9
   number of 28, 45
   and numeral classifiers 184–5
   opaque semantics of 63
   origin of 368–9, 372–5, 377–9, 384, 386, 395–6
   overt 44, 56–9, 61, 63, 84, 91–5, 322, 325, 358, 373, 422, 448
   and person 252–5
   and possession 258–60
   productivity 58
   pronominal 37, 67–77, 184, 192, 205, 226, 230, 246, 259, 283, 380–1, 398
   resolution 50, 52–4

   semantics of 342, 275–83, 345
   size of 6
   suprasegmental realization of 60
   variable assignment of 28, 68–9, 267
   see also gender
noun class systems, *see* noun class
noun classifier, *see* classifier, noun
noun incorporation 150–1, 160–1, 165, 295, 360, 394, 430
   body part incorporation and classificatory 151, 165, 355
   classificatory 150–1, 160, 202, 227
   and lexical compounding 151
noun phrase 20, 22
number 18–19, 24, 52, 57, 74, 242, 279, 368, 377, 379–80, 388–9, 392-3, 436–7, 449
   interaction with classifiers 243, 248–52, 254–5, 263–4, 268–70
   and numeral classifiers 117
numeral, numbers 2, 17, 20, 31, 40, 59, 61, 67, 69, 75, 114, 199–200, 399, 418
numeral classifier, *see* classifier, numeral
numeral system 99–100

O (direct object of a transitive verb) 3, 15, 17, 34, 73, 74, 149–50, 152–8, 160–8, 184, 196–7, 200–1, 209, 250–1, 256–7, 265, 287, 306, 325, 327, 363–5, 406, 426–7, 437–9, 449, 451
object, direct 3, 33–4
   see also O
object marker 35
obsolescence of language, *see* language obsolescence
omission of classifiers 335
open class 37, 411, 447
   classifiers in possessive constructions as 129, 141
   numeral classifiers as 98, 101, 103
orientation as a semantic parameter 18, 149, 153, 158–9, 166, 175–6, 178, 287, 289, 298–9, 305–6, 406, 448.
   see also position in space
origin of classifier 1, 18, 196, 203, 226, 352, 361, 450

paucal 248, 437
perception, perceptual features 307, 337–8, 421–2
peripheral arguments 162
person 21, 52, 392
   interaction with classifiers 245, 252–5, 263–4, 268–70
personal pronouns 39, 68–9
phonological reduction of classifiers 357, 371, 376, 395

pidginization 382, 388–9, 391
  see also creolization of languages
plural 21–2, 24, 45–6, 48, 50, 74, 77, 100,
    187, 221, 240, 243–9, 251, 253–6, 263,
    377, 388–9, 413
  in numeral classifier languages 100–1
plural marking, see plural
polarity, see negation
politeness 21, 102, 143, 260–2, 268–70, 436
polygrammaticalization 363, 370, 374–6,
    402–3
polysemy 271, 316
polysynthetic languages 99, 108, 248, 447
position in space 149, 153, 158–9, 166,
    175–6, 178
  as a semantic parameter 17, 250, 277, 296,
    406
  see also orientation as a semantic
    parameter
possessed noun 2, 15, 31–2, 59–60, 66, 125,
    294–5
possessee 125
  see also possessed noun
possession:
  alienable 126–46.
    see also possession type
  direct 133
    see also possession, inalienable
  inalienable 33, 126, 146
    see also inalienably possessed nouns
  indirect 133
    see also possession, alienable
possession type 243, 257–9, 268–70, 438, 449
  and noun class agreement 258–9
  possession type and type of classifier
    137–9, 126–46
  see also possessive construction, type of
possessive construction, type of 2, 5, 31, 125,
    137–9, 126–46, 449
possessive noun phrase 31
possessives 19, 417
possessor 2, 15, 32, 294–5
postposition, see adpositions
posture verbs 153, 159, 182, 299, 362–3,
    406
predicate 20, 39
  categories 242
predicate classifier systems, see classifier,
    verbal
predicate-argument agreement type 29, 37,
    40, 59, 70, 76, 193–4, 197, 306, 392,
    422
preposition, see adpositions
productivity of classifier systems 334
proficiency in:
  noun classifiers 83

numeral classifiers 83, 98, 113
pronominal noun class, see noun class,
    pronominal
pronominalization 13, 252
pronouns 21, 35–7, 39, 70, 79, 194, 210, 228,
    252–6, 262, 358, 368, 373, 392–3, 398,
    415, 439, 451
prototype 8, 14, 308–9, 314–15, 317, 325,
    403, 421, 425, 432–3
  and continuum approach 14

quanta as a semantic parameter 274, 285,
    293, 299, 304, 422
quantifier 2, 17, 49, 107, 115, 249
quantifiers and classifiers 115–20, 249
quantity:
  of an entity 115
  expression of 98

rarity of classifiers 5
rational gender 22–3
realization of noun classes and classifiers
    6–7, 15, 17, 20–1
reanalysis in noun categorization 186, 249,
    352, 370, 373, 377–9, 392, 399
reclassification 267, 320, 328
  with classifiers in possessive
    constructions 137–41, 143
  in languages with more than one classifier
    type 196
  in multiple classifier systems 223, 267
  with noun classes 43, 267
  with noun classifiers 83, 267
  with verbal classifiers 267
reduplication 59, 109, 430
reference management 321
referent tracking 157, 192, 211, 321, 326
referentiality 333, 335
relative clauses 88–9, 221–3, 231, 327
relative pronoun 39
relativizer 35, 92, 327, 392, 396
  classifiers as 219, 221, 225, 333
repeaters 5, 3, 15, 17, 59, 103, 353, 361–2,
    370, 376, 384, 397, 423, 430, 434–5
  as classifiers in possessive
    constructions 128, 136, 141–2
  in languages with more than one classifier
    type 187
  in multiple classifier systems 222–7
    see also multiple classifier systems
  as noun class agreement markers 61–3
  as noun classifiers 91
  as numeral classifiers 99, 103–4, 110
residual class 79
residue classifier 274, 279, 281, 293, 304
  see also default classifier

S (intransitive subject) 3, 15, 17, 33, 34, 37, 60, 71, 74, 149–50, 152–4, 162–3, 165–8, 184, 194, 196–7, 200–1, 209, 250–1, 256–7, 265, 306, 327, 363–5, 405, 426, 437, 439, 449, 451
sample 4
Sapir–Whorf hypothesis 340
scope 6, 15, 20, 81, 95, 243, 258, 425–6
self-classifiers, or autoclassifiers, *see* repeaters
semantic basis of categorization 4, 13, 21
semantic change 18, 352, 357, 361
semantic extension 83, 307, 309, 311, 338, 346, 403–4, 408–11, 421, 445
   see also extension, semantic
semantic function 8, 84
semantic groups of nouns 24
semantic opacity 20, 196, 275, 280, 283, 307–8, 315, 347, 400, 407–8
   see also semantic transparency
semantic residue 28
semantic transparency 20, 196, 275, 280, 283, 307–8, 315, 347, 407, 409, 416
   see also semantic opacity
semantically transparent choice of noun classifier 82
semi-repeaters, or partial repeaters 110
serial verbs as a source for classifiers 363
sex as a semantic parameter 1, 17, 19–22, 25, 44, 58, 68, 102, 185, 187, 275, 283–4, 286–8, 304, 341, 347, 350, 358, 396, 428
sex-differentiable 23, 26, 42, 43
shape as a semantic parameter 2, 3, 17, 249–50, 256, 266, 268, 272–3, 275, 277–8, 281–3, 288–93, 295–7, 299–307, 315–18, 337–40, 350, 356, 366, 384–5, 404–6, 409, 411, 418, 423, 446, 448–9
   in classifiers in possessive constructions 125–7, 131, 146
   in deictic classifiers 177
   in genders and noun classes 21, 42, 45, 69, 76
   in languages with more than one classifier type 185, 187, 191, 197, 200
   in locative classifiers 172
   in multiple classifier systems 200
   see also multiple classifier systems
   in noun classifiers 82
   in numeral classifiers 98, 101–2, 105, 113–5, 117, 121, 123
   in verbal classifiers 149, 152–4, 156, 161, 163
singular 21, 24, 45–6, 240, 243–52, 255, 263, 377, 388–9, 413
singular marking, *see* singular

size as a semantic parameter 185, 273, 277–9, 282–3, 289, 295, 405, 418, 449
   in classifiers in possessive constructions 126, 131, 146
   in genders and noun classes 21, 43, 58, 69
   in languages with more than one classifier type 185, 187
   in numeral classifiers 98, 117
   in verbal classifiers 149, 152
social status as a semantic parameter in noun categorization 260, 271–2, 280, 284, 288, 305–6, 315, 335, 342, 350–1
   in noun classifiers 82, 84
   in numeral classifiers 98
socio-cultural changes 311, 347–50
socio-cultural parameters in categorization 16–17, 307
specific classifier, *see* unique classifier
specificity 215, 321–4, 333
speech register 187, 260–2, 342, 366–7, 423
split agreement 30, 67, 76
split systems of noun classes 15, 66, 283
structure as a semantic parameter 17, 281
   in classifiers in possessive constructions, 126–7, 131
   in noun classifiers 82
   in numeral classifiers 98
   in verbal classifiers 149
style 349, 423
subgender 48
subject 33–4, 37, 39, 194, 200, 422, 440
superclassing 43, 48–9, 53, 55, 70, 228–9, 248
superordinate-subordinate relation in classifier systems 316–17, 349, 370, 401
suppletion 59, 252
suppletive classificatory verbs 11, 205
   see also classificatory verb
syntactic function 39

target of agreement 36
target gender, *see* gender, target
tense 242, 263–4
topic continuity 321
topical constituent 34
topicality 34, 37, 39, 197, 321
transitive construction 73–4
tua, classifier in Thai 314–15, 349, 411, 422, 442
type, agglutinative, *see* agglutinating languages
type, fusional, *see* fusional languages
type, isolating, *see* isolating languages
type, polysynthetic, *see* polysynthetic languages

unclassified nouns 249, 272, 297, 324

unique classifier 98, 166, 185, 273, 275, 293, 300–1, 344
unit counters 353–4, 360–1
universal 4, 10, 244, 272, 338, 388.
  see also universal parameter in noun categorization
universal parameter in noun categorization 15, 22, 388

value as a semantic parameter 135, 274, 294, 302, 307
variable classification, *see* reclassification
vegetable gender or noun class 66, 79, 278–9, 281, 350, 366, 372–3, 408
verbal classifier, *see* classifier, verbal

verbal classifiers:
  in Athabaskan tradition 9, 167, 169, 265
  in Australianist tradition 9
  in South and Southeast Asian tradition 9
verb, noun class agreement on 22, 35, 47, 69, 72
verb-argument agreement, *see* predicate-argument agreement type
verbal categories, *see* predicate categories
verbs, stative, semantic groups of 165
verbs, telic 165
visibility as a semantic parameter 181, 266, 280, 363

word order, *see* constituent order